Ancient Scholars
about the Turks and the Turkic Nations

Volume 2.

Copyright © 2022 A. Sanducci

All rights reserved. No part of this book may be reproduced or transmitted in any form or by any means, electronic or mechanical, including photocopying, recording or by any information storage and retrieval system without permission in writing from the publisher.

For feedback, please email at AncientTurks@gmail.com

Imprint—World Scholarly Press, Trabuco Canyon, USA
ISBN: 979-8-9859237-3-5
Library of Congress Control Number: 2022936297
Title: *Ancient Scholars about the Turks and the Turkic Nations. Volume 2.*
Author: A. Sanducci
Digital distribution | 2022
Paperback | 2022

A. Sanducci

Ancient Scholars about the Turks and the Turkic Nations

Volume 2.

TABLE OF CONTENTS.

THE TURKIC ALPHABET	1

VOLUME 1.

CHAPTER I.
§1. THE BIBLICAL ORIGINS OF THE TURKIC NATIONS.
§2. THE ANCIENT TURKIC NATION OF AZ AND THE BIBLICAL LAND OF UZ.
§3. THE BIBLICAL TYRIANS AND THE MEDES ARE THE ANCIENT TURKS.
§4. THE TURKIC ORIGIN OF THE BIBLICAL HITTITES, THE KHETA, THE KHITAI OF CENTRAL ASIA AND CHINA.
§5. THE AKKADIANS, THE SUMERIANS, THE SUSIANS, THE KASSITES, THE CAANITES – THE TURKIC NATIONS OF BIBLICAL PROPORTIONS.
§6. THE BIBLICAL PHILISTINES' TIES TO THE TURKIC NATIONS.

CHAPTER II.
§1. THE TURKIC PEDIGREE OF THE ARIAN NATIONS.
§2. THE TURKIC ORIGIN OF ODIN – THE GOD OF ALL GODS.
§3. TROY, THE SAME AS ASGARD – THE ANCIENT LAND OF THE TURKS.
§4. THE TURKIC NATIONS — AZ, ASIR, AZERI, AND AZERBAIJANIS.
§5. THE STRIKING SIMILARITIES BETWEEN THE GERMANIC AND TURKIC PEOPLES.

CHAPTER III.
§1. THE TATARS AND THE MONGOLS ARE CLOSELY RELATED TO EACH OTHER TURKIC NATIONS.
§2. THE GENETIC RESEARCH THAT ESTABLISHED THE TURKIC FOREFATHER OF A BILLION HUMANS WORLDWIDE.

CHAPTER IV.
§1. THE MEDES AND MEDIA.
§2. THE TURKIC NAMES OF THE MEDIAN CITIES WITH THE CAPITAL OF MEDIA – AKBATANA.
§3. THE NATIONS AND TRIBES OF MEDIA.
§4. THE TURKIC NAMES OF THE MEDES.
§5. THE MEDIAN LANGUAGE OF TURKIC ORIGIN – THE ANALYSIS BASED ON THE BEHISTUN INSCRIPTION.
§6. 65 GRAMMATICAL POINTERS, ATTESTING THAT MEDIAN WAS A TURKIC LANGUAGE.

CHAPTER V.
§1. THE SCYTHIANS AND SCYTHIAN TRIBES.
§2. THE PRIMARY SCYTHIAN TRIBES, LOCATED IN SCYTHIA.
§3. THE AS TRIBE AND ITS DERIVATIVES.
§4. THE SACAI AND THEIR DERIVATIVE TRIBES.
§5. THE PARTHIANS, THE BACTRIANS, AND THEIR SUBSIDIARY TRIBES.
§6. THE HUN, AKA THE KHOUNOI.
§7. THE SARMATAI AND THE SARMATIAN TRIBES, INCLUDING THE TURCAE.
§8. THE GETAI FAMILY.
§9. THE CELTS, THE GAULS, THE IBERIANS, AND THE GERMANIC TRIBES.
§9-1. THE CELTIC, THE IBERIAN, THE KELTO-SCYTHIAN TRIBES AND NATIONS.

§9-2. THE GAULS, AKA THE GALLIAE, AKA THE GALLI.
§9-3. THE GERMANIC TRIBES.
§10. THE THRACIANS.

BIBLIOGRAPHY

VOLUME 2.

§11. THE TROJAN NATIONS.	2
§11-1. THE DARDANII AND THE ILLYRIAN TRIBES.	8
§11-2. THE TEUCRI, OR THE TEUCRIANS, AND THEIR DERIVATIVES.	15
§11-3. THE LELEGES AND THEIR DERIVATIVES.	20
§11-3-1. 45 GRAMMATICAL POINTERS, ATTESTING THAT ETRUSCAN WAS A TURKIC LANGUAGE.	66
§11-4. THE PHRYGIANS AND THEIR DERIVATIVE TRIBES.	78
§11-4-1. THE LEXICO-GRAMMATICAL SIMILARITIES BETWEEN THE PHRYGIAN AND THE TURKIC LANGUAGES.	80
§11-4-2. 37 GRAMMATICAL POINTERS, ATTESTING THAT PHRYGIAN WAS A TURKIC LANGUAGE.	121
§11-4-3. THE PHRYGIAN TRIBES: THE BERECYNTES, CERBESII, PELOPONNESIANS, DORIANS, LEUCADIANS, LACEDEMONIANS, ARMENIANS.	134
§11-5. THE PELASGI AND THEIR POSTERITY.	172
§11-5.1. PELASGIAN CITIES AND DISTRICTS.	232
§11-5.2. PELASGIAN ORIGINS OF THESEUS, HERCULES, ACHILLES, AND ALEXANDER THE GREAT.	237
§11-5-3. PELASGIAN MYTHOLOGY AND PANTHEON OF GODS.	244
§11-5-4. THE TURKIC WORD TATAR, OR TARTAR, USED BY THE GREEKS, ROMANS, HITTITES, ARMENIANS.	255
§11-6. THE SOLYMI, MILYAE, TERMILAE, LYCIANS, XANTHIOI, APHNEII.	263
§11-7. THE PAPHLAGONIANS, CAUCONIANS, MARIANDYNI, LIGUES, MATIENOI, CAPPADOCIANS, HENETI.	266
§11-8. THE HALIZONES, CHALYBES, ARMENOCHALYBES, AMAZONES.	273
§11-9. THE CILICIANS, OR HYPACHAEANS, TRACHEIOTAE, PISIDIANS, SELGEIS, SAGALASSEIS, CLITAE.	278
§11-10. MITOCHONDRIAL DNA DATA CONNECT THE TROJANS, THE SCYTHIANS, THE ETRUSCANS, THE TURRENIANS, THE PELASGIANS TO THE TURKIC NATIONS.	284

CHAPTER VI.

THE ANCIENT TURKIC ALPHABET AND ITS CLOSE SIMILARITY TO THE PELASGIAN, LYDIAN, LYCIAN, PHRYGIAN, CARIAN, ETRUSCAN/TURRENIAN, SCYTHIAN SCRIPTS.	288

CHAPTER VII.

§1. THE ANCIENT TURKIC TAMGAS.	315
§2. THE POLITICAL TAMGAS, INDICATING STATEHOOD, LEVEL OF INDEPENDENCE OF A STATE, AND ITS SUBJECTS.	323
§3. THE RELIGIOUS TAMGAS, INDICATING MYSTICAL, MAGICAL, SPIRITUAL SIGNS.	325
§4. THE TAMGAS, INDICATING MILITARY AND STATE ATTRIBUTES.	331
§5. THE TAMGAS, REPRESENTING NATURE AND ANIMALS.	335

CHAPTER VIII.

§1. THE TURKIC NATIONS IN THE AMERICAS.	340

§2. THE NAMES OF THE NATIVE AMERICAN TRIBES THAT HAVE A TURKIC ORIGIN.	344
§3. RELIGION AND THE KURGAN BUILDING CULTURE OF THE NATIVE AMERICANS.	355
§4. THE GEOGRAPHICAL NAMES OF THE TURKIC ORIGIN IN THE AMERICAS.	356
§5. THE TURKIC ETYMOLOGY OF THE MAYAN VOCABULARY.	360
§6. THE NATIVE AMERICAN WORDS OF TURKIC ORIGIN.	362
§7. THE TURKIC TAMGAS, PETROGLYPHS AND NATIVE AMERICAN ARTIFACTS.	364
BIBLIOGRAPHY	378

Despite of many years, countless hours of research and development, significant financial injections from private sources, and in an effort to continue a glorious tradition of the ancient scholars who did not charge for their works, this book is offered free to make the information accessible to everyone. As some platforms do not allow free distribution, any proceeds from the sale of the book will be given to charity.

"The Central Intelligence Agency has not approved or endorsed the contents of this publication."

The Turkic alphabet.

TURKIC LETTER	ENGLISH SOUND AND EXAMPLE
A a	[ɑ] **A**rm
B b	[b] **B**oy
C c	[dʒ] **J**ohn
Ç ç	[tʃ] **Ch**ild
D d	[d] **D**awn
E e	[ɛ] **E**dward
Ə ə	[æ] **A**pple
F f	[f] **F**ire
G g	[gʲ] **G**uess
Ğ ğ	[ɣ] doesn't exist in English. Similar to **R** in French as in Pa**r**don.
H h	[h] **H**ot
X x	[kʰ] doesn't exist in English. Similar to German **Ch** as in Da**ch** or Russian **X** as in **Х**олод.
I ı	[ɨ] doesn't exist in English. Similar to Russian **Ы**, which is a retracted variety of [i] pronounced with the root of the tongue blocking the throat, as in **Ы**ргак.
İ i	[i] S**i**t
J j	[ʒ] Dé**j**à vu
K k	[k] **K**ite
Q q	[g] **G**oal
L l	[l] **L**emon
M m	[m] **M**other
N n	[n] **N**ice
Ŋ ŋ	[ŋ] Meeti**ng**
O o	[o] **O**racle
Ö ö	[ø:] B**ir**d
P p	[p] **P**lum
R r	[r] **R**un
S s	[s] **S**on
Ş ş	[ʃ] **Sh**ow
T t	[t] Time
U u	[u] P**u**t
Ü ü	[y:] does not exist in English. Similar to German K**ü**che.
V v	[v] **V**ictory
Y y	[j] **Y**ellow
Z z	[z] **Z**ebra

§ 11. The Trojan nations.

There was a fascinating nation of antiquity that rose to stardom and, due to the legendary poet *Homer*, got etched in the minds and hearts of the past and present generations of humanity. It was the nation of the *Trojans*, the natives of the kingdom *Troy* – "drawn from the high blood of Heaven", as called them *Virgil* [5.56].

Sadly, most of the modern world either does not know who these *Trojans* were or erroneously thinks that they were the *Greeks*. Only a small fraction of the academic world accepted the truth – the people of *Troy* were the ancestors of modern *Turkic* nations, in general, and *Turkish*, in particular. The name *Troy*, or as the *Greeks* called it *Troia* (Τροία), is of *Turkic* origin. It comprises of two elements:

Tr > *Tur* '1.powerful, eternal; 2.*Tur* – a male name' + *Oi* > *Öi* 'home', meaning "powerful home" or "house of *Tur*" in *Turkic*.

Tur, aka *Tros* (Τρώς), aka *Turos*, was a great-grandson of *Zeus*, after whom the land of *Troy* and its people *Trojans* acquired their names. His name means "powerful leader" in *Turkic* (*Tr* > *Tur* 'powerful; eternal' + *Os* > *Us* 'chief, master').

The legendary *Homer* in "The Iliad" announced the genealogy of *Tros's* family presented directly by the offspring of this *Trojan* dynasty – *Aeneas*:

> "In the beginning *Dardanos* was the son of *Zeus*, and founded *Dardania*, for *Ilion* was not yet established on the plain for men to dwell in, and her people still abode on the spurs of many-fountained *Ida*. *Dardanus* had a son, king *Erichthonius*, who was wealthiest of all men living...*Erichthonius* begat *Tros*, king of the *Trojans*, and *Tros* had three noble sons, *Ilos*, *Assaracos*, and *Ganymede* who was comeliest of mortal men; wherefore the gods carried him off to be *Zeus's* cupbearer, for his beauty's sake, that he might dwell among the immortals. *Ilos* begat *Laomedon*, and *Laomedon* begat *Tithonos*, *Priam*, *Lampos*, *Klytios*, and *Hiketaon* of the stock of *Ares*. But *Assaracos* was father to *Kapys*, and *Kapys* to *Anchises*, who was my father, while *Hektor* is son to *Priam*." [2.20.199-339]

The biblical sources also mentioned *Tur*, aka *Tros*, aka *Turos*, as *Tiras*, the youngest son of prophet *Japheth*, known among the *Turkic* nations as *Turk*. ["The Book of Genesis." 10.2] The *Jewish* intellectual *Flavius Josephus* identified *Thiras* as the progenitor of the *Thracians*, from which the *Trojan* nations, with their kinship to the *Scythians* and the *Medes*, were derived:

> "*Thiras* also called those whom he ruled over *Thirasians*, but the *Greeks* changed the name into *Thracians*..." ["The Genuine Works of *Flavius Josephus* the *Jewish* Historian." 1.6.1]

The name *Tur* ("1.nation of the *Turs*, *Turks*; 2.eternal; 3.powerful; 4.ascending") is a very ancient *Turkic* name that has been in use, primarily, as a component of the archaic male and female names by the *Turkic* nations of the past and the present:

- ❖ *Turalp* "eternal hero", "powerful hero", "*Turkic* hero" (*Tur* + *Alp* 'hero').
- ❖ *Turbay*, *Turbəy* "eternal noble", "powerful noble" (*Tur* + *Bay*, *Bəy* 'noble').
- ❖ *Turel* "1.nation of the *Turs*, *Turks*; 2.eternal nation; 3.powerful nation" (*Tur* + *El* 'nation').
- ❖ *Turğay*, *Turqay* "eternally great", "great *Tur* or *Turk*" (*Tur* + *Ğay*, *Qay* 'great'). *Qay* was the first part in the name of *Gaius Julius Caesar*. This is a male name.
- ❖ *Turğayə*, *Turqayə* "eternally great", "great *Tur* or *Turk*". It is a female name.
- ❖ *Turxan* "1.ruler of the country of the *Turs*; 2.King *Tur*; 3.eternal or powerful king" (*Tur* + *Xan* 'ruler, king, khan').

- *Turqut* "1.eternal happiness; 2.eternal spirit" (*Tur* + *Qut* '1.happiness; 2.spirit"). The *Germanic* nation of the *Goths* derived their name from this *Turkic* word *Qut*.
- *Turay* "ascending Moon" (*Tur* 'ascending' + *Ay* 'Moon'). This is a male name.
- *Turayə* "ascending Moon". This one is a female name.
- *Bağatur* "a royal *Tur* or *Turk*" (*Bağa* 'high dignity' + *Tur*).
- *Batur* "1.a royal *Tur*; 2.a hero". This is a shortened version of *Bağatur*.
- *Turgeş* "a *Tur* man", "a *Turkic* man" (*Tur* '*Turkic*' + *Geş* 'man'). This was both a personal name and the name of the ancient *Turkic* tribe.
- *Turğan* "1.from the *Turs*' blood; 2.of *Turkic* blood" (*Tur* + *Ğan* 'blood'). It was both a personal name and the name of a *Turkic* tribe.
- *Turan* "1.the land of the *Turs*; 2.the *Turs*". This name was in use both by males and females. *Turan* was also the name of the *Turkic* country in *Central Asia*.
- *Turk, Türk* "1.we are the *Turs*; 2.we are powerful; 3.we are eternal" (*Tur* + *-K* (*-Ük*) 'an affix, equivalent to the *English* words *We Are*').

"Drevneturkskiy slovar" and "Opit slovaria turkskikh narechiy" by *Radlov V.V.* provided a number of ancient *Turkic* personal names and ethnonyms that contained the name *Tur*, such as *Tura Tutuq, Turçı, Turçı Baqşı, Yigin Alp Turan*.

This very name *Tur* was a core component in the name of the founder (*Turrenos* = Τυρρηνός,) of a *Trojan* nation – the *Turrenoi* (Τυρρηνοί), as well as a country he established in *Italy* – *Turrenia* (Τυρρηνία):

- *Turrenos*: *Tur* + *En* > *-An* 'a *Turkic* affix, indicating plurality' + *Os* > *Us* 'chief', meaning "head of the *Turs*" in *Turkic*.
- *Turrenoi*: *Tur* + *En* > *-An* 'a *Turkic* affix, indicating plurality' + *-Oi* 'a *Greek* ending', meaning "the *Turs*", "the *Turks*".

Strabo gave an interesting account about the creation of the *Turrenian* or *Tyrrhenian* state and nation:

> "The *Tyrrheni* have now received from the *Romans* the surname of *Etrusci* and *Tusci*. The *Greeks* thus named them from *Tyrrhenus* the son of *Atys,* as they say, who sent hither a colony from *Lydia. Atys,* who was one of the descendants of *Hercules* and *Omphale*, and had two sons, in a time of famine and scarcity determined by lot that *Lydus* should remain in the country, but that *Tyrrhenus,* with the greater part of the people, should depart. Arriving here, he named the country after himself, *Tyrrhenia,* and founded twelve cities, having appointed as their governor *Tarcon*,[1] from whom the city of *Tarquinia* [received its name], and who, on account of the sagacity which he had displayed from childhood, was feigned to have been born with hoary hair. Placed originally under one authority, they became flourishing; but it seems that in after-times, their confederation being broken up and each city separated, they yielded to the violence of the neighbouring tribes. Otherwise they would never have abandoned a fertile country for a life of piracy on the sea, roving from one ocean to another; since, when united they were able not only to repel those who assailed them, but to act on the offensive, and undertake long campaigns. After the foundation of *Rome, Demaratus* arrived here, bringing with him people from *Corinth*. He was received at *Tarquinia,* where he had a son, named *Lucumo,* by a woman of that country. *Lucumo* becoming the friend of *Ancus Marcius,* king of the *Romans,* succeeded him on the throne, and assumed the name of *Lucius Tarquinius Priscus*. Both he and his father did much for the embellishment of *Tyrrhenia,* the one by means of the numerous artists who had followed him from their native country; the other having the resources of *Rome*. It is said that the triumphal costume of the consuls, as well as that of the other magistrates, was introduced from the

---

[1] The name *Tarcon* or *Tarcan* is of *Turkic* origin, meaning "governor, ruler".

Tarquinii, with the fasces, axes, trumpets, sacrifices, divination, and music employed by the *Romans* in their public ceremonies. His son, the second *Tarquin*, named *Superbus*, who was driven from his throne, was the last king [of *Rome*]." [5.2.2.-5.2.3]

It took hundreds of years for the *Turs*, or ancient *Trojans* and *Turrenoi*, to reclaim their native land, once taken from them – known nowadays as *Turkey*.

It was the second and last time in the history of the world when the formidable *Roman Empire* was brought to its knees by a nation of *Turkic* extraction, after the *Hun* and the *Goths*. This time, it was the *Byzantine Empire* with its capital *Constantinople*, modern-day *Istanbul*, conquered by a 21-year-old young *Turkish* sultan *Mehmed the Conqueror*, or *Mehmed II*. He brought to an end this Eastern *Roman Empire* in 1453, established the *Ottoman Empire*, and added the title *Caesar* to his other titles. "We do not conquer the lands. We conquer the hearts", he memorably said. He restored the Ecumenical Orthodox Patriarchate and established a *Jewish* Grand Rabbinate and *Armenian* Patriarchate of Constantinople in the capital to prove his words. Considering himself and his *Turkish* people as the descendants of the *Trojans*, sultan *Mehmed II* said: "After the passage of so many years, God appointed me to be the avenger of this city, of its inhabitants…" Another *Turkish* statesman, the founder of modern *Turkey* – *Mustafa Kemal Ataturk*, was reported to say: "Now, we have taken revenge for *Hector*" after winning the *Greco-Turkish* War of 1919-1922.

The fact that the people of *Troy* were ancient *Turks* was attested by the 800-year-old, highly esteemed *Icelandic* saga "The Prose *Edda*." This artistic tribute to the heavenly entity *Odin* and his nation from *Turkland* affirms:

> "Near the earth's centre was made that goodliest of homes and haunts that ever have been, which is called *Troy*, even that which we call *Turkland*." [Prologue. 3]

To further confirm that the people of *Troy* were the *Turks*, the *Icelandic* saga narrates about the *Turkic* order of the society, established by *God Odin* in *Europe*:

> "There he established chieftains in the fashion, which had prevailed in *Troy*…" [Prologue. 5]

There are various scholars who claimed that the story about *Troy* and the *Trojans*, written by *Homer*, was nothing but just a myth. However, *Strabo*, invoking *Herodotus*, asserted that not only the *Trojans* did exist in history, but they also branched out into 8 or 9 main divisions:

> "The poet implies that it was the *Trojans* chiefly who were divided into eight or even nine bodies of people, each forming a petty princedom, who had under their sway the places about *Aesepus*, and those about the territory of the present *Cyzicene*, as far as the river *Caïcus*…That *Priam* was king of all these countries the words with which *Achilles* addresses him clearly show: "We have heard, old man, that your riches formerly consisted in what *Lesbos*, the city of *Macar*, contained, and *Phrygia* above it and the vast *Hellespont*."" [13.1.7]

However, with due respect to *Strabo*, *Homer* did not imply that the *Trojans* were partitioned into 8 or 9 derivative groups. In book 2 of "The Iliad", *Homer* enumerated exactly 12 principal *Trojan* nations, comprising a large *Trojan* confederation: *Dardanians*, aka *Dardanii*, *Lycians*, *Mysians*, *Cilicians*, *Paeonians*, *Paphlagonians*, *Halizones*, *Phrygians*, *Maeonians*, *Carians*, *Thracians*, *Ciconians*, *Pelasgi*. Meanwhile, *Strabo* confirmed that the designation *Trojan* applied to all the confederates:

> "Even the people, who in the Catalogue are said to be commanded by *Hector*, are called *Trojans*; "*Hector*, the mighty, with the nodding crest, commanded the *Trojans*"…" [13.1.7]

The *Icelandic* saga "The Prose *Edda*" by *Sturluson* also corroborates the existence of 12 rulers of *Troy*:

> "There he established chieftains in the fashion which had prevailed in *Troy;* he set up also twelve head-men to be doomsmen over the people and to judge the laws of the land; and he ordained also all laws as there had been before in *Troy,* and according to the customs of the *Turks.*"
> [Prologue. 5]

While taking into consideration all these 12 *Trojan* nations, depicted by *Homer,* as well as the post-*Homeric* development of these nations of *Troy,* a need emerges to enumerate their derivatives as well. With that goal in mind, we present a new classification of the *Trojan* nations, provided below, based on the knowledge of the ancient *Greek* and *Latin* authors, including *Homer, Strabo, Euripides, Ovid,* and others.

The Trojan nations.

1. *Dardanii = Dardanians* ⟷ *Illyrians*

Autariatai; Autarieis; Taulantioi; Perraiboi; Enchelees; Parthenoi; Dassaretioi; Darsioi; Ardiaioi; Palarioi; Skordiskoi; Triballi; Atintanoi; Mædi = Maidoi = Arioi = Arians; Istroi; Liburnoi; Dalmatai = Dalmates = Dalmatian

2. *Teucri = Teucrians* ⟷ *Pelasgi; Thracians*

Pæonians = Paiones = Pannonioi   *Cicones = Ciconians*   *Gergithes*

Siriopaiones; Paioplai; Doberes; Agrianes

3. *Leleges* ⟷ *Pelasgi*

Carians = Kares   *Meones*   *Locri = Lokroi*

Mysians = Musoi ⟷ *Getae; Thracians; Olympians;*   *Locri Epicnemidii;*
Thyni; Bithynians = Bithyni;   *Locri Narycii;*
Olympeni = Hellespontii   *Locri Epizephyrii;*
Kabelees = Lasonoi   *Locri Opuntii;*
Ozolian Locri;
Lydians = Ludoi   *Amphisseian Locri;*
Locri Thronium

Asii = Asioi ⇔ *Scythians*   *Turreni = Turrenoi*

Asmanoi; Asiotai; Attasioi;   *Troskoi; Etrusci; Etrurians; Touskoi = Tusci;*
Aspisioi Skythai; Asiades;   *Rasenna; Raeti = Raitoi*
Auseis; Assyrani; Asturoi;
Ausigdoi; Astelebaioi;
Auskhitai = Auskhisai;
Lankiatoi; Brigaikinoi;
Bedounisioi; Orniakoi;

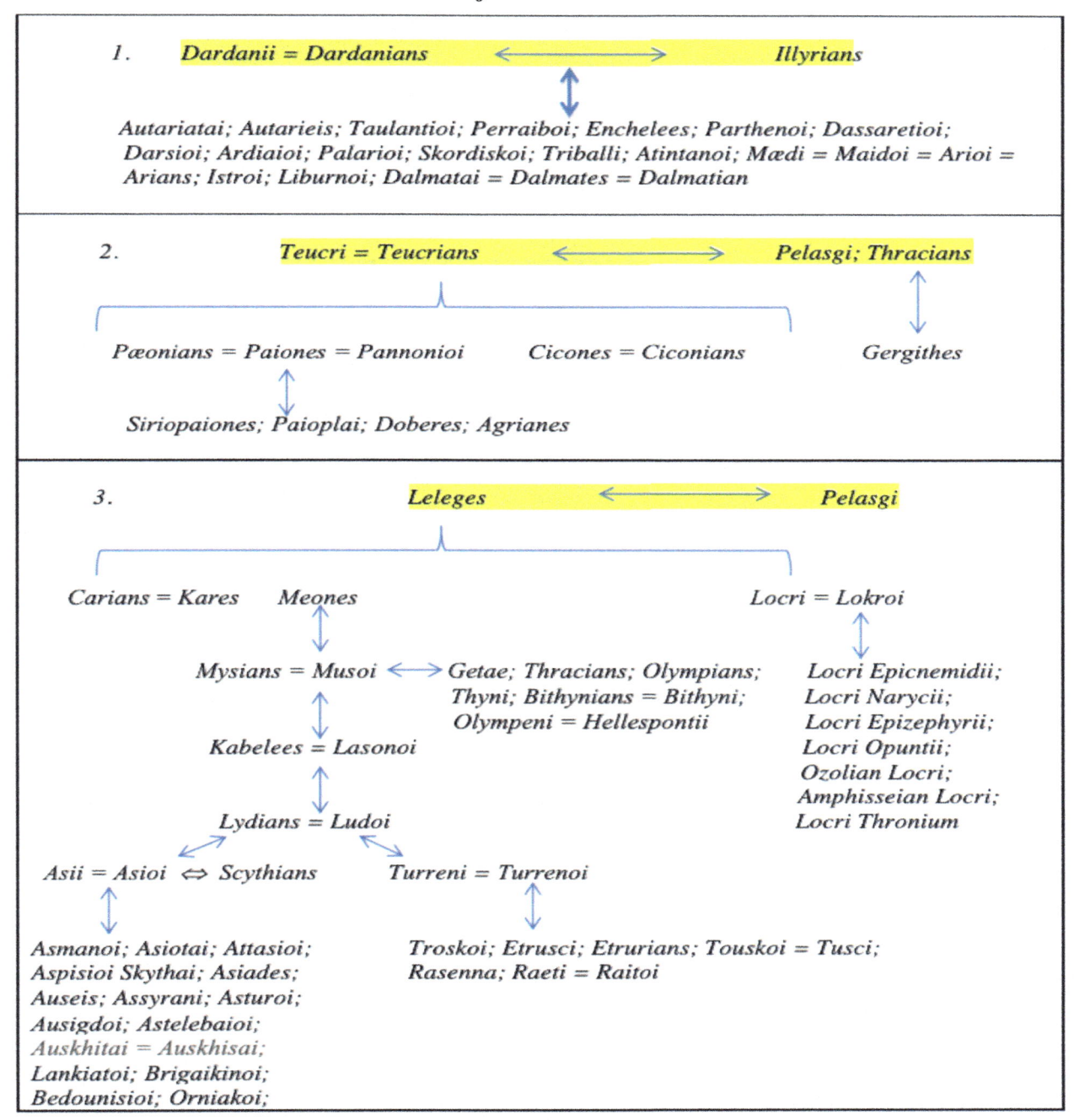

Loungonoi; Sailinoi;
Souperatioi; Amakoi;
Teibouroi; Egourroi;
Gigourroi; Pesici;
Lancieses; Zoelae;
Libyan Auseis = Maxyes = Maxytani = Mazax = Amaziq;
Tuareg = Tuaryk; Aghadez; Tagazi; Tibbo

---

4. ==*Phrygians = Fruks = Brugoi = Bruges = Briges* ⟵⟶ *Thracians; Pelasgi*==

Berecyntes;   *Peloponnesians* ⇔ *Dorians*   *Armenians* (not modern *Armenians*)
Cerbesii
                          ↕
           Leucadians; Lacedaemonians, aka *Spartans;*
                          Argives

---

5.   ==*Pelasgi*==

Peloponnesians, *Dorians* →	→ *Argives* + *Eginetans* + *Spartans, Lacedaemonians* ↓ *Mycenaeans* + *Danaans* + *Heracleidae* → *Rhodians* + *Oenotrians* → *Italians; Sicels; Morgetes; Chones* + *Achaeans* → *Crotonians; Placians; Sybarites* *Æolians; Tarantini; Melians; Minyai; Sabini* *Boeotians; Phocians; Magnetes* *Claudi; Hernici; Marsi; Marrucini; Picentes; Sabelli; Vestini; Peligni; Samnites* ↙↘ *Hirpini; Leucani; Bruttii; Frentani*
Phrygians, *Thessalians*	→ *Armenians* + *Caucasian Albanians* + *Pheraeans* + *Iberians* (not modern *Armenians*) *Caucasian Iberians* ↓ *Scythians* *Western Iberians* ↓ *Ibersi*
Arcadians	→ *Orchomenians*

Ionians	Athenians = Cranian Pelasgians = Cecropians = Attikoi = Ægialeans; Eretrians; Keïans; Chians; Naxians; Siphnians; Seriphians; Cynurians; Islanders; Hellespontii
Tyrrheni	Turrenoi; Tursenoi; Troskoi; Etrusci; Etrurians; Touskoi = Tusci; Rasenna; Raeti
Curetes	Cretans

6. **Solymi = Solumoi**

Milyae ⇔ Termilae ⇔ Lukioi = Lycians ⇔ Aphneioi = Aphneian Trojans ⇔ Xanthioi
                                                                                             Scythians Thracians

7. **Paphlagonians** ⟷ **Thracians**

Caucones; Mariandyni;   Heneti = Veneti
Cappadocians = Leucosyri;
Ligues; Matienoi
                                        Medes   Galatians = Galatai

8. **Halizones = Alizones** ⟶ Scythians

Alazones; Amazones; Alubes = Khalubes; Chaldeans

Armenochalybes

9. **Cilicians**

Hypachaeans + Clitae + Pisidians ⟶ Selgeis; Sagalasseis

7

§11-1. THE DARDANII AND THE ILLYRIAN TRIBES.

The *Dardanians*, called by the *Latins* the *Dardanii* and known amongst the *Greeks* as the *Dardanoi*, were the first *Trojan* nation mentioned by *Homer* when enumerating the *Trojan* forces against the *Greeks*. It is important to note that they were not just allies to the people of *Troy*. They were related to the *Trojans* by blood as well, in the opinion of *Strabo*:

> "…then those under *Æneas,*
> the brave son of *Anchises* had the command of the *Dardanii,*
> and these were *Trojans,* for the poet says,
> "Thou, *Æneas,* that counsellest *Trojans*"…" [13.1.7]

The beautiful goddess of love *Aphrodite,* or *Venus* – daughter of *Zeus,* who favored the *Trojans,* was the mother of *Aeneas,* the commander of the *Dardanii,* as claimed by *Homer:*

> "The *Dardanians* were led by brave *Aeneas,* whom *Venus* bore to *Anchises,* when she, goddess though she was, had lain with him upon the mountain slopes of *Ida.*" [2.2.800-839]

In addition to the *Asian Dardanii,* who lived in *Asia Minor,* there were also the *European Dardani,* from whom, according to *Procopius,* the famous *Emperor* of *Byzantine Justinian* took his origin ["On the Buildings." 4.1.17]. *Pliny the Elder* located the *Dardanii* in *Moesia,* while *Ptolemy* was more precise by placing them in *Upper Moesia* [3.9]:

> "Joining up to *Pannonia* is the province called *Mœsia,* which runs, with the course of the *Danube,* as far as the *Euxine.* It commences at the confluence previously mentioned. In it are the *Dardani,* the *Celegeri,* the *Triballi,* the *Timachi,* the *Mœsi,* the *Thracians,* and the *Scythians* who border on the *Euxine.*" [*Pliny the Elder.* "The Natural History." 3.29(26)]

Strabo characterized the *Dardanii* as ferocious yet very artistic people:

> "The *Dardanii* are entirely a savage people, so much so that they dig caves beneath dung heaps, in which they dwell; yet they are fond of music, and are much occupied in playing upon pipes and on stringed instruments." [7.5.7]

Homer described the *Dardanii* as a war-like nation - "*Dardanians,* fighters in close combat" [17.184], and king *Priam* as a "son of *Dardanus*" [11.165], an "offspring of *Dardanus*" [24.171].
 As it was believed, *Dardanus, Zeus's* son by the *Pleiad Electra,* a native of *Arcadian Pheneus,* was the ancestor of the *Trojan* people. Hence, the name of the *Dardanii* originated from their founding father, *Dardanus.* On the same note, a *Greek* historian, who lived between 60 to 30 BCE, *Diodorus Siculus,* aka *Diodorus of Sicily,* in his "Library of History" pointed out that *Dardanus* was the king of the *Scythians:*

> "…for *Phineus* having married (besides his former wife) *Idea* the daughter of *Dardanus* king of *Scythia,* was so enslaved by an inordinate affection to her, that he humoured her in everything that she required…" [4.3]

Though the king of *Scythians* and the founder of the *Dardanians* were two different persons, the name *Dardanus* carried by both, pointed to their common *Scythian* ancestry. The name can easily be deduced from the *Turkic* source:

Dardanus, aka *Dardanos* = Δάρδανος: *Dar* > *Dər* 'amass' + *Dan* 'glory, fame' + *Os* > *Us* 'master', meaning "ruler who garnered glory" in *Turkic*.

By the way, the *Dardanelle* strait, known among the *Greeks* as the *Hellespont,* got its name after the fabled *Trojan Dardanos.*

According to *Diodorus Siculus, Dardanus* was the first to cross in a hand-made boat from the *Samothrace* Island to the land in *Asia Minor* (modern *Turkey),* where he established a city, then kingdom with the people – all named after him:

"Afterwards one *Saon,* an islander, the son, (as some say), of *Jupiter* and *Nympha,* but (as others, of *Mercury* and *Rhena*), gathered the inhabitants (before living scattered and dispersed) into a body; and made laws for their better government, and divided them into five tribes, calling them after the names of his sons, but named himself *Saon,* after the name of the island. The government being thus settled, it is said, that *Dardanus, Jasion,* and *Harmonia,* the children of *Jupiter* and *Electra,* one of the daughters of *Atlas,* were born among them. Of these, *Dardanus,* (being a bold and brave spirited man) passed over in a pinnace into *Asia,* and first built the city *Dardanus,* and erected the kingdom of *Troy,* (so called, from *Troy* built afterwards), and called the people *Dardanians*. He reigned, they say, over many other nations besides in *Asia* and that the *Dardanians* above *Thrace,* were a colony settled there by him." [5.3]

On the word of *St. Jerome,* the city of *Dardanus,* or *Dardania,* was founded by *Dardanus* in 1477 BCE. The ancient *Roman* poet *Virgil,* or *Publius Vergilius Maro,* corrected *Diodorus Siculus* by stating that *Dardanus* initially was from the shores of *Tuscany,* and from there he moved to *Phrygia,* then to *Thracian Samos,* or *Samothrace,* with the final destination at the *Trojan* coast:

"And now my mind recals, (thou lapse of time
Obscures the tale,) th' *Aurunean* Elders told
How *Dardanus,* in these our regions born,
To *Phrygian Ida's* cities urg'd his way,
And *Thracian Samos,* now call'd *Samothrace.*
He, from his *Tuscan* seat in *Corythus*
Hence gone, in the gold courts of starry Heav'n
Sits thron'd, and, while his altars here on earth
Arise, there swells the number of the Gods." [7.271-279]

This means that the *Trojans* initially hailed from the land known later as *Turrenia,* or *Tyrrhenia,* currently *Tuscany* in *Italy*. In his epic poem "The *Aeneid*", *Ovid* explained why the people of *Troy,* including the *Dardanii,* chose the country, known today as *Italy,* as their new place of habitation after they left *Troy:*

"There is a place by *Greeks Hesperia* call'd,
An ancient land, martial, and rich in glebe;
Th' *Oenotrians* till'd the soil; but rumour tells
The region they in younger ages born
Have stil'd *Italia* from their leader's name.
These are our destin'd seats; hence *Dardanus,*
And hence the Sire *Iasius* sprung, that Prince
From whom our lineage comes." [3.238-245]

Based on this assertion of the ancient man of letters, an inference emerges to the surface that the *Turkic* nation of *Troy* was the autochthonous native of the *Italian* land long before a younger race – the *Italians* arrived there.

Ovid in *"Fasti"* went even further and presented a detailed lineage of the founders of *Rome* – *Romulus* and *Remus* that proved the unexpected. They had a *Trojan* origin. *Turkic* blood reigned in the veins of the *Roman* founders, as well as in many famous *Roman* emperors, such as *Julius Caesar*:

> "...*Dardanus'* was born of *Electra*, the daughter of *Atlas*? And that *Electra* shared the bed of *Jove*? His son was *Ericthonius*; from him *Tros* sprung: he was the father of *Assaracus*, *Assaracus* of *Capys*. This last begot *Anchises*, with whom, *Venus* did not disdain to hold the name of parent in common. Hence was born *Æneas*; his piety well proved, bore the sacred relics and his father sitting on his shoulders, a second pious charge, through the flames of *Troy*. At length we have arrived at the blessed name of *Iülus*, from which point the *Julian* house is connected with its *Trojan* ancestors.
>
> His son was *Postumus*, who, because he was born in the deep sylvan shades, was called *Silvius*, among the *Latian* nation. And he, *Latinus*, is thy sire; *Alba* succeeds *Latinus*, *Epytus* succeeds to thy dignity, O *Alba*. He gave to *Capys* the revived name of *Troy*; he, too, became thy grandsire, O *Calpetus*. And while, in succession to him, *Tiberinus* was occupying the throne of his father, he is said to have been drowned in the eddy of the *Etrurian* stream. And yet he had lived to see *Agrippa*, his son, and *Remulus*, his grandson. They say that against *Remulus* the thunderbolts were hurled. After these came *Aventinus*, from whom the place and the hill, too, derived its name. After him the sovereignty passed to *Procas*; him *Numitor* followed, the brother of the cruel *Amulius*; *Ilia* and *Lausus* were the children of *Numitor*. *Lausus* falls by his uncle's sword; *Ilia* is beloved by *Mars*, and produces thee, *Quirinus*, with *Remus*, thy twin brother."
> [Translated by *H.T. Riley*. 4.21-60]

To make this genealogy more digestible, it is better to demonstrate it as a scheme below:

Electra + *Jupiter*
↓
Dardanus – the founder of the Trojan nation
↓
Ericthonius
↓
Tros
↓
Assaracus of *Capys*
↓
Anchises + *Venus*
↓
Æneas
↓
Iülus – the Teucrian, or Trojan, founder of the house of Julius Caesar
↓
Postumus, aka *Silvius*
↓
Latinus
↓
Alba
↓
Epytus
↓
Capys
↓
Calpetus
↓
Tiberinus
↓
Agrippa
↓
Remulus
↓
Aventinus
↓
Procas
↓
Numitor
↓
Ilia + *Mars*
↓
Quirinus, aka *Romulus* and *Remus* – the founders of Rome, the twin brothers

The great *Latin* poet of 50-15 BCE, *Sextus Propertius* in "The Elegies" gave a perfect summary to this ancestry:

"…*Troia cades, et Troica Roma, resurges*…" [4.1.17]

"…*Troy* will fall, and *Trojan Rome* will rise!" [2]

Strabo classified the *Dardanii* as an *Illyrian* nation that had kin tribes: "the *Autariatæ, Ardiæi,* and *Dardanii,* among the *Illyrians*" [7.5.6]. Expectedly, the names of the *Dardanii* and cognate tribes reveal their *Turkic* breed:

➤ *Dardanii,* aka *Dardani,* aka *Dardanoi,* aka *Dardanians:* Dar > Dər 'amass' + Dan 'glory, fame', meaning "nation that builds up its glory" in *Turkic*.

➤ *Illyrian,* aka *Illurioi* = Ἰλλυριοί: Ill > İllə 'create confederation, union' + Uri > Uru 'tribe', meaning "create a union of tribes" in *Turkic*. According to *Appian*, the *Illyrians* obtained their name after their founder *Illyrius*, or *Illurios* (Ἰλλυριός: Ill > Illə 'create a union' + Uri > Uru 'tribe' + Os > Us 'chief', meaning "chief creator of the tribal union) – a son of the *Cyclops*. The author gave a rather interesting account about the origination of the tribal and country name, though not entirely sure of its authenticity:

"They say that the country received its name from *Illyrius*,[3] the son of *Polyphemus;* for the *Cyclops Polyphemus* and his wife, *Galatea,* had three sons, *Celtus, Illyrius,* and *Galas,* all of whom migrated from *Sicily;* and the nations called *Celts, Illyrians,* and *Galatians* took their origin from them. Among the many myths prevailing among many peoples this seems to me the most plausible. *Illyrius* had six sons, *Encheleus, Autarieus, Dardanus, Mœdus, Taulas,*[4] and *Perrhœbus,* also daughters, *Partho, Daortho, Dassaro,* and others, from whom sprang the *Taulantii,* the *Perrhœbi,* the *Enchelees,* the *Autarienses,* the *Dardani,* the *Partheni,* the *Dassaretii,* and the *Darsii. Autarieus* had a son *Pannonius,* or *Pæon,* and the latter had sons, *Scordiscus* and *Triballus,* from whom nations bearing similar names were derived. But I will leave these matters to the archæologists." ["*Illyrian* Wars." 3.1.2]

The story sounds healthy but contradicts the account provided by *Diodorus Siculus* about the *Celts* and the *Galatai,* insisting that they were born from *Hercules* [5.24], and opposes *Dardanus's* genealogy derived from *Zeus,* according to *Ovid*. However, in general, all three men of letters were right, as all the nations described by *Appian,* also known as the *Trojan, Germanic, Galatai, Celtic,* and alike peoples, were of *Scythian* extraction and related to each other.

According to *Appian,* the notion '*Illyrian*' was used as a common denominator of the inhabitants of *Illyria,* without proper attention to their kinship:

"These peoples, and also the *Pannonians,* the *Rhærtians,* the *Noricans,* the *Mysians of Europe,* and the other neighboring tribes who inhabited the right bank of the *Danube,* the *Romans* distinguished from one another just as the various *Greek* peoples are distinguished from each other, and they call each by its own name, but they consider the whole of *Illyria* as embraced under a common designation. Whence this idea took its start I have not been able to find out, but it continues to this day, for they farm the tax of all the nations from the source of the *Danube* to the *Euxine Sea* under one head, and call it the *Illyrian* tax." [3.1.6]

➤ *Autariatai* = Αὐταριάται: Autari > Autariei 'name of the founder of the tribe' (Aut > At 'horse' + Ari > Əri > Ər 'warrior' + -İ 'an affix of possession') + Atai 'father, patriarch', meaning "tribe of the patriarch *Autariei*" and "main tribe of the warrior horsemen" in *Turkic*. Though *Appian* did not indicate specifically *Autariei*, or *Autarieus,* as the eponymous father of the *Autariatai* by assigning

---
[2] The *Latin* text was translated into *English* by the author of the present work.
[3] In the original *Greek* text, it is *Illurios* = Ἰλλυριός.
[4] It should be *Taulanta* (Ταύλαντα in the original *Greek* text).

11

him only to the tribe of the *Autarieis*, it is obvious that this *Illyrian* tribe also acquired its name after the same founder.

The *Roman* writer *Justin* gave a short account about the *Autariatai* (incorrectly translated into *English* as *Antariatae*), who abandoned their country, overwhelmed by rodent infestation:

"During these transactions, *Cassander*, returning from *Apollonia*, fell in with the *Antariatae*, who, having abandoned their country on account of the vast number of frogs and mice that infested it, were seeking a settlement. Fearing that they might possess themselves of *Macedonia*, he made a compact with them, received them as allies, and assigned them lands at the extremity of the country." [15.2]

➢ *Autarieis* = Αὐταριεῖς: *Autari* > *Autariei* 'name of the founder of the tribe' (*Aut* > *At* 'horse' + *Ari* > *Əri* > *Ər* 'warrior' + *I* > *-İ* 'an affix of possession') + *Eis* > *İs* 'trace', meaning "remnants of *Autariei*" in *Turkic*. Judging by the name, it seems that the *Autarieis* and the *Autariatai* were leaves from the same branch. Compare:
  - *Autariatai*: *Aut* > *At* 'horse' + *Ari* > *Əri* 'warrior' + *Atai* 'father, patriarch'.
  - *Autarieis*: *Aut* > *At* 'horse' + *Ari* > *Əri* 'warrior' + *Eis* > *İs* 'trace'.

Appian depicted the *Autarieis* as impious people who got punished by *Apollo* for that sin:

"The *Autarienses*[5] were overtaken with destruction by the vengeance of *Apollo*. Having joined *Molostimus* and the *Celtic* people called *Cimbri* in an expedition against the temple of *Delphi*, the greater part of them were destroyed by storm, hurricane, and lightning just before the sacrilege was committed. Upon those who returned home there came a countless number of frogs, which filled the streams and polluted the water. The noxious vapors rising from the ground caused a plague among the *Illyrians* which was especially fatal to the *Autarienses*. At last they fled from their homes, and as the plague still clung to them (and for fear of it nobody would receive them), they came, after a journey of twenty-three days, to a marshy and uninhabited district of the *Getæ*, where they settled near the *Bastarnæ*." ["*Illyrian* Wars." 3.1.4]

➢ *Taulantii*, aka *Taulantioi* = Ταυλάντιοι > *Taulanta* = Ταύλαντα: *Taul* > *Taulı* 'fat, heavy' + *Anta* > *Endi* 'wide', meaning "heavy and wide-shouldered" in *Turkic*. As claimed by *Appian*, this *Illyrian* tribe was named after *Taulanta* (incorrectly transcribed as *Taulas*) – one of six sons of *Illyrius*. *Thucydides* characterized these people as barbarians:

"*Epidamnus* is a city situated on the right hand to such as enter into the *Ionian Gulf*. Bordering upon it are the *Taulantii*, barbarians, a people of *Illyris*." ["History of the *Peloponnesian* War."]

➢ *Perrhæbi*, aka *Perraiboi* = Περραιβοὶ > *Perraibon* = Περραιβὸν: *Perra* > *Pərü* 'gift, present' + *Ai* > *Aya* 'the best' + *Bon* > *Bən, Ben* 'I', meaning "I am the best gift" in *Turkic*. This *Illyrian* tribe was also created and named after its founding father *Perraibon* (incorrectly translated into *English* as *Perrhæbus*), son of *Illyrius*. However, the name of the tribe itself has a slightly different meaning: *Perrhæbi, Perraiboi*: *Perra* > *Pərü* 'gift, present' + *Ai* > *Aya* 'the best' + *Bi, Boi* > *Boi* 'tribe', meaning "tribe as the best gift" or "*Perraibon's* tribe" in *Turkic*.

➢ *Enchelees*, aka *Enkhelees* = Ἐγχέλεες > *Enkhelea* = Ἐγχέλεα: *En* > *Ən* 'most' + *Chel, Khel* > *Xal* 'power', meaning "the most powerful" in *Turkic*. This tribal name owes its origination to the founder *Enkhelea*, erroneously translated into *English* as *Encheleus*, a son of *Illyrius*, as stated by *Appian*.

➢ *Partheni*, aka *Parthenoi* = Παρθηνοὶ > *Partho* = Παρθὼ > *Pərtəv* "ray of light; light" in *Turkic*. This *Illyrian* tribe acquired the name of its female founder – *Partho*, a daughter of *Illyrius*, and means "house of *Partho*" (*Partheni, Parthenoi*: *Parth* > *Partho* + *En* 'house') in *Turkic*.

---

[5] In the original *Greek* text, it is *Autarieis* = Αὐταριεῖς.

➢ *Dassaretii,* aka *Dassaretioi* = *Δασσαρήτιοι* > *Dassaró* = *Δασσαρὼ*: *Das > Tasa* 'real' [6] + *Saró > Sará* 'power, might; bravery', meaning "real power" in *Turkic*. Another daughter of *Illyrius* – *Dassaró* was the founder of this *Illyrian* tribe, as claimed by *Appian*. The tribal name has the meaning "be powerful" (*Dassaretii, Dassaretioi: Das > Tasa* 'real' + *Saró > Sará* 'power, might; bravery' + *Et* 'make, create').

➢ *Darsii,* aka *Darsioi* = *Δάρσιοι* > *Daortho* = *Δαορθὼ*: *Da > Dəü* 'great' + *Ortho > Ört* 'fire', meaning "great fire" in *Turkic*. As asserted by *Appian*, this tribe also owes its appellation to its founding mother – *Daortho,* a daughter of *Illyrus*. However, the name of the tribe has a modified meaning – "tribe of *Daortho*" (*Darsii, Darsioi: Dar > Daortho + Sii, Soi > Soi* 'tribe') in *Turkic*.

➢ *Ardiaioi* = *Ἀρδιαῖοι,* aka *Ardiæi: Ardi > Arda* 'ruin, destroy' + *Ai, Aei > Ai* 'order', meaning "tribe that brings disorder" in *Turkic*. *Appian* mentioned this *Illyrian* tribe along with another kin tribe – the *Palarioi* in his work "The *Illyrian* Wars":

"The *Ardei* and the *Palarii,* two other *Illyrian* tribes, made a raid on *Roman Illyria,* and the *Romans,* being otherwise occupied, sent ambassadors to scare them." [3.2.10]

➢ *Palarioi* = *Παλάριοι,* aka *Palarii: Pal > Pəl* 'hill' + *Ari > Əri* 'man, warrior' (*Ər* 'warrior' + *-İ* 'an affix of possession'), meaning "warrior tribe of mountaineers" in *Turkic*. Another *Turkic* word – *Pal* "wildfowl," could also be used to provide the meaning of the tribal name. However, the first variant seems more suitable when considering a *Turkic* tribe with a similar name construction – *Suvari*. Compare:
- *Palarii: Pal* 'hill' + *Ari* 'man, warrior', meaning "mountain man".
- *Suvari: Suv* 'river' + *Ari* 'warrior, man', meaning "river man".

➢ *Scordiscoi,* aka *Skordiskoi* = *Σκορδίσκοι,* aka *Scordisci,* aka *Skordistes* = *Σκορδίστες*:
  o *Scordiscoi, Skordiskoi, Scordisci: Sc, Sk > Sık* 'packed, overcrowded' + *Ordi > Ordu* 'army' + *Isco > İskə* 'tear apart', meaning "tribe that tears apart a large army" in *Turkic*.
  o *Scordistes: Sc > Sık* 'packed, overcrowded' + *Ordi > Ordu* 'army' + *Istes > Eş Tuş* 'comrades' (*Is > Eş* 'brother-in-arms' + *Tes > Tuş = Taş* 'fellow'), meaning "fellow soldiers of a large army" or "*Skordiskon's* brothers in arms" in *Turkic*.

As reported by *Appian,* the *Scordiscoi* (and other variants of the name) were named after their founding father – *Skordiskon* (*Σκορδίσκον*), who was a great-great-grandson of the *Cyclops Polyphemus*. His name consists of the following *Turkic* words:

Skordiskon: Sk > Sık 'packed, overcrowded' + *Ordi > Ordu* 'army' + *Isk > İskə* 'tear apart' + *On > -Ən, -Yən* 'an affix, denoting constant action', meaning "the one who tears apart large armies" in *Turkic*.

Earlier, it was determined that the *Skordiskoi,* known also the *Scordisci, Scordistes,* were a *Kelto-Scythian* nation. The etymological analysis of the derivative names also proved their *Turkic* root. Their classification as an *Illyrian* tribe by *Appian* is a testament to the kinship of *Scythian, Celtic, Illyrian,* and *Trojan* nations.

➢ *Triballi,* aka *Triballoi* = *Τριβαλλοί*: *Tri > Tiri* 'agile' + *Balli, Balloi > Bəlli* 'powerful; distinguished', meaning "agile and powerful tribe" or "people of *Triballon*" in *Turkic*. Despite *Strabo,* who presented the *Triballi* as a *Thracian* tribe [7.5.6; 7.3.13], *Appian* considered them as an *Illyrian* tribe that obtained its name after *Triballon* (*Τριβαλλόν*) – a son of *Pannonion,* or *Pannonius,* or *Pæon,* who was a son of *Autariei,* who was a son of *Illyrius* and a grandson of the *Cyclops Polyphemus* [3.1.2]. The founding father's name originated from the *Turkic* roots:

---

[6] *Ashmarin N.I.* [13.225].

Triballon: Tri > Tırı 'agile' + *Ballon > Bəllən* 'be famous', meaning "the one famous for his agility" in *Turkic*.

➤ *Mœdi,* aka *Maidoi = Μαῖδοι,* aka *Medoi = Μῆδοι,* aka *Arioi = Ἄριοι,* aka *Arians:*
  o *Mœdi, Maidoi, Medoi > Matı* "wonderful" in *Turkic*.
  o *Arioi, Arians > Ar* "warrior, man, hero" in *Turkic*.
This was a colony of the *Medes,* introduced later as a *Thracian* nation by *Strabo* [7.5.7], closely related to the *Scythians,* and classified as the *Illyrian* people by *Appian:*
  "Such was the punishment which the god visited upon the *Illyrians* and the *Celts* for their impiety. But they did not desist from temple robbing, for again, in conjunction with the *Celts,* certain *Illyrian* tribes, especially the *Scordisci,* the *Mœdi,* and the *Dardani* again invaded *Macedonia* and *Greece* together, and plundered many temples, including that of *Delphi,* but losing many men this time also." [3.1.5]

➤ *Atintanoi = Ἀτιντανοί,* aka *Atintani: Atin > Atın* 'his/her name' (*At* 'name, glory' + *-In* 'an affix, denoting possession') + *Tan* 'reject', meaning "tribe careless about its glory" in *Turkic*. *Appian* presented this tribe as an *Illyrian* people:
  "While the *Romans* were engaged in a three years' war with the *Gauls* on the river *Po, Demetrius,* thinking that they had their hands full, set forth on a piratical expedition, brought the *Istrians,* another *Illyrian* tribe, into the enterprise, and detached the *Atintani* from *Rome*." [3.2.8]

➤ *Istroi = Ἴστροι,* aka *Istrians > Ister: Is > İs* 'trace' + *Ter > Törə* 'create', meaning "pathmaker" in *Turkic*. The *Istroi,* or the *Istrians,* obtained their name from the river *Ister* "pathmaker" – a *Thracian* appellation of the river *Danube*.

➤ *Dalmatai = Δαλμάται,* aka *Dalmates = Δαλμάτης,* aka *Delmateis = Δελματεῖς,* aka *Dalmatians:* *Dalm, Delm > Dəlim* 'many, much' + *At* 'glory', meaning 'tribe vast in its glory" in *Turkic*. According to *Appian,* the *Dalmates* acquired their name first as the *Delmateis* (incorrectly transcribed as *Delmatenses*) from the city *Delminion* (Δελμίνιον, translated into *English* as *Delminium*), aka *Dalminion* (Δαλμίνιον):
  "The *Dalmatians,* another *Illyrian* tribe, made an attack on the *Illyrian* subjects of *Rome,* and when ambassadors were sent to them to remonstrate they were not received...Nevertheless, he drove them into the city of *Delminium,* from which place they first got the name of *Delmatenses,* which was afterward changed to *Dalmatians*." [3.2.11]
The name of the city of *Delminion* (Δελμίνιον) translates as "many houses" in *Turkic* (*Delm > Dəlim* 'many, much' + *In > İn* 'house' + *Ion > -Ən* 'an affix of plurality'). Obviously, the city was famous for having many buildings in it.

➤ *Liburnoi = Λιβυρνοί: Lib > Lap* 'suddenly and a lot' + *Burn > Buran* 'emasculating' (*Bur* 'emasculate' + *-An* 'an affix, denoting constant action'), meaning "tribe that emasculates many foes" in *Turkic*. *Appian* mentioned this *Illyrian* tribe in his work "*Illyrian* Wars":
  "At the time when *Cæsar* held the command in *Gaul* these same *Dalmatians* and other *Illyrians,* who were then in a very prosperous condition, took the city of *Promona* from the *Liburni,* another *Illyrian* tribe." [3.3.12]

§ 11-2. THE TEUCRI, OR THE TEUCRIANS, AND THEIR DERIVATIVES.

One of the founders of the *Trojan* people – the *Teucrians*, was *Teucer* of *Crete*. From him sprung *Aeneid*, the ancestor of the *Romans*. *Ovid* surfaced this circumstance in "Metamorphoses":

"Then, recollecting how the *Trojans* had
derived their origin from *Teucer's* race,
they sailed to *Crete*…" [13.705-707]

Virgil stated that *Teucer* was the first to inhabit the *Trojan* land:

"My father, long revolving in his mind
The race and lineage of the *Trojan* kind,
Thus answer'd their demands: "Ye princes, hear
Your pleasing fortune, and dispel your fear.
The fruitful isle of *Crete,* well known to fame,
Sacred of old to *Jove's* imperial name,
In the mid ocean lies, with large command,
And on its plains a hundred cities stand.
Another *Ida* rises there, and we
From thence derive our *Trojan* ancestry.
From thence, as 't is divulg'd by certain fame,
To the *Rhœtean* shores old *Teucrus* came;
There fix'd, and there the seat of empire chose,
Ere *Ilium* and the *Trojan* towers arose.
In humble vales they built their soft abodes"…" ["The *Aeneid*." *John Dryden's* translation. 3]

However, *Virgil* did not forget to mention the first founding father of the *Trojan* people, described earlier – *Dardanus,* who established the kingdom of *Troy:*

"Old *Dardanus,* th' Original and Sire
Of *Troy,* whom *Atlas'* child *Electra* bare…" [8.181-182]

The name *Teucer* has an obvious *Turkic* origin. In *Greek* orthography, it is Τεῦκρος, in *Latin* - *Teucrus: Teukros, Teukrus, Teucer: Teuk, Teuc > Tek* 'one; alone' + *R, Er > Er* 'warrior, man' + *Os, Us > Us* 'master, chief', meaning "one-of-a-kind noble warrior" in *Turkic*. The name *Teucer* is still in use, mainly in the *USA* as *Tucker*.

Initially from *Crete*, the *Teucri* sought refuge on the shores of *Sicily,* as testified by *Ovid* in his work "Metamorphoses":

"…they sailed to *Crete* but there could not endure
ills sent by *Jove,* and, having left behind
the hundred cities, they desired to reach
the western harbors of the *Ausonian* land…
They set their sails then for the neighboring land
of the *Phaeacians,* rich with luscious fruit:
then for *Epirus* and to *Buthrotos,*
and came then to a mimic town of *Troy,*
ruled by the *Phrygian* seer. With prophecies
which *Helenus,* the son of *Priam,* gave,

they came to *Sicily,* whose three high capes
jut outward in the sea." [13.707-733]

Ancient authors would use the words *Trojani,* or *Trojans,* and *Teucri* as complementary synonyms. The language of the *Trojans* was not *Indo-European. Virgil* confirmed that the language of the *Trojans* utterly differed from the language of the *Latins.* In her plea to "the king of almighty *Olympus*" *Jupiter,* his wife *Juno* asked him to destroy the identity and the language of the *Trojans,* aka the *Teucrians:*

"This let me beg (and this no fates withstand)
Both for myself and for your father's land,
That, when the nuptial bed shall bind the peace,
(Which I, since you ordain, consent to bless,)
The laws of either nation be the same;
But let the *Latins* still retain their name,
Speak the same language which they spoke before,
Wear the same habits which their grandsires wore.
Call them not *Trojans:* perish the renown
And name of *Troy,* with that detested town." ["The *Aeneid.*" John Dryden's translation. 12]

The wish was granted, as the gods deemed worthy to demolish *Asia*'s dominant power and *Priam*'s white-handed nation, and the *Trojans*' names disappeared from the maps and histories; however, their deeds surpassed all expectations. As it is from their race came the founder of *Rome* – *Romulus* and the renowned leader of ancient *Rome* from the *Julian* dynasty – *Julius Caesar:*

"This is his time prefix'd. *Ascanius* then,
Now call'd *Iulus,* shall begin his reign
He thirty rolling years the crown shall wear,
Then from *Lavinium* shall the seat transfer,
And, with hard labor, *Alba Longa* build.
The throne with his succession shall be fill'd
Three hundred circuits more: then shall be seen
Ilia the fair, a priestess and a queen,
Who, full of *Mars,* in time, with kindly throes,
Shall at a birth two goodly boys disclose.
The royal babes a tawny wolf shall drain:
Then *Romulus* his grandsire's throne shall gain,
Of martial towers the founder shall become,
The people *Romans* call, the city *Rome.*
To them no bounds of empire I assign,
Nor term of years to their immortal line
Ev'n haughty *Juno,* who, with endless broils,
Earth, seas, and heav'n, and *Jove* himself turmoils;
At length aton'd, her friendly power shall join,
To cherish and advance the *Trojan* line
The subject world shall *Rome's* dominion own,
And, prostrate, shall adore the nation of the gown.
An age is ripening in revolving fate
When *Troy* shall overturn the *Grecian* state,
And sweet revenge her conqu'ring sons shall call,
To crush the people that conspir'd her fall
Then *Cæsar* from the *Julian* stock shall rise…" ["The *Aeneid.*" John Dryden's translation. 1]

All three components of the name – *Gaius Julius Caesar* were derived from the *Turkic* source:
> *Gaius* > *Gəi, Gəy* 'great' + *Us* 'chief'
> *Julius* > *Iulus, Iuluş* "rescue"
> *Caesar: Cae* > *Ki* 'earth, place' + *Sar* > *Şər* 'ruler, monarch'

Very surprisingly, *Homer* in "The Iliad" did not even hint at the existence of the *Teucrians* and their founder *Teucer*, and moreover, *Homer* named *Teucer* a war chief, fighting against the *Trojans*. However, *Homer* alluded to the derivatives of the *Teucrians* – the *Paeonians* and the *Gergithes*:

> "*Pyraechmes* led the *Paeonian* archers from distant *Amydon*, by the broad waters of the river *Axius*, the fairest that flow upon the earth." ["The Iliad." Translated by *Samuel Butler*. 2]

The names of the *Trojan* tribes in this second group also prove to be of *Turkic* origin:

➤ *Teucri*, aka *Teucrians*: *Teuc* > *Tek* 'one; alone' + *Er* 'warrior, man, hero', meaning "tribe of the exceptional warriors" in *Turkic*.

➤ *Gergithes* = Γέργιθες: *Gergith* > *Qorqit* 'frighten' + *Thes* > *Taş* 'fellow', meaning "frightening tribe" in *Turkic*. This *Teucrian* tribe obtained its name after the *Trojan* prince, son of *Priam Gorguthion* (Γοργυθίων) that proceeds from the *Turkic* word *Qorqitan* "the one who instills fear" (*Qorqit* 'frighten' + *-An* 'an affix, denoting constant action').
Without directly naming the *Gergithes*, *Homer* forthbrought the name of their founder – *Gorgythion*:
"As he spoke he aimed another arrow straight at *Hector*, for he was bent on hitting him; nevertheless he missed him, and the arrow hit *Priam's* brave son *Gorgythion* in the breast."
["The Iliad." Translated by *Samuel Butler*. 8]
Unlike *Homer*, *Herodotus* pointed out that "the *Gergithes* were the only remaining people of the ancient *Teucrians*…" [5.122]
As a reminiscence of this nation, *Strabo* recounted their old places of habitation:
"In *Lampsacene* is a place well planted with vines, called *Gergithium*, and there was a city *Gergitha*, founded by the *Gergithi* in the *Cymæan* territory, where formerly was a city called *Gergitheis*, (used in the plural number, and of the feminine gender,) the birthplace of *Cephalon* the *Gergithian*, and even now there exists a place in the *Cymæan* territory called *Gergithium*, near *Larissa*." [13.1.19]

➤ *Pæonians*, aka *Paiones* = Παίονες, aka *Pæones*, aka *Pannonioi* = Παννόνιοι, aka *Pannonians*, aka *Paioplai* = Παιόπλαι, aka *Pæoplians*, not *Paeoplas*, aka *Siriopaiones* = Σιριοπαίονές, not *Seiropæonians*:
  o *Pæonians, Pæones, Paiones* > *Paiona* = Παίονα > *Paiana* "benevolent spirit" in *Turkic*. In addition to listing this *Turkic* word with the indicated meaning, *Radlov V.V.* also determined the integral parts of the word *Paiana* as *Pai* 'lord' + *Ənə* 'lady' [4.2.1139]. According to *Appian*, the *Paeonians* were named after their founder *Paiona* (translated into *English* as *Pæon*), aka *Pannonion* (Παννόνιον, translated into *English* as *Pannonius*), who was a son of *Autarieus*, a grandson of *Illyrius*, and a brother to two other founding fathers – *Skordiskon* and *Triballon* [3.1.2].

  o *Pannonioi, Pannonians* > *Pannonion*: *Panno* > *Paiana* 'benevolent spirit' + *Nion* > *-Nın* 'an affix of possession', meaning "be in the hands of the benevolent spirit" in *Turkic*.

  o *Paioplai, Pæoplians*: *Pai* 'lord' + *Oplai* 'make wealthy' (*Öp* 'wealth' + *-La, -Lə* 'an affix, converting a noun into a verb'), meaning "noble tribe that creates wealth" in *Turkic*.

Interestingly, on one occasion, *Herodotus* considered them to be the same people – the *Paiones*, while on a different setting, he presented them as a derivative tribe:

> "*Xerxes* then marched through the country of the *Paeonian* tribes — the *Doberians* and the *Paeoplas* — which lay to the north of *Pangaeum*, and, advancing westward, reached the river *Strymon* and the city *Eion*..." [7.113]

- o *Siriopaiones*: *Sirio* > *Siri* 'source, origin' + *Paiones* > *Paiana* 'benevolent spirit', meaning "the original *Paiones*" in *Turkic*.

According to *Appian*, the *Paeonians* were known as the *Pæones* by the *Greeks* and were recognized as the *Pannonioi* (translated into *English* incorrectly as *Pannonians*) by the *Romans*:

> "The *Pæones* are a great nation on the *Danube*, extending from the *Iapydes* to the *Dardani*. They are called *Pæones* [7] by the *Greeks*, but *Pannonians* [8] by the *Romans*. They are counted by the *Romans* as a part of *Illyria*, as I have previously said, for which reason it seems proper that I should include them in my *Illyrian* history. They have been renowned from the *Macedonian* period through the *Agrianes*, who rendered very important aid to *Philip* and *Alexander* and are *Pæones* of *Lower Pannonia* bordering on *Illyria*. When the expedition of *Cornelius* against the *Pannonians* resulted disastrously, so great a fear of those people came over all the *Italians* that for a long time afterwards none of the consuls ventured to march against them." [3.3.14]

Herodotus offered an extensive account of this *Teucrian* nation:

> "About the same time, by means of a certain accident, *Darius* took a resolution to command *Megabyzus* to transplant the *Pæonians* out of *Europe* into *Asia*. For *Pigres* and *Mastyes*, two *Pæonians*, being desirous to become masters of *Pæonia*, came to *Sardis* after the return of *Darius*, accompanied by their sister, who was a tall and beautiful person. And observing *Darius* one day sitting in the suburbs of the *Lydians*, they dress'd their sister in the best manner they could, and sent her down to the river, carrying a pitcher on her head, leading a horse by a bridle hanging upon her arm, and at the same time spinning a thread from her distaff. *Darius* looking upon the maid with attention as she pass'd by, because her manner was altogether different from the customs, not only of the *Persian* and *Lydian* women, but of any other in *Asia*, order'd some of his guards to observe what she would do with the horse. The guards follow'd her, and found that when she came down to the river, she water'd the horse, and having fill'd her pitcher, return'd again by the same way; carrying the water on her head, leading her horse, and spinning, as she had done before. *Darius* no less surpriz'd with the account they gave, than with what he himself had seen, commanded her to be brought into his presence...when *Darius* ask'd who she was, the young men made answer, that they were *Pæonians*, and that the maid was their sister,…that they came to put themselves under his protection; that *Paonia* is situated upon the river *Strymon*, not far from the *Hellespont*; and that the people are a colony of *Teucrians*, from the city of *Troy*. When they had given account of these particulars, *Darius* farther demanded, if all the women of that country were as industrious as their sister. And the *Pæonians*, who had contriv'd the whole design to no other end, readily anwer'd, they were. Upon which a messenger was dispatch'd on horseback, with letters from the King to *Megabyzus*, general of his forces in *Thrace*, requiring him to compel the *Pæonians* to leave their country, and pass into *Asia* with their wives and children. When the *Pæonians* heard that the *Persians* were coming to invade them, they drew all their forces towards the sea, thinking the *Persians* would attempt to enter that way and prepar'd to dispute their passage. But *Megabyzus*, understanding that the whole strength of *Pæonia* was in a readiness to receive him on that side, took his way, by the direction of his guides, towards the upper part of the country. And concealing his march from the enemy, fell in upon their cities empty of men, and easily possess'd himself of all. The *Pæonians* no sooner heard that their cities were surpriz'd, than they dispers'd themselves; and every man

---

[7] In the original *Greek* text, it is *Paiones* = Παίονες.
[8] It should be *Pannonioi* = Παννόνιοι.

returning home, the whole country submitted to the *Persians*. And in this manner all those *Pæonians*, who were known by the names of *Seiropæonians* and *Pæoplians* together with the people of those parts that descend towards the lake of *Prasias*, were expell'd from their ancient seats, and transported into *Asia*." [5.12-15]

The *Pæonians* had a couple of derivative tribes – the *Doberes* and the *Agrianes*.

➢ <u>*Doberes* = Δόβηρες, aka *Doberians:*</u> *Dobe* > *Döbə* 'hill' + *Er* 'warrior, man', meaning "mountaineer" in *Turkic*.

➢ <u>*Agrianes* = Ἀγριᾶνες, aka *Agrianians:*</u> *Agri* > *Ağrı* 'get stronger' + *Ian* > -*Yan* 'an affix, denoting constant action', meaning "tribe that gets stronger" in *Turkic*. This was a chief *Paeonian* tribe that served in the army of *Alexander the Great* and led him to the victory:

> "He then advanced into the land of the *Agrianians* and *Paeonians*, where messengers reached him, who reported that *Clitus*, son of *Bardylis*, had revolted, and that *Glaucias*, king of the *Taulantians*, had gone over to him. They also reported that the *Autariatians* intended to attack him on his way. He accordingly resolved to commence his march without delay. But *Langarus*, king of the *Agrianians*, who, in the lifetime of *Philip*, had been an open and avowed friend of *Alexander*, and had gone on an embassy to him in his private capacity, at that time also came to him with the finest and best armed of the shield-bearing troops, which he kept as a bodyguard." [*Arrian of Nicomedia*. "The Anabasis of *Alexander*." 1.5]

Here comes the intriguing part. The country of the *Paeonian* tribes – *Paeonia* lied in *Thrace*, which proves that the *Pæonians* were no one else but the *Thracians*. The logical chain of thoughts leads to the conclusion: as the *Pæonians* were the descendants of the *Trojan* nation of the *Teucrians*, then they should be considered the *Thracians*. This is additional proof that *Homer's* "horse-taming *Trojans*" were a *Thracian* progeny, directly connected to a greater *Scythian* family.

➢ <u>*Cicones, Kikones* = Κίκονες, aka *Ciconians:*</u> *Ci, Ki* > *Kıy* 'loud speech' + *Con, Kon* > *Kon* 'live', meaning "tribe that lives vociferously" in *Turkic*. As the name suggests, this *Thracian* nation was clamorous. Apropos of that, there were two *Turkic* tribes with similar names – *Kıy* "loud speech" and *Kıybik* "very loud speech" [*Radlov*. 2.1.687, 701]. The *Cicones* were a *Thracian* tribe that sided with the *Trojans* in the *Trojan* War, as reported by *Homer* in "The Iliad":

> "*Euphemus*, son of *Troezenus*, the son of *Ceos*, was captain of the *Ciconian* spearsmen."
> [Translated by *Samuel Butler*. 2]

William Smith, adverting to many scholars of antiquity, characterized the *Cicones* as a *Thracian* nation:

> "...a *Thracian* people inhabiting the coast district between the rivers *Hebrus* in the E. and *Lissus* in the W., where they appear to have lived from very remote times. (Hom. Il. 2.846, Od. 4.39; Hdt. 7.59,110; Orph. Arg. 77; Steph. Byz. s. v. Μαρώνεια; Mela, 2.2, 8; Plin. Nat. 4.18; Verg. G. 4.520; Sil. Ital. 11.477; Ov. Met. 10.2, 15.313.) [*Cicones*].

The fact that both the *Thracian* and the *Trojan* nations shared the same heritage is not shocking. *Strabo* was one of the first to mention the uniting them characteristics, such as common ethnonyms, demonyms, endonyms, autonyms, and toponyms:

> "There was also in *Lesbos* a city called *Arisba*, the territory belonging to which was possessed by the *Methymnæans*. There is a river *Arisbus* in *Thrace*, as we have said before, near which are situated the *Cabrenii Thracians*. There are many names common to *Thracians* and *Trojans*, as *Scei*, a *Thracian* tribe, a river *Sceus*, a *Scæn* wall, and in *Troy*, *Scæan* gates. There are *Thracians* called *Xanthii*, and a river *Xanthus* in *Troja*; an *Arisbus* which discharges itself into the *Hebrus*, and an *Arisbe* in *Troja*; a river *Rhesus* in *Troja*, and *Rhesus*, a king of the *Thracians*. The poet mentions also another *Asius*, besides the *Asius* of *Arisbe*, who was the maternal uncle of the hero

Hector, own brother of *Hecuba,* and son of *Dymas* who lived in *Phrygia* on the banks of the *Sangarius.*" [13.1.21]

As we already know, the *Thracian* tribe *Xanthii* were a *Scythian* tribe *Dahæ,* surnamed *Xanthii.*

There is one more crucial fact left to discuss before wrapping up this paragraph. The *Pæonians,* just like their primogenitors, the *Teucrians,* as well as their derivatives, were considered not only as the *Thracians* and a branch of the *Scythians.* They were also known as the *Pelasgi:*

> "*Macedonia* was formerly called *Emathia,* from the name of king *Emathion,* of whose prowess the earliest proofs are extant in those parts. As the origin of this kingdom was but humble, so its limits were at first extremely narrow. The inhabitants were called *Pelasgi,* the country *Paeonia.* But in process of time, when, through the ability of their princes and the exertions of their subjects, they had conquered, first of all, the neighbouring tribes, and afterwards other nations and peoples, their dominions extended to the utmost boundaries of the east. In the region of *Paeonia,* which is now a portion of *Macedonia,* is said to have reigned *Pelegonus,* the father of *Asteropaeus,* whose name we find, in the *Trojan* war, among the most distinguished defenders of the city. On the other side a king named *Europus* held the sovereignty in a district called *Europa.*" [*Justin.* 7.1]

This testimonial is yet another piece of the large mosaic picture that vividly demonstrates the indivisible kin ties between the most distinguished nations of the ancient world – the *Scythians,* the *Thracians,* the *Trojans,* and the *Pelasgi.*

§ 11-3. THE LELEGES AND THEIR DERIVATIVES.

The third branch of the *Trojan* nations is comprised of the *Leleges* (Λέλεγες) and closely related to them big and small nations and tribes: the *Carians,* the *Locri* and their branched off tribes, the *Meonians,* later known as the *Lydians,* the *Mysians,* as well as the *Asii* with their numerous branches, the *Turreni,* aka the *Etrusci,* and the like.

The *Leleges* were not just *Trojans* – they represented the third *Trojan* dynasty, as stated by *Strabo:*

> "The third dynasty is that of the *Leleges,* which is also a *Trojan* dynasty;
> "of *Altes,* the king of the war-loving *Leleges,*"
> by whose daughter *Priam* had *Lycaon* and *Polydorus.*" [13.1.7]

Herodotus proclaimed that the name *Leleges* was the ancient, original name of the *Carians,* who shared common blood ancestry with the *Mysians* and the *Lydians:*

> "The *Carians* came from the islands to inhabit on the continent. They were anciently call'd *Leleges,* and liv'd in the islands under the protection of *Minos,* paying no kind of tribute, that I could ever find by enquiring into the remotest times. But when he had occasion for mariners, they assisted him with their ships in the great conquests he made, and raised themselves to a higher degree of reputation than any other nation. They were the inventors of three things now in use among the *Grecians.* For the *Carians* were the first who wore a crest upon their helmets; adorn'd their shields with various figures; and invented the handle, by which they are managed; whereas, before this invention, the shield hung about the soldier's neck by a thong of leather, and descended by the left shoulder. After a long time, the *Dorians* and *Ionians*

abandon'd the islands likewise, as the *Carians* had done, and settled on the continent. And this account the *Cretans* give of the *Carians*. But the *Carians* not assenting to these things, affirm they were originally inhabitants of the continent, and always went under the same name. In testimony of which they show an ancient temple at *Mylasa,* dedicated to the *Carian Jupiter;* where the *Mysians* and *Lydians* are admitted to participate with the *Carians* in their worship, as nations of the same blood. For, say they, *Lydus* and *Mysus* were brothers to *Cares,* and on that account the use of this temple is communicated to their posterity, and not to to any other people, through the same language with the *Carians*." [1.171]

The etymological research of the ethnic names of this *Trojan* group, including the *Leleges* and their derivatives, revealed their well-expected *Turkic* origin:

> *Leleges* = Λέλεγες > Leilek, Ləilək "stork" in *Turkic*. The wandering nature of the *Leleges* and their peculiar way of settlement was similar to their *Pelasgians* forefathers, who were also called "storks", or *Pelargi,* by the *Athenians* due to "their settling like birds in any place where they chanced to come", according to *Strabo*. This name of the ancient *Trojan* nation is still in use in the *Turkic Republic of Kyrgyzstan,* denominating the *Leilek* district.
> According to *Pausanias,* the *Leleges* acquired their tribal name after *Lelex* (Λέλεξ), who was the great-grandson of *Io,* or *Isis* – the *Pelasgian* flame of *Zeus* turned into a heifer and later worshipped as a goddess in *Egypt. Pausanias* also clarified that *Lelex* was a son of *Libya,* who was a daughter of *Io's* son *Apis,* aka *Epaphos* – the ruler of *Egypt*:
>> "Below the citadel near the sea is the tomb of *Lelex,* who they say arrived from *Egypt* and became king, being the son of *Poseidon* and of *Libya,* daughter of *Epaphus*."
>> ["Description of *Greece*." 1.44.3]
>
> Having confirmed that the *Leleges* were named after their founder *Lelex, Pausanias* asserted that he arrived in the region of *Greece* – *Laconia* from *Egypt* and became its first indigenous sovereign:
>> "In the twelfth generation after *Car* the son of *Phoroneus* the *Megarians* say that *Lelex* arrived from *Egypt* and became king, and that in his reign the tribe *Leleges* received its name. *Lelex* they say begat *Cleson, Cleson Pylas* and *Pylas Sciron,* who married the daughter of *Pandion* and afterwards disputed with *Nisus,* the son of *Pandion,* about the throne, the dispute being settled by *Aeacus,* who gave the kingship to *Nisus* and his descendants, and to *Sciron* the leadership in war. They say further that *Nisus* was succeeded by *Megareus,* the son of *Poseidon,* who married *Iphinoe,* the daughter of *Nisus,* but they ignore altogether the *Cretan* war and the capture of the city in the reign of *Nisus*." [1.39.6]
>
>> "After the figures of *Hermes* we reach *Laconia* on the west. According to the tradition of the *Lacedaemonians* themselves, *Lelex,* an aboriginal was the first king in this land, after whom his subjects were named *Leleges. Lelex* had a son *Myles,* and a younger one *Polycaon. Polycaon* retired into exile, the place of this retirement and its reason I will set forth elsewhere. On the death of *Myles* his son *Eurotas* succeeded to the throne. He led down to the sea by means of a trench the stagnant water on the plain, and when it had flowed away, as what was left formed a river-stream, he named it *Eurotas*." [Idem. 3.1.1.]

> *Locri,* aka *Lokroi* = Λοκροί, aka *Locrians:* Loc, Lok > Loka 'wanderer, vagabond' + R > Ər 'man, warrior', meaning "wandering warrior" in *Turkic*. Previously known as the *Leleges,* the *Locri* were named after their chieftain *Locros* (Λοκρός "chief wandering warrior" in *Turkic*), whose name was confirmed by *Strabo* in line with *Hesiod:*
>> "On the subject of the *Ætolian* polity, he calls the present *Locri, Leleges,* and observes that they occupy *Boeotia*. He repeats the same remark on the subject of the polity of the *Opuntians* and *Megareans*.
>> But we should chiefly rely upon *Hesiod,* who thus speaks of them:

"For *Locrus* was the leader of the nation of the *Leleges,* whom *Jupiter,* the son of *Saturn,* in his infinite wisdom, once gave as subjects to *Deucalion,* a people gathered from among the nations of the earth."

For it seems to me to be obscurely intimated by the etymology of the name, *Leleges,* that they were a mixed people anciently collected together, which had become extinct." [7.7.2]

The name of the *Locrian* leader calls attention to the lifestyle of the *Leleges* that *Aristotle* called "a wandering nation":

"The fact of the association of these people with the *Carians* may be regarded as a proof of their being barbarians, and *Aristotle,* in his Politics, shows that they were a wandering nation, sometimes in company with the *Carians,* sometimes alone, and that from ancient times; for, in speaking of the polity of the *Acarnanians,* he says that the *Curetes* occupied a part of the country, and the *Leleges* (and after them the *Teleboæ*) the western side." [*Strabo.* 7.7.2]

The *Locri* were the first men to create written laws for their society:

"The *Locri* are believed to have been the first who committed their laws to writing…" [6.1.8]

Besides their judicial acumen, these people were acknowledged for their military prowess after destroying an army of 130,000 *Crotoniatæ* by a 13 times smaller force of 10,000 *Locrians:*

"After the *Locri* is the [river] *Sagras,* in the feminine gender, on which is situated the altar of the *Dioscuri,* near which ten thousand *Locrians,* with a small body of *Rhegians* gained a victory over 130,000 *Crotoniatæ,* whence they say arose the proverb applied to incredulous people, "It is more true than the victory of the *Sagras.*" Some people add to the mysterious account, that it was announced the same day at the *Olympic* games to the people there assembled, and this speedy news was found perfectly correct. They say that this mischance was so unfortunate an event to the *Crotoniatæ,* that after it they did not long remain as a nation, on account of the number of citizens who fell in the battle." [*Strabo.* 6.1.10]

The *Locri* were split into several tribes throughout *Greece* and *Italy,* each of which had an additional appellation specifying their location, such as the *Locri Epicnemidii,* the *Locri Epizephyrii,* the *Locri Narycii,* the *Locri Opuntii,* the *Locri Ozolae,* the *Amphisseian Locri,* and the *Locrians* from *Thronium:*

"On either side of *Phocis* the *Locrians* dwelt; to the west the *Locri Ozolae,* to the east the *Locri Epicnemidii* and *Opuntii.* It was over these last, as appears from *Homer,* that *Ajax* the son of *Oileus* reigned: they were situated between *Phocis* and the *Euboean* gulph, with *Boeotia* to the southeast, and *Thessaly* to the north-west. The *Epicnemidii* possessed the parts near the *Maliac* bay; the *Opuntii* dwelt higher up, on the *Euripus.* As for the *Locri Ozolae,* they were placed on the other side of *Phocis,* in a very small territory between *Phocis* and *Attica,* and in time were incorporated with the *Aetolian* people. The name of *Locrians* was attributed to them all, because originally they were one people, those of the east and west having had a communication one with the other by those mountains which divide *Thessaly* from the rest of *Greece.* And it is likely that the *Ozolae* and *Opuntians* were colonies of the *Locri Epicnemidii,* as these were the only *Locrians* who had a right to send deputies to the *Amphictyonic* council. The *Opuntians* had their appellation from the city *Opus* on the *Euboean* gulph, and the *Epicnemidii* from the mountain *Cnemis.* The *Ozoleans* sought the etymology of their name in antient fable: it was derived, say they, from a word which in *Greek* signifies to stink, because this whole country was infected by the putrid smell of the carcass of the monster *Python;* for it was here *Apollo* slew him. — To *Locris Epicnemidia* belonged the straights of *Thermopylae,* that famed pass, the scene of one of the greatest actions that ever people durst perform. It lieth between mount *Oeta* and the *Maliac* bay, and was named *Thermopylae,* the gates of the hot baths, from the narrowness of the passage, and the hot springs that were in the neighbourhood of it."

[*John Gast*. Archdeacon of *Glandelagh*. "The History of *Greece* to the Accession of *Alexander of Macedon*." 1.2.1.159-160]

- *Locri Epicnemidii*, aka *Locri Epicnemidij*, were initially identified as the *Leleges*, according to *Pliny the Elder*:
    "After them come the *Locrians*, surnamed *Epicnemidii*, formerly called *Leleges*, through whose country the river *Cephisus* passes, in its course to the sea." [4.12]
  Pausanias called them "the *Locrians* under *Mount Cnemis*":
    "*Herodotus* does not give the number of the *Locrians* under *Mount Cnemis*, but he does say that each of their cities sent a contingent. It is possible, however, to make an estimate of these also that comes very near to the truth. For not more than nine thousand *Athenians* marched to *Marathon*, even if we include those who were too old for active service and slaves; so the number of *Locrian* fighting men who marched to *Thermopylae* cannot have exceeded six thousand." [10.20.2]

- *Locri Narycii*, aka *Narycian Locri*, aka *Italian Locrians*, were surnamed after the *Italian* city of *Narycia*. *Virgil* in "The *Aeneid*" mentioned them as the founders of the city:
    "The *Narycian Locri* [9] have built a city here, and *Lyctian Idomeneus* has filled the plain with soldiers: here is that little *Petelia*, of *Philoctetes*, leader of the *Meliboeans*, relying on its walls." [3.356-462]
  Most likely, *Pausanias* called this tribe of the *Locri* "the *Italians Locrians*" that occupied the land near the *West Point*:
    "*Euthymus* was by birth one of the *Italian Locrians*, who dwell in the region near the headland called the *West Point*, and he was called son of *Astycles*." [6.6.4]

- *Locri Epizephyrii*, aka *Locroi Epizephurioi* = Λοκροί Ἐπιζεφύριοι, had their surname from *Greek* *epi-Zephyros* "under the West Wind", as stated by *Strabo*:
    "After the *Herculeum Promontorium* is the headland of *Locris*, which is called *Zephyrium*, possessing a haven exposed to the west winds, whence is derived its name. Then is the state of the *Locri Epizephyrii*, a colony of *Locrians* transported by *Evanthes* from the *Crissæan* gulf, shortly after the foundation of *Crotona* and *Syracuse*. *Ephorus* was not correct in stating that they were a colony of the *Locri Opuntii*." [6.1.7]

- *Locri Opuntii*, aka *Opuntian Locrians*, aka *Opuntii*, aka *Opuntians*, accepted their additional cognomen after the city *Opus* that was their capital. *Pausanias* in "Description of *Greece*" made a note that the *Opuntii* and the *Locri* were related:
    "The first to sail thither legend says was *Leonymus of Crotona*. For when war had arisen between the people of *Crotona* and the *Locri* in *Italy*, the *Locri*, in virtue of the relationship between them and the *Opuntians*, called upon *Ajax* son of *Oileus* to help them in battle. So *Leonymus* the general of the people of *Crotona* attacked his enemy at that point where he heard that *Ajax* was posted in the front line. Now he was wounded in the breast, and weak with his hurt came to *Delphi*. When he arrived the *Pythian* priestess sent *Leonymus* to *White Island*, telling him that there *Ajax* would appear to him and cure his wound." [3.19.12]

- *Ozolian Locri*, aka *Locroi Ozolai* = Λοκροὶ Ὀζόλαι, were registered by *Pausanias* along with two other *Locrian* tribes – the one that dwelled in the land opposite to the island of *Euboea*, and another was from this island:
    "The *Ozolian Locrians*, and the *Locrians* opposite *Euboea*, send one each; there is also one from *Euboea*. Of the *Peloponnesians*, the *Argives*, *Sicyonians*, *Corinthians* and *Megarians* send one, as *Nicopolis* send deputies to every meeting of the *Amphictyonic*

---

[9] In the original *Latin* text, it is *Locri Narycii*.

League; but each city of the nations mentioned has the privilege of sending members in turn after the lapse of periodic intervals." [10.8.5]

- *Amphisseian Locri,* aka *Amphisses Locroi = Ἀμφίσσης Λοκροί,* were also known as the *Locrians* from *Amphissa* that *Pausanias* pointed out when describing their land dispute with the *Phocians:* "But those who first openly started the war were the *Locrians* from *Amphissa*. For there happened to be a piece of land the ownership of which was a matter of dispute between the *Locrians* and the *Phocians*. Egged on by *Ismenias* and his party at *Thebes,* the *Locrians* cut the ripe corn in this land and drove off the booty. The *Phocians* on their side invaded *Locris* with all their forces, and laid waste the land." [3.9.9]

- *Locroi* from *Thronium = Λοκροί τε ἐκ Θρονίου* drew *Pausanias's* attention due to the fact that they found the city of *Thronium* along with the *Abantes* from *Euboea:*
  "When the *Greek* fleet was scattered on the voyage home from *Troy, Locrians* from *Thronium,* a city on the river *Boagrius,* and *Abantes* from *Euboea,* with eight ships altogether, were driven on the *Ceraunian* mountains. Settling here and founding the city of *Thronium,* by common agreement they gave the name of *Abantis* to the land as far as they occupied it." [5.22.4]

As it was determined with the assistance of the ancient men of letters, the *Leleges,* being a part of the *Thracians,* belonged to the *Pelasgian* family. Surprisingly, *Homer* did not mention the *Leleges* in "The Iliad", just noted one of their branches – the *Carians* combating on the side of the *Trojans:*

"*Nastes* lead the *Carians,* men of a strange speech. These held *Miletus* and the wooded mountain of *Phthires,* with the water of the river *Maeander* and the lofty crests of *Mt. Mycale*. These were commanded by *Nastes* and *Amphimachus,* the brave sons of *Nomion*."
["The Iliad." Translated by *Samuel Butler*. 2]

Even more unexpectedly, *Homer* entered a *Lelegian* tribe of the *Locri* as a fighting side for the *Greeks:*

"*Ajax,* the fleet son of *Oileus,* commanded the *Locrians*. He was not so great, nor nearly so great, as *Ajax* the son of *Telamon*. He was a little man, and his breastplate was made of linen, but in use of the spear he excelled all the *Hellenes* and the *Achaeans*. These dwelt in *Cynus, Opous, Calliarus, Bessa, Scarphe,* fair *Augeae, Tarphe,* and *Thronium* about the river *Boagrius*. With him there came forty ships of the *Locrians* who dwell beyond *Euboea*." [Idem ibid]

Here comes an intriguing moment that has never been mentioned by any scholar or a historian – in the *Trojan* war, certain groups ethnically were related to the *Trojans,* but fought against them, such as the *Pelasgian Argives* and the *Myrmidons* led by *Achilles,* a *Pelasgian* by origin, as well as the *Lacedaemonians,* the *Spartans,* and the *Athenians,* who also belonged to the *Pelasgian* family:

"Those again who held *Pelasgic Argos, Alos, Alope,* and *Trachis;* and those of *Phthia* and *Hellas* the land of fair women, who were called *Myrmidons, Hellenes,* and *Achaeans;* these had fifty ships, over which *Achilles* was in command." [Idem ibid]

"And those that dwelt in *Lacedaemon,* lying low among the hills, *Pharis, Sparta,* with *Messe* the haunt of doves; *Bryseae, Augeae, Amyclae,* and *Helos* upon the sea; *Laas,* moreover, and *Oetylus;* these were led by *Menelaus* of the loud battle-cry, brother to *Agamemnon,* and of them there were sixty ships, drawn up apart from the others. Among them went *Menelaus* himself, strong in zeal, urging his men to fight; for he longed to avenge the toil and sorrow that he had suffered for the sake of *Helen*." [Idem ibid]

> "And they that held the strong city of *Athens*, the people of great *Erechtheus*, who was born of the soil itself, but *Jove's* daughter, *Minerva*, fostered him, and established him at *Athens* in her own rich sanctuary. There, year by year, the *Athenian* youths worship him with sacrifices of bulls and rams. These were commanded by *Menestheus*, son of *Peteos*. No man living could equal him in the marshalling of chariots and foot soldiers." [Idem ibid]

> "For the *Opuntian Locrians*, whom *Homer* represents as coming to *Troy* with bows and slings, we know were armed as heavy infantry by the time of the *Persian* wars." [*Pausanias*. 1.23.4]

When enumerating the participants on the side of the *Greeks, Homer* openly declared them "the chiefs and princes of the *Danaans*", not *Greeks*:

> "And now, O Muses, dwellers in the mansions of *Olympus*, tell me – for you are goddesses and are in all places so that you see all things, while we know nothing but by report – who were the chiefs and princes of the *Danaans?*" ["The Iliad." Translated by *Samuel Butler*. 2]

The *Danaans* were a branch of the *Pelasgians* and obtained their name after the famed *Pelasgian* hero *Danaos*, who, according to *Strabo*, "made a law that those who had before borne the name of *Pelasgiotæ* throughout *Greece* should be called *Danai*", or *Danaans*. [5.2.4]

As it was determined, the *Pelasgians* did not have *Indo-European* origin and did not share the same lifestyle or language that the *Greeks* had. It was the *Pelasgians*, who were the first aboriginal nation of *Greece* long before the arrival of the *Greeks* into this land, who established the country *Pelasgia*, built numerous cities, including *Athens*, only later to abandon their own ethnic identity and language under the duress or goodwill. *Herodotus* testified in favor of this fact and provided several examples of this ethnic transformation, including the *Attikoi* (Ἀττικοι), the *Athenians*, aka the *Athenaioi* (Ἀθηναῖοι), previously known as the *Cranian Pelasgians*, aka the *Pelasgoi Kranaoi* (Πελασγοί Κραναοί), aka *Ægialean Pelasgi*, aka *Pelasgoi Aigialees* (Πελασγοὶ Αἰγιαλέες), aka the *Cecropians*, aka the *Kekropidai* (Κεκροπίδαι), aka the *Iones* (Ἴωνες), aka the *Ionians*:

> "If therefore all the *Pelasgian* race was such as these, then the *Attic* race, being *Pelasgian*, at the same time when it changed and became *Hellenic*, unlearnt also its language." [1.57]

> "When the *Pelasgians* possess'd those countries, which now go by the name of *Greece*, the *Athenians* were called *Cranian Pelasgians*. Under the reign of *Cecrops*, they had the name of *Cecropians;* which in the time of their king *Erechtheus*, they changed for that of *Athenians*, and lastly were named *Ionians* from *Ion*, the son of *Xuthus*, who was their general." [Idem. 8.44]

> "The *Ionians* furnished a hundred ships, and were armed like the *Greeks*. Now these *Ionians*, during the time that they dwelt in the *Peloponnese* and inhabited the land now called *Achaea* (which was before the arrival of *Danaus* and *Xuthus* in the *Peloponnese*), were called, according to the *Greek* account, *Ægialean Pelasgi*, or "*Pelasgi* of the Sea-shore," but afterwards, from *Ion* [10] the son of *Xuthus*, they were called *Ionians*." [Idem. 7.94]

All the converted branches of the *Pelasgi*, such as the *Attikoi*, the *Athenians*, and the *Ionians*, got recognized by the *Greeks* as the highly regarded *Grecians*, or the citizens of *Greece*:

> "For in that time, the *Pelasgians* inhabited part of the *Athenian* territories; and, because the *Athenians* were accounted among the nations of *Greece*, came likewise to be esteem'd *Grecians*.

---

[10] The name *Ion* is of *Turkic* origin and proceeds from *Iən, Yən* "great, huge".

> Whoever is initiated in the *Cabirian* mysteries of the *Samothracians*, which they receiv'd from the *Pelasgians*, knows what I say." [Idem. 2.51]

Meanwhile, *Strabo* pointed out the foreign origin of the *Greek* royal names and asserted that the *Pelasgi* were "said to be the most ancient people that were sovereigns in *Greece*":

> "Some names show their barbarous origin, as *Cecrops, Codrus, Oeclus, Cothus, Drymas,* and *Crinacus*.[11] *Thracians, Illyrians,* and *Epirotæ* are settled even at present on the sides of *Greece*. Formerly the territory they possessed was more extensive, although even now the barbarians possess a large part of the country, which, without dispute, is *Greece*. *Macedonia* is occupied by *Thracians*, as well as some parts of *Thessaly;* the country above *Acarnania* and *Ætolia*, by *Thesproti, Cassopæi, Amphilochi, Molotti,* and *Athamanes, Epirotic* tribes." [7.7.1]

Getting back to the etymological analysis of the names of the related *Trojan* nations, unified into a group under the *Leleges*, we can easily detect their *Turkic* roots:

> *Carians*, aka *Kares* = Κᾶρες > *Kara, Qara* "great, magnificent", meaning "magnificent people" in *Turkic*. The nation of the *Carians* got its name after *Karos* (Καρὸς), one of three *Lelegian* brothers. This very name *Kara*, or *Qara*, (in the *Turkic* languages, the letters *K* and *Q* are interchangeable) has been an integral part of the *Turkic* proper and tribal names, as well as of *Turkic* toponyms and hydronyms:
> - *Kara Bölük* "great division" – a *Turkic* tribe.
> - *Kara Yağma* "great assailant" – a *Turkic* tribe.
> - *Karaçay* "great river" – a *Turkic* people in the *Caucasus,* and a name of the river in the *Ural* mountains.
> - *Kara Khan* "great ruler" – a male name.
> - *Kara Kan* "great blood" – a male name.
> - *Qarabala* "great son" – a male name.
> - *Qarabudaq* "great branch" – a male name.
> - *Qarabuğa* "great bull", "hero" – a male name.
> - *Qaraqaya* "great rock" – a male name.
> - *Qaradağ* "great mountain" – a male name, a name of a region and of a mountain in *Azerbaijan*.
> - *Qarabağ* "great garden" – the *Karabakh* region of the *Azerbaijan Republic*.
> - *Karakum* "great or countless sand" – a desert in *Central Asia*.
>
> *Strabo* used several ancient authors' opinions for comparison purposes when describing the *Leleges* and the *Carians*. Similar to other *Trojans*, they were forced to leave their native lands:
> "Some writers conjecture that the *Leleges* and *Carians* are the same people; others, that they were only joint settlers, and comrades in war, because there are said to be some settlements called *Settlements of the Leleges* in the *Milesian* territory, and in many parts of *Caria* there are burial-places of the *Leleges*, and deserted fortresses, called *Lelegia*. The whole country called *Ionia* was formerly inhabited by *Carians* and *Leleges;* these were expelled by the *Ionians*, who themselves took possession of the country. In still earlier times, the captors of *Troy* had driven out the *Leleges* from the places about *Ida* near the rivers *Pedasus* and *Satnioeis*." [7.7.2]

> *Meiones* = Μηίονες, aka *Maiones* = Μαίονες, aka *Mæones*, aka *Meones* = Μήονες, aka *Meonas* = Μήονας, aka *Kabelees* = Καβηλέες, aka *Lasonioi* = Λασόνιοι, aka *Mysians*, aka *Musoi* = Μυσοὶ, aka *Lydians*, aka *Ludoi* = Λυδοί:

---

[11] The names in the *Greek* text are indicated as follows: *Cecrops*=Κέκροψ, *Codros*=Κόδρος, *Aiklos*=Ἄικλος, *Cothos*=Κόθος, *Drymas*=Δρύμας, *Crinacos*=Κρίνακος.

- *Meiones, Maiones, Meones, Meonas* > *Məin* "brain" in *Turkic*. Most likely that the *Meiones*, translated into *English* as the *Mæonians*, acquired their name from their king *Meïon* = *Μήων*. As his name testifies, the king was brainy, intellectually gifted. *Diodorus Siculus* acknowledged that "in ancient times *Meïon* became king of *Phrygia* and *Lydia*." [3.58.1]
  Homer named the *Meiones* among the *Trojan* nations, who came to defend *Troy* against the *Greek* invaders:
  > "*Mesthles* and *Antiphus* commanded the *Meonians*, sons of *Talaemenes*, born to him of the *Gygaean* lake. These led the *Meonians*, who dwelt under *Mt. Tmolus*."
  > ["The Iliad." Translated by *Samuel Butler*. 2].

  Based on the language peculiarities, *Strabo* made a note of the close kinship between the *Mæones*, the *Lydians*, and the *Phrygians*:
  > "The *Lydians* also, and the *Mæones*, whom *Homer* calls *Meones*, are in some way confounded with these people and with one another; some authors say that they are the same, others that they are different, nations. Add to this that some writers regard the *Mysians* as *Thracians*, others as *Lydians*, according to an ancient tradition, which has been preserved by *Xanthus the Lydian*, and by *Menecrates of Elæa*, who assign as the origin of the name *Mysians*, that the *Lydians* call the beech-tree (Oxya) *Mysos*, which grows in great abundance near *Olympus*, where it is said decimated persons were exposed, whose descendants are the later *Mysians*, and received their appellation from the *Mysos*,[12] or beech-tree growing in that country. The language also is an evidence of this. It is a mixture of *Lydian* and *Phrygian* words, for they lived some time in the neighbourhood of *Olympus*." [12.8.3]

- *Kabelées* (translated as *Cabalians*): *Kab* 'archetype, specimen'[13] + *Elé* > *Elí* 'people' (*El* 'people, nation' + *-İ* 'an affix of possession'), meaning "exemplary nation" in *Turkic*. *Herodotus* asserted that the *Mæonians* used to be called the *Kabelees* (*Cabalians*), as well as the *Lasonioi* (*Lasonians*):
  > "The *Cabalians*, who are *Maeonians*, but are called *Lasonians*, had the same equipment as the *Cilicians*..." [7.77]

- *Lasonioi* (rendered as *Lasonians*): *Las* > *Ləs* 'pine tree'[14] + *Oni* > *Öni* 'trunk of' (*Ön* 'trunk' + *-İ* 'an affix, equivalent to the preposition *Of*'), figuratively meaning "strong support" in *Turkic*. *Radlov V.V.* presented an example that perfectly matches the name of the *Lasonioi* – both by the definition and their lexical construction [1.2.1214]. Compare:
  - *Ləs Öni* "trunk of a pine tree".
  - *Ağaştıng Önü* "trunk of a tree".

  Based on the name, it is easy to deduce that the *Lasonioi* lived in an area populated by pine trees. As an aside, pine trees are the dominant plants on *Turkey's Anatolian* peninsula, which the *Lasonioi* presumably used to inhabit many a time ago.

> *Mysians*, aka *Mœsi*, aka *Moisoi*=*Μοισοί*, aka *Musoi* = *Μυσοί*, aka *Mysi* > *Muş* "strong, sturdy" in *Turkic*. Named after their leader *Mysus*, or properly *Muson* (*Μυσὸν*), the *Mysians* were previously known as the *Meiones*, aka the *Maiones*, aka the *Meones*, aka the *Meonas*, aka *Getae*. According to *Strabo*,
> "...*Mysi, Maeones*, and *Meones*[15] are the same people." [12.3.20]

---

[12] The name of a beech tree in *Lydian* as *Mysos* = *Μυσός* proceeds after the *Turkic Muş* "strong". The beech always had a reputation as a sturdy tree with a lifespan of 150 to 400 years.
[13] *Egorov V.G.* "Etimologicheskiy slovar chuvashskogo yazika." [89].
[14] Ibid [127].
[15] In the original *Greek* text, it is *Musoi* = *Μυσοὶ*, *Maiones* = *Μαίονες*, *Meones* = *Μήονες*.

Though *Herodotus* proclaimed that the *Mysians* were the brotherly nation to the *Carians* and the *Lydians*, he also later noted that the *Mysians* were a colony of the *Lydians*, and were also identified as the *Olympienoi*:

> "The *Mysians* had upon their heads native helmets, and they bore small shields and used javelins burnt at the point. These are settlers from the *Lydians*, and from mount *Olympos* [16] they are called *Olympienoi*. Of the *Lydians* and *Mysians* the commander was *Artaphrenes* the son of *Artaphrenes*, he who invaded *Marathon* together with *Datis*." [7.74]

Strabo considered the *Mysians* to be a *Scythian* nation of the *Getæ*, who spoke the same language as the *Thracians*:

> "It is but just too that *Apollodorus* should give some explanation respecting the *Mysians* mentioned in the epic poems of *Homer*, whether he takes them to be but people of his feigning, when the poet says, "Of the close-fighting *Mysians* and the illustrious *Hippemolgi*", or would he regard them as the *Mysians* of *Asia*? Now if he should declare that he considers them to be those of *Asia*, he will misinterpret the poet, as has been before observed; but if he should say they were but an invention, as there were no *Mysians* in *Thrace*, he will be guilty of a palpable misstatement, for even in our own times *Ælius Catus* has removed from the opposite side of the *Danube* into *Thrace* fifty thousand *Getæ*, who speak a language cognate with the *Thracian*. They still inhabit the very spot, and pass by the name of *Moesi*." [17] [7.3.10]

Let us keep in mind that *Gotus Iordanus* identified the *Getae* both as a *Gothic* and a *Scythian* nation. *Ptolemy* distinguished two *Mysian* lands – *Upper Mysia* and *Lower Mysia*, where, along with the *Mysians*, numerous kin tribes lived, such as a *Scythe-Getae-Dacian* tribe of the *Pikensioi* (Πικηνσιοι), a *Trojan-Illyrian* tribe of the *Dardanoi*, a *Thracian* tribe of the *Triballi*, the *Scythian Troglodytes*, a *Scythe-Sarmate-Germanic* tribe of the *Peukinoi*, a *Thracian* tribe of the *Krobuzoi* (Κρόβυζοι η Κρυβυζοί), and many more [3.9-10].

Pliny the Elder also acknowledged the *Thracians* and the *Scythians*, living in *Mysia* (or *Mœsia*) along with the *Mysians*:

> "Joining up to *Pannonia* is the province called *Mœsia*, which runs, with the course of the *Danube*, as far as the *Euxine*. It commences at the confluence previously mentioned. In it are the *Dardani*, the *Celegeri*, the *Triballi*, the *Timachi*, the *Mœsi*, the *Thracians*, and the *Scythians* who border on the *Euxine*." [3.29]

On a related note, *Ptolemy* called the country of the *Mysians Mysia*, while *Pliny the Elder* knew it as *Mœsia*.

Relying on the opinion of a fellow scholar *Poseidonius*, *Strabo* characterized the *Mysians* as peaceful vegetarians and ascetics, abstaining from carnal pleasures, yet resilient warriors, skilled in martial arts and hand-to-hand combat:

> "*Poseidonius* goes on to say of the *Mysians* that in accordance with their religion they abstain from eating any living thing, and therefore from their flocks as well; and that they use as food honey and milk and cheese, living a peaceable life, and for this reason are called both "god-fearing" and "capnobatae";[18] and there are some of the *Thracians* who live apart from woman-kind; these are called "*Ctistae*",[19] and because of the honor in which they are held, have been dedicated to the gods and live with freedom from every fear; accordingly, *Homer* speaks collectively of all these peoples as "proud *Hippemolgi*, *Galactophagi* and *Abii*, men most just," but he calls them "*Abii*" more especially for this reason, that they live apart from women, since

---

[16] In the original *Greek* text, it is *Olumpos* = Ολυμπος.

[17] It is *Moisoi*=Μοισοί in the original *Greek* text.

[18] Translated as "those who walk on/in smoke/clouds" or "intoxicated by inhaling smoke", this is a *Turkic* word: *Capnobatae, Kapnobatas*=Καπνοβάτας: *Cap, Kap* > *Köp* 'foam, bubbles, fizz' + *No* > *-Qa* 'into' + *Bat* 'immerse, place' + *Ae, As* > *-Ai* 'an affix, denoting a noun', meaning "the one who is immersed (placed) into bubbles" in *Turkic*.

[19] The *Thracian* word *Ctistae* or *Ktistai*=Κτίσται "founders, creators" has an obvious *Turkic* origin: *Ctis, Ktis* > *Katış* 'become stronger' + *Tae, Tai* > *Atai* 'founder, patriarch', meaning "strong in spirit patriarchs or founders" in *Turkic*.

he thinks that a life which is bereft of woman is only half-complete (just as he thinks the "house of *Protesilas*" is only "half complete", because it is so bereft); and he speaks of the *Mysians* as "hand-to-hand fighters" because they were indomitable, as is the case with all brave warriors; and *Poseidonius* adds that in the Thirteenth Book one should read "*Moesi*, hand-to-hand fighters" instead of "*Mysi*, hand-to-hand fighters".

Nevertheless it would perhaps be superfluous to change the text [of *Homer*], which has stood the test of so many years. For it appears more probable to suppose that the people were anciently called *Mysians*, but that their name is now altered." [7.3.3-4]

In addition to being recognized as the *Scythians*, Strabo considered the "lordly *Mysians*", as *Homer* put it, later known also under the name of the *Bithynians* and the *Thyni*, to be a colony of the *Thracians*:

"It is generally acknowledged by writers, that the *Bithynians*, who were formerly *Mysians*, received this name from *Bithynians* and *Thyni*, *Thracian* people, who came and settled among them. They advance as a proof of their statement, first as regards the *Bithynians*, that there still exists in *Thrace* a people called *Bithynians*, and then, as regards the *Thyni*, that the seashore, near *Apollonia* and *Salmydessus*, is called *Thynias*. The *Bebryces*, who preceded them as settlers in *Mysia*, were, as I conjecture, *Thracians*. We have said that the *Mysians* themselves were a colony of those *Thracians* who are now called *Maesi*." [20] [12.3.3]

Let us not forget the statements by *Herodotus*, agreeing with *Strabo's* inference about the *Thracians*, first known as the *Strymonians*, who renamed themselves into the *Bithynians* after resettling in *Asia* [7.75].

➢ *Olympians, aka Olympienoi, aka Olumpienoi = Ὀλυμπιηνοί, aka Olympenoi = Ὀλυμπηνοί, aka Olympeni, aka Hellespontii, aka Hellespontins, aka Ellespontioi = Ἑλλησπόντιοι:*
  o *Olym, Olum > Olum* 'immortal' [21] + *Pi* 'ruler' + *Ien > Ian, Yan* 'near', meaning "near the immortal rulers" or "near the *Mount Olympus*" in *Turkic*. The lexical construction of this name with the preposition of place at the end identifies its pure *Turkic* origin, as it does not exist in the *Indo-European* languages. The *Mount Olympus* was known as the home of 12 ancient *Olympian* gods – *Zeus* and his spouse *Hera*, as well as *Athena, Aphrodite, Artemis, Apollo, Demeter, Hephaestus, Hester, Hermes, Poseidon,* and *Ares*. Due to this fact, the name of the *Mount Olympus* is translated from *Turkic* as "immortal ruler", specifying the inhabitants of the mountain.
  o *Hellespontii, Hellespontins, Ellespontioi: Helles, Elles > Ellas = Ἑλλάς > Elləş* '1.a female name; 2.make peace' in *Turkic* + *Pontii, Pontins, Pontioi > Pontos* 'sea' in *Greek*, meaning "strait of *Ellas*".

According to *Strabo*, the *Olympenoi* (translated into *English* as *Olympeni*) were also known as the *Hellespontii*:

"To the south of the *Bithynians* are the *Mysians* round *Olympus* (who by some are called the *Olympeni* and by others the *Hellespontii*) and the *Hellespontian Phrygia*..." [12.4.10]

➢ *Lydians, aka Ludoi = Λυδοὶ, aka Lydi > Lutı* "wayfarer, wanderer" in *Turkic*. The *Lydians* were known formerly as the *Meonians*, just like the *Mysians*, and later changed their name to honor their prince *Lydus*, or correctly *Ludos* (*Λυδός*), according to the testimony provided by *Herodotus*:

"The *Lydians* were arm'd more like to the *Grecians* than any other people of the army. They had been formerly known by the name of *Meonians*; but were afterwards call'd *Lydians* from *Lydus*, the son of *Atys*." [7.74]

Strabo supported *Herodotus's* assertion about the *Lydians* by confirming their previous and subsequent names:

---

[20] In the original *Greek*, it is *Moisoi=Μοισοί*.
[21] *Olum* has other meanings as well – "existence; immortality". Compare to the *Turkic* word *Ölüm* "mortal; mortality, death".

"Those who had been kings of this country before *Argon*, were descended from *Lydus*, the son of *Atys*, who gave his name to the whole nation, which before his time were call'd *Meones*..." [*Herodotus*. 1.7]

"The next tract of country was occupied by... *Lydians*, who were then called *Mæonians*, and by the survivors of the *Mysians*, who were formerly governed by *Telephus* and *Teuthoras*." [*Strabo*. 13.1.8]

Pliny the Elder called them the *Lydi* and noted that they were later renamed as the *Turreni* (*Tyrrheni*) and *Tusci*:

"At an early period the *Umbri* were expelled from it by the *Pelasgi;* and these again by the *Lydians*,[22] who from a king of theirs were named *Tyrrheni*, but afterwards, from the rites observed in their sacrifices, were called, in the *Greek* language, *Tusci*." [3.8]

Herodotus portrayed the *Lydians* as a very resourceful nation, who were the first to create gold and silver coins and use them for trade, and who invented different types of games for entertainment:

"Now the *Lydians*...were the first of men, so far as we know, who struck and used coin of gold or silver; and also they were the first retail-traders. And the *Lydians* themselves say that the games which are now in use among them and among the *Hellenes* were also their invention. These they say were invented among them at the same time as they colonized *Tyrsenia*..." [1.94]

However, the *Lydians* were a humble nation with extremely high morals, "for among the *Lydians* as also among most other Barbarians it is a shame even for a man to be seen naked." [1.10]

➢ *Asii*, aka *Asaioi* = Ασαιοι, aka *Assaioi* = Ἀσσαῖοι, aka *Asioi* = Ἄσιοι, aka *Auseis* = Αὐσεῖς, aka *Ausees* = Αὐσέες, aka *Asiades* = Ἀσιάδης, aka *As*, aka *Az*:
  o *Asii, Asaioi, Assaioi, Asioi, As, Az > Əs, Ös* "lord, noble" in *Turkic*.
  o *Auseis, Ausees: Aus > As* 'the *As* tribe' + *Eis, Ees > İs* 'trace', meaning "remnants of the *As* tribe" in *Turkic*.
  o *Asiades: As* '*Asias*' + *Ade > Ada* 'father', meaning "tribe of the forefather *Asias*" in *Turkic*.

The *Asii* were related to the *Lydians*. The tribe of the *Asii* that inhabited the royal capital of *Lydia Sardis* since ancient times coexisted with the *Lydians* as a kin tribe. Based on the assertion of the *Lydians*, *Herodotus* stated that both the continent of *Asia* and the *Lydian* tribe acquired their names after the prince of *Lydia* – *Asias*:

"*Libya* indeed is said by most of the *Hellenes* to have its name from *Libya* a woman of that country, and *Asia* [23] from the wife of *Prometheus*: but this last name is claimed by the *Lydians*, who say that *Asia* has been called after *Asias* [24] the son of *Cotys* the son of *Manes*,[25] and not from *Asia* the wife of *Prometheus*; and from him too they say the *Asian* [26] tribe in *Sardis* [27] has its name." [4.45]

Homer in "The Iliad" did not specifically bring up the name of the *Asii* but clearly indicated that these *Trojan* people were led to the *Trojan* War by *Asias* – the same name that was assigned to the continent of *Asia* after the *Lydian* leader of the *Asiades*:

"They that dwelt about *Percote* and *Practius*, with *Sestos*, *Abydos*, and *Arisbe* – these were led by *Asius*, son of *Hyrtacus*, a brave commander – *Asius*, the son of *Hyrtacus*, whom his powerful dark bay steeds, of the breed that comes from the river *Selleis*, had brought from *Arisbe*." [Translated by *Samuel Butler*. 2]

Strabo also adverted to *Homer* when describing this nation and confirmed that

---

[22] In the original *Latin* text, it is *Lydi*.
[23] *Asie* = Ἀσίη in the original *Greek* text.
[24] *Asias* = Ἀσίας.
[25] *Manes* = Μάνης.
[26] *Asiades* = Ἀσιάδης.
[27] *Sardeis* = Σάρδεις in *Greek*, present-day *Sart* in western *Turkey*.

"The people, also, who lived between the *Æsepus* and *Abydos* were *Trojans,* for the country about *Abydos* was governed by *Asius*…" [13.1.7]

This *Trojan* tribe of the *Asii,* or *Auseis,* is the same as a *Scythian* tribe – the *Asaioi* and the *Turkic* tribe of the *As,* or *Az,* or *Uz,* well-documented in the numerous historical works by the ancient historians and geographers, such as *Ptolemy, Strabo, Juvaini,* in ancient and medieval *Turkic* inscriptions carved in stone, such as on a *Gobustan* rock dated 12th - 8th century BCE in *Azerbaijan,* on *Central Asian* monuments – *Bilge Kagan, Kultegin* as a pictograph ⿰, meaning "*Az*", as well as in the *Icelandic* saga "The Prose *Edda*" as *Asir.*

Besides leaving its traces in the names of the countries, cities, places, such as *Azerbaijan, Kyrgyzstan, Uzbekistan; Nizhniye Azy, Astrakhan, Azgyr, Aza, Yukhary Aza, Azaru, Astara;* the nations – the *Azerbaijani, Kyrgyz, Uzbek, Oguz,* this *Trojan-Scythe-Turkic* tribe also made its contribution to the names of the water bodies, such as the *Sea* of *Azov,* as well as to the ancient name of the river in *Tuscany, Italy – Ausar,* aka *Aisar* (Αἴσαρ), aka *Auser* "an *As* warrior" or "royal warrior", currently known as *Serchio.* According to *William Smith,*

"*Auser* or *Ausar* (Αἴσαρ, Strab.: *Serchio*), a considerable river of *Etruria,* rising in the *Apennines* on the borders of *Liguria,* and flowing near the city of *Luca,* is evidently the same with the modern *Serchio,* though that river now flows into the *Tyrrhenian Sea* by a separate mouth, seven miles N. of that of the *Arno,* while all ancient writers represent the *Auser* as falling into the *Arnus.* The city of *Pisae* was situated at the point of their junction: and the confluence of the two streams was said to give rise to a violent agitation of their waters. (*Strab.* v. p.222; *Plin. Nat.* 3.5. s. 8; *Rutil. Itin.* 1.566.) The *Auser* appears to have retained its ancient course till about the 12th century; but the exact period of the change is unknown; the whole space between it and the *Arnus,* in the lower part of their course, is so flat and low that it is said that their waters still communicate during great floods. A canal or ditch between the two streams still retained the name of *Osari* in the days of *Cluverius.* The modern name of *Serchio* is supposed to be a corruption of *Auserculus,* a form which is found in documents of the middle ages. (*Cluver. Ital.* p. 462; *Müller, Etrusker,* p. 213; *Targioni-Tozzetti, Viaggi* in *Toscana,* vol. ii. p. 146--178.) [*Auser*]

This tribe of the *Asii,* or the *Asaioi,* was among the most celebrated tribes of the *Scythians*. In the opinion of *Strabo,* the *Asii* had "the common appellation of *Scythians*". It was one of few *Scythian* tribes "who deprived the *Greeks* of *Bactriana*".

The *Asii, Asaioi, Auseis, Asiades* expanded into numerous branches – the *Astelebaioi, Asmanoi, Asiotai, Attasioi, Aspisioi Skythai, Asiades, Auseis, Assyrani, Asturoi, Lankiatoi, Brigaikinoi, Bedounisioi, Orniakoi, Loungonoi, Sailinoi, Souperatioi, Amakoi, Teibouroi, Egourroi, Gigourroi, Pesici, Lancieses, Zoelae,* and others. The etymological analysis of these tribal names proved their *Turkic* origin.

➢ *Astelebaioi* = Ἀστελεβαῖοι: As + Tel 'free' + Eb 'house' + Bai 'lord', meaning "nobles of the free house of the *As*" in *Turkic*. This branch of the *Asioi* tribe was *Lydian* as well. According to *Stephanus of Byzantium,* it inhabited the city of *Astelebe* (As + Tel 'free' + Eb 'house') in *Lydia*.

Most of the *Asioi* and their offshoots were scattered all over *Asia* and *Europe*. However, one derivative took the *African* direction and branched out there into a number of *African* tribes that still exist in *North Africa* and the *Sahara* Desert. *Herodotus* recorded them as the *Libyan Auseis*.

➢ <u>*Auseis* = Αὐσεῖς, aka *Ausees* = Αὐσέες, aka *Ausigdoi* = Αὔσιγδοι, aka *Auskhitai* = Αὐσχῖται, aka *Auskhisai* = Αὐσχίσαι, aka *Maxyes,* aka *Maksues* = Μάξυες, aka *Mazues* = Μάζυες, aka *Mazices,* aka *Maxitani,* aka *Maxytani,* aka *Tuaryk,* aka *Tuareg,* aka *Aghadez,* aka *Tagazi,* aka *Amaziq*</u>:

- *Auseis, Ausees: Aus > As* 'the *As*' + *Eis, Ees > İs* 'trace', meaning "remnants of the *As* tribe" in *Turkic*. *Stephanus of Byzantium* asserted *Herodotus*'s testimony: "Αὐσεῖς, ἔθνος Λιβύης." – "*Auseis*, a *Libyan* ethnos" [28].

- *Ausigdoi: Aus > As* 'the *As*' + *Igd > İgid* 'hero, man of courage', meaning "brave *As* men" in *Turkic*. This was another branch of the *Auseis* that made *Libya* their home, as stated by *Stephanus of Byzantium*:
    "Αὔσιγδα, πόλις Λιβύης… Ἑκαταῖος δὲ νῆσον οἶδε. τὸ ἐθνικὸν Αὔσιγδοι." –
    "*Ausigda*, a city in *Libya*…*Hecataeus* knows the island. The *Ausigdoi* tribe."

- *Auskhitai, Auskhisai:*
    - *Auskhitai: Aus > As* 'the *As*' + *Khitai > Xıtay, Qıtay* 'the name of the *Turkic* tribe', meaning "the *As* and the *Khitai*" in *Turkic*.
    - *Auskhitai: Aus > As* 'the *As*' + *Khitai > Katı* 'strong, powerful', meaning "powerful *As* tribe" in *Turkic*.
    - *Auskhisai: Aus > As* 'the *As*' + *Khisai > Küsəy* 'the name of a *Turkic* tribe',[29] meaning "the *As* and the *Khisai*" in *Turkic*.
    - *Auskhisai: Aus > As* 'the *As*' + *Khis > Xız, Küs* 'strength, power', meaning "powerful *As* tribe" in *Turkic*.

    Ancient scholars were at variance about the name of this *Libyan* tribe. While *Stephanus of Byzantium* recognized them as the *Auskhitai*:
    "Αὐσχῖται, ἔθνος Λιβύης ὑπὲρ Βάρκης." –
    "*Auskhitai*, a tribe in *Libya* above *Barca*",
    Herodotus called them the *Auskhisai*:
    "Next after the *Asbystai* on the West come the *Auchisai*: these dwell above *Barca* and reach down to the sea by *Euesperides*…" [4.171]

    In either case, there was a *Turkic* tribe with the matching name and its definition. There is a high probability that this *Libyan* tribe was a result of a mixture of the *Turkic Khitai* from the *Kashgar* region of *Turkestan* (the land of the *Uyghurs*, presently known as *Xinjiang* in *China*) and the *Lydian As* tribes. In our early chapters, we discussed the *Turkic* tribe of the *Khitai* (𐰴𐰃𐱃𐰞), or *Qıtay*,[30] based on the reports of the renowned scholars of the 19th c., and established a kin relationship of this *Turkic* tribe with the *Hittites* (aka the *Kheta* of *Syria*), the *Scythian* tribes – the *Khattai*, the *Matuketai*, the *Germanic* tribes – the *Chatti*, (aka the *Kháttai*) and their derivative – the *Khattourioi*, (aka the *Khaitouoroi*), and the *Turkic* tribes – the *Kataul*, the *Katağan*.

    Nowadays, the *Libyan Auseis*, or the *Mazues*, are known as the members of a greater *Berberian* family under a number of names, stemming from the same root – *Az*, or *As*, such as *Ama<u>z</u>igh*, *Ima<u>z</u>ighen*, and *Tama<u>z</u>ight*.

- *Maxyes, Maksues, Mazues, Mazices: M > Mən* 'great' + *Ax, Aks, Azic, Az > As* 'the *As*' + *Yes, Ues, Es > İs* 'trace', meaning "remnants of the great *As* tribe" in *Turkic*. Both names – *Ausees* and *Mazues* were derived from the same root – *Əs*, or *As*. The *Mazues* modified their name by adding *M* at the beginning. This is a rather frequent phenomenon observed in the words of *Turkic* origin, such as *Ares > Maris, Mars* "the god of war", *Az > Az-maz* "a little". In some cases, the letter *M* at the beginning stands for the reduced word *Mən* "grand, great" in *Turkic*: *Ama* "mother" > *Məmə* "grandmother", *Aça* "father" > *Maçi* "grandfather".

---

[28] All the texts by *Stephanus of Byzantium* in this present book were translated into *English* from *Greek* by the author of the present work.
[29] *Uraksin Z.G.* [855].
[30] "Drevneturkskiy slovar." [449].

Furthermore, according to the testimony of *William Smith,* the name of the tribe was misspelled in *Greek* as *Maxyes:*

> "The gentile name of the *Berbers – Amazigh,* "the noble language" is found, according to an observation of *Castiglione,* even in *Herodotus* (4.191, ed. *Bähr*), where the correct form is *Mazyes* (Μαζύες, *Hecataeus,* ap. Steph. B. sub voce s. u.), which occurs in the MSS., while the printed editions erroneously give Μαξύες (Niebuhr, Lect. on Anc. Ethnog. and Geog. vol. ii. p. 334), as well as in the later *Mazices* of *Ammianus Marcellinus* (29.5; Le Beau, Bas Empire, vol. iii. p. 471; comp. Gibbon, c. xxv.)" [*Mauretania*]

Ammianus Marcellinus introduced this tribe as the *Mazices,* a modified version of the *Mazues:*

> "Leaving this place, our general, advancing by long marches, reached *Tiposa,* where, with great elation, he gave answers to the envoys of the *Mazices,* who had combined with *Firmus,* and now in a suppliant tone implored pardon, replying to their entreaties that he would at once march against them as perfidious enemies." [29.5.17]

Initially known as the *Asiades,* "the progenitor of the *As*", this *Trojan* tribe was introduced by *Herodotus* as the *Ausees,* aka the *Maxyes,* who resettled in distant *Libya:*

> "The west side of the river *Triton* is inhabited by the *Libyan Auses,*[31] who being husbandmen, and accustom'd to live in houses, are call'd *Maxyes.* They wear long hair on the right side of the head, and shave the left. They paint the body with vermilion, and pretend to be of *Trojan* extraction. Their country, with all the rest of the western parts of *Libya* abounds more in woods and wild beasts, than those of the nomads." [4.191]

Herodotus gave a broad account about the *Libyan Ausees,* translated into *English* as the *Auseans:*

> "Next to these *Machlyes* are the *Auseans;* these and the *Machlyes,* separated by the *Triton,* live on the shores of the *Tritonian* lake. The *Machlyes* wear their hair long behind, the *Auseans* in front. They celebrate a yearly festival of *Athena,* where their maidens are separated into two bands and fight each other with stones and sticks, thus (they say) honoring in the way of their ancestors that native goddess whom we call *Athena.* Maidens who die of their wounds are called false virgins. Before the girls are set fighting, the whole people choose the fairest maid, and arm her with a *Corinthian* helmet and *Greek* panoply, to be then mounted on a chariot and drawn all along the lake shore. With what armor they equipped their maidens before *Greeks* came to live near them, I cannot say; but I suppose the armor was *Egyptian;* for I maintain that the *Greeks* took their shield and helmet from *Egypt.* As for *Athena,* they say that she was daughter of *Poseidon* and the *Tritonian* lake, and that, being for some reason angry at her father, she gave herself to *Zeus,* who made her his own daughter. Such is their tale. The intercourse of men and women there is promiscuous; they do not cohabit but have intercourse like cattle. When a woman's child is well grown, the men assemble within three months and the child is adjudged to be that man's whom it is most like." [4.180]

o *Maxitani, Maxytani: Max* 'great *As* tribe', 'great nobles' (*M + ∂s* 'lord, noble') + *Itan, Ytan* > *İtən* 'doer; maker', meaning "great *As* nation that produces noble men" in *Turkic.*

William Smith and *Justin* mentioned a king of the *Libyan* tribe of the *Maxitani – Hiarbas:*

> "They were probably the same people as those mentioned by *Justin* (18.7), and called *Maxytani,* whose king is said to have been *Hiarbas* (Verg. A. 4.36, 196, 326), and to have desired *Dido* for his wife. (Heeren, African Nations, vol. i. p. 34, trans.; Rennell, Geog. of Herod. vol. ii. p. 303.). [*William Smith. Maxyes*]

---

[31] In the original *Greek* text, it is *Ausees* = Αὐσέες.

"When the power of the *Carthaginians*, from success in their proceedings, had risen to some height, *Hiarbas*, king of the *Maxitani*, desiring an interview with ten of the chief men of *Carthage*, demanded *Elissa* in marriage, denouncing war in case of a refusal." [*Justin*. 18.6] However, *Virgil* ["The *Aeneid*." 4.31-54] and *Dante* ["The Divine Comedy." 31.70-90] introduced this *Libyan* ruler as King *Iarbas*. The name of *Iarbas*, or the corrupted version – *Hiarbas*, has *Turkic* roots: *Iar, Hiar > Yar* 'split, crack' + *Bas* 'head', meaning "the one who crashes enemies".

o *Tuareg, Tuaryk > Türük, Türk* "Turk" in *Turkic*. This *Libyan* tribe was a progeny of the *Trojan Asii*, resettled in *Libya* and renamed into *Mazues*, currently the *Tuaryk*. William Smith distinguished common features, inherent to their ancestors, as described by *Herodotus*, and retained by the descendant tribe, such as shaving the left side of the head and leaving hair on the right side to grow:

"…a *Libyan* tribe, and a branch of the nomad *Ausenses Herodotus* places them on the "other side," i. e. the W. bank, of the river *Triton:* reclaimed from nomad life, they were "tillers of the earth, and accustomed to live in houses." They still, however, retained some relics of their former customs, as "they suffer the hair on the right side of their heads to grow, but shave the left; they paint their bodies with red lead:" remains of this custom of wearing the hair are still preserved among the *Tuaryks,* their modern descendants. (*Hornemann*, Trav. p. 109.) They were probably the same people as those mentioned by *Justin* (18.7), and called *Maxytani,* whose king is said to have been *Hiarbas* (Verg. A. 4.36, 196, 326), and to have desired *Dido* for his wife. (Heeren, African Nations, vol. i. p. 34, trans.; Rennell, Geog. of Herod. vol. ii. p. 303.)" [*Maxyes*]

The *Tuaryk* were also divided into two main tribes – the *Aghadez* and the *Tagazi*, according to the 18th c. geographer and scientist *Alexander von Humboldt*:

"These two nations, which inhabit the desert between *Bornou, Fezzan,* and *Lower Egypt,* were first made more accurately known to us by the travels of *Hornemann* and *Lyon*…The *Tuaryks* are subdivided into two tribes — the *Aghadez* and the *Tagazi*. These are often caravan leaders and merchants. They speak the same language as the *Berbers,* and undoubtedly belong to the primitive *Lybian* races. They present the remarkable physiological phenomenon that, according to the character of the climate, the different tribes vary in complexion from a white to a yellow, or even almost black hue; but they never have woolly hair or negro features."

["Views of Nature Or Contemplations on the Sublime Phenomena of Creation, with Scientific Illustrations." 50-51]

o *Aghadez: Agh > Ağ* 'white' + *Adez > Ediz* '1.tall; 2.exalted; 3.high place', meaning "tribe of white-skinned, tall (or exalted) people" or "white-skinned tribe from a high place" in *Turkic*. This subsidiary tribe of the *Tuaryk* has a remarkably distinct *Turkic* name. Currently, they live in the *Agadez* region of *Niger* with the capital *Agadez*. Strikingly, there was a *Turkic* tribe of the *Ediz* – a subdivision of the *Oguz* confederation, indicated in "Drevneturkskiy slovar" [163].

o *Tagazi: Tag > Təg* 'race, origin' + *Azi > Az* 'the *Asii*', meaning "from the race of the *Az* or the *Asii*" in *Turkic*. The name of this *Tuaryk* tribe points to their remote *Trojan* roots.

o *Tibbo, Tibbou, Tibbos, Tibbous: Tib > Tip* 'foundation' + *Bo, Bou, Bos, Bous > Boi* 'tribe', meaning "essential tribe" in *Turkic*. The tribe of the *Tibbo* belonged to the *Berber* family, just like the *Tuaryk* and their derivatives. The *French* scientist and writer of the 19th c., *Louis Figuier*, classified them as a *Berber* tribe:

"The *Tibbous,* who wander over the country to the east of the *Sahara,* have been looked upon as belonging to the *Berber* family, but their complexion is darker and they do not speak the *Arab* tongue. Their noses are aquiline, their lips but slightly thick, they have intelligent faces, and are of slender build. Their activity is very great and they are addicted to robbing caravans." ["The Human Race." 363]

Interestingly, they were characterized like their ancient *Trojan* ancestors as "the birds" due to their constant change of habitation:

"The *Tibbos* or *Tibbous* occupy the eastern, and the *Tuaryks* (*Tueregs*) the western portion of the great sandy ocean. The former, from their habits of constant moving, were named by the other tribes "birds." [*Humboldt A.* "Views of Nature Or Contemplations on the Sublime Phenomena of Creation, with Scientific Illustrations." 50]

Though *Herodotus* took with a large grain of salt the claims of the *Mazues,* about their ancestral lineage connecting them straight to the *Trojan Asii,* or the *Ausees,* there are many factors that confirm their statements. First of all, etymologically, their names are of *Turkic* origin.

Secondly, there were cultural resemblances, such as the religious customs and traditions, including worship of the *Pelasgian* goddess *Athena.*

Thirdly, anatomically, their descendants – the *Tuaryk,* the *Aghadez,* the *Tagazi,* and the *Tibbo* are different from the *African* race, as they do not have "woolly hair or negro features", as stated by *Alexander von Humboldt.*

Fourthly, the mtDNA analysis confirmed that the *Tuaryk,* or the *Tuareg,* have a *European* origin and arrived in *Libya* 8-9 thousand years ago:

"The *Tuareg* of the *Fezzan* region (*Libya*) are characterized by an extremely high frequency (61%) of haplogroup H1, a mitochondrial DNA (mtDNA) haplogroup that is common in all *Western European* populations. Coalescence time estimates suggest an arrival of the *European* H1 mtDNAs at about 8,000–9,000 years ago, while phylogenetic analyses reveal three novel H1 branches, termed H1v, H1w and H1x, which appear to be specific for *North African* populations, but whose frequencies can be extremely different even in relatively close *Tuareg* villages."

[*Claudio Ottoni,* et al. "Mitochondrial Haplogroup H1 in *North Africa:* An Early Holocene Arrival from *Iberia.*" doi:10.1371/journal.pone.0013378]

The fact that the common ancestor of Haplogroup H emerged in the *Caucasus* and the *Middle East* around 18,000 years ago, from where the descendants dispersed all over *Europe* and the *Iberian Peninsula,* proves that the *Tuaryk* and their *Berber* forefathers did not belong to the *African* race.

Figure 1. A Tuaryk man.
Credit: FreeImages.com/Luisa Russo.

Figure 2. An aged Turkish man portrait captured during after-coup night demonstration of President Erdogan supporters. Istanbul, Turkey, Eastern Europe and Western Asia. 22 July 2016.
Credit: Mstyslav Chernov (CC BY-SA 4.0). Cropped.

Fifthly, the structure of their society decidedly matches that of the *Trojan* and *Turkic* nations, such as confederation, matrilineality, nomadism. The *Tuaryk* clans always get united into a confederation. They adhere to a kinship system, in which ancestral descent is traced through maternal instead of paternal lines, similar to the *Akkadians,* the *Etruscans,* the *Lycians*. And just like their *Trojan* and *Turkic* ancestors, the *Tuaryk* maintained a nomadic lifestyle.

And lastly, *Trojan, Turkic,* and *Tuaryk* nations used the ancient alphabet, emanating from a common *Turkic* source. The table below comparing the alphabets of the *Ancient Berber,* [32] used by all the *Berber* tribes before the common era and later modified into the *Tifinagh* script, and the ancient *Turkic,* revealed stunning similarities between these two sets of letters.

ANCIENT BERBER	ANCIENT TURKIC
⊙ ⊡	⊙ ⊙ ⬦
Γ V ∧	∧ ∧ ⌐⌐
⊓ ⊐ ⊏	⊓ ⌒
‖‖‖	∣
= ‖	⦁ ⫞
—	∣
X	8 8
○ ☐	☐ ○
⋛ M ⋚	M ⋛
+ ×	×
⊐ ⊔	⩓ ⩓ ⩓ ⩓
⋒	Ɛ
⊁	Ψ
I	I
Z N	⇞ N
⊢ ⊤ ⊤	⊣⊢
H	H H
⊠	⊠ ⋈
⊔ U ⊓	⊃ ⊓ ⊃

---

[32] See www.omniglot.com/writing/berber.htm

This table vividly illustrates and confirms the declared postulates about the close connection between the *Trojan Asii*, the *Libyan Auseis*, including their *Berber* derivatives, and the *Turkic* nations (mostly *Turks* and *Azerbaijanis*) on all major levels – cultural, societal, genetic, anatomical, and linguistic. It is also a testament that the *Turkic* nations, being very ancient, represent a unique family of people that has a multiracial background, as one group of *Turkic* nations are *Asians*, the second one – *Caucasians* and *Europeans*, the third one – more deeply and timewise remotely related *Africans* and *Native Americans*.

At this point, it has been determined that two *Trojan* nations were of *Scythian* extraction – the *Asii* and the *Mysians*. The latter are also considered to be the *Thracians*. Now, a mind-boggling conclusion begs to emerge: if the *Asii*, related to the *Lydians*, aka the *Meonians*, aka the *Mysians*, kin to the *Carians*, aka the *Leleges*, aka the *Trojans*, are of *Scythian* extraction, then all other *Trojan* nations belong to the greater *Scythian* family by default. The kinship with the *Scythians* automatically applies to the remaining *Trojan* nations in this group, as they all were related by blood. This includes another major part of the present group – the *Turreni*, aka the *Etrusci*, aka the *Etrurians*, aka the *Tusci*.

> *Tyrrheni*, aka *Turreni*, aka *Turrenoi* = Τυρρηνοὶ, aka *Tursenoi* = Τυρσηνοί, aka *Troskoi* = Τροσκοι, aka *Etrusci*, aka *Etrouskoi* = Ἐτροῦσκοι, aka *Etrurians*, aka *Touskoi* = Τόυσκοι, aka *Toskoi* = Τοσκοι, aka *Tusci*, aka *Thusci*, aka *Rasenna* = Ῥασέννα, aka *Rasena* = Ῥασένα, aka *Raeti*, aka *Rhaeti*, aka *Raitoi* = Ῥαιτοί:
  o *Tyrrheni, Turreni, Turrenoi, Tursenoi*: *Tyrr, Turr, Turs > Tur* 'ascend' + *En > -An* 'an affix, denoting constant action', meaning "ascending" in *Turkic*. As it was traditional in the ancient world to set the name of a tribe or nation after its leader, the *Tyrreni* also acquired their name after *Turren*. However, this name of the *Trojan-Lydian* prince was spelled differently by the *Greek* scholars. *Herodotus* introduced him as *Tursenos* = Τυρσηνός (*Tursen > Tursun* 'ascend' + *Os > Us* 'master'), while *Strabo* presented him as *Turrenos* = Τυρρηνός (*Turren > Turan* 'ascending' + *Os > Us* 'master'). As a result, the name of the nation also varied from *Turrenoi* to *Tursenoi*. Both names are valid, as they both proceed from the same root *Tur* that has several meanings – "powerful" as an adjective and "ascend" as a verb, just like in other kindred nations' names – *Trojans, Thracians, Treres,* and *Turks*. Moreover, these two *Etruscan* names have their *Turkic* counterparts that are still in usage by the modern *Turkic* nations:
    ▪ *Turenos, Turrenos > Turan* – a *Turkic* male and female name, means "ascending" in *Turkic*. This name is currently used in *Northern* and *Southern Azerbaijan*.
    ▪ *Tursenos > Tursun* – a *Turkic* male name, means "ascend; long live" in *Turkic*. Nowadays, it is mostly used among the *Uzbeks, Tatars, Uyghurs,* and *Kazakhs*.

"Drevneturkskiy Slovar" detected the appellation *Turan* in a *Turkic* male name – *Yigin Alp Turan* [260] and a *Turkic* country name – *Turanlıq* [33] "the inhabitants of *Turan*", "*Turks*" [587]. There is a very crucial point that has to be addressed here in reference to the country of *Turan* and its misinterpretation by some pro-*Persian* proponents. The latter always claim, without even properly consulting the source, that the country *Turan* was named after the *Persian* prince *Tur* and refer to the 10th - 11th c. poet *Ferdowsi*, or *Firdousi*, and his poem "Shahnameh" ("The Epic of Kings"). However, the *Persian* verseman did not state anything even close to that. The poet clearly indicated that the *Persian* king *Feridoun* divided the world, three parts of which he assigned to his sons: *Roum* (*Rome*) and the *West* (روم و خاور) – to *Salem*; the domain of the *Turks* (ترک) – the land of *Turan* (توران زمین), the lands of the *Salar Turks* [34] (سالار ترکان), and *China* (چین) – to *Tur*; and *Iran* with the *Nizhvaran* plain (دشت نیزهوران) – to *Iraj*:

---

[33] *Turanlıq > Turan* 'name of the *Turkic* country' + *-Lıq* 'an affix, equivalent to the word *Having*' in *Turkic*.
[34] Currently known as the *Salar*, these *Turkic* people of the *Oguz* branch reside in *China*.

"Then having read the secrets of Fate, *Feridoun* parted the world and gave the three parts unto his sons in suzerainty. *Roum* and *Khaver*, [35] which are the lands of the setting sun, did he give unto *Silim*. *Turan* and *Turkistan* [36] did he give unto *Tur*, and made him master of the *Turks* and of *China*, but unto *Irij* [37] he gave *Iran*, with the throne of might and the crown of supremacy." [Translated by *Helen Zimmern*. "*Feridoun*." 5]

به سه بخش کرد آفریدون جهان	نهفته چو بیرون کشید از نهان
سیم دشت گردان و ایران‌زمین	یکی روم و خاور دگر ترک و چین
همه روم و خاور مر او را سزید	نخستین به سلم اندرون بنگرید
گرازان سوی خاور اندر کشید	به فرزند تا لشکری برگزید
همی خواندندش خاور خدای	به تخت کیان اندر آورد پای
ورا کرد سالار ترکان و چین	دگر تور را داد توران زمین
کشید آنگهی تور لشکر به راه	یکی لشکری نامزد کرد شاه
کمر بر میان بست و بگشاد دست	بیامد به تخت کنی برنشست
همی پاک توران شهش خواندند	بزرگان بر او گوهر افشاندند
مر او را پدر شاه ایران گزید	از ایشان چو نوبت به ایرج رسید
هم آن تخت شاهی و تاج سران	هم ایران و هم دشت نیزه‌وران
همان کرسی و مهر و آن تخت عاج	بدو داد کو را سزا بود تاج
چنان مرزبانان فرخ نژاد	نشستند هر سه به آرام و شاد

[*Ferdowsi*. "*Shahname*" in *Persian*. – *Feridoun*. 5]

As we see, the author specifically pointed out that *Tur* was assigned to rule the country of the *Turks* – *Turan* and the lands of the *Chinese* and the *Salar Turks*. Nowhere did he mention the unfounded claim that the country of *Turan* acquired its name after the *Persian* prince *Tur*. If that were the case, then the same principle should have applied to *China*, as well as to *Roum*, or *Rome*, to which the *Persian* king appointed his other sons as the rulers. In fact, *Firdousi* asserted that *Turan* was the country of the *Turks*.

Nobody in their right mind can say that *Rome* and the *West* were named after the *Persian* prince *Silim* (*Salem*) or *Iran* – after the *Persian* prince *Iraj*.

Obviously, *Turan*, *Turkestan*, or the lands of the *Salar Turks*, *China*, *Roum*, and *Iran* had already been established as countries under the corresponding names long before even the *Persian* princes were born, and *Firdousi*, in his compilation of the poetic fairy tales, full of monsters and evil spirits, distinctly affirmed that.

Remarkably, the *Arabic* writer of the 9th c. *Ibn Khordadbeh*, who lived one century before *Ferdowsi*, asserted in "The Book of Roads and Kingdoms" that *Turan* was the ruler of the country of the *Turks*:

"The monarchs, whom *Ardashir* called "Shah": *Buzurg Kushan-Shah, Kilan-Shah, Buz Ardashiran-Shah*, which means "[a ruler] of *Mosul*", *Maysan-Shah, Buzurg Armaniyan-Shah, Azarbazgan-Shah, Sijistan-Shah, Marv-Shah, Badashvarkar-Shah, Yaman-Shah, Taziyan-Shah, Kazash-Shah, Burjan-Shah, Amukan-Shah, Sabiyan-Shah, Mushkizdan-Shah* (in *Khorasan*), *Allan-Shah* (in *Mugan*), *Barashkan-Shah* (in *Azerbaijan*), *Kufs-Shah* (in *Kirman*), *Makran-Shah* (in *Sind*), **Turan**-*Shah* (in [the country] of the *Turks*), *Hinduvan-Shah, Kabulan-Shah, Shiryan-Shah* (in *Azerbaijan*), *Raykhan-Shah* (from *Hind*), *Gigan-Shah* (in *Sind*), *Balashajan-Shah, Davarkhan-Shah* (in *Davar* country), *Nakhshaban-Shah,*

---

[35] It means "the *Western* countries", or "the *West*".
[36] In the original *Persian* text, it is "*Salar Turkan*", or the *Salar Turks*.
[37] It should be *Iraj* ایرج

Kashmiran-Shah, Bakardan-Shah, Kuzafat-Shah – all these are the names of the sovereigns." [38] [11]

The *British* scholar, who translated the genealogical history of the *Turkic* nations, written by *Abul Ghazi Bahader Khan*, the king of *Khowarazm*, also emphasized the cases of intentional misrepresentation of the historical facts by the *Persian* chronologers:

"The *Persian* historians make *Tur,* the founder of the *Turkish* nation, to have been a son of one their first monarchs, and represent the *Tartar* princes as often overcome and made tributary by their heroes; which runs counter to what has been advanced by our *Tartar* historian. The *Persian* writers consider *Afrasiab* king of *Turkestan* as a great hero, and conqueror of *Persia;* whereas, according to the *Khan* of *Khowarazm, Afrasiab Khan* was at the head only of an inferior monarchy, and is not placed in the line of *Mogul* or *Tartarian* emperors." [Preface]

o *Tusci, Thusci, Touskoi, Troskoi* > *Tuskan* "a relative" in *Turkic* (*Tu* 'be born' + *-S* 'an affix, denoting an order' + *-Kan* 'an affix, converting a verb into a noun'). By the way, *Ptolemy* mentioned the *Tusci* as the inhabitants of the area "between the *Caucasus* mountains and the *Ceruani* mountains", who were the remnants of the magnificent *Etruscan* nation.

o *Etrusci, Etrouskoi: Etr* > *Er* 'warrior, man' + *Trusci, Trouskoi* > *Tusci* > *Tuskan* 'a relative', meaning "warrior kinsman" in *Turkic*. In this case, a consonant rearrangement between *R* and *T* took place. This is a very frequent phenomenon in the *Turkic* languages. Compare:
Kirpik = Kiprik, Ördək = Ödirək.

o *Etrurians: Etr* > *Er* 'warrior, man' + *Trur* > *Tur* 'the *Tur* nation', meaning "warrior nation of the *Tur*" in *Turkic*. Actually, the name of the *Etrurians* is known as such only in *English* and is based on the name of the *Italian* district *Etruria*. *Pliny the Elder* called it *Hetruria*.

o *Rasenna, Rasena: Ra* 'reputation' + *Sen* > *San* 'respect, esteem' + *Na* > *-Ni* 'an affix, similar to the word *Having*', meaning "highly esteemed" or "having an esteemed reputation" in *Turkic*. There is a *Turkic* equivalent of this name, existing as a set expression in *Azerbaijani* – *Ad-Sanlı* "having an esteemed reputation" [39]. In addition to a multitude of other appellations, this nation also named itself after their leader *Rasenna* to indicate a separate branch of the *Etruscan* people, according to *Dionysius of Halicarnassus:*

"The *Romans* give them different appellations: For, from the country they once inhabited, named *Etruria,* they call them *Etrusci,* and from their knowledge in the ceremonies relating to divine worship, in which they excel all others, they call them, at this time, though less accurately, *Tusci,* but formerly, with the same accuracy, as the *Greeks,* they called them *Thyscoi:* However, they call themselves from the name of one of their leaders, *Razenua*." [40] ["*Roman* antiquities." 1.30.3]

o *Raeti, Rhaeti, Raitoi* > *Riayət* "esteem, honor" [41] in *Turkic*. Following their cultural tradition, the *Etruscans* again renamed themselves after their leader when they got displaced by the *Gauls*. This time they called themselves "the nation of *Rhaetia*", according to *Justin:*

"*Tusci* quoque duce *Raeto* avitis sedibus amissis *Alpes* occupavere et ex nomine ducis gentem *Raetorum* condiderunt." [20.5.9]

---

[38] Translated into *English* by the author of the present book.
[39] *Orujev O.I.* [487].
[40] In the original *Greek* text, it is *Rasenna* ('Ρασέννα).
[41] Not to confuse with the *Arabic* word *Raıyat* "people". According to *Radlov V.V., Riayət* is a *Turkic* word [3.1.720].

"The *Etruscans*,[42] too, when they were driven from their old settlements, betook themselves, under a captain named *Rhaetus*, towards the *Alps*, where they founded the nation of *Rhaetia*, so named from their leader." [20.5]

This *Trojan* nation of the *Turreni*, with numerous name variations derived from the *Scythian* and *Pelasgian* roots, was a founder of the *Roman Empire*. A senator and historian of the *Roman* Empire, who lived in 56-120 CE, *Publius Cornelius Tacitus* disclosed in his work "The Annals" how the *Tyrrhenians* emerged as a nation:

"The *Sardians*[43] read out a decree linking them by blood to the *Etruscans*: since *Lydus* and *Tyrrhenus*, sons of King *Atys*, had divided the nation, *Lydus* retaining the land of his fathers, *Tyrrhenus* being given the task of founding a new colony; and the two leaders gave their names to their territories in *Asia Minor* (*Lydia*) and *Italy* (*Tyrrhenia*) respectively. *Lydia* added further to its power, by sending colonists to that peninsula which later took its name from *Pelops* (the *Peloponnese*)." [4.55]

His asseveration was initially announced by *Herodotus*:

"The customs of the *Lydians* differ little from those of the *Grecians*...They were the first of all the nations we know, who introduc'd the art of coining gold and silver to facilitate trade, and first practis'd the way of retailing merchandize. They pretend to be the inventors of divers games, which are now common to them with the *Grecians*. And, as they say, were found out about the time they sent a colony to *Turrenia* on this occasion. During the reign of *Atys*, the son of *Manes* – king of *Lydia*, a scarcity of provisions spread over the kingdom, which the people for a time supported with patience and industry. But when they saw the evil still continuing, they applied themselves to find out a remedy; and some inventing one game, and others another, they gradually introduced dice, balls, tables, and all other plays, chess only excepted, of which the *Lydians* do not challenge the invention. And to bear this calamity better, they us'd to play one whole day without intermission, that they might not be disquieted with the thoughts of food; eating and drinking on the next day, without amusing themselves with any kind of game. After they had continued this alternate manner during eighteen years, and found their wants rather increasing than abating, the king divided the people into two parts, and order'd them to determine by lot, which division should relinquish the country and which should remain in possession; he himself designing to reign over those who should have the fortune to stay, and appointing his son *Tyrrhenus* to command that part which should be oblig'd to remove. Those who by lot were constrain'd to depart, march'd down to *Smyrna*, where having built a sufficient number of ships, and put all things necessary on board, they set sail in search of food, and of a new habitation; till having pass'd by many nations, they arriv'd in *Umbria*, and built divers cities, which they inhabit to this day. There they chang'd their ancient name, and were no longer call'd *Lydians* but *Tyrrhenians*, from their leader *Tyrrhenus*,[44] the son of their king." [1.94]

Strabo also confirmed that "the *Lydians*...had taken the name of *Tyrrheni*..." after the *Trojan* prince from *Lydia Tyrrenus*, a son of King *Atys*, who was a progeny of the world-famous hero *Hercules*:

"The *Greeks* thus named them from *Tyrrhenus*[45] the son of *Atys*, as they say, who sent hither a colony from *Lydia*. *Atys*, who was one of the descendants of *Hercules* and *Omphale*, and had two sons, in a time of famine and scarcity determined by lot that *Lydus* should remain in the

---

[42] In the original *Latin* text, it is *Tusci*.
[43] The *Trojans* who lived in the capital of *Lydia* – *Sardis*.
[44] In the original *Greek* text, it is *Tursenos* = Τυρσηνός.
[45] In the original *Greek* text, it is *Turrenos* = Τυρρηνός.

country, but that *Tyrrhenus*, with the greater part of the people, should depart. Arriving here, he named the country after himself, *Tyrrhenia*, and founded twelve cities, having appointed as their governor *Tarcon*,[46] from whom the city of *Tarquinia*[47] [received its name], and who, on account of the sagacity which he had displayed from childhood, was feigned to have been born with hoary hair. Placed originally under one authority, they became flourishing; but it seems that in after-times, their confederation being broken up and each city separated, they yielded to the violence of the neighbouring tribes. Otherwise they would never have abandoned a fertile country for a life of piracy on the sea, roving from one ocean to another; since, when united they were able not only to repel those who assailed them, but to act on the offensive, and undertake long campaigns." [5.2.2]

According to *Ptolemy*, the *Tyrrenoi* were the same *Touskoi*:

"…the *Touskoi* who in *Greek* are called *Turrenoi*…" [3.1] [48]

Strabo shared *Ptolemy's* view about the *Touskoi* and the *Turrenoi* being the same:

"The *Turrenoi* have now received from the *Romans* the surname of *Etrouskoi* and *Touskoi*." [5.2.2][49]

Plutarch also called them the *Turrenoi*, (though it was translated into *English* as the *Tuscans*), who were originally from the *Lydian* city *Sardis*:

"And of the *Tuscans*, the people of *Veii*, who possessed much territory and dwelt in a great city, were the first to begin war with a demand for *Fidenae*, which they said belonged to them…For the *Tuscans* are said to be colonists from *Sardis*, and *Veii*[50] is a *Tuscan* city." [1. *Romulus*. 25]

Justin characterized them as the *Tusci* from *Lydia*, erroneously translated into *English* as the *Etrurians*:

"Many *Italian* cities, indeed, after so long a lapse of time, still exhibit some traces of *Greek* manners; for the *Etrurians*,[51] who occupy the shore of the *Tuscan* Sea, came from *Lydia*; and *Troy*, after it was taken and overthrown, sent thither the *Veneti* (whom we see on the coast of the *Adriatic*), under the leadership of *Antenor*." [20.1]

Both the land *Etruria*, or *Hetruria*, and its resilient inhabitants frequently changed their names throughout history, as it was asserted by *Pliny the Elder*:

"The coast of *Liguria* lieth between the Rivers *Varus* and *Macra*, 211 miles. To it is adjoined the seventh, wherein is *Hetruria*, from the river *Macra*: and itself, with the names often changed. In old time the *Pelasgi* drove the *Umbri* from thence: and by them the *Lydi* did the like, of whose King they were named *Tyrrheni*: but soon after, of their ceremonies in sacrificing, in the *Greek* language *Thusci*." ["*Pliny's* Natural History." 3.5]

Tacitus also chipped in and presented the *Trojan* capital *Ilium* as "the parent of *Rome*", confirming the commonly accepted *Lyde-Turrenian* connection:

---

[46] The word *Tarcon (Tarkon = Τάρκων)* has a *Turkic* origin from *Tarcan* and means "governor".
[47] In the original *Greek* text, it is *Tarkunia = Ταρκυνία*.
[48] Translated into *English* by the author of the current work.
[49] This excerpt was rendered into *English* by the creator of this book.
[50] A purely *Tuscan* city of *Etruria*, known as *Oueioi = Οὐήιοι, Ouioi = Οὐιοί* in *Greek*.
[51] In the original *Latin* text, it is *Tusci*.

"Even *Ilium*,[52] though it recalled *Troy*, the parent of *Rome*, held no significance except its glorious past." ["The Annals." 4.55]

In spite of the overwhelming chorus of the ancient historians and men of science, asserting that the *Turreni* were the *Trojan* nation of the *Lydians,* one of the *Greek* portrayers of the antique life – *Dionysius of Halicarnassus* went against the grain and tried to prove everyone wrong — from the prominent patriarch of history *Herodotus* to the illustrious geographer *Strabo* on this matter, claiming that the *Turreni* had no connection to the *Lydians:*

"For this reason, I am persuaded that the *Tyrrhenians,* and the *Pelasgi* are a different people. However, I do not think that the *Tyrrhenians* were a colony of the *Lydians:* For they do not use the same language with the latter; neither can it be alleged that, though they agree, no longer, in that respect, they, still, retain some other indications of their mother country. For, they neither worship the same gods as the *Lydians,* nor make use of the same laws, or institutions: but, in these, they differ more from the *Lydians,* than from the *Pelasgi:* And those seem to come nearest to the truth, who do not look upon them as a foreign people, but as natives of the country; since they are found to be a very ancient nation, and to agree with no other, either in their language, or in their manner of living: And there is no reason why the *Greeks* may not be supposed to have called them by this name, both from their living in towers, and from the name of their kings." [1.30]

Dionysius of Halicarnassus reminds us of some hoary and modern scholars who, in their big strife of distinguishing themselves from the crowd by any means, are ready to provide shocking but unsubstantiated statements. *Dionysius of Halicarnassus's* false conjecture got easily refuted by the *Italian* professor *Piazza* and his colleagues in their reputable genetic research. Based on this genetic research, the article "Ancient *Etruscans* were immigrants from *Anatolia*, or what is now *Turkey*", presented by the *European* Society of Human Genetics in 2007, supported both *Strabo's* and *Herodotus's* claims about the origin of the *Etruscans,* or the *Turreni*. According to this article, the archeological sites of ancient *Etruscan* cities reveal their continuous occupation since the Iron Age and stand silent witnesses to the fact that the *Etruscan* history in *Etruria* started with the arrival of the ancient *Lydians* from the present-day south coast of *Turkey,* as it was asserted by *Herodotus* and *Strabo* [*European* Society of Human Genetics. "Ancient *Etruscans* Were Immigrants from *Anatolia,* Or What Is Now *Turkey*." ScienceDaily. 18 June 2007. www.sciencedaily.com/releases/2007/06/ 070616191 637.htm].

Despite the available genetic research and affirmations from reputable academic sources, there are quite a few ignorant pseudo-experts who refer to *Dionysius of Halicarnassus's* baseless claims to prove their false conjectures. The author's assertion about the *Lydians* and the *Turreni* not using the same language reveals his ignorance about the historical facts, such as nations switching their language or unlearning their own language, in particular, a *Pelasgian* tribe of *Attica* – the *Attikoi;* the *Cranian Pelasgians,* renamed into the *Cecropians,* then into the *Athenians,* and then into a *Greek* tribe of the *Ionians;* a division of a *Trojan* tribe of the *Leleges,* later recognized as a *Greek* tribe of the *Locrians,* all of which assumed the language and identity of the *Greeks,* as stated by *Herodotus* [8.44;1.57], *Strabo* [12.4.6], and even by *Dionysius of Halicarnassus* himself in the passing about the *Leleges-Locrians:*

"After they had remained there five generations, during which, they arrived to the greatest prosperity, enjoying the most fertile plains in *Thessaly,* in the sixth generation, they were driven out of it by the *Curetes,* and *Leleges,* who are now called *Aetoli,* and *Locri,* and by many others,

---

[52] Modern day *Hisarlik* in *Turkey*.

who inhabit near *Parnassus,* their enemies being commanded by *Deucalion,* the son of *Prometheus* and *Clymene,* the daughter of *Oceanus.*" [1.17]

By the time of *Dionysius of Halicarnassus* — 1st century BCE, the language of the *Turreni* most definitely had changed, if counting from the moment they landed on the *Etrurian* soil back on the 12th century BCE. Slowly but surely, the *Turreni* assimilated among the *Latins* and switched their language. However, one must not forget that these *Turreni* brought the alphabet to the *Latin* nation, equivalent to the *Lydian* and similar to the *Pelasgian* script.

A *Roman* poet *Virgil* poetically described the divine intervention that facilitated the vanishing of the *Trojans,* known later as the *Etrusci,* on the *Roman* soil, in the dialogue between *Jupiter* and his sinister wife *Juno,* who pled against the *Trojans* to lose their identity, language, and culture:

> "Then thus the founder of mankind replies
> (Unruffled was his front, serene his eyes):
> "Can *Saturn's* issue, and heaven's other heir,
> Such endless anger in her bosom bear?
> Be mistress, and your full desires obtain;
> But quench the choler you foment in vain.
> From ancient blood th' *Ausonian* people [53] sprung,
> Shall keep their name, their habit, and their tongue.
> The *Trojans* to their customs shall be tied:
> I will, myself, their common rites provide;
> The natives shall command, the foreigners subside.
> All shall be *Latium; Troy* without a name;
> And her lost sons forget from whence they came.
> From blood so mix'd, a pious race shall flow,
> Equal to gods, excelling all below."
> ["The *Aeneid.*" Translated by *John Dryden.* 12]

Other two claims brought forward by *Dionysius of Halicarnassus,* such as the *Turreni* "neither worship the same gods as the *Lydians,* nor make use of similar laws, or institutions" are also false, as both the *Turreni* and the *Lydians* worshipped the same pantheon of gods, such as *Apulu/Aplu,* or *Apollo, Hercle,* or *Hercules, Nethuns,* or *Neptune.* And both of the nations instituted a similar manner of living and structure of the society – established a confederation of 12 tribes and cities, founded cities, and built walls:

> "[They add that the *Tyrrheni*] built there twelve cities, and named the metropolis *Capua.* But luxury having made them effeminate, in the same way that they had formerly been driven from the banks of the *Po,* they were now forced to abandon this country to the *Samnites;* who in their turn fell before the *Romans*…In the interior is the metropolis, *Capua,*[54] being, as the etymon of the name signifies, 'the head'; for in regard to it all the other cities appear small, excepting *Teanum – Sidicinum,* which is a very considerable place." [*Strabo.* 5.4.3]

Pliny the Elder also gave a short description of some of the *Etruscan* cities:

> "The first towne of *Hetruria,* is *Luna,* famous for the haven; then the Colonie *Luca,* lying from the sea: and neerer unto it, is *Pisæ,* betweene the river *Auser* and *Arnus,* which tooke the beginning from *Pelops* and the *Pisians,* or *Atintanians* a *Greeke* nation. *Vada Volaterranea,* the

---

[53] The *Latins.*
[54] In the original text, it is *Capo* = Καπω and proceeds from the *Turkic* – *Kapa,* meaning "a head" [*Radlov.* 2.1.404]. It is still in use in contemporary *Turkish* as *Kafa* and *Azerbaijani* as *Qafa.*

river *Cecinna. Populonium* of the *Tuscanes* in times past, situate onely upon this coast. After these, the rivers *Prille,* and another after *Umbro,* navigable, and of it tooke name; so forward the tract of *Umbria,* and the port towne *Telamon: Coassa Volscientium,* a colonie planted there by the people of *Rome, Graviscæ, Castrum Novum; Pyrgi,* the river *Cæretanus,* and *Cære* itself, standing foure miles within, called *Agylla* by the *Pelasgians* who built it: *Alsium* and *Frugenæ.* The river *Tiberis,* distant from *Macra* 284 miles. Within-forth are these colonies, *Falisca* descended from *Argi* (as *Cato* saith) and for distinction it is called *Hetruscorum.*" [3.8]

Interestingly, some *Roman* historians did not discriminate the *Trojan* nations from the *Greeks,* wrongfully considering them all as the *Greek* nation, including *Justin:*

"Many *Italian* cities, indeed, after so long a lapse of time, still exhibit some traces of *Greek* manners; for the *Etrurians,* who occupy the shore of the *Tuscan* Sea, came from *Lydia;* and *Troy,* after it was taken and overthrown, sent thither the *Veneti* (whom we see on the coast of the *Adriatic*), under the leadership of *Antenor. Adria,* too, which is near the *Illyrian* Sea, and which gave name also to the *Adriatic,* is a *Greek* city; and *Diomede,* being driven by shipwreck, after the destruction of *Troy,* into those parts, built *Arpi. Pisae,* likewise, in *Liguria,* had *Grecian* founders; and *Tarquinii,* in *Etruria,* as well as *Spina* in *Umbria,* has its origin from the *Thessalians; Perusia* was founded by the *Achaeans.* Need I mention *Caere?* Or the people of *Latium,* who were settled by *Aeneas?* Are not the *Falisci,* are not *Nola* and *Abella,* colonies of the *Chalcidians?* What is all the country of *Campania?* What are the *Bruttii* and *Sabines?* What are the *Samnites?* What are the *Tarentines,* whom we understand to have come from *Lacedaemon,* and to have been called *Spurii?* The city of *Thurii* they say that *Philoctetes* built; and his monument is seen there to this day, as well as the arrows of *Hercules,* on which the fate of *Troy* depended, laid up in the temple of *Apollo.*" [20.1]

Having arrived in *Italy* 10-12 centuries prior to *Common Era*, the *Etrusci* became a prominent nation, who founded the glorious *Roman* race and dominion, gave the existing *Latin* race their alphabet, which is currently known as *Latin* and has been used as such worldwide without any credit to its creators – the *Etrusci,* aka the *Turreni.*

The indubitable *Turkic* origin of the *Etrusci* was triumphantly proved, on the base of the philological and mythological evidence, by the outstanding linguist of the 19th c. *Isaac Taylor,* in his book "*Etruscan Researches*". This was done after all the unsuccessful attempts by other authors to decipher the *Etruscans* sepulchral inscriptions:

"*Latin, Greek, Oscan, Hebrew, Phoenician, Arabic, Ethiopic, Chinese, Coptic*, and *Basque* have all been tried in turn. *Sir W. Betham* believed the *Etruscan* to be a *Keltic* dialect. *Dr. Donaldson* and the Earl of *Crawford* have attempted to show that it is *Gothic. Mr. Robert Ellis* has expended much ingenuity and learning in the attempt to prove its *Armenian* affinities. *Dr. Steub* maintains that it is a *Rhaeto-Romansch* speech. It may be safely affirmed that none of these attempts have been regarded as satisfactory by any person except their authors." [3]

The location of the main monuments, tombs, and artifacts of *Etruscan* art and civilization, collected predominantly in the twelve *Etrurian* cities, pointed to the fact that the *Etrusci,* aka the *Etruscans,* preferred to dwell in the cities without proper mingling with the rural population – a race of the conquered, speaking a different language. *Isaac Taylor* compared the *Etruscan* society to the *Turkish* Empire of the 19th c. and correctly predicted the same demise and language disappearance of the ruling nation:

"At the present time we have in the *Turkish* empire a pretty exact parallel to the state of society which must have existed in ancient *Etruria.* The *Turks,* like their kinsmen the *Turrhenna,* constitute an aristocracy of conquest, a ruling class, dwelling almost exclusively in the great cities, and having no tendency to amalgamate with the subject-races. Throughout *Turkey, Syria, Egypt, Tunis,* and *Tripoli,* the language of the court, of the law, of the bureaucracy, and of the aristocracy, is the *Osmanli;* [55] various *Greek, Slavonic, Arabic,* and *Berber* dialects being spoken by the artisans and the villagers, who constitute the great bulk of the population. If the *Turkish* empire were overthrown, the *Turkish* language would speedily fall into disuse, and the elements of the *Turkish* nationality would rapidly be absorbed. These considerations may help to account for the rapid and complete disappearance of the *Etruscan* language from *Etruria,* and also for the fact that in the present speech of *Tuscany* few, if any, *Etruscan* elements can be detected." [17]

The *Etruscans,* aka the *Turreni,* were famous for a number of accomplishments, encompassing different area of life – great seafarers, city builders who gained outstanding artistic achievements, reflected in the well-preserved tombs:

"It may be said that the ceramic art of the *Etruscans* has been the one great permanent legacy which they have bequeathed to the world. The suggestion may perhaps be allowed that the art of modern *Europe* owes much to the hereditary transmission of the *Etruscan* instinct for form and colour. Geographically, ancient *Etruria* is modern *Tuscany.* The blood of the mediaeval *Florentines* was probably *Etruscan,* with but small alien admixture. It was at *Florence* that the arts instinctively revived at the earliest possible moment after the *European* cataclysm. The earliest homes of art, the leading schools of colour, were at *Bologna, Florence, Perugia, Siena, Lucca,* and *Parma* — cities which belonged, all of them, to the old *Etruscan* dominion. All the greatest colourists have come from this region. *Titian* is an apparent exception, but the name of *Titian* is one of the commonest of the names in the ancient *Etruscan* sepulchres. *Giotto, Fra Angelico, Ghirlandajo, Masaccio, Perugino, Fra Bartolemmeo, Leonardo, Coreggio, Garofalo, Michael Angelo, Eaphael, Francia, Guido Eeni, Domenichino,* and the *Caracci,* were all *Tuscans*, and in all reasonable probability may have been ultimately of *Etruscan* lineage. It may almost be affirmed that, beyond the area once occupied by the *Etruscan* race, no colourist of the highest rank has ever been born." [Idem. 66]

In stark contrast to the government systems with the tendency to a theocracy in a *Semitic* society and an elected or hereditary chief in *Indo-European* states, the *Etruscan* realm was based on confederation structure with twelve tribe overlords:

"The *Etruscan* nation was familiarly known to the *Romans* as the 'twelve tribes' of *Etruria, duodecim Etruriee populi.* When the *Etruscan* dominion was extended beyond the *Apennines,* it was thought necessary to organise the newly acquired territory on the same twelvefold tribal plan as the parent state. Each of the twelve tribal cities was ruled by its *Lucumo,*[56] and the *Etruscan* league was the confederation of these tribal despots. When we come to examine the etymology of the word *Lucumo* we shall find that it is a *Turkic* word meaning simply 'the great khan'." [Idem. 84]

By the way, *Strabo* gave a comprehensive account of *Lucumo's* origin and his state-building and art-creating accomplishments:

"After the foundation of *Rome, Demaratus* arrived here, bringing with him people from *Corinth.* He was received at *Tarquinia,* where he had a son, named *Lucumo,* by a woman of that country.

---

[55] The scholar meant the *Turkish* language.
[56] *Lucumo: Lu > Ulu* 'great' + *Cumo > Kan, Xan* 'khan' in *Turkic*.

Lucumo becoming the friend of *Ancus Marcius,* king of the *Romans,* succeeded him on the throne, and assumed the name of *Lucius Tarquinius Priscus*. Both he and his father did much for the embellishment of *Tyrrhenia,* the one by means of the numerous artists who had followed him from their native country; the other having the resources of *Rome*. It is said that the triumphal costume of the consuls, as well as that of the other magistrates, was introduced from the *Tarquinii,* with the fasces, axes, trumpets, sacrifices, divination, and music employed by the *Romans* in their public ceremonies. His son, the second *Tarquin,* named *Superbus,* who was driven from his throne, was the last king [of *Rome*]. *Porsena,* king of *Clusium,* a city of *Tyrrhenia,* endeavoured to replace him on the peace with the *Romans,* and departed in a friendly way, with honour and loaded with gifts." [5.2.2]

The government structure of the *Etruscans* and the *Trojans* had a genetic blueprint and was the invention, inherent exclusively to the *Turkic* nations, starting from the *Hittites,* or the *Khatti,* with their 12 kings forming confederacy in *Syria,* the *Akkadian* confederacy in 28th c. BCE in *Babylon,* the *Hun* with the *Hunnic* confederacy, the *Medes* with the union of six nations, and later in *Europe* – the union of the *Norse,* and in *Central Asia* and the *Caucasus* – numerous *Turkic* confederations, including the *Oguz* alliance of the *Turkic* tribes in the 6th - 7th centuries, the *Qizilbash* Confederation of 7 powerful *Turkic* tribes ruled by the *Safavid* dynasty in *Persia* from the 16th through 18th centuries, all the way to the *Native American* confederations, such as *Powhatan* confederacy of around 30 *Algonquian*-speaking tribes, the *Iroquois* Confederacy, and many more. The union of the *Norse,* described in the age-old *Icelandic* saga "The Prose *Edda*", was created as a copy of the *Trojan* state structure:

"There he established chieftains in the fashion which had prevailed in *Troy;* he set up also twelve head-men to be doomsmen over the people and to judge the laws of the land." [Prologue. 5]

Confederation of the *Turkic* tribes or nations was established by the leaders of the tribes responsible for summoning their warriors in case of war to fight along with the rest of the confederate nations against a common enemy. The selection of the *Turkic* chieftains was centered on two primary principles – birth and merit. The *Turkic* tribes would allow a progeny of a distinguished man to rule until he/she proved to be incapable or unworthy. In that case, the merit factor would step in and play a major role. Moreover, the excellence in military skills, ability to lead and win wars were the most critical elements deciding the leadership future of any *Turkic* person, not being rich or poor, a male or a female.

Unlike any other ancient nations who erected buildings for the living, the *Etruscans* were mostly preoccupied with the construction of the dwellings for the dead in the form of mounds. *Isaac Taylor* noted that these burial mounds, or kurgans, were the essential part of the non-*Indo-European* culture:

"But, scattered over the world, from *Algiers* to *Kamtschatka,* from the *Orkneys* to *Ceylon,* we find everywhere the conspicuous and unmistakable monuments of a great ancient tomb-building race. This race seems to form the ethnological substratum of the whole world; it is like the primary rock which underlies the whole series of subsequent formations. There can be no hesitation as to the existing stock to which these ancient non-*Aryan* tomb-builders belonged. The great *Turanian* race, which was the first to spread beyond the cradle of mankind, and of which the *Chinese,* the *Mongols,* the *Tatars,* and the *Finns* are existing representatives, is pre-eminently the race of the tomb-builders. The vast and numerous monuments which constitute the tombs of this race can always be recognized; they exhibit a most remarkable and most significant unity of design and purpose. These tombs are all developments of one hereditary type; they are all the expressions of one great hereditary belief, and they all serve the purposes of one great hereditary cultus. The type on which they are modelled is the house. The belief which they express is the fundamental truth which has been the great contribution of the *Turanian* race to the religious thought of the world — the belief in the deathlessness of souls. The cultus which they serve is the worship of the spirits of ancestors, which is the *Turanian* religion. The creed of the *Turanians* was animism. They believed that everything, animate or inanimate, had its soul or spirit; that the spirits of the dead could still make use of the spirits of the weapons, ornaments, and utensils which they had used in life, and could be served by the spirits of their slaves, their horses, and their dogs, and needed for their support the spirits of those articles of food on which they had been used to feed. Hence when we open these ancient *Turanian* sepulchres we find that the resting-places for the dead have been constructed on the exact model of the abodes of the living — the dead have been carefully provided with the necessaries of life — the warrior is buried with his spear and his arrows, the woman with her utensils and her ornaments; by the side of the infant's skeleton we find the skeleton of the faithful house-dog — slaughtered in order that the soul of the brave and wise companion might safely guide the soul of the helpless little one on the long journey to the unknown land. In all respects the tomb is the counterpart of the house, with the sole difference that it is erected in a manner more durable and more costly." [34-36]

Under "*Turanian*", the author meant the *Turkic* nations and their derivatives predominantly. The author also emphasized that the *Turkic* nations were the ancient tomb-builders and trendsetters:

"The ancient *Turkic* graves in *Siberia* are, moreover, constructed on the same type. The traveller *Bell* describes them as existing in public domain in thousands near *Tomsk*. There is a passage and a central chamber covered with a mound of earth, within which are found the skeletons of the deceased, buried with all their weapons and ornaments." [46]

Unlike the *Egyptian* mausoleums, the *Turkic* tombs, in general, and the *Etruscan*, in particular, were built as family sepulchers and were constructed in two designs – in the form of the tents, similar to *Siberian* yurts or *Native American* wigwams, as well caves, carved out from the cliffs like the cliff-dwellings of the *Etrusci* and the *Anasazi* – a *Native American* tribe. The construction of the tent-tomb was vividly depicted by *Isaac Taylor*:

"When a man died, he was left, with all his possessions, in his tent. To keep the body from the wolves the tent was covered with a mound of earth or stones, preserving the original pyramidal form. This is doubtless the origin of the sepulchral tumulus. That the model of the tumulus was the tent is, moreover, indicated by a very curious and widely-spread survival. The tent was necessarily surrounded, as is still the case in *Greenland* and *Siberia,* with a circle of heavy stones, which were needed to keep down by their weight the skins of which the tent was composed. Long after the origin of the sepulchral tumulus had been forgotten, long after the tumulus-builders had ceased to dwell in tents, this circle of stones continued to be erected around the base of the funeral mound." [42-43]

Figure 3. A modern Turkic – Uyghur yurt on Karakul Lake. Kashgar Region, China.
© Credit: Fernando Tatay/ shutterstock.com

Figure 4. Yurts, or tents, in Mongolia. Credit: Susanne Wunderlich from FreeImages.

Another anonymous scholar of the *Turkic* Studies, who introduced himself as "the Translator", wrote in his opus "An Account of the Present State of the *Northern Asia,* Relating to the Natural History of *Grand Tatary* and *Siberia* and the Manners, Customs, Trade, Laws, Religion and Polity of the Different People Inhabiting the Same together with Some Observations Concerning *China, India, Persia, Arabia, Turky,* and *Great Russia*", *London,* 1729:

> "Notwithstanding we are sure that the people who inhabit this continent at present have always led an unfix and wandering life: yet there are two things which puzzle the curious a little. The first is, that in many places of *Grand Tatary* towards the frontiers of *Siberia,* there are to be seen little hills, under which are found skeletons of men, accompany'd with the skeletons of horses, and many sorts of small vessels and jewels of gold and silver. There also found there skeletons of women with gold rings on their fingers…and inasmuch as the greatest part of the pagan *Tatars* have at present the custom, when any of their own people dies, to bury with him his best horse and moveables for his use in the other world, they did not fail to bury vessels of gold and silver with their dead so long as they had any left. So that all the difference between the aforesaid graves, and those of the present pagan *Tatars,* consists in this: that now there remains no more of those riches among them: what they inter with their dead usually consists of some wooden porringers, and such like utensils, which tho in themselves of little value, yet on account of the use they are of in their little houses, are of no small consideration. Add to this, that considering the extraordinary veneration which all the pagan *Tatars* generally have for those graves, as the graves of their ancestors; the opposition which the *Callmaks* gave to those who went to search them, may be taken as a certain sign, that they look'd upon them as the tombs of their ancestors, since no other consideration could have moved so peaceable a people as the *Callmaks* naturally are, to take a course on the like occasion." [2.8.1]

This type of tombs was found everywhere that a *Turkic* foot stepped on – from *North Africa, Algeria* to *China, Siberia, Mongolia* all the way through *Central Asia* to the *Caucasus,* where it was called "kurgan", meaning "burial tomb; structure" in *Turkic,* also in the *Middle East – Syria* and *Israel,* in *Europe – Sweden, Ireland, England, Germany,* as well as in the *Americas.*

Figure 5. Etruscan mound tomb (8th century BCE) in Cerveteri Rome Province, Italy.

© Credit: Massimo Salesi/ Shutterstock.com

Figure 6. Neolithic mound tombs in Boyne Valley, Ireland.

© Credit: SunFreez/Shutterstock.com

Figure 7. Native American Indian mound at Hopewell Culture National Historical Park. Ohio, USA.

© Credit: NPS/Hopewell Culture NHP.

Figure 8. Native American burial mound at the Bynum Site, built between 100 BCE and 100 CE. Mississippi, USA.

© Credit: Natchez Trace Parkway/National Park Service.

Figure 9. Burial mound of a Scythian king.

© Credit: Boris Rezvantsev/Shutterstock.com

Figure 10. Burial Mounds of Sumerian civilization. Date to Dilmun era (5000 BCE - 100 BCE). A'ali town area. Bahrain.

© Credit: Authentic travel/Shutterstock.com

Figure 11. Old Uyghur tombs in Kashgar, Xinjiang, China.

© Credit: Yu Zhang/Shutterstock.com

Figure 12. Royal Viking mounds in Gamla Uppsala village, Uppland, Sweden.

© Credit: Nadezhda Kharitonova/ Shutterstock.com

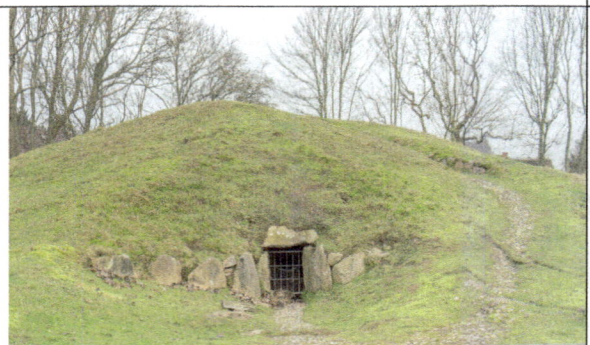

Figure 13. Stone Age burial mound on the island of Sylt in Germany.

© Credit: Cora Mueller/Shutterstock.com

Figure 14. Thracian burial tomb (3rd Century CE) in Pomorie, Bulgaria. © Credit: Nenov Brothers Images/ Shutterstock.com

Figure 15. The grave mound of the Gepidae and the Goths in Poland.

© Credit: Artur Henryk/stock.adobe.com

Figure 16. The burial mound of Midas, the king of Phrygia in Turkey.

© Credit: Cinar/stock.adobe.com

50

The second type of the *Etruscan* tombs – caves were carved out from the cliffs and built into a city of the dead:

> "At *Castel d'Asso,* at *Cervetri,* at *Norchia,* and at many other places in *Etruria,* there are hundreds of tombs hollowed out in the low cliffs, the tombs facing each other like the houses in the streets of a town, with lanes of tombs branching out right and left. In one place we have a square or piazza, surrounded by tombs instead of houses. These cities of the dead are constructed on the precise model of the cities of the living. The tombs themselves are exact imitations of the house. There is usually an outer vestibule, apparently appropriated to the annual funeral feast; from this a passage leads to a large central chamber, which is lighted by windows cut through the rock. This central hall is surrounded by smaller chambers, in which the dead repose. On the roof we see carved in stone the broad beam or roof-tree, with rafters imitated in relief on either side, and even imitations of the tiles. These chambers contain the corpses, and are furnished with all the implements, ornaments, and utensils used in life. The tombs are in fact places for the dead to live in. The position and surroundings of the deceased are made to approximate as closely as possible to the conditions of life. The couches on which the corpses repose have a tri-clinial arrangement, and are furnished with cushions carved in stone; and imitations of easy chairs and footstools are carefully hewn out of the rock. Everything, in short, is arranged as if the dead were reclining at a banquet in their accustomed dwellings. On the floor stand wine-jars, and the most precious belongings of the deceased — arms, ornaments and mirrors — hang from the roof, or are suspended on the walls. The walls themselves are richly decorated, usually being painted with representations of festive scenes; we see figures in gaily embroidered garments reclining on couches, while attendants replenish the goblets or beat time to the music of the pipers."
> [*Isaac Taylor.* 46-48]

In spite of the stunning similarity of this type of *Etruscans* tombs with the *Egyptian* ones, the crucial difference between them was in usage and designation of these tombs. Unlike the *Egyptians,* who would build a mausoleum for one individual and seal off the access to it from everyone else, the *Etruscan* tombs were constructed for several members of a family with one purpose in mind – to turn these tombs into a place of worship and reverence of the ancestors like temples, where religious ceremonies were held. Interestingly, the modern *Turkic* nations have preserved this ancient tradition by attending the graves of their loved ones during each significant holiday and leave food and beverages on or near a burial lot for the deceased.

The *Etruscan* tombs were mirrors reflecting everyday lives, customs, and traditions of the *Etrusci*. A female, especially a wife in the *Etruscan* society, had an exalted position. She was her husband's helpmate, a companion, who equally participated at the parties, sitting at the same table next to her husband, drinking wine and having a good time. Even a wife's tomb was usually more magnificent than her husband's. It was an innate, customary phenomenon for all the *Turkic* nations of the pre-*Islamic* era to treat a woman and a wife with high esteem and respect. It was already mentioned in this book, but some things worth repeating – even nowadays, in the modern *Azerbaijani* society, a wife or a husband is typically introduced and called as *Həyat Yoldaşım* "my friend in life", "my life partner" to underline the equal rights of the spouses. Usually, it is considered rude to present one's wife or husband as *Arvadım* "my wife" or *Ərim* "my husband" correspondingly.

The sepulchers of the *Etruscans* bore witness to their religion and were a crucial part of their spiritual trifecta. The *Etruscans*, as well as all the *Turkic* nations from the *Scythians, Pelasgians* to the *Medes*, even including most if not all the *Native Americans*, practiced the religion known as *Tengriism* in the *Turkic* world, which was based on threefold belief – in heavenly spirits, earthly spirits, and ancestral spirits. According to *I. Taylor,* these divine beings were revered in the following order:

> "1 – The powers of heaven: namely, the spirits of the sun, of the moon, of the stars, of the sky, of the clouds, and of the thunder.

2 – The powers of earth: the deathless terrestrial spirits, which represent or inhabit the mountains, the stones, the rivers, the fields, and the trees.

3 – The ancestral powers: the spirits of the departed, who are believed to retain an interest in the concerns of their descendants, and to be able to influence their fortunes." [89-90]

And it was the ancient *Turkic* nations that introduced this religion to all other nations worldwide, including the *Greeks* and the *Romans*. The faith of the *Turks* survived persecution by other major religions that followed – Christianity, Islam and still exists around the world under different names – Shamanism, Paganism.

Ancient *Turkic* mythology was well represented in paintings on the walls and sarcophagi of the *Etruscans*. According to *Isaac Taylor,* among the deities and spirits depicted inside the *Etruscans* tombs, the most frequented spirits were *Kulmu, Vanth, Hinthial,* and *Nathum*. In addition to the images, their names were provided along with a *Latin* translation. The inferences deduced below draw a straight parallel between these names and *Turkic* words, confirming their *Turkic* etymology:

←←←*Kulmu* →→→

Let us cross-reference the following *Turkic* names of spirits in comparison to *Kulmu*:

- *Kulmu* "spirit of death": *Kul* > *Qul* 'spirit' + *Ulm* > *Ölüm* 'death' + -*U* 'an affix of possession, equivalent to the *English* preposition *Of*' in *Turkic*.
- *Qulyabanı* "spirit of the steppe": *Qul* 'spirit' + *Yaban* 'steppe' + -*I* 'an affix of possession, equivalent to the *English* preposition *Of*' in *Turkic*.
- *Mayğıl* "young female spirit": *May* 'child; female child' + *Ğıl* = *Qul* 'spirit' in *Turkic*.

As we already know, the *English* word *Ghoul* has its origin from the *Turkic Qul, Ğıl*.

←←←*Vanth* →→→

- *Vanth* 'spirit of destruction': *Vanı* > *Fanı* 'destroy' + -*Th* > -*T* 'an affix, converting a verb into a noun', meaning "destruction" in *Turkic*.

The difference between these two spirits, both being the angels of death, is that *Kulmu* haunts the graves, while *Vanth* instigates death and destruction. In the picture below, *Vanth* is depicted as a winged spirit instructing *Achilles*, or *Achle* in *Etruscan,* to slay a helpless *Trojan* prisoner on the ground.

←←←*Hinthial* →→→

- *Hinthial: Hin* > *Jin* 'body' + *T* > -*D* 'an affix, converting a noun into a verb' + *Hial* > *Hayal* 'specter', meaning "embodied ghost" in *Turkic*.

Incidentally, *Isaac Taylor* considered the word *Hayal*, or *Khayal*, "specter, ghost" to be of *Turkic* origin. *Hinthial Patrukles*, or "a ghost of *Patroclus*", standing next to *Achilles,* was portrayed in the drawing "The sacrifice of the *Trojan* prisoners".

THE SACRIFICE OF THE TROJAN PRISONERS.

1. ACHMENRUN (Agamemnon).
2. HINTHIAL-PATRUKLES (Ghost of Patroklos).
3. VANTH (Death).
4. ACHLE (Achilleus).
5. TRUIALS (a Trojan).
6. CHARU (Charon).
7. AIVAS TLAMUNUS (Ajax Telamonius).
8. TRUIALS (a Trojan).
9. AIVAS VILATAS (Ajax Oileus).
10. TRUIALS (a Trojan).

Figure 17. "Etruscan Researches." by Isaac Taylor, 1874.

←←←Nathum →→→

o *Nathum*: *Na* > *Ina* 'to wish, to desire' + *Ath* > *At* 'break, destroy' + *-Um* 'an affix, converting a verb into a noun', meaning "the one who desires destruction" in *Turkic*.

This *Etruscan* divinity, or fury, most likely does not share much with the ancient *Turkic God Natagai*, aka *Natigay, Nogat, Itoga*, as *Isaac Taylor* suggested. The *Turkic* nations, including the *Tatars* in *China*, *Siberia*, and *Central Asia*, used to worship God of the *Earth* called *Natagai* (*Natagai*: *N* > *In* 'Earth' + *At* > *∂t, Et* 'create, make' + *Agai* 'master, lord', meaning "the Lord, who created the *Earth*"). In the book "A Voyage round the World in six parts" by *Dr. John Francis Gemelli Careri*, containing testimony about the lands inhabited and ruled by the *Turkic* nations in the 17-18th cc., the author mentioned this *Tatar* deity as a religion in the empire of *China*, governed by a *Tatar* Emperor (not *Chinese*, by the way):

> "There are several religions profess'd in the Empire of *China*, according to the variety of people in it. To begin with the Emperor, he being a *Tartar*, follows the idolatry of his nation, which as in the main it agrees with the religion of the *Chineses* and *Japoneses*, yet they all differ in sects, wherein the *Tartars* do not agree among themselves, much less with the *Chineses* and *Cochinchineses*, as neither they do among themselves. This difference arises from the several idols, which everyone takes for his tutelar God. The *Tartars* of *Great Tartary* adore a deity, they call *Natagai*, whom they esteem the God of the *Earth*, and they have so great a veneration for him, that no man is without his image in his house; and being persuaded that *Natagai* had a wife, they place her on his left, with little idols before them, as if they were their children. They pay adoration, and make obeisance to them, especially when they are going to dinner or supper, anointing the mouths of the images with the fat of the meat that is dress'd, and lay some of their dinner or supper at the door, believing they feed on it." [2.4]

As we see, the *Turkic God Natagai's* primary mission was to create and protect the *Earth*, while *Nathum* – the *Etruscan* equivalent of the *Greco-Pelasgian* fury *Ate*, who, according to the ancient mythology, was hell-bent on tracking and annihilating a culprit, shared the same functions with the latter – to find and destroy the killers of the innocent.

The *Etruscan* ossuaries contained plenty of artifacts and drawings full of mythological creatures, akin to ancient *Turkic* beliefs, such as guardian spirits, grave spirits. All these spiritual notions later migrated into other major world religions, such as Christianity and Islam.

Numerous paintings on the *Etruscan* tomb walls illustrate dark monsters who torture the evildoers with a hammer or mallet in their hands. These grave spirits were very well-known in *Turkic* mythology as two demons questioning a deceased after s/he was buried and, if found guilty in committing any crimes, beating up the dead with a hammer. The same testimony is given in the book by *Isaac Taylor:*

> "*Pococke,* the *Oriental* traveller, tells that the *Turkic* tribes which he visited a century and a half ago had a curious superstition. They believed that two black demons dwell in the sepulcher with the dead, and if he be found guilty of any crime, they punish him with hammers. Unfortunately *Pococke* does not mention the name of these demons; but the black complexion, the hammer, and the office, agree so precisely with the representations of the *Etruscan Charu,* that we can hardly refuse to admit the identification." [117]

These ancient *Turkic* demons of black color, known as the *Etruscan Charu,* or *Kharu* (from *Xara (Khara), Kara* "black" in *Turkic*) transited later to *Islam,* where they are called *Inkir, Minkir,* who serve as two inquisitors welcoming a departed person in his/her grave to the netherworld and perform pretty much the same functions as their *Turkic* undead colleagues, including the mauling part if warranted.

Another fascinating group of spirits, reflected inside the *Etruscan* sepulchers, involves none other than *Jinns,* those good old genies. By the way, the name of these spiritual beings has a pure *Turkic* origin, later adopted by the *Chinese* as *Shin* and the *Arabs* as *Jinn.* The *German* etymologist of the 19th c. *Radlov V.V.* wholeheartedly confirmed the *Turkic* origins of the word *Jin,* aka *Chin* "evil spirit, demon" [4.1.208], and *Isaac Taylor* provided the linguistic analysis that reached the same conclusion:

> "In the *Turanian* spirit-world a prominent place is taken by the guardian spirits who were believed to be the constant protectors of the persons to whom they were attached. This doctrine also takes its place in the *Etruscan* mythology, and from thence it penetrated into the *Roman* system. Every human being was believed to have his protecting spirit, whose sex corresponded to the sex of the protected person. Every man had his *Genius,* and every woman had her *Juno.* These words have not yet been recognized on the monuments; we only possess them in their *Latin* guise, and they are evidently accommodated in form to an assumed *Latin* etymology. But if these words were, as is doubtless the case, borrowed from the *Etruscans,* there is no difficulty in detecting a *Turanian* source. We have seen that in *Chinese* the word *Shin* or *Jin* means 'spirits'. These *Shin* are of three classes — celestial, terrestrial, and ancestral. The ancestral spirits, the spirits of kings, sages, and families, are called *Jin Kwei.* This word *Jin* pervades all the *Ugric* languages. The *Jinns* of the 'Arabian Nights' are probably to be regarded as ultimately not *Semitic,* but *Turanian.* The word *Jinn* in modern *Turkish* denotes the '*Genii,*' the spirits of nature, a race of intelligent beings with unsubstantial bodies of the nature of smoke. The *Turkish Jan* 'soul,' and other related words, have already been enumerated, and will suffice to explain the *Etrusco-Latin* word *Genius,* which denotes a man's soul, or his protecting and inspiring spirit." [126-127]

Denoting the same supreme deities, the names of the ancient *Etruscan* divine beings also had a noticeable similarity and, at the same time, distinction from their *Greco-Roman* counterparts:

ETRUSCAN Pantheon	GRECO-ROMAN Pantheon
Tin, Tina, Tinia – the king of gods	*Zena, Jupiter, Zeus, Jove*
Thana – the goddess of maternity	*Diana, Janus, Artemis, Hekate*
Menrva – the goddess of wisdom	*Minerva, Athena*
Turan – the goddess of love	*Urania, Venus, Aphrodite*
Nethuns – the sea god	*Neptune, Poseidon*
Sethlans – the god of fire and metal	*Vulcan, Hephaestus*
Phuphluns – the god of wine, health, happiness	*Baccus, Liber, Iacchus, Zagreus, Dionysos*
Thesan – the goddess of the dawn	*Eos, Aurora*
Thalna – the goddess of childbirth	*Juno, Hera, Regina*
Turms – the messenger between people and gods	*Hermes, Mercury*
Apulu, Aplu – the god of the Sun	*Apollo, Apollon, Phoebus*
Hercle – the hero god	*Hercules, Heraclea*
Aesar "God"	*Deus* "God"

Without getting into a detailed analysis of all the names of *Etruscan* heavenly divinities, a few names will suffice to show the striking match between the *Etruscan* and *Turkic* immortals.

The *Etruscan* king of the gods *Tin* is *Tenri*, aka *Tengri* – the *Turkic* king of gods. Both names have the same *Turkic* root with numerous variants *Tin, Ten, Teng, Tan* "1.sky; 2.spirit". In the *Turkic* languages, *Tin, Ten* turned into *Tenri, Tanri, Tengri, Tangri, Tangara* due to the added *Turkic* word *Ar* 'warrior, man', that brought the meaning of the whole word to "sky man, sky warrior".

Aesar – this *Etruscan* god was not represented in the divine assemblage of the *Roman* and *Greek* immortals. *Gaius Suetonius Tranquillus* first revealed it in "The Lives of The First Twelve *Caesars*":

> "About the same time, the first letter of his name, in an inscription upon one of his statues, was struck out by lightning; which was interpreted as a presage that he would live only a hundred days longer, the letter C denoting that number; and that he would be placed among the Gods, as *Aesar,* which is the remaining part of the word *Caesar,* signifies, in the *Tuscan* language, a God." ["*Caesar Augustus.*" 95]

Aesar, aka *Asar*, aka *Azar*, is a *Turkic* word in its purest form: *Aes, As, Az* > *Əs, Ös, As* 'lord' + *Ar* 'warrior, man', meaning "supreme being; God" in *Turkic*.

Dated back to the time of *Ptolemy,* there were a number of geographical locations with the names matching or close to *Azar,* such as the city of *Azara* in *Sarmatia,* the city *Azara* with the river *Araxes* flowing nearby [*Strabo*. 11.14.3], the city of *Ausara* in *Arabia Felix,* the town *Auzara* in *Mesopotamia,* the *Azar* Mountain in *Marmarica,* the town of *Azora* in *Armenia,* the city of *Asseros* in *Pelasgia,* as well as a famous temple of *Diana,* called *Azara* in the land of the *Elymæi* that was plundered by a *Parthian* king, according to *Strabo:*

> "In after-times the king of *Parthia* heard that the temples in their country contained great wealth, but knowing that the people would not submit, and admonished by the fate of *Antiochus,* he invaded their country with a large army; he took the temple of *Minerva,* and that of *Diana,* called *Azara,* and carried away treasure to the amount of 10,000 talents." [16.1.18]

The word-formation of *Azara* ideally matches that of another *Turkic* word with the same meaning "God" – *Tangar, Tangara, Tengri,* or *Tanri:*
   Azara > *Az* 'lord' + *Ar*, meaning "supreme being, God".
   Tangara > *Tang* 'sky' + *Ar,* meaning "sky being, God".

The assertions of some biased linguists trying to connect this word *Azar,* or *Azara,* with the *Persian Azar* (meaning "insult, sorrow"), do not withstand any criticism. Other etymologists, such as *Egorov V.G.* attempted to play the *Indian* card by pulling the origin of *Azar* from *Asura* "lord" in *RigVeda* (1.24.14) and *Ahuro-Mazda,* meaning "the wise lord" without any justifying archeological artifacts or linguistic proof. This theory was recently strongly refuted by a *Finish* Indologist and Sindologist, professor *Asko Parpola,* who presented sound archaeological and linguistic evidence in his book "The Roots of *Hinduism:* the Early *Aryans* and the *Indus* Civilization", in favor of the *Uralic* root *Asera* "lord, prince". This, practically, confirms the *Turkic* origin of the word *Azar,* or *Aser,* due to the kinship of the *Uralic* and the *Turkic* languages and peoples. It has been established on a genetic level that the *Uralic* peoples shared a common affinity with the *Turkic* ones ["Genes reveal traces of common recent demographic history for most of the *Uralic*-speaking populations." *Kristiina Tambets, Bayazit Yunusbayev,* et al. (Genome Biology, volume 19, Article number: 139 (2018))].

Furthermore, *Asura* in later *Vedic* texts meant "a class of demonic beings", known in *Turkic* as *Asurı,*[57] who embodied the notion of the chaos-creating evil in *Hindu, Turkic,* and *Persian* mythology. Therefore, there is no reason to believe that the cities and places of the antique world were named after the demonic beings to honor evil forces opposing God or a pantheon of gods.

Moreover, the same name in a slightly modified form – *Asir* – was mentioned in the *Icelandic* saga by *Sturluson* to denote a divine race.

Going back to the main subject on hand, the epitaphs and the inscriptions in the *Etruscan* tombs proved the point that the names of the ancient heroes and regular folks, known among the *Etruscans,* were practically the same as the slightly modified *Greek* and *Latin* ones:

- *Achmenrun* [*Agamemnon*]
- *Achle* [*Achilles*]
- *Aivas Tlamunus* [*Ajax Telamonius*]
- *Truials* [*Trojan*]
- *Uthuze* [*Odysseus*]
- *Thurms* [*Hermes*]
- *Aitas* [*Hades*]
- *Terasias* [*Tiresias*]
- *Pentasila* [*Penthesilea* – queen of the *Amazons*]

---

[57] "Drevneturkskiy slovar." [61].

- *Uruzthe* [*Orestes*]
- *Kluthumustha* [*Clytemnestra*]
- *Lekne* [*Licini*]
- *Velimna* [*Volumnius*]
- *Titi* [*Titius*]
- *Unata* [*Otacilius*]
- *Phulni* [*Folnius*]

Isaac Taylor gave a masterful analysis of the *Etruscan* names by deriving their origin from the *Turkic* sources due to their *Latin* translation, inscribed on the sarcophagi. With our few additions and changes, some examples are provided below:

- *Kahati* "violent" > *Qəhər* "anger".

- *Vari* "red" > *Valə* "violet"; *Lal, Ləl, Al* "red".

- *Kiarthi* "swarthy": *Kiar* > *Kara* 'black' + *Thi* > *Teri* 'skin'.

- *Thapiri* "very dark" = *Thap-thara* > *Kap-kara* "very dark".

- *Vani* "frail, perishable" > *Fani* "frail, perishable".

- *Aelche* "quince-apple" > *Alça* "cherry plum" in *Turkic*.

- *Ath* > *At, Otho* "horse" in *Turkic*. This name was translated into *Latin* as *Marcus* "horse". *Isaac Taylor* asserted that from this *Etruscan* name originated the word *Ottoman*:
  "It seems also to form the first portion of the name of *Oth-man*, the great *Turkic* sultan from whom the *Otto-man* empire and the *Os-manli* language take their name." [267]

- *Vele* had a *Latin* equivalent of *Caius* that itself was a *Turkic* word *Gəi, Gəy* "great, big". Therefore, *Vele* is another form of the *Turkic* word *Bəli, Bəlli* "famous".

- *Arth* also had the same *Latin* equivalent – *Caius* "great". Its *Turkic* root is irrefutable: *Arth* > *Artık* "exceeding, superior, great" in *Turkic*.

- *Tarquin* > *Tarkan* "governor", "royal dignity" from *Tark* = *Tərğə* 'gather, unite' + *Kan* 'khan, king' in *Turkic*.

The inscriptions with *Latin* translation on the *Etruscan* sarcophagi and many sepulchral offerings in the *Etruscan* tombs, such as dishes, statues, vases helped us reveal the *Turkic* origin of the *Etruscan* words, for instance, *Klan* > *Oğlan* "son; tribe" in *Turkic*. It became an international word with the central meaning of "tribe": *Clan* in *English, German, French, Albanian, Afrikaans, Yiddish*; *Cliens* in *Latin*; *Clann* in the *Scottish Gaelic*; *Klan* in *Russian, Basque, Bulgarian, Urdu, Hungarian, Norwegian*; *Klaani* in *Finnish*, while in the *Turkic* languages it is both *Klan* "clan" and *Oğlan* "son, boy".

The following list of the *Etruscan* words was carefully analyzed by *Isaac Taylor* and, with our adjustments or additions, is presented here. To derive or confirm the *Turkic* etymology of the *Etruscan* words, we utilized the time-tested, reputable etymological works by *Radlov V.V., Egorov V.G.*, and the book "Drevneturkskiy slovar", collectively created by the scholars of the former *USSR* Academy of Science.

ETRUSCAN	TURKIC
1. *Suthina* "an offering", 2. *Suthil* "a thing offered, an offering".	*Sitil* "vessel".
3. *Suthi* "tomb".	*Sitil* "vessel".
4. *Mi* "I am".	*Min, Mən* "I", "I am".
5. *Kana* "statue".	*Kən* "ornament".
6. *Phleres, Phieres* "gift".	*Peru, Veriş* "gift, offering".
7. *Turk, Turke, Turuke, Turce.*	*Türk, Türük* "ethnic name", "a *Turk*."
8. *Akil* "ashes".	*Kül, Köl* "ashes".
9. *Ape, Ipe, Ipi* "1.sister; 2.elder sister".	*Apa* "elder sister".
10. *Arke* "husband".	*Erkək* "male"; *Ər* "husband".
11. *Arth* "great".	*Artık* "great, exceeding, superior"; *Arlıq* "powerful, wealthy"; *Arta* "live in abundance".
12. *Larth, Larthi, Larthia, Lar* "1.great; 2.lord, lady".	*L > Al* 'powerful, mighty' + *Art, Ar > Ar* 'man', meaning "powerful man (person)" in *Turkic*.
13. *Lares* "1.lords, the great ones; 2.spirits of virtuous ancestors".	*Lar > Al + Ar + Es > Əs* 'lord', meaning "powerful, noble men" in *Turkic*.
14. *Larvae* "spirits of the evil men".	*Lar > Al + Ar + Vae > Vai* 'grief, woe', meaning "powerful, distressing men" in *Turkic*.
15. *At, Ath, Oto* "1.horse; 2.horseman".	*At, Ot* "horse".
16. *Ataison* "climbing vine".	*At > Ot* 'plant' + *Aison > Üzüm, İsöm, Yözöm* 'grape', meaning "vine" in *Turkic*.

ETRUSCAN	TURKIC
17. *Capys* "falcon".	*Cap* > *Kap* 'snatch' + *Us* 'fly', meaning "catch and fly away", "bird that catches a prey" in *Turkic*.
18. *Toga* "national *Roman* garb adopted from the *Etruscans*".	*Tağas* "garment, garb"; *Tiku* "garment".
19. *Lucumo, Laukane* "1.chief of an *Etruscan* tribe: 2.great prince".	*Lu, Lau* > *Ulu* 'great' + *Cumo, Kane* > *Kan, Xan* 'king, chief', meaning "great king" in *Turkic*.
20. *Laukanesa* "wife of a chief".	*Lau* > *Ulu* 'great' + *Kane* > *Kan, Xan* 'king, chief' + *Esa* > *-Iş* 'an affix, denoting the word *Wife*', meaning "wife of a khan" in *Turkic*. There was a *Turkic* word *Kanış* "wife of a khan" [*Radlov.* 2.1.117].
21. *Asa, Esa, Isa* "1.wife; 2. madam; 3.noble".	*Əçə* "wife"; *Es, Əs* "lord, noble".
22. *Al, El, Ul, Nal* "1.maternal clan; 2.title of a mother; 3. child of". This word in any variants always followed a name of the mother's clan in the *Etruscan* epitaphs, such as AU: KVENLE: MÉTHL NAL *Au* (an abbreviation of *Aules*) – the name of a deceased man; *Kvenle* – his father's family name; *Methl Nal* – "the *Methle* clan" – his mother's family name. This word also can indicate the title of a mother of a deceased in an epitaph: VEILIA: SURTI: VELKZNAL: SEK *Veilia:* widow: *Velkzni* mother: daughter "*Veilia,* a widow, daughter of *Velkzni* mother." The third use employs the general notion "child of", such as *Trui AL* "child of *Troy*" (*Troy Ulı* in *Turkic*).	*El, Əl* "tribe, clan"; *Aila* "title of the elder women".

ETRUSCAN	TURKIC
23. **Ril** "year".	**İl, Yıl** "year".
24. **Avil, Aivil** "age".	*A, Ai > Ai, Ay* 'month' + *Vil > İl* 'year', meaning "date; age" in *Turkic*.
25. **Camillus** "1.messenger of gods; 2.messenger of priests; 3.*Mercury*".	**Hammal** "porter, carrier".
26. **Celer** "1.patrician horseman; 2.bodyguard".	*Cel > Kələ* 'bull' + *Er* 'warrior', meaning "strong as a bull warrior" in *Turkic*.
27. **Eka** "here".	**Egə, Egei, Tega** "here, thither".
28. **Etera** "1.young; 2.young son; 3.younger son".	**Edder, Ödər** "young"; **Oti** "younger child".
29. **Agalletora** "boy".	*Agall > Oğul* 'boy' + *Etora > Edder* 'young', meaning "young boy" in *Turkic*.
30. **Klan** "1.son; 2.child".	**Oğlan, Ulan** "son, boy, child".
31. **Hel** "son".	**Ul, Uol, Uul** "son, boy".
32. **Subulo** "flute-player".	*Sub > Çubuk* 'tube' + *Ulo > Ul* 'boy', meaning "flute-player" in *Turkic*.
33. **Sekh, Sek, Sak** "daughter".	**Kıs** "girl, daughter". This is a rearranged form of the *Etruscan Sekh, Sek, Sak*. This letter rearrangement phenomenon is frequently observed in *Turkic*, such as *Ua > Au* "poison"; *Şu > Uş* "this"; *Əru = Uri* "progeny".
34. **Kecha** "little".	**Kişi, Kiçik** "little, small".
35. **Kechase** "died".	**Keçiril** "pass away, die"; **Keçindi** "died".
36. **Ken, Kehen, Anken, Ekn** "1.here; 2.this".	**Kunta, Kin** "here"; **Ənə, An** "this".

ETRUSCAN	TURKIC
37. *Kizi* "body".	*Kizi* "human, man".
38. *Naper* "soul".	*Nəfər* "man, person".
39. *Ras* "head".	*Bas* "head".
40. *Tene* "piece".	*Dane* "piece"; *Denə, Tən* "body".
41. *Tepae* "hill".	*Təpə, Tepe* "hill".
42. *Arno* "name of an *Etruscan* river".	*Arna* "water-course", "channel".
43. *Soracte* "name of an *Etruscan* limestone crag".	*Sorac > Şorak* 'snow-white' + *Te > Ta, Tu* 'mountain', meaning "snow-white mountain" in *Turkic*. There is a mountain in *Siberia* called *Aktu* "white mountain" (*Ak* 'white' + *Tu* 'mountain' in *Turkic*).
44. *Tina* "heaven".	*Taŋ* "sky, heaven".
45. *Tinskvil* "a bronze offering".	*Tins > Tünç* 'bronze' + *Kvil > Kobur* 'vessel', meaning "bronze vessel" in *Turkic*.
46. *Truial* "son of *Troy*", "child of *Troy*".	*Trui* 'house of *Tur*' (*Tr > Tur* + *Ui > Öi* 'house') + *Al > Ul* 'son', meaning "son of *Troy*" in *Turkic*.
47. *Lautni* "freedman". To indicate the social status of a person, who was freed from slavery, the *Etruscans* used the word *Lautni* "freedman" on the epitaphs: 1) AULE: ALFNIS: LAUTNI "*Aules Alfenis*, a freedman". 2) LARTH: AULES: LATN "*Lars Aules*, a freedman". 3) APIUNI: CUMERES: LAU "*Apiuni Kumeres*, a freedman".	*Laut > Lutı* 'vagrant, free' + *Ni > Olan* 'being', meaning "the one who is free" in *Turkic*. The word order of *Lautni* is pure *Turkic*. *Lutı* "wayfarer, vagabond".

ETRUSCAN	TURKIC
48. **Ludio** "dancer".	**Lutı** "person, who leads a party lifestyle, such as a dancer, a singer".
49. **Ludus** "dance".	*Lud > Lutı* 'dancer' + *Us > -Uş* 'an affix, creating another noun from a noun', meaning "dance" in *Turkic*.
50. **Lusni, Losna, Luna** "light, flame".	**Yalın** "flame".
51. **Manim** "I myself", "I am".	**Mənəm** "I am".
52. **Ma** "land".	**Maŋ** "land, area".
53. **Manes** "deified spirits of the underworld".	*Man > Maŋ* 'land, area' + *Es > Əs* 'lord', meaning "master of a land" in *Turkic*.
54. **Mantus** "King of the underworld".	*Man > Maŋ* 'land, area' + *Tus > Tuş* 'mate, partner', meaning "co-host of the land" in *Turkic*. **Tuzak** "hell, underworld".
55. **Mania** "Queen of the underworld".	*Man > Maŋ* 'land, area' + *Ia > İə* 'master, host', meaning "hostess of the land" in *Turkic*.
56. **Parkhis** "ancestor".	*Pa > Apa* 'father' + *Ar* 'man' + *Khis > Kişi* 'man', meaning "father of a man", "patriarch" in *Turkic*. There is an ancient *Turkic* word *Ər kişi* "man" [*Radlov.* 1.1.751] that matches the *Etruscan* counterpart in its meaning and sequential order of the components. Furthermore, the *Turkic* word *Apa* was noted to come at the beginning of a word, such as *Apa Tarkan* "commander in-chief" [*Egorov.* 30].
57. **Vlssi** "his wife".	*Vl > Evli* 'married' + *Ssi > -Si* 'an affix, denoting a pronoun *His/Her*", meaning "his wife" in *Turkic*.
58. **Porcus** "pig".	**Tonquz** "pig"; **Porsuk** "badger".

ETRUSCAN	TURKIC
59. **Puia** "1.child; 2.daughter; 3.maiden".	*Pəyak* "child".
60. **Puiak** "1.little daughter; 2.little child".	*Pəyak* "child".
61. **Puiam** "1.my daughter; 2.my child".	*Pui > Pəyak* 'child' + *Am > -Am (-Im)* 'an affix, denoting a noun in the 1st p. sing.', meaning "my child" in *Turkic*.
62. **Puius, Fuius** "1.his daughter; 2.his child".	*Pui, Fui > Pəyak* 'child' + *Us > -Si* 'an affix, denoting a pronoun *His/Her*', meaning "his child" in *Turkic*.
63. **Sagitta** "arrow".	*Sag > Sak* 'strike', 'inject' + *Itta > İtən* 'maker, doer', meaning "the one that strikes" in *Turkic*.
64. **Semna** "priestess".	*Sem > Kam* 'shaman' + *Na > Ana* 'female', meaning "a female shaman" in *Turkic*. *Samdal* "be devoted", "devotee"; *Şaman* "shaman".
65. **Sethlans** "the Fire God".	*Seth > Ot, Ut* 'fire' + *Lans > Olan* 'becoming', meaning "the one that turns into a fire" in *Turkic*.
66. **Sians** "guests".	*Çün* "meeting of people".
67. **Teke, Theke** "1.gave; 2.presented".	*Tek, Thek > Takı* 'donate, give' (or *Tak* 'put, hang') + *E > -Dı, -Ti* 'an affix, denoting the past tense in the 3rd p. sing', meaning "he/she put" in *Turkic*.
68. **Tul** "tomb".	*Tura* "edifice, structure".
69. **Turan** "1.Urania; 2.Venus; 3.heaven".	*Tura* 'God', *Tori* 'heaven' + *An > Ana* 'female; goddess', meaning "goddess of heaven" in *Turkic*. *Ama*, another variant of *Ana*, was known among the ancient *Turkic* people as a goddess – a mother of the whole world [*Ashmarin*. 1.186].

ETRUSCAN	TURKIC
70. **Thesan** "1.sunrise; 2.Aurora".	**Tasan** "the one that rises".
71. **Usil** "rising Sun".	**Ucalan** "rising".
72. **Vel, Vol** "town". The *Greek* form of this word is *Ouol* [Ουολ]. *I.Taylor* enumerated many *Etruscan* towns starting with this word: *Velathri* (*Volaterræ*, *Vol terra*), *Volci* (*Vulci*), *Velsuna* (*Volsinii*, *Vulsinii*, *Bolsena*), *Velsina* (*Felsina*, *Bologna*), *Voltumnae*, *Vulturnum*, *Velitrae*, *Velumnas*, *Falerii*.	**Aul** "settlement", "village".
73. **Onia, Enna, Ena, Ina, Una** "town". *I.Taylor* indicated these words as suffixes, being an integral part of the *Etruscan* town names, such as *Vetulonia*, *Clavenna*, *Chiavenna*, *Ravenna*, *Capena*, *Velsina*, *Velsuna*.	**İn** "house".
74. **Zilakh** "sarcophagus".	*Zil* > *Çul* 'stone' + *Akh* > *Ak* 'tears', meaning "stone coffin" in *Turkic*.
75. **Makh** "one".	**Maka, Makka** "one". According to *I.Taylor*, "In all languages the most widely spread names of numerals are those denoting one, two, and five, the names of which almost universally denote, as we have seen, finger, arms, and hand. To denote 'one' a finger was held up, to signify 'two' the arms, while 'five' was indicated by the expanded hand. So far there is a general agreement among almost all races." ["*Etruscan* Researches." 170] Unaware of the *Turkic* word *Maka*, the scholar derived it as a component of the *Turkic* *Barmak* "finger".
76. **Ki, Ke** "two".	**İki, İke, Eki** "two".
77. **Zal** "three".	**Oza, Üz** "three".

ETRUSCAN	TURKIC
78. *Sa, Za* "four".	*Se, Sə* "four". This numeral is a forgotten part of another *Turkic* one – *Sekiz*: *Se* 'four' + *Ekiz* 'twin', meaning "four twos", "eight" in *Turkic*.
79. *Thu, Thun* "five".	*Ton* "hand"; *Tutam* "handle, handful". I. Taylor noticed that "Throughout the *Turanian* region we find that this word for 'hand' has been the source of the numeral used to denote 'five', though the dialectic changes are often so great as to leave unchanged no single letter of the root." [163]. In *Chuvash*, for instance, the word *Pilök* denotes five, which also means "a lower part of the arm" [*Egorov*. 160]. In *Turkic*, "hand" is a part of the numeral 50 – *Əlig, Elig, Əllik, Əlli* (*Əl, El* 'hand' + *-İg, - Lik, -Li* 'an affix, denoting the word *Ten*'), meaning "five tens" in *Turkic* [*Egorov*. 24].
80. *Huth* "six".	*Ut, Ult, Ulta, Altı, Olti* "six". Egorov V.G. indicated *Utməl* "sixty": *Ut* 'six' + *-Məl* 'an affix, denoting the numeral *Ten*' in *Chuvash* [279].
81. *Sem* "seven".	*Sette, Siç, Siçö* "seven".
82. *Kis* "eight".	*Sekiz* "eight" (*Se* 'four' + *Ekiz* 'twin'), meaning "four twos", "eight" in *Turkic*.
83. *Tivr* "ten". *Thr* "an abraded form of *Tivr*".	*Ti, Thu, Thun > Ton* 'hand, five' + *Ivr > İgirə* 'twin', meaning "five twos", "ten" in *Turkic*. The *Turkic* numerals, containing the words *Ekiz, İgirə* "twin", also include *İgirmi* (*İgirə* 'twin' + *-Mi* 'an affix, denoting the number 10'), meaning "two tens" in *Turkic*.

ETRUSCAN	TURKIC
84. **Thunesi** "nine".	*Thun > Ton* 'hand, five' + *Esi > Se* 'four', meaning "nine" in *Turkic*. *I.Taylor* gave a very convincing breakdown of the *Etruscan* word and its *Turkic* etymology: "The first syllable is apparently *thu-* or *thun-*, which we have seen means 'five'. It is just possible that *-esi*, the latter part of the word, may be an abnormal form of the ordinal suffix, but there seems to be a much greater likelihood in identifying it with *se, zia,* or *sa,* 'four'. The digit *Thunesi* would therefore be 'nine', or 5 + 4. This analysis is confirmed by a comparison with the *Turkic* words for nine, 'togus and tohus', which are, apparently, abraded forms of *tong – usa,* or 5 + 4." [180].
85. **Tivr Sa** "1.ten and four; 2.fourteen".	*Ti, Thu, Thun > Ton* 'hand, five' + *Ivr > İgirə* 'twin' + *Sa > Se* 'four', meaning "five twos and four", "ten and four", "fourteen". The *Etruscan* numeral order is the same as in *Turkic,* such as *On dörd* "ten and four".
86. **Zathrm** "1.four ten-ones; 2.forty".	*Za > Se* 'four' + *Thr* (*Ton* 'hand, five' + *İgirə* 'ten') + *M > Maka* 'one', meaning "four ten-ones", "forty" in *Turkic*. The *Etruscan* order of numerals found its perfect match in the *Turkic* ones: *Tört On* ("four tens", "forty"), *Üç On* ("three tens", "thirty"), *Bəş On* ("five tens", "fifty") [*Radlov.* 1.2.1042, 1872].

§ 11.3-1. 45 GRAMMATICAL POINTERS, ATTESTING THAT ETRUSCAN WAS A TURKIC LANGUAGE.

NOUNS.

1. *Etruscan* and *Turkic* nouns do not have a gender. Additions at the end modify them.

2. The masculine and feminine gender of the nouns can be determined by their definition:

    - *Sek* "daughter", *Klan* "boy" in *Etruscan*.
    - *Kız* "girl, daughter", *Oğlan* "boy" in *Turkic*.

3. The gender of the *Etruscan* and *Turkic* noun can be ascertained by another noun, following or preceding it:

    - *Klens Puia* "female child" in *Etruscan*.
    - *Kız Bala* "female child" in *Turkic*.

4. Both in *Etruscan* and *Turkic*, masculine nouns can turn into feminine ones with the addition of the words or affixes:

    - *Semna* "priestess" (*Sem* > *Kam* 'shaman' + *Na* > *Ana* 'female; dame') in *Etruscan*.
    - *Ama Çelen* "female snake" (*Ama* 'female' + *Çelen* 'snake') in *Turkic*.
    - *Laukanesa* "wife of a king" (*Lau* > *Ulu* 'great' + *Kan* 'king, chief' + *-Esa* > *-Iş* 'an affix, denoting the word *Wife*') in *Etruscan*.
    - *Kanış* "wife of a king" (*Kan* 'king' + *-Iş* 'an affix, denoting the word *Wife*') in *Turkic*.

5. Compound nouns in *Etruscan* and *Turkic* are formed in several, similar ways:

    > When two nouns are united:
    - *Klan Puiak* "boy child", "small boy" in *Etruscan*.
    - *Oğul Kıs* "boy girl", "children" in *Turkic*.

    - *Klan Kizi* "boy man", "young man" in *Etruscan*.
    - *Ir Kizi* "warrior man", "man" in *Turkic*.

    > When two nouns are joined:
    - *Semna* "priestess" (*Sem* > *Kam* 'shaman' + *Na* > *Ana* 'female, dame') in *Etruscan*.
    - *Turan* "Urania; goddess" (*Tura* 'God' + *An* > *Ana* 'female') in *Etruscan*.
    - *Qayınana* "mother-in-law" (*Qayın* 'son-in-law' + *Ana* 'mother') in *Turkic*.
    - *Xörama* "virgin mother" (*Xör* 'virgin' + *Ama* "mother; goddess") in *Turkic*.

    > When an adjective and a noun are joined:
    - *Lucumo, Laukane* "great king" (*Lu, Lau* > *Ulu* 'great' + *Cumo, Kane* > *Kan* 'king') in *Etruscan*.
    - *Aksakal* "elder" (*Ak* 'white' + *Sakal* 'beard') in *Turkic*.

6. The plural number of the nouns is formed by adding the affixes *-Ar, -Tr, -Lan* in *Etruscan* or *-Lar, -Lər* in *Turkic*:

    - *Klenar* > *Oğlanlar* "sons".
    - *Tular* > *Turalar* "tombs, structures".
    - *Puantrn* > *Pəyaklarına* "to her children".
    - *Suthurlan* > *Sitillər* "vessels".

7. The plural can take the possessive affix *-Asi* after the affix of plurality *-Ar* in *Etruscan* and *-I, -İ* after the affixes of plurality *-Lar, -Lər* in *Turkic*:

    - *Klenarasi* > *Oğlanları* "his/her sons".

8. Both in *Etruscan* and *Turkic*, the plural, followed by the possessive affix, can have case-endings, such as the dative case-ending in the 3rd person *-N* in *Etruscan* and *-Na* in *Turkic*:

    - *Puantrn* "to her children" in *Etruscan*.
    - *Pəyaklarına* "to her children" in *Turkic*.

9. The dative case of substantives is formed by the affixes *-N, -E, -A* in *Etruscan* and *-Na, -Ə* in *Turkic*:

    - *Puantrn* in *Etruscan* > *Pəyaklarına* in *Turkic* = "to her children".
    - *Turke* in *Etruscan* > *Türkə* in *Turkic* = "to Turk".
    - *Aulesa* in *Etruscan* > *Aulesə* in *Turkic* = "to Aules".

10. Diminutives of nouns are formed by adding affixes *-Ik, -K* in *Etruscan* and *-Ak, -Çak* in *Turkic* to the root:

    - *Suthik* "small tomb" > *Suthi* "tomb" in *Etruscan*.
    - *Turaçak* "small structure" > *Tura* "structure" in *Turkic*.

    - *Puiak* "little girl or child" > *Puia* "girl, child" in *Etruscan*.
    - *Oğlanak* "small boy" > *Oğlan* "boy" in *Turkic*.

11. Nouns can transform into adjectives or participles without changing any form in both languages:

    - *Suthil* "offering" [n], *Suthil* "offered" [part.] in *Etruscan*.
    - *Qızıl* "gold" [n], *Qızıl* "red" [adj] in *Turkic*.

12. Both in *Etruscan* and *Turkic*, substantives use the affix *-Lik* to denote the abstract function or quality of a thing:
    - *Khiselik* "effigy" in *Etruscan*: *Khise* > *Kişi* 'man' + *-Lik*.
    - *Kişilik* "manhood" in *Turkic*: *Kişi* 'man' + *-Lik*.

13. Nouns can reshape into another noun by adding the affix *-Us* in *Etruscan* and *-Uş, -Iş* in *Turkic*:

    - *Ludio* "dancer" > *Ludus* "dance" (*Lud* > *Lutı* 'dancer' + *Us* > *-Uş*) in *Etruscan*.
    - *Bağ* "rope" > *Bağış* "ligament" in *Turkic*.

14. Nouns can designate the object possessed with the help of the possessive affixes, such as *-M* in the 1st person sing. in *Etruscan* and *-Im, -Am* in *Turkic*, which act as possessive pronouns:

    - *Puiam* "my child" in *Etruscan*.
    - *Pəyakım* "my child" in *Turkic*.

15. Nouns with the possessive affixes in the 3rd person singular can be formed by *-Si, -S, -As* in *Etruscan* and *-I, -Si* in *Turkic*, which function as possessive pronouns:

    - *Klensi* in *Etruscan* > *Oğlanı* in *Turkic* = "his son".
    - *Puius, Fuius* in *Etruscan* > *Pəyakı* in *Turkic* = "his daughter (child)".
    - *Aiseras* in *Etruscan* > *Tengrisi* in *Turkic* = "his god".

16. When two nouns are in apposition, only the second one has the termination:

    - *Alpan Turke* in *Etruscan* > *Alban Türkə* in *Turkic* = "<u>to</u> the *Albanian Turk*".

17. Both in *Etruscan* and *Turkic*, titles as a sign of respect follow the name of a female or a male. *Etruscan* titles *Isa, Esa, Asa,* and the abbreviated *S* "madam" (from *Es, Əs* "lord; great" in *Turkic*) are equivalent to the *Turkic Xanım* "madam" and consistently come after a female's name, not before it as in the *Indo-European* languages:

    - *Pravna <u>Isa</u>* "<u>Madam</u> *Pravna*" in *Etruscan*.
    - *Pravna <u>Xanım</u>* "<u>Madam</u> *Pravna*" in *Turkic*.

18. Patronymic names are followed by *Ul* "child, son" in *Etruscan* and *Turkic:*

    - *Jeputr <u>Ul</u>* "<u>son</u> of *Jupiter*" in *Etruscan*.
    - *Tanrı <u>Ulı</u>* "<u>son</u> of God" in *Turkic*.

19. One and the same word or name can have several variations in *Etruscan* and *Turkic* languages, also observed in *Median* and *Phrygian*.

    Isaac Taylor noted the orthographic and lexical irregularities of the *Etruscan* speech: "The speech represented by the inscriptions was obviously in an unfixed condition. In the same tomb, nay, even in the same inscription, we find perplexing variations in the formation of the letters; and the powers of the letters are so uncertain that the same name is not uniformly spelt in the same way. We have, for instance, in the same inscription, such variations as *Lart* and *Larth*, or *Arnt* and *Arnth*. The punctuation is also most irregular; and the words are constantly undivided, or divided wrongly. There is no system in the abbreviations; vowels are thrown out or retained in a haphazard and unreasonable fashion." [358]

    - *Teke, Theke* "presented" in *Etruscan*.
    - *Zilakh, Zilath, Zilc* "coffin" in *Etruscan*.
    - *U, Oğul, Oğl* "son, boy" in *Turkic*.
    - *Ana, Ama, Anne* "mother" in *Turkic*.

PRONOUNS.

20. There are two types of pronouns in *Etruscan* and *Turkic:* independent and dependent. Independent pronoun stands alone, while dependent one is represented by a relevant affix attached to a noun.

21. Independent personal pronoun of the 1st person singular in *Etruscan Mi* "I" is allied to *Min, Men, Mən* in *Turkic:*

    - <u>MI</u>:   THANAS   (in *Etruscan*).
    - <u>Min</u>: *Tanas*   (in *Turkic*).
    - <u>I</u>:   *Thanas*
    - "I am *Thanas*."

22. Independent pronouns can take verbal affixes, such as *-Im* in *Etruscan* and *-Əm* in *Turkic*:

    - MAN<u>IM</u>: ARKE: RIL: LXVII (in *Etruscan*).
    - Mən<u>əm</u>: ər[i]: il[im]: 67 (in *Turkic*).
    - <u>I am</u>: husband: year: 67
    - "<u>I am</u> a 67-year-old husband."

23. Dependent possessive pronouns are represented by affixes attached to nouns, such as the affixes in the 1st person, singular *-M* in *Etruscan* and *-M, -Im, -İm* in *Turkic*:

    - *Puia<u>m</u>* "<u>my</u> daughter" in *Etruscan*.
    - *Pəyakı<u>m</u>, Bala<u>m</u>* "<u>my</u> child" in *Turkic*.

24. Dependent possessive pronouns in the 3rd person singular can be formed by the possessive affixes *-S, -Si, -Shi, -Asi* in *Etruscan* and *-Si, -I* in *Turkic*, attached to nouns:

    - *Klen<u>si</u>* "<u>his</u> son"; *Klenar<u>asi</u>* "<u>his</u> sons" in *Etruscan*.
    - *Bala<u>sı</u>* "<u>his</u> child"; *Balalar<u>ı</u>* "<u>his</u> children" in *Turkic*.
    - *Avil<u>s</u>* "<u>his</u> age" in *Etruscan*.
    - *Oğlan<u>ı</u>* "<u>his</u> son"; *Oğlanlar<u>ı</u>* "<u>his</u> sons" in *Turkic*.

25. The possessive affix in possessive plural pronouns, such as *-Asi* in *Etruscan* and *-I* in *Turkic*, always follows the plural ending *-Ar* in *Etruscan* and *-Lar* in *Turkic*:

    - *Klen<u>arasi</u>* "his sons" in *Etruscan*.
    - *Oğlan<u>ları</u>* "his sons" in *Turkic*.

26. Demonstrative pronouns can act as adjectives or adverbs of place, such as *Ken, Kehen, Anken, Eka* "this, here" in *Etruscan* and *Ənə, An, Ku* "this, here" in *Turkic*:

    - *Eka suthik* "<u>this</u> little tomb" in *Etruscan*; *Ku pəyak* "<u>this</u> child" in *Turkic*. [adj]
    - *Eka suthis* "<u>Here</u> is his tomb" in *Etruscan*; *Ku pəyaktı* "<u>Here</u> is a child" in *Turkic*. [adv]

NUMERALS.

27. The ordinal numerals in *Etruscan* are formed from cardinals by means of the affixes *-S, -Sk* and in *Turkic* – with the help of the affixes *-Se, -Ske, -Eske, -Nç, -Nc, -İnç, -Inc, -Nşi, -Nti, -Ndi*:

    - *Makh<u>s</u>* "first" in *Etruscan* = *Beren<u>se</u>, Birin<u>çi</u>, Birin<u>şi</u>* "first" in *Turkic*.
    - *Ki<u>s</u>* "second" in *Etruscan* = *İken<u>se</u>, İkin<u>ç</u>, İkin<u>ti</u>, İkin<u>di</u>, İkin<u>çi</u>, Ikin<u>ci</u>* "second" in *Turkic*.

28. The *Etruscan* system of numeration was a combination of decimal and vigesimal methods, employing *Alkhl* "twenty" – a reduplicated form of the affix *-Lkh* "ten", similar to the *Turkic* affixes *-Lik, -Lig, -Lık, -Lıq* "ten":
    - *Ke-A<u>lkh</u>l* "two twenties", "forty" in *Etruscan*.
    - *El<u>lik</u>, Əl<u>lik</u>* "five tens", "fifty" in *Turkic*.

29. In the cardinal numbers from 11 to 19, the lower number follows the higher in *Etruscan* and *Turkic* in contrast to *English, Russian, Persian,* and other *Indo-European* languages:

    - *Tivr Sa* "ten and four", "fourteen" in *Etruscan*.
    - *On Dörd* "ten and four", "fourteen" in *Turkic*.

30. The *Etruscan* numeral adjuncts, or noun classifiers, that stand between a number and certain names of persons, animals, or objects to be counted – *Ras* "head", *Naper* "soul", *Tane* "corn, piece", match closely *Baş* "head", *Nefer* "person, soul", *Dane* "piece", which are *Turkic* in origin, not *Persian* or *Arabic,* as they were first recorded in *Etruscan* – a *Turkic* language:

    - *Sa Ras* = *Se Baş* "four heads".
    - *Hut Naper* = *Ut Nefer* "six souls".
    - *Sa Tene* = *Se Dane* "four pieces".

31. Both the *Etruscan* and *Turkic* numeral adjuncts do not accept plural form:

    - *Sa Ras* = *Se Baş* "four heads" (literally, "four head").
    - *Hut Naper* = *Ut Nefer* "six souls" (literally, "six soul").
    - *Sa Tene* = *Se Dane* "four pieces" (literally, "four piece").

POSTPOSITIONS.

32. Similar to other kindred *Turkic* languages, such as *Median* and *Phrygian, Etruscan* did not have prepositions. The available ancient texts, including the *Etruscan* epitaphs, revealed the dependent type of postpositions, represented by the affixes *-N, -E, -I* in *Etruscan* and *-Na, -Ə* in *Turkic*, equivalent to the preposition *To, For*:

    - *Puantrn* in *Etruscan* > *Pəyaklarına* in *Turkic* = "to her children" (literally, "her children to").

        - LARTHIA: ATEINEI: PHLERES: PUANTRN: SL: TURKE (in *Etruscan*).
        - *Lartiə: Ateinei:* peru: pəyaklarına: əsilli: *Türkə* (in *Turkic*).
        - *Larthia: Ateinei:* gift: children to: adults: *Turk* to.
        - "*Larthia Ateinei's* gift to her adult children, the *Turks*."

        NOTE:
        1. The *Turkic* word *Əsilli* is the counterpart of the *Etruscan* abbreviation *SL*. It means "adult" and "anyone above 10 years old" [*Radlov*. 1.1.879].
        2. The word *Türk* could be both in singular and as a collective noun without the added affix of plurality, as it was asserted by *Mahmud Kashgari* ["Divanü Lügat-it-Türk" ("The Corpus of the *Turkic* Lexicon"). 1.177].

    - *Aulesi* in *Etruscan* > *Aulesə* in *Turkic* = "to *Aules*" (literally, "*Aules* to").

        - AULESI: METELLIS: VE: VESIAL: KLENSI: TEKE (in *Etruscan*).
        - *Aulesə: Metellis: Ve[le]: Vesia* aila: oğlı: takıdı (in *Turkic*).
        - *Aules* to: *Metellis: Ve[le]: Vesia* mother: son: gave
        - "*Vele*, son of madam *Vesia*, gave to *Aules Metellis*."

- *Turce* in *Etruscan* > *Türkə* in *Turkic* = "to Turk" (literally, "Turk to").

    o [I]N: TURCE: RAMT: ALF: U[H]TAVI: SELVAN (in *Etruscan*).
    o [I]nı: *Türkə*: *Ramt[ə]*: *Albı*: *U[h]tavi*: sevilən (in *Turkic*).
    o Younger brother: *Turk* <u>to</u>: *Ramtus*: *Albus*: *Octavia*: beloved.
    o "<u>To</u> the beloved younger brother *Ramtus Albus*, the *Turk*, whose mother is *Octavia*."

PARTICIPLES.

33. Some *Etruscan* and *Turkic* participles do not differ from substantives in their form:

    o *Suthil* "offering" [n], *Suthil* "offered" [p] in *Etruscan*.
    o *Thesan* "sunrise" [n], "rising (sun)" [p] in *Etruscan*.
    o *Tasan* "the one that rises" [n]; "rising" [p] in *Turkic*.

34. Present participles can be formed by the affix *-An* in *Etruscan* and *Turkic*:

    o *Thesan* "sunrise", "rising (sun)" in *Etruscan*.
    o *Tasan* "the one that rises"; "rising" in *Turkic*.

35. Past participles utilize the affixes *-Thas, -As, - Eis* in *Etruscan* and *-As, -Bas, -Pas, -Mas* in *Turkic*. The *Turkic* affix *-Mas* and its variants *-Mıs, -Mış* originally belonged to the *Oguz* group of the *Turkic* languages, that primarily includes *Azerbaijani* and *Turkish*:

    o *Zilakhnthas* "having been coffined" in *Etruscan*.
    o *Basdırılmış* "having been coffined" in *Turkic*.

36. Past participles can employ the affix *-N* in *Etruscan* and *Turkic* to create a passive form. This affix is followed by one of the affixes *-Thas, -As, - Eis* in *Etruscan* and *-Mış, -As, -Bas, -Pas, -Mas* in *Turkic*:

    o *Zilakhnthas* "having been coffined" in *Etruscan*.
    o *Aldanmış* "having been tricked" in *Turkic*.

VERBS.

37. Verbs usually stand at the end of a sentence in *Etruscan* and *Turkic*.

    o LARIS : PUMPUS: ARNTHAL: KLAN: <u>KECHASE</u> (in *Etruscan*).
    o *Larıs*: *Pumpus*: *Arnti* aila: oğlı: <u>keçindi</u> (in *Turkic*).
    o *Larth*: *Pompey*: *Arnthi* mother: son: <u>passed away</u>
    o "*Laris Pumpus* (*Larth Pompey*), son of madam *Arnthi*, <u>passed away</u>".

    o AULESI: METELLIS: VE: VESIAL: KLENSI: <u>TEKE</u> (in *Etruscan*).
    o *Aulesa*: *Metellis*: *Ve[le]*: *Vesia* aila: oğlı: <u>takıdı</u> (in *Turkic*).
    o To *Aules*: *Metellis*: *Ve[le]*: *Vesia* mother: son: <u>donated</u>
    o "*Vele*, son of madam *Vesia*, donated to *Aules Metellis*."

38. Verbs can form from other parts of speech in *Etruscan* and *Turkic* by means of affixes:

    o *Zilakhnu* "he was coffined": *Zilakh* 'coffin' + *-N* 'an affix, denoting the passive voice' + *-U* 'an affix, denoting the past tense in the 3rd p. sing.' in *Etruscan*.
    o *Aldandı* "he was tricked": *Al* 'trick' + *-Da* 'an affix, converting a noun into a verb' + *-N* 'an affix, denoting the passive voice' + *-Dı* 'an affix, denoting the past tense in the 3rd p. sing.' in *Turkic*.

39. The *Etruscan* verbal affix *-M* and the *Turkic* *-M, -Üm* create verbs in the 1st person sing., in the past tense:
    o *Lupum* "I died" in *Etruscan* = *Öldüm* "I died" in *Turkic*.

40. The past tense of a verb in the 3rd person singular is formed by the addition of the affixes *-Thi, -E, -U* in *Etruscan* and *-Ti, -Di, -Dı, -Dü* in *Turkic*:

    o *Veithi* "gave" in *Etruscan* = *Verdi* "gave" in *Turkic*.
    o *Theke, Teke* "gave, donated" in *Etruscan* = *Takıdı* "gave" in *Turkic*.
    o *Lupu* "died" in *Etruscan* = *Ölüp, Öldü* "died" in *Turkic*.

41. Both *Etruscan* and *Turkic* verbs utilize the affixes *-N, -Un* to create the passive voice:

    o *Kurikhunte* "was made": *Kurikh* > *Kürə* 'do' + *-Un* > *-N* 'an affix, denoting the passive voice' + *-Te* > *-Ti* 'an affix, denoting the past tense' in *Etruscan*.
    o *Kürəndi* "was made": *Kürə* 'do' + *-N* 'an affix, denoting the passive voice' + *-Di* 'an affix, denoting the past tense' in *Turkic*.

    o ANK[E]N: SUTHI: KURIKHUNTHE: MATUNAS: LARISALISA (in *Etruscan*).
    o *An: sitil: kürəndi: Matunas[a]: anası Larisa xanım* (in *Turkic*).
    o This: tomb: was made: Matunas [for]: [whose] mother [is] Larisa Madam
    o "This tomb was made for *Matunas*, the child of Madam *Larisa*."

42. The affix, indicating the past tense, always follows the affix of the passive voice in both languages:

    o *Zilakhnu, Kurikhunte* in *Etruscan*.
    o *Aldandı, Kürəndi* in *Turkic*.

43. The verbs can transform into adjectives, participles, and nouns with the help of the affixes, such as *-Uk* in *Etruscan* and *-Ük* in *Turkic*:

    o *Lupu* "died" [58] > *Lupuke* "deceased" [adj., part.], "a deceased" [noun] in *Etruscan*.
    o *Tez* "run" > *Tezük* "runaway" [adj., noun] in *Turkic*.

44. The structural composition of a sentence in *Etruscan* completely matches the *Turkic* one:

    o AULESI: METELLIS: VE: VESIAL: KLENSI: TEKE (in *Etruscan*).
    o *Aulesa: Metellis: Ve[le]: Vesia aila: oğlı: takıdı* (in *Turkic*).
    o *Aules* to: Metellis: Ve[le]: Vesia mother: son: gave
    o "*Vele*, son of madam *Vesia*, gave to *Aules Metellis*."

---

[58] *I. Taylor* did not indicate the infinitive of this verb.

45. The ethnonym *Turk,* or *Turke,* was a frequent phenomenon in the *Etruscan* artworks that decorated the tombs of the *Etruscans.*

This should not come as a surprise due to one obvious fact – the *Etrusci* belonged to a larger *Scythian* family, including the *Medes* and their *Sarmatian* derivative tribes, one of which was the *Tyrcae,* aka *Turkae,* aka *Turks.* This fact was distinctly affirmed by *Pliny the Elder* when describing the *Sarmates* and their derivative tribes.

The following lexical analysis of the *Etruscan* inscriptions with this word *Turke,* or *Turce,* left on the variety of the sepulchral offerings, was carried on the base of the material, gathered by *Isaac Taylor* in his book "*Etruscan* Researches", as well as of the work "Corpus inscriptionum italicarum antiquioris aevi ordine geographico digestum, et glossarium italicum in quo omnia vocabula continentur ex umbricis, sabinis, oscis, volscis, etruscis aliisque monumentis quae supersunt collecta... cura et studio." by the *Italian* archeologist *Ariodante Fabretti,* published in *Latin* in 1867.

The *Etruscan* tombs exposed a rather unusual feature exclusively characteristic to them: in addition to indicating the names of the dead along with their close relatives, such as a mother, a father, the *Etruscans* also listed their status in the society (*Lautni* "freedman", *Asa, Esa, Isa* "noblewoman"), as well as their ethnic affiliation.

In the following examples, the *Etruscans* not only pinpointed their ethnicity as *Turk* but, in some cases, were more specific to indicate even the area of origin, such as *Alpan Turk.* When indicated as *Turke,* the ending affix –*E* is equivalent to the *English* preposition *To,* thus meaning "to *Turk*":

1.   VIPIA: ALSINAI: TURKE: VERSENAS: KAIIA
Turkic: Vipia: Alsinai[dan]: Türkə: Versenaz: Qəiyə.
Verbatim: *Vipia: Alsinai: Turk* to: *Versenas: Kaiia.*
Loose translation: "From *Vipia Alsinai* to *Versenas Kaiia,* the *Turk.*"
Note: *Kaiia: Kai > Gəi, Gəy* 'great' + *Ia > -İə, -Yə* 'an affix, equivalent to the *English* preposition *To*' in *Turkic.*

2.   IN: TURK[E]: VEL: SVEITUS
Turkic: Inı: *Türk[ə]:   Vəli: Sveitus.*
Verbatim: Younger brother: [to] *Turk: Veli: Sveitus.*
Loose translation: "To a younger brother *Vel Sveitus,* the *Turk.*"
Note: 1) *In > Inı* "junior brother" in *Turkic.* ["Drevneturkskiy slovar." 210]
   2) As the *Etruscan* tongue was agglutinative, like all the *Turkic* languages, the word construction was made with affixes added at the end of the words. Prepositions were represented by affixes, such as in the word *Turke, Turce* (*Turk, Turc* + -*E* 'an affix, equivalent to the preposition *To*').

3.   [I]N: TURCE: RAMT: ALF: U[H]TAVI: SELVAN
Turkic: [I]nı: Türkə: Ramt[ə]: Albı: U[h]tavi: sevilən.
Verbatim: Younger brother: *Turk* to: *Ramt: Albi: U[h]tavi* (*Octavia*): beloved.
Loose translation: "To the beloved younger brother *Ramt Albi* (*Ramtus Albus*), the *Turk,* whose mother is *Uhtavi* (*Octavia*)."
Note: *Selvan > Sevilən* "beloved" in *Turkic.*

4.   MI: SUTHIL: VELTHURI: THURA: TURKE: AU: VELTHURI: PHNISKIAL
Turkic: Mən: sitil[i]:   *Velturi:*   türə[di]:   Türkə: Au[les]: *Velturi:*   Fniski aila.
Verbatim: I: vessel: *Velturi:* placed: *Turk* for: *Au[les]: Velturi:* [his] mother *Fniski.*
Loose translation: "I, the vessel, was placed by *Velturi* for *Aules Velturi,* the *Turk,* whose mother's name is *Fniski.*"
Note: 1) *Thura > Tür* "to place" in *Turkic.*

74

2) *Phniskial: Phniski* 'a female name' + *-Al* 'an affix, indicating a matronymic name', 'madam' in *Etruscan*.

5.   LARKE: LEKN[E]: TURKE: PHLERE: SUTHURLAN: VEITHI
<u>Turkic</u>:   Larkə: Lekn[ə]:   Türkə: peru: sitillar: verdi.
<u>Verbatim</u>: Larke: Lekn[e]:   Turk to: gift: vessels: gave.
<u>Loose translation</u>: "*Larke* gave a gift of vessels to *Lekne* (*Licini*), the *Turk*."
<u>Note</u>: 1) *Phlere* > *Peru* "gift" in *Turkic* [*Egorov*. 143].
   2) *Suthurlan: Suthur* > *Sitil* 'vessel' + *Lan* > *-Lar* 'an affix of plurality', meaning "vessels" in *Turkic*.
   3) *Veithi* > *Verdi* "gave" in *Turkic*. Like in *Turkic*, a predicate verb stands at the end of a sentence in *Etruscan*.

6.   UTNI: THUPHULTH: ASA: TURKE
<u>Turkic</u>:   Utni: Tupult: aça: Türkə.
<u>Verbatim</u>: Utni: Thuphulth: father: Turk to.
<u>Loose translation</u>: "To *Utni*, the *Turk*, whose father's name is *Thuphulth*."
<u>Note</u>: 1) *Thuphulth* > *Tupul* "large, fat" in *Turkic*.
   2) *Asa* > *Aça* "father" in *Turkic* [*Egorov*. 35]

7.   THUKER: HERMEN: AS: TURUKE
<u>Turkic</u>:   Tükər: Hərmən: aça: Türükə.
<u>Verbatim</u>: Tucker: Hermen: father: Turk to.
<u>Loose translation</u>: "To *Tucker* (*Tocerus*), the *Turk*, whose father is *Hermen*."
<u>Note</u>: 1) *Turk, Turuk* > *Türk, Türük*. Both in *Etruscan* and *Turkic*, the name of the *Turkic* ethnicity has the same variations.
   2) *Hermen: Her* > *Er* 'warrior, man, hero' + *Men* 'I', meaning "I am the warrior/man/hero" in *Turkic*. This *Etruscan* male name is equivalent to *Herman* and *Erman* in *Turkic*, *Armand* in *French*, and *Herman* in *German*.

8.   A: VELSCUS: THUPLTH: AS: ALPAN: TURKE
<u>Turkic</u>:   A[ules]: Velskus: Tupult: aça: Alpan: Türkə.
<u>Verbatim</u>: A[ules]: Velscus: Thuphulth: father: Alpan: Turk to.
<u>Loose translation</u>: "To *Aules Velscus*, the *Albanian Turk*, whose father is *Thuphulth*."
<u>Note</u>: 1) *Alpan* "Albania – a name of the place in *Italy*", mentioned by *Ptolemy* as such.
   2) *Alpan* > *Alp* 'hero' + *-An* 'an affix of plurality', meaning "heroes" in *Turkic*.

The conducted analysis of lexical composition of the *Etruscan* words and their grammatical structure left no doubt in their affinity to the ancient *Turkic* language. This is not a far-fetched fantasy to assert that *Etruscan* is, in fact, a *Turkic* language. The authority of *I. Taylor* seems decidedly preferable on this point:

"Now the mode in which the *Etruscans* employed the suffixes *-al* and *-isa* is beyond all question distinctly agglutinative. It may be confidently asserted that the mere existence of such a word as TLESN-AL-ISA or VAR-NAL-ISA is of itself sufficient to establish the agglutinative character of *Etruscan* grammar, and thus to set at rest forever the question of the linguistic affinities of the *Etruscan* tongue. It is an inexplicable marvel that this obvious and unmistakable feature of the *Etruscan* language should have so long escaped recognition." [247]

Figure 18. An Etruscan woman, carrying a child. 5th c. BCE. The Metropolitan Museum of Art, USA. [OA] Credit: Rogers Fund, 1917.

It is noteworthy to mention that early *Etruscan* works of art, including statuettes on top of sarcophagi, reveal some *Mongoloid* features, such as squinted or almond-shaped eyes and high cheekbones, similar to those of the *Turkic* nations of *Central Asia*.

The *Etruscans* shared close affinity with their *Scythian* and *Phrygian* brethren, which was delightfully confirmed by the great multitude of the *Etruscans* artwork, such as a terracotta cinerary urn, illustrating a *Phrygian* cap with wings on a head of a bizarre creature, or a statuette of a *Scythian* mounted archer, wearing a typical *Phrygian* cap with a *Scythian* fitted jacket.

Figure 19. Etruscan terracotta cinerary urn. 2nd c. BCE. The Metropolitan Museum of Art, USA. [OA] Credit: Purchase, 1896

Figure 20. Bronze statuette of a Scythian mounted archer. 5th c. BCE. The Metropolitan Museum of Art, USA. [OA] Credit: Gift of Norbert Schimmel Trust, 1989.

The ancient *Turkic* culture, language, and religion paved the way for the rise of the *Roman* nation and culture. As *Isaac Taylor* once famously said:

> "*Roman* history is the history of an *Aryan* civilization based upon a substratum of *Turanian* culture. The earliest structure which exists at *Rome* is constructed on an *Etruscan* model, and was probably built by *Etruscan* skill. At the earliest period at which *Rome* emerges into the light of authentic history we find her ruled by an *Etruscan* dynasty. The beginnings of her culture, her art, and her religion were, to a great extent, of *Etruscan* origin, and her social and her political institutions are not without traces of *Etruscan* influence.
> For some centuries the history of *Italy* is the history of the gradual uprising to political power and social importance of the hitherto subject *Aryan* element – *Latin, Umbrian,* or *Oscan* – which at *Rome* first emancipated itself from *Etruscan* sovereignty, and then, gradually asserting its supremacy over all *Etruria,* succeeded finally in absorbing or superseding the arts, the laws, the language, and the nationality of the once dominant race."
> ["*Etruscan* Researches." 6-7]

The *Etruscans,* similar to other kindred *Trojan* nations, endured numerous invasions into their lands both by their kin and foreigners, that resulted in their language and name replacement, according to *Strabo:*

> "But the present changes have produced many differences in consequence of the continual succession of governors of the country, who confounded together people and districts, and separated others. The *Phrygians* and *Mysians* were masters of the country after the capture of *Troy;* afterwards the *Lydians;* then the *Aeolians* and *Ionians;* next, the *Persians* and *Macedonians;* lastly, the *Romans,* under whose government **most of the tribes have lost even their languages and names**, in consequence of a new partition of the country having been made. It will be proper to take this into consideration when we describe its present state, at the same time showing a due regard to antiquity." [12.4.6]

It is only left to say that fate was crueler to some *Turkic* nations than others, such as the ancestors of the modern *European* nations – *Germanic, Icelandic, Celtic,* and the like. Their native *Turkic* language faded away, entirely replaced by the languages of *Indo-European* origin. Furthermore, their genuine *Turkic* origins are currently ignored, dismissed as a fairy tale by these very nations, who not only forfeited their true roots a long time ago but also lost the desire to claim back their original ancestry.

However, there is a wonderful *English* saying: "Better late than never!" As long as there is hope in the heart, nothing is lost. Hope is like a sapling that sooner or later can blossom into a fruit-bearing tree. Let us plant together these seedlings alongside the long-forgotten road back to our *Turkic* ancestors and cherish their glorious deeds and triumphs as ours!

xxxxxxxxxxxxxxxxx   xxxxxxxxxxxxxxxxx

§ 11-4. THE PHRYGIANS AND THEIR DERIVATIVE TRIBES.

The *Phrygians* were ruled to be the first humans to populate the *Earth,* after the argument between them and the *Egyptians* ended in their favor, according to *Herodotus:*

"Now the *Egyptians,* before the time when *Psammetichos* became king over them, were wont to suppose that they had come into being first of all men; but since the time when *Psammetichos* having become king desired to know what men had come into being first, they suppose that the *Phrygians* came into being before themselves, but they themselves before all other men." [2.2]

However, according to the *Latin* historian *Justin*, this argument of antiquity was settled between the *Egyptians* and the *Scythians:*

"The nation of the *Scythians* was always regarded as very ancient; though there was long a dispute between them and the *Egyptians* concerning the antiquity of their respective races; the *Egyptians* alleging that, "In the beginning of things, when some countries were parched with the excessive heat of the sun, and others frozen with extremity of cold, so that, in their early condition, they were not only unable to produce human beings, but were incapable even of receiving and supporting such as came from other parts (before coverings for the body were found out against heat and cold, or the inconveniences of countries corrected by artificial remedies), *Egypt* was always so temperate, that neither the cold in winter nor the sun's heat in summer, incommoded its inhabitants; and its soil so fertile, that no land was ever more productive of food for the use of man; and that, consequently, men must reasonably be considered to have been first produced in that country, where they could most easily be nourished." The *Scythians,* on the other hand, thought that the temperateness of the air was no argument of antiquity; "because Nature, when she first distributed to different countries degrees of heat and cold, immediately produced in them animals fitted to endure the several climates, and generated also numerous sorts of trees and herbs, happily varied according to the condition of the places in which they grew; and that, as the *Scythians* have a sharper air than the *Egyptians,* so are their bodies and constitutions in proportion more hardy. But that if the world, which is now distinguished into parts of a different nature, was once uniform throughout; whether a deluge of waters originally kept the earth buried under it; or whether fire, which also produced the world, had possession of all the parts of it, the *Scythians,* under either supposition as to the primordial state of things, had the advantage as to origin. For if fire was at first predominant over all things, and, being gradually extinguished, gave place to the earth, no part of it would be sooner separated from the fire, by the severity of winter cold, than the northern, since even now no part is more frozen with cold; but *Egypt* and all the east must have been the latest to cool, as being now burnt up with the parching heat of the sun. But if originally all the earth were sunk under water, assuredly the highest parts would be first uncovered when the waters decreased, and the water must have remained longest in the lowest grounds; while the sooner any portion of the earth was dry, the sooner it must have begun to produce animals; but *Scythia* was so much higher than all other countries, that all the rivers which rise in it run down into the *Lake Maeotis,* and then into the *Pontic* and *Egyptian* seas; whereas *Egypt,* (which, though it had been fenced by the care and expense of so many princes and generations, and furnished with such strong mounds against the violence of the encroaching waters, and though it had been intersected also by so many canals, the waters being kept out by the one, and retained by the other, was yet uninhabitable, unless the *Nile* were excluded) could not be thought to have the most ancient population; being a land, which, whether from the accessions of soil collected by its kings, or those from the *Nile,* bringing mud with it, must appear to have been the most recently formed of all lands." The *Egyptians* being confounded with these arguments, the *Scythians* were always accounted the more ancient." [2.1.1]

Both testimonies allow us to assert that the *Egyptians* recognized the *Phrygians* and the *Scythians* as a nation of one stock, which was more ancient than them.

Like most of the *Trojans*, the *Phrygians* (Φρύγες, Βρίγες in *Greek*) were *Thracians*, and *Troy* was also known as *Phrygia*. This was attested by *Euripides* (c. 480 - 406 BCE) in his tragedy "*Hecuba*", who was a *Phrygian* wife of the king of *Troy Priam*:

"...I *Polydore*, a son of *Hecuba* the daughter of *Cisseus* and of *Priam*. Now my father, when *Phrygia's* capital was threatened with destruction by the spear of *Hellas*, took alarm and conveyed me secretly from the land of *Troy* unto *Polymestor's* house, his friend in *Thrace*..." [Translated by *Edward Philip Coleridge*.]

As the *Thracians* were related to the *Scythian* nation, unsurprisingly, the *Phrygians* were also of *Scythian* extraction. *Strabo* repeatedly asserted that the *Phrygians* and the *Thracians* shared the same pedigree:

"It is difficult to define the boundaries of the *Bithynians, Mysians, Phrygians*, of the *Doliones* about *Cyzicus,* and of the *Mygdones* and *Troes;* it is generally admitted that each of these tribes ought to be placed apart from the other. A proverbial saying is applied to the *Phrygians* and *Mysians,* "The boundaries of the *Mysi* and *Phryges* are apart from one another," but it is difficult to define them respectively. The reason is this; strangers who came into the country were soldiers and barbarians; they had no fixed settlement in the country of which they obtained possession, but were, for the most part, wanderers, expelling others from their territory, and being expelled themselves. All these nations might be supposed to be *Thracians*, because *Thracians* occupy the country on the other side, and because they do not differ much from one another." [12.4.4-5]

"Even the *Phrygians* themselves are the same as the *Briges,* a people of *Thrace*...All these people quitted *Europe* entirely, the *Mysians* alone remaining." [Idem. 7.3.2]

"...nor is it at all improbable that, as the *Phrygians* themselves are a colony of *Thracians,* so they brought from *Thrace* their sacred ceremonies, and by joining together *Dionysus* and the *Edonian Lycurgus* they intimate a similarity in the mode of the worship of both." [Idem. 10.3.17]

"Somewhere in this neighbourhood is the mountain *Bermius,* which was formerly in the possession of the *Briges,* a *Thracian* nation, some of whom passed over to *Asia* and were called by another name, *Phrygians (Phryges).*" [Idem. Fragments. 25]

According to *Strabo*, "*Thracians*...do not differ much from one another." This means that the *Phrygians* spoke the same language as the *Getae*, the *Mysians*, the *Teucrians*, the *Asii,* and other *Thracian* nations, as well as the *Medes* and the *Scythians* did, – which was a non-*Indo-European* language – the *Turkic* language.

Following the elaborated facts that both the *Thracian* and *Scythian* nations shared the same *Turkic* roots, we determined that the *Phrygians,* as a *Thracian* nation, exhibited similar signs confirming their *Turkic* heritage. The most compelling evidence is the lexico-grammatical similarities between *Phrygian* and *Turkic*.

§ 11-4-1. THE LEXICO-GRAMMATICAL SIMILARITIES BETWEEN THE PHRYGIAN AND THE TURKIC LANGUAGES.

The glossary of the *Phrygian* words and their *Turkic* counterparts, provided below, as well as the analysis of the texts obtained from many *Greco-Phrygian* inscriptions,[59] firmly and unequivocally refute a widely distributed belief that *Phrygian* belonged to the *Indo-European* language family and affirm its *Turkic* origin.

The *Phrygian* section displays the words with their definition, which was taken from the ancient works or assumed by modern scholars. The assumed meanings do not always match the context. Therefore, we offer our interpretation of the *Phrygian* words, supported by the works of highly esteemed etymologists and *Turkologists*.[60]

PHRYGIAN	TURKIC	INDO-EUROPEAN
1.-Abberet "will bring, carry, bear". Other forms: **Abretoy, Abberetoi, Abberetor, Abbireto, Abereti, Beret** BOC translation: "bear, produce".	*Abberet, Abretoy, Abberetoi, Abberetor, Abbireto, Abereti*: *Abber/Abr/Abbir/Aber > Appar, Apar* 'bear, carry' [*Schwarz*.2] + *-Et* 'an affix, equivalent to *Will*', meaning "will bring" in *Turkic*. According to *Radlov V.V.*, the word *Apar*, or *Appar*, is a constricted union of two *Turkic* words – *Alip* 'take' + *Bər* 'bring' [R.1.1.613]. *Beret*: *Ber > Bər* 'bring, give' [R.4.2.1224] + *Et > -Et* 'an affix of the future tense', meaning "will bring, give" in *Turkic*. The affix *-Et* that denominates the future tense in the 3rd p. sing. is still in use in the modern *Kyrgyz* language: *Al bilet* – "He/She will know".	PIE *Bher* "bear, carry".
2.-Ad "its, him, her; his". Other forms: **A, As, At, Ot** BOC translation: *Ad, At, Ot* "to, at, by"; *As* "in, at, by".	*Anın* "its, his, her" in *Turkic*. *Anı* "him, her, it" in *Turkic* [R.1.1.226]. 1.*titetikmenos*: <u>at</u>: *tie*: *adeitou*. 2.*titetikmenos*: <u>as</u>: *tian*: *eitou*. Tormented: <u>him/her</u>: Zeus: will do. (verbatim) "Zeus will torment <u>him/her</u>." 3.*[i]os*: *ni*: *semon*: *knoumane*: *kakon*: *adaket*: *aini*: <u>a</u>: *teamas*: Whoever: any: this very: enclosed resting place: harm: will do: or: <u>its</u>: chamber. (verbatim) "Whoever does any harm to this enclosed resting place or <u>its</u> chamber."	PIE *Hens, a preposition
3.-Adamna "friend"	*Adaş* "friend" [R.1.1.484] in *Turkic*.	N/A

---

[59] The glossary and the texts were mostly obtained from the doctoral dissertation by *Bartomeu Obrador Cursach* (indicated as BOC thereafter) "Lexicon of the *Phrygian* Inscriptions", 2018. Barselona, Spain.
[60] Some names or works will be abbreviated, such as *R.* for *Radlov V.V., Dr.Sl.* for "Drevneturkskiy slovar".

PHRYGIAN	TURKIC	INDO-EUROPEAN

4.-Adaket
"will do, make, create, produce".
 	
Other forms:
Addaket, Adoket, Addakek, Adaken, Ada Ke, Addakem, Addaketor, Adda Kettor, Ddakett, Daket, Dakor, Dedasitiy, Dakaren, Odeketoy, Tedatoy, Edaes, Edae, Edes, Daes, Edatoy, Eitou=K'egedou=Egedou= Adeittnou.
 	
BOC translation:
"do, put".
	Adaket, Adoket, Addakek, Adaken, Ada Ke, Addakem, Ddakett, Daket:
	Adak, Ada, Ado, Adda, Dda, Da, De, Ode, Te, Ed, Eda, Eit, Eged 'do, create' > *Et, Eti, Ət, Əd, Ədə, Edgü* 'do, make, create, build, produce' [Dr.Sl.186] + *Et* > *-Et* 'an affix of the future tense', meaning "will do, make" in *Turkic*.
	
	Addaketor, Adda Kettor: Addak > Edgü 'do, make, create, build, produce' + *Ettor, Etor > Etor* 'will do' (*Et* 'do, make' + *Or* > *-Ar, -Ər* 'an affix of the future tense in the 3rd p. sing.'), meaning "will create" in *Turkic*.
	
	These *Phrygian* words are similar to the *Turkic* paired verbs, which can have the same or different meanings to signify one definition, for instance, in *Khakass* — *Imne-Tomna* "cure" (literally, "cure-cure"), *Ala-Sula* "bless" ("bless-bless"), *Uula-Ala* "howl" ("howl-howl"), in *Azerbaijani* — *Düzüb-Qoşar* "will fix" (literally, "put in order-will fix"), *Yanıb-Yakılar* "will be distressed" (literally, "burnt-will spread").
	
	Dakor: Dak > Edgü 'do, make, create, build, produce' + *Or > -Ar, -Ər* 'an affix of the future tense in the 3rd p. sing.', meaning "will do, create, make" in *Turkic*.
	
	Edaes, Edes, Daes: Ed, D > Et 'do, make, create, build, produce' + *-Es > -Miş, -Mız* 'an affix of the past tense in the 3rd p. sing.', meaning "did, made, created, produced, built" in *Turkic*.
	There is a similar *Turkic* example:
	    Ol evkə barmış ol.
	    "He went home."
	    [Dr.Sl.658].
		PIE *$d^h eh_1$-
		'to do, put, place'

PHRYGIAN	TURKIC	INDO-EUROPEAN

	Odeketoy, Tedatoy, Edatoy, Dedasitiy: *Odeke, Teda, Eda, Dedasi* > *Əd, Ədə, Edgü* 'do, create, build, produce' + *Toy, Tiy* > *-Ti, -Tı* 'an affix, denoting a verb in the 3rd p. sing. in the past tense', meaning "[he] made, created, did" in *Turkic*.
	
	Eitou, K'egedou, Egedou, Adeittnou: *Eit, K'eged, Eged, Adeittn* > *Et, Edgü* 'do, make, create, build, produce' + *Ou* > *-Ö, -Uo* 'an affix of the future tense in the 3rd p. sing.', meaning "will do, make, create, produce" in *Turkic*.
	
	The affix *-Ö* survived in the *Chuvash* language, i.e. *Vəl təvö* "he will do", *Vəl Kayö* "he will go". The affix *-Uo* as an indicator of the future tense in the 3rd p. sing. is still widely utilized in the *Yakut* language, i.e. *Anar ırıahıt buoluo* "Anar will be a singer"; *Onu ongoruo* "he will do it".
	
	Similar to *Phrygian*, in *Turkic* there are numerous other derivatives from the *Turkic* root *Et/Ət/Əd*: *Etiglig* "active", *Etgəli* "creation", *Etig* "deed", *Etindi* "did, made", *Etgü kerək* "must be done" [Dr.Sl.186]; *Ətkən* "made", *Ətti* "made", *Ədip* "made", *Ədər* "makes, will make, does, will do", *Ədəkli* "creating, forming, generating", *Ətmək, Etmək* "do, make, create", *Ədə bilmədi* "couldn't do". [R.1.1.835-839]; *Edəmiş, Etmiş* "having done" [Dr.Sl.658].
	Both in *Phrygian* and *Turkic*, the verb *Ed* or its other forms always come at the end of a sentence, act as a component of the complex verb construction with the affixes attached to it at the end to show its tense, person, number, and are always preceded by a noun, an adverb, an adjective, or a pronoun:
	   Tura ətti "s/he built a house".
	   Ot ətti "s/he set up the fire".	

PHRYGIAN	TURKIC	INDO-EUROPEAN
	Yoğ ətti "s/he turned smth. into nothing". *Uluq ətti* "s/he increased". *Kəndi ətti* "s/he personally did it". Now, compare these *Turkic* expressions to the *Phrygian* ones: *Kake Adaket* "will do harm" (verbatim: "harm will do"). *Keneman Edaes* "made the enclosed place" (verbatim: "the enclosed place made").	
5.-*Akaragayun* "upper rock", "altar". BOC translation: N/A	*Akaragayun: Akara > Ağarı* 'upper' + *Gayu > Qaya* 'rock' + *N > -Nı* 'an affix, denoting the accusative case', meaning "upper rock", "altar" in *Turkic*.	N/A
6.-*Akristin* "female slave, bakeress".	*Akristin: Akr > Ağır* 'heavy, difficult; heavily' [R.1.1.157] + *Is > İs* 'work, job' [R.1.2.1523] + *Tin > Tiyən* 'an affix, denoting constant action', meaning "the one who does heavy work" in *Turkic*.	N/A
7.-*Anar* 1."smart, sharp-witted man"; 2."husband". BOC translation: "man, husband"	*Anar* "smart man/warrior" [R.1.1.229] in *Turkic*. *Anar: An* 'intellect' + *Ar* 'man, warrior', meaning "smart man/warrior" in *Turkic*. *Anar* is an ancient *Turkic* male name, frequently used by the modern *Azerbaijanis* [Dr.Sl.43]. The old *Icelandic* saga "The Prose *Edda*" also mentioned a hero *Anarr*. *Anar* was also a root word in the name of a *Scythian* tribe *Anareoi*.	N/A
8.-*Areyastin* "from *Areyas* or *Arias*". BOC translation: "from (the mountain) *Areya*".	*Areyastin: Areyas > Arias* 'an island name' + *Tin > -Tın* 'an affix, denoting a preposition *From*', meaning "from *Areyas*" in *Turkic*.	N/A

PHRYGIAN	TURKIC	INDO-EUROPEAN
	This is a typical *Turkic* word formation that ends with an affix *-Tın*, equivalent to the preposition *From*. *William Smith* in the "Dictionary of *Greek* and *Roman* Geography" specified two variants of the name – *Arias* and *Aretias* and indicated that it was the name of "a small island on the coast of *Pontus*, 30 stadia east of *Pharnacia* (*Kera sunt*), called "*Apeos vigos*" by *Scymnus* (*Steph. B. s.v.* "*Apeos viaos*") and *Scylax*. Here (*Apollon. Rhod. ii. 384*) the two queens of the *Amazons*, *Otrere* and *Antiope*, built a temple to *Ares*. *Mela* (*ii. 7*) mentions this place under the name of *Area* or *Aria*, an island dedicated to *Mars*, in the neighbourhood of *Colchis*." [*Aretias*], [*Arias*]. The word-formation with a preposition attached as an affix to a noun at the end, as observed in the *Phrygian Areyastin*, does not exist in the *Indo-European* languages.	
9.-Arkiaevais "head of the *Arkia* house (family)". BOC translation: "son of *Arkias*".	*Arkiaevais*: *Arkia* > *Arka* 'backbone, support' + *Ev* 'family, clan, house' + *Ais* > *Əs* 'master, lord', meaning "head of the *Arkia* family" in *Turkic* [R.1.1875]. This *Phrygian* word combination *Evais* in the form of *Ev Yəsi* "head of the house" is still in usage in several *Turkic* languages, including *Azerbaijani*. As male names, *Arkia* and *Arka* share the same *Turkic* origin and meaning. The *Phrygian* word *Arkiaevais* was built on the *Turkic* word-formation principles, totally different from the *Indo-European* ones.	From *Greek Αρκιας*. No explanation was given for *Evais*.
10.-Ates Arkiaevais "*Ates*, the head of the *Arkia* family". BOC translation: "*Ates*, son of *Arkias*."	*Atış* "1.shootout; 2.an ancient *Turkic* male name". Both meanings were provided by *Mahmud Kashgari* more than 1 thousand years ago [Dr.Sl.67].	N/A

PHRYGIAN	TURKIC	INDO-EUROPEAN
<u>*11.-Memevais*</u> "head of the *Meme* house, family". BOC translation: "son of *Meme(s)*".	*Memevais*: *Meme* > *Mamay* 'giant' [R.4.2.2064] + *Ev* 'family, clan, house' + *Ais* > *Əs* 'master, lord', meaning "head of the *Meme* family" in *Turkic*. The male name *Mamay* has been used among the *Turkic* nations, and even nowadays, it functions as a surname for many *Ukrainians*.	N/A
<u>*12.-Kanutieivais*</u> "head of the *Kanuti* family". BOC translation: "son of *Kanuti*".	*Kanutieivais*: *Kanuti* > *Kanat* 'wing' + *Ev* 'family, clan, house' + *Ais* > *Əs* 'master, lord', meaning "head of the *Kanuti* family" in *Turkic*. Even nowadays, this *Turkic* male name *Kanat* is popular among the *Turkic* nations, especially the *Kazakhs*. They interpret the name as "wing of good luck, happiness, support, and help".	N/A

<u>*13.-At*</u>
1."to a fault, very much";
2."him, her, his".
 	
BOC translation:
1."his, her";
2."to, at, by".
	Ət "to a fault, very much" in *Turkic*.
	
	This *Turkic* word stands at the end of a sentence or a clause in *Turkic* [R.1.1.839]:
	    Əlik ma anındı törü arttı <u>ət.</u>
	    "The ruler issued laws that got disseminated <u>to a fault</u>."
	
	Compare to *Phrygian*:
	    Ioi bekos: me: bere[t] <u>at:</u>
	    Tie: ke: tittetikm[e]nos: eitou.
	    "His/her bread and everything <u>to a fault</u> will be torn up to pieces by Zeus."
	
	Anı, Anın "him, her, his" in *Turkic*.
		PIE *Hed —
		a preposition

<u>*14.-Ata*</u> "father, patriarch". Other forms: *Atai, Atas*	*Ata, Atai* "father" in *Turkic*. *Atası* "his/her father". *Atas*: *Ata* 'father' + *S* > *-Sı* 'an affix of possession') in *Turkic*.	N/A

85

PHRYGIAN	TURKIC	INDO-EUROPEAN

BOC translation:
N/A
	Neither of these words has reasonable equivalents in the *Indo-European* languages. Therefore, no translation was provided by the proponents of the IE doctrine.
	But a quick glance at these *Phrygian* words by any *Turkic* speaker will bring up an immediate, meaningful association with the native vocables. These very ancient *Turkic* base words still exist in all three forms in most *Turkic* languages [R.1.1.449].
	The *Phrygian Atai* matches the *Turkic Atai* perfectly. The addition of *-İ* to the end of a noun was an ancient *Turkic* phenomenon, observed in some *Turkic* words, such as in
	    Ana > Anai "mother" [R.1.1.227],
	    Baba > Babai "father" [R.4.2.1564],
	    Bəbi > Bəbəi "baby" [R.4.2.1637].
	The inscriptions, containing *Ata, Atai*, or *Atas*, were detected on the bottom of a cup dated the 5th-4th c. BCE, currently in the *Gordion Museum* inv. No. I 484; on an 8th c. BCE bronze plain omphalos bowl found in a tumulus in *East Lycia*, currently in the *Antalya Museum*, inv. No.17-21-87.	

15.-Atatas "from the same father". BOC translation: N/A	*Atadaş* "from the same father". *Atatas: Ata* 'father' + *Tas > Daş, Taş* 'companion') in *Turkic* [R.1.1.457]. This word was found incised on a *Phrygian* stone block dated to 850 BCE in *Karkemiş, Turkey*.	N/A
16.-Teama "chamber". Other forms: **Tiama, Tiamas, Teamas, Ateamas, Ateama** BOC translation: "burial plot".	*Tamuğ* "chamber" in *Turkic*. The *Phrygian* word was presented in a number of variations that all point to one source – to a *Turkic* word *Tamuğ* "chamber" [R.3.1.1002].	Luwian *Tiiamm(i)* "earth" > PIE *Dgh-em-

PHRYGIAN	TURKIC	INDO-EUROPEAN
17.-Atses "unnamed, unknown". BOC translation: N/A	*Atsiz* "unnamed, unknown". *Atses: At* 'name' + *Ses* > *-Sız* 'an affix, equivalent to the preposition *Without*' in *Turkic*.	N/A
18.-Ay "if, or". Other forms: **Ai, Ain', Aini, Ayniy, Ain**	*Ya* "or" [R.4.1.1] in *Turkic*. The *Phrygian Ay* is the same as the *Turkic Ya* due to a typical *Turkic* word rearrangement, when one word exists in two or more modified forms, such as *Ua > Au* "poison", *Şu > Uş* "this", *Uya > Yuva* "nest". Just like in *Phrygian*, there are several *Turkic* variants of this word, such as *Ya nə; Ya da; Yəni* "or"; *Eyhana* "if". *Ya nə, Yəni* "or" in *Turkic*. *Ayniy, Ain, Aini: Ai, Ay > Ya* 'or' + *Niy, N, Ni > Ni* 'whatever') in *Turkic*.	PIE *Ehi.
19.-Baba 1."father, patriarch"; 2."grandfather"; 3.a male name with the same meanings. Other forms: **Bba, Babas.** BOC translation: N/A	*Babá* "father, ancestor, patriarch, grandfather" in *Turkic* [R.4.2.1563]. This male name *Babá* was detected in both the *Phrygian* inscriptions and the bilingual *Phrygian-Greek* texts. It was a very common name throughout *Anatolia*. As a male name, *Baba* is still popular among the modern *Azerbaijanis*. Furthermore, only in *Azerbaijani*, both meanings exist. However, *Babá* as "grandfather" is in use in the *Azerbaijan Republic*, while *Baba* as "father" is in full swing in *Southern Azerbaijan*. In other *Turkic* languages, such as *Turkish*, it is accepted as "father", whereas in *Uzbek, Tatar, Uyghur* it means "grandfather". *Babası* "his/her father" in *Turkic*.	N/A

PHRYGIAN	TURKIC	INDO-EUROPEAN
	Babas: *Baba* 'father, ancestor, patriarch' + *S* > -*Sı* 'an affix of possession', meaning "his/her father" in *Turkic*.	
20.-*Balen* "king".	*Bölən* "dignitary, nobleman" in *Turkic* [R.4.2.1701].	*Belo* "power, strength".
21.-*Bas* 1."cropland"; 2."an affix of negation in the 3rd p. sing. in the future tense". BOC translation: "the name of a deity".	*Basau* "cropland" [R.4.2.1528]. -*Bas* "an affix of negation in the 3rd p. sing., in the future tense" in *Turkic*. Though in most modern *Turkic* languages, this affix -*Bas* got replaced by -*Mas*, -*Maz*, -*Mes*, -*Mez*, -*Məz*, -*Pes*, -*Pas*, in *Khakass* and *Kazakh*, it continues to stay in demand in the form of -*Bas*. In *Kazakh*, the affix -*Bas* and its forms are used with the pronouns of both in singular and plural, i.e. *Ol jazbas, körmes, oynamas, istemes, kespes, koçpas.* – "He/she/they will not write, see, play, want, cut, move". However, in *Khakass*, it is strictly employed after the pronouns in the 3rd p. sing.: *Ol sanabas, kilbes, atpas, itpes, toğınmas, sinmes.* – "He/she will not count, come, shoot, do, work, decrease". Just like in *Turkic*, where the word *Bas* can function both as an affix and a noun, carrying several meanings, such as "head", "ruler", the *Phrygian Bas* also conveyed several meanings and acted both as a noun and an affix: *totoss eitibas bekos.* "Forever will not produce bread". *bas: ioi: bekos: me: bere[t] at:tie: ke: tittetikm[e]nos: eitou.* "His/her cropland, bread, and everything else, in return, will be torn up to pieces by *Zeus*."	PIE *Bheh* "to shine". *Bas* "the shining one" is an epiclesis of *Zeus*, who presides over the fertility of the fields [BOC.156].
22.-*Batan* "will slay". BOC translation:	*Bat* 'slay' + *An* > -*A*, -*Ar* 'affix, denoting the future tense' [Dr.Sl.667], meaning "will slay" in *Turkic*.	See *Bas*.

PHRYGIAN	TURKIC	INDO-EUROPEAN
"the name of a deity", aka *Bas*.	*Batan* has nothing to do with any imaginary *Bas* or *Bat*, as claimed by BOC. Compare our verbatim and loose translation with the translation offered by BOC below: *Me: ddeo: me: zemelos: titetikmenos: eitou: as: batan: orouenan: ke.* "And: god: and: people: torn up into pieces: will do: him/her: will slay: in place: too." (verbatim) "Then god and people will torment and slay him/her at the spot as well." "Let him be cursed among gods and men by *Bat* and the father." (BOC.)	
23.-Bédu "water".	*Bu* "water gas, vapor" [R.4.2.1799]. *Bulak, Bulağ* "spring" [R.4.2.1837] in *Turkic*.	*Wed-, Wod-* "wet, water".
24.-Bekós "bread".	*Boğúz* "bread, grain" [Dr.Sl.110] in *Turkic*. There were numerous variations of this ancient *Turkic* word: 1. *Boğás, Boğáz, Boğúz, Buğúz, Buğáz* "food" [R.4.2.1807, 1649, 1652]; 2. *Buğdai, Boğdai* "wheat" [R.4.2.1654]; 3. *Buğaça, Boğaça* "puff pastry" [R.4.2.1805]; 4. *Böksəmət, Böksimək* "some sort of bread" [R.4.2.1695]; 5. *Bökmö* "pie" [R.4.2.1717]; 6. *Bapa* "bread" [R.4.2.1563]; 7. *Baklava* "*Turkic* pastry with nuts and honey" [R.4.2.1444]; 8. *Bakla* "*Turkic* unit of volume to measure dry wheat" [R.4.2.1443]; 9. *Pəkənd* "bread" [R.4.2.1216] The *Turkic* poet, statesman, and philosopher of the 11th c., *Yusuf Balasaqunlu* mentioned this *Turkic* word *Boğuz* (*Boğzi* in the accusative case) in his book "*Kutadgu Bilig*":	*PIE Bheh* "to warm".

PHRYGIAN	TURKIC	INDO-EUROPEAN
	"*Bodun tevşiqi barça <u>boğzı</u> üçün, Telim xalqlar öldi bu <u>boğzı</u> üçün.*" [256.3.4] "All the efforts of the people are for the sake of a piece of <u>bread</u>, Many nations perished because of this <u>bread</u>." [Translated into *English* by the author of the present book]	
25.-Bendos 1."stele"; 2."a stone plate with an inscription"; 3."eternal stone". BOC translation: "statue, image".	*Ben > Beŋü, Bengü* 'statue; eternal' + *Dos > Daş, Toş, Taş* 'stone', meaning "1.stele; 2.stone plate with an inscription; 3.eternal stone" in *Turkic*. There is an ancient *Turkic* word combination, closely related to the *Phrygian Bendos*: *Beŋü Taş* "stele; a stone plate with an inscription." [Dr.Sl.95] Additionally, the word *Beŋü, Bengü* (a letter '*ŋ*' stands for '*ng*') functioned as a stand-alone unit with 2 meanings and had numerous modified forms in *Turkic*: *Beŋkü, Beŋgü, Beŋigü, Meŋü, Meŋkü, Meŋgü, Meŋigü, Meŋi.* [Idem. 94]	*PIE Bheudh-os* "perception".
26.-Beret "all, everything". BOC translation: See *Abberet*	*Bəri, Barı* "all, everything" in *Turkic* [R.4.2.1598-1599]. According to BOC, the word *Beret* was a verb with the definition "produce", and combined with the preceding *Me*, was translated as "let not produce". There is a huge flaw in this type of interpretation of the survived *Phrygian* texts. Most if not all of them are *Phrygian* curses, inscribed to repel any potential evildoer and consist of 2 clauses as a rule. The first clause contains a verb that always ends in *-Et*, such as *Adak<u>et</u>, Dak<u>et</u>*, while the second clause is completed by a verb that ends in *-Ou*, such as *Eit<u>ou</u>*. As the first clause is conditional and states any future actions by any culprit, the affix *-Et* in the verb is a denominator of the conditional future	See *Abberet*.

PHRYGIAN	TURKIC	INDO-EUROPEAN
	tense, while the second clause presents a verdict of the future punishment, where a verb ends in an affix *-Ou* that signifies the future tense. With *Me Beret,* the meaning gets lost in translation. There are two main examples with the usage of *Beret* – in the second clause, following the first one after the verb *Adaket:* ios: <u>adaket</u>: bas: ioi: bekos: me: <u>beret</u> Whoever: <u>will do</u>: cropland: his/her: bread: and: <u>everything</u> (verbatim) "Whoever <u>will do</u>, his/her cropland, bread, and <u>everything</u>…" ios: ni: semoun: k[nou]mani: kakoun: <u>add[a]ket</u> aini: mankes bas[c]: ioi bekos: me: <u>bere[t]</u> at:tie: ke: tittetikm[e]nos: <u>eitou.</u> Whoever: whatever: this very: enclosed resting place: harm: <u>will do</u>: or: stele its: top: His/her bread: and: everything to a fault: *Zeus*: in return: torn to pieces: <u>will make</u>. (verbatim) "Whoever does any harm to this enclosed resting place or its stele, its top, His/her bread and everything else, in return, will be torn to pieces by *Zeus*." Logically, if *Beret* was a verb, then it should have ended in *-Ou,* similar to *Eitou,* instead of *-Et* in one text, while in another text *-T* was absent but added by BOC to prove his point. There are *Phrygian* texts that carry two verbs in the second clause of the curse, and both of them end in *-Ou,* such as *Adeitou* and *K'egedou:* ios: ni: semoun: knoumanei: kakoun: <u>adoket</u>: seirai: titetikmenos: at: ti: <u>adeitou</u>: gegreimenon: <u>k'egedou</u>: orouenos: outon.	

PHRYGIAN	TURKIC	INDO-EUROPEAN
	Moreover, the modified form of *Beret – Abbireto* stands at the end of the first clause as it is expected: *ios: ni: semoun: knoumani: kakoun: <u>abbireto</u>: aini: mmura: tos: ni: d[ios z]imelos: ti: meka: t[ie] tittetikmenos: <u>eitou</u>.* This example also vouches in favor of different verb affixes located in the first or the second clause of the *Phrygian* curses that define the cause and effect.	
27.-Deos 1."Zeus"; 2."deity, deities". Other forms: **Ddeo, Dios, Denos, Denun, Duos.** BOC translation: "God"	*Deos > Zeús (Ζεύς)*: *Ziya* 'light' + *Us* 'master', meaning "master of light" in *Turkic*. The letters *D* and *Z* are interchangeable in *Turkic*, such as in *Adak = Azak* "leg" [R.1.1.477] There is also an archaic *Turkic* equivalent of *Deos – Diyü* "good and evil spirits" [R.3.2.1758]	PIE Dh-s-ó- "God", cognate of *Greek Theos*.
28.-Deton 1."safekeeper, holder, depository"; 2."enclosed place"; 3."camp". BOC translation: "(funerary) monument, inscription".	*Deton: Det > Dut, Tut* 'safekeep, make, hold, use' [R.3.2.1792,1475-1479] + *On > -An* 'an affix, denoting constant action', meaning "holder, safekeeper, container" in *Turkic*. There is also another *Turkic* word that fits the description: *Tut* "camp; enclosed place" [R.3.2.1475].	Dheh "to do, put"; *Greek Thetos* "placed, set".
29.-Devos "its enclosure". BOC translation: "God"	*Devos: Devo > Devəə* 'enclosure, yard, grounds' + *S > -Si* 'an affix, denoting possession', meaning "its enclosure" in *Turkic*. The *Phrygian* word *Devos (Devo)* retained its presence only in the modern *Tuva* language [Tatarintsev B.I. "Etimologicheskiy slovar tuvinskogo yazika." 2.116]	N/A

PHRYGIAN	TURKIC	INDO-EUROPEAN
30.-*Duman* "community, area". BOC translation: "community, association".	*Tuman* "community, area" in *Turkic* [R.3.2.1518]. Though there are two other *Turkic* words, such as *Dümən* "protection, wheel" [R.3.2.1822] and *Duman* "hill" [R.3.2.1518], the most probable source for the *Phrygian Duman* was *Tuman*, as there was also a *Phrygian* derivative *Dumasta* "leader of a community or area" in *Turkic*. By the way, the letters *D* and *T* in *Turkic* words always interchange, such as in *Duman* = *Tuman* [R.3.2.1518], *Ad* = *At* "name", *Kadın* = *Katun* "lady", *Ədil* = *Ətil* "the ancient *Turkic* name of the *Volga* River".	PIE Dheh "put".
31.-*Dumasta* 1. "leader of a tuman"; 2. a title.	*Dumasta*: *Dum* > *Tuman* 'community, area' + *Asta* > *Usta* 'master, leader, teacher' [R.1.2.1749], meaning "leader of a community" in *Turkic*. The letters *A* and *U* can replace each other in *Turkic* without altering the meaning of a word, such as in *Aba* = *Abu* "father", *An* = *Ul* "s/he", *Konak* = *Konuk* "guest", *Ağız* = *Üs* "mouth".	See *Duman*.
32.-*Eiroi* "hero, man, warrior". BOC translation: "hero".	*Er* "hero, man, warrior" in *Turkic*. This is a very ancient *Turkic* word [R.1.1.751; Dr.Sl.175].	Greek Eros, Eroos "deceased".
33.-*Gegreimenon* "gnarled". Other forms: ***Gegreimenan, Gegeimenan.*** BOC translation: "written".	*Gegreimenon*: *Gegrei* > *Kəkirəi* 'gnarl, twist' [R.2.2.1061,1062] + *Menon* > *-Miş* 'an affix, indicating the past participle', means "gnarled" in *Turkic*. Both in *Phrygian* and *Turkic*, a participle comes in front of a verb: Phr. – Gegrei<u>menon</u> k'egedou. Turk. – Kəkirəi<u>miş</u> edəcək. Eng. – <u>Gnarled</u> will make. (verbatim)	PIE Ghrei(H) "strike".

PHRYGIAN	TURKIC	INDO-EUROPEAN
	Phr. – Tite<u>kmenos</u> adeitou *Turk.* – Titil<u>miş</u> edəcək. *Eng.* – <u>Torn into pieces</u> will make. (verbatim) This is a classic example of the *Turkic* word order that rarely if ever gets utilized in the *Indo-European* languages. Moreover, the *Phrygian* word *Gegreimenon* has its modified version – *Kəkrəit*, combined with a verb and without an affix *-Menon* in *Turkic*, recorded by Radlov V.V. Compare: *Kəkrəit* "make gnarled": *Kəkirə* 'gnarled, twisted' + *İt* 'make, do'. *Gegreimenon* 'gnarled' + *K'egedou* 'will make'. The *Turkic* verb *İt* (*Et, Əd*) shares the same root with the *Phrygian K'ege<u>d</u>ou* and the related *E<u>d</u>aes, E<u>d</u>ae, E<u>d</u>es, E<u>d</u>atoy, Eitou, A<u>d</u>aket*.	
34.-Iman 1."shrine"; 2."dwelling in the enclosed place". Other forms: **Inmeney, Imenan.**	*Iman: I > Ü* 'dwelling' [R.1.2.1797] + *Man* 'enclosed place' [R.4.2.2015], meaning "dwelling in the enclosed place", "shrine" in *Turkic*.	PIE *Men "stand fast, remain".
35.-Ios "who, whoever, anyone, person, somebody". Other forms: **[I]os, Ois, Eios, Yos, Yosyos, Is, Isos, Ion, Ian.** BOC translation: "who, whoever".	*Ös, Kəs, O* "who, whoever, anyone, person, somebody" in *Turkic* [R.1.2.1290].	PIE *(H)i-o- "id".
36.-Ioi "his, her, him". Other forms: **Oy, Oi.**	*Onı* "him, her, that" in *Turkic*.	PIE *He(i)/*Hi — an anaphoric pronoun.

PHRYGIAN	TURKIC	INDO-EUROPEAN
BOC translation: "him, her".		
37.-Kan "fence, wall, enclosure". BOC translation: "somehow, whatever".	*Kana* "fence, wall, enclosure" in *Turkic* [R.4.2.108]. The suggested by BOC meaning "somehow" or "whatever" does not completely agree with the following *Phrygian* text: *Ois: ni: semun: knumanei: kakun: addaket: ai: kan:* Whoever: whatever: [to] this very: enclosed resting place: harm: will do: or: [to its] fence (verbatim) "Whoever, whatever will do harm to this enclosed resting place or [its] fence." "Whoever does harm to this tomb or whatever" [BOC]	PIE *Kue/o* "somehow".
38.-Kake "harm" (noun). Other forms: **Kaka, Kakey, Kakin, Kakoun, Kakon, Kakou, Kaken, Kakin, Kakun.** BOC translation: "ill" (adverb).	*Kik, Kek* "harm" in *Turkic* [*Egorov*.112; R.2.2.1058]. This word always functions with another *Turkic* word *Et* "do, make". Unlike most *Indo-European* languages, in *Turkic*, an object precedes a verb. Compare: *Kek et* "harm do" (verbatim) or "do harm". The exact same situation is observed in the *Phrygian* texts, where *Kake* is followed by the verb *Adaket* "will do": *Ios: ni: semon: knoumanei: kake: adaket:* Whoever: whatever: this very: enclosed resting place: harm: will do:	N/A
39.-Ke 1. "and" (conj.); 2. "and, also, too" (adverb) 3. "in return"; 4. "then".	*Kin* "then" in *Turkic* [R.2.2.1073, 1345-1346]. *Də, Da, Ta, Tə* 1. "a conjunction *And*"; 2. "an adverb *And, Too*"; 3. "in return", such as *Tanrı da* "and God", "God in	PIE *Kue* "and".

PHRYGIAN	TURKIC	INDO-EUROPEAN

Other forms: **K, Key, Ti.**
 	
BOC translation: "and".
	return" for emphasis, mostly in *Turkic* curses or prayers. For instance,
	
	    Kim: bu: yeri: dağıtsa: Tanrı: da: onu: didik-didik: edəcək.
	    Whoever: this: place: destroys if: God: <u>in return:</u> him/her: tormented: will make. (verbatim).
	    "If anyone destroys this place, <u>in return,</u> God will torment him/her".
	
	Now, compare to *Phrygian*:
	
	    Ioi bekos: me: bere[t] at:tie: <u>ke</u>: tittetikm[e]nos: eitou.
	    His/her bread: and: everything to a fault: Zeus: <u>in return</u>: torn to pieces: will make. (verbatim)
	    "His/her bread and everything else, <u>in return,</u> will be torn to pieces by *Zeus*."
	
	In *Turkic*, letters K, D, T can be interchangeable in many words, such as
	    Ə<u>k</u>ə = A<u>d</u>a = A<u>t</u>a "father",
	    Ut<u>k</u>a = Ot<u>d</u>a = Ot<u>t</u>a "in the fire".
	    [R.3.1.79]
	Therefore, the *Phrygian* conjunction *Ke* was a more ancient form of the *Turkic Da, Ta.*
	Both in *Phrygian* and *Turkic,* the same word order was detected: *Ke* (*Turkic Da, Də*) comes after a noun, not in front of it, as in the *Indo-European* languages, and participates in the constructions *Ke...ke* (*Da...Də, Da...Da*) "Both...and":
	
	    zemelos: <u>ke</u>: deos: <u>ke</u>: titetikmenos: eitou. (Phr.)
	    adamlar: <u>da</u>: diyülər: <u>də</u>: didik-didik: edər. (Turkic)
	    People: <u>and</u>: deities: <u>and</u>: tormented: will do. (verbatim for *Phrygian* and *Turkic*)
	    "Will be tormented by <u>both</u> the people <u>and</u> deities".	

PHRYGIAN	TURKIC	INDO-EUROPEAN

	Ke plays the function of the adverb *Too, Also*:
	   me: ddeo: me: zemelos: titetikmenos: eitou: as: batan: orouenan: ke. (*Phr.*)
	   me: tın: me: sımıl: ditik-ditik (titilmiş): etər: anı: bata: ornın: da. (*Turkic*)
	 And: god: and: people: torn up into pieces: will do: him/her: will slay: in place: too. (verbatim)
	 "And god and people will tear him/her to pieces and slay at the spot, too."
	 "Let him be cursed among gods and men by *Bat* and the father."
	 (BOC's translation. *Ke* at the end was not translated).
	
	 The *Phrygian Ke* was observed to follow the conjunction *Me* "and":
	   me ke: oi: totoss eiti bas: bekos. (*Phr.*)
	   me də: ona: tutaşi: etməz (edbas): boğuz. (*Turkic*)
	 And then: for him/her: forever: will not produce: bread. (verbatim)
	 "And then, he/she will be forever deprived of bread."
	 "And let *Bas* not give bread to him."
	 (BOC)
	 In this case, *Ke* had a different source of origination and meaning: *Kin* "then" in *Turkic*.	

40.-Keneman "wide, enclosed place". BOC translation: "niche".	*Keneman: Kene > Kən* 'wide, spacious' [R.2.2.1074] + *Man, Mane > Man* 'enclosed place' [R.4.2.2015], meaning "wide, enclosed place" in *Turkic*. Both in *Phrygian* and *Turkic*, the noun *Man* follows the adjective *Kene* (*Kən*).	PIE *Keh, Sanscrit Khánati "to dig".
41.-Kfiyanaveyos "very much loved". BOC translation: N/A	*Kfiyanaveyos: Kf > Kip* 'very' + *Yan* 'great' + *Ave > Ava* 'passion, love' + *Yos > -Sa* (*-Saq*) 'an affix, converting a noun into an adjective', meaning "very greatly (much) loved".	N/A

PHRYGIAN	TURKIC	INDO-EUROPEAN
	This *Phrygian* word exhibits a typical *Turkic* construction: adverb + adjective + adjective (noun + affix).	
42.-Knoumane "enclosed place of rest". Other forms: **Knoumanei, Knoumen, K[nou]mani, Knoumani, Knouman, Knumanei, Knoum, Knouma, Kino Ma, Kno, Knou, Kn, K Noum Manei, Kn Mmanei.** BOC translation: "tomb, memorial".	*Knoumane: Knou > Kon* 'place of rest, resting place' [R.2.1.535] + *Mane > Man* 'enclosed place' [R.4.2.2015], meaning "enclosed resting place" in *Turkic*. The *Phrygian* word consisted of two independent lexemes, used together or separately, such as *Kino Ma, Kno, Knou, Kn, K Noum Manei, Kn Mmanei*, etc.	PIE *KneuH- "scratch, dig".
43.-Knais "woman, wife". Other forms: **Knaus, Knayke, Knaikan, Knaiko[s].**	*Kanış* "lady, wife of a khan, queen" [R.2.1.117] in *Turkic*.	PIE *Gwneh- "woman".
44.-Korou "plot, piece of ground". BOC translation: "a definite space, piece of ground, place".	*Kora* "plot, piece of ground" in *Turkic* [R.2.1.551].	Greek *Xoros* "a definite space, piece of ground, place".
45.-Koroumane "plot-enclosed place". Other form: **Koro[u] Mane** BOC translation: "a definite space".	*Koroumane: Korou > Kora* 'plot, piece of ground' + *Mane > Man* 'enclosed place' [R.4.2.2015], meaning "plot-enclosed place" in *Turkic*. This *Phrygian* word was observed both as a whole word – *Koroumane* and split into two words – *Koro[u] Mane*.	See *Korou*.
46.-Kos "someone, somebody, something".	*Kəs* "someone, whoever" [R.2.2.1154] in *Turkic*. *Kim* "whoever, who" in *Turkic* [Dr.Sl.307; R.2.2.1402].	PIE *Kuo/Kui-, *Kui-m.

PHRYGIAN	TURKIC	INDO-EUROPEAN
Other form: **Kin.**	**Kini** "he, she, it" in *Yakut*.	
47.-Kuryan "ruler"; **Eyon** "subduer". BOC translation: Kuryaneyon "ruler".	**Kuran** "ruler" (*Kur* 'rule, establish, organize, institute' [R.2.1.919] + *Yan* > -*An* 'an affix, denoting constant action'). *Әyən* "subduer" (*Әy* 'subdue, subjugate' [R.1.1.658] + -*Әn* 'an affix, denoting constant action') in *Turkic*. BOC treated these two *Phrygian* words as one – *Kuryaneyon* "ruler".	PIE *Kor-io- "army, war".
48.-Ataniyen 1. a male name; 2. "shooter, subduer".	*Ataniyen*: *Atan* 'shooter' (*At* 'shoot' [Dr.Sl.65] + -*An* 'an affix of constant action') + *Iyen* > *İyən* 'subduer' (*İy* 'subdue, subjugate' [R.1.2.237] + -*Әn* 'an affix, denoting constant action'), meaning "shooter, subduer" in *Turkic*. Astonishingly, both in *Phrygian* and *Turkic* there were alike variations of the same word – *Әy*, *İy*.	N/A
49.-Tataniyen 1. a male name; 2. "founder".	*Tat* > *Tət* 'found, establish' + -*An* 'an affix of constant action' + *Iyen* > *İyən* 'subduer' (*İy* 'subdue, subjugate' + -*Әn* 'an affix, denoting constant action'), meaning "founder, subduer" in *Turkic*.	N/A
50.-Meka "laudable, praiseworthy, all-praised". Other form: **Mek An.** BOC translation: "big, great".	**Mak** "laudable, praiseworthy, all-praised" [R.4.2.1993] in *Turkic*. This *Phrygian* word *Meka* should not be confused with *Mekas*, which is a verb in the 3rd person sing., in the past tense: d[ios z]imelos: ti: <u>meka</u>: t[ie] tittetikmenos: eitou. d[eities]: [p]eople: and: <u>all-praised</u>: Z[eus]: tormented: will do. (verbatim)	PIE *Meg-h- "big, great".
51.-Mekas "did put in place; engaged".	*Mekas, Mekais*: *Mek* > *Mauk* 'put in place; engage in' [R.4.2.1993] + *As, Ais* > -*Miş*, -*Mız* 'an affix of the past tense',	PIE *Meg-h- "big, great".

PHRYGIAN	TURKIC	INDO-EUROPEAN

Other forms:
Mekas, Mekais.
 	
BOC translation:
"big, great".
	meaning "did put in place", "engaged" in *Turkic*.
	Compare:
	    vasous: iman: <u>mekas:</u>
	    kanutievais:
	    devos: ke: <u>mekas:</u>
	    Vasous: shrine: <u>put in place</u>:
	    Kanuti family head:
	    Its enclosure: too: <u>put in place</u>.
	    (verbatim)
	    "*Vasos Iman* the <u>great</u> (the son) of *Kanuti* and the <u>great</u> god." (BOC)	

52.-Manes 1. a male name; 2. "great chief". BOC translation: a name of a person.	*Manes:* Man 'great, big' [*Egorov*.130] + *Es > Us* 'master', meaning "great chief" in *Turkic*. This male name was widely used among the *Trojan* nations. *Manes* was known as a leader of the *As* tribe in *Sardis*, the capital of *Lydia*, as a king of *Lydia* whose son *Atys* sent his own offspring, *Tyrrhenus*, out of the country to establish a colony elsewhere. *Manes* was a popular name among the *Phrygians* to the point that the people of *Attica* would name all their *Phrygian* slaves by the name either *Manes* or *Midas*. [*Strabo*.7.3.12] Both the *Cappadocians* and the *Paphlagonians* extensively used this male name, while *Strabo* put emphasis on the fact that this was a *Paphlagonian* name [12.3.25]. Among the *Carians*, the name turned into *Mane*. In the bilingual *Lydian-Aramaic* inscription, this name was rendered as *Mny* in *Aramaic* and *Manelid* in *Lydian*. The name *Manes* left its trace in the names of the *Turkic* settlements and villages: *Manış* village in *Turkmenistan*, *Manış* town in *Perm* region of *Russia*, as well as in the last names – *Manyshev, Manyshkin*.	N/A Stated as a word of "unknown origin" by BOC.
53.-Manka "stele with inscription". Other forms:	*Məŋkü* "stele with inscription" in *Turkic* [R.4.2.2082]. *Məŋküsi* "his/her/its stele".	PIE *Men "remain".

100

PHRYGIAN	TURKIC	INDO-EUROPEAN
Mankes, Mankai, Mankan, M[ank]e. BOC translation: "stele".	*Mankes: Manke > Maŋkü + S > -Si* 'an affix of possession, equivalent to the pronouns *His/Her/Its*'. *Mankai: Manka > Maŋkü* 'stele' *+ I > -İa* 'an affix, equivalent to the prepositions *To, Towards*', meaning "towards/to a stele" in *Turkic*.	
<u>54.-Mank</u> "surrounding; enclosed place". Other form: *Manka.* BOC translation: "stele".	*Mang* "a surrounding" [R.4.2.2006]. *Manka: Mank > Mang + A > -A* 'an affix, equivalent to the preposition *To*', meaning "to the surrounding".	*PIE *Men* "remain".

<u>55.-Me</u>
1."and";
2."in return, then";
3."because, as";
4."even";
5."also".
 	
BOC translation:
1."not";
2."before, in the sight of, among".
	Me "and", "also", "in return, then", "because, as", "even" in *Turkic* [Dr.Sl.340].
	
	It got preserved as *Men* only in the modern *Kazakh* language. The *Phrygian Me* bears the contextual meaning "in return, then", similar to the *Turkic Me* in curses and prayers:
	   ios: sa: tou: sorou: kake: addaket: <u>me</u>: zemelos: ot: tittetikmenos: eitou.
	   Whoever: this: clay: honorary place: harm: will do: <u>and</u>: people: him/her: torn into pieces: will do. (verbatim)
	   "Whoever does harm to this honorary place made of clay, <u>in return</u>, he/she will be torn into pieces by people."
	   "Whoever does harm to this coffin, let him be accursed in the sight of men." (BOC)
	
	In some *Phrygian* texts, *Me* is used twice, similar to the "then...and" structure:
	   <u>me</u>: *ddeo:* <u>me</u>: *zemelos: titetikmenos: eitou:*
	   <u>Then</u>: god: <u>and</u>: people: tormented: will do. (verbatim)
	   "<u>Then</u> god <u>and</u> people will torment."
		PIE *Me;
		PIE *Meh.

PHRYGIAN	TURKIC	INDO-EUROPEAN
	The meaning "before, in the sight of, among" offered by BOC does not hold water, especially in the following *Phrygian* text where BOC completely omitted the word: *titetikmenos: as: tian: eitou: me ke: oi: totoss: eiti bas: bekos.* Him/her: *Zeus:* will do: <u>and</u> also: for him/her: forever: will not produce: bread. (verbatim) "He/she will be torn up into pieces by *Zeus* <u>and</u> moreover, he/she will be deprived of bread." "Let him become accursed by *Zeus* and let *Bas* not give bread to him." (BOC) The suggested by *BOC* translation of *Me* as a negation *Not*, preceding *Beret*, doesn't make sense, and the reasons were provided earlier. See *Beret > Bəri, Barı* "all, everything".	
56.-Mmura "hill, kurgan". Other forms: *Mou[rou]n, Mourou[n].* BOC translation: "stupid action, mistreatment".	*Mar* "hill, kurgan" [R.4.2.2025] in *Turkic*. The hesitantly suggested by BOC meaning is not a good fit for the following *Phrygian* text, translated into *English* with some words ignored: *ios: ni: semoun: knoumani: kakoun: abbireto: aini: mmura: tos: ni:* Whoever: whatever: this very: enclosed place of rest: harm: will bring: or: kurgan: base: anything. (verbatim) "Whoever brings any harm to this enclosed place of rest or <u>kurgan</u>, its base or anything..." "Whoever brings harm or <u>mistreatments</u> to this tomb..." (BOC)	*Greek Moros* "dull, stupid".
57.-Nana 1."mother"; 2."grandmother".	*Nənə* "1.mother; 2.grandmother" in *Turkic*.	N/A

PHRYGIAN	TURKIC	INDO-EUROPEAN
Other form: *Inas.* BOC translation: N/A	*Inas: Ina > İnə* 'mother' [R.1.2.241] + *S > -Si* 'an affix of possession, equivalent to the pronouns *His, Her*', meaning "his/her mother" in *Turkic*. The existence of these *Phrygian* words, denoting "mother" along with another one – *Matar* "mother", points out that *Nana* and *Ina* were the indigenous *Phrygian* words of the *Turkic* root in contrast to the *Indo-European* loanword *Matar*. The *Turkic* origin of these words is further confirmed by the *Phrygian* derivative *Nanavata* or *Nənə Ata* "parents" in *Turkic*.	
58.-*Nana vata* 1."mother, father"; 2."parents". BOC translation: "nana & vata".	*Nənə Ata* "mother, father; parents" in *Turkic*. [*Egorov*.37]. This word combination is still frequently used in modern *Turkic* languages as *Ana-ata, Ata-ana* "parents". The existence of the synonym *Patres* "parents" in some *Phrygian* texts demonstrates its loaned nature.	N/A
59.-*Nev* 1."grandchild, grandson, granddaughter, offspring"; 2."human being". Other forms: *Nevos, Nevotan.* BOC translation: "son, descendant".	*Nəvə* "offspring, grandchild, grandson, granddaughter" [*Musayev*.437]. *Nəbə* "human being" in *Turkic* [R.3.1.688]. *Nevos: Nevo > Nəvə* 'grandchild' + *S > -Si* 'an affix, equivalent to the pronouns *His, Her*', meaning "his/her grandchild" in *Turkic*. *Nevotan: Nevo > Nəvə* 'grandchild' + *Tan > -Tən* 'an affix, equivalent to the preposition *From*', meaning "from a grandchild" in *Turkic*.	PIE *Nepot- "nephew, grandson, descendant".
60.-*Ni* "whatever, anything". BOC translation: A particle.	*Ni* "whatever, any" in *Turkic* [R.3.1.697].	N/A "…its origin is not at all clear…" [BOC]

PHRYGIAN	TURKIC	INDO-EUROPEAN
61.-Ni se "the living" BOC considered *Se* a part of *Semin, Semon, Semoun, Semun, Semou, Simoun, <S>imun* "this"	*Ne ersə, Nersə* "the living" in *Turkic* [Dr.Sl.356, 358].	
62.-Onenin "his, her, its". BOC translation: "his own".	*Onun, Anın* "his, her, its" in *Turkic* [R.1.1.232].	N/A
63.-Oip-Eis "house-property". BOC translation: *Oi Petes* "feet".	*Öp* "house" [R. 1.2.1308]. *İs* "property" [R.1.2.1525]. *Oip-Eis: Oip > Öp* "house" + *Eis > -İs* "property", meaning "house-property" in *Turkic*. There were different readings of these *Phrygian* words among the experts, when some considered them as one word, such as *Oipeis* (*Ramsay* 1887), or two words – *Akeoi Peies* (*Ramsay* 1905, *Calder*), *Oi Peies* (*Haas, Orel*), *Oi Petes* (BOC). Contextually, the *Phrygian* curse is very close to the malediction of the survived *Lydian-Aramaic* inscription, where a potential wrongdoer is cursed along with his/her "court, house, property, soil, and water." ["*Sardis.*" Publications of the American Society for the Excavation of *Sardis* by *Enno Littmann*. 1916. 6.1.24]. Therefore, the second part of the *Phrygian* curse should be transcribed and translated as follows:	PIE *Ped- "feet".

PHRYGIAN	TURKIC	INDO-EUROPEAN
	zeira: ke: oip eis: ke: tittetikmena: at: tie: adeittnou. Mind: and: house-property: and: torn into pieces: him/her: *Zeus:* will do. (verbatim) "*Zeus* will tear into pieces his/her mind and house and property." "Let his hands and feet become accursed by *Zeus*." (BOC) Here, the word *Oip-Eis* acts as a set expression, similar to the *Turkic Ev-Eşik* "house-property". This word combination is still in use in *Azerbaijani* [*Musayev*.183].	
64.-Orouan "place". Other forms: **Orou An, Orouenan, Orouenos.** BOC translation: "keeper, protector".	**Orun, Orın** "place" in *Turkic* [R.1.2.1055, 1058]. *Orouenan* > *Ornun* "his/her place" (*Orın* 'place' + *-Un* 'an affix, denoting a pronoun *His/Her/Its*'). Radlov V.V. provided an example of usage of this *Turkic* word in a sentence: *Da karğadım ornun anın.* – "And I cursed his place." [R.1.2.1058].	PIE *Ser- "to bind, to tie together, thread". Greek – *Ouros* 'watcher, guard'.
65.-Ouelas "people". BOC translation: "relatives".	**Ulus** "people" [R.1.2.1696] in *Turkic*. Its root is from *Oul* "son" in *Turkic* [R.1.2.988].	PIE *Suel-eh-es "relatives" (likely translation).
66.-Ouranion 1."ascending"; 2."heavenly". BOC translation: "heavenly".	**Uran, Turan** "ascending" in *Turkic*. **Turə** "God" [*Egorov*.259] in *Turkic*. The *Phrygian* word *Ouranion* was most likely akin to the *Etruscan Turan* – the *Etruscan* goddess of love, known in the *Greco-Roman* pantheon as *Urania, Venus, Aphrodite.* Interestingly, among the *Tuva* people the female name *Uran* is still widely used.	PIE *Uors-. Greek *Ouranos* "heaven". However, according to BOC, the etymology of this *Greek* word "is not at all clear" [262].

PHRYGIAN	TURKIC	INDO-EUROPEAN
	There was also a *Turkic* tribe of *Uran*, recorded existing until the 19th c. [*Uraksin*. 864].	
67.-Outon "always, eternally". Other form: **Outan**. BOC translation: "punishment, word, spell".	*Ötün* "always, eternally" [R.1.2.1281] in *Turkic*.	PIE *Uéth-r, *Uth-én-s.
68.-Par "all"; **69.-Tes** "spirit". Other forms: **Par Tan, Par Tus**. BOC translation: *Partes* – N/A	*Par* "all" in *Turkic* [R.4.2.1144]. *Tös* "spirit" in *Turkic* [R.3.2.1264]. These *Phrygian* words were handled as one word *Partes* by *Orel, Haas,* BOC without any provided translation. Compare: *tetiokmenos: eitou: dios: ke: zemelos: ke: par: tes*. Tormented: will do: deities: and: people: and: <u>all: spirit</u>. (verbatim) "He/she will be tormented by the deities and people and all the spirits." "Let him be accursed (in the sight of) gods and men <u>partes</u> (?)." (BOC) By the way, similar to the *Phrygian Par Tes*, the *Turkic* word *Par* "all" was also used in conjunction with a noun in a singular form, following it: *Par Yər* "all the land" [R.4.2.1144].	N/A
70.-San "amount". BOC translation: "this".	*San* "amount" [R.4.1.296; *Shwarz*.465] in *Turkic*. The translation of *San* as "this" by BOC does not seem plausible. Compare: *ios: ni: <u>san</u>: kakoun: ad[da]ke: mankai:* Whoever: any: <u>amount (this–BOC)</u>: harm: will do: stele…(verbatim)	See *Semon*.

106

PHRYGIAN	TURKIC	INDO-EUROPEAN
	"Whoever does any <u>amount</u> of harm to the stele…" "Whoever does harm to <u>this</u> stele…" (BOC) Moreover, in all the *Phrygian* texts *Semoun* "this" is followed by *Knoumanei* "enclosed place of rest". In the provided above text, *San* is followed by *Kakoun* "harm". If we follow BOC's translation of *San* as "this", then *San Kakoun* "this harm" will render the text incoherent: "Whoever does <u>this harm</u> to stele…"	
<u>71.-*Si*</u> "this". Other forms: ***S, Sa, Ses, Sas, Sos, Esai, Sai, Sin, San.***	*So, Şu* "this" [R.4.1.512,1094] in *Turkic*.	PIE *So- "to" or *Ki-.
<u>72.-*Min*</u> "this" Other forms: ***Mon, Moun, Mun, Mou.*** BOC considered it a part of *Semin, Semon, Semoun, Semun, Semou, Simoun, <S>imun*.	*Mına* "this" in *Turkic* [R.4.2.2140].	See *Si*.
<u>73.-*Panta*</u> "whole, all, every". Other form: ***Pantes.***	*Panta* > *Bütün* "whole, all, every" [R.4.2.1898] in *Turkic*. Here, word rearrangement and consonant sonorization–desonorization, typical for *Turkic*, take place. Compare: *Pan<u>t</u>a* = *Bü<u>t</u>ün.* *<u>P</u>alta* = *<u>B</u>alta* "axe". *Kör<u>p</u>ü* = *Kö<u>b</u>ür* "bridge". *A<u>q</u>ban* = *A<u>b</u>a<u>k</u>an* = *A<u>b</u>ğan* (name of a river). *To<u>b</u>rak* = *Tor<u>p</u>ak* "land".	PIE *Ph-ent- "all".

PHRYGIAN	TURKIC	INDO-EUROPEAN

74.-*Sk* "tomb";
 	
75.-*Eledriai*
"around", "surroundings".
 	
BOC translation:
Skeledriai – N/A
	Süki "tomb" [R.4.1.798] in *Turkic*.
	
	Əyləndərə "around" in *Turkic*.
	
	The word *Əyləndərə* got preserved only in the *Chulym* language:
	   Meni əyləndərə sas polğan.
	   "There was a swamp around me." [1]
	
	Sk Eledriai: *Sk* > *Süki* 'tomb' + *Eledriai* > *Əyləndərə* 'around', meaning "around tomb" or "tomb surroundings" in *Turkic*.
	
	Incorrectly deciphered as one word – *Skeledriai*, it should be considered as two independent words: *Sk* and *Eledriai*.
		N/A

76.-*Proitanos* "person from the same house". BOC translation: N/A	*Proitanos*: *Pr* > *Pir* 'one, same' + *Oi* > *Öi* 'house' + *Tan* > -*Tən* 'an affix, equivalent to the preposition *From*' + *Os* > *Ös* 'person', meaning "person from the same house" in *Turkic*.	N/A
77.-*Euge* "God, deity". Other forms: *Eugi, Eygi.* BOC translation: See *Totosseti*.	*Egə* "God, deity" in *Turkic* [R.1.1.695]. The suggested explication of the *Phrygian* word channels *Ramsay's Euge Sarna*. There were several interpretations of *Euge*, mostly as a word component in *Eugesarnai* (*Ramsay* 1887); *Eugisarnan* (*Haas*), *Eygisarnan* (*Orel*), *Seugisarnan* (*Friedrich*), *Seygisarnan* (*Ramsay* 1905), or even deciphered differently as *Totosseiti* (BOC). However, none of them made sense, as in that case no deity or people were mentioned in the text, which was an absolute must in the *Phrygian* curses to show who will punish the malefactor. For that purpose, BOC came up with a mysterious *Sarnan*.	N/A

---

[1] See *Bashbug Firat*. "Osobennosti poslelojnix konstruktsiy v chulimskom yazike." [5:9-20.16].

PHRYGIAN	TURKIC	INDO-EUROPEAN
78.-*Sarna* "will stop" Other forms: **Sarnai, Sarnan.** BOC translation: *Sarnan* "the name of a deity".	*Sarna, Sarnai, Sarnan*: *Sarn > Sərin* 'stop, discontinue, block' [R.4.1.461] + *A, Ai, An > -A, -Ə* 'an affix, denoting a verb in the 3rd p. sing., in the future tense", meaning "will stop" in *Turkic*: aini: kos: semoun: knoumanei: kakoun: addaket: aini: manka: be[k]os: ioi: me: totoss: eugi: <u>sarnan</u>. Or: whoever: this very: enclosed place of rest: harm: will do: or stele: bread: his/her: in return: forever: God: <u>will block</u>. (verbatim) "Or whoever does harm to this enclosed place of rest or stele, in return, God <u>will block</u> his/her livelihood (bread)." "If someone does harm to this tomb or to the stele, let <u>Sarnan</u> not give him bread." (BOC) The *Turkic* affix *-A*, specifying the 3rd person singular, in the future tense, retained its functionality mostly in the *Yakut* language, i.e. *Kini barıa* – "he/she <u>will go</u>" [Korkina.53], as well as in *Bashkir*, i.e. *Ber aznanan ulımdın tuyı bula.* – "In a week, it <u>will be</u> my son's wedding"; *Kərim məktəptən kayta.* – "*Karim* <u>will come back</u> from school." [Usmanova.116].	N/A
79.-*Sorou* "honorary place". Other form: **Soroi.** BOC translation: "cinerary urn, sarcophagus".	*Sorun* "honorary place" in *Turkic* [R.4.1.545].	Greek *Sorós* "cinerary urn".

PHRYGIAN	TURKIC	INDO-EUROPEAN
80.-Tian "Zeus", "God", "Spirit". Other forms: **Ti, Tie, Tiei, Tios.**	**Tın, Tin** "spirit" in *Turkic* [R.3.2.1312]. This is a very ancient *Turkic* word, recorded by *Radlov V.V.* in a number of expressions: 　*Ata Dağı, oğul dağı, arı tın.* – "Father, son, Holy spirit". Another derivative of *Tın* is *Tenrı* along with its variants: *Tengri, Tanri, Tangri, Tangara* "God", "sky man", "spirit man". All these versions were available in the *Akkadian* language: 　*Ti, Til, Tin* "living, life". 　*Dingir, Dimir* "God, life-maker, creator". *Phrygian Tian, Ti* "Zeus", *Etruscan Tin, Tina, Tinia* "Zeus", even *Chinese Ti* "God" contained the *Turkic* root *Tın*. According to *J.G.R. Forlong*, the *Polynesian* god of heaven and light *Tangaroa*, or *Tangaloa*, also took its origin from the *Turkic* "*Tangri*, or *Tengri* for the god of heaven), who may as well be compared with the "supreme *Tangara*" of *America* (Bradford, Americ.Antiq., p.400). The name *Tangaroa* appears to mean "the god on high". ["Faiths of Man: A Cyclopedia of Religions." 3.400]	*PIE *Di-éu-* "sky".
81.-Tiara 1."circle"; 2."headband, crown, diadem". BOC translation: "a kind of cap".	**Dairə** "circle" [*Schwarz.257*] in *Turkic*. This word has a *Turkic* origin and should not be considered a loanword, as both the word and the object it signified, were invented by the *Medes*. Both the *Phrygians* and the *Medes* shared *Turkic* roots. Later, this *Turkic* word was borrowed by the *Persians*, according to *Herodotus* [7.62]. BOC also acknowledged that the word *Tiara* belonged to a non-*Indo-European* language:	N/A

110

PHRYGIAN	TURKIC	INDO-EUROPEAN
	"In any case, although the etymology of tiara (Gr. τιαρα, τιερης, and τιαρις) is unknown, it is considered an oriental word (related to the *Persian* world) borrowed from a non-*IE* language (see EDG,1481), so there are no grounds for claiming a *Phrygian* origin." [338]	

82.-Tetikmenos "tormented, torn to pieces". Other forms: **Titetikmenos, Tittetikmena, Titetoukmenoun, Tittetikmenos, Tetiokmenos, Teittetikmenos, Tetikme, Tittetikmena, Titetikm, Tittetikmenoi, Atetikmenos, Ettetikmenos, Thitetikmeno, Tetio Kmenos, Titeteikmenos.** BOC translation: "accursed".	*Tetikmenos: Tetik* > *Titik, Didik, Ditik* 'torn up to pieces, tormented' [R.3.2.1770, 1771] + *Menos* > *-Miş* 'an affix, indicating the past participle', meaning "torn up to pieces" in *Turkic*.
	
	There are several similarities between the *Phrygian Tetikmenos* and *Turkic Didilmiş* or *Ditik-ditik* that could not be brushed off as a coincidence:
	1. The *Phrygian* word *Tetikmenos* is very similar to the *Turkic Didilmiş* both in form and meaning.
	2. Both words share the same *Turkic* root *Tit, Dit, Did* "tear to pieces".
	3. Both the *Phrygian* and *Turkic* languages follow strict word order where participle comes first, followed by verb, and never the other way around:
	    Tetikmenos Eitou
	    Ditik-ditik Etər; Didilmiş Etər
	    "Torn into pieces will do." (verbatim)
	4. The word order with participle, followed by verb, is a natural occurrence in both *Phrygian* and *Turkic*, which was not detected in the *Indo-European* languages.
	5. In *Turkic*, there is also another derivative from the root *Tit, Did*, that resembles the *Phrygian* counterpart. Compare:
	    Tur. *Didik-didik*
	    Phr. *Titetikm*
	This is a pure *Turkic* phenomenon when the same lexeme is used twice in one word: *Didik-didik, Bölek-bölek,*
		PIE *Deik- "to point, indicate".

PHRYGIAN	TURKIC	INDO-EUROPEAN
	Cırığ-cırığ and carry the same definition "torn up to pieces". In *Phrygian*, the trace of this *Turkic* occurrence is also observed in various forms: *Tittetikmena, Titeteikmenos,* and the like. 6. Both in *Phrygian* and *Turkic*, this set expression *Tetikmenos Eitou = Ditik-ditik Etər* was always employed in the curses, which is still valid in the modern *Azerbaijani* language. For instance: *Didik-didik olasan!* "Become tormented!"; *Tanrı səni didik-didik eləsin!* "Let God torment you!" ("[Let] God you tormented make!" – Verbatim).	
83.-Tou "clay, earthen". Other forms: **To, Tono, Ti, T, Tai, Ta, Tan.** BOC translation: "this, that".	*Toi* "clay, earthen" [R.3.1.1141] in *Turkic*. The suggested by BOC translation of *Tou* as "this" does not fit in the logical frames; for instance, in the following text, it happens to follow another *Phrygian* word *Semoun* "this" ("this very"), which was omitted by BOC in the translation: *ios: semoun: tou: knoumanei: kakou: adaket:* Whoever: this very: clay (this – BOC): to enclosed place of rest: harm: will do: (verbatim) "Whoever will do harm to this clay tomb (enclosed place of rest)..." "Whoever does harm to this tomb..." (BOC)	*PIE* anaphoric **To-*.
84.-Tos "bottom, base". BOC translation: "this, that".	*Tos* "bottom, base" [R.3.2.1264] in *Turkic*. The suggested translation by BOC as "this, that" does not match either grammatical or lexical order of the *Phrygian* text, for instance:	*PIE* anaphoric **To-*.

PHRYGIAN	TURKIC	INDO-EUROPEAN
	ios: ni: semoun: knoumani: kakoun: abbireto: aini: mmura: tos: ni: Whoever: whatever: this very: enclosed place of rest: harm: will bring: or: kurgan: base (this – BOC): anything... (verbatim) "Whoever brings any harm to this enclosed place of rest or kurgan, its base or anything..."	
85.-Totos "always, constantly, forever". Other form: **Totoss.** BOC translation: *Totosseiti* "give".	*Tutaşı* "always, constantly, forever" in *Turkic* [Dr.Sl.592]. BOC saw this word as a component of *Totosseiti*. However, the analysis of the *Phrygian* texts leads us to believe that these were two separate words – *Totoss* and *Eiti*: *titetikmenos: as: tian: eitou: me ke: oi: totoss: eiti bas: bekos.* Torn up to pieces: him/her: Zeus: will do: and moreover: for him/her: forever: will not produce: bread. (verbatim) "...he/she will be torn up into pieces by *Zeus* and moreover, he/she will forever be deprived of livelihood (bread)." "...let him become accursed by *Zeus* and let *Bas* not give bread to him." (BOC)	PIE *Deh- "to give".
86.-Upsodan "from the top". Other forms: **Upso Dan, [Ou] Psodan.** BOC translation: "above, on the top".	*Ucadan* "from the top" (*Uca* 'top, high' + *-Dan* 'an affix, equivalent to the preposition *From*') in *Turkic*. There is also *Ucada* "on the top, on the high" in *Turkic*.	PIE *Up-s- "above".
87.-Zeirai "mind, intellect". Other forms: **Zeira, Tsirai.**	*Zerəi* "mind, intellect" [R.4.1.890] in *Turkic*.	PIE *Ghes-r- "hand".

PHRYGIAN	TURKIC	INDO-EUROPEAN
BOC translation: "hands".		
88.-Zémelo "dynasty, tribe, family, kinfolk, people". Other forms: ***Zemelen, Zemelos, Szemelos, Zemelosi, Zimelos.*** BOC translation: "human beings".	*Sımıl* "dynasty, tribe, family, kinfolk, people" [R.4.1.676] in *Turkic*.	PIE *Dhghe-m- "earth".

Now, let us analyze two dozen of ancient *Phrygian* inscriptions that reveal uncanny *Turkic* word order:

1 – <u>***baba: memevais: proitanos: kɸiyanaveyos: si: keneman: edaes.***</u>
Turkic:
    Baba: Meme ev yəsi[nə]: pir öitən ös: kip yan avasaq: so: kən man: edip (etmiş).
Verbatim translation:
    Baba: Meme family head [for]: same house from person: very great loved: this: spacious, enclosed place of rest: made.
Loose translation:
    "*Baba* made this spacious, enclosed place of rest for the very much beloved human being *Meme*, the head of the family from the same house (dynasty)."
Translated by BOC:
    "*Baba* the son of *Meme*(s), the proitanos, the kɸiyanaveyos, made this niche."

2 – <u>***bba: memevais: proitano[s]: kτiyanaveyos: akara gayun (akaragayun – BOC): edaes.***</u>
Turkic:
    Baba: Meme ev yəsi[nə]: pir öitən ös: kip yan avasaq: ağarı qayanı: edip (etmiş).
Verbatim translation:
    Baba: Meme family head [for]: same house from person: very great loved: upper rock: made.
Loose translation:
    "*Baba* made the altar (upper rock) for the very much beloved human being *Meme*, the head of the family from the same house (dynasty)."
Translated by BOC:
    "*Baba* the son of *Meme*(s), the proitanos, the kτiyanaveyos, made the akaragayun."
NOTE:
    This inscription was etched "on a vertical side of an outcrop of rock "altar". [BOC. 351].

3 – **_ios: ni se: mon (ni semon – BOC): knoumanei: kake: adaket: titetikmenos: as: tian: eitou: me ke: oi: totoss: eiti bas: bekos._**

Turkic:
>Ös (kəs): nersə: mına: kon mana: kek: edəcək (kılat): ditik-ditik (titilmiş): anı: tanrı: etər: me də: ona: tutaşi: etməz (edbas): boğuz.

Verbatim translation:
>Whoever: the living: this: enclosed place of rest to: harm: do will: torn up to pieces: him/her: *Zeus:* do will: and then: him/her for: forever: produce will not: bread.

Loose translation:
>"Whoever in existence does harm to this enclosed place of rest, he/she will be torn up into pieces by *Zeus,* and moreover, he/she will forever be deprived of livelihood (bread)."

Translated by BOC:
>"Whoever does harms to this tomb, let him become accursed by *Zeus* and let *Bas* not give bread to him."

NOTE:
>*Knoumanei > Knouman + -Ei, -E, -I > -A* 'an affix, equivalent to the preposition *To*', meaning "to the enclosed place of rest" in *Turkic*.

4 – **_ios: ni se: mon (ni semon - BOC): knoumanei: kakin: adaket: ain': ad: ateamas: titetikmenos: as: tian: [eito]u._**

Turkic:
>Ös: nersə: mına: kon mana: kek: edəcək (kılat): ya: anın: tamuğı[na]: ditik-ditik (titilmiş): anı: tanrı: etər.

Verbatim translation:
>Whoever: the living: this: enclosed place of rest to: harm: do will: or: [to] its: chamber: torn up to pieces: him/her: *Zeus:* do will.

Loose translation:
>"Whoever in existence does harm to this enclosed place of rest or its chamber, *Zeus* will tear him/her up to pieces."

Translated by BOC:
>"Whoever does harm to this tomb or to this plot, let him be accursed by *Zeus*."

NOTE:
>*Ateamas > Ateama, Teama + -S > -Sı* 'a possessive affix, equivalent to the word *Its*', meaning "its chamber" in *Turkic*.

5 – **_ios: ni se: moun (ni semon - BOC): k[nou]mani: kakoun: add[a]ket: aini: mankes: bas: ioi: bekos: me: bere: at: tie: ke: tittetikm[e]nos: eitou._**

Turkic:
>Ös: nersə: mına: kon mana: kek: edəcək (kılat): ya: məngküsınə:
>Basau: anın: boğuzı: me: bəri: ət: tanrı: da: ditik-ditik (titilmiş): etər.

Verbatim translation:
>Whoever: the living: this: enclosed place of rest to: harm: do will: or: stele its:
>Cropland: his/her: bread: and: everything: to a fault: *Zeus:* in return: tormented: make will.

Loose translation:
>"Whoever does any harm to this enclosed place of rest or its stele,
>His/her cropland, bread, and everything else will be torn up to pieces by *Zeus*."

Translated by BOC:
>"Whoever does harm to this tomb or to this stele, let *Bas* not produce bread to him and let him become accursed by *Zeus*."

NOTE:
> *Mankes: Manke > Məŋkü + -S > -Si* 'an affix of possession, equivalent to the word *Its*', meaning "its stele" in *Turkic*.

6 – **[i]os: ni se: mon (ni semon - BOC): knoumane: kakon: adaket: aini: a: teamas: me: deos: tie: tittetikmenos: eitou.**

Turkic:
> Ös: nersə: mına: kon mana: kek: edəcək (kılat): ya: anın: tamuğına:
> Me: tın: Tanrı: ditik-ditik (titilmiş): etər.

Verbatim translation:
> Whoever: the living: this: enclosed place of rest to: harm: do will: or: its: chamber: Then: deities: *Zeus:* torn up to pieces: make will.

Loose translation:
> "Whoever in existence does harm to this enclosed place of rest or its chamber, then the deities, *Zeus* will tear him/her up into pieces."

Translated by BOC:
> "Whoever does harm to this tomb or the plot, let him become accursed by *Zeus* among gods."

7 – **aini: kos: [ni] se: moun (semon - BOC): knoumanei: kakoun: addaket: aini: manka: be[k]os: ioi: me: totoss: euge: sarnan.**

Turkic:
> Ya: kəs: nersə: mına: kon mana: kek: edəcək (kılat): ya: manga:
> Boğuzı: anın: me: tutaşı: Egə: sərina.

Verbatim translation:
> Or: whoever: the living: this: enclosed place of rest: harm: do will: or: the surrounding to: bread: his/her: then: forever: God: block will.

Loose translation:
> "Or whoever in existence does harm to this enclosed place of rest or its surrounding, in return, God will block his/her livelihood (bread) forever."

Translated by BOC:
> "If someone does harm to this tomb or to the stele, let *Sarnan* not give him bread."

8 – **knoumane: kaken: addaket: me: zemelos: ke: deos: ke: titetikmenos: eitou.**

Turkic:
> Kon mana: kek: edəcək (kılat): me: sımıl: da: tın: da: ditik-ditik (titilmiş): etər.

Verbatim translation:
> Enclosed place of rest to: harm: do will: then: people: both: deities: and: tormented: do will.

Loose translation:
> "Whoever does harm to the enclosed place of rest, in return, both people and gods will torment him/her."

Translated by BOC:
> "Whoever does harm to th[is] tomb, let him be accursed in the sight of men and gods."

9 -   *ios: ni se: moun (semon - BOC): knoumane: kakoun: addaket: me: ddeo: me: zemelos: titetikmenos: eitou: as: batan: orouenan: ke.*

Turkic:
> Ös: nersə: mına: kon mana: kek: edəcək (kılat): me: tın: me: sımıl: ditik-ditik (titilmiş): etər: anı: bata: ornın: da.

Verbatim translation:
> Whoever: the living: this: enclosed place of rest to: harm: do will: then: god: and: people: torn up into pieces: do will: him/her: destroy will: his/her place: too.

Loose translation:
> "Whoever in existence harms this enclosed place of rest, then god and people will tear him/her to pieces, destroy his/her place, too."

Translated by BOC:
> "Whoever afflicts harm to this grave, let him be cursed among gods and men by *Bat* and the father."

10 –   *ois: ni se: mun (semun - BOC): knumanei: kakun: addaket: ai: kan: at: tie : ke: deos: ke: tittetikmenos: eitou.*

Turkic:
> Ös: nersə: mına: kon mana: kek: edəcək (kılat): ya: kan[a]:
> Anı: Tanrı: da: tın: da: ditik-ditik (titilmiş): etər.

Verbatim translation:
> Whoever: the living: this: enclosed place of rest to: harm: do will: or: enclosure:
> Him/her: Zeus: and: deities: and: tormented: do will.

Loose translation:
> "Whoever in existence does harm to this enclosed place of rest or the enclosure, he/she will be tormented by *Zeus* and deities."

Translated by BOC:
> "Whoever does harm to this tomb or whatever, let him be accursed by *Zeus* and the gods."

11 -   *ios: ni se: mon (semon - BOC): knoumanei: kakon: addaket: tetiokmenos: eitou: dios: ke: zemelos: ke: par: tes.*

Turkic:
> Ös: nersə: mına: kon mana: kek: edəcək (kılat):
> Ditik-ditik (titilmiş): etər: tın: da: sımıl: da: par: tös.

Verbatim translation:
> Whoever: the living: this: enclosed place of rest to: harm: do will:
> Torn into pieces: do will: deities: and: people: and: all: spirit.

Loose translation:
> "Whoever in existence does harm to this enclosed place of rest, he/she will be tormented by the deities and people, and all the spirits."

Translated by BOC:
> "Whoever does harm to this tomb, let him be accursed (in the sight of) gods and men partes."

12 –   *ios: ni se: moun (semon - BOC): knoumane: kakev: addaketor: deos: zemelos: ke: titetikmenos: eitou.*

Turkic:
>   Ös: nersə: mına: kon mana: kek: etgü-etər: tın: sımıl: da: ditik-ditik (titilmiş): etər.

Verbatim translation:
>   Whoever: the living: this: enclosed place of rest to: harm: do-cause will: deities: people: and: torn into pieces: do will.

Loose translation:
>   "Whoever in existence does harm to this enclosed place of rest, he/she will be torn up to pieces by the deities and people."

Translated by BOC:
>   "Whoever does harm to this tomb, let him be accursed (in the sight of) gods and men."

13 -   *ios: ni se: mon (semon - BOC): knoumanei: kakon: adaket: aini: sa: t∫o∫u: teamas: tie: tittetikmenos: eitou.*

Turkic:
>   Ös: nersə: mına: kon mana: kek: edəcək (kılat): ya: so: toi: tamuğı[na]:
>   Tın: ditik-ditik (titilmiş): etər.

Verbatim translation:
>   Whoever: the living: this: enclosed place of rest to: harm: do will: or: this: clay: chamber: *Zeus:* tormented: do will.

Loose translation:
>   "Whoever in existence does harm to this enclosed place of rest or this clay chamber, *Zeus* will torment him/her."

Translated by BOC:
>   "Whoever does harm to this tomb or to this plot, let him be accursed."

14 -   *ios: ni se: mon (semon - BOC): knoumane: kakon: adaket: deos: zemelos: titetikmenos: eitou.*

Turkic:
>   Ös: nersə: mına: kon mana: kek: edəcək (kılat): diyü: sımıl: ditik-ditik (titilmiş): etər.

Verbatim translation:
>   Whoever: the living: this: enclosed place of rest to: harm: do will: spirits: people: tormented: do will.

Loose translation:
>   "Whoever in existence does harm to this enclosed place of rest, the spirits and people will torment him/her."

Translated by BOC:
>   "Whoever does harm to this tomb, let him be accursed (in the sight of) gods and men".

15 -   *ios: ni se: moun (semon - BOC): knoumani: kakoun: abbireto: aini: mmura: tos: ni: d[ios z]imelos: ti: meka: t[ie] tittetikmenos: eitou.*

Turkic:
>   Ös: nersə: mına: kon mana: kek: beret: ya nə: mara: tos: ni:
>   t[ı s]ımıl: da: mak: T[in]: ditik-ditik (titilmiş): etər.

Verbatim translation:
>   Whoever: the living: this: enclosed place of rest to: harm: bring will: or: to kurgan: base: whatnot:
>   D[eities p]eople: and: the all-praised: Z[eus]: tormented: do will.

118

Loose translation:
> "Whoever in existence brings harm to this enclosed place of rest or the kurgan, its base, or whatnot, will be tormented by the deities, people, and the all-praised *Zeus*."

Translated by BOC:
> "Whoever brings harm or mistreatments to this tomb, let him be accursed by the great *Z[eus]* (in the sight of) g[ods and m]en."

16 - *ios: ni se: mon (semon - BOC): knoumane: kakon: daket: aini: manka: tie: tittetikmenos: eitou.*

Turkic:
> Ös: nersə: mına: kon mana: kek: edəcək (kılat): ya: manga:
> Tin: ditik-ditik (titilmiş): etər.

Verbatim translation:
> Whoever: the living: this: enclosed place of rest to: harm: do will: or: the surrounding to: *Zeus:* tormented: do will.

Loose translation:
> "Whoever in existence does harm to this enclosed place of rest or the surrounding, will be tormented by *Zeus*."

Translated by BOC:
> "Whoever does harm to this tomb or stele, let him be accursed (by) *Zeus*."

17 - *eios: ni se: moun (semon - BOC): knoumani: kakon: addaket: zeira: ke: oipeis: ke: tittetikmena: at: tie: adeittnou.*

Turkic:
> Ös: nersə: mına: kon mana: kek: edəcək (kılat):
> Zerəi: də: öp-is: də: ditik-ditik (titilmiş): anı: Tin: etər.

Verbatim translation:
> Whoever: the living: this: enclosed place of rest to: harm: do will:
> Mind: and house-property: and: tormented: him/her: *Zeus:* do will.

Loose translation:
> "Whoever in existence does harm to this enclosed place of rest, *Zeus* will destroy his/her mind and house-property."

Translated by BOC:
> "Whoever does harm to this tomb, let his hands and feet become accursed by *Zeus*. Zeira-hands? Petes – feet?"

18 - *ios: [ni] se: moun (semon - BOC): tou: knoumanei: kakou: adaket: titetikmenos: at: tie: adeitou.*

Turkic:
> Ös: nersə: mına: toi: kon mana: kek: edəcək (kılat):
> Ditik-ditik (titilmiş): anı: Tin: etər.

Verbatim translation:
> Whoever: the living: this: clay: enclosed place of rest to: harm: do will:
> Tormented: him/her: *Zeus:* do will.

Loose translation:
> "Whoever in existence does harm to this enclosed place of rest, made of clay, *Zeus* will torment him/her."

Translated by BOC:
> "Whoever does harm to this tomb, let him be accursed by *Zeus*."

19 -   *ios: sa: ti: sk eledriai (skeledriai – BOC): kakoun: daket: atetikmenos: at: ti: adeitou.*
Turkic:
    Ös: so: toi: süki əyləndərəyə: kek: edəcək (kılat): ditik-ditik (titilmiş): anı: Tin: etər.
Verbatim translation:
    Whoever: this: clay: tomb around: harm: do will: tormented: him/her: *Zeus:* do will.
Loose translation:
    "Whoever does harm to this clay tomb and its surrounding, *Zeus* will torment him/her."
Translated by BOC:
    "Whoever does harm to this skeledriai, let him become accursed by *Zeus*."

20 -   *ios: ni se: moun (semon - BOC): knoumanei: kakoun: adoket:*
    seirai: titetikmenos: at: ti: adeitou: gegreimenon: k'egedou: orouenos: outon.
Turkic:
    Ös: nersə: mına: kon mana: kek: edəcək (kılat):
    Sırai: ditik-ditik (titilmiş): anı: Tanrı: etər: kəkiri (kəkirəmiş): etər: ornın: ötün.
Verbatim translation:
    Whoever: the living: this: enclosed place of rest to: harm: do will:
    Completely: torn into pieces: him/her: *Zeus:* do will: gnarled: do will: on the spot: eternally.
Loose translation:
    "Whoever in existence does harm to this enclosed place of rest, he/she will be utterly tormented and gnarled by *Zeus* right then and there for eternity."
Translated by BOC:
    "Whoever does harm to this tomb with [his] hand, let him become accursed by *Zeus* and let him suffer the written curse of the keeper."

21 –   *ios: ni: san: kakoun: ad[da]ke: mankai:*
    geg[re]imenan: egedou: tios: outan.
Turkic:
    Ös: ni: san: kek: edəcək (kılat): məŋküyə:
    Kəkiri (kəkirəmiş): etər: Tın: ötün.
Verbatim translation:
    Whoever: any: amount: harm: do will: to stele:
    Gnarled: do will: *Zeus:* eternally.
Loose translation:
    "Whoever does any amount of harm to this stele, *Zeus* will make him/her gnarled forever."
Translated by BOC:
    "Whoever does harm to this stele, let him suffer the written curse of *Zeus*."

22 –   *ios: sa: tou: sorou: kake: addaket:*
    me: zemelos: ot: tittetikmenos (ottittetikmenos – BOC): eitou.
Turkic:
    Ös: so: toi: sorun: kek: edəcək (kılat):
    Me: sımıl: anı: ditik-ditik (titilmiş): etər.
Verbatim translation:
    Whoever: this: clay: honorary place: harm: do will:
    And: people: him/her: torn to pieces: do will.
Loose translation:
    "Whoever harms this honorary place, made of clay, in return, people will torment him/her."

Translated by BOC:

"Whoever does harm to this coffin, let him be accursed in the sight of men."

NOTE:

Suggested by BOC *Ottittetikmenos* should be read as two separate words: *Ot* "him/her", *Tittetikmenos* "torn to pieces".

23 - **_vasous: iman: mekas:_**
kanutievais:
devos: ke: mekas:

Turkic:

Vasous: ü manı: maukmış:
Kanuti ev yəsi[nə]:
Devəəsini: də: maukmış.

Verbatim translation:

Vasous: shrine: put in place:
Kanuti family head [for]:
Enclosure its: too: put in place.

Loose translation:

"*Vasous* set up this shrine and its enclosure for *Kanuti* – the head of the family (house)."

Translated by BOC:

"*Vasos Iman* the great (the son) of *Kanuti* and the great god."

§11-4-2. 37 GRAMMATICAL POINTERS, ATTESTING THAT PHRYGIAN WAS A TURKIC LANGUAGE.

Based on the analysis of 88 attested *Phrygian* words and 23 ancient *Phrygian* texts, it was determined that *Phrygian* was never a part of the *Indo-European* family. The following grammatical, morphological, phonetic, and lexical facts speak loud and clear in favor of the *Turkic* origin of the *Phrygian* language.

NOUNS.

1. 88 *Phrygian* words, ideally matching the *Turkic* counterparts, without any established *Indo-European* equivalents.

While the *Indo-European* proponents struggle to find any evidence linking the *Phrygian* words to the *Proto-Indo-European* source, we found 88 *Phrygian* words that easily matched their *Turkic* counterparts without any shenanigans.

First and foremost, attested to be the most ancient word in the world by *Herodotus*, – the *Phrygian Bekós* and *Turkic Boğás* look very similar and share the same meaning – "bread". Even a stress mark falls on the exact location in both words – the second syllable. As a rule, in all the *Turkic* languages, the accent of a word always lies on the last syllable.

The following 27 *Phrygian* words also do not have any truly attested *Indo-European* origin but perfectly match *Turkic* words both in form and meaning:

1) *Akristin* "female slave, bakeress" > *Ağır + İs + Tin* "the one who does heavy work".
2) *Anar* "husband; smart man" > *Anar* – a *Turkic* male name that means "smart man".
3) *Ates* – a male name > *Atış* – an ancient *Turkic* male name that means "shootout".
4) *Meme* – a male name > *Mamay* – a *Turkic* male name that means "giant".
5) *Kanuti* – a male name > *Kanat* – a *Turkic* male name that means "wing".
6) *Baba* – a male name > *Baba* – a *Turkic* male name that means "father, patriarch".
7) *Manes* – a male name > *Manış* – a *Turkic* male name from *Man + Us* "great chief".
8) *Ata, Atai* > *Ata, Atai* "father" in *Turkic*.
9) *Atatas* > *Atadaş* "from the same father" in *Turkic*.
10) *Nana* > *Nənə* "mother; grandmother" in *Turkic*.
11) *Nana vata* > *Nənə Ata* "mother, father; parents" in *Turkic*.
12) *Duman* "community" > *Tuman* "community" in *Turkic*. Compare to *PIE Dheh* "put".
13) *Dumasta* "leader of community": *Tuman + Usta* "leader of a community".
14) *Eiroi* "hero" > *Er* "hero, man, warrior" in *Turkic*.
15) *Kake* "harm" > *Kik, Kek* "harm" in *Turkic*.
16) *Kos, Kin* "someone, whoever" > *Kəs, Kim* "someone, whoever" in *Turkic*.
17) *Manka* "stele" > *Məŋkü* "stele with the inscription" in *Turkic*. (Compare to *PIE *Men* "remain".)
18) *Ni* > *Ni* "whatever, anything, any" in *Turkic*.
19) *Onenin* > *Onun, Anın* "his, her, its" in *Turkic*.
20) *Par* > *Par* "all" in *Turkic*.
21) *Tes, Tan, Tus* > *Tös* "spirit" in *Turkic*.
22) *Skeledriai: Süki + Əylənderə* "around tomb" in *Turkic*.
23) *Proitanos: Pir + Öi + Tən + Ös* "person from the same house" in *Turkic*.
24) *Euge* > *Egə* "God, deity" in *Turkic*.
25) *Tiara* > *Dairə* "circle" in *Turkic*.
26) *Zeirai* > *Zerəi* "mind, intellect" in *Turkic*. (Compare to *PIE *Ghes-r-* "hand".)
27) *Zemelo* "human beings" > *Sımıl* "dynasty, tribe, family, kinfolk, people" in *Turkic*. (Compare to *PIE *Dhghe-m-* "earth".)

2. Nouns do not have gender in *Phrygian* and *Turkic*.

   As nouns do not have gender in *Phrygian* and *Turkic*, their modifications are implemented by the affixes at the end:
   - *Nev* "grandchild, granddaughter, grandson" in *Phrygian*;
   - *Nəvə* "grandchild, granddaughter, grandson" in *Turkic*.
   - *Knais* "wife" in *Phrygian* = *Kanış* "wife" in *Turkic* (*Kan* 'king' + *-Iş* 'an affix, denoting the word 'Wife').

3. Gender of masculine and feminine nouns revealed by their definition in *Phrygian* and *Turkic*.

   - *Nana* "mother; grandmother" in *Phrygian*;
   - *Nənə* "mother; grandmother" in *Turkic*.
   - *Ata, Atai, Baba* "father, patriarch" in *Phrygian*;
   - *Ata, Atai, Baba* "father, patriarch" in *Turkic*.

4. Formation of the plural with the help of the affixes both in *Phrygian* and *Turkic*.

   The plural is formed by adding the affix *-As* in *Phrygian* and *-Us* in *Turkic* to a substantive:
   - *Ouelas* "people" in *Phrygian* (*Ouel* > *Oul* 'son, young man' + *-As* > *-Us* 'an affix of plurality' in *Turkic*).

- *Ulus* "people" in *Turkic* (*Ul, Oul* 'son, young man' + *-Us* 'an affix of plurality'). This ancient *Turkic* affix *-Us* has left its trace mostly in *Turkish* as a verbal affix *-Uz, -Iz*, attached to a noun, such as *Oğluz* "we are sons", *Evlatız* "we are children". A similar situation is observed in the *Turkic* archaism *Türük* "Turks", "Turk" > *Tür=Tur* + *-Ük* 'an affix of plurality, equivalent to the words *We Are*', meaning "we are Turs; we are Turks".

5. Declension of nouns in *Phrygian* and *Turkic* is implemented with the help of the affixes.

    ➢ Dative case affixes *-A, -I* in *Phrygian* and *-A, -Yə* in *Turkic*:
    - *Manka* "to the surrounding" in *Phrygian* = *Manka* "to the surrounding" in *Turkic* (*Mank* > *Mang* 'a surrounding' + *-A* 'an affix, equivalent to the preposition *To*').
    - *Mankai* "towards/to a stele" in *Phrygian* = *Maŋküyə* "towards/to a stele" in *Turkic* (*Manka* > *Maŋkü* 'stele' + *-I* > *-Yə* 'a *Turkic* affix, equivalent to the prepositions *To, Towards*').
    - *Knoumanei* "to the enclosed resting place" in *Phrygian* (*Knou* > *Kon* 'place of rest, resting place' + *Mane* > *Man* 'enclosed place' + *-I* > *-A* 'a *Turkic* affix, equivalent to the preposition *To, Towards*' in *Turkic*).

    ➢ Accusative case affix *-N* in *Phrygian* and *-Nı* in *Turkic*:
    - *Akara Gayun Edaes* "made the upper rock" in *Phrygian* = *Ağarı Qayanı Etmiş* "made the upper rock" in *Turkic* (*Gayun: Gayu* > *Qaya* 'rock' + *-N* > *-Nı* 'an affix, denoting the accusative case'). In both languages, the accusative case of a noun is used to mark the direct object (*Gayun* = *Qayanı*) of the transitive verb (*Edaes* = *Etmiş*).

    ➢ Genitive case affixes *-Ton, -Tin, -Dan* in *Phrygian* and *-Tən, -Dən, -Dan* in *Turkic*:
    - *Nevotan* "from a grandchild" in *Phrygian* (*Nevo* > *Nəvə* 'grandchild' + *Tan* > *-Tən* 'an affix, equivalent to the preposition *From*'), meaning "from a grandchild" in *Turkic*.
    - *Nəvədən* "from a grandchild" in *Turkic* (*Nəvə* 'grandchild' + *-Dən* 'an affix, equivalent to the preposition *From*').
    - *Areyastin* "from *Arias*" in *Phrygian* (*Areyas* > *Arias* 'an island name' + *Tin* > *-Tın* 'a *Turkic* affix, denoting a preposition *From*', meaning "from *Arias*" in *Turkic*).
    - *Upsodan* "from the top" in *Phrygian* (*Upso* > *Uca* 'top, high' + *-Dan* 'a *Turkic* affix, equivalent to the preposition *From*', meaning "from the top" in *Turkic*).

6. Nouns with the possessive affixes.

    Both in *Phrygian* and *Turkic*, substantives take possessive affixes, such as *-S* in *Phrygian* and *-Si, -Sı* in *Turkic*:
    - *Atas* "his/her father" in *Phrygian* = *Atası* "his/her father" in *Turkic* (*Ata* 'father' + *-S* = *-Sı* 'an affix, equivalent to the pronouns *His, Her*' in *Turkic*).
    - *Mankes* "his/her/its stele" in *Phrygian* = *Məŋküsi* "his/her/its stele" in *Turkic* (*Manka* = *Maŋkü* + *-S* = *-Si* 'an affix of possession, equivalent to the pronouns *His, Her, Its*' in *Turkic*).
    - *Nevos* "his/her grandchild" in *Phrygian* = *Nəvəsi* "his/her grandchild" in *Turkic* (*Nevo* = *Nəvə* 'grandchild' + *-S* = *-Si* 'an affix, equivalent to the pronouns *His, Her*' in *Turkic*).

- *Inas* "his/her mother" in *Phrygian* = *İnəsi* "his/her mother" in *Turkic* (*Ina* > *İnə* 'mother' + -*S* = -*Si* 'an affix of possession, equivalent to the pronouns *His, Her*' in *Turkic*.
- *Devos* "its enclosure" in *Phrygian* = *Devəəsi* "its enclosure" in *Turkic* (*Devo* = *Devəə* 'enclosure' + -*S* = -*Si* 'an affix, denoting possession' in *Turkic*).

7. Nouns with the affixes, denoting affection.

In order to demonstrate affection, some *Phrygian* and *Turkic* nouns add the affix -*I* in *Phrygian* and -*İ* in *Turkic*:
- *Atai* in *Phrygian* and *Turkic* "dear father" (*Ata* 'father' + -*I* = -*İ* 'an affix, equivalent to the word *Dear*' in *Turkic*).
- *Babai* in *Phrygian* and *Turkic* "dear father" (*Baba* 'father' + -*I* = -*İ* 'an affix, equivalent to the word *Dear*' in *Turkic*).
- *Anai* in *Phrygian* and *Turkic* "dear mother" (*Ana* 'mother' + -*I* = -*İ* 'an affix, equivalent to the word *Dear*' in *Turkic*).

8. Paired words.

The *Phrygian* and *Turkic* languages have a peculiar lexical occurrence that hardly any *IE* languages possess. This phenomenon entails the arrangement of words in pairs. These words can be verbs, nouns, adjectives, participles, adverbs that function as set expressions. Depending upon their meaning, there are two major groups of the paired words distinguished:

- Both components in the paired word relay the same meaning:
  - *Addaketor* "will do" (literally, "do-do will") in *Phrygian* (*Addak* > *Edgü* 'do, make, create' + *Etor* > *Etər* 'will do', literally, 'do will' (*Et* 'do, make, create' + *Or* > -*ər* 'an affix of the future tense in the 3rd p. sing., similar to *Will*').
  - *Yaratar-Etər* "will do" (literally, "do will-do will") in *Turkic* [Dr.Sl.240] (*Yarat* 'do, create' + -*Ar* 'an affix of the future tense in the 3rd p. sing., similar to *Will*' + *Etər* 'will do', literally, 'do will').

  There are numerous *Turkic* examples matching the *Phrygian* counterparts, such as: *Usta-Pasta* "lead someone" (lead-lead), *Gözəl-Göyçək* "beautiful" (beautiful-beautiful), *Alay-Alay* "regiment after regiment" (regiment-regiment), *Tanış-Biliş* "acquaintance" (acquaintance-acquaintance), *Al-Qırmizi* "bright red" (red-red), *Asta-Asta* "slowly" (slow-slow), *Qırıq-Qırıq* "broken" (broken-broken).

- Both components carry slightly different semantic content:
  - *Oip-Eis* "house-property" in *Phrygian* (*Oip* > *Öp* 'house' + *Eis* > -*İs* 'property' in *Turkic*).
  - *Ev-Eşik* "house" (literally, "house-property") in *Turkic* (*Ev* 'house' + *Eşik* 'property').

  There are countless *Turkic* paired words of this category that could be enumerated, just to name few: *Gör-Götür* "learn" (see-take), *Qırar-Tökər* "will kill" (exterminate-throw away), *Basar-Kəsər* "will threaten" (conquer-cut).

9. Compound nouns.

Phrygian and *Turkic* use compound nouns very frequently. There are several types of the compounds:

- When two (or more) substantives unite:
    - *Nana vata* "mother, father; parents" in *Phrygian* = *Nənə-ata, Ana-ata* "mother, father; parents" in *Turkic*.
- When two (or more) nouns join:
    - *Atatas* "from the same father" in *Phrygian* = *Atadaş* "from the same father" in *Turkic* (*Ata* 'father' + *Tas* = *Daş, Taş* 'companion').
    - *Koroumane* "plot-enclosed place" in *Phrygian* (*Korou* > *Kora* 'plot, piece of ground' + *Mane* > *Man* 'enclosed place' in *Turkic*).
    - *Knoumane* "enclosed place of rest" in *Phrygian* (*Knou* > *Kon* 'place of rest' + *Mane* > *Man* 'enclosed place' in *Turkic*).
- When an adjective and a noun are joined:
    - *Keneman* "wide, enclosed place" in *Phrygian* (*Kene* > *Kən* 'wide, spacious' + *Man* 'enclosed place' in *Turkic*).
    - *Akkoş* "swan" in *Turkic* (*Ak* 'white' + *Koş* 'bird').
- When an adverb is combined with a particle:
    - *Akristin* "female slave" in *Phrygian* (*Akr* > *Ağır* 'heavily' + *Istin* > *İstiyən* 'working' in *Turkic*).
- When a pronoun unites with or joins a noun:
    - *Ni se* "the living" in *Phrygian* = *Nersə* "the living" (*Ni* = *Ne* 'what' + *Se* = *Ersə* 'all the living' in *Turkic*).
- When two participles are merged:
    - *Ataniyen* "subduer" in *Phrygian* (*Atan* 'shooter; shooting': *At* 'shoot' + *-An* 'an affix of constant action') + *Iyen* > *İyən* 'subduer; subduing' (*İy* 'subdue, subjugate' + *-Ən* 'an affix, denoting constant action' in *Turkic*).

10. In *Phrygian* and *Turkic,* only the second component of compound nouns takes a termination.

    - *Akaragayun, Akara Gayun:* *Akara* > *Ağarı* 'upper' + *Gayun* > *Qayanı* 'rock' (*Gayu* > *Qaya* 'rock' + *N* > *Nı* 'an affix, denoting the accusative case' in *Turkic*).
    - *Knoumanei* "to the enclosed resting place" in *Phrygian* (*Knou* > *Kon* 'place of rest, resting place' + *Mane* > *Man* 'enclosed place' + *-I* > *-A* 'a *Turkic* affix, equivalent to the preposition *To, Towards*' in *Turkic*).

11. Collective nouns, following the pronoun *Par* "all" both in *Phrygian* and *Turkic,* can be in a singular number.

    - *Par Tes* "all the spirits", literally – "all spirit" in *Phrygian* (*Par* 'all' + *Tes* > *Tös* 'spirit' in *Turkic*);
    - *Par Yər* "all the lands", literally – "all land" in *Turkic* (*Par* 'all' + *Yər* 'land' in *Turkic*).

12. Nouns can form from participles without any modification.

    Some *Phrygian* and *Turkic* nouns do not differ from participles in their form:
    - *Kuryan* "ruler; ruling" in *Phrygian* = *Kuran* "ruler; ruling" in *Turkic* (*Kur* 'rule, establish, organize, institute' + *-Yan* > *-An* 'an affix, denoting constant action' in *Turkic*).
    - *Eyon* "subduer; subduing" in *Phrygian* = *Əyən* "subduer; subduing" in *Turkic* (*Ey* > *Əy* 'subdue, subjugate' + *-On* > *-Ən* 'an affix, denoting constant action' in *Turkic*).
    - *Ataniyen* "subduer; subduing" in *Phrygian* (*Atan* 'shooter; shooting': *At* 'shoot' + *-An* 'an affix of constant action') + *Iyen* > *İyən* 'subduer; subduing': *İy* 'subdue, subjugate' + *-En* > *-Ən* 'an affix, denoting constant action' in *Turkic*).

- *Tataniyen* "founder; founding; subduer; subduing" in *Phrygian* (*Tatan* 'founder; founding': *Tat* > *Tət* 'found, establish' + *-An* 'an affix of constant action' + *Iyen* > *İyən* 'subduer; subduing': *İy* 'subdue, subjugate' + *-En* > *-Ən* 'an affix, denoting constant action' in *Turkic*).
- *Deton* "safekeeper; safekeeping" in *Phrygian* (*Det* > *Dut, Tut* 'safekeep' + *On* > *-An* 'an affix, denoting constant action' in *Turkic*).

13. One and the same word can have several variations in *Phrygian* and *Turkic*.

Similar to *Turkic* and other related to it languages, such as *Median* and *Etruscan*, *Phrygian* demonstrates words having numerous variants:
- *A, As, At, Ot* "its, him, her; his" in *Phrygian* = *Anın, Onun, Uning, Əna, Kinini, Ul* "its, his, him, her" in *Turkic*.
- *Ios, Ois, Eios, Yos, Yosyos, Is, Isos, Ion, Ian* "who, whoever" in *Phrygian* = *Ös, Kəs, O* "who, whoever" in *Turkic*.

ADJECTIVES.

14. Adjectives can be created from nouns with the help of affixes.

The *Phrygian* affix *-Ses* and the *Turkic* affix *-Sız*, added to a noun, can create adjectives:
- *At<u>ses</u>* "unnamed" in *Phrygian* = *At<u>sız</u>* "unnamed" in *Turkic* (*At* 'name' + *Ses* > *-Sız* 'an affix, equivalent to the preposition *Without*' in *Turkic*).

VERBS.

15. Both in *Phrygian* and *Turkic*, verbs stand at the end of a sentence.

- *Baba: memevais: proitanos: kɸiyanaveyos: si: keneman: <u>edaes</u>.* – in *Phrygian*.
- "Baba <u>made</u> this spacious, enclosed place of rest for the very much beloved human being *Meme*, the head of the family from the same house (dynasty)."
- *Təngri mening işim <u>etti</u>.* – in *Turkic*.
- "God <u>put</u> my affairs in order." [Dr.Sl.186].

16. *Phrygian* and *Turkic* verbs create the past and future tenses with the help of the affixes.

17. The future tense of verbs is created by the *Phrygian* affixes *-Et, -Or, -Ou, -A, -An* and the *Turkic* affixes *-Ar, -Ər, -Ö, -Uo, -A*.

Unlike the *IE* languages, where the future tense is formed by the auxiliaries (i.e., *Will, Shall* in *English*), preceding the verbs, or by prefixes, infixes, suffixes, and internal stem changes – on separate occasions or all at once, such as in *Russian* – <u>идти</u> "to go" > <u>пойду</u> "I will go" (<u>по</u> – prefix; <u>йд</u> – the stem changed from <u>ид</u>; <u>у</u> – the ending in the 1st p. sing.), both in *Phrygian* and *Turkic*, the future tense is created exclusively by adding a corresponding affix to a verb at its end, while retaining the verbal stem unchanged.

There are five forms of the future tense in *Phrygian* that correspond to their *Turkic* analogues. All of them were constructed with the help of the affixes, such as *-Et, -Or, -Ou, -A, -An* in *Phrygian* and *-Et, -Ar, -Ər, -Ö, -Uo, -A* in *Turkic*:

- *Abberet* "will bring" in *Phrygian* (*Abber* > *Appar, Apar* 'bear, carry' + *-Et* 'an affix, equivalent to *Will* in the 3rd p. sing.' in *Turkic*);
- *Al bilet –* "s/he will know" in *Turkic* (*Bilet: Bil* 'know' + *-Et* 'an affix, equivalent to *Will* in the 3rd p. sing.').

- *Dakor* "will make" in *Phrygian* (*Dak* > *Edgü* 'make' + *-Or* > *-Ar, -Ər* 'an affix of the future tense in the 3rd p. sing' in *Turkic*);
- *Etər* "will make" in *Turkic* (*Et* 'make' + *-Ər* 'an affix of the future tense in the 3rd p. sing') [Dr.SL.186].

- *Eitou* "will do, make, create, produce" in *Phrygian* (*Eit* > *Et* 'do, make, create, build, produce' + *-Ou* > *-Ö, -Uo* 'an affix of the future tense in the 3rd p. sing.' in *Turkic*);
- *Onu ongoruo* "he will do it" in *Turkic* (*Ongor* 'do' + *-Uo* 'an affix of the future tense in the 3rd p. sing.').

- *Sarna* "will stop" in *Phrygian* (*Sarn* > *Sərin* 'stop' + *-A* 'an affix of the future tense in the 3rd p. sing.' in *Turkic*);
- *Kini barıa* - "s/he will go" in *Turkic* (*Barıa: Barı* 'go' + *-A* 'an affix of the future tense in the 3rd p. sing.').

- *Batan* "will slay" in *Phrygian* (*Batan: Bat* > *Batır* 'slay' + *-An* > *-A* 'an affix of the future tense in the 3rd p. sing.' in *Turkic*);
- *Kərim məktəptən kayta.* "Karim will return from school" (*Kayta: Kayt* 'return' + *-A* 'an affix of the future tense in the 3rd p. sing.').

18. The past tense of the verbs is formed by the *Phrygian* affixes *-Toi, -Tiy, -Es* and *Turkic* affixes *-Ti, -Tı, -Miş*.

The *Phrygian* verbs of the past tense were constructed on the same principles and by similar affixes as in *Turkic*:
- *Edatoi* "s/he made, built" in *Phrygian* (*Eda* > *Ədə* 'do, make, build' + *Toi* > *-Ti* 'an affix of the past tense in the 3rd p. sing.' in *Turkic*);
- *Ətti* "s/he made, built' in *Turkic* (*Ət* 'do, make, build' + *-Ti* 'an affix of the past tense in the 3rd p. sing.').

- *Edaes* "s/he did, made" in *Phrygian* (*Eda* > *Ədə* 'do, make' + *-Es* > *-Miş* 'an affix of the past tense in the 3rd p. sing.' in *Turkic*);
- *Ol evkə barmış ol* "he went home" in *Turkic* (*Bar* 'go' + *-Miş* 'an affix of the past tense in the 3rd p. sing.').

19. Negation in *Phrygian* and *Turkic* verbs is created with the help of an affix *-Bas*.

Precisely like in *Turkic*, *Phrygian* negative sentences were constructed with the help of affixes, such as *-Bas,* attached to a verb it modifies:
- *Eitibas* "s/he will not produce" in *Phrygian* (*Eiti* > *Et* 'make, produce' + *-Bas* 'an affix of negation in the 3rd p. sing., in the future tense' in *Turkic*);
- *Jazbas* "s/he will not write" in *Turkic* (*Jaz* 'write' + *-Bas* 'an affix of negation in the 3rd p. sing., in the future tense').

None of the *IE* languages has this kind of capability of expressing the negation by means of affixation.

20. In *Phrygian* and *Turkic,* an object stands in front of a verb instead of following it.

   It is an established rule in the *IE* languages that an object should follow a transitive verb. In some *IE* languages, such as *Russian,* an object as a noun can stand in front of a verb. However, in that case, it is frequently subject to the rules of declension.
   In contrast to the *IE* languages, both *Phrygian* and *Turkic* must have an object in front of a verb. And this object or a noun retains its neutral form. Compare the languages with verbatim translation into *English:*
   - *English:* He built a <u>school</u>. (Not: He a school built)
   - *Russian:* On shkol<u>u</u> postroil. – "He a <u>school</u> (in sing., acc. case) built."
   - *Phrygian: Baba* ... <u>keneman</u> *edaes.* – "*Baba* …a <u>wide, enclosed place</u> made."
   - *Turkic: O* <u>tura</u> *ətti.* – "He a <u>house</u> built."

PARTICIPLES.

21. Participles in *Phrygian* and *Turkic* are also formed with the help of affixes.

22. Present participles are created with the addition of the *Phrygian* affixes *-An, -Yan, -Yen* and the *Turkic* affixes *-Yan, -Yən* to verbs.

   - *Kur<u>yan</u>* "ruling; ruler" in *Phrygian = Kur<u>an</u>* "ruling; ruler" in *Turkic* (*Kur* 'rule, establish, organize, institute' + *-Yan* > *-An* 'an affix, denoting constant action' in *Turkic*).
   - *Ey<u>on</u>* "subduing; subduer" in *Phrygian = Əy<u>ən</u>* "subduing; subduer" in *Turkic* (*Ey* > *Əy* 'subdue, subjugate' + *-On* > *-Ən* 'an affix, denoting constant action' in *Turkic*).
   - *Atan<u>iyen</u>* "subduing; subduer" in *Phrygian* (*Atan* 'shooting; shooter': *At* 'shoot' + *-An* 'an affix of constant action' + *Iyen* > *İyən* 'subduing; subduer': *İy* 'subdue, subjugate' + *-En* > *-Ən* 'an affix, denoting constant action' in *Turkic*).
   - *Tatan<u>iyen</u>* "founding; founder; subduing; subduer" in *Phrygian* (*Tatan* 'founding; founder': *Tat* > *Tət* 'found, establish' + *-An* 'an affix of constant action' + *Iyen* > *İyən* 'subduer; subduing': *İy* 'subdue, subjugate' + *-En* > *-Ən* 'an affix, denoting constant action' in *Turkic*).
   - *Det<u>on</u>* "safekeeping; safekeeper" in *Phrygian* (*Det* > *Dut, Tut* 'safekeep' + *-On* > *-An* 'an affix, denoting constant action' in *Turkic*).

23. Past participles are formed by the affixes *-Menos, -Menon* in *Phrygian* and *-Miş, -Mış* in *Turkic*.

   - *Gegrei<u>menon</u>* "gnarled" in *Phrygian* (*Gegrei* > *Kəkirəi* 'gnarl, twist' + *Menon* > *-Miş* 'an affix, forming the past participle' in *Turkic*).
   - *Tetik<u>menos</u>* "torn up to pieces, tormented" in *Phrygian* (*Tetik* > *Titik, Didik* 'tormented' + *-Menos* > *-Miş* 'an affix, forming the past participle', meaning "tormented", "torn up to pieces" in *Turkic*);
   - *Didil<u>miş</u>* "torn up to pieces, tormented" in *Turkic* (*Didil* 'tormented' + *-Miş* 'an affix, forming the past participle').

24. Both in *Phrygian* and *Turkic,* past participles can have the passive voice with the help of the affixes *-Ik, -İk,* added to verbs.

- *Tetikmenos* "torn to pieces" in *Phrygian*: Tet > Tit 'tear to pieces' + -Ik > -İk 'an affix, denoting the passive voice of the participle' + -Menos > -Miş 'an affix, indicating the participle in the past perfect tense'.
    - *Titik, Didik* "torn to pieces" in *Turkic*: Tit, Did 'tear to pieces' + -İk 'an affix, denoting the passive voice of the participle'.

25. Both in *Phrygian* and *Turkic*, a participle comes in front of a verb and is frequently used with specific verbs, such as *Eitou, K'egedou, Adeitou* (and the like) in *Phrygian* and *Edər, Edəcək* (and the like) in *Turkic*.

    The structure Past Participle + *Eitou, K'egedou, Adeitou* in *Phrygian* is equivalent to the *Turkic* one, as the *Phrygian* verbs share the same root with the *Turkic* verbs İt, Et, Əd "do".
    This unique combination is used in the *Turkic* curses, predominantly in the *Azerbaijani* ones. Compare the *Phrygian* curse *Titetikmenos Eitou* "torn up to pieces do will" (verbatim) to a plethora of similar *Azerbaijani* combinations:

    Didik-didik eləsin
    Parça-parça eləsin   "[let him/her] torn up to pieces do".
    Cırığ-cırığ eləsin

    - *Phr.* – Gegreimenon: k'egedou.
    - *Turk.* – Kəkirəimiş: edəcək.
    - *Eng.* – Gnarled: make will. (verbatim)

    - *Phr.* – Titekmenos: adeitou.
    - *Turk.* – Titilmiş: edəcək.
    - *Eng.* – Torn into pieces: make will. (verbatim)

26. Created with the help of affixes, participles can function as nouns in *Phrygian* and *Turkic*:

    - *Kuryan* "ruler; ruling" in *Phrygian* = *Kuran* "ruler; ruling" in *Turkic* (*Kur* 'rule, establish, organize, institute' + -Yan > -An 'an affix, denoting constant action').

PRONOUNS.

27. Pronouns do not have gender in *Phrygian* and *Turkic*:

    - *Ioi, Oy, Oi* "him, her" in *Phrygian* = *Onı* "him, her" in *Turkic*.

28. Pronouns can be independent and dependent in *Phrygian* and *Turkic*.

    Independent pronouns in *Phrygian* – *Ad* "its, his, her", *Ios* "who, whoever", *Ioi* "him, her", *Ni* "whatever, any" and their *Turkic* counterparts *Anın* "its, his, her", *Ös* "who, whoever", *Onı* "him, her", *Ni* "whatever, any" differ from dependent pronouns, which are represented by the affixes, such as -S in *Phrygian* and -Si in *Turkic*, -An in *Phrygian* and -Un in *Turkic*, attached to substantives:
    - *Devos* "its enclosure" in *Phrygian*: Devo > Devəə 'enclosure' + -S > -Si 'an affix, denoting possession', meaning "its enclosure" in *Turkic*.

- *Atas* "his/her father" in *Phrygian* = *Atası* "his/her father" in *Turkic* (*Ata* 'father' + *-S* = *-Sı* 'an affix, equivalent to the pronoun *His/Her*' in *Turkic*).
- *Mankes* "his/her/its stele" in *Phrygian* = *Məŋküsi* "his/her/its stele" in *Turkic* (*Manka* = *Maŋkü* 'stele' + *-S* = *-Si* 'an affix, equivalent to the pronouns *His/Her/Its*' in *Turkic*).
- *Nevos* "his/her grandchild" in *Phrygian* = *Nəvəsi* "his/her grandchild" in *Turkic* (*Nevo* = *Nəvə* 'grandchild' + *-S* = *-Si* 'an affix, equivalent to the pronouns *His, Her*' in *Turkic*).
- *Inas* "his/her mother" in *Phrygian* = *İnəsi* "his/her mother" in *Turkic* (*Ina* > *İnə* 'mother' + *-S* = *-Si* 'an affix, equivalent to the pronouns *His, Her*' in *Turkic*).
- *Orouenan* "his/her place" in *Phrygian* = *Ornun* "his/her place" in *Turkic* (*Orouen* > *Orın* 'place' + *-Un* 'an affix, denoting a pronoun *His/Her*' in *Turkic*).

Not a single *IE* language can brag about having dependent pronouns created by affixes.

29. Types of *Phrygian* pronouns and their striking match to *Turkic* ones.

Among the detected *Phrygian* pronouns, we could single out possessive, demonstrative, interrogative, generalizing, indefinite ones that have *Turkic* equivalents, matching them in form and meaning:
- Possessive pronouns:
  - *Ad, As, At* "his, her" in *Phrygian* = *Anın* "his, her" in *Turkic*.
  - *Onenin* "his, her" in *Phrygian* = *Onun, Anın* "his, her" in *Turkic*.
- Demonstrative pronouns:
  - *Si, Sa, Sos* "this" in *Phrygian* = *So, Şu* "this" in *Turkic*.
  - *Min* "this" in *Phrygian* = *Mına* "this" in *Turkic*.
- Interrogative pronouns:
  - *Ios* "who" in *Phrygian* = *Ös* "who" in *Turkic*.
- Generalizing pronouns:
  - *Beret* "all, everything" in *Phrygian* = *Bəri, Barı* "all, everything" in *Turkic*.
  - *Par* "all" in *Phrygian* and *Turkic*.
  - *Panta* "whole, all, every" in *Phrygian* = *Bütün* "whole, all, every" in *Turkic*.
- Indefinite pronouns:
  - *Ios* "whoever, anyone" in *Phrygian* = *Ös* "whoever, anyone" in *Turkic*.
  - *Ni* "whatever, any" in *Phrygian* and *Turkic*.

CONJUNCTIONS.

30. *Phrygian* and *Turkic* conjunctions can link homogenous parts of a sentence by following them.

Usually, in *IE,* it is customary for a conjunction to stand between the words that it connects. However, that is not always the case in both *Phrygian* and *Turkic*. A *Phrygian* conjunction *Ke* "and" (similar to the *Turkic De, Də, Da* "and") connects homogeneous substantives by following them instead of being between them:

- deos: zemelos: ke: titetikmenos: eitou. (Phr.)
- diyü: sımıl: da: titilmiş: etər. (Turk.)
- deities: people: and: torn into pieces: do will.
- "will be torn into pieces by the deities and people".

31. A conjunction can be both coordinating and adverbial in *Phrygian* and *Turkic*.

The coordinating conjunction *Ke* "and" in *Phrygian* and *Da* "and" in *Turkic* can also assume the function of the adverbial conjunction with the meaning "in return":
- *Bas: ioi: bekos: me: bere[t] at: tie: <u>ke:</u> tittetikm[e]nos: eitou.* (*Phr.*)
- Basau: anın: boğuzı: me: bəri: ət: tanrı: <u>da:</u> titilmiş: etər. (*Turk.*)
- Cropland: his/her: bread: and: everything to a fault: *Zeus*: <u>in return:</u> torn into pieces: will make.
- "<u>In return</u>, his/her cropland, bread, and everything to a fault will be torn into pieces by *Zeus*."

- *<u>Da</u> kılar kləştorlar yat tənrilərə ki tanır.* [R.2.2.1532] in *Turkic*.
- "<u>In return,</u> s/he will worship foreign gods that s/he knows."

32. Both *Phrygian* and *Turkic* conjunction *Me* "and" can begin a sentence or a clause.

The conjunction *Me*, standing at the beginning of a sentence or a clause, bears the meaning "and", "then", "in return":
- *Knoumane: kaken: addaket: <u>me:</u> zemelos: ke: deos: ke: titetikmenos: eitou.* (*Phr.*)
- Kon mana: kek: kılat: <u>me:</u> sımıl: da: tın: da: titilmiş: etər. (*Turk.*)
- Enclosed place of rest to: harm: do will: <u>then:</u> people: both: deities: and: tormented: do will.
- "[Whoever] does harm to the enclosed place of rest, <u>then</u> both people and gods will torment him/her."

- *<u>Me</u> boldı qamuq tilədi.* (*Turk.*)
- "<u>Then</u> everything appeared as he wanted." [Dr.Sl.340]

33. *Phrygian* conjunctions can create correlative structures *Ke...ke* "Both...and", *Me...me* "Both...and", "Then...and", similar to the *Turkic* ones – *Da...da, Də...də* "Both...and", *Me...me* "Both...and", "Then...and".

- *Knoumane: kaken: addaket: me: <u>zemelos: ke: deos: ke:</u> titetikmenos: eitou.* (*Phr.*)
- Kon mana: kek: kılat: me: <u>sımıl: da: tın: da:</u> titilmiş: etər. (*Turk.*)
- Enclosed place of rest to: harm: do will: then: <u>people: both: deities: and:</u> tormented: do will.
- "[Whoever] does harm to the enclosed place of rest, then <u>both people and deities</u> will torment him/her."

- *Ios: ni se: moun: knoumane: kakoun: addaket: <u>me: ddeo: me: zemelos:</u> titetikmenos: eitou.* (*Phr.*)
- Ös: nersə: mına: kon mana: kek: kılat: <u>me: tın: me: sımıl:</u> titilmiş: etər. (*Turk.*)
- Whoever: the living: this: enclosed place of rest to: harm: do will: <u>then: god: and: people:</u> torn up into pieces: do will.
- "Whoever in existence harms this enclosed place of rest, <u>then god and people</u> will tear him/her to pieces."

In this example, the conjunction *Me* "and" starts a clause, bearing the meaning "then" in *Phrygian* and *Turkic*.

The *IE* languages also have similar constructions. However, one crucial fact sets both *Phrygian* and *Turkic* apart from them – these correlative conjunctions, such as *Ke...ke,* follow a word, not precede it.

34. The conjunctions can act as conjunctive adverbs.

    Both the *Phrygian* conjunctions *Ke, Me* "and" and the *Turkic* conjunctions *Da, Də* "and" can act as conjunctive adverbs "too", "then":

    - *Me: ddeo: me: zemelos: titetikmenos: eitou: as: batan: orouenan: ke. (Phr.)*
    - *Me: tın: me: sımıl: titilmiş: etər: anı: bata: ornın: da. (Turk.)*
    - And: god: and: people: torn up into pieces: do will: him/her: destroy will: place his/her: too.
    - "Whoever in existence harms this enclosed place of rest, then god and people will tear him/her to pieces, destroy his/her place, too."

    - *Aini: kos: se: moun: knoumanei: kakoun: addaket: aini: manka: be[k]os: ioi: me: totoss: Euge: sarnan. (Phr.)*
    - *Ya: kəs: se: mına: kon mana: kek: kılat: ya: maŋküyə: boğuz[ını]: onı: me: tutaşı: Egə: sərinə. (Turk.)*
    - Or: whoever: this very: enclosed place of rest: harm: will do: or stele: bread: his/her: then: forever: God: will block.
    - "Or whoever does harm to this enclosed place of rest or stele, then God will block his/her livelihood (bread) forever."

POSTPOSITIONS.

35. Absence of prepositions in *Phrygian* and *Turkic.*

    Both in *Phrygian* and *Turkic*, prepositions do not exist. Postpositions replace them. Similar to kin *Turkic* languages, *Phrygian* has two kinds of postpositions – independent and dependent.
    An independent postposition follows a word it governs instead of standing in front of it as *IE* prepositions do:
    - *Eledriai > Əyləndərə* "around" in *Turkic.*
    - *Sk Eledriai* - "around tomb" (literally, "tomb around") in *Phrygian (Sk > Süki* 'tomb' + *Əyləndərə* 'around' in *Turkic).*

    A dependent postposition in *Phrygian* and *Turkic* functions as an affix attached to a noun it governs. Most if not all the *IE* languages exhibit dissimilar behavior (rare exceptions can apply, such as *Westward* in *English),* as in all of the languages of this group, prepositions govern and lead a noun. The following affixes, acting as postpositions, were observed in *Phrygian* – *-Ton, -Tin, -Dan* "from" and in *Turkic -Tən, -Dən, -Dan* "from", as well as *-I* "to, towards" in *Phrygian* and *-Yə, -A* "to, towards" in *Turkic:*

    - *Nevotan* "from a grandchild" in *Phrygian (Nevo > Nəvə* 'grandchild' + *Tan > -Tən* 'a *Turkic* affix, equivalent to the preposition *From*' in *Turkic);*
    - *Nəvədən* "from a grandchild" in *Turkic (Nəvə* 'grandchild' + *-Dən* 'an affix, equivalent to the preposition *From*').
    - *Areyastin* "from *Arias*" in *Phrygian (Areyas > Arias* 'an island name' + *Tin > -Tın* 'a *Turkic* affix, denoting a preposition *From*' in *Turkic).*

- *Upsodan* "from the top" in *Phrygian* (*Upso* > *Uca* 'top, high' + *-Dan* 'an affix, equivalent to the preposition *From*' in *Turkic*).
- *Manka* "to the surrounding" in *Phrygian* = *Manga* "to the surrounding" in *Turkic* (*Mank* > *Mang* 'a surrounding' + *-A* 'an affix, equivalent to the preposition *To*' in *Turkic*).
- *Mankai* "towards/to a stele" in *Phrygian* = *Maŋküyə* "towards/to a stele" in *Turkic* (*Manka* > *Maŋkü* 'stele' + *-I* > *-Yə* 'an affix, equivalent to the prepositions *To, Towards*' in *Turkic*).
- *Knoumanei* "to the enclosed resting place" in *Phrygian* (*Knou* > *Kon* 'place of rest, resting place' + *Mane* > *Man* 'enclosed place' + *-I* > *-A* 'an affix, equivalent to the preposition *To, Towards*' in *Turkic*).

SYNTAX.

36. Free syntactic order both in *Phrygian* and *Turkic*.

In *IE*, basic declarative sentences typically have the structure subject–verb–object (SVO). Both in *Phrygian* and *Turkic*, subjects, objects, and verbs have a free-for-all right to roam around in a sentence in any order. Aside from the usual SVO structure, in both languages, a subject can come after the main verb; an object can stand in front of the modifying verb; a pronoun can follow the object it modifies:

- *tetiokmenos: eitou: dios: ke: zemelos: ke: par: tes.* (Phr.)
- torn into pieces: do will: deities: and: people: and: all: spirit.

- *zeira: ke: oip eis: ke: tittetikmena: at: tie: adeittnou.* (Phr.)
- mind: and: house-property: and: torn into pieces: his/her: Zeus: do will.

- *Da: karğadım: ornun: anın.* (Turk.)
- And: I cursed: place: his/her. (verbatim)
- "And I cursed his place." [R.1.2.1058]

However, there are exceptions to the rule in *Phrygian* and *Turkic*: an adjective can rarely if ever come after the modifying noun unless it converts into a verb by affixation. Compare:
- *Phrygian*: *Meka Tie* "all-praised *Zeus*".
- *Turkic*: *Mak Tin* "all-praised God".

By the way, in *Persian* and *French*, an adjective always follows a noun it modifies.

PHONETICS.

37. Consonant and vowel harmony in *Phrygian* and *Turkic*.

The words in a sentence are subject to vowel harmony and consonant change in *Turkic*. The same situation is observed in *Phrygian*.
For instance, nouns in the dative case are formed with the help of the affixes that depend on the preceding consonant or vowel to use the appropriate one. If a noun ends in the consonant *K*, the dative case ending will be *-A*. If a substantive has the vowels *A, E* at the end, then it takes the termination *-I*, equivalent to the *Turkic -Yə*:

- *Manka* "to the surrounding" in *Phrygian* = *Manga* "to the surrounding" in *Turkic* (*Mank* > *Mang* 'a surrounding' + *-A* 'an affix, equivalent to the preposition *To*').

- *Mankai* "towards/to a stele" in *Phrygian* = *Maŋküyə* "towards/to a stele" in *Turkic* (*Manka* > *Maŋkü* 'stele' + *-I* > *-Yə* 'an affix, equivalent to the prepositions *To, Towards*').
- *Knoumanei* "to the enclosed resting place" in *Phrygian* (*Knou* > *Kon* 'place of rest, resting place' + *Mane* > *Man* 'enclosed place' + *-I* > *-A* 'an affix, equivalent to the preposition *To, Towards*').

To sum this all up, it is important to add that many *Phrygian* texts contained either a *Greek* passage, sentence, or loanwords. However, it will be futile to seek the kinship of *Phrygian* and *Greek*. Taking aside the fact that even the written mode was incompatible: the *Phrygian* text is sinistroverse, while the *Greek* one is dextroverse, the difference between *Greek* and *Phrygian* was so deep that the ancient *Greek* and *Latin* authors related *Phrygian* to "barbarian" *Thracian*:

> "The original language of the *Phrygians* must have been *Thracian*, as they came from *Thrace*. But *Thracian* was regarded as a barbarian dialect by the *Greeks*, and so was the *Phrygian*. *Demosthenes*, in his oration "de Corona," reproaches *Æschines* with using barbarous *Phrygian* exclamations; and how different the *Thracian* was from the *Greek* may be seen from *Ovid's Tristia*, from the works of *Lucian*, and even from *Ammianus Marcellinus*, who says that in ancient times the *Thracians* followed barbarian customs and used a variety of barbarian dialects. *Dio Cassius* also draws a distinction between *Thracian* and *Greek*. *Lucian* also speaks of *Thracian* as being as different a language from *Greek* as *Persian, Scythian,* or *Celtic*. "By *Jupiter*," says *Hermes*, "everybody does not understand *Greek*; I too am not a polyglot, nor do I speak nor understand *Scythian, Persian, Thracian,* nor *Celtic*." That the *Phrygian* tongue was not a dialect of the *Greek* may be seen from what *Herodotus* records, that the *Egyptians* regarded the *Phrygians* as a more ancient people than themselves."
> ["The Theatre of *St. Paul's* Activity." The *Dublin* University Magazine. 75.505-506]

§11-4-3. THE PHRYGIAN TRIBES:
THE BERECYNTES, CERBESII, PELOPONNESIANS, DORIANS, LEUCADIANS, LACEDEMONIANS, ARMENIANS.

Initially known as the *Briges*, or *Bruges*, the *Phrygians* were considered much more ancient than the *Trojans*. *Herodotus* noted their close resemblance to another *Trojan* nation – the *Paphlagonians*:

> "The dress of the *Phrygians* closely resembled the *Paphlagonian*, only in a very few points differing from it. According to the *Macedonian* account, the *Phrygians*, during the time that they had their abode in *Europe* and dwelt with them in *Macedonia*, bore the name of *Brigians*;[61] but on their removal to *Asia* they changed their designation at the same time with their dwelling-place." [7.73]

As mentioned in the chapter about the *Paphlagonians*, the latter wore helmets, resembling tiaras of the *Medes*, and the native boots, similar to the *Scythian* footwear, reaching halfway to the knee. *Strabo* was in agreement with *Herodotus* about the old names of the *Phrygians*:

---

[61] In the original *Greek* text, it is Βρίγες = Briges.

> "Thus also *Brygi*, *Briges*, and *Phryges*[62] are the same people." [12.3.20]

and also constated that

> "The accounts respecting the *Phrygians* and the *Mysians* are more ancient than the *Trojan* times." [Idem. 12.8.4]

> "But when the *Phrygians* passed over from *Thrace,* and put to death the chief of *Troy* and of the country near it, they settled here, but the *Mysians* established themselves above the sources of the *Caicus* near *Lydia*." [Idem. 12.8.4]

Interestingly, a *Phrygian* city *Ankyra* (the capital of modern *Turkey* – *Ankara*) was found by the world-famous *Phrygian* king *Midas*, who according to *St. Jerome,* reigned in *Phrygia* in 1310 BCE:

> "Now this people occupied the country on the farther side of the river *Sangarius* capturing *Ancyra*, a city of the *Phrygians*, which *Midas* son of *Gordius* had founded in former time. And the anchor, which *Midas* found, was even as late as my time in the sanctuary of *Zeus*, as well as a spring called the *Spring of Midas*, water from which they say *Midas* mixed with wine to capture *Silenus*." [*Pausanias*. 1.4.5]

Though the *Phrygians* were not the derivatives of the *Trojans,* they were related to each other nevertheless – both being a *Thrace-Pelasgian* nation of the *Scythian* roots and *Turkic* blood. The *Asiatic* origin of the *Thracians* was indirectly exposed by *Strabo* when he affirmed the *Asiatic* nature of the *Thracian* music [10.3.17]. Thuswise, the *Phrygians,* being a part of the *Thracian* nation, were not *Indo-Europeans*, though they were among the first nations, if not the first to populate *Europe* and from there went back to their *Asiatic* roots – to *Asia Minor*. There the *Phrygians* put a stake in the *Trojan* ground and established their country *Phrygia* under the auspices of the *Trojan* king, as it was deduced from the words of the heroic warrior *Achilles* to the king of *Troy Priam* in *Homer's* "The Iliad":

> "…your riches formerly consisted in what *Lesbos*, the city of *Macar,* contained, and *Phrygia* above it and the vast *Hellespont*." [*Strabo*. 13.1.8]

And this was an additional reason (besides the fact that King *Priam's* wife *Hecuba* had a *Phrygian* origin) why the *Phrygians*, under the leadership of their heroes *Ascanius* and *Phorcys,* came to defend the *Trojan* land from the *Greco-Danaan* army. By the way, the name *Ascanius* and its cognate *Ascania* as the name of the country, lake, and river were characteristic to both the *Phrygians* and the *Mysians,* according to *Strabo:*

> "But as far as we are able to conjecture, we may place *Mysia* between *Bithynia* and the mouth of the *Aesepus*, contiguous to the sea, and nearly along the whole of *Olympus*. Around it, in the interior, is the *Epictetus,* nowhere reaching the sea, and extending as far as the eastern parts of the *Ascanian* lake and district, for both bear the same name. Part of this territory was *Phrygian*, and part *Mysian;* the *Phrygian* was further distant from *Troy;* and so we must understand the words of the poet, when he says, "*Phorcys*, and the god-like *Ascanius,* were the leaders of the *Phryges* far from *Ascania,*" that is, the *Phrygian Ascania;* for the other, the *Mysian Ascania,* was nearer to the present *Nicaea*, which he mentions, when he says, "*Palmys, Ascanius,* and *Morys,* sons of *Hippotion*, the leader of the *Mysi,* fighting in close combat, who came from the fertile soil of *Ascania,* as auxiliaries." It is not then surprising that he should speak of an *Ascanius,* a

---

[62] "Βρῦγοι καὶ Βρύγες καὶ Φρύγες" in the original *Greek* text.

leader of the *Phrygians,* who came from *Ascania,* and of an *Ascanius,* a leader of the *Mysians,* coming also from *Ascania,* for there is much repetition of names derived from rivers, lakes, and places." [12.4.5-6]

This is not just a coincidence that the root of the words *Ascania, Ascanius* derives its origin from the *Turkic* words *As* 'the *As* tribe' and *Can* 'blood' with the self-explanatory meaning – "of the *As* blood". Let us not forget the statement by *Herodotus* about whom the continent of *Asia* owes its name to – the nation of the *As* that used to inhabit the *Trojan* capital *Sardis.* And it is no wonder to find out that the name of the *Phrygian* nation and its derivative tribes came from the *Turkic* source:

➤ *Phryges* = Φρύγες, aka *Fruks* = Φρύξ, aka *Brugoi* = Βρῦγοι, aka *Bruges* = Βρύγες, aka *Briges* = Βρίγες > *Berik* "strong, firm" in *Turkic.* By assertion of *Strabo,* the *Phrygians* had many cognate tribes, including the *Berecyntes* and the *Cerbesii:*
> "But the *Berecyntes,* a tribe of *Phrygians,* the *Phrygians* in general, and the *Trojans,* who live about *Mount Ida,* themselves also worship *Rhea,* and perform orgies in her honour; they call her mother of gods, *Agdistis,* and *Phrygia,* the Great Goddess." [10.3.13]

➤ *Berécyntes,* aka *Berékuntes* = Βερέκυντες: *Beréc, Berék* > *Berík* 'strong, firm' + *Yn* > *Ün* 'fame' + *Tes* > *-Tı* 'an affix, equivalent to the word *Having',* meaning "having strong, fast-paced fame" in *Turkic.* By the time of *Strabo,* neither *Berecyntes* nor *Cerbesii* existed any longer:
> "The names of some *Phrygian* tribes, as the *Berecyntes* and *Cerbesii,* are mentioned, which no longer exist. And *Alcman* says, "He played the *Cerbesian,* a *Phrygian* air." They speak also of a *Cerbesian* pit which sends forth destructive exhalations; this however exists, but the people have no longer the name of *Cerbesii.*" [12.8.21]

➤ *Cerbesii,* aka *Kerbesioi* = Κερβήσιοι: *Cer, Ker* > *Kər* 'crucify' + *Bes* > *Bas* 'destroy', meaning "tribe that kills by crucifying its foes" in *Turkic.*

➤ *Peloponnesian,* aka *Peloponnesioi* = Πελοποννήσιοι: *Pelopon* '*Pelop's*' (*Pelop* + *On* > *-Un, -In* 'an affix, denoting possession' in *Turkic*) + *Nesos* 'island' in *Greek,* meaning "*Pelop's* island". The name of the nation was acquired after the *Phrygian* founder of the island *Peloponnesus* – *Pelop,* aka *Pelops* (Πέλοψ), who had the name of *Turkic* origin:
$$Pelop > Pil \text{ 'rule'} + Op \text{ 'seize'}.$$
Judging by the name of the island and this *Phrygian* nation, it gets clear that the actual name of their founder was *Pelop,* not *Pelops.* Otherwise, it should have been *Pelopsonnesus,* not *Peloponnesos* (Πελοπόννησος). Moreover, the affix *-On* added to the name in *Pelopon* openly marks its *Turkic* pedigree. This is a screaming indication that the first portion of the name was preserved according to the *Turkic* grammatical rule of affixation, while the second one – the *Greek* part (*Nesos*), was simply added to it. It also explains the existence of two *N-s* in the name:
$$Pelopon > Pelopın \text{ '}Pelop's\text{'} + Nesos \text{ 'island'}.$$
Strabo indicated that a colony of the *Phrygians* was brought by their leader *Pelops* to a new country that received his name – the *Peloponnesos,* or *Peloponnesus:*
> "For *Pelops* brought colonists from *Phrygia* into the *Peloponnesus,* which took his name." [7.7.1]

As attested by *St. Jerome, Pelops* reigned the *Peloponnesus* for 59 years from 1397 BCE. Intriguingly, *Pindar* acknowledged *Pelops* as a *Lydian:*

> "The lord of *Syracuse,* whose courses' fame
> Shines in the land where *Lydian Pelops* came,
> New home to found – *Pelops,* of ocean's king,
> *Poseidon,* loved – whom *Clotho* drew from out the laver's cleansing dew

With ivory shoulder glistening." [Translated by *F.D. Morice*. O.1.25]

However, this was not a mistake. The *Lydians* and the *Phrygians* were kindred *Trojan* nations, a part of the greater *Thrace-Scythian* family. And this was acknowledged by some ancient scholars, such as *Sophocles*, who considered *Lydia* and *Troy* to be *Phrygia*:

"For some writers transfer this quarrel, *Sophocles*, for example, to *Cilicia*, which he, following the custom of tragic poets, calls *Pamphylia*, just as he calls *Lycia* "*Caria*" and *Troy* and *Lydia* "*Phrygia*."" [*Strabo*. 14.5.16]

The kurgan-building culture was inherent to the *Phrygians* as well. This is an additional fact connecting the *Phrygians* with the *Thracians*, the *Scythians*, and the *Turkic* nations. There is still a tumulus standing in honor of the *Phrygian* king *Midas* in the territory of modern *Turkey*.

Pausanias took a note of this ancient funeral tradition of burying the dead in grave mounds when mentioning a story about *Pelops*:

"There is also a story that *Pelops* made here an empty mound in honor of *Myrtilus*, and sacrificed to him in an effort to calm the anger of the murdered man, naming the mound *Taraxippus* (Frightener of horses) because the mares of *Oenomaus* were frightened by the trick of *Myrtilus*." [6.20.17]

- *Dorians*, aka *Doriees* = Δωριέες, aka *Pelasgi*, aka *Pelasgoi* = Πελασγοί, aka *Argives*, aka *Argivus*, aka *Argeioi* = Ἀργεῖοι:

  - *Doriees* > *Dor* "clan, dynasty" in *Turkic*. After the *Phrygians* got a new denomination – the *Peloponnesians*, they later renamed themselves into the *Dorians*. According to *Herodotus*,

    "The *Dorians* of *Asia* furnish'd thirty ships; and as they were *Peloponnesians* by descent, appeared in all points, arm'd like the *Grecians*." [7.93]

  - *Pelasgi*, *Pelasgoi*: *Pelas* > *Pilis* 'knowledge' + *Gi*, *Goi* > -*Gə* 'an affix, converting a noun into a verb', meaning "teach, provide knowledge" in *Turkic*. Besides being of *Phrygian* and *Peloponnesian* extraction, the *Dorians* were considered to belong to the *Pelasgian* family, who also were the *Thracians*, and by default, the *Scythians*. *Herodotus* detected the connection between the *Pelasgians*, the *Dorians*, and the *Lacedemonians*:

    "…the *Lacedemonians* and *Athenians* were the principal nations of *Greece*, the first being of *Dorian*, and the other of *Ionian* descent. They were in ancient time esteem'd the most considerable, when they went under the names of *Pelasgians* and *Hellenians*…" [1.56]

    The *Pelasgi* were also known under numerous other names that they acquired after the names of new leaders who set out new colonies, such as the *Argive*, the *Arcadians*, the *Lacedaemonians*, the *Turrenians*, the *Etruscans*, the *Tusci*, the *Pæonians*, or *Paiones*. For the sake of avoiding the repetition, we are not going to provide further discourse about the *Pelasgi* here, as a separate chapter devoted to this fascinating nation along with its numerous derivatives follows shortly.

  - *Argives*, *Argivus*, *Argeioi* > *Argos* (Ἄργος): *Ar* 'warrior, man, hero' + *Gos* > *Qos*, *Qus* 'erupt, disgorge', meaning "the one who produces warriors" in *Turkic*. Both the region *Argos*, or *Argeia*, and the nation of the *Argives*, aka the *Arcadians*, acquired their corresponding names after the *Pelasgian* hero *Argos*, aka *Argus*:

    "But *Argus* received the kingdom and called the *Peloponnese* after himself *Argos*; and having married *Evadne*, daughter of *Strymon* and *Neaera*, he begat *Ecbasus*, *Piras*, *Epidaurus*, and *Criasus*, who also succeeded to the kingdom."
    [*Apollodorus*. "Library." 2.1.2]

    By the way, there is a popular *Turkish* name *Erdogan* that by its structure and meaning "the one who produces warriors" matches the name of *Argos*, or *Argus*:

$$Argos > Ar + Gos$$
$$Erdogan > Er + Doğan$$

In line with the general testimony of antiquity, *Argos*, previously known as the *Peloponnesus*, was originally inhabited by the *Pelasgians*. *Homer* called it "pasture-land of horses" [2.3.75], *Pausanias* named it "horse-breeding *Argos*" [9.36.7], and *Euripides* appealed to it as "*Argos*, city of *Pelasgia*" ["*Phoenissae*." 250] and "city of horses" ["*Orestes*." 1598].

➤ <u>*Leukadioi* = Λευκάδιοι, aka *Leucadians*:</u> *Leuká, Leucá* > *Loká* 'wanderer, vagabond' + *Ad* 'walk', meaning "wandering vagrant" in *Turkic*. This *Dorian* tribe added a new connotation to its name to showcase its free-spirited nature. *Herodotus* confirmed the *Dorian* heritage of the *Leucadians*:
> "The *Megarians* furnished the same complement as at *Artermision*; the *Amprakiots* came to the assistance of the rest with seven ships, and the *Leucadians* with three, these being by race *Dorians* from *Corinth*." [8.45]

➤ <u>*Lacedaemonians*, aka *Lakedaimónioi* = Λακεδαιμόνιοι, aka *Lacedemonians*, aka *Spartans*, aka *Spartiatai* = Σπαρτιαται:</u>
  o *Lakedaimónioi, Lacedaemonians, Lacedemonians*: *Lace, Lake* > *Leke,Ləkə* 'stain' + *Daemon, Demon, Daimon* > *Dəymiyən* 'untouchable' (*Dae, Dai* > *Dəy* 'touch' + *M* > *-Mi* 'an affix, denoting negation' + *On* > *-Yən* 'an affix, denoting constant action', meaning "spotless, stain-free" (literally, "the one that stain does not touch") in *Turkic*. The word-formation principle with a noun followed by a participle, observed in this name, certifies its *Turkic* background. There is a multitude of *Turkic* words constructed on this lexical principle. Compare:
    ▪ *Lake* + *Daimon* = *Lakedaimon*.
    ▪ *Lakə aparmayan* "the one that does not remove a stain".
    ▪ *Lakə aparan* "the one that removes a stain".
    ▪ *Lakə tutan* "the one that gets a stain".

  o *Spartiatai, Spartans*: *Sparti, Sparta* > *Sparta* 'female name' + *At* 'glory', meaning "glory of *Sparta*" in *Turkic*. *Sparta* (*Sp* > *Səp* 'love' + *Arta* 'live in abundance', meaning "love and live in abundance" in *Turkic*) was the name of the *Pelasgian* princess *Sparta* who also had blood ties to the *Trojan* nation of the *Leleges*, as her great-grandfather *Leleges* (Λέλεγες), or *Lelex*, was the one who founded it.
  The *Turkic* people also were not strangers when it came to naming their tribes in honor of a female. For instance, there were *Turkic* tribes that survived until the 20th c. under the appellation of the *Kankis* (Xankıs) "daughter of a *Khan*", the *Yilkisi* (Yılkısı) "daughter of the nation".[63]
  Testified by *Herodotus* as having the *Dorio-Pelasgian* lineage, the *Lacedaemonians* and their land were named after their king *Lacedaemon*. According to the legend, his mother was a mountain nymph *Taygete*, aka *Taygetes* (*Taugetes*=Ταϋγέτης: *Tau* 'mountain' + *Get* > *Ket, Kət* "mighty" in *Turkic*) and his father was *Zeus*:
  > "Having no male issue, he left the kingdom to *Lacedaemon*, whose mother was *Taygete*, after whom the mountain was named, while according to report his father was none other than *Zeus*." [*Pausanias*. 3.1.2]

  Lacedaemon married *Sparta*, a daughter of the *Pelasgian* king *Eurotas* whose grandfather was *Lelex*, after whom the *Leleges* got their appellation:
  > "*Lacedaemon* was wedded to *Sparta*, a daughter of *Eurotas*. When he came to the throne, he first changed the names of the land and its inhabitants, calling them after himself, and next he founded and named after his wife a city, which even down to our own day has been called *Sparta*." [Idem. 3.1.2]

---

[63] *Uraksin Z.G.* "Bashkirsko-russkiy slovar." [860, 863].

> "After the figures of *Hermes* we reach *Laconia* on the west. According to the tradition of the *Lacedaemonians* themselves, *Lelex*, an aboriginal was the first king in this land, after whom his subjects were named *Leleges*. *Lelex* had a son *Myles*, and a younger one *Polycaon*. *Polycaon* retired into exile, the place of this retirement and its reason I will set forth elsewhere. On the death of *Myles* his son *Eurotas* succeeded to the throne. He led down to the sea by means of a trench the stagnant water on the plain, and when it had flowed away, as what was left formed a river-stream, he named it *Eurotas*." [Idem. 3.1.1]

As we remember, this *Thracian* nation of the *Leleges* was directly related to the *Carians, Lydians* (*Asii, Turreni, Etrusci*), *Mysians* (*Getae, Bithynians, Thyni, Olympians*), and the *Locrians*. *Strabo* classified the *Leleges* as the 3rd *Trojan* dynasty. This assertion categorically and unconditionally solidifies the argument that the *Spartans* and the *Lacedaemonians* were the *Pelasgians* of the *Thracian* extraction with straight ties to other *Trojan* nations. They were recognized as the *Greeks* due to their citizenship, not ethnicity. The *Pelasgian* lineage of the *Lacedaemonians* was also strongly supported by *Herodotus*:

> "…the *Lacedemonians* and *Athenians* were the principal nations of *Greece*, the first being of *Dorian*, and the other of *Ionian* descent. They were in ancient time esteem'd the most considerable, when they went under the names of *Pelasgians* and *Hellenians*; of which the latter constantly continued in one country, while the former very often chang'd their seat." [1.56]

Similar to the *Etruscans,* or the *Turrenians,* as well as many *Turkic* people, the *Spartans* highly respected females who controlled many aspects of their society, as *Aristotle* pointed it out:

> "For it appears that the original teller of the legend had good reason for uniting *Ares* with *Aphrodite,* for all men of martial spirit appear to be attracted to the companionship either of male associates or of women. Hence this characteristic existed among the *Spartans,* and in the time of their empire many things were controlled by the women; yet what difference does it make whether the women rule or the rulers are ruled by the women?" ["Politics". 1269b.25]

Going back to *Herodotus*, we need to note that the historian exposed a critical point to be discussed further. As we see, the leading nations of *Greece* were the *Lacedaemonians* and the *Athenians*. None of them were originally *Greek*, as both of them were of *Pelasgian* extraction. According to *Dionysius of Halicarnassus*, the *Dorians* and the *Ionians* spoke the same language with a slight difference in words:

> "There is little difference in their language, and they still borrow many words from one another, like the *Ionians* and *Dorians*." ["*Roman* Antiquities." 1.28]

Herodotus was one of the first to point to the language spoken by the *Pelasgi* (aka the *Dorians*, who were the *Phrygians*), which was foreign to *Greek:*

> "What language however the *Pelasgians* used to speak I am not able with certainty to say. But if one must pronounce judging by those that still remain of the *Pelasgians* who dwelt in the city of *Creston* above the *Tyrsenians*, and who were once neighbours of the race now called *Dorian*, dwelling then in the land which is now called *Thessaliotis,* and also by those that remain of the *Pelasgians* who settled at *Plakia* and *Skylake* in the region of the *Hellespont,* who before that had been settlers with the *Athenians,* and of the natives of the various other towns which are really *Pelasgian*, though they have lost the name, if one must pronounce judging by these, the *Pelasgians* used to speak a Barbarian language." [1.57]

The *Dorians* are the connecting link that puts the *Phrygians* and the *Pelasgi* under one roof, as the *Dorians* derive their origin from both of these kindred nations.

Meanwhile, *Herodotus* clearly related the well-forgotten truth about the *Ionians*, aka *Iones*, who were originally the *Pelasgians:*

"When the *Pelasgians* possess'd those countries, which now go by the name of *Greece*, the *Athenians* were called *Cranian Pelasgians*. Under the reign of *Cecrops*, they had the name of *Cecropians;* which in the time of their king *Erechtheus*, they changed for that of *Athenians*, and lastly were named *Ionians* from *Ion*, the son of *Xuthus*, who was their general." [8.44]

"Now the *Ionians*, so long time as they dwelt in the *Peloponnese*, in the land which is now called *Achaia*, and before the time when *Danaos* and *Xuthos* came to the *Peloponnese*, were called, as the *Hellenes* report, *Pelasgians* of the coast-land, and then *Ionians* after *Ion* the son of *Xuthos*." [Idem. 7.94]

As we see, both the *Dorians* and the *Ionians* belonged on the same *Pelasgian* stock. Furthermore, there was one nation, which was considered to be the colony of both the *Ionians* and the *Dorians* – the *Hellespontii*, aka *Hellespontins*, aka *Ellespontioi* = Ἑλλησπόντιοι:

"All the *Hellespontins* (except the *Abydenians*, who were ordered by the king to stay at home for the guard of the bridges) furnished one hundred sail; and being colonies of the *Ionians* and *Dorians*, appeared in *Grecian* arms." [Idem. 7.95]

This very nation of the *Hellespontins* had one more appellation – the *Olympenoi*, which was none other than an offshoot of the *Thracian* nation of the *Leleges*, known as the *Mysians*, who later went under the name of the *Bithynians* and the *Thyni*, acknowledged as a colony of the *Thracians* [*Strabo*. 12.4.10].

If we take into account the similarity of the *Phrygian* and *Pelasgian* languages, justice will be served by giving the *Phrygians* a surname – *Pelasgians*.

The *Phrygians* had one more derivative tribe, called the *Armenians*, that populated the land of *Armenia*. To prevent any confusion, it is important to note that these ancient *Armenians* have nothing to do with the modern *Armenians*.

> *Armenians*, aka *Armenioi* = Ἀρμένιοι: *Ar* 'warrior' + *Men* 'I', meaning "I am a warrior" in *Turkic*. The names of the nation *Armenians*, aka *Armenioi*, the male name *Armenus*, and the country of *Armenia* have a pure *Turkic* origin. Furthermore, both in ancient *Greek* (except for the termination *-Oi*) and in the *Turkic* languages, even nowadays, the names look similar:
>   *Armenioi* – in *Greek*.
>   *Ermeni* – in *Turkish*.
>   *Ermәni* – in *Azerbaijani*.
> There are plenty of *Turkic* ethnonyms built on the same word construction principle. Moreover, the same pattern is observed in the names of some *Scythian, Sarmatian, Germanic,* and *Paphlagonian* tribes. Compare:
> - *Armenioi* > *Ar* + *Men* (a *Phrygian* tribe).
> - *Turkmen, Turkman* > *Turk* + *Men, Man* (a *Turkic* nation in *Central Asia*).
> - *Turkoman* > *Turko* + *Man* (a *Turkic* nation in *Syria*).
> - *Ottoman* > *Otto* + *Man* (a *Turkish* dynasty).
> - *Naiman* > *Nai* + *Man* (an ancient *Turkic* tribe of the *Uzbeks*).
> - *Burman* > *Bur* + *Man* (a *Turkic* tribe).
> - *Asmanoi* > *As* + *Man* (a *Scythian* tribe).
> - *Cicimeni* > *Cici* + *Men* (a *Sarmatian* tribe).
> - *German* > *Ger* + *Man* (a *Germanic* tribe).
> - *Alamanoi* > *Ala* + *Man* (a *Germanic* tribe).
> - *Markamanoi* > *Marka* + *Man* (a *Germanic* tribe).

- *Pylaemenes* > *Pylae* + *Men* (a *Trojan* tribe of the *Paphlagonian* branch).

As a side note, the ethnonym *Turkmen* (*Türkmən*) was formed from *Türk*=*Turk* + *Mən*=*Men*, meaning "I am a *Turk*". Mahmud Kashgari explained how this ethnicon was created and noted that the word *Türk*=*Turk* would remain unchanged both in singular and plural:

"They say: *Kim Sən*? 'Who are you?' and respond *Türk Mən* 'I am a *Turk*.'…*Türk* as the name of *Noah's* son is singular, but (when it denotes his offspring), it is a collective name…" [64]

["Divanü Lügat-it-Türk." ("The Corpus of the *Turkic* Lexicon.") 1.177]

By the way, this renowned *Turkic* linguist specified that the *Turkic* nations obtained their name after *Turk*, the son of the prophet *Noah*:

"*Türk* (*Turk*) – the name of *Noah's* son, may *Allah's* blessings be upon him. This is the name by which the almighty *Allah* called the progeny of *Turk*, the scion of *Noah*…

As we have said, *Türk* is the name bestowed (to *Turks*) by the almighty *Allah*. The esteemed Sheikh and Imam, *al-Husayn Ibn Khalaf al-Kashgari* told us that *Ibn al-Gharqi* had informed him…with his chain of transmitters going back to the Prophet, may *Allah* bless him and acknowledge, who said:

"*Allah*, glorious and almighty, declares, "I have an army that I named *Türk* and lodged in the East: when I get infuriated by any people, I give them (*Turks*) power over them.""

This is (why *Turks* have) superiority over all (other) humans, as the almighty and glorious *Allah* himself took the trouble to name them, situated them in the highest place on Earth with the fine climate and called them his own army. Additionally, they are endowed with beauty, decency, respect for elders, keeping their promises. Devoid of arrogance, haughtiness, they have courage deserving praise and (other commendable virtues) impossible to enumerate them all." [65] [Idem ibid.]

In ancient times, usually a tribe, a nation, as well as their land, town, country, rivers, and mountains they inhabited or conquered would obtain the names after their leaders. For instance, *Pelasgia* > *Pelias*, *Turrenia* > *Turrenus*, *Lydia* > *Lydus*, *Peloponnesus* > *Pelop*, *Persia* > *Persus* or his son *Perses*, *Europa* > *Europus*, *Media* > *Medea*, *Greece* > *Græcus*, *Troy* > *Tros*, *Turkey* > *Turk*, *Hayastan* > *Haik*; *Argive* > *Argos*, *Arcadians* > *Arcas*, *Achaneans* > *Achaeus*, *Phthiotis* > *Phthius*, *Lacedaemonians* > *Lacedaemon*, *Spartans* > *Sparta*, *Ionians* > *Ion*, and the like.

This was the case with *Armenia*. The latter owes its name to a *Pelasgian* man – *Armenos* = Ἄρμενος with the surname *Thessalian* (after the land of the *Pelasgians* – *Thessaly*), who originally hailed from the *Pelasgian* city of *Armenium*. According to *Strabo*, the *Armenians* as a nation and *Armenia* as a land acquired their denomination after the *Pelasgian Armenos*, or *Armenus*, who was one of the *Argonauts*:

"It is said that when *Jason*, accompanied by *Armenus* the *Thessalian*, undertook the voyage to the *Colchi*, they advanced as far as the *Caspian Sea*, and traversed *Iberia*, *Albania*, a great part of *Armenia*, and *Media*, as the *Jasoneia* and many other monuments testify. *Armenus*, they say, was a native of *Armenium*, one of the cities on the lake *Boebeis*, between *Pheræ* and *Parisa*, and that his companions settled in *Acilisene*, and the *Suspiritis*, and occupied the country as far as *Calachene* and *Adiabene*, and that he gave his own name to *Armenia*." [Strabo. 11.4.8]

The voyage of the *Argonauts* took place in 1265 BCE, as claimed by *St. Jerome*. This means that *Armenia* was named after *Armenos* in the 13th c. BCE.

Strabo specifically pointed out that *Armenium* was a *Thessalian* city – the city of the *Pelasgi*:

"There exists an ancient account of the origin of this nation to the following effect. *Armenus* of *Armenium*, a *Thessalian* city, which lies between *Pheræ* and *Larisa* on the lake *Bœbe*,

---

[64] The text was translated into *English* by the author of the present book.
[65] The excerpt was rendered into *English* by the author of the current work.

accompanied *Jason*, as we have already said, in his expedition into *Armenia*, and from *Armenus* the country had its name, according to *Cyrsilus the Pharsalian* and *Medius the Lariscæan*, persons who had accompanied the army of *Alexander*. Some of the followers of *Armenus* settled in *Acilisene*, which was formerly subject to the *Sopheni;* others in the *Syspiritis*, and spread as far as *Calachene* and *Adiabene*, beyond the borders of *Armenia*." [11.14.12]

For the colonies getting established on new lands, it was traditional to transfer the name of their native toponyms, oronyms, even ethnic names to a new place of habitation, as the *Thracians* did in *Troy*, for instance, a city called *Arisba* (Ἄρίσβα) in *Lesbos* and a river *Arisbos* (Ἄρισβος) in *Thrace;* the *Thracians* called *Skaioi* (Σκαιοί), a river *Skaios* (Σκαιός), a *Skaion* (Σκαιόν) wall in *Thrace*, and in *Troy, Skaiai* (Σκαιαί) gates; a river *Arisbos* in *Thrace* and *Arisbe* (Ἄρίσβη) in *Troja;* a river *Resos* (Ῥῆσος) in *Troja*, and *Resos*, a king of the *Thracians* [*Strabo*. 13.1.21]. This phenomenon would occur either out of nostalgic feelings or due to the resemblance of the natural environment. *Dionysius of Byzantium*, in his work "Anaplus of the *Bosporos*", shows a similar example:

"*Kanopos* is a name brought from *Egypt*, from the similarity of the life here. For a large river, permanent but not navigable, cuts to the sea, from which the name for the gulf." [29]

The similitude of nature was the cause of naming the river *Araxes*, too. *Strabo* noted that the river *Araxes* obtained its name from *Armenus* and his compatriots:

"It is supposed that *Armenus* and his companions called the *Araxes* by this name on account of its resemblance to the *Peneius*, for the *Peneius* had the name of *Araxes* from bursting through *Tempe*, and rending *Ossa* from *Olympus*. The *Araxes* also in *Armenia*, descending from the mountains, is said to have spread itself in ancient times, and to have overflowed the plains, like a sea, having no outlet; that *Jason*, in imitation of what is to be seen at *Tempe*, made the opening through which the water at present precipitates itself into the *Caspian Sea;* that upon this the *Araxenian* plain, through which the river flows to the cataract, became uncovered. This story which is told of the river *Araxes* contains some probability; that of *Herodotus* none whatever. For he says that, after flowing out of the country of the *Matiani*, it is divided into forty rivers, and separates the *Scythians* from the *Bactrians*." [11.14.13-14]

The river *Araxes* (Ἀράξης) is known nowadays as the river *Araks*, aka *Aras*, aka *Araz*, flowing along the borders of *Turkey, Azerbaijan, Armenia,* and *Iran:*

"The *Araxes*, after running to the east as far as *Atropatene*, makes a bend towards the west and north. It then first flows beside *Azara*, then by *Artaxata*, a city of the *Armenians;* afterwards it passes through the plain of *Araxenus* to discharge itself into the *Caspian Sea*." [Idem. 11.14.3]

From *Strabo's* testimony, the meaning of *Araxes* (*Araz, Aras, Araks*) becomes obvious as "an outlet cutting through a land".
Meanwhile, *Stephanus of Byzantium* defined the meaning of the name as "tear":

"Ἀράξης, ποταμὸς Ἀρμενίας. καὶ Θετταλίας· οὕτως γὰρ ὁ Πηνειὸς ἐκαλεῖτο ἐκ τοῦ ἀράξαι. τὸ τοπικόν Ἀράξιον ὕδωρ."
"*Araxes* – a river in *Armenia* and the other one in *Thessaly*, as that's how the *Pineios* was called – from the word *Araksai* "tear". The local meaning is "the *Araxian* water". [66]

---

[66] The translation into *English* was provided by the author of the present book.

As we see, the river was known both as *Araxes* and *Araksai* with the meaning "tear" and "the *Araxian* water".

The etymological analysis of these names reveals their pure *Turkic* origin:
- *Araxes* = Ἀράξης, Araks, Araz, Aras: *Ar* 'tear, split, cut through' [R.1.1.244] + *Axes, Aks, Az, As* > *Ağz, Auz, As* 'opening, outlet, passage' [R.1.1.179,180], meaning "outlet that cuts through" in *Turkic*.
- *Araksai* = Ἀράξαι: *Araks* '*Araxes*' + *Sai* 'river', meaning "the *Araxian* river" in *Turkic*. Radlov V.V. pointed out that the *Turkic* people would call any large flowing river *Sai* [4.1.219].

The second component of the name – *Aks* or *Axes* has several variants in *Turkic* languages – *Ağz, Auz, As, Ağız, Ağıs, Aus, Oz, Us*. As a result, the word *Araks* reflects a number of variations:
- *Araks* > *Ar* + *Ağz*
- *Araz* > *Ar* + *Auz*
- *Aras* > *Ar* + *As*

The *Thessalian Armenus* gave his name not only to the land and country of *Armenia* but also, by default, to its inhabitants – the *Armenians,* who were a *Pelasgian* colony of the *Phrygians*. Strabo also added that the *Armenians* were the descendants of the *Thessalian*, aka *Pelasgian, Jason*:

> "I have spoken of *Medeia* in the account of *Media,* and it is conjectured from all the circumstances that the *Medes* and *Armenians* are allied in some way to the *Thessalians,* descended from *Jason* and *Medeia*." [11.14.14]

The *Greek* geographer also underlined the fact that these *Armenians* would dress in accordance with the *Thessalian* traditions:

> "The dress of the *Armenian* people is said to be of *Thessalian* origin; such are the long tunics, which in tragedies are called *Thessalian;* they are fastened about the body with a girdle, and with a clasp on the shoulder. The tragedians, for they required some additional decoration of this kind, imitate the *Thessalians* in their attire. The *Thessalians* in particular, from wearing a long dress, (probably because they inhabit the most northerly and the coldest country in all *Greece,*) afforded the most appropriate subject of imitation to actors for their theatrical representations. The passion for riding and the care of horses characterize the *Thessalians,* and are common to *Armenians* and *Medes*." [Idem. 11.14.12]

It is important to bring attention to the passion of horse-riding noticed by *Strabo* in both the *Armenians* and the *Medes*. This love of horses was very characteristic not only to the *Armenians* and the *Medes* but to all other nations directly related to them as well, such as the *Scythians,* the *Thracians,* the *Trojans,* the *Turkic* nations, and even the *Native Americans*. This adoration of horses played a detrimental role in the destruction of the *Trojans,* as knowing their weak spot, the *Greco-Danaans* built nothing else but a horse to make sure that the *Trojans* would bring it into their city.

Marcus Junianus Justinus supported *Strabo's* assertions about the *Pelasgian* founder of *Armenia,* whose name he recorded as *Armenius:*

> "But since we here make a transition to *Armenia,* we must look a little farther back into its origin; for it is not right that so great a kingdom should be passed in silence, since its territory, next to that of *Parthia,* is of greater extent than any other kingdom. *Armenia,* from *Cappadocia* to the *Caspian Sea,* stretches over a space of eleven hundred miles, and is seven hundred miles in breadth. It was founded by *Armenius,* the companion of *Jason of Thessaly.* King *Pelias,* wishing to procure *Jason's* death from dread of his extraordinary ability, which was dangerous to his throne, ordered him to go on an expedition to *Colchis,* to bring home the fleece of the ram so celebrated throughout the world; hoping that the man would lose his

life, either in the perils of so long a voyage, or in war with barbarians so remote. But *Jason*, having spread abroad the report of so glorious an enterprise, at which the chief of the youth from almost all the world came flocking to him, collected a band of heroes, who were called *Argonauts*. Having brought his troop back safe, and being again driven from *Thessaly* by the sons of *Pelias*, he set out on a second voyage for *Colchis*, accompanied by a numerous train of followers (who, at the fame of his valour, came daily from all parts to join him), by his wife *Medea*, whom, having previously divorced her, he had now received again from compassion for her exile, and by his step-son *Medus*, whom she had by *Aegeus* king of the *Athenians;* and he re-established his father-in-law *Aeetes* who had been driven from his throne." ["History of the World, Extracted from *Trogus Pompeius*." 42.2]

As if it was not enough, *Justin* made it a point to repeat once more again that the founder of *Armenia* as a country was *Armenus* from *Thessaly* – the *Pelasgian* country:

"*Armenius*, too, who was himself a *Thessalian*, and one of the captains of *Jason*, having re-assembled a body of men, who, after the death of *Jason* were wandering about, founded *Armenia*, from the mountains of which the river *Tigris* issues, at first with a very small stream, but after running some distance, is lost in the earth, and then, flowing five and twenty miles underground, rises up a great river in the province of *Sophene;* and thus it is received into the marshes of the *Euphrates*." [Idem. 42.3]

It appears that in addition to the *Pelasgians*, the name of *Armenos*, aka *Armenius*, was used by other kindred nations, such as the *Germanic* tribe of the *Cherusci*. *Tacitus* narrated about a distinguished *Cheruscan* prince *Arminius*, which is a modified name of *Armenus* ["The Annals." 2.9]. This male name continues to be in use in some modern *Turkic* languages, such as *Ərmən* in *Azerbaijani*.

Actually, *Herodotus* was the first to deduce the origin of the *Armenians* from the *Phrygians*, who, as it was earlier established, were a *Thracian* people related to the *Pelasgians* – a non-*Indo-European* nation of *Turkic* roots:

"The *Phrygians*, as the *Macedonians* say, were called *Briges* as long as they were *Europeans* and lived as neighbors of the *Macedonians;* but when they moved over into *Asia*, they changed their name to *Phrygians* at the same time as they changed their place of residence. The *Armenians* were equipped like the *Phrygians*, being indeed colonists of the *Phrygians*." [7.73]

By referring to *Eudoxus*, *Stephanus of Byzantium* also confirmed *Herodotus's* testimony about the *Phrygian* origin of the *Armenians:*

"Οἱ οἰκήτορες Ἀρμένιοι, ὡς Εὔδοξος πρώτῃ γῆς περιόδου Ἀρμένιοι δὲ τὸ μὲν γένος ἐκ Φρυγίας καὶ τῇ φωνῇ πολλὰ φρυγίζουσι. Παρέχονται δὲ λίθον τὴν γλύφουσαν καὶ τρυπῶσαν τὰς σφραγῖδας."
"The inhabitants are called the *Armenioi* (Armenians), as *Eudoxus* states in the 1st book of "Description of Land": "The *Armenians* hail from *Phrygia*, and there are many *Phrygian* words in their language; stone is mined there to be used for cutting out and drilling seals.""[67]

These *Armenians* – a *Phryge-Pelasgian* colony of the *Turkic* origin, who acquired their ethnic name after their founder *Armenus*, had no relation or ties to the modern *Indo-European Armenians*. The name of the modern *Armenians* derives its etymology from the *Arabic* word *Aramean*, aka *Arammaean* – "related to *Aram*", as they are considered to be the people of *Aram*. It was either a

---

[67] The translation into *English* from the *Greek* text was done by the author of the present book.

pure coincidence of the names, similar to the state of *Georgia* in the *USA* and the country of *Georgia,* or a deliberate action to converge these names with the purpose to confuse and build historically incorrect and false assumptions. Here comes to mind a wise statement made by *Pausanias:*

> "All through the ages, many events that have occurred in the past, and even some that occur today, have been generally discredited because of the lies built up on a foundation of fact."
> ["Description of *Greece.*" 8.2.6]

The *Aramean* name of the modern *Armenians* was confirmed by the 18th c. *French* researcher and translator of *Herodotus, Pierre Henri Larcher:*

> "*Stephanus of Byzantium,* under the word "*Armenia*", says likewise, that the *Armenians* came from *Phrygia,* and that their language greatly resembled that of the *Phrygians.*
> But we shall perhaps do better to refer to *Mar Ibas Cathina,* a *Syrian* author, who flourished about 130 years before our era. This writer, who had been recommended by *Valasarces,* king of *Armenia,* to *Arsaces,* king of the *Parthians,* the conqueror of *Antiochus Sidetes,* had access to the royal archives, and brought back to this prince a history of *Armenia* from the earliest times, written in the *Chaldean* language, and translated into *Greek* by order of *Alexander the Great.* This history makes no mention of a *Phrygian* colony, but that *Hai'cus,* who is considered as the father and the founder of the *Armenians',* passed with his partisans from *Babylonia* into the country which has been since called *Armenia,* where his successors reigned down to *Aramus,* his sixteenth descendant, who gave to his people the name of *Arameans,* or *Armenians,* and to the country, that of *Armenia. Josephus* is of the same opinion. "From *Aramus,*" says he, "came the *Armenians,* whom the *Greeks* call *Syrians.*" This *Aramus* was, according to *Moses Chorenensis,* contemporary with *Abraham.* To these authorities may be added that of *Strabo.* "The *Armenians,* the *Syrians,* and the *Arabians,*" says he, "have considerable affinity in their language, in their manner of living, and in the characteristic form of the body, more especially in those districts which border on each other..." The *Assyrians,* the *Arianians,* and the *Arameans* (*Armenians*), have a resemblance not only to one another, but to the *Mesopotamians.* We may also say that there is some affinity in their names; for those whom we call *Syrians,* are by the *Syrians* called *Armenians* and *Arameans.*"
> ["*Larcher*'s notes on *Herodotus,* Historical and Critical Comments on the History of *Herodotus.*" Edited by *W.D. Cooley.* 282.1844.]

About 400 years after *Herodotus,* in the time of *Strabo,* the *Greek* historian recorded two *Armenian* nations: the *Armenians,* aka *Armenioi* (Αρμενιοι), – the descendants of the *Pelasgian Armenos* and the posterity of the *Syrian Aram* – the *Arammaioi* (Αραμμαιοι), translated into *English* as the *Arameans,* or the modern *Armenians,* whom the *Greeks* used to call the *Syrians,* while the *Syrians* recognized them as the *Arameans.*

Strabo was very precise in distinguishing two *Armenians* – the *Armenians* of the *Phryge-Pelasgian* extraction and the *Arammaioi,* later called the *Armenians* of the *Syrian* descent – the forefathers of the modern *Armenians,* who also acknowledge themselves as the *Hai.* The *Greek* geographer clearly enunciated the fact that the *Arammaioi* (Αραμμαιοι), aka the *Arameans,* were acknowledged by the *Greeks* as the *Syrians:*

τοὺς γὰρ ὑφ' ἡμῶν Σύρους καλουμένους ὑπ' αὐτῶν τῶν Σύρων Ἀραμμαίους καλεῖσθαι: τούτῳ δ' ἐοικέναι τοὺς Ἀρμενίους καὶ τοὺς Ἄραβας καὶ Ἐρεμβούς...

"Those whom we call *Syrians* style themselves *Arammaioi*,[68] names greatly like those of the *Armenioi*, *Arabs*, and *Eremboi*." [1.2.34]

Referring to the authority of another ancient scholar – *Posidonius*, *Strabo* enumerated the factors that united the *Armenians*, aka *Arammaioi*, with the *Syrians* and the *Arabs*:

"But there is no occasion to tamper with the text, which is of great antiquity; it is a far preferable course to suppose a change in the name itself, which is of frequent and ordinary occurrence in every nation: and in fact certain grammarians establish this view by a comparison of the radical letters. *Posidonius* seems to me to adopt the better plan after all, in looking for the etymology of names in nations of one stock and community; thus between the *Armenians*, *Syrians*, and *Arabians* there is a strong affinity both in regard to dialect, mode of life, peculiarities of physical conformation, and above all in the contiguity of the countries. *Mesopotamia*, which is a motley of the three nations, is a proof of this; for the similarity amongst these three is very remarkable." [1.2.34]

The *Syrian-Arabic* origin of the modern *Armenians*, asserted by *Strabo* thousands of years ago, was supported by the recent genetic research "Origin and Expansion of Haplogroup H, the Dominant Human Mitochondrial DNA Lineage in West Eurasia: The *Near Eastern* and *Caucasian* Perspective", published in Molecular Biology and Evolution, 2007. This research came to the same conclusion as *Strabo*:

"The populations from the southern *Caucasus* are more similar to *Levantine* populations, a trend that was particularly evident from the closeness of *Syrians* and *Armenians*."

In the world of 440 BCE described by *Herodotus*, there was not an independent country under the name of *Armenia* stretching from sea to sea. *Armenia* portrayed by *Herodotus* was not situated in the territory of modern *Armenia*. This land belonged to a *Scythian* tribe of the *Saspeires*, who lived next to other three nations from the *Red Sea* to the *Black Sea* – the *Medes*, the *Persians*, and the *Colchians*:

"The land where the *Persians* live extends to the southern sea which is called *Red*; beyond these to the north are the *Medes*, and beyond the *Medes* the *Saspires*, and beyond the *Saspires* the *Colchians*, whose country extends to the northern sea [69] into which the *Phasis* river flows; so these four nations live between the one sea and the other." [4.37]

"But what is beyond the *Persians*, and *Medes*, and *Saspires*, and *Colchians*, east and toward the rising sun, this is bounded on the one hand by the *Red Sea*, and to the north by the *Caspian Sea* and the *Araxes* River, which flows toward the sun's rising." [Idem. 4.40]

"It is a thirty days' journey for an unencumbered man from the *Maeetian* lake to the river *Phasis* and the land of the *Colchi*; from the *Colchi* it is an easy matter to cross into *Media*: there is only one nation between, the *Saspires*; to pass these is to be in *Media*." [Idem. 1.104]

Meanwhile, *Herodotus* did not say even a word about the *Hai*, the *Arameans*, the *Arammaioi*, or the *Armenians* from *Babylon* living either in *Armenia* or *Babylon*.

By the time of *Strabo* – 63 BCE-23 CE, the country of *Armenia*, established by *Armenos* the *Thessalian*, was conquered, in turn, by either the *Persians*, the *Macedonians*, or the *Medes*:

---

[68] In the original *Greek* text, it is *Arammaioi (Αραμμαιοι)*. This excerpt was translated by the author of the current book due to the incorrect *English* translation done by the other translator.
[69] The *Black Sea*.

146

"This is the ancient account, but the more recent, and extending from the time of the *Persians* to our own age, may be given summarily, and in part only (as follows); *Persians* and *Macedonians* gained possession of *Armenia*, next those who were masters of *Syria* and *Media*." [*Strabo*. 11.14.15]

After *Armenia* was seized from the last *Persian* ruler by *Artaxias* and *Zariadris*, these high-ranking officers of the *Macedonian* king *Antiochus the Great*, unable to govern the country as a whole, split *Armenia* into two parts – the *Greater* and the *Lesser Armenia*:

"The last was *Orontes*, a descendant of *Hydarnes*, one of the seven *Persians*: it was then divided into two portions by *Artaxias* and *Zariadris*, generals of *Antiochus the Great*, who made war against the *Romans*. These were governors by permission of the king, but upon his overthrow they attached themselves to the *Romans*, were declared independent, and had the title of kings. *Tigranes* was a descendant of *Artaxias*, and had *Armenia*, properly so called. This country was contiguous to *Media*, to the *Albani*, and to the *Iberes*, and extended as far as *Colchis*, and *Cappadocia* upon the *Euxine*." [Idem. 11.14.15]

Cappadocia was named the *Lesser Armenia* by the *Romans*, according to *Appian*:

"*Mithridates* withdrew into the country which the *Romans* now call *Lesser Armenia*, taking all the provisions he could and spoiling what he could not carry, so as to prevent *Lucullus* from getting any on his march." ["The *Mithridatic* Wars." 13.90]

Initially, *Armenia* as a country was small in size. As a result of conquering other nations' lands and adding them to *Armenia*, it swelled into a large kingdom:

"According to historians, *Armenia*, which was formerly a small country, was enlarged by *Artaxias* and *Zariadris*, who had been generals of *Antiochus the Great*, and at last, after his overthrow, when they became kings, (the former of *Sophene*, *Acisene*, (*Amphissene?*) *Odomantis*, and some other places, the latter of the country about *Artaxata*,) they simultaneously aggrandized themselves, by taking away portions of the territory of the surrounding nations: from the *Medes* they took the *Caspiana*, *Phaunitis*, and *Basoropeda*; from the *Iberians*, the country at the foot of the *Paryadres*, the *Chorzene*, and *Gogarene*, which is on the other side of the *Cyrus*; from the *Chalybes*, and the *Mosynœci*, *Carenitis* and *Xerxene*, which border upon the *Lesser Armenia*, or are even parts of it; from the *Cataones*, *Acilisene*, and the country about the *Anti-Taurus*; from the *Syrians*, *Taronitis* – hence they all speak the same language." [*Strabo*. 11.14.5]

The most notable kings of *Armenia* after *Zariadris* and *Artaxias*, according to *Strabo*, were *Artanes*, crushed by *Tigranes*, who previously was a hostage of the *Parthians*, followed by *Artavasdes*, who was later carried in chains through the city of *Alexandria* and executed for his treachery against the *Romans*:

"*Artanes* the *Sophenian* was the descendant of *Zariadris*, and had the southern parts of *Armenia*, which verge rather to the west. He was defeated by *Tigranes*, who became master of the whole country. He had experienced many vicissitudes of fortune. At first, he had served as a hostage among the *Parthians*; then by their means he returned to his country, in compensation for which service they obtained seventy valleys in *Armenia*. When he acquired power, he recovered these valleys, and devastated the country of the *Parthians*, the territory about *Ninus*, and that about *Arbela*. He subjected to his authority the *Atropatenians*, and the

Gordyæans; by force of arms he obtained possession also of the rest of *Mesopotamia,* and, after crossing the *Euphrates,* of *Syria* and *Phœnicia.* Having attained this height of prosperity, he even founded near *Iberia,* between this country and the *Zeugma* on the *Euphrates,* a city, which he named *Tigranocerta,* and collected inhabitants out of twelve *Grecian* cities, which he had depopulated. But *Lucullus,* who had commanded in the war against *Mithridates,* surprised him, thus engaged, and dismissed the inhabitants to their respective homes. The buildings which were half finished he demolished, and left a small village remaining. He drove *Tigranes* both out of *Syria* and *Phœnicia.*

Artavasdes, his successor, prospered as long as he continued a friend of the *Romans.* But having betrayed *Antony* to the *Parthians* in the war with that people, he suffered punishment for his treachery. He was carried in chains to *Alexandria,* by order of *Antony,* led in procession through the city, and kept in prison for a time. On the breaking out of the *Actiac* war he was then put to death." [Idem. 11.14.15]

The *Romans* could easily appoint or remove the kings of *Armenia* whom they selected out of many nations, including the *Medes:*

"Next, *Artavasdes III* was imposed on the country, by order of *Augustus,* and ejected again not without discredit to us. *Gaius Caesar* was then delegated to settle *Armenian* affairs. He granted the *Armenian* crown to *Ariobarzanes,* a *Mede* by origin (he also ruled as *Ariobarzanes II of Media Atropatene*), who was welcomed by the *Armenians* for his good looks and noble qualities. *Ariobarzanes* meeting an accidental death, his son was not long tolerated; and after experiencing government by the woman called *Erato,* who was shortly expelled, the weak and wavering people, masterless rather than free, accepted *Vonones* the fugitive as their king." [Idem. 2.4]

It is imperative to remind that the *Greek* historians of antiquity, such as *Herodotus* and *Strabo,* were objective in their opinions and would verify their point of view through the testimonies of other esteemed scholars when stating the facts. There was not any hidden agenda in their works to aggrandize themselves or their nation. As such, there is no reason to doubt their assertions and conclusions about the *Phrygian* origin of *Armenians* and the *Syrian* roots of the *Arameans,* aka the *Arammaioi,* or the present-day *Armenians.* It is highly probable that in the times of *Herodotus,* the modern *Armenians* were either still living in *Babylon* and known as the *Syrians,* or they had left the country and gained a new name of the *Hai,* or people of *Haik,* after their leader and country of *Haikh.*

Stunningly, another genetic research, "Genetic evidence for an origin of the *Armenians* from Bronze Age mixing of multiple populations", indirectly confirmed the *Babylonian* origin of the modern *Armenians* by positioning them in *Turkey,* a major part of which was the *Babylonian* Empire:

"The position of the *Armenians* within global genetic diversity appears to mirror the geographical location of *Turkey,* which forms a bridge connecting *Europe,* the *Near East,* and the *Caucasus.*" [*Marc Haber, Massimo Mezzavilla, Yali Xue, David Comas, Paolo Gasparini, Pierre Zalloua, Chris Tyler-Smith.* "*European* Journal of Human Genetics." volume 24, pages 931–936 (2016)]

Furthermore, the genetic study was unable to determine the exact population from which the modern *Armenians* derived their origin by asserting that they were the product of a mixture of different peoples:

"The *Armenians* show signatures of an origin from a mixture of diverse populations occurring from 3000 to 2000 BCE. This period spans the Bronze Age, characterized by extensive use of metals in farming tools, chariots, and weapons, accompanied by development of the earliest writing systems and the establishment of trade routes and commerce. Many civilizations such as in ancient *Egypt, Mesopotamia,* and the *Indus* valley grew to prominence. Major population expansions followed, triggered by advances in transportation technology and the pursuit of resources. Our admixture tests show that *Armenian* genomes carry signals of an extensive population mixture during this period." [Idem ibid]

Now, let us trace the chronological timeline of *Armenian* history. *Homer,* born sometime between 12th – 8th BCE, did not bring up any *Armenians* or *Armenia,* though the events in his works took place in the regions including *Armenia* of *Strabo* and *Ptolemy.*

Herodotus, who lived around the 5th c. BCE, was the first known historian who mentioned the *Armenians* as a subsidiary ethnic group derived from the *Phrygians:*

"The *Phrygians* carried arms little differing from those of the *Paphlagonians*. This people, if we may believe the *Macedonians,* went under the name of *Brygians* during all the time they inhabited in *Europe* within the territories of *Macedonia;* but upon their arrival in *Asia,* chang'd their name with their country, and have ever since been call'd *Phrygians*. The *Armenians,* being a colony of the *Phrygians,* appear'd in the same accoutrements; and both these nations were commanded by *Artochmes,* who had married a daughter of *Darius*." [7.73]

The *Armenians* of *Herodotus,* aka the *Phrygians,* lived on the land known today as *Turkey,* where the river *Euphrates* took its course from:

"*Babylon* then was walled in this manner; and there are two divisions of the city; for a river whose name is *Euphrates* parts it in the middle. This flows from the land of the *Armenians* and is large and deep and swift, and it flows out into the *Erythraian* sea." [1.180]

Herodotus specified the location of the *Armenian* territory between the *Cilicians* and the *Matienians:*

""And the nations moreover dwell in such order one after the other as I shall declare: the *Ionians* here; and next to them the *Lydians,* who not only dwell in a fertile land, but are also exceedingly rich in gold and silver," and as he said this he pointed to the map of the Earth, which he carried with him engraved upon the tablet, "and here next to the *Lydians,*" continued *Aristagoras,* "are the *Eastern Phrygians,* who have both the greatest number of sheep and cattle of any people that I know, and also the most abundant crops. Next to the *Phrygians* are the *Cappadokians,* whom we call *Syrians;* and bordering upon them are the *Kilikians,* coming down to this sea, in which lies the island of *Cyprus* here; and these pay five hundred talents to the king for their yearly tribute. Next to these *Kilikians* are the *Armenians,* whom thou mayest see here, and these also have great numbers of sheep and cattle. Next to the *Armenians* are the *Matienians* occupying this country here; and next to them is the land of *Kissia* here, in which land by the banks of this river *Choaspes* is situated that city of *Susa* where the great king has his residence, and where the money is laid up in treasuries."" [5.49]

The *Cilicians,* or the *Kilikians,* located on what is today the southern coast of *Turkey,* and the *Matienians* resided in the lands of the ancient *Mannaean* kingdom, presently known as *Southern Azerbaijan* in *Iran*. A tiny territory between these two nations – the *Cilicians* and the *Matienians,* belonged to the *Armenians* – the *Phrygian* colonists, who resettled from *Phrygia* to this small patch of the land. We want to reiterate that this was the first known location of *Armenia,* recorded in the 5th c. BCE.

By the time of *Strabo* – 1st c. BCE, two distinct peoples – the *Armenians* of the *Phrygian* extraction and the *Arammaioi,* or the *Armenians* of the *Syrian* origin, were reported.

In the 1st c. CE, *Pliny the Elder* recognized *Greater* and *Lesser Armenia* without acknowledging the existence of the *Armenians:*

> "*Greater Armenia,* beginning at the mountains known as the *Paryadres,* is separated, as we have already stated, from *Cappadocia* by the river *Euphrates,* and, where that river turns off in its course, from *Mesopotamia,* by the no less famous river *Tigris.* Both of these rivers take their rise in *Armenia,* which also forms the commencement of *Mesopotamia,* a tract of country which lies between these streams; the intervening space between them being occupied by the *Arabian Orei.* It thus extends its frontier as far as *Adiabene,* at which point it is stopped short by a chain of mountains which takes a cross direction; whereupon the province extends in width to the left, crossing the course of the *Araxes,* as far as the river *Cyrus;* while in length it reaches as far as the *Lesser Armenia,* from which it is separated by the river *Absarus,* which flows into the *Euxine,* and by the mountains known as the *Paryadres,* in which the *Absarus* takes its rise.
>
> The river *Cyrus* takes its rise in the mountains of the *Heniochi,* by some writers called the *Coraxici;* the *Araxes* rises in the same mountains as the river *Euphrates,* at a distance from it of six miles only; and after being increased by the waters of the *Usis,* falls itself, as many authors have supposed, into the *Cyrus,* by which it is carried into the *Caspian Sea.* The more famous towns in *Lesser Armenia* are *Caesarea, Aza,* and *Nicopolis;* in the *Greater Arsamosata,* which lies near the *Euphrates, Carcathiocerta* upon the *Tigris, Tigranocerta* which stands on an elevated site, and, on a plain adjoining the river *Araxes, Artaxata.* According to *Aufidius,* the circumference of the whole of *Armenia* is five thousand miles, while *Claudius Caesar* makes the length, from *Dascusa* to the borders of the *Caspian Sea,* thirteen hundred miles, and the breadth, from *Tigranocerta* to *Iberia,* half that distance. It is a well-known fact, that this country is divided into prefectures, called "Strategies," some of which singly formed a kingdom in former times; they are one hundred and twenty in number, with barbarous and uncouth names. On the east, it is bounded, though not immediately, by the *Ceraunian Mountains* and the district of *Adiabene.* The space that intervenes is occupied by the *Sopheni,* beyond whom is the chain of mountains, and then beyond them the inhabitants of *Adiabene.* Dwelling in the valleys adjoining to *Armenia* are the *Menobardi* and the *Moscheni.* The *Tigris* and inaccessible mountains surround *Adiabene.* To the left of it is the territory of the *Medi,* and in the distance is seen the *Caspian Sea;* which, as we shall state in the proper place, receives its waters from the ocean, and is wholly surrounded by the *Caucasian Mountains.* The inhabitants upon the confines of *Armenia* shall now be treated of." [6.9-6.10]

> "Beyond the *Gates of Caucasus,* in the *Gordyaean Mountains,* the *Walli* and the *Suani,* uncivilized tribes, are found; still, however, they work the mines of gold there. Beyond these nations, and extending as far away as *Pontus,* are numerous nations of the *Heniochi,* and, after them, of the *Achaei.* Such is the present state of one of the most famous tracts upon the face of the earth." [Idem. 6.12]

Pliny the Elder stated the existence of the *Armenochalybes,* inhabiting the land next to the *Ceraunian Mountains,* located in the modern country of *Albania* in *Europe:*

> "The whole plain which extends away from the river *Cyrus* is inhabited by the nation of the *Albani,* and, after them, by that of the *Iberi,* who are separated from them by the river *Alazon,* which flows into the *Cyrus* from the *Caucasian* chain. The chief cities are *Cabalaca,* in *Albania, Harmastis,* near a river of *Iberia,* and *Neoris;* there is the region also of *Thasie,* and that of *Triare,* extending as far as the mountains known as the *Paryadres.* Beyond these are the deserts of *Colchios,* on the side of which that looks towards the *Ceraunian Mountains*

dwell the *Armenochalybes;* and there is the country of the *Moschi,* extending to the river *Iberus,* which flows into the *Cyrus;* below them are the *Sacassani,* and after them the *Macrones,* upon the river *Absarus.* Such is the manner in which the plains and low country are parcelled out. Again, after passing the confines of *Albania,* the wild tribes of the *Silvi* inhabit the face of the mountains, below them those of the *Lubieni,* and after them the *Diduri* and the *Sodii.*" [6.12]

However, the *Armenochalybes* were not the ancestors of the modern *Armenians.* They were a derivative branch of the *Chalybes,* described by *Homer* as a kindred nation to the *Trojans,* who fought at their side against the *Greeks* in the famous *Trojan* war. Most likely, to honor *Armenos,* a *Pelasgian* from *Thessaly,* the *Chalybes* added an attribute *Armenian* to their name and became the *Armenochalybes.*

By the 2nd c. CE, another scholar – *Ptolemy* also did not make a note of any *Armenians* in *Armenia* or anywhere else, in his fundamental work "The Geography", where the author enumerated all the regions and cities of *Greater Armenia* but never left a word about the *Armenians* as the inhabitants of these or any other lands:

"In the region of *Armenia* which is included between the *Euphrates* River, the *Cyrus* and the *Araxes,* is *Cortazena* which is near the *Moschici* mountains above that which is called *Bochae* near the *Cyrus* River, and *Tobarena* and *Totene* near the *Araxes* River and *Colthene,* and *Soducene* which are below this: then along the *Paryardes* mountains is *Siracene* and *Sacapene…*
In the section which is below this up to that river which flows into the *Euphrates* in the northern country are the regions, commencing in the west, *Basilisene, Bolbene* and *Arsesa,*[70] below these *Acilisene* and *Astaunitis* and *Sophene* near the same bend of the river…
Moreover toward the east from the sources of the *Tigris* River is *Bagranandene,* and *Gordyene* which is below this, from which to the east is *Cotaea* and below this *Mardi.*" [5.12]

Being a very detail-oriented geographer, who would not miss an opportunity to catalog each and every tribe in the described region, for instance, the *Arabs* in *Syria* [5.14], the multitude of the *Scythian* people [5.8], or the *African* tribes [4.3], *Ptolemy* surprisingly did not specify the peoples of *Greater Armenia*. Judging by the names of the boroughs, however, it is easy to deduce what tribes lived there:

- *Basilisene* = Βασιλισηνή: Basileia = βασιλήια 'a *Scythian* tribe' + *Ene* > *En* 'region, territory', meaning "land of the *Basileia*" in *Turkic* (*Basileia: Bas* 'head; main' + *Il* 'nation, people', meaning "leading nation" in *Turkic*). By the way, there was a *Pelasgian* town *Basilis* in the district of *Parrhasia,* on the *Alpheius,* said to have been founded by the *Pelasgian* king *Cypselus.*
- *Siracene, Sarakene* = Σαρακηνή > *Sirakenoi* = Σιρακηνοί' 'a *Scythian* tribe' (*Sirak* > *Sırak* 'wood strip' + *En* 'house', meaning "tribe that has houses made from wood strips" in *Turkic*).
- *Arsia* = Αρσία: *Ar* 'warrior, man' + *Sia* > *Sıı* 'respect, honor', meaning "honor to warriors" or "honorable men" in *Turkic*. From this name of the region emerged the waterbody *Arsene* (*Ars* > *Arsia* 'honorable men' + *Ene* > *En* 'abode' in *Turkic*), later known as the lake *Van. William Smith* also reported other ancient names of this lake:
    "(Αρσηνή: *Ván*), a large lake situated in the S. of *Armenia. Strabo* (xi. p.529) says that it was also called *Thonitis* (Θωνῖτις), which *Groskurd* corrects to *Thospitis* (Ξωσπῖτις, comp. Ptol. 5.13.7; Plin. Nat. 6.27. s. 31). The lake *Arsissa,* which *Ptolemy* (l.c.) distinguishes from *Thospitis* has been identified with *Arsene,* and the name is said to survive in the

---

[70] It should be *Arsia* = Αρσία.

fortress *Arjísh*, situated on the N. of the lake (St. Martin, Mém. sur l'Armenie, vol. i. p. 56)." [*Arsene*]

- *Acilisene* = Ακιλισηνή: *Ac* 'pure' + *Ilis* > *İlis* 'honor' + *Ene* > *En* 'abode', meaning "abode of the highly honored" in *Turkic*.

  Strabo indicated that the inhabitants of *Acilisene* were the progeny of the *Thessalian Armenus's* friends, who planted their roots in this *Armenian* land:

  > "Some of the followers of *Armenus* settled in *Acilisene*, which was formerly subject to the *Sopheni*; others in the *Syspiritis*, and spread as far as *Calachene* and *Adiabene*, beyond the borders of *Armenia*." [11.14.12]

  > "It is said that when *Jason*, accompanied by *Armenus* the *Thessalian*, undertook the voyage to the *Colchi*, they advanced as far as the *Caspian Sea*, and traversed *Iberia*, *Albania*, a great part of *Armenia*, and *Media*, as the *Jasoneia* and *Armenus*, they say, was a native of *Armenium*, one of the cities on the lake *Bœbeis*, between *Pheræ* and *Parisa*, and that his companions settled in *Acilisene*, and the *Suspiritis*, and occupied the country as far as *Calachene* and *Adiabene*, and that he gave his own name to *Armenia*." [Idem. 11.4.8]

  The ancient *Greek* scholar also acknowledged these colonists from *Thessaly* as the *Armenians*, who adopted the religious rites of the *Persians* and erected houses of worship in honor of their deities, mostly in *Acilisene*:

  > "Both the *Medes* and *Armenians* have adopted all the sacred rites of the *Persians*, but the *Armenians* pay particular reverence to *Anaïtis*, and have built temples to her honour in several places, especially in *Acilisene*. They dedicate there to her service male and female slaves; in this there is nothing remarkable, but it is surprising that persons of the highest rank in the nation consecrate their virgin daughters to the goddess. It is customary for these women, after being prostituted a long period at the temple of *Anaïtis*, to be disposed of in marriage, no one disdaining a connexion with such persons." [11.14.16]

- *Kotarzene* = Κοταρζηνή: *Ko* 'wonderful' + *Tarz* > *Tərzi* 'tailor' + *Ene* > *En* 'abode', meaning "abode of the wonderful tailors" in *Turkic*. Evidently, the land was famous for its highly-skilled dressmakers.
- *Tosarene* = Τωσαρηνή: *Tos* > *Tös* 'highland' + *Ar* 'warrior, man' + *Ene* > *En* 'abode', meaning "abode of the mountain men" in *Turkic*.
- *Otene* = Ωτηνή: *Ot* 'fire; grass' + *Ene* > *En* 'abode', meaning "land of fire" or "grassy land" in *Turkic*.
- *Kolthene* = Κολθηνή: *Kolthe* > *Kolti* 'base, bottom' + *Ene* > *En* 'abode', meaning "lowland" in *Turkic*.
- *Sodoukene* = Σοδουκηνή: *Sodouk* > *Soğuk* 'cold' + *Ene* > *En* 'abode', meaning "cold land" or "land with the cold climate" in *Turkic*.
- *Sakapene* = Σακαπηνή: *Sak* > *Sağ* 'untouched' + *Apene* > *Apaina* 'pristine field', meaning "untouched, pristine filed" in *Turkic*.
- *Sophene* = Σωφηνή: *Soph* > *Sof* 'end' + *Ene* > *En* 'abode', meaning "borderland" in *Turkic*. As the name suggests, *Sophene* was a part of *Greater Armenia*, located at the border with *Mesopotamia*, formed by the *Taurus* mountains, otherwise known as the *Gordyæan* mountains:

  > "The southern mountains on the other side of the *Euphrates*, extending towards the east from *Cappadocia* and *Commagene*, at their commencement have the name of *Taurus*, which separates *Sophene* and the rest of *Armenia* from *Mesopotamia*, but some writers call them the *Gordyæan* mountains." [*Strabo*. 11.12.4]

  According to *Strabo*, *Sophene* was ruled by the royalty, occasionally united with the rulers of other parts of *Armenia*:

  > "The *Lesser Armenia* is sufficiently fertile. Like *Sophene* it was always governed by princes who were sometimes in alliance with the other *Armenians*, and sometimes acting independently." [11.14.28]

- *Gordyene* = Γορδυηνή: *Gordy* > *Qurd* 'wolf' + *Ene* > *En* 'abode', meaning "abode of the *Gordyæans*" in *Turkic*. This *Turkic* name was assigned after the *Phrygian* king *Gordius* to the region in *Greater Armenia*, its inhabitants – the *Gordyæans*, as well as to the *Thracian* town *Gordion*, aka *Gordium*, as well as to the *Gordyene* mountains, aka *Gordyaean*, aka *Gordyaei*, aka *Gorduaia* (Γορδυαῖα), aka *Ceraunian* mountains, later renamed into *Ağrıdağ* and *Ararat*.
- *Anzetene* = Ανζητηνή: *An* > *Ən* 'wide' + *Zeta* > *Sət* 'terrace' + *Ene* > *En* 'abode', meaning "district with wide horizontal shelflike formations" in *Turkic*. There was also a city *Anzeta* (Ανζητα), most likely the capital of this district.
- *Cotaea* = Κωταία, aka *Cotiaeum*, aka *Kotiaeion* = Κοτιάειον, aka *Kotiaeus* = Κοτιαεύς, aka *Kutahiyah* > *Köt* "pleasure, festivity" in *Turkic*. Most likely, this region of *Armenia* was named after the *Phrygian* city of *Cotiaeum*.
- *Mardoi* = Μάρδοι: *Mar* 'hill' + *Doi* > *Da* 'mountain', meaning "mountainous region" in *Turkic*.

Shockingly, the etymological analysis of the cities and villages in *Greater Armenia* (except *Babila*), listed by *Ptolemy*, also revealed their *Turkic* origin:

- *Sala* = Σάλα > *Səl* "rest" in *Turkic*. There is a district and a city in the *Azerbaijan Republic* – *Salyan*=*Səlyan* ("place of rest") that contains the same *Turkic* root.
- *Baraza* = Βάραζα: *Bar* 'rich' + *Aza* > *Az, As* 'a Trojan and a Turkic nation', meaning "the rich *Az* nation" in *Turkic*. Besides *Armenia Major*, *Ptolemy* also indicated other cities containing the name of the *Az, As* nation, in *Asian Sarmatia* – *Azara* "an *Az* warrior, an *Azeri*"; *Azaraba* "the place of the *Azeri*" [5.8]; in *Cappadocia* – *Arasaza* "the *Az* from the *Araxes* area"; *Aza*; *Asiba* "the place of the *As*" [5.6.]. As it was stated earlier in the present book, from this *Az* nation many *Turkic* peoples took their origin, such as the *Azerbaijanis*, or the *Azeri*, the *Kirghiz*, as well as the *Turkic* confederation of the *Oguz*.
- *Ascoura* = Ασκουρα: *As* 'a Trojan and a Turkic nation' + *Coura* > *Kürə* 'place of celebration', meaning "celebration place of the *As* people" in *Turkic*.
- *Azata* = Αζάτα: *Az* + *Ata* > *Atau* 'island, landmass', meaning "land of the *Az* people" in *Turkic*.
- *Azora* = Αζόρα or *Ozara* = Οζάρα: *Az, Oz* 'the *Az*' + *Or, Ar* 'warrior', meaning "an *Az* warrior; an *Azeri*" in *Turkic*. *Ptolemy* was not sure about the correct spelling of the city name and, for that purpose, provided two variants.
- *Santouta* = Σάντουτα: *San* 'multitude' + *Touta* > *Tut* 'crowd, people', meaning "populous city" in *Turkic*.
- *Lala* = Λάλα > *Lələ* "small" in *Turkic*.
- *Satafara* = Σαταφάρα > *Sadəf* 'mother of pearl; pearl' + *Ara* > *Yər* 'land', meaning "land of pearls" in *Turkic*.
- *Toga* = Τώγα > *Toğai* "1.meadow; 2.lowland covered with forest" in *Turkic*.
- *Sourta* = Σούρτα, aka *Surta* > *Sürt* "1.hill; 2.higher ground" in *Turkic*.
- *Cozala* = Κοζάλα or *Kozola* = Κόζολα > *Közöl, Gözəl* "beautiful" in *Turkic*. *Ptolemy* was unsure about the spelling of the name and furnished its alternative as well, and strikingly both of the variants exist in *Turkic*.
- *Cotomana* = Κοτομάνα: *Coto* > *Kət* 'wonderful' + *Mana* > *Man* 'walled place', meaning "wonderful city, surrounded by walls" in *Turkic*.
- *Dizaka* = Δίζακα: *Diz* > *Dizi* 'village' + *Aka* 'master', meaning "main village" in *Turkic*.
- *Kholoua* = Χολούα: *Khol* > *Köl* 'lake' + *Oua* > *Öv* 'house, home', meaning "lakeside community" in *Turkic*.
- *Kholouata* = Χολουάτα: *Khol* > *Köl* 'lake' + *Ou* > *Öv* 'house, home' + *Ata* > *Atau* 'island, landmass', meaning "lakeside community in an island" in *Turkic*.
- *Sakalbina* = Σακάλβινα: *Saka* > *Sacai* 'a Scythian tribe' + *Alb* 'hero' + *Ina* > *İn* 'house, home', meaning "home of the *Sacai* hero" in *Turkic*.

- *Tareina* = *Τάρεινα*: *Tare* > *Tərə* 'fresh' + *Ina* > *İn* 'house, home', meaning "new home" in *Turkic*.
- *Thalina* = *Θαλίνα*: *Thal* > *Tala* 'flatland' + *Ina* > *İn* 'house, home', meaning "place on a flatland" in *Turkic*.
- *Koubina* = *Κούβινα*: *Koubi* > *Kobı* 'ravine' + *Ina* > *İn* 'house, home', meaning "town near or in the ravine" in *Turkic*.
- *Dosoata* = *Δοσοάτα*: *Doso* > *Tos* 'dust' + *Ata* > *Atau* 'island, landmass', meaning "sandy landmass" in *Turkic*.
- *Arsarata* = *Αρσαρατα*: *Arsar* 'wild' + *Ata* > *Atau* 'island, landmass', meaning 'wild place" in *Turkic*. As it so happens, according to *Radlov V.V.*, there used to be a *Turkic* tribe *Arsari* [1.1.326].
- *Arsamosata* = *Αρσαμόσατα*: *Arsamós* > *Arsımás* 'the one who does not act foolishly' (*Arsa* > *Arsı* 'act foolishly' + *Mos* > *Mas* 'an affix of negation') + *Ata* > *Atau* 'island, landmass', meaning "place where nobody fools around" in *Turkic*. Interestingly, there is a city in *Russia*, founded in the 16th c., the name of which – *Arzamás* closely matches that of the ancient city in *Greater Armenia*, without its last component – *Ata*. Even a stress mark falls on the same syllable.
- *Brepos* = *Βρεπός*: *Br* > *Bir* 'blessed' + *Ep* > *Əp* 'house, home' + *Os* > *Ös* 'motherland', meaning "blessed homeland" in *Turkic*.
- *Brizaka* = *Βρίζακα*: *Br* > *Bir* 'blessed' + *Zaka* > *Sacai* 'a *Scythian* tribe', meaning "city of the blessed *Sacai*" in *Turkic*.
- *Khasira* = *Χασίρα* > *Xasır* "container, bag, sack" in *Turkic*.
- *Khorsa* = *Χόρσα* > *Körüsə* "wish to see" in *Turkic*.
- *Armaouria* = *Αρμαουρία*: *Arma* > *Ərim* 'rest area' + *Our* > *Ör* 'highland', meaning "resting place on a highland" in *Turkic*.
- *Artaksata* = *Ἀρταξάτα*, aka *Artaksiasata* = *Ἀρταξιάσατα*: *Artaks* > *Artaxias* (*Ar* 'warrior' + *Taks* > *Tağıs* 'destroy') + *Ata* > *Atau* 'landmass', meaning "city of *Artaxias*" in *Turkic*. The city *Artaksiasata*, or *Artaksata* for short, were named after the king *Artaxias*, according to *Strabo* and *Plutarch*:

    "The cities of *Armenia* are *Artaxata*, called also *Artaxiasata*, built by *Hannibal* for the king *Artaxias*, and *Arxata*, both situated on the *Araxes*; *Arxata* on the confines of *Atropatia*, and *Artaxata* near the *Araxenian* plain; it is well inhabited, and the seat of the kings of the country." [*Strabo*. 11.14.6]

    "It is said that *Hannibal the Carthaginian*, after *Antiochus* had been conquered by the *Romans*, left him and went to *Artaxas the Armenian*, to whom he gave many excellent suggestions and instructions. For instance, observing that a section of the country which had the greatest natural advantages and attractions was lying idle and neglected, he drew up a plan for a city there, and then brought *Artaxas* to the place and showed him its possibilities, and urged him to undertake the building. The king was delighted, and begged *Hannibal* to superintend the work himself, whereupon a very great and beautiful city arose there, which was named after the king, and proclaimed the capital of *Armenia*."
    [*Plutarch*. "Lucullus." 31.3-4]
- *Naksouána* = *Ναξουάνα*: *Nak* 'Noah' + *Souána* > *Sıván* 'caress, embrace', meaning "land that embraced the prophet *Noah*" in *Turkic*. The *Azerbaijanis* preserved this name as *Nakhchiván* that denotes the whole region and its capital in the *Azerbaijan Republic*.
- *Athoua* = *Αθούα*: *At* 'horse' + *Oua* > *Ova* 'flatland; wide place', meaning "flatland to raise horses" in *Turkic*.
- *Tinissa* = *Τίνισσα*: *Ti* 'always' + *Nissa* > *Nəs* 'marvel', meaning "everlastingly marvelous city" in *Turkic*. There were several cities in *Greater Armenia* with *Nissa* in their names – *Tinissa*, *Dara<u>nissa</u>*. *Nissa*, or *Nisa*, was the first capital of the *Parthians*, located in what is now modern *Ashgabat*, the capital of *Turkmenistan*.

- *Daranissa* = Δαράνισσα: *Dara* > *Dərə* 'valley' + *Nissa* > *Nəs* 'marvel', meaning "marvelous city in a valley" in *Turkic*.
- *Zoriga* = Ζώριγα: *Zor* 'great' + *Iga* > *Igə* 'master', meaning "great master city" in *Turkic*.
- *Sana* = Σάνα > *San* "honor" in *Turkic*.
- *Zogokara* = Ζογοκάρα and *Sogokara* = Σογοκάρα: *Zogo, Sogo* > *Sok* 'cold' + *Kara* 'land', meaning "land with the cold climate" in *Turkic*. Both these city names with a slight difference share the same *Turkic* etymology.
- *Kodana* = Κόδανα: *Kod* > *Köd* 'protect, defend' + *Ana* 'strip of land', meaning "protected land" in *Turkic*.
- *Zarouana* = Ζαρούανα: *Zarou* > *Zərua* 'jackal' + *Ana* 'strip of land', meaning "land full of jackals" in *Turkic*.
- *Siauana* = Σιανάνα: *Si* 'treat, regale' + *Au* > *Av* 'hunt' + *Ana* 'strip of land', meaning "land of treat and hunt" in *Turkic*.
- *Bouana* = Βουάνα: *Bou* > *Böi* 'grass' + *Ana* 'strip of land', meaning "grassland' in *Turkic*.
- *Dauduana* = Δαυδυάνα: *Dau* > *Dəü* 'big' + *Udu* > *Üdə* 'rest' + *Ana* 'strip of land', meaning "large place of rest" in *Turkic*.
- *Sagauana* = Σαγανάνα: *Saga* > *Sağa* 'estuary' + *Ana* 'strip of land', meaning "land near an estuary" in *Turkic*.
- *Matoustana* = Ματουστανα: *Mato* > *Matı* 'wonderful' + *Usta* 'artisan' + *Ana* 'strip of land', meaning "place of wonderful artisans" in *Turkic*.
- *Thelbalane* = Θελβαλάνη: *Thel* > *Telə* 'light brown' + *Bal* 'honey' + *Ane* > *Ana* 'strip of land', meaning "land of golden honey" in *Turkic*.
- *Astakana* = Ἀστακάνα: *As* 'the As or Az tribe' + *Tak* > *Tək* 'race, origin' + *Ana* 'strip of land', meaning "land of the As race" in *Turkic*. The name of this city in *Greater Armenia* was similar to the one in *Bactria* and closely matched the *Parthian* city name – *Artacana* (*Ar* 'warrior, man, hero' + *Tak* 'race, origin' + *Ana* 'strip of land', meaning "land of the warrior race" in *Turkic*.)
- *Siai* = Σίαι: *Si* > *Sıy* 'honor, respect' + *Ai* 'order, law', meaning "honorable and law-abiding city" in *Turkic*.
- *Kakhoura* = Καχούρα: *Kakh* > *Kak* 'stiff' + *Oura* > *Ur, Ör* 'hill; highland', meaning "town on a stiff hill" in *Turkic*.
- *Phausua* = Φαύσυα > *Pəs* 'fog',[71] meaning "misty land" in *Turkic*. Perhaps, this town was always immersed into mist.
- *Phandalia* = Φανδαλία: *Phanda* > *Fanta* 'sparrow' + *Lia* > *-Lı* 'an affix, denoting the word Having', meaning "place full of sparrows" in *Turkic*.
- *Kitamon* = Κίταμον: *Kit* > *Kıt* 'sparse, low-density' + *Amon* > *Amın* 'dwelling; location', meaning "place with few dwellings" in *Turkic*.
- *Anarion* = Ανάριον: *Anar* > *Aŋar* 'red-breasted duck, merganser' + *Ion* > *Yan* 'place, side', meaning "place full of ducks" in *Turkic*.
- *Sigoua* = Σιγούα: *Sig* > *Siğ* 'low, shallow, flat' + *Oua* > *Ova* 'flatland; wide place', meaning "low flatland" in *Turkic*.
- *Teroua* = Τερούα: *Ter* 'God' + *Oua* > *Öv* 'house, habitation', meaning "divine habitat" in *Turkic*.
- *Zourzoua* = Ζουρζούα or *Zourgoua* = Ζουργούα: *Zourz, Zourg* > *Zor* 'big, great' + *Oua* > *Öv* 'house, habitation', meaning "great place" in *Turkic*.
- *Sardeoua* = Σαρδηούα: *Sarde* > *Sart* 'merchant' + *Oua* > *Öv* 'house, habitation', meaning "marketplace" in *Turkic*.
- *Balisbiga* = Βαλισβίγα: *Balis* > *Beləs* 'hill' + *Biga* > *Bigə*[72] 'sturdy', meaning "inaccessible city on a hill" in *Turkic*.

---

[71] *Egorov V.G.* "Chuvashskiy etimologicheskiy slovar." [149].
[72] *Pekarskiy E.K.* "Slovar yakutskogo yazika." [459].

- ❖ *Elegerda* = Ηλέγερδα: *Ele* > *El* 'people' + *Gerda* > *Kərtə* 'trace, mark', meaning "national landmark" in *Turkic*. The second part of the name *Gerda* has other variants – *Kerta, Certa, Garta*, as in *Tigrano<u>kerta</u>* or *Artagi<u>garta</u>*. The *Parthians* mainly used the component *Kerta/Certa* in the names of their cities; for instance, *Pliny the Elder,* aka *C. Plinius Secundus,* testified that the *Parthian* king *Vologesus* founded a city called after himself – *Vologesocerta* "*Vologesus's* mark", just like *Tigranes* named *Tigranokerta*:

  "The *Parthi* again, in its turn, founded *Ctesiphon,* for the purpose of drawing away the population of *Seleucia,* at a distance of nearly three miles, and in the district of *Chalonitis; Ctesiphon* is now the capital of all the *Parthian* kingdoms. Finding, however, that this city did not answer the intended purpose, king *Vologesus* has of late years founded another city in its vicinity, *Vologesocerta* by name." [6.30]

  This testimony strongly confirms our etymological deduction that *Kerta* was a *Turkic* word, as the *Parthians* were of *Turkic* extraction.

- ❖ *Tigranokerta* = Τιγρανοκέρτα: *Tigrano* > *Tigran* 'the name of the king in *Greater Armenia*' + *Kerta* > *Kərtə* 'trace, mark', meaning "*Tigran's* mark" in *Turkic*. By the way, the first component of the toponym was observed in the names of the city *Tigrana* in *Media* and the river *Tigris*. All three names share a lexeme *Tigran* that originated from *Tigris* "shaft, arrow" in the language of the *Medes*:

  "When its course becomes more rapid, it assumes the name of *Tigris,* given to it on account of its swiftness, that word signifying an arrow in the *Median* language."
  [*Pliny the Elder*. 6.31].

  "The *Tigris* passes through this lake after issuing from the mountainous country near the *Niphates,* and by its rapidity keeps its stream unmixed with the water of the lake, whence it has its name, for the *Medes* call an arrow, *Tigris*." [Idem. 11.14.8]

  With the references to the ancient works, *William Smith* noticed that the word *Tigris* had several variants, such as *Tigres, Tigridis, Tigridem*:

  "We find various forms of its name, both in *Greek* and *Latin* writers. The earlier and more classical *Greek* form is ἡ Τίγρης, gen. Τίγρητος (Hdt. 6.20; Xen. Anab. 4.1. 3; Arr. Anab. 7.7, &c.), whilst the form ὁ Τίγρις, gen. Τίγριδος, and sometimes Τίγριος, is more usual among the later writers. (Strab. ii. p.79, xv. p. 728; Ptol. 5.13.7; Plut. Luc. 22, &c.) Amongst the *Romans* the nom. is constantly *Tigris,* with the gen. *Tigris* and acc. *Tigrin* and *Tigrim* among the better writers (Virg. Eel. 1.63; Lucan 3.261; Plin. vi. s. 9; Curt. 4.5, &c.); but sometimes *Tigridis, Tigridem* (Lucan 3.256; Eutrop. 9.18; Amm. Marc. 23.6.20, &c.)"
  [*Tigris*]

  As the *Median* language is a part of the *Turkic* language family, it was an extremely easy task to find several counterparts to the word *Tigris* in *Turkic*:

  Tığı "arrow", *Təgir* "move in one direction", *Tirig* "weapon", *Terk* "fast", *Türğən* "swift". There was also *Tügər* (*Tüg, Tığı* 'arrow' + *Ər* 'warrior', meaning "archer") – an ancient *Turkic* tribe of the *Oguz* branch.

  That being said, the male name *Tigran,* or *Tigranes,* has, without any doubt, *Turkic* roots, corresponding to an ancient *Turkic* male name *Tegrənç*, listed in "Drevneturkskiy slovar" [549]. According to *Strabo*, *Tigranes* was the king of the *Armenians,* who were the *Phrygians,* aka the *Pelasgians* from *Thessaly* [11.14.14]. Therefore, neither *Tigranes* nor the *Armenians* he ruled were related in any shape or form to the modern *Armenians*. This is a pure case of mistaken identity. Furthermore, even the *Turkic* name of another city *Tigranoama* (*Ama* "mother" in *Turkic*), found by *Tigranes,* confirms the stated fact.

  Assuming that *Tigranes* was of the *Aramean* (*Arammaioi*), or modern *Armenian* extraction, both his name and his cities would carry appellations of *Armenian,* not *Turkic* origin. No reason or force could have prevented the mighty King *Tigranes* from exercising his God-given right to use his mother tongue when naming the places he built. He used the same *Turkic* word *Kerta* that the *Parthian* King *Vologesus* utilized to name his respective cities. As such, this is an additional confirmation that *Tigranes* was a *Phrygian*, aka a *Pelasgian*, whose ancestors originally hailed from *Thessaly*.

- *Karkathiokerta* = Καρκαθιόκερτα: *Kar* > *Kara* 'great' + *Kathio* > *Kat* 'riverside' + *Kerta* > *Kərtə* 'trace, mark', meaning "great landmark at the riverside" in *Turkic*. This city was the capital of *Sophene* – a canton of *Greater Armenia*, and it was situated at the shore of the river *Tigris*, to which the name of this city points. Though omitted by *Ptolemy*, this *Sophenian* city was brought up by *Strabo* and *Pliny the Elder*, who considered it to be a part of the *Lesser Armenia*:

    "The royal city of *Sophene* is *Carcathiocerta*." [*Strabo*. 11.14.2]

    "The more famous towns in *Lesser Armenia* are *Cæsarea*, *Aza*, and *Nicopolis*; in the Greater *Arsamosata*, which lies near the *Euphrates*, *Carcathiocerta* upon the *Tigris*, *Tigranocerta* which stands on an elevated site, and, on a plain adjoining the river *Araxes*, *Artaxata*." [*Pliny the Elder*. 6.10]

- *Artagigarta* = Αρταγιγάρτα: *Artagi* > *Ərtəği* 'ancient' + *Garta* > *Kərtə* 'mark', meaning "ancient landmark" in *Turkic*.
- *Tigranoama* = Τιγρανοάμα: *Tigrano* > *Tigran* + *Ama* 'mother', meaning "mother of *Tigranes*" in *Turkic*. Evidently, King *Tigranes* found a city to honor his mother's memory.
- *Mazara* = Μαζάρα: *Maz* > *Məz* 'joy' + *Ara* > *Yəri* 'place' (*Yər* 'place' + *-İ* 'an affix of possession'), meaning "place of joy" in *Turkic*.
- *Artemita* = Αρτέμιτα > *Artemis*: *Ar* 'warrior, hero' + *Temis* 'pure, virgin', meaning "virgin warrior" in *Turkic*. The city in *Greater Armenia* was named after the *Pelasgian* goddess *Artemis*.
- *Babila* = Βαβίλα = *Babil* in *Turkic*. Though this is a *Semitic* name of the ancient city of *Babylon*, it was created as a calque from the *Akkadian* *Ka-dingirra* "gate of God",[73] which is a *Turkic* expression: *Ka* > *Kapu* 'gate' + *Dingirra* > *Tengri* 'God'.
- *Anzeta* = Ανζητα: *An* > *Ən* 'wide' + *Zeta* > *Sət* 'terrace', meaning 'city with wide terraces" in *Turkic*.
- *Soeita* = Σόειτα > *Söit* 'willow' in *Turkic*. Evidently, the city had many willows growing around to earn this name.
- *Belkania* = Βελκανία: *Bel* > *Bəl* 'hill' + *Kan* > *Kən* 'ornament' + *Ia* > *-İ* 'an affix of possession', meaning "decoration, ornament on the hill" or "beautiful town on a mountain" in *Turkic*.
- *Seltia* = Σελτία: *Sel* 'torrent' + *Tia* > *Tu* 'mountain', meaning "town with a torrent from a mountain" in *Turkic*.
- *Thospia* = Θωσπία: *Thos* > *Tös* 'highland' + *Pia* > *Pi* 'edge', meaning "town located at the edge of a highland" in *Turkic*.
- *Kolkis* = Κολκίς: *Kol* 'valley' + *Kis* 'yurt; nomad's tent', meaning "place with yurts in a valley" in *Turkic*.
- *Kolsa* = Κόλσα: *Kol* 'valley' + *Sa* > *Sai* 'river', meaning "town in a valley with a river" in *Turkic*.
- *Korra* = Κόρρα: *Kor* > *Kör* 'bridge' + *Ra* > *-Rı* 'an affix, equivalent to the word *Having*', meaning "city with a bridge" in *Turkic*.
- *Taska* = Τάσκα: *Tas* 'bare; plain; smooth' + *Ka* > *Kaia* 'cliff', meaning "town set on a bare cliff" in *Turkic*.
- *Phora* = Φώρα > *Por* "chalk-stone" in *Turkic*.
- *Maipa* = Μαϊπα: *Mai* 'side'[74] + *Pa* > *Pai* 'portion', meaning "small town on a side" in *Turkic*.
- *Kapouta* = Καπούτα: *Kapo* > *Kapu* 'gate' + *Uta* > *Ut* 'grass', meaning "gated town with a meadow" in *Turkic*.

---

[73] "Faiths of Man: a Cyclopædia of Religions." by *J.G.R .Forlong* [1.224].
[74] "Slovar chuvashskogo yazika." by *Ashmarin N.I.* [1.151].

- ❖ *Kholimma* = Χολίμμα: *Khol* > *Köl* 'lake' + *Imma* > *Ömnö* 'in front of',[75] meaning "city along the lakeside" in *Turkic*.
- ❖ *Terebia* = Τερεβία: *Tere* > *Tərə* 'fresh, new' + *Bia* 'mare, horse', meaning "town full of fresh horses" in *Turkic*.
- ❖ *Pherendis* = Φερενδις: *Pheren* > *Parən* 'dependable' + *Dis* > *Dizi* 'village', meaning "well-guarded village" in *Turkic*.

In the 2nd – 3rd c. of the common era, the *Armenians*, or the *Arammaioi*, were recorded living together with the *Arabs* in *Mesopotamia*, in modern days roughly corresponding to *Iraq, Kuwait*, the eastern parts of *Syria, Southeastern Turkey*:

"Now *Mesopotamia* is bordered on one side by the *Tigris*, and on the other by the *Euphrates*, rivers which flow from *Armenia* and from the lowest slopes of *Taurus*; but they contain a tract like a continent, in which there are some cities, though for the most part only villages, and the races that inhabit them are the *Armenian* and the *Arab*. These races are so shut in by the rivers that most of them, who lead the life of nomads, are so convinced that they are islanders, as to say that they are going down to the sea, when they are merely on their way to the rivers, and think that these rivers border the earth and encircle it." [*Philostratus*. "The Life of *Apollonius of Tyana*." 1.20]

The *Roman* historian *Publius Cornelius Tacitus* (1st-2nd c. CE) was among the last to mention the *Armenians* of the *Pelasgi-Phrygian* origin. He stated that the *Armenians* were continuously under the control of the *Romans*:

"The general, although he was overcome by the despair of his army, first wrote a letter to *Vologeses*, not a supliant petition, but in a tone of remonstrance against the doing of hostile acts on behalf of the *Armenians*, who always had been under *Roman* dominion, or subject to a king chosen by the emperor." ["The Annals of *Tacitus*." 15.13]

The *Roman* chronicler and senator also brought forward the assertion that the *Armenians* and the *Parthians* were related, which is not surprising, provided their common *Scythian* roots:

"Added to that, the *Armenians*, of dubious loyalty, were invoking the aid of both sides, though by their geography, and the similarity of their way of life, they were closer to the *Parthians*, with whom they intermarried, and under whom, being ignorant of true freedom, they were more inclined to accept servitude." [Idem. 13.34]

This kinship of the *Armenians* (Αρμένιοι) of the *Pelasgi-Phrygian* extraction with the *Parthians* was also confirmed by *Procopius of Caesaria*:

"…since after this the *Armenians* had no hope of ever reaching an agreement with the *Romans*, and since they were unable to prevail over the emperor in war, they came before the *Persian* king led by *Bassaces*, an energetic man. And the leading men among them came at that time into the presence of *Chosroes* and spoke as follows: "Many of us, O Master, are *Arsacidae*, descendants of that *Arsaces* who was not unrelated to the *Parthian* kings when the *Persian* realm lay under the hand of the *Parthians*, and who proved himself an illustrious king, inferior to none of his time.""
["History of the Wars." 2.3.32-33]

---

[75] "Etimologicheskiy slovar chuvashskogo yazika." by *Egorov V.G.* [274].

Figure 21. *Armenian* foot soldiers wearing *Phrygian* caps. (CC BY-SA 3.0) Credit: *Gevork Nazarian*.

After the *Parthians*, the *Armenian* kings fell into subordination to the *Romans*, according to *Strabo*:

"Many kings reigned after *Artavasdes*, who were dependent upon *Cæsar* and the *Romans*. The country is still governed in the same manner." [11.14.16]

"The *Lesser Armenia*, which was in the possession of different persons at different times, according to the pleasure of the *Romans*, was at last subject to *Archelaus*." [12.3.29]

From thereon, the history leaves us in the dark as to the manner in which the *Armenians* of the *Pelasgi-Phrygian* extraction ceased to exist.

Fast-forwarding eight centuries to the 10th c. of our common era, *Armenia* was documented as a province located in what is now *Southern Azerbaijan* (currently, a part of *Iran*), heretofore the lands of the *Matienians*, anciently known as the kingdom of *Mannae*. In the manuscript "Hudud al-Alam." – "The Boundaries of the World.", compiled in the year of 982, the anonymous author enumerated around a dozen of towns and cities of *Armenia*, spelled as *Arminiya*:

"Report about the provinces of *Adharbadhagan*, *Arminiya*, and *Arran* [76] and their cities.
These three provinces are adjoining to each other. Their rural areas permeate each other. To the east of this land are the boundaries of *Gilan;* to the south of it – the borders of *Iraq* and *Jazira;* to the west of it are the borders of *Rum* and the *Sarir;* to the north of it – the borders of *Sarir* and *Khazars* (spelled: *Ghazaran*). These places are the loveliest of the Islamic lands…*Greek*, *Armenian*, *Pecheneg*, *Khazar*, and *Slavic* (*Saqlabi*) slaves are brought there. 1.*Ardavil* – the capital of *Adharbadhagan*, a large city surrounded by the wall…This is the seat of the rulers of *Adharbadhagan*.[77] 2.*Asna, Sarav, Miyana, Khuna, Jabruqan* – small but fine, well-designed, and crowded towns. 3.*Tabriz* – a small town, lovely and well-designed…4.*Maragha* – a big city, blossoming and fine, with flowing waters and blossoming gardens. 5.*Barzand* – a thriving and

---

[76] *Arran*, or *Aran* means "meadow, lowland; a country with moderate climate" in *Turkic* [R.1.1.251]. Currently, it is a part of *Azerbaijan Republic*, except for *Tiflis* – a capital of modern *Georgia*.
[77] Also known as *Azerbaijan*.

well-maintained city with flowing waters... 6.*Muqan* is a city with a district located on the seacoast...7.*Vartan* – a very well-designed city...

All these cities that we have listed belong to *Adharbadhagan*.

Arminiya and *Arran*.

8.*Duvin* (*Dwn*) – a large city and the capital of *Arminiya*, surrounded by a wall. 9.*Dakharraqan* (spelled: *Dakhartab*), is a prosperous city with flowing waters near Lake *Kabudhan*. 10.*Urmiya* (spelled: *Armana*) is a big city, very well-designed and very pleasant. 11.*Salamas* (now: *Salmas*) is a prosperous and crowded city...12.*Khoy, Bargri, Arjij, Akhlat, Nakhchuvan, Bidlis* (spelled: *Budlais*) – all these are cities, small and large, thriving, nice, crowded, having wealth and merchants...13.*Malazgird* – a frontier post against the *Rumiyans*.[78] 14.*Qaliqala* (usually, *Qaliqala, Erzurum*) – a city inside of which there is a reliable fortress...15.*Mayyafariqin* (spelled: *Miyafariqin*) – a city inside a fortress...16.*Marand* is a small town, well-designed, nice, and crowded... 17.*Mimadh* – renowned district, well-designed, fine, and crowded. 18.*Ahar* – the main place of *Mimadh*...19.*S.ngan* (*Sungan*?) – a city with a large district belonging to the kingdom of *Sunbat*.

All these cities that we have listed appertain to *Arminiya*.

20.*Qaban* – a thriving city, producing a lot of good quality cotton. 21.*Barda* – a big city, very lovely. It is the capital of *Arran* and the seat of the ruler of this province...22.*Baylaqan* – a very nice city, producing large quantities of striped fabrics...23.*Bazhgah* ("Duty [collection] house") – a city on the bank of the *Aras* [*Araxes*] river, producing fish. 24.*Ganja, Shamkur* – cities with vast fields, well-designed, nice, and producing woolen fabrics of all kinds. 25.*Khunan* – a district on the banks of the *Kur*[79] river, which forms the border between *Arminiya* and *Arran*. 26.*Varduqiya* (*Barduj*) – a small and sparsely peopled town in *Hunan*. 27.*Qala* – a large fortress... on the border between *Arminiya* and *Arran*. 28.*Tiflis* – a big city, prosperous, sturdy, well-designed, and very nice...It is a frontier post against infidels. 29.*Shakki* – a district in *Arminiya*, well-designed and nice...The inhabitants are Muslims, as well as the infidels. 30.*Mubaraki* – a large village at the gates of *Barda*...31.*Suq Al-Jabal* – a town in *Shakki*, not far from *Barda*. 32.*Sunbatman* (?) – a city in the distant end of *Shakki* with a secure fortress...33.*Sanar* – a district with a length of 20 farsangs and located between *Shakki* and *Tiflis*...34.*Qabala* – a city between *Shakki, Barda*, and *Shirvan*, well-designed and lovely. 35.*Bardij* – a small town, well-designed and nice. 36.*Shirvan, Khursan, Lizan* (*Layzan*?) – three provinces under one ruler. He is called *Shirvan–shah, Khursan-shah*, and *Lizan-shah*. He lives in a military camp at a farsang distance from *Shamakhi*. 37.*Khursan* – a borough (located between?) *Darband* and *Shirvan*, next to *Mount Qabk* (*Caucasus*). 38.*Kurdivan* – a well-designed and nice city. 39.*Shavaran* – the capital of *Shirvan*, is located by the sea...40.*Darband-i Khazaran* – a city on the seaboard...Slaves from all kinds of infidels who live nearby are brought there. 41.*Baku* – a city, located on the seashore near the mountains. All the naphtha used in the *Daylaman* country comes from there."[80] [35-36]

As a side note, there was an ancient city *Armine* in *Paphlagonia*, according to *Pliny the Elder*, that resonates with *Arminiya* in "Hudud-al-Alam.":

"There was formerly also a town of the same name, and another near it called *Armene*;[81] we now find there the colony of *Sinope*, distant from *Mount Cytorus* one hundred and sixty-four miles." [6.2]

All the names of the boroughs and towns in *Armenia* of the 10th c. point to their *Turkic* origin:

---

[78] *Romans,* or the people of *Rome*.
[79] Also known as the river *Cyrus*.
[80] The text was translated into *English* by the author of the present book.
[81] In the original *Latin* text, it is *Armine*.

- *Duvin (Dwn) > Dawan* "mountain pass" in *Turkic*.
- *Dakharraqan: Dakh > Dağ* 'mountain' + *Arra > Ara* 'middle' + *Qan > Qon* 'settlement', meaning "settlement between the mountains" in *Turkic*.
- *Urmiya: Ur* 'hill' + *Miya > May* 'side', meaning "hillside" in *Turkic*. This city is still in existence under the same name in *Southern Azerbaijan (Iran)*.
- *Salamas, Salmas: Sala, Sal > Sal* 'drop, bring down' + *-Mas* 'an affix, denoting negation in the future tense', meaning "city that will not disappoint" in *Turkic*. Known nowadays as *Salmas*, it is a city in *Southern Azerbaijan*.
- *Khoy > Xoy* "narrow passage" in *Turkic*. This city in *Southern Azerbaijan* has not changed its name as of today.
- *Bargri: Bar* 'wealthy' + *Gri > Gır* 'highland', meaning "wealthy highlands" in *Turkic*. There were a number of *Turkic* cities with the similar names: *Barçuq, Barçan* [Dr.Sl. 83]
- *Arjij > Arğış* "farmer's market" in *Turkic*.
- *Akhlat > Ağlat* "make someone cry" in *Turkic*. Incidentally, there was a *Turkic* region under similar name *Ağlasun* "let him/her cry", mentioned by *Radlov V.V.* [1.1.177].
- *Nakhchuván, aka Naksouána = Naχουάνα: Nakh, Nak* 'Noah' + *Chuvan, Soána > Sıván* 'caress, embrace', meaning "land that embraced the prophet *Noah*" in *Turkic*. According to the *Azerbaijanis, Noah* settled on this land after the Flood. The name has not dramatically changed – nowadays, it is *Nakhchiván (Naxçıván)* and applies both to the city and the region in the *Azerbaijan Republic*.
- *Bidlis (Budlais): Bidl, Budl > Budal* 'place' + *Is > İs* 'soot', meaning "town covered in soot" in *Turkic*.
- *Malazgird: Malaz* 'marshy, muddy place' + *Gird > Girdə* 'round, circular', meaning "circular-shaped, muddy place" in *Turkic*.
- *Qaliqala: Qali > Qalı* 'soar' + *Qala* 'citadel', meaning "soaring citadel, fortress" in *Turkic*.
- *Mayyafariqin: Mayya > Meyi* 'brain, head' + *Fariqin > Fərğana* 'damp, swampy place', meaning "main swampy place" in *Turkic*. The name itself suggests that this town is one of the similar marshy places, including *Malazgird* and *Fergana (Fərğana)* city, with the latter located in the modern-day *Turkic* country of *Uzbekistan*.
- *Marand: Mar* 'hill' + *And > Əndə* 'outspread', meaning "town that outspread the hill" in *Turkic*. The same city under the uncorrupted name still exists in *Southern Azerbaijan*.
- *Mimadh: Mi > Mı* 'marshy place' + *Madh > Mədə* 'mark', meaning "small area with marshy place" in *Turkic*.
- *Ahar > Əhər > Akhar = Axar* "stream" in *Turkic*. The city acquired its name after the river *Ahar = Əhər*, at the left shore of which it was situated. This city and the river still persist under the same ancient name in *Southern Azerbaijan*.
- *S.ngan (Sungan?): Sun* 'pheasant' + *Gan > Qon* 'settlement', meaning "place full of pheasants" in *Turkic*.

Now, it is the best opportune time to give the floor to the age-old *Armenian* scholars and historians to introduce their interpretation of their countrymen's – modern *Armenian* people's origin.

The *Arabic* origin of the name *Armenian*, or properly *Arammaioi*, was attested by the reputable etymologist and linguist of the 19th c., Professor *Lazar Budagov*, an ethnic *Armenian* himself ["Sravnitelniy slovar turetsko-tatarskikh narechiy." 1.33].

The *Armenian* historian of the disputed date of existence – the 5th or 9th c., *Movses Khorenatsi*, aka *Moses Chorenensis*, aka *Moses of Khorens*, whom the modern *Armenians* call "the father of the *Armenian* history", gave an account about the birth of the word *Armenian* from *Aram* during the timeframe that correlated with the lifespan of the biblical figure *Abraham*. According to *Movses Khorenatsi*, the ancestors of modern *Armenians*, who originally hailed from *Babylon* (!), at first did not call themselves *Armenians* or their country *Armenia*. They were known as the *Hai* after their leader *Haik*, and the country where they resettled was named *Haikh*. For the record, even nowadays, the *Armenians* continue to identify each other as *Hai* and their country as *Haiastan* (*Haia* > *Haik* + -*Stan* 'country' in *Persian*):

> "*Haik*, not wanting to obey him, after the birth of his son *Aramanaak* in *Babylon*, starring along with his sons, daughters, sons of his sons, powerful men numbering about three hundred and other family members and strangers to him and all the people and belongings, goes to the land of *Ararad,* located in the northern edges. On the way, he settled at the foot of the mountain, on the plain, where few of the people had settled down earlier and lived. Having subjugated them, *Haik* builds a house there – the Lord's dwelling – and gives it to *Cadmos*, the son of *Aramananeac* for the hereditary possession." [82] [1.10]

> "*Haik* builds a settlement on the battlefield and in honor of the victory in the battle gives it the name *Haikh*. For this reason, the region is now called *Hayots Dzor*. The hill, on which *Bel* fell with his brave warriors, *Haik* called *Gerezmank,* which is now pronounced as *Gerezmanakk*. But *Bel's* body, covered with potions, *Haik,* says (the chronicler), orders to be taken to *Khark* and buried on a hill in the sight of his wives and sons. Our country, by the name of our ancestor, is called *Haikh*." [1.11]

As a side note, from the words of *Movses Khorenatsi,* it becomes clear that the land of *Ararad* already existed under that name and in the stipulated location prior to the arrival and its occupation by *Haik* and his colony. However, neither *Roman* historian *Pliny the Elder* nor *Greek* geographers *Ptolemy* and *Strabo* ever mentioned the existence of this land *Ararad* or the mountain *Ararat,* though both stated that there were *Gordyaean,* aka *Gordyaia* (Γορδυαια ορος), aka *Ceraunian* Mountains (*Ceraunij*):

> "The noted mountains of *Armenia* are the *Moschici* extending along that part if *Pontus Cappadocia,* which is above them, and the *Paryardes* mountains, the terminal positions of which are 75 43 20 and 77 42 and the *Udacespes* mountains, the central part of which is in 80 30 40 and a part of the *Antitaurus* mountains located on this side of the *Euphrates,* the middle of which is 72 41 40 and that which is called *Abas* mountains, the middle part of which is in 77 41 10 and the *Gordyaei* mountains, the middle of which is located in 75 39 40." [*Ptolemy*. 5.12]

> "According to *Aufidius,* the circumference of the whole of *Armenia* is five thousand miles, while *Claudius Cæsar* makes the length, from *Dascusa* to the borders of the *Caspian Sea,* thirteen hundred miles, and the breadth, from *Tigranocerta* to *Iberia,* half that distance. It is a well-known fact, that this country is divided into prefectures, called "Strategies," some of which singly formed a kingdom in former times; they are one hundred and twenty in number, with barbarous and uncouth names. On the east, it is bounded, though not immediately, by the *Ceraunian* Mountains and the district of *Adiabene*. The space that intervenes is occupied by the *Sopheni,* beyond whom is the chain of mountains, and then beyond them the inhabitants of *Adiabene*. Dwelling in the valleys adjoining to *Armenia* are the *Menobardi* and the *Moscheni*. The *Tigris* and inaccessible mountains surround *Adiabene*. To the left of it is the territory of the *Medi,* and in the distance is seen the *Caspian Sea;* which, as we shall state in the proper place, receives its waters from the ocean, and is wholly surrounded by the *Caucasian* Mountains." [*Pliny the Elder*. 6.10]

> "The rivers *Tigris* and *Euphrates* flowing from *Armenia* towards the south, after having passed the *Gordyæan* mountains, and having formed a great circle which embraces the vast country of

---

[82] This and all other excerpts were translated into *English* by the author of the present book, based on the translation made by *Troy Azelli* "The History of Armenia", USA. 2020, and the *Russian* version – "Istoriya Armenii", translated by *G. Sarkisian*. Erevan. 1990.

Mesopotamia, turn towards the rising of the sun in winter and the south, particularly the *Euphrates,* which, continually approaching nearer and nearer to the *Tigris,* passes by the rampart of *Semiramis,* and at about 200 stadia from the village of *Opis,* thence it flows through *Babylon,* and so discharges itself into the *Persian Gulf.*" [*Strabo.* 2.1.26]

These *Gordyæan* mountains were called after the famous *Phrygian* King *Gordius* ("wolf" in *Turkic*), connected to the fable about *Alexander the Great's* solution of the riddle with the *Gordian* knot. The mountains were later renamed into the *Ararat* mountains by the *Armenians* and *Ağridağ* mountains by the *Turkish* people.

It's worth mentioning that *Movses Khorenatsi* named his book "History of the *Hai.*" However, after his passing, it was renamed to "History of the *Armenians.*", and then – "History of *Armenia.*"

Movses Khorenatsi's testimony about *Babylon* as the fatherland of the *Armenians,* as well as their original name as the *Hai,* was confirmed by another *Armenian* historian of the 7th c., the bishop *Sebeos* in his work "History of the Emperor *Irakl.*":

"These are the names of the husbands of the ancestors, the first-born in *Babylon,* and those who departed to the countries of the north, to the land of *Ararad.* Haik moved from *Babylon* with his wife, children, and all his belongings. He went and settled in the land of *Ararad,* at the foot of the mountain, in the house that Father *Zervan* had previously built with his brothers.
Thereafter, *Haik* left this possession to his grandson *Cadmium,* son of *Aramaniac.* He himself moved from there, and went to the north, and settled on one high glade. This field is called *Hark* "fathers" in honor of fathers. Additionally, on the same occasion, the country received the name *Haik* and all [the countrymen – an appellation] the *Hai.*" [83] [ch.1].

Later, the country *Haikh,* or *Haik,* as well as other lands that the people of *Haik* conquered, were renamed to *Armenia* in honor of their ancestor *Aram,* who forcefully occupied the lands of other nations, as per the testimony of *Movses Khorenatsi:*

"*Harm,* after living years, gave birth to *Aram.* They say that *Aram* made many valiant feats in battles and that he pushed *Armenia's* borders in all directions. All nations call our country by his name, for example, the *Greeks – Armen,* the *Persians,* and *Syrians – Armenikk.*" [1.12]

The assertion of the *Armenian* annalist about how his nation and country acquired its name after *Aram* solidifies *Strabo's* statements about the *Arameans* (aka the *Arammaioi*), later modified into the *Armenians.*

However, it seems that *Armenia* under such name existed long before even the founder of the *Armenian* people *Haik* was born, according to the statements of *Beros Sibyl* – a diviner, highly esteemed by *Movses Khorenatsi:*

"But now I will be happy to begin the forthcoming narration with (the words) respected by me and exceeding many in her truthfulness *Beros Sibyl.* "Before (the construction) of the tower", she says, "and before the division of the human race into many languages, and after sailing *Xisuthra* to *Armenia,* the rulers of the earth were *Zrvan, Titan* and *Iapetoste.*" It seems to me that this is *Shem, Ham,* and *Japheth.*" [1.6]

Hereon, *Movses Khorenatsi* pointed out one crucial fact: whatever new place *Haik's* descendants, later renamed into the *Arameans,* or the *Armenians,* went to resettle in after leaving *Babylon* – their motherland, they would find out that each and every land had already been populated by other

---

[83] The excerpt was translated into *English* by the author of the present book from "Istoriya imperatora Irakla. Sochinenie episkopa Sebeosa, pisatelia 7-go veka.", translated from *Armenian* into *Russian* by *Patkanian K.*

nations, including the land of *Ararad* that existed under that name prior to the arrival of *Haik* and his colonists:

> "But the chronicler reports something amazing: in many places of our country, even before the arrival of our indigenous ancestor, *Haik*, a small number of people had lived scattered." [1.12]

Hereby, *Movses Khorenatsi* strongly confirmed that his *Armenian* brethren were not the autochthonous inhabitants of *Armenia* (currently located in the vicinity of the *Caucasus*). Moreover, the *Armenian* chronologist made a note of a very interesting fact – the ruler of *Armenia* ordered all the native inhabitants of *Armenia* to learn the *Armenian* language:

> "He himself leaves one of his relatives in the country by the name of *Mshak* with ten thousand troops and returns to *Armenia*. However, he orders the residents of the country to learn *Armenian* speech and language. That is why the *Greeks* still call this country Pro-*Armenia*, which means "First *Armenia*". The indigenous people of this country, not knowing how to pronounce it correctly, called the settlement "*Mazhak*", built and surrounded by a low wall and named by *Aram's* alderman *Mshak* in his own name, until later others built up and expanded it and called it *Caesarea*." [1.14]

This is another proof provided by *Movses Khorenatsi* that *Armenia* was not the motherland of his people. There were indigenous tribes who had lived in *Armenia* long before the *Armenian* arrivals and were not of *Armenian* stock; consequently, they did not know the *Armenian* language.

From the narration by *Movses Khorenatsi*, it appeared that the notable *Armenians* were mostly the vassals to other kings, appointed by the latter as officials and governors of the *Armenian* people:

> "For the exploits of *Nebuchadnezzar's* father were recorded by their custodians of the memorial notes, and (the deeds) of ours, who had not thought of such things, were mentioned only last. If you ask, how do we know so well the names of our ancestors, and in many cases their deeds, I will answer: from the ancient *Chaldean, Assyrian,* and *Persian* archives; for their names and deeds, as officials, governors, and great satraps appointed by the kings, were included in their records." [1.21]

The *Armenian* chronicler honestly and openly revealed that his countrymen, being of small number, mostly lived in servitude to more dominant nation-states:

> "For although we are a small garden, and are very limited in number, and deprived of power, and have been conquered by other nations many times, still in our country there have been many feats of courage worthy of being immortalized in writing, which, however, none of them cared to record in books." [1.3]

A considerable portion of his book *Movses Khorenatsi* devoted to the foreign rulers appointed over the *Armenian* people, mostly to *Arsaces* (*Arshak*) and *Valarsaces* (*Valarshak*):

> "Now, in the Second Book, I will describe to you in the orderly fashion the affairs related to our country, starting from the reign of *Alexander* (*Macedonian*) and up to the reign of the holy and valiant man *Trdat the Great* – all the brave and courageous deeds and reasonable institutions of each (of those who ruled) after the *Persian King Arshak* and his brother *Valarshak*, appointed by him to reign over our people; (in a word) everything that concerns the kings of our country (originated) from his seed, who, passing power from father to son, began to be called by the name of *Arshak Arshakuni*, (moreover) the only one ascended the throne in succession, and the rest replenished and multiplied the royal family." [2.1]

The fact that *Arsaces* and his brother *Valarsaces* were of *Parthian*, aka *Scythian* extraction, not *Persian*, was confirmed by *Movses Khorenatsi* in his first book:

> "They say that *Arshak the Great*, King of *Persia* and *Parthia* and by birth a *Parthian*, having separated himself from the *Macedonians*, reigned over the whole *East* and *Assyria*, and, having killed King *Antiochus* in *Nineveh*, subdued the whole universe to his power. He appoints his brother *Valarshak* as a king in *Armenia*, considering it favorable for maintaining the inviolability of his reign. He designates *Mtsbin* as its capital and adds to his (state) a part of western *Syria*, *Palestine*, *Asia*, all Middle-earth, and *Tetalia*, from the *Pontine Sea* to the place where the *Caucasus* ends at the *Western Sea*, as well as *Atrpatakan* "and so on, what your thought and courage will achieve, for the boundaries of the brave", he says, "are determined by their sword: how many it cuts off, so many they own."" [1.8]

Procopius in "History of the Wars" was in agreement with the historical fact that the *Persian* empire was governed by the *Parthians* of *Scythian* descent, not *Persian:*

> "...*Arsaces* who was not unrelated to the *Parthian* kings when the *Persian* realm lay under the hand of the *Parthians*, and who proved himself an illustrious king, inferior to none of his time." [2.3.32]

It was sure as daylight that *Arsaces* was a *Scythian*. First of all, the name *Arsaces* gives a solid reason to deduce its origin from a *Scythian* tribe of *Sacae*:
 Ar 'warrior, hero' + *Saces* > *Sacae*, meaning "*Sacae* warrior, or hero" in *Turkic*.
This is proved by one crucial fact mentioned by *Strabo* – out of all the neighboring nations, *Arsaces* sought refuge among his kindred – the *Apasiacai*, who were a branch of the *Sacae* nation:

> "...*Arsaces* afterwards fled from *Seleucus Callinicus*, and retreated among the *Aspasiacæ*." [84] [11.8.8]

Furthermore, and most importantly, *Strabo* openly declared that *Arsaces* was a *Scythian:*

> "Afterwards *Arsaces*, a *Scythian*, (with the *Parni*, called nomades, a tribe of the *Dahæ*, who live on the banks of the *Ochus*,) invaded *Parthia*, and made himself master of it." [11.9.2]

Arsaces built a city for the *Parthians* with the *Turkic* name *Dara* that means "ravine; valley, surrounded by hills or mountains" – exactly how *Justin* described its location:

> "*Seleucus* being then recalled into *Asia* by new disturbances, and respite being thus given to *Arsaces*, he settled the *Parthian* government, levied soldiers, built fortresses, and strengthened his towns. He founded a city also, called *Dara*, in *Mount Zapaortenon*, of which the situation is such, that no place can be more secure or more pleasant; for it is so encircled with steep rocks, that the strength of its position needs no defenders; and such is the fertility of the adjacent soil, that it is stored with its own produce. Such too is the plenty of springs and wood, that it is amply supplied with streams of water, and abounds with all the pleasures of the hunt." [41.5]

Arsaces was a notable son of the *Scythian* people, whose name became glorious among the *Parthians* to the point that they would apply it as a royal title to their subsequent rulers, as stated by *Justin*:

---

[84] There is a spelling error in the name. It should be *Apasiacai* = Ἀπασιάκαι.

> "Thus *Arsaces*, having at once acquired and established a kingdom, and having become no less memorable among the *Parthians* than *Cyrus* among the *Persians, Alexander* among the *Macedonians*, or *Romulus* among the *Romans*, died at a mature old age; and the *Parthians* paid this honour to his memory, that they called all their kings thenceforward by the name of *Arsaces*. His son and successor on the throne, whose name was also *Arsaces*, fought with the greatest bravery against *Antiochus*, the son of *Seleucus*, who was at the head of a hundred thousand foot and twenty thousand horse, and was at last taken into alliance with him. The third king of the *Parthians* was *Priapatius*; but he was also called *Arsaces*, for, as has just been observed, they distinguished all their kings by that name, as the *Romans* use the titles of *Caesar* and *Augustus*. He, after reigning fifteen years, died, leaving two sons, *Mithridates* and *Phraates*, of whom the elder, *Phraates*, being, according to the custom of the nation, heir to the crown, subdued the *Mardi*, a strong people, by force of arms, and died not long after, leaving several sons, whom he set aside, and left the throne, in preference, to his brother *Mithridates*, a man of extraordinary ability, thinking that more was due to the name of king than to that of father, and that he ought to consult the interests of his country rather than those of his children." [41.6.5]

Movses Khorenatsi noted that in some cases, when left without a ruler, his *Armenian* compatriots would seek a foreign king to rule over them instead of electing someone from their own, such as in the given occasion – to the *Persian* King *Khosrow*:

> "When the *Armenian* dignitaries saw that the *Greeks* did not put a king over them, and found it difficult to live without a leader, they decided to submit to *King Khosrow* voluntarily." [3.48]

The *Armenian* historian *Movses Khorenatsi* left a few words about the *Turkic* nations and names as well. He used the ancient *Turkic* military title *Nukar* "man-at-arms" when describing a *Mede* from *Media*:

> "Shortly before *Nin* became the ruler of *Assyria, Aram*, pressed by the surrounding peoples, gathers many brave fellow tribesmen – archers and most skillful spearmen, young men and mature, dexterous in fights, bold in heart and ready for battle – numbering about fifty thousand. At the borders of *Armenia*, he meets the young *Medes* under the leadership of a certain *Nukar*, nicknamed *Mades*, a proud and warlike man, as the same chronicler notes. Similar to an outlaw, like the *Kushans*, trampling *Armenia's* borders with the hooves of horses, he oppressed (the country) for two years." [1.13]

The *Turkic* nation of the *Bulgars* – indigenous to the *Caucasus*, was also known to *Movses Khorenatsi*:

> "In the days of *Arshak*, great troubles arose around the great *Caucasus Mountain*, in the Land of the *Bulgars*; many of them, having separated, came to our country and settled for a long time below *Kol*, on fertile land, in places rich in bread." [2.9]

With all due respect to the *Armenian* author, there were numerous occasions when his statements contradicted other reputable sources, even the Bible. This was done deliberately, without passing the information through a filter of truth, as the writer himself disclosed:

> "But more often, the elders from the *Aram* tribe narrate this all from memory in songs, accompanied by the play on a pandirn (a stringed musical instrument) with performances and dances. Whether these legends hold the truth or the falsehood, we don't care. After all, in this

book, I cite everything completely: both what the ear hears and what is written in the books, so that you know everything and become convinced of the purity of my motives towards you." [1.6]

Movses Khorenatsi insisted that the founder of the *Hai,* aka the modern *Armenians, Haik* was the son of *Torgom,* the descendent from *Tiras* – the son to *Gamer* (or *Gomer*) and the grandson to *Japheth:*

"Such was *Haik,* the son of *Torgom,* the son of *Tiras,* the son of *Gamer,* the son of *Japheth,* the ancestor of the *Armenians,* and such are his family and descendants and the country of their dwelling." [1.12]

However, this avowal is seriously flawed. First of all, *Torgom,* or *Togarmah,* was not the son of *Tiras. Togarmah* was the son of *Gomer.* Secondly, *Tiras* was not the son of *Gamer* (*Gomer*), as *Movses Khorenatsi* declared. Actually, *Tiras* was the son of *Japheth* and the brother of *Gomer:*

"And the sons of *Gomer; Ashkenaz,* and *Riphath,* and *Togarmah.*" ["Genesis." KJB. 10:3.]

"The sons of *Japheth; Gomer,* and *Magog,* and *Madai,* and *Javan,* and *Tubal,* and *Meshech,* and *Tiras.*" [Idem. 10:2.]

Thirdly, nowhere in the Bible can one find the name of *Haik,* let alone being the son of *Torgom* (*Togarmah*). Fourthly, according to the *Jewish* chronicles and medieval rabbinical works, such as "The Chronicles of *Jerahmeel*" [31.6] and "The Book of *Jasher*" [10.10], as well as "*Khazar* Correspondence" between the *Khazarian* King of the *Turkic* origin *Joseph ben Aaron* and *Hasdai ibn Shaprut,* foreign secretary to the *Caliph of Cordoba* [227-232], *Togarmah* was linked to the *Turkic* nations and had 10 sons, from whom 10 *Turkic* peoples originated, as shown below:

The Chronicles of Jerahmeel	***The Book of Jasher***	***Khazar Correspondence***	***Originated People***
Cuzar	*Buzar*	*Khazar*	*Khazar* – a *Turkic* people
Paşinaq	*Parzunac*	*Bizal*	*Pecheneg* – a *Turkic* people
Alan	*Elicanum*	*Avar*	*Alani* – a *Scythian* tribe
Bulgar	*Balgar*	*Bulgar*	*Bulgari* – a *Scythian* and a *Turkic* tribe
Kanbina	*Ragbib*	*Janur*	*Yanilar* – a *Turkic* tribe [*Uraksin.* 862]
Turq	*Tarki*	*Tarna*	*Turks*
Buz	*Bid*	*Uauz*	*Oguz* – a *Turkic* people
Zakhukh	*Zebuc*	*Sawir*	*Saviri* – a *Scythian* tribe
Ugar	*Ongal*	*Ujur*	*Hunni,* or *Hunuguri* – a *Scythian* tribe
Tulmeş	*Tilmaz*	*Tauris*	*Tauri* – a *Scythian* tribe

Before wrapping up the discussion about the ancestors of the modern *Armenians,* there is a need to address some extremely gross inaccuracies in the account presented by *Movses Khorenatsi* about the *Persian* kings:

> "Now, let us move on to the enumeration of the kings from the clan of *Artashes,* up to the abolition of their power. After *Arshavir,* as we said, *Artashes* reigns thirty-four years, *Darius* – thirty years, *Arshak* – nineteen years, *Artashes* – twenty years, *Peroz* – thirty-four years, *Valarsh* – fifty years, *Artabanus* – thirty-one years. *Artashir of Stakhr,* son of *Sasan,* kills him, abolishes the kingdom of the *Parthians,* and takes their hereditary country away from them." [2.69]

Without getting into a lengthy discussion about all the enumerated kings and whether or not they should be considered such, the example of *Artabanus* will suffice to serve the purpose. *Artabanus* was not the king of *Parthia,* and he did not rule it for 31 years, as asserted by the *Armenian* annalist. He was the commander of the royal bodyguard in the *Persian* court who killed the *Persian* King *Darius* and then his son *Xerxes.* "*Artashir of Stakhr*", aka *Artaxerxes,* avenged the murder of his royal father and grandfather by putting to death *Artabanus.* The *Latin* intellectual *Justin,* in his work "Epitome of *Pompeius Trogus*", confirmed this fact:

> "*Xerxes,* king of *Persia,* once the terror of the nations around him, became, after his unsuccessful conduct of the war against *Greece,* an object of contempt even to his own subjects. *Artabanus,* his chief officer, conceiving hopes of usurping the throne, as the king's authority was every day declining, entered one evening into the palace (which from his intimacy with *Xerxes* was always open to him), accompanied by his seven stout sons, and, having put the king to death, proceeded to remove by stratagem such of the king's sons as opposed his wishes. Entertaining little apprehension from *Artaxerxes,* who was but a boy, he pretended that the king had been slain by *Darius,* who was of full age, that he might have possession of the throne the sooner, and instigated *Artaxerxes* to revenge parricide by fratricide. When they came to *Darius's* house, he was found asleep, and killed as if he merely counterfeited sleep. But seeing that one of the king's sons was still uninjured by his villainy, and fearing a struggle for the throne on the part of the nobles, he took into his councils a certain *Bacabasus,* who, content that the government should remain in the present family, disclosed the whole matter to *Artaxerxes,* acquainting him "by what means his father had been killed, and how his brother had been murdered on a false suspicion of parricide; and, finally, how a plot was laid for himself." On this information, *Artaxerxes,* fearing the number of *Artabanus'* sons, gave orders for the troops to be ready under arms on the following day, as if he meant to ascertain their strength, and their respective efficiency for the field. *Artabanus,* accordingly, presenting himself under arms among the rest, the king, pretending that his corslet was too short for him, desired *Artabanus* to make an exchange with him, and, while he was disarming himself, and defenseless, ran him through with his sword, ordering his sons, at the same time, to be apprehended. Thus this excellent youth at once took revenge for his father's murder, and saved himself from the machinations of *Artabanus.*" [3.1]

Furthermore, *Artabanus* was not an ethnic *Persian* – he was a *Scythian* and directly related to *Arsaces* the *Parthian,* as follows from *Tacitus:*

> "Accordingly they summoned *Artabanus,* an *Arsacid* by blood, who had grown to manhood among the *Dahae,* and who, though routed in the first encounter, rallied his forces and possessed himself of the kingdom." ["Annals of *Tacitus.*" 2.3]

There is a need to dissect another absolutely ridiculous claim stated as a historical fact by *Movses Khorenatsi,* who referenced some obscure and unknown names of historians, perhaps fabulated, such as *Scamadros,* in contrast to the well-established and reputable *Herodotus, Plutarch,* and other

Greek scholars. *Movses Khorenatsi* asserted that it was *Artashes the Parthian* who ruled the world and defeated the *Lydian* king *Croesus*. However, a simple calculation of the dates makes this assertion null and void. The comparison of the lifespan dates of *Cyrus, Solon,* and *Croesus* reveals that all three of them were contemporaries of each other:

Cyrus: 600 BCE – 530 BCE
Solon: 640 BCE – 558 BCE
Croesus: 595 BCE – 547 BCE

From *Movses Khorenatsi's* own statements, it becomes evident that *Artashes the Parthian* lived 400 years after *Cyrus, Solon,* and *Croesus:*

> "Besides, they tell about the encounter of *Croesus* and *Nectaneb,* and *Nectaneb,* described by *Manephon,* is the last *Egyptian* king, whom some considered *Alexander's* father. We know that *Cyrus* lived two hundred years earlier than *Nektaneb* and *Nectaneb* – more than two hundred years earlier than *Artashes the First*, King of *Armenia*." [2.13]

As such, there is no way to take the following story relayed by *Movses Khorenatsi* seriously:

> "*Skamadros* writes: "The proud *Lydian* king *Croesus* was deceived by the response of the Oracle of *Pythia*: '*Croesus*, crossing the river *Alis*, will destroy the state.' Assuming this refers to strangers, he ruined himself, for *Artashes the Parthian* fettered him and put him on an iron brazier. *Croesus,* remembering the words of *Solon of Athens,* began to speak in his own language: "O *Solon, Solon!* You wisely said that a person should not be considered happy until his death." Those, who were nearby and heard, told *Artashes* that *Croesus* was invoking some new deity. *Artashes* relented and ordered him to be brought to him. After asking and finding out what he was shouting about, he ordered to stop his torture."" [2.13]

The *Greco-Roman* biographer *Plutarch's* testimony that coincides with *Herodotus's* account on this matter seems much closer to the truth:

> "At this time, then, *Croesus* held *Solon* in a contempt like this; but afterwards he encountered *Cyrus,* was defeated in battle, lost his city, was taken alive and condemned to be burnt; and then, as he lay bound upon the pyre in the sight of all the *Persians* and of *Cyrus* himself, with all the reach and power of which his voice was capable, he called out thrice: "O *Solon!*" *Cyrus,* then, astonished at this, sent men to ask him what man or god this *Solon* was on whom alone he called in his extremity. And *Croesus,* without any concealment, said: "This man was one of the sages of *Greece,* and I sent for him, not with any desire to hear or learn the things of which I stood in need, but in order that he might behold, and, when he left me, bear testimony to the happiness I then enjoyed, the loss of which I now see to be a greater evil than its possession was a good. For when it was mine, the good I derived from it was matter of report and men's opinion, but its departure from me issues in terrible sufferings and irreparable calamities, which are real. And that man, conjecturing this future from what he then saw, bade me look to the end of my life, and not let insecure conjectures embolden me to be proud and insolent." When this was reported to *Cyrus,* since he was a wiser man than *Croesus,* and saw the word of *Solon* confirmed in the example before him, he not only released *Croesus,* but actually held him in honour as long as he lived. And thus *Solon* had the reputation of saving one king and instructing another by means of a single saying." ["*Solon.*" 1.28.2-4]

One would agree with the *Armenian* researcher *A.O. Sarkissian* who admitted that *Movses Khorenatsi's* "History of *Armenia*" was full of fables and myths yet consecrated into existence ["On the Authenticity of *Moses of Khoren's History*." Journal of the American Oriental Society. 1940.60.1.81].

On some occasions, being intolerant to other scholars' opinions contradicting his viewpoint, *Movses Khorenatsi* categorically refused to accept any affirmations made by the *Greeks* or other nations about the *Armenians* by stating:

"Anything else, asserted by the *Greeks*, is unacceptable to us; others (let them think) as they want." [1.14]

He also applied harsh words to his own *Armenian* countrymen – dead and alive when criticizing their scientific inaptitude, arrogant and lawless character:

"And it seems to me that both the current and ancient *Armenians* had no attraction to science and the collection of wise songs. Therefore, it is unnecessary to continue our talk about people who are unreasonable, stupid, and wild." [Idem. 1.3]

"But they can say: (it happened) because of the absence of script and literature at that time, or because of various wars that frequently followed one after another. But this opinion is untenable, for there were intervals between the wars, as well as *Persian* and *Greek* scripts, used to write numerous books, that have been stored by us to this day, containing information about property in villages and regions, and in every house, about community litigation and transactions, especially about the inheritance of ancestral estates." [Idem ibid]

"But I want to note the hardheartedness and arrogance of our people from the beginning to the present. Not being committed to good and indisposed to truth, or distinguished by the arrogant and headstrong character, they opposed the king's will regarding *Christian* faith, following the will of wives and concubines." [Idem. 2.92]

"Here, I am ashamed to reveal the truth, especially about the lawlessness and nefariousness of our people and their deeds, worthy of great sorrow and tears." [Idem ibid]

"Therefore, while mourning my people, I will say as *Paul* said about his enemies and the foes of the cross of *Christ,* using not my own, but the *Holy Spirit's* words. A flawed and disappointing clan, the clan unsettled in heart and unfaithful to God in its spirit! People of *Aram*! How long will you be hard-hearted, why do you love vanity and godlessness? Do you not realize that the Lord has magnified his saint and that the Lord will not hear when you call to him? For you have become hardened in the Fall and do not repent on your lounges, for you make unlawful sacrifices and despise those who trust in God. Therefore, you will encounter a trap that you do not recognize and will fall into this trap, and the beast that you will hunt will seize you." [Idem. 2.92]

Remarkably, these statements of the medieval *Armenian* historian about his people echoed in the 21st c. through the president and later, the prime minister of *Armenia Nikol Pashinyan,* who wrote the following about his *Armenian* ancestors:

"Let us stop praising our ancestors and ask ourselves a very pragmatic question: what did these ancestors bequeath to us, what did they leave behind? Nothing, more than nothing. Because "nothing" is when you have to start from scratch, but we have to start from, I don't know, which minus, because our ancestors left us only such a stock of genocides, humiliation, betrayal, and immorality, which, as it turns out, is difficult, extremely difficult to overcome.
I condemn our ancestors, I curse them because they did nothing to make us live more dignifiedly and more proudly today. Our ancestors did not care for their descendants, even as much as

animals instinctively care. I condemn all those who praise our ancestors. [85]
[https://haqqin.az/news/185456]

By the 19th c., the ancestors of the modern *Armenians* were known as a people without a country:

> "The *Armenians* are chiefly known, at the present day, not as a nation having a home and country of their own, but as a scattered race — citizens of the world. This is so far from surprising, that one cannot read the history of *Armenia* without wondering that any trace of its ancient inhabitants remains. At an early date, they were carried or driven to *Mesopotamia* and *Cilicia*. In later times, the *Turkish* conquest caused many of them to emigrate to *Constantinople. Shah Abbas,* as we have seen, forcibly removed many thousands to *Persia*. The *Saracens* and *Greeks,* while contending for the possession of *Armenia,* took away multitudes of captives. *Toghrul Beg* and *Timour* carried thousands into unknown regions. The *Mamelukes* removed sixty thousand *Armenians* to *Egypt;* and it is known that the *Persians,* in every war — even in the last with *Russia* — carried away their captives into servitude. In addition to these causes of depopulation, multitudes have, at various periods, been induced, by oppression at home, to seek voluntarily an asylum in distant countries. The *Armenians,* therefore, are found not only in almost every part of *Turkey* and *Persia,* but in *India, Russia, Poland,* and many other parts of *Europe*. Thousands migrate, every year, from their native mountains to the large cities of *Turkey,* where they practise, for years, the humble occupations of porters and water-carriers; but, almost invariably, they or their children work their way into the ranks of trade. Some begin with the calling of a mechanic, ascending gradually to that of a merchant, and finally the more able or fortunate reaching the dignity of a banker — which is the highest summit of their ambition."
> [*Goodrich S.G.* "A History of All Nations, from the Earliest Periods to the Present Time; Or, Universal History in which the History of Every Nation, Ancient and Modern, Is Separately Given." 1.130.257]

And it was the *Bolsheviks,* who in the 1st quarter of the 20th c. put together a territory for the scattered *Armenians* on the lands of the *Irevan Khanate,* founded by the *Azerbaijanis,* called it *Armenia,* and joined it as the *Soviet Socialist Republic of Armenia* to the *Union of the Soviet Socialist Republics,* or the *USSR*. After the dissolution of the *USSR* in 1991, an independent *Armenian* country emerged – the Republic of *Armenia*.

The best way to end this chapter is to invoke *Strabo* with his wise words:

> "Indeed it becomes immediately evident that they have woven together a tissue of myths not through ignorance of the real facts, but merely to amuse by a deceptive narration of the impossible and marvellous." [1.2.35]

---

[85] Translated from *Russian* into *English* by the author of the current book.

§ 11-5. THE PELASGI AND THEIR POSTERITY.

The next *Trojan* nation to be discussed is the "noble *Pelasgi*," as *Homer* put it. *Pelasgi* fought against the *Greeks* to defend *Troy* and the *Trojans* in the *Trojan* war:

"To the seaward lie the *Carians,* the *Paeonian* bowmen, the *Leleges,* the *Cauconians,* and the noble *Pelasgi*." ["The Iliad". Translated by *S. Butler*. 2]

The *Pelasgi* were the most ancient, aboriginal, *Thrace-Scythian* nation that inhabited *Greece* prior to the *Greeks*, as well as some regions of *Italy*. From them issued forth many nations of *Greece, Rome, Troy*. The *Pelasgi* were very closely related to the *Trojans*, being of the same stock and *Turkic* blood. After the *Trojan* war, they left, along with the remnants of the defeated *Trojans*, for new land, established the kingdom of *Turrenia*, aka *Tyrrhenia*, and changed their names from the *Pelasgi* to the *Turrenians* in honor of their *Trojan* leader *Turrenus* (*Turan*).

With the references to other fellow writers of antiquity, *Strabo* asserted the non-*Greek* origin of the *Pelasgi*:

"Almost everyone is agreed that the *Pelasgi* were an ancient race spread throughout the whole of *Greece*, but especially in the country of the *Æolians* near to *Thessaly*. *Ephorus*, however, says that he considers they were originally *Arcadians*, who had taken up a warlike mode of life; and having persuaded many others to the same course, imparted their own name to the whole, and became famous both among the *Greeks*, and in every other country where they chanced to come. *Homer* informs us that there were colonies of them in *Crete*, for he makes *Ulysses* say to *Penelope* —
 "Diverse their language is; *Achaians* some,
 And some indigenous are; *Cydonians* there,
 Crest-shaking *Dorians*, and *Pelasgians* dwell."
And that portion of *Thessaly* between the outlets of the *Peneius* and the *Thermopylæ*, as far as the mountains of *Pindus*, is named *Pelasgic Argos*, the district having formerly belonged to the *Pelasgi*... *Anticlides* says, that they first colonized about *Lemnos* and *Imbros*, and that some of their number passed into *Italy* with *Tyrrhenus*, the son of *Atys*. And the writers on the *Athenian Antiquities*, relate of the *Pelasgi*, that some of them came to *Athens*, where, on account of their wanderings, and their settling like birds in any place where they chanced to come, they were called by the *Athenians Pelargi*." [5.2.4]

The ancient *Greek* tragedian *Aeschylus* (463-7 BCE), in his play "Suppliant Women", confirmed *Strabo's* discourse by the narration of the *Pelasgian* king *Pelasgus* (or *Pelasgos*) – the king of *Argos* about himself and his people:

"For I am *Pelasgus*, offspring of *Palaechthon*, whom the earth brought forth, and lord of this land; and after me, their king, is rightly named the race of the *Pelasgi*, who harvest the land. Of all the region through which the pure *Strymon* flows, on the side toward the setting sun, I am the lord. There lies within the limits of my rule the land of the *Perrhaebi*, the parts beyond *Pindus* close to the *Paeonians*, and the mountain ridge of *Dodona;* the edge of the watery sea borders my kingdom. I rule up to these boundaries.
The ground where we stand is *Apian* land itself, and has borne that name since antiquity in honor of a healer. For *Apis*, seer and healer, the son of *Apollo*, came from *Naupactus* on the farther shore and purified this land of monsters deadly to man, which Earth, defiled by the pollution of bloody deeds of old, caused to spring up — plagues charged with wrath, an ominous colony of swarming serpents.

Of these plagues *Apis* worked the cure by sorcery and spells to the content of the *Argive* land, and for reward thereafter earned for himself remembrance in prayers." [250-270]

Aeschylus emphasized that the *Pelasgians* had a "barbarian tongue":

Pelasgus (King of *Argos*): "I invoke *Apia's* hilly land — for well, O land, you understand my barbarous speech..." [Idem. 117]

As it was enunciated in earlier chapters, the *Pelasgians*, or the *Pelasgi*, branched out into a multitude of nations – small and big, famous and obscure. They shared close ties with the *Trojan* people of *Pæones*, who were a colony of the *Teucrians* [*Herodotus*. 5.12] – a *Thrace-Scythian* nation founded by *Teucer*, who begot *Aeneid*, the ancestor of the *Romans*.

According to *Justin*, the *Pelasgi* were the natives of *Macedonia*, known previously as *Pæonia*:

"*Macedonia* was formerly called *Emathia*, from the name of king *Emathion*, of whose prowess the earliest proofs are extant in those parts. As the origin of this kingdom was but humble, so its limits were at first extremely narrow. The inhabitants were called *Pelasgi*, the country *Paeonia*." [7.1]

Obviously, the *Pelasgi* were renamed to the *Pæonians* after the country they populated. They were also ethnically and culturally connected to another *Trojan* nation – the *Phrygians* and, consequently, to their derivatives – the *Peloponnesians*, the *Lacedaemonians*, the *Spartans*, the *Hellespontii*, the *Armenians* (these were not the ancestors of modern *Armenians*), as all of them were united by the *Dorian* heritage.

Additionally, the *Pelasgi* were kith and kin with the *Leleges*, subsequently, with their offshoot nations – the *Carians*, the *Lydians*, the *Locri*, the *Asii*, the *Turreni*, the *Etrusci*, or the *Tusci*, the *Mysians*, who also were considered to be the *Getae*, or the *Thracians*.

Just like their *Scythe-Thracian* brethren, the *Pelasgi* remained fluid in the places they inhabited and in the names they carried. Let us have an excursion into the *Pelasgian* world and meet most if not all of the *Pelasgian* nations:

> *Pelasgi*, aka *Pelasgoi* = Πελασγοί, aka *Pelasgiotae*, aka *Pelasgiotai* = Πελασγιῶται:
> o *Pelasgi, Pelasgoi: Pelas > Pilis* 'knowledge' + *Gi, Goi > -Gə* 'an affix, converting a noun into a verb', meaning "teach, provide knowledge" in *Turkic*.
> o *Pelasgiotae, Pelasgiotai: Pelasgi* 'teach, train' (*Pelas > Pilis* 'knowledge' + *Gi > -Gə* 'an affix, converting a noun into a verb') + *Otae, Otai > Otau* 'dwelling, camp', meaning "training camp" or "abode of the *Pelasgi*" in *Turkic*. The *Pelasgiotai* were named as such after the district *Pelasgiotis* (Πελασγιῶτις).

Both *Strabo* and *Pausanias* affirmed that the nation and the country of the *Pelasgi* attained their name from their founder. However, they differed in the interpretation of the name, as for *Strabo*, it was *Pulaios* (Πύλαιος), while *Pausanias* spelled it as *Pelasgos* (Πελασγὸς):

"That the *Pelasgi* were a great nation history, it is said, furnishes other evidence. For *Menecrates* of *Elæa*, in his work on the foundation of cities, says, that the whole of the present *Ionian* coast, beginning from *Mycale* and the neighbouring islands, were formerly inhabited by *Pelasgi*. But the *Lesbians* say that they were commanded by *Pylæus*, who is called by the poet the chief of the *Pelasgi*, and that it was from him that the mountain in their country had the name of *Pylæum*." [*Strabo*. 13.3.3]

"The *Arcadians* say that *Pelasgus* was the first inhabitant of this land. It is natural to suppose that others accompanied *Pelasgus*, and that he was not by himself; for otherwise he would have been a king without any subjects to rule over. However, in stature and in prowess, in beauty and

in wisdom, *Pelasgus* excelled his fellows, and for this reason, I think, he was chosen to be king by them. *Asius* the poet says of him:
> "The godlike *Pelasgus* on the wooded mountains Black earth gave up, that the race of mortals might exist." [*Pausanias*. "Description of *Greece*." 8.1.4]

"*Pelasgus* on becoming king invented huts that humans should not shiver, or be soaked by rain, or oppressed by heat. Moreover, he it was who first thought of coats of sheep-skins, such as poor folk still wear in *Euboea* and *Phocis*. He too it was who checked the habit of eating green leaves, grasses, and roots always inedible and sometimes poisonous." [Idem. 8.1.5]

"But he introduced as food the nuts of trees, not those of all trees but only the acorns of the edible oak. Some people have followed this diet so closely since the time of *Pelasgus* that even the *Pythian* priestess, when she forbade the *Lacedaemonians* to touch the land of the *Arcadians*, uttered the following verses:
> "In *Arcadia* are many men who eat acorns,
> Who will prevent you; though I do not grudge it you."

It is said that it was in the reign of *Pelasgus* that the land was called *Pelasgia*." [Idem. 8.1.6]
In spite of divergence in interpretation, both variants of the name of the *Pelasgian* nation's founder bear the same *Turkic* root – *Pilis*:
- *Pulaios* > *Pilis* "knowledge" in *Turkic*.
- *Pelasgos*: *Pilis* + *G* > *-Gə* 'an affix, converting a noun into a verb' + *Os* > *Us* 'master', meaning "master who provides knowledge" in *Turkic*.

In the *Turkic* languages, there is also a shortened version of *Pelasgos*, an archaic word derived from the same root – *Pilgə* "wise man" [*Radlov*. 4.2.1341].
According to *Pausanias*, wisdom, among other merits, was the deciding factor why *Pelasgos* was selected as the king of his people. His name reflected his virtue. He was an inventor, a teacher, and a highly respected leader to whom people would listen and follow.
The *Athenians* altered the name of the *Pelasgi* into a *Grecian* word *Pelargós*=Πελαργός "stork" to distinguish their transient lifestyle that, actually, matched in meaning the appellation of another *Pelasgi-Trojan* nation – the *Leleges* "stork" in *Turkic*:
> "And the writers on the *Athenian* antiquities, relate of the *Pelasgi*, that some of them came to *Athens*, where, on account of their wanderings, and their settling like birds in any place where they chanced to come, they were called by the *Athenians Pelargi*." [*Strabo*. 5.2.4]

Herodotus stated that the *Pelasgi*, or *Pelasgians*, spoke a language different from *Greek*, and they were the first to take up the lands of *Greece*. Later, they went under the name of the *Dorians* and the *Lacedemonians*:
> "What language however the *Pelasgians* used to speak I am not able with certainty to say. But if one must pronounce judging by those that still remain of the *Pelasgians* who dwelt in the city of *Creston* above the *Tyrsenians*, and who were once neighbours of the race now called *Dorian*, dwelling then in the land which is now called *Thessaliotis*, and also by those that remain of the *Pelasgians* who settled at *Plakia* and *Skylake* in the region of the *Hellespont*, who before that had been settlers with the *Athenians*, and of the natives of the various other towns which are really *Pelasgian*, though they have lost the name, if one must pronounce judging by these, the *Pelasgians* used to speak a Barbarian language." [1.57]

While insisting that the *Pelasgi* spoke "a barbarous language", *Herodotus* also pointed out that a group of the *Pelasgi* assimilated with the *Greeks* and switched to their language:
> "If, I say, adding to these such other *Pelasgian* cities as have alter'd their name, I may be permitted to give my conjecture, the *Pelasgians* spoke a barbarous language. And if the whole *Pelasgian* body did so; the people of *Attica*, who are descended from them, must have unlearnt their own mother tongue, after they took the name of *Grecians*. For the language of the *Crotonians* and of the *Placians* is the same; but different from that of all their neighbors. By

> which it appears they have taken care to preserve the language they brought with them into those places. But the *Hellenians*, as I think, have from the time they were people, us'd the same language they now speak. And tho', when separated from the *Pelasgians*, they were at first of no considerable force; yet from a small beginning they advanc'd to a mighty power, by the conjunction of many nations, as well barbarians as others. Whereas, on the other hand, the *Pelasgians* being a barbarous nation, seem to me never to have risen to any considerable grandeur." [1.57]

Strabo's testimony is in harmony with the statement of *Herodotus* about the *Pelasgi* being the first nation to inhabit *Greece:*

> "This oracle, according to *Ephorus*, was established by *Pelasgi*, who are said to be the most ancient people that were sovereigns in *Greece*." [7.7.10]

He even went further by asserting that the nations and tribes other than the *Greeks* initially inhabited *Greece:*

> "Perhaps even the whole of *Greece* was, anciently, a settlement of barbarians, if we judge from former accounts. For *Pelops* brought colonists from *Phrygia* into the *Peloponnesus*, which took his name; *Danaus* brought colonists from *Egypt; Dryopes, Caucones, Pelasgi, Leleges*, and other barbarous nations, partitioned among themselves the country on this side of the isthmus. The case was the same on the other side of the isthmus; for *Thracians*, under their leader *Eumolpus*, took possession of *Attica; Tereus of Daulis* in *Phocæa;* the *Phoenicians*, with their leader *Cadmus*, occupied the *Cadmeian* district; *Aones*, and *Temmices*, and *Hyantes, Boeotia. Pindar* says, "there was a time when the *Boeotian* people were called *Syes*." Some names show their barbarous origin, as *Cecrops, Codrus, Oeclus, Cothus, Drymas,* and *Crinacus*.[86] *Thracians, Illyrians,* and *Epirotæ* are settled even at present on the sides of *Greece*. Formerly the territory they possessed was more extensive, although even now the barbarians possess a large part of the country, which, without dispute, is *Greece. Macedonia* is occupied by *Thracians*, as well as some parts of *Thessaly;* the country above *Acarnania* and *Ætolia*, by *Thesproti, Cassopæi, Amphilochi, Molotti,* and *Athamanes, Epirotic* tribes." [Idem. 7.7.1]

The *Pelasgi*, just like their relatives — the *Scythians*, and later the *Turkic* nations, were constantly on the move. They also were the rulers of *Peloponnesus*, aka *Pelasgia*, aka *Apia:*

> "*Peloponnesus*, called beforetime *Apia* and *Pelasgia*, is a demie island, worthie to come behind no other land foer excellencie and name; lying betweene two seas, *Ægeum* and *Ionium:* like unto the leafe of a plaine tree, in regard of the indented creekes and cornered noukes thereof: it beareth a circuit of 563 myles, according to *Isidorus*."
>
> [*C.Plinius Secundus.* "The History of the World." Translated by *Philemon Holland.* 4.4]

It is worth mentioning that the name *Apia* existed as *Api* — the goddess of *Earth* in *Scythian* religion. The name originated from *Apa* "mother" in *Turkic*.

This proves a critical point here that the *Pelasgi*, aka the *Lacedemonians*, aka the *Dorians*, aka the *Peloponnesians*, aka the *Phrygians*, by "changing their country, came to inhabit in *Peloponnesus*, where they were call'd *Dorians*," as *Herodotus* believed. The *Dorians* lived in *Lacedaemon* for centuries, as *Plutarch* noted:

> "For a period of no less than six hundred years the *Dorians* had been living in *Lacedaemon*, and this was the first time in all that period that enemies had been seen in the country; before this, none had ventured there." [5.31]

As a further matter, it is necessary to point out that *Homer* mostly used the word *Pelasgian* to denominate the warriors of the *Pelasgi*, fighting against the *Greco-Danaans* on the side of the *Trojans:*

---

[86] In the original *Greek* text it is *Kekrops=Κέκροψ, Kodros=Κόδρος, Aiklos=Ἄικλος, Komos=Κόθος, Drumas=Δρύμας, Krianos=Κρίνακος.*

"At this moment *Hippothous* brave son of the *Pelasgian Lethus,* in his zeal for *Hector* and the *Trojans,* was dragging the body off by the foot through the press of the fight, having bound a strap round the sinews near the ankle…" [17]

However, the *Latin* poets *Ovid, Virgil,* even *Homer* with *Euripides* used the word *Pelasgian* extensively, applying that to all the *Greeks*.

Unlike the *Latin* authors, *Homer* used the word *Pelasgian* also in the meaning "of *Pelasgian* heritage". When describing the *Greco-Danaan* contingent ready for the *Trojan* war, *Homer* declared that a part of it came from *Pelasgian Argos*:

"Those again who held *Pelasgic Argos, Alos, Alope,* and *Trachis;* and those of *Phthia* and *Hellas* the land of fair women, who were called *Myrmidons, Hellenes,* and *Achaeans;* these had fifty ships, over which *Achilles* was in command." ["The Iliad." 2]

To which *Euripides* in "The *Phoenician* Maidens" exclaimed:

"O *Argos,* city of *Pelasgia!* I dread thy prowess…" [255].

The dual meaning of the word *Pelasgian* used by the ancient authors, applying to both the *Greeks* and the *Pelasgians,* was explained by *Herodotus,* who attested to the fact that both the *Grecian* nations, such as the *Athenians* and the *Ionians,* used to be the *Pelasgians* (a non-*Indo-European* nation), who later assimilated with the *Greeks,* switched their language and ethnic identity to the *Grecians*:

"When the *Pelasgians* possess'd those countries, which now go by the name of *Greece,* the *Athenians* were called *Cranian Pelasgians.* Under the reign of *Cecrops,* they had the name of *Cecropians;* which in the time of their king *Erechtheus,* they changed for that of *Athenians,* and lastly were named *Ionians* from *Ion,* the son of *Xuthus,* who was their general." [8.44]

To the *Pelasgian* origin of the *Greeks, Ovid* did testify in his "Metamorphoses", where he called the *Greeks* "the *Pelasgian* nation":

"But soon afterwards,
he brought into that land a ravished wife,
Helen, the cause of a disastrous war,
together with a thousand ships, and all
the great *Pelasgian* nation." [12.7-11]

As it was reported earlier, the *Pelasgi* were a wandering nation, like other kindred nations, such as the *Trojan Leleges,* the *Carians,* the *Scythians,* and their posterity — *Turkic* nations in stark contrast to the domiciled, non-migratory nations, such as the *Greeks, Persians,* and related *Indo-Europeans. Strabo* corroborated this transient spirit of the *Pelasgi* by saying:

"Inroads and migrations took place chiefly about the period of the *Trojan* war, and subsequently to that time, *Barbarians* as well as *Greeks* showing an eagerness to get possession of the territory of other nations. This disposition, however, showed itself before the time of the *Trojan* war; for there existed then tribes of *Pelasgi, Caucones,* and *Leleges,* who are said to have wandered, anciently, over various parts of *Europe.* The poet represents them as assisting the *Trojans,* but not as coming from the opposite coast." [12.8.4]

"The *Pelasgi,* however, were a nation disposed to wander, ready to remove from settlement to settlement, and experienced both a great increase and a sudden diminution of strength and numbers, particularly at the time of the *Æolian* and *Ionian* migrations to *Asia.*" [Idem. 13.3.3]

After living in *Samothracia* for some time, the *Pelasgians* decided to resettle in *Attica,* as asserted by *Herodotus*:

"…*Pelasgians* were inhabitants of *Samothracia,* before they came into the country of *Attica*…" [2.51]

By the way, the name *Samothracia,* aka *Samothrace,* aka *Samothráke* (Σαμοθράκη), aka *Samothreike* (Σαμοθρηίκη), is of *Turkic* origin:

- *Samo > Səmah* 'desire, wish' + *Thracia, Thrake, Threike* (*Tr > Tur* 'powerful, eternal' + *Acia, Ake, Eike > Əkə* 'patriarch'), meaning "desired *Thrace*" or "the desired land of the powerful founders" in *Turkic*.

However, according to *Diodorus Siculus*, *Samothrace* attained its name from the queen of the *Amazons Myrina*:

> "Whilst she was busy in taking other islands, she was endangered by a storm at sea, where, offering up her prayers to the mother of the gods for deliverance, she was driven upon a certain desert island, which she consecrated to the beforementioned goddess, being admonished so to do by a dream; and there she erected altars, and offered magnificent sacrifices. This island is called *Samothracia*, which, according to the *Greek* dialect, signifies the Sacred Island. But there are some historians that say, it was formerly called *Samos*, and from some *Thracians* that came to inhabit there, *Samothracia*. After that the *Amazons* were returned into the continent, they fabulously report, that the mother of the gods (being delighted with this island) placed there her sons, called the *Corybantes*. In the records of their sacred mysteries, it is declared who was their father; and she herself (they say) taught them the rites and mysteries that are now in use in that island, and instituted and appointed a sacred grove, and an inviolable sanctuary." [3.4]

Both listed options of the name *Samothrace* signal its non-*Indo-European* origin, namely, its *Turkic* root. *Diodorus Siculus* gave the translation of this word into *Greek* as a "sacred island" that confirms its non-*Greek* etymology:

- *Samothrake = Σαμοθράκη: Samo > Suma* 'revere'[87] + *Othrake > Otruğ* 'island', meaning "revered or sacred island" in *Turkic*.

Of course, not always the *Pelasgi* left their lands on their own accord – from some places, they were dispelled by force, according to *Herodotus*:

> "The *Pelasgians* had been already driven out of *Attica* by the *Athenians*; whether justly or unjustly I shall not determine, having nothing more to say than what is reported on both sides. *Hecatæus*, the son of *Hegesander*, affirms they were unjustly expell'd. For, says he, when the *Athenians* saw that the lands about *Hymessus*, which they had given to the *Pelasgians* in payment for the wall they had built about the *Acropolis*, were improv'd from a barren and unprofitable soil into a fertile and well-cultivated region, they grew envious of their prosperity and coveting to resume the country, drove out the *Pelasgians* without any other pretence whatever. On the other hand, the *Athenians* affirm, that they were justly ejected on account of the injuries they had done. For they saw that while the *Pelasgians* continued to inhabit under mount *Hymessus*, they frequently left their habitations and in contempt of the *Athenians* offer'd violence to their sons and daughters who were sent for water to the place call'd the Nine Fountains, because in those times neither they nor any other people of *Greece* were furnish'd with slaves. That the *Pelasgians* not contented with these attempts, were at last manifestly detected to have form'd a design against *Athens* and that the *Athenians*, to show themselves as generous as the others had been base, when they had the power of punishing these offenders for their manifest treachery, chose rather to command them only to depart the country which the *Pelasgians* obeying possessed themselves of *Lemnos*, and other places." [6.137]

Homer, in his turn, contended that the *Pelasgi* rushed to *Troy* to render military assistance "from deep-ploughed *Larisa*", which was the capital of *Thessaly*, while the *Greco-Danaans* came from *Pelasgian Argos*. As ancient records show, *Thessaly* used to be a part of *Thrace*. In the opinion of *Strabo*, "some understood *Pelasgian Argos* to be a *Thessalian* city, formerly situated near *Larisa*, but now no longer in existence. Others do not understand a city to be meant by this name, but the *Thessalian* plain, and to have been so called by *Abas*, who established a colony there from *Argos*." [9.5.5]

During *Strabo*'s time, *Thessaly* was partitioned into four districts, and the *Pelasgi* were called *Pelasgiotæ*:

---

[87] *Egorov V.G.* "Etimologicheskiy slovar chuvashskogo yazika." [195].

"Such then is *Thessaly*, which is divided into four parts, *Phthiotis, Hestiæotis, Thessaliotis,* and *Pelasgiotis. Phthiotis* comprises the southern parts, extending along *Oeta* from the *Maliac* and (or) *Pylaïc Gulf* as far as *Dolopia* and *Pindus,* increasing in breadth to *Pharsalia* and the *Thessalian* plains. *Hestiæotis* comprises the western parts and those between *Pindus* and *Upper Macedonia;* the rest is occupied by the inhabitants of the plains below *Hestiæotis,* who are called *Pelasgiotæ,* and approach close to the *Lower Macedonians;* by the [*Thessalians*] also, who possess the country next in order, as far as the coast of *Magnesia.* The names of many cities might here be enumerated, which are celebrated on other accounts, but particularly as being mentioned by *Homer;* few of them, however, but most of all *Larisa,* preserve their ancient importance." [9.5.3]

The *Pelasgians* were the founding fathers, the originators of two principal nations of *Greece,* later acknowledged as the *Hellenes* – the *Athenians,* aka the *Ionians,* and the *Dorians,* aka the *Lacedaemonians* [*Herodotus.* 1.56].

The name of the *Hellenes* and their land *Hellas,* or *Ellada* (Ἑλλάδα), was imparted by the *Pelasgian* king *Hellenos* (Ἕλληνος).[88] It is recognizably of *Pelasgian* origin and can effortlessly be deduced from the *Turkic* word *Ellən* "union, confederation" [Dr.Sl.171] in *Turkic:*

- *Hellenos: Helle > Ellə* 'create a union of tribes, or confederation' + *N > -N* 'an affix, converting a verb into a noun' + *Os > Us* 'master', meaning "unifying leader", "leader of the confederation" in *Turkic.*

Similar word alterations under the influence of the affix *-N* (and its variations *-In, -İn, -An*) were recorded in "Drevneturkskiy Slovar", such as *Yığ* "collect" > *Yığın* "collection, pile"; *Ter* "gather" > *Terin* "crowd"; *Yal* "flame (verb)" > *Yalan* "flame (noun)" [658].

Remarkably, the name of *Hellenos,* as its meaning implied, became a unifying blanket of all the tribes of *Pelasgia,* later known as *Greece.* It replaced the *Pelasgian* identity. Further down in the history lane, the appellation – *Hellenes* began to denote the people of *Greek* descent exclusively, and the word *Hellenic* stood for *Greek.* Nevertheless, the etymology of this name was ruled unknown, implying that the appellation *Hellenos* and its derivatives did not have *Greek* origin.

Thucydides recounted the emergence of the *Hellenes* after the *Trojan* war:

"For before the *Trojan* War, nothing appeareth to have been done by *Greece* in common; nor indeed was it, as I think, called all by that one name of *Hellas;* nor before the time of *Hellen,* the son of *Deucalion,* was there any such name at all. But *Pelasgicum* (which was the farthest extended) and the other parts, by regions, received their names from their own inhabitants. But *Hellen* and his sons being strong in *Phthiotis,* and called in, for their aid, into other cities; these cities, because of their conversing with them, began more particularly to be called *Hellenes:* and yet could not that name of a long time after prevail upon them all."

["The History of the *Grecian* War." 1].

Intriguingly, *Herodotus* considered the *Hellenes* a race apart from the *Pelasgians,* only starting the count after *Perseus.* Prior to that, he traced the origin of the *Hellenes* from the *Pelasgian-Argive* dynasty, leading to the *Thraco-Pelasgian* queen *Io* in *Egypt:*

"...if one enumerates their ancestors in succession going back from *Danae* the daughter of *Acrisios,* the rulers of the *Dorians* will prove to be *Egyptians* by direct descent."

[*Herodotus.* 7.53]

Moreover, *Herodotus* explicitly emphasized that the *Hellenes* and the *Pelasgi* were one nation that later split into two independent entities, speaking two different languages:

"As for the *Hellenic* race, it has used ever the same language, as I clearly perceive, since it first took its rise; but since the time when it parted off feeble at first from the *Pelasgian* race, setting

---

[88] Not to be confused with a female name *Helen* (*Helene*=Ἑλένη) and a male name *Helenos* (he was the *Trojan* king *Priam's* son), signifying "torch, blaze" in *Greek.* Both of them point to their *Turkic* origins from the ancient word *əlaŋü* "blaze" [Henry G. Schwarz. "An *Uyghur-English* Dictionary." 303.].

forth from a small beginning it has increased to that great number of races which we see, and chiefly because many Barbarian races have been added to it besides." [1.58]

It seems clear that the *Hellenes* began to speak *Greek* from the moment they parted ways with their *Pelasgian* kin, and all the descending tribes followed the *Hellenic* suit by unlearning their *Pelasgian* language, such as the *Ionians*, the *Attikoi*. *Herodotus* kept us in the dark by not providing more details about how and why the *Hellenes* switched from the *Pelasgian* to the *Greek* language. One can conjecture from his own words that many *Greek* tribes joined the *Hellenes*, and not only did they increase their numbers but also managed to change their language to *Greek*.

Attested by many renowned historians, *Hellenos* was genealogically connected to the *Pelasgians* by being a great-grandson of the *Titan Iapetus* (brother of *Cronus*, who was, in his turn, the father of *Zeus*), a grandson of two brothers *Prometheus* and *Epimetheus*, and the son of *Deucalon* (from the union of *Prometheus* and *Clymene*) and *Pyrrha* (from the union of *Epimetheus* and *Pandora*).

On the authority of *Apollodorus* and *Strabo*, it appears that *Hellenos* issued three male offsprings: *Dorus* (properly, *Doros*=Δῶρος), *Aelous* (properly, *Aiolos*=Αἴολος) и *Xuthus* (properly, *Xouthos*=ξουθός). From the first two scions, the *Dorians* and the *Aeolians* took their origin, and from the sons of *Xuthus* – *Achaeus* (Ἀχαιός) and *Ion* (Ἴων) sprung the *Achaeans* and the *Ionians*:

"*Hellen* [89] had *Dorus*, *Xuthus*, and *Aeolus* by a nymph *Orseis*. Those who were called *Greeks* he named *Hellenes* after himself, and divided the country among his sons. *Xuthus* received *Peloponnese* and begat *Achaeus* and *Ion* by *Creusa*, daughter of *Erechtheus*, and from *Achaeus* and *Ion* the *Achaeans* and *Ionians* derive their names. *Dorus* received the country over against *Peloponnese* and called the settlers *Dorians* after himself. *Aeolus* reigned over the regions about *Thessaly* and named the inhabitants *Aeolians*." [*Apollodorus*. "Library." 1.7.3]

"The *Ionians*, who were descendants of the *Athenians*, were, anciently, masters of this country. It was formerly called *Ægialeia*, and the inhabitants *Ægialeans*, but in later times, *Ionia*, from the former people, as *Attica* had the name of *Ionia*, from *Ion* the son of *Xuthus*.

It is said, that *Hellen* was the son of *Deucalion*, and that he governed the country about *Phthia* between the *Peneins* and *Asopus*, and transmitted to his eldest son these dominions, sending the others out of their native country to seek a settlement each of them for himself. *Dorus*, one of them, settled the *Dorians* about *Parnassus*, and when he left them, they bore his name. *Xuthus*, another, married the daughter of *Erechtheus*, and was the founder of the *Tetrapolis of Attica*, which consisted of *Œnoe*, *Marathon*, *Probalinthus*, and *Tricorythus*.

Achæus, one of the sons of *Xuthus*, having committed an accidental murder, fled to *Lacedæmon*, and occasioned the inhabitants to take the name of *Achæans*.

Ion, the other son, having vanquished the *Thracian* army with their leader *Eumolpus*, obtained so much renown, that the *Athenians* intrusted him with the government of their state. It was he who first distributed the mass of the people into four tribes, and these again into four classes according to their occupations, husbandmen, artificers, priests, and the fourth, military guards; after having made many more regulations of this kind, he left to the country his own name.

It happened at that time that the country had such an abundance of inhabitants, that the *Athenians* sent out a colony of *Ionians* to *Peloponnesus*, and the tract of country which they occupied was called *Ionia* after their own name, instead of *Ægialeia*, and the inhabitants *Ionians* instead of *Ægialeans*, who were distributed among twelve cities.

After the return of the *Heracleidæ*, these *Ionians*, being expelled by the *Achæans*, returned to *Athens*, whence, in conjunction with the *Codridæ*, (descendants of *Codrus*) they sent cut the *Ionian* colonists to *Asia*. They founded twelve cities on the seacoast of *Caria* and *Lydia*, having distributed themselves over the country into as many parts as they occupied in *Peloponnesus*. The *Achæans* were *Phthiotæ* by descent, and were settled at *Lacedæmon*, but when the *Heracleidæ* became masters of the country, having recovered their power under *Tisamenus*, the son of

---

[89] In the original *Greek* text, it is *Hellenos* = Ἕλληνος.

Orestes, they attacked the *Ionians,* as I said before, and defeated them. They drove the *Ionians* out of the country, and took possession of the territory, but retained the same partition of it which they found existing there. They became so powerful, that, although the *Heracleidæ,* from whom they had revolted, occupied the rest of *Peloponnesus,* yet they defended themselves against them all, and called their own country *Achæa.*" [*Strabo.* 8.7.1]

➢ *Dorians, aka Doriees = Δωριέες, aka Phrygians, aka Peloponnesians* > *Doros=Δῶρος: Dor* 'clan, dynasty' + *Os* > *Us* 'master', meaning "head of the dynasty" in *Turkic.* The nation was named after their leader *Doros,* the son of the *Pelasgian* king *Hellen,* who according to some ancient accounts, was the son of *Zeus,* not *Deucalion* [*Apollodorus.* 1.7.2]. The word construction of this name – *Doros* insistently invites us to accept its *Turkic* roots. The structural and lexical resemblance of *Doros* to *Turkic* names *Elxan, Elbəy, Elbaşı* is very credible:
- o *Doros: Dor* 'clan' + *Os* > *Us* 'master'.
- o *Elxan: El* 'people' + *Xan* 'king'.
- o *Elbəy: El* 'people' + *Bəy* 'chief, head'.
- o *Elbaşı: El* 'people' + *Başı* 'head'.

It is important to emphasize that the second component -*Os* in the name *Doros* and in similar *Pelasgian* names was not a *Greek* termination, as in that case, all the *Pelasgian* appellations should have had an added termination. The *Pelasgian* names, such as *Deucalion* (Δευκαλίων), *Ion* (Ἴων), *Lycaon* (Λυκάων), beg to agree. As such, the word *Os, Us* at the end of the *Pelasgian* names signified the elevated position of their carriers as a "master, chief". This structure with the title added at the end of the name is inherently *Turkic.* Most likely than not, the *Greek* names also acquired this termination -*Os* from the *Pelasgians.* There is another variation of it – -*Ar, -Er, -Ir, -Or* "warrior, man, hero", added to a name at the end that can be observed both in the ancient *Turkic* names (*Yabing er, Azmas er, Yangilmaz er, Kugir, As er, Pogu er, Uz er, En Ergu er, Barchi er, Apa er, Kemgchi er*), in the olden *Icelandic* saga "The Prose *Edda*" in the names of the sons of *Odin* and the *Asir,* or the *As* people: *Rerir, Sigmundar, Gunnar, Gudrunar, Jolnar, Hamdir, Okunar, Asir.* Even the original last name of the author *Snorri Sturluson* was *Sturlusonar,* and in the *Pelasgian* names – *Agenor, Gelenor* [*Pausanias.* 2.16]

Being true to their *Pelasgian* nature, the *Dorians* were predisposed to wanderings:
"For under the reign of *Deucalion,* the *Pelasgians* inhabited the country of *Pthiotis;* and in the time of *Dorus,* the son of *Hellenes* possess'd that region which is called *Istiæotis,* lying at the foot of the mountains *Ossa* and *Olympus.* From thence being expell'd by the *Cadmœans,* they betook themselves to *Macednum* on mount *Pindus,* which place they afterwards abandon'd for another settlement in *Dryopis;* and again changing their country, came to inhabit in *Peloponesus,* where they were call'd *Dorians.*" [*Herodotus.* 1.56]

According to *Pausanias,* the *Dorians* came from *Oeta* – a region of the *Pelasgian Thessaly* to *Peloponnesus,* where they renamed themselves into the *Dorians* and founded magnificent cities:
"The rest of *Peloponnesus* belongs to immigrants. The modern *Corinthians* are the latest inhabitants of *Peloponnesus,* and from my time to the time when they received their land from the *Roman* Emperor is two hundred and seventeen years. The *Dryopians* reached the *Peloponnesus* from *Parnassus,* the *Dorians* from *Oeta.*"
[*Pausanias.* "*Description of Greece.*" 5.1.2]

"The remaining races, four in number, have come in from without, namely the *Dorians, Aitolians, Dryopians* and *Lemnians.* Of the *Dorians* there are many cities and of great renown; of the *Aitolians, Elis* alone; of the *Dryopians, Hermion* and *Asine,* which latter is opposite *Cardamyle* in the *Laconian* land; and of the *Lemnians,* all the *Paroreatai.*" [*Herodotus.* 8.73]

Herodotus considered the *Peloponnesian* region of *Dryopis* to be the motherland of the *Dorians:*
"When these words were reported, then the *Thessalians,* moved with anger against the *Phokians,* became guides to the Barbarian to show him the way: and from the land of *Trachis* they entered

> *Doris;* for a narrow strip of the *Dorian* territory extends this way, about thirty furlongs in breadth, lying between *Malis* and *Phokis,* the region which was in ancient time called *Dryopis;* this land is the mother-country of the *Dorians* in *Peloponnese.*" [*Herodotus.* 8.31]

The esteemed *Greek* historian traced the genealogy of the *Dorians,* aka the *Argives,* to their *Thrace-Pelasgic* roots although by his time, they were *Hellenized* and regarded as the *Hellenes,* acknowledged later as the *Greeks:*

> "This is the report given by the *Lacedemonians* alone of all the *Hellenes;* but this which follows I write in accordance with that which is reported by the *Hellenes* generally, I mean that the names of these kings of the *Dorians* are rightly enumerated by the *Hellenes* up to *Perseus* the son of *Danae* (leaving the god out of account), and proved to be of *Hellenic* race; for even from that time they were reckoned as *Hellenes.* I said "up to *Perseus*" and did not take the descent from a yet higher point, because there is no name mentioned of a mortal father for *Perseus,* as *Amphitryon* is for *Heracles.* Therefore with reason, as is evident, I have said "rightly up to *Perseus*"; but if one enumerates their ancestors in succession going back from *Danae* the daughter of *Acrisios,* the rulers of the *Dorians* will prove to be *Egyptians* by direct descent." [*Herodotus.* 7.53]

By *Egyptians, Herodotus* meant the progeny of the *Pelasgian* princess *Io,* who resettled in *Egypt* and established a royal dynasty. The diagram below introduces the *Thrace–Pelasgian* lineage issued from the *Pelasgian* king *Inachus* and *Melia* – parents of *Io.*

The *Thrace-Pelasgian* genealogy of the *Argives.*

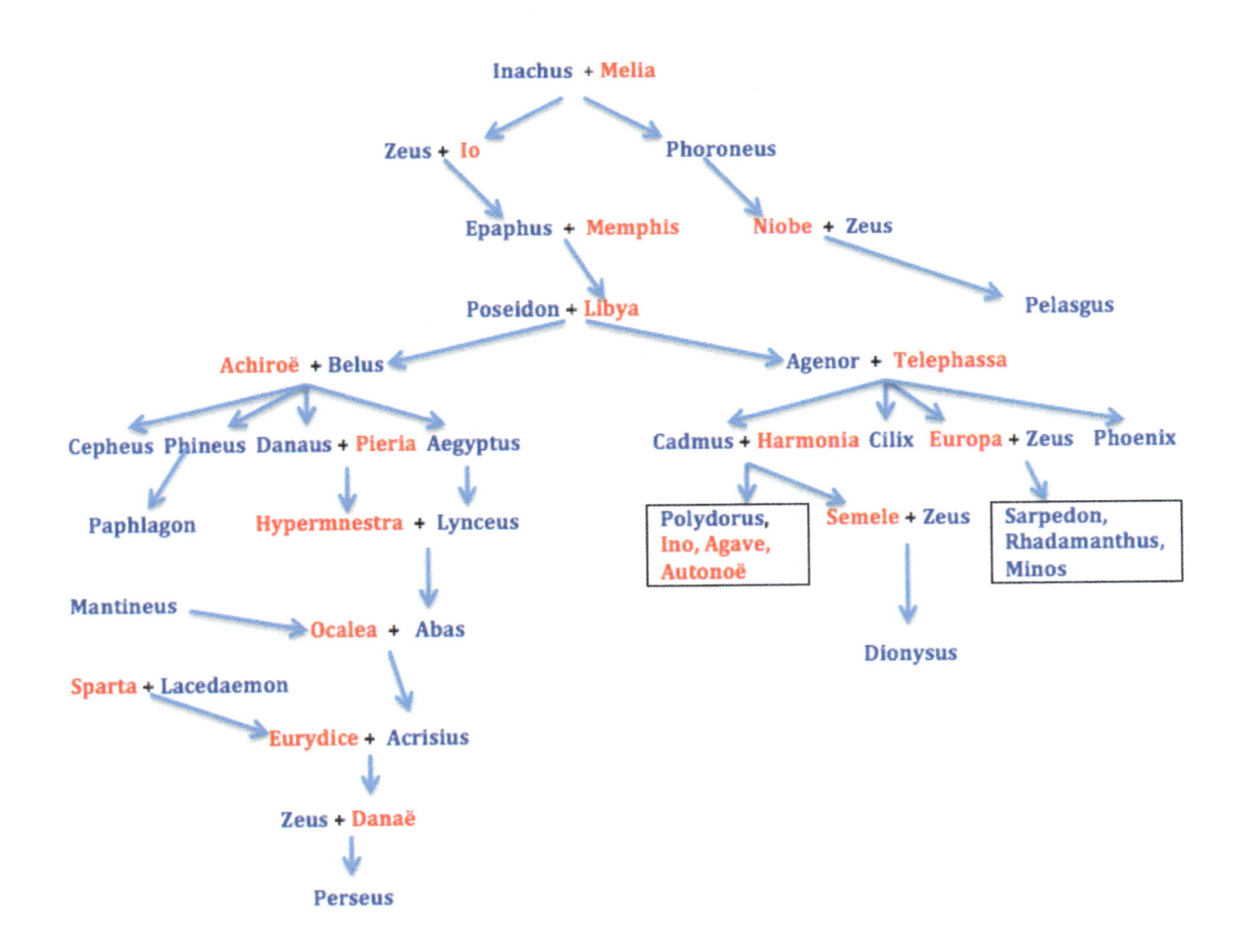

Interestingly, the *Dorians* were fashion trendsetters whom other people of *Greece* would follow. *Herodotus* narrated a rather somber story that served as a confirmation of this fact, as well as the reason why later the *Athenian* women switched to the *Ionian*, or correctly, the *Carian* style of clothes:

> "This is the report which is given by the *Argives* and *Eginetans* both, and it is admitted by the *Athenians* also that but one alone of them survived and came back to *Attica*: only the *Argives* say that this one remained alive from destruction wrought by them upon the army of *Athens*, while the *Athenians* say that the divine power was the destroyer. However, even this one man did not remain alive, but perished, they say, in the following manner: when he returned to *Athens* he reported the calamity which had happened; and the wives of the men who had gone on the expedition to *Egina*, hearing it and being very indignant that he alone of all had survived, came round this man and proceeded to stab him with the brooches of their mantles, each one of them asking of him where her husband was. Thus he was slain; and to the *Athenians* it seemed that the deed of the women was a much more terrible thing even than the calamity which had happened; and not knowing, it is said, how they should punish the women in any other way, they changed their fashion of dress to that of *Ionia*, for before this the women of the *Athenians* wore *Dorian* dress, very like that of *Corinth*, they changed it therefore to the linen tunic, in order that they might not have use for brooches." [5.87]

> "In truth however this fashion of dress is not *Ionian* originally but *Carian*, for the old *Hellenic* fashion of dress for women was universally the same as that which we now call *Dorian*." [Idem. 5.88]

➤ *Argives*, aka *Argivus*, aka *Argeioi* = Ἀργεῖοι > *Argos*=Ἄργος, *Argus*: *Ar* 'warrior, man, hero' + *Gos*, *Gus* > *Qos*, *Qus* 'erupt, disgorge', meaning "the one who produces warriors" in *Turkic*. As it was earlier said, this *Dorian* issue, as well as the region they inhabited – *Argos*, or *Argeia*, came into possession of their corresponding names after the *Pelasgian* hero *Argos*, aka *Argus*:

> "But *Argus* received the kingdom and called the *Peloponnese* after himself *Argos*..."
> [*Apollodorus*. "Library." 2.1.2]

Pausanias repeatedly mentioned that the *Argives* were of *Dorian* extraction, and wherever they went, they would introduce or practice their *Dorian* customs and traditions:

> "Subsequently a division of the *Argives* who, under *Deiphontes*, had seized *Epidaurus*, crossed to *Aegina*, and, settling among the old *Aeginetans*, established in the island *Dorian* manners and the *Dorian* dialect." [2.29.5]

> "When *Agesipolis* grew up and came to the throne, the first *Peloponnesians* against whom he waged war were the *Argives*. When he led his army from the territory of *Tegea* into that of *Argos*, the *Argives* sent a herald to make for them with *Agesipolis* a certain ancestral truce, which from ancient times had been an established custom between *Dorians* and *Dorians*. But *Agesipolis* did not make the truce with the herald, but advancing with his army proceeded to devastate the land." [Idem. 3.5.8]

➤ *Mycenaeans*, aka *Mukenaioi* = Μυκηναίοι > *Mukene*=Μυκήνη > *Mukan* "delicate, fragile" in *Turkic*. On the authority of *Pausanias*, it seems certain that out of many other versions, the nation of the *Mycenaeans* and their country obtained their name from the eponymous *Thrace-Pelasgian* heroine *Mycene*, daughter of *Inachus*:

> "*Homer* in the *Odyssey* mentions a woman *Mycene* in the following verse: "*Tyro* and *Alcmene* and the fair-crowned lady *Mycene*." She is said to have been the daughter of *Inachus* and the wife of *Arestor* in the poem which the *Greeks* call the *Great Eoeae*. So they say that this lady has given her name to the city." [2.16.4]

Under the leadership of their king *Agamemnon*, who was the grandson of *Pelops* and, consequently, was of the *Phryge-Thrace-Pelasgian* extraction, the *Mycenæans* were the leading force against the *Trojans* in the *Trojan* War [*Homer*. 2.484-580].

- *Danaans,* aka *Danaoi* = Δαναοί > *Danaos*=Δαναός: *Dana* 'smart, intelligent' + *Os* > *Us* 'master', meaning "bright ruler" in *Turkic*. The *Danaioi* carried the appellation after their king *Danaos*, or *Danaus*, who was a great-grandson of the *Egyptian* king *Epaphus* – the son of the *Pelasgian* princess *Io*. According to the legend, *Danaos* fled *Egypt* from his brother *Aegyptus*, who wanted to marry 50 daughters of *Danaos* to his sons forcefully. He arrived in *Argos*, demanded and took the throne from *Pelasgus*, and ordered all the inhabitants to be called the *Danaioi*:

    "Likewise *Æschylus* in his Suppliants, or *Danaids*, makes their race to be of *Argos* near *Mycenæ*. *Ephorus* likewise says that *Peloponnesus* was named *Pelasgia;* and *Euripides*, in the Archelaus, says,

    "*Danaus*, who was the father of fifty daughters, having arrived in *Argos* inhabited the city of *Inachus*, and made a law that those who had before borne the name of *Pelasgiotæ* throughout *Greece* should be called *Danai*."" [*Strabo*. 5.2.4]

    Interestingly, both the *Latin* historian *St. Jerome* in his "The Chronicle" ("Chronicon") and *Pausanias* mentioned the name of King *Gelanor* (*Gelan* > *Gülen* 'laughing' + *Or* > *Ör* 'man', meaning "laughing man" in *Turkic*, as *Gelanor* was laughing at *Danaos's* claim to the throne of *Argos*) instead of King *Pelasgus*:

    "After *Iasus*, *Crotopus*, the son of *Agenor*, came to the throne and begat *Sthenelas*, but *Danaus* sailed from *Egypt* against *Gelanor*, the son of *Sthenelas*, and stayed the succession to the kingdom of the descendants of *Agenor*." [*Pausanias*. 2.16.1]

    St. Jerome also acknowledged that *Danaos* acquired the kingship in 1475 BCE and killed the sons of his brother *Aegyptus*, except for one, through his daughters in 1467 BCE.

    As an important note, *Homer* called the attacking contingent against the *Trojans* in the *Trojan* War – the *Danaans* (not *Greeks*), who were, as we know, *Pelasgians* in essence:

    "He thought that on that same day he was to take the city of *Priam*, but he little knew what was in the mind of *Jove*, who had many another hard-fought fight in store alike for *Danaans* and *Trojans*." ["The Iliad." 2]

- *Heracleidae,* aka *Hrakleides* = Ἡρακλείδης: *Heracl, Hrakl* '*Hercules*' + *Eid* > *Ed* 'assets, heritage', meaning "lineage of *Hercules*" in *Turkic*.

    As far as the name of *Hercules*, it has a very ancient *Turkic* origin, detected in a number of kin languages, carrying the same meaning "powerful warrior, hero":

    o *Akkadian* – *Er-gal* "great man": *Er* 'warrior, hero' + *Gal* > *Kal* 'power' in *Turkic*.
    o *Etruscan* – *Erkle* "great man": *Er* 'warrior, hero' + *Kle* > *Kal* 'power' in *Turkic*.
    o *Median* – *Hraklea* "powerful man": *Hr* > *Er* 'warrior, hero' + *Aklea* >*Akkala* 'overpower' in *Turkic*.

    The second component of the name as an independent word was observed in *Hittite* – *Gal, Kal* "great", in *Akkadian* – *Gal* 'great', in *Susian* – *Khal* "great", in *Turkic* – *Kal* "power".

    However, according to *Diodorus Siculus*, *Hercules* first was known as *Alkaios* = Ἀλκαῖος (translated into *English* as *Alcides*): *Al* 'huge, powerful, great' + *Kaio* > *Kaia* 'rock' + *Os* > *Us* 'master', meaning "leader, large as a huge rock" in *Turkic*. Due to his heroic feat as a toddler, *Hercules* acquired the second name that perpetuated him for ages:

    "Afterwards *Juno* [*Hera*] sent two serpents to devour the child: but he took them with both his hands by their throats, and strangled them. Upon which account the *Argives* (coming to understand what was done) called him *Hercules*, because *Juno* was the occasion of his glory and fame, for he was before called *Alcides*. Others are named by their parents, but he gained his name by his valour." [4.1]

    Even this interpretation of the name provided by *Diodorus Siculus* points to its *Turkic* source. The attempt to derive the name of *Hercules*, or *Hrakles* (Ἡρακλῆς), from *Greek Kleos*=Κλέος "glory" seems far-fetched, as *Herodotus* recorded the name of *Hercules* as *Hraklea* (Ἡρακλέα). However, both variants inevitably point to one and the same *Turkic* direction:

- *Hrakles: Hra* 'Hera, wife of *Zeus*' + *Akles* > *Akla* 'glorify, elevate', meaning "glorify *Hera*" in *Turkic*.
- *Hraklea: Hr* > *Er* 'warrior, hero' + *Aklea* > *Akkala* 'overpower', meaning "powerful hero/warrior" in *Turkic*.

It was likely that after *Hercules,* all the *Turkic* males in antiquity opted to have two names – one given after birth and another after the military or heroic achievement. For instance, the famous emperor *Chingis Khan* was initially known as *Tamuzin*:

"At his birth his father called him *Tamuzin,* but when he was declar'd Khan, he took the name of *Chingis.*"

[*Abul Ghazi Bahader.* "A General History of the *Turks, Moguls,* and *Tatars*…".1.3.1]

Furthermore, the name *Hera* also has *Turkic* roots. The *Pelasgian* goddess *Hera's* appellation was explained as "lovely" by *Plato:*

"…*Hera* is a lovely one (ἐρατή), as indeed, *Zeus* is said to have married her for love." [404c]

And yet again, the etymology of *Hera's* name as *Erate* (ἐρατή) has distinctive *Turkic* features:

Erate "lovely" > *Yüratu* "love" (noun), *Yürat, Yarat* "love" (verb) [90] in *Turkic*. There is also a *Turkic* word *Yürǝk, Ürǝk* "heart" that shares the same root – *Yür, Ür.*

The second exegesis of *Hera's* name (in *Greek,* it is *Hra* = Ἥρα) comes from the idea of her being a protectress, a heroess. In this case, again, the name of the *Pelasgian* deity emanated from a *Turkic Er* "hero, warrior".

It is no wonder that all the variants and components of *Hercules's* name originated from the *Turkic* foundation. As a *Thrace-Pelasgian* with the *Argive* lineage, stemming from King *Inachus, Hercules* was the founder of many nations related to the *Turkic* people, such as the *Scythians* [*Herodotus.* 4.10], the *Agathursoi,* the *Gelonoi* [*Herodotus.* 4.104], the *Lydians,* the *Turreni,* the *Etruscans* [*Strabo.* 5.2.2], the *Germanic* tribes [*Diodorus Siculus.* 5.24], the *Medes* [*Flavius Arrianus.* 4.7]. As far as the *Scythian* nation of the *Agathursoi, Herodotus* noticed the stunning similarity in customs and traditions between them and the *Thracians:*

"The *Agathyrsians* are the most luxurious of men and wear gold ornaments for the most part…In their other customs they have come to resemble the *Thracians.*" [4.104]

The same analogy can be extended to the kin nation of the *Sabines* – a *Pelasgian* branch of the *Spartans:*

"*Fabius,* the historian, says that the *Romans* first knew what wealth was when they became masters of this nation." [*Strabo.* 5.3]

"The custom of wearing rings was believed to have been introduced into *Rome* by the *Sabines,* who are described in the early legends as wearing gold rings with precious stones (gemmati anuli) of great beauty (Liv. 1.11; Dionys. A. R. 2.38)." [*William Smith. Sabini.*]

"For, at that time, the *Sabines* wore ornaments of gold, and were, in no degree, inferior to the *Tyrrhenians* in elegance." [*Dionysius of Halicarnassus.* 2.38]

The *Heracleidae* were the *Pelasgian* posterity of the legendary hero, also known as *Heracles.* As pure *Argives,* they came to *Peloponnesus* together with the *Dorians* to stake their claim to their fatherland and its royal seat:

"It was in the reign of this *Tisamenus* that the *Heracleidae* returned to the *Peloponnesus;* they were *Temenus* and *Cresphontes,* the sons of *Aristomachus,* together with the sons of the third brother, *Aristodemus,* who had died. Their claim to *Argos* and to the throne of *Argos* was, in my opinion, most just, because *Tisamenus* was descended from *Pelops,* but the *Heracleidae* were descendants of *Perseus.*" [*Pausanias.* 2.18.7]

---

[90] *Egorov V.G.* "Etimologicheskiy slovar chuvashskogo yazika." [350].

As noted by *St. Jerome*, the *Heracleidae* arrived in the *Peloponnesus* in 1098 BCE. And it was the *Spartan* King *Lysander*, who issued a decree to elect a king based on valor and excellence instead of heritage:

> "Of the *Heracleidae* who united with the *Dorians* and came down into *Peloponnesus*, there was a numerous and glorious stock flourishing in *Sparta;* however, not every family belonging to it participated in the royal succession, but the kings were chosen from two houses only, and were called *Eurypontidae* and *Agiadae*. The rest had no special privileges in the government because of their high birth, but the honours which result from superior excellence lay open to all who had power and ability. Now *Lysander* belonged to one of these families, and when he had risen to great fame for his deeds, and had acquired many friends and great power, he was vexed to see the city increased in power by his efforts, but ruled by others who were of no better birth than himself. He therefore planned to take the government away from the two houses, and restore it to all the *Heracleidae* in common, or, as some say, not to the *Heracleidae*, but to the *Spartans* in general, in order that its high prerogatives might not belong to those only who were descended from *Heracles*, but to those who, like *Heracles*, were selected for superior excellence, since it was this which raised him to divine honours. And he hoped that when the kingdom was awarded on this principle, no *Spartan* would be chosen before himself." [*Plutarch*. "*Lysander*." 24.3-5]

Many *Turkic* nations shared *Lysander's* view and acted likewise by electing the leaders and sovereigns based on their heroism and military acumen.

➢ *Rhodians,* aka *Rodioi* = ′Ρόδιοι > *Rodos*=′Ρόδος: *Ro* > *Ru* 'dynasty, clan' + *Odos* > *Ödüs* 'succor', meaning "carer of the family" in *Turkic*. As attested by *Diodorus Siculus*, the *Rhodians* and their island *Rhodos* acquired their name after the daughter of *Poseidon Rodos*:

> "The island of *Rhodes* was antiently inhabited by those called *Telchines;* who, (as an old story goes), were the offspring of *Thalassa,* and with *Caphira,* the daughter of *Oceanus,* brought up *Neptune,* who was committed to their care by *Rhea*. It is said they invented several arts, and found out many other things useful and conducive to the well-being of man's life. It is reported, they were the first that made statues of the gods, and that some of the antient images were denominated from them; for amongst the *Lindians, Apollo* is called *Apollo Telchinius:* amongst the *Ialysians, Juno* and the nymphs were called *Telchiniœ;* and amongst the *Camirœans, Juno,* was called *Juno Telchinia*. But these *Telchines* were likewise reported to be conjurers, for they could raise storms and tempests, with rain, hail, and snow, whenever they pleased; which the magicians, (as is related in history), were used to do. They could likewise transform themselves into other shapes, and were envious at all who learned their art. *Neptune,* they say, fell in love with *Halia,* the sister of the *Telchines,* and of her begat several children, six sons, and one daughter, called *Rhode,* from whom the island was called *Rhodes*." [5.3]

In the opinion of *St. Jerome*, *Telchines* founded *Rhodes* in 1737 BCE.

The *Rhodians* were an *Argive-Dorian* branch of the *Pelasgi*, an offshoot of the *Heracleidae*, who participated in the *Trojan* War against the *Trojans* led by the offspring of *Heracles*:

> "*Tlepolemus,* son of *Hercules,* a man both brave and large of stature, brought nine ships of lordly warriors from *Rhodes*. These dwelt in *Rhodes,* which is divided among the three cities of *Lindus, Ielysus,* and *Cameirus,* that lies upon the chalk…" [*Homer*. 2]

> "The *Rhodians* and *Cytherians, Dorique* both, by constraint, bore arms; one of them, namely the *Cytherians,* a colony of the *Lacedaemonians,* with the *Athenians* against the *Lacedaemonians* that were with *Gylippus;* and the other, that is to say, the *Rhodians,* being by descent *Argives,* not only against the *Syracusians,* who were also *Dorique,* but against their own colony, the *Gelans,* which took part with the *Syracusians*."
> [*Thucydides*. "The History of the *Grecian* War." 7]

- *Oenotrians, aka Oinotroi = Οἰνωτροί, aka Oinotrioi = Οἰνώτριοι, aka Oenotri, aka Aezii, aka Aizeoi = Αιζεοι, aka Lycaones, aka Lukaones = Λυκαονες:*
  - Oenotrians, Oinotroi, Oinotrioi > Oinotros=Οἴνωτρος: Oeno, Oino > Öyün 'be famous' + Tr > Tur 'powerful, strong, eternal' + Os > Us 'master', meaning "famous, powerful leader" in *Turkic*. By the way, the name *Oinotros* consists of two main components: *Oino + Tros,* whereas *Tros,* or *Turos* "strong leader", was a great-grandson of *Zeus,* after whom the land *Troia* and its people *Trojans* acquired their names.
  - Aezii, Aizioi > Aizeo=Αιζεο > Az, As > Əs "lord" in *Turkic*.
  - Lukaones > Lukaonos=Λυκαονος: Luka > Lükə 'raindrop' + Aon > Yan 'soul', meaning "soul, pure as a raindrop" in *Turkic*.

This *Pelasgian* colony of the *Dorian-Argive* breed was known under three appellations after its leaders: *Oinotros, Aizeo, Lukaonos,* as stated by *Dionysius of Halicarnassus:*

"And all the country he possessed, which was very large, was called *Oenotria;* and all the people under his command, *Oenotrians;* which was the third time they changed their name. For, in the reign of *Æzius,* they were called *Æzii;* when *Lycaon* succeeded to the command, *Lycaonians;* and, after *Oenotrus* led them into *Italy,* they were, for a while, called *Oenotrians.*" [1.1.12]

Pausanias also confirmed that these people established their presence in *Italy* under the appellation of their founder *Oenotrus,* who was the son of the king of *Arcadia – Lycaon (Λυκάων),* the grandson of *Pelasgus,* leading all the way to the *Thrace-Pelasgian* patriarch – *Inachus:*

"But *Oenotrus,* the youngest of the sons of *Lycaon,* asked his brother *Nyctimus* for money and men and crossed by sea to *Italy;* the land of *Oenotria* received its name from *Oenotrus* who was its king. This was the first expedition despatched from *Greece* to found a colony, and if a man makes the most careful calculation possible he will discover that no foreigners either emigrated to another land before *Oenotrus.*" [*Pausanias.* 8.3.5]

William Smith referred to the opinion of many outstanding scholars of antiquity by asserting that the *Oenotrians* were the first and most ancient *Pelasgian* colonists of *Italy:*

"There seems no doubt that the *Oenotrians* were a *Pelasgic* race, akin to the population of *Epirus* and the adjoining tract on the E. of the *Adriatic.* This was evidently the opinion of those *Greek* writers who represented *Oenotrus* as one of the sons of *Lycaon,* the son of *Pelasgus,* who emigrated from *Arcadia* at a very early period. (Pherecydes, ap. Dionys. 1.13; Paus. 8.3.5.) The statement of *Pausanias,* that this was the most ancient migration of which he had any knowledge, shows that the *Oenotrians* were considered by the *Greeks* as the earliest inhabitants of the *Italian* peninsula. But a more conclusive testimony is the incidental notice in *Stephanus of Byzantium,* that the *Greeks* in *Southern Italy* called the native population, whom they had reduced to a state of serfdom like the *Penestae* in *Thessaly* and the *Helots* in *Laconia,* by the name of *Pelasgi.* (Steph. Byz. s. v. Χῖοι.) These serfs could be no other than the *Oenotrians*. Other arguments for their *Pelasgic* origin may be deduced from the recurrence of the same names in *Southern Italy* and in *Epirus,* as the *Chones* and *Chaones, Pandosia,* and *Acheron,* &c. *Aristotle* also notices the custom of συσσίτιαι, or feasting at public tables, as subsisting from a very early period among the *Oenotrians* as well as in *Crete.* (Arist. Pot. 7.10.)" [*Oenotria*]

Dionysius of Halicarnassus on the authority of *Antiochus of Syracuse* averred that after the *Oenotrian* leaders of the *Pelasgian* extraction – *Italos (Ἰταλός)* and *Sicelos (Σικελός), Italy* and *Sicily* acquired their respective names:

"And *Antiochus of Syracuse,* a very old historian, in his account of the planting of *Italy,* enumerates the most ancient inhabitants, in the order, in which each of them possessed themselves of any part of it; and says that the first, who are recorded in history to have inhabited that country, were the *Oenotri.* His words are these:

"*Antiochus,* the son of *Xenophanes,* has given this account of *Italy,* which is the most credible and certain, out of the ancient histories: That country, which is now called *Italy,* was formerly possessed by the *Oenotri.*"

Then, he relates in what manner they were governed, and that, in the process of time, *Italus* came to be their king, from whom, changing their name, they were called *Italians;* that he was succeeded by *Morges,* from whom they were called *Morgetes:* And that *Sicelus,* being received as a guest by *Morges,* and, setting up for himself, divided the nation. After which he adds this, "Thus were the *Oenotri* called *Siceli, Morgetes,* and *Italians.*"" [1.1.12]

➢ *Italians,* aka *Italoi* = Ἰταλοί > *Italos*=Ἰταλός: *Italo* > İtələ 'lead forward; push forward' (*It* > İt 'push, pushed' + *Alo* > Ələ, Elə 'do') + *Os* > Us 'master', meaning "pushing forward chief" in *Turkic.* As a side note, the *Turkic* word İtələ still exists without any change in shape or meaning. According to *Dionysius of Halicarnassus* and *Antiochus of Syracuse,* the *Italians* became known under this name due to the *Pelasgic-Oenotrian* king *Italos,* or *Italus:*

> "But, in process of time, it was called *Italy,* from a man of great power; who, according to *Antiochus, the Syracusian,* being both a wise and good prince, and, having prevailed on some of his neighbours by his eloquence, and subdued the rest by force, he made himself master of all that country, which lies between the *Lametine* and *Scylletic* bays; which part, he says, was the first, that was called *Italy* from *Italus.* After he had possessed himself of this tract, and had many subjects under his command, he, immediately, aimed at subduing those nations, that lay contiguous, and united many cities under his government; he says, also, that *Italus* was an *Oenotrian.* But *Hellanicus,* the *Lesbian,* says, that, when *Hercules* was driving *Geryon's* cows to *Argos,* and, already, in *Italy,* a calf left the herd; and, running away, wandered over all that coast; and that it swam over the intermediate streight, and went into *Sicily;* that *Hercules,* following the calf, inquired of the inhabitants wherever he came, if they had seen it; and that they, understanding but little *Greek,* and, from the description he gave them of the animal, calling it by the name of *Vitulus,* by which it is still known, he, from that animal, called all the country the calf had wandered over, *Vitalia;* and he adds, that it is no wonder the name has been changed by time, since the like alteration has, also, happened to many *Greek* names. But, whether, as *Antiochus* says, the country took this name from a commander, which, perhaps, is the most probable; or, according to *Hellanicus,* from the calf, yet, this, at least, is manifest from both their accounts, that, in *Hercules* time, or very little before, it was called *Italia:* For, before this, the *Greeks* called it *Hesperia,* and *Ausonia,* and the people of the country, *Saturnia,* as I said before." [1.35]

The ancient *Athenian* historian and general *Thucydides* also was in favor of the legend that *Italy* owed its name to *Italos,* whom he called a ruler of the *Sicels:*

> "But the *Siculi* passed out of *Italy,* (for there they inhabited) flying from the *Opici,* having, as is most likely and as it is reported, observed the Straight, and with a fore-wind gotten over in boats which they made suddenly on the occasion, or perhaps by some other means. There is at this day a people in *Italy,* called *Siculi.* And *Italy* itself got that name after the same manner, from a King of *Arcadia,* called *Italus.* Of these a great army crossing over into *Sicily,* overthrew the *Sicanians* in battle, and drove them into the South and West parts of the same; and instead of *Sicania,* caused the island to be called *Sicilia,* and held and inhabited the best of the land for near 300 years after their going over, and before any of the *Grecians* came thither. And till now they possess the Midland, and North parts of the island." ["The History of the *Grecian* War." 6]

➢ *Sicels,* aka *Siculi,* aka *Sikeloi* = Σικελοί > *Sikelos*=Σικελός: Sıkıla 'subdue' (*Sik* > Sık 'subdued' + *El* > Ələ, Elə 'do') + *Os* > Us 'master', meaning "subduing chief" in *Turkic.* As stated earlier, the *Sicels* were called after their *Pelasgic* ruler *Sikelos,* whose name was lexically akin to his brother's. Compare:
- *Italos*: *It* > İt 'pushed' + *Al* > Ələ, Elə 'do' + *Os* > Us 'master', meaning "leading forward chief" in *Turkic.*
- *Sikelos*: *Sik* > Sık 'subdued' + *El* > Ələ, Elə 'do' + *Os* > Us 'master', meaning "subduing chief" in *Turkic.*

Furthermore, the *Turkic* word *Sıkıla* still exists without having any semantic changes or alterations.

➢ *Morgetes* = Μόργητες: *Morge* > *Mərğə* 'courageous' + *Tes* > *Taş* 'fellow, partner', meaning "courageous fellows", "partners of *Morges*" in *Turkic*. The first part of the ethnic group's appellation – *Morge* represents a truncated form of the name of the *Pelasgic* prince *Morges* (Μόργης), followed by a *Turkic* word *Taş*, which is a frequent component of the *Turkic* words, added at the end. Remarkably, the same word construction pattern with the word *Taş* or its modified variants at the end is observed in the *Scythian, Celtic, Trojan,* and even the *Native American* tribal names: *Borustheneitas* – a *Scythian* tribe, *Scordistes* – a *Kelto-Scythian* tribe, *Tauristes* – a *Kelto-Scythian* tribe, *Gergithes, Krotoniates, Sybarites* – *Trojan* tribes, *Tsistsistas,* or *Dzitsistas* – a *Native American* tribe.

Under the authority of *Strabo* and *Dionysius of Halicarnassus, William Smith* emphasized that the *Morgetes,* named after their royal, joined their *Pelasgic* brethren – the *Sicels* and coinhabited *Sicily*:
"*Antiochus of Syracuse* (ap. Dionys. 1.12) represented the *Siculi, Morgetes* and *Italietes* as all three of *Oenotrian* race; and derived their names, according to the favourite *Greek* custom, from three successive rulers of the *Oenotrians,* of whom *Italus* was the first, *Merges* the second, and *Siculus* the third. This last monarch broke up the nation into two, separating the *Siculi* from their parent stock; and it would seem that the *Morgetes* followed the fortunes of the younger branch; for *Strabo,* who also cites *Antiochus* as his authority, tells us that the *Siculi* and *Morgetes* at first inhabited the extreme southern peninsula of *Italy,* until they were expelled from thence by the *Oenotrians,* when they crossed over into *Sicily.*" (Strab. vi. p.257.)" [*Morgetes*]

➢ *Khones*, aka *Chones*, aka *Xones* = Χῶνες > *Kon* "abiding place" in *Turkic*. As it appears to be, the *Chones,* the people of *Southern Italy,* became known under this appellation due to the city of *Chone*:
"*Apollodorus,* in his description of the ships [of the *Greeks*], narrates concerning *Philoctetes,* that, according to certain writers, this prince having disembarked in the district of *Crotona,* settled on the promontory of *Crimissa,* and built the city of *Chone* above it, from which the inhabitants were called *Chones;* and that certain colonists being sent by him into *Sicily,* to the neighbourhood of *Eryx,* with *Ægestus* the *Trojan,* founded *Ægesta.*" [*Strabo*. 6.1.3]

Quoting *Antiochus, Strabo* confirmed the descendance of the *Chones* from the *Œnotrians*:
"*Antiochus,* in his treatise on *Italy,* says that this district, which he intended to describe, was called *Italy,* but that previously it had been called *Œnotria*…He says that afterwards the names of *Italy* and of the *Œnotrians* were extended as far as *Metapontium* and the *Siritis;* the *Chones,* a people of *Œnotrian* descent, and highly civilized, inhabited these districts, and called their country *Chone.*" [6.1.4]

➢ *Achaeans*, aka *Achaians,* aka *Akhaioi* = Ἀχαιοί: *Ach, Akh* > *Ak, Ağ* 'white' + *Ae, Ai* > *Ai* 'Moon', meaning "white Moon", "bright Moon" in *Turkic*. The *Achæans* as a nation, as well as *Achæa* – the region they inhabited, were named after the *Pelasgian* hero *Achæus,* or *Akhaios* (Ἀχαιός). The name *Akai* "white Moon" was also an ancient *Turkic* tribal name [*Uraksin*. 857] and the appellation of a male hero, recorded by *Radlov V.V.* [1.1.89]. There is a striking resemblance in the structural and lexical construction when comparing the *Pelasgian* names to the *Turkic* ones:
  o *Achæus,* or *Akhaios* > *Ak, Ağ* 'white' + *Ai* 'Moon' + *Os* 'master'.
  o *Actaeus,* or *Aktaios* > *Ak, Ağ* 'white' + *Tai* 'stallion' + *Os* 'master'.
  o *Akai* > *Ak, Ağ* 'white' + *Ai* 'Moon'.

There is a vivid connection between the *Pelasgian Achaeans,* or the *Akhaioi,* and the *Scythe-Sarmatian* tribe of the *Achaei. Ammianus Marcellinus* presented them as "the most ferocious of all the nations" [22.8.25]; *Strabo* detected their *Pelasgian* heritage and situated these people at a seacoast, subsisting by piracy [11.2.12], while *Pomponius Mela* classified them as a *Scythian* tribe [1.13].

The ancient historians were seemingly at variance when recounting different backgrounds of *Achæus* and determining which one should take the credit for naming the nation of the *Achæans* after himself. To *Dionysius of Halicarnassus,* he was a *Pelasgian* from the *Argive* dynasty [1.17]. *Pausanias,* however, insisted that *Achæus* belonged to the *Hellen's* dynasty by being a grandson of *Hellen* and a son of *Xuthus:*
> "Later on, after the death of *Hellen, Xuthus* was expelled from *Thessaly* by the rest of the sons of *Hellen,* who charged him with having appropriated some of the ancestral property. But he fled to *Athens,* where he was deemed worthy to wed the daughter of *Erechtheus,* by whom he had sons, *Achaeus* and *Ion.*" [7.1.2]

And the *Achæans* denominated themselves after this *Hellenic Achæus:*
> "When the sons of *Achaeus* came to power in *Argos* and *Lacedaemon,* the inhabitants of these towns came to be called *Achaeans.* The name *Achaeans* was common to them; the *Argives* had the special name of *Danai.*" [Idem. 7.1.7]

The confusion between the two contradicting postulates is easy to clarify if we track the timeline and whereabouts of the *Pelasgians,* drawn by *Dionysius of Halicarnassus* [1.17.1]. The *Achæans* were named first after the *Pelasgian* ruler *Achæus* of the *Argive* dynasty. Having established their presence in *Thessaly,* they lived there for five generations. Then they were expelled by *Deucalion,* who happened to be the father of *Hellen,* the grandfather of *Xuthus,* and the great-grandfather of *Achæus,* after whom the *Achæans* were allegedly named, according to *Pausanias.*

The *Achaeans* were the main indigenous nation, in addition to the *Arcadians,* who inhabited the *Peloponnesus,* according to *Pausanias* in "Description of *Greece.*":
> "The *Greeks* who say that the *Peloponnesus* has five, and only five, divisions must agree that *Arcadia* contains both *Arcadians* and *Eleans,* that the second division belongs to the *Achaeans,* and the remaining three to the *Dorians.* Of the races dwelling in *Peloponnesus* the *Arcadians* and *Achaeans* are aborigines. When the *Achaeans* were driven from their land by the *Dorians,* they did not retire from *Peloponnesus,* but they cast out the *Ionians* and occupied the land called of old *Aegialus,* but now called *Achaea* from these *Achaeans.* The *Arcadians,* on the other hand, have from the beginning to the present time continued in possession of their own country." [5.1.1]

Apparently, *Peloponnesus* was previously known as *Pelasgia,* according to *Ephorus:*
> "*Ephorus* likewise says that *Peloponnesus* was named *Pelasgia*…" [*Strabo.* 5.2.4]

From the words of *Pausanias,* it became evident that his *Achæus* – the descendant of *Hellen* was also a *Pelasgian,* who went back to *Thessaly* and reclaimed the land of his ancestors:
> "Of his sons, *Achaeus* with the assistance of allies from *Aegialus* and *Athens* returned to *Thessaly* and recovered the throne of his fathers…" [7.1.3]

The *Pelasgian* origin of the *Achæans* is revealed through the political and urban structure of their society. Amazingly similar to the kin *Pelasgian* nations – the *Tyrennians,* the *Trojans,* and the *Ionians,* the *Achæans* had exactly 12 cities and were united into a confederation style of government:
> "When the *Ionians* were gone the *Achaeans* divided their land among themselves and settled in their cities. These were twelve in number, at least such as were known to all the *Greek* world; *Dyme,* the nearest to *Elis,* after it *Olenus, Pharae, Triteia, Rhypes, Aegium, Ceryneia, Bura, Helice* also and *Aegae, Aegeira* and *Pellene,* the last city on the side of *Sicyonia.* In them, which had previously been inhabited by *Ionians,* settled the *Achaeans* and their princes." [*Pausanias.* 7.6.1]

> "At this time the *Achaeans* brought the *Lacedaemonians* into the *Achaean* confederacy, exacted from them the strictest justice, and razed the walls of *Sparta* to the ground. These had been built at haphazard at the time of the invasion of *Demetrius,* and afterwards of the *Epeirots* under *Pyrrhus,* but under the tyranny of *Nabis* they had been strengthened to the greatest possible degree of safety. So the *Achaeans* destroyed the walls of *Sparta,* and also repealed the laws of

Lycurgus that dealt with the training of the youths, at the same time ordering the youths to be trained after the *Achaean* method." [Idem. 7.8.5]

The *Achæans* extended into several branches, such as the *Crotonians*, the *Placians*, and the *Sybarites*.

➤ *Crotonians*, aka *Crotoniats*, aka *Krotoniates* = Κροτωνιάτης, aka *Krotonietai* = Κροτωνιῆται, aka *Krestonetai* = Κρηστωνιῆται:
  o *Crotonians* > *Croton, Kroton*=Κροτών: *Crot, Krot* > *Korut* 'patronize, favor, shelter' + *On* > -*An* 'an affix, denoting constant action', meaning "the one who provides shelter, favor" in *Turkic*. On the authority of many ancient writers, *William Smith* concluded that the *Crotonians* derived their name from a man *Croton*, who provided shelter and hospitality to *Hercules*:
    "Its name was derived, according to the current legend, from a person of the name of *Croton*, who afforded a hospitable reception to *Hercules* during the wanderings of that hero; but having been accidentally killed by him, was buried on the spot, which *Hercules* foretold would eventually become the site of a mighty city. (Diod. 4.24; Iambl. Vit. Pyth. 50; Ovid, Ov. Met. 15.12-18, 55; Etym. M. v. Κρότων.) Hence we find *Croton* sometimes called the founder of the city, while the *Crotoniats* themselves paid peculiar honours to *Hercules* as their tutelary divinity and *Oekist*. (Heraclid. Pont. 36; Iambl. Vit. Pyth. 40; Eckhel, vol. i. p. 172.)" [*Croton*]
  o *Crotoniats, Krotoniates*: *Crotonia, Krotonia* '*Kroton*' + *Ts, Tes* > *Taş* 'fellow, partner', meaning "*Kroton's* partners", "fellows that do favors" in *Turkic*.
  o *Krotonietai*: *Krotoni* '*Kroton*' + *Etai* > *Atai* 'father', meaning "sons of *Kroton*" in *Turkic*.
  o *Krestonetai*: *Kreston* '*Kreston*' + *Etai* > *Atai* 'father', meaning "sons of *Kreston*" in *Turkic*.
Herodotus called the *Crotonians* both as *Krotonietai* = Κροτωνιῆται (translated into *English* as "men of *Croton*") and *Krestonetai* = Κρηστωνιῆται ("people of *Creston*" in *English* translation):
    "Now the men of *Croton* are by descent *Achaians*." [8.47]

"For the people of *Creston* do not speak the same language with any of those who dwell about them, nor yet do the people of *Plakia*, but they speak the same language one as the other: and by this it is proved that they still keep unchanged the form of language which they brought with them when they migrated to these places." [Idem. 1.57]
Herodotus's statement about the identical language used both by the *Crestonians*, aka the *Crotonians*, and the *Placians* was in harmony with the views of *Dionysius of Halicarnassus*:
    ""For neither the *Crotoniats*," says *Herodotus*, "nor the *Placians* agree in language with any of their present neighbours, although they agree with each other; and it is clear that they preserve the fashion of speech which they brought with them into those regions." However, one may well marvel that, although the *Crotoniats* had a speech similar to that of the *Placians*, who lived near the *Hellespont*, since both were originally *Pelasgians*, it was not at all similar to that of the *Tyrrhenians*, their nearest neighbours." [1.29.1-4]

➤ *Placians, aka Plakienoi* = Πλακιηνοί: *Plac, Plak* > *Pələk* 'gift' + *Ian, Ien* > *İn* 'home', meaning "bestowed home" in *Turkic*. Most likely, an *Achæan* tribe relocated to the *Hellespont*, where they became known under the appellation of the *Placians* in honor of their hometown in *Mysia*:
    "*Pla'cia* (Πλακίη: Eth. Πλακιανός), an ancient *Pelasgian* town in *Mysia Olympene*, at the foot of *Mount Olympus*, and on the east of *Cyzicus*. The place seems to have decayed or to have been destroyed at an early time, as it is not mentioned by later writers. (Hdt. 1.57; Scylax, p. 35; Dionys. i. p. 23: Steph. B. sub voce Πλάκη.)" [*William Smith. Placia*]

➤ *Sybarites, aka Subarites* = Συβαρίτης: *Sybari, Subari* > *Sybaris, Súbaris*=Σύβαρις (*Sy, Su* 'water' + *Baris* > *Barısı* 'everyone') + *Tes* > *Taş* 'fellow, partner', meaning "fellows of public water" or "fellows with water for everyone" in *Turkic*. Both the *Achæan* tribe of the *Subarites* and their city *Sybaris* with the river were named after a public fountain called *Sybaris*:

> "It is said, that from the fountain *Sybaris* which is there, the river *Sybaris* in *Italy* had its name." [*Strabo*. 8.7.5]

The *Sybarites* rose to extraordinary power and riches due to their bountiful land, a busy port, and relaxed laws allowing citizenship to the immigrants from other nations:

> "It rose rapidly to great prosperity, owing in the first instance to the fertility of the plain in which it was situated. Its citizens also, contrary to the policy of many of the *Greek* states, freely admitted settlers of other nations to the rights of citizenship, and the vast population of the city is expressly ascribed in great measure to this cause. (Diod. 12.9.) The statements transmitted to us of the power and opulence of the city, as well as of the luxurious habits of its inhabitants, have indeed a very fabulous aspect, and are without doubt grossly exaggerated, but there is no reason to reject the main fact that *Sybaris* had in the sixth century B.C. attained a degree of wealth and power unprecedented among *Greek* cities, and which excited the admiration of the rest of the *Hellenic* world." [*William Smith. – Sybaris*]

The exorbitant level of affluent luxury, extreme pleasure-seeking, excesses in feasts, and self-indulgence exhibited by the *Sybarites* became proverbial and turned their name into a symbol of hedonism and excess.

> *Aiginetai = Αἰγινῆται, aka Eginetans:* Ai 'Moon' + Gine > Günə 'to Sun' (Gün 'Sun' + -ə 'an affix, denoting a preposition *To*') + *Tai* 'similar', meaning "tribe similar to Moon and Sun" in *Turkic*. Remarkably, the construction of the name *Aiginetai* also conforms to the *Turkic* word structure. Any *Turkic*-speaking modern individual can effortlessly derive the same conclusion.

The *Aiginetai*, or as it was rendered into *English* – the *Eginetans*, were a *Dorian* stock, as corroborated by *Herodotus*:

> "Of the islanders the *Eginetans* furnished thirty; these had also other ships manned, but with them they were guarding their own land, while with the thirty which sailed best they joined in the sea-fight at *Salamis*. Now the *Eginetans* are *Dorians* from *Epidauros,* and their island had formerly the name of *Oinone*." [8.46]

> *Lacedaemonians, aka Lacedemonians, aka Lakedaimónioi = Λακεδαιμόνιοι, aka Spartans, aka Spartiatai = Σπαρτιαται:*
>   o *Lacedaemonians, Lacedemonians, Lakedaimónioi:* Lace, Lake > Lǝkǝ 'stain' + *Daemon, Demon, Daimon* > Dǝymiyǝn 'untouchable' (Dǝy 'touch' + -Mi 'an affix, denoting negation' + -Yǝn 'an affix, denoting constant action', meaning "spotless, stain-free", literally, "the one that stain does not touch") in *Turkic*.
>   o *Spartans > Sparta* (Sp > Sǝp 'love' + *Arta* 'live in abundance', meaning "love and live in abundance" in *Turkic*) was the name of a daughter of the king of *Laconia – Eurotas,* and the great granddaughter of *Leleges,* the first king of *Laconia* and the founder of the third *Trojan* dynasty. Furthermore, *Leleges* was a great-grandson of *Io*, or *Isis –* the daughter of the *Pelasgian* King *Inachus*.
>   o *Spartiatai: Sparti = Sparta* 'a female name' + *At* 'glory', meaning "glory of *Sparta*" in *Turkic*.

Considered as a *Dorian* posterity, the *Lacedæmonians* and the *Spartans* were one *Pelasgian* nation under two different names to honor their founder and king *Lacedæmon* and *Sparta* – his wife, the princess of *Laconia* and daughter of the king *Eurotas* respectively:

> "After the figures of *Hermes* we reach *Laconia* on the west. According to the tradition of the *Lacedaemonians* themselves, *Lelex,* an aboriginal was the first king in this land, after whom his subjects were named *Leleges*. *Lelex* had a son *Myles,* and a younger one *Polycaon*. *Polycaon* retired into exile, the place of this retirement and its reason I will set forth elsewhere. On the death of *Myles* his son *Eurotas* succeeded to the throne.

Having no male issue, he left the kingdom to *Lacedaemon,* whose mother was *Taygete,* after whom the mountain was named, while according to report his father was none other than *Zeus. Lacedaemon* was wedded to *Sparta,* a daughter of *Eurotas.* When he came to the throne, he first changed the names of the land and its inhabitants, calling them after himself, and next he founded and named after his wife a city, which even down to our own day has been called *Sparta.*" [*Pausanias.* 3.1.1-2]

It was the *Thrace-Pelasgian,* as well as the *Scythian* and *Turkic* tradition to treat women equally with men. As a result, throughout history, not only cities and towns, rivers and creeks but also the nations were named after notable females:

"The citadel they call *Larisa* after the daughter of *Pelasgus.* After her were also named two of the cities in *Thessaly,* the one by the sea and the one on the *Peneus.*" [Idem. 2.24.1]

As a side note, the main heroine of *Homer*'s "The Iliad", over whom the famous *Trojan* war started and caused the destruction of the whole country – *Helen* was a *Pelasgian,* aka *Lacedemonian.* When describing *Helen's* concern about her brothers' non-participation in the *Trojan* war out of fear of ridicule or hate, *Homer* indicated that *Helen* hailed from *Lacedaemon:*

""I see, moreover, many other *Achaeans* whose names I could tell you, but there are two whom I can nowhere find, *Castor,* breaker of horses, and *Pollux* the mighty boxer; they are children of my mother, and own brothers to myself. Either they have not left *Lacedaemon,* or else, though they have brought their ships, they will not show themselves in battle for the shame and disgrace that I have brought upon them."

She knew not that both these heroes were already lying under the earth in their own land of *Lacedaemon.*" [3]

Surprisingly, *Helen* classifies her brothers as the *Achaeans.* However, this can be explained by the fact that they were *Pelasgians* as well and obtained the new name after their leader *Achæus,* or *Akhaios* ("bright Moon" in *Turkic*).

In general, the *Lacedæmonians* were described by *Herodotus* as the law-abiding, freedom-loving, fearless warriors who would never flee the battlefield:

"So also the *Lacedemonians* are not inferior to any men when fighting one by one, and they are the best of all men when fighting in a body: for though free, yet they are not free in all things, for over them is set Law as a master, whom they fear much more even than thy people fear thee. It is certain at least that they do whatsoever that master commands; and he commands ever the same thing, that is to say, he bids them not flee out of battle from any multitude of men, but stay in their post and win the victory or lose their life." [7.104]

Diodorus Siculus also noticed that the *Lacedæmonians* were eager to fight and glad to accept their death if victory could not be attained [8.27.2].

There were legends sung about the free-spirited *Lacedemonians,* one of which *Herodotus* decided to leave to us as a cautionary tale:

"But after the bad reception they gave to the heralds of *Darius,* they could not sacrifice happily for a long time; and being much disturb'd at this calamity, they met together often, and by public proclamation, made inquiry, "If any *Lacedemonian* would die for *Sparta.*" Upon which notification, *Sperthies,* the son of *Anerlstus,* and *Bulis,* the son of *Ncolaus,* both *Spartans,* of eminent dignity and interest, voluntarily offered their lives to make satisfaction to *Xerxes,* the son of *Darius,* for the death of his heralds. And accordingly, these *Lacedemonians* sent these persons to the *Medes,* as to certain death. But as their courage deserved admiration, so their words were no less memorable. For when, in their way to *Susa,* they came to *Hydarnes,* the *Persian* general of the maritime parts of *Asia,* he receiv'd and treated them with great magnificence; and among other discourse ask'd them this question; "Men of *Lacedæmon,* why have you such an aversion for the king's friendship? You may see by my example, and the dignities I possess, how well the king understands the value of a brave man. He has already a high opinion of your courage; and if you will comply with his desires, he will certainly confer the government of some part of *Greece* upon every one of your nation." They answer'd:

"*Hydarnes*, you are not a proper person to give us counsel in this affair, for you determine concerning two things not equally understood by you. How to be a servant, you know perfectly well; but you have neither tried whether liberty be valuable, or not. If you had ever experienced the worth of liberty, you would counsel us to defend it, not only with lances, but even with hatchets.'" [7.134-135]

Following the ancient tradition inherent to the *Scythian, Thracian, Trojan, Pelasgian,* and then *Turkic, Native American* nations, the *Lacedæmonians* built their state on the principles of confederation by uniting all the kin tribes. *Pausanias* mentioned the *Lacedæmonian* confederacy during his narration of the *Dorian* affairs:

"Fate decreed that the *Thebans* should restore the *Mantineans* from the villages to their own country after the engagement at *Leuctra,* but when restored they proved far from grateful. They were caught treating with the *Lacedaemonians* and intriguing for a peace with them privately without reference to the rest of the *Arcadian* people. So through their fear of the *Thebans* they openly changed sides and joined the *Lacedaemonian* confederacy, and when the battle took place at *Mantineia* between the *Lacedaemonians* and the *Thebans* under *Epaminondas,* the *Mantineans* joined the ranks of the *Lacedaemonians*." [8.8.10]

Being in tune with *Herodotus, Plutarch* also noted the highly disciplined nature of the *Lacedæmonians,* greatly admired by all other nations. He would use the names *Spartan* and *Lacedemonian* interchangeably:

"For men will not consent to obey those who have not the ability to rule, but obedience is a lesson to be learned from a commander. For a good leader makes good followers, and just as the final attainment of the art of horsemanship is to make a horse gentle and tractable, so it is the task of the science of government to implant obedience in men. And the *Lacedaemonians* implanted in the rest of the *Greeks* not only a willingness to obey, but a desire to be their followers and subjects. People did not send requests to them for ships, or money, or hoplites, but for a single *Spartan* commander; and when they got him, they treated him with honour and reverence, as the *Sicilians* treated *Gylippus;* the *Chalcidians, Brasidas;* and all the *Greeks* resident in *Asia, Lysander, Callicratidas,* and *Agesilaüs*. These men, wherever they came, were styled regulators and chasteners of peoples and magistrates, and the city of *Sparta* from which they came was regarded as a teacher of well-ordered private life and settled civil polity." ["*Lycurgus.*" 30.4-5]

In addition to their leadership and commanding characteristics that other nations were longing to acquire, the *Spartans* had a great aptitude for music and poetry as well:

"In short, if one studies the poetry of *Sparta*, of which some specimens were still extant in my time, and makes himself familiar with the marching songs which they used, to the accompaniment of the flute, when charging upon their foes, he will conclude that *Terpander* and *Pindar* were right in associating valour with music. The former writes thus of the *Lacedaemonians:*

"Flourish there both the spear of the brave and the *Muse's* clear message, In short, if one studies the poetry of *Sparta,* of which some specimens were still extant in my time, and makes himself familiar with the marching songs which they used, to the accompaniment of the flute, when charging upon their foes, he will conclude that *Terpander* and *Pindar* were right in associating valour with music. The former writes thus of the *Lacedaemonians*

Justice, too, walks the broad streets."

And *Pindar* says:

"There are councils of *Elders,*
And young men's conquering spears,
And dances, the *Muse,* and joyousness."

The *Spartans* are thus shown to be at the same time most musical and most warlike;

"In equal poise to match the sword hangs the sweet art of the harpist," as their poet says. For just before their battles, the king sacrificed to the *Muses*, reminding his warriors, as it would seem, of their training, and of the firm decisions they had made, in order that they might be prompt to face the dread issue, and might perform such martial deeds as would be worthy of some record." [Idem. 21.3-4]

Meanwhile, *Pausanias* emphasized that the *Spartans* (like their *Scythian, Thracian, Turkic* brethren) cared less about aggrandizing themselves by creating literary works, describing their heroic accomplishments:

"The *Spartans* seem to me to be of all men the least moved by poetry and the praise of poets. For with the exception of the epigram upon *Cynisca,* of uncertain authorship, and the still earlier one upon *Pausanias* that *Simonides* wrote on the tripod dedicated at *Delphi,* there is no poetic composition to commemorate the doings of the royal houses of the *Lacedaemonians.*" [3.8.2]

Unfortunately, the dominant nation of the *Spartans* and the *Lacedæmonians,* conquered by no human being, destroyed themselves by greed and vice, just like their *Pelasgian* brethren – the *Turrhenians,* aka the *Tyrrhenians:*

"The *Lacedaemonians,* by observing the laws of *Lycurgus,* from a lowly people grew to be the most powerful among the *Greeks* and maintained the leadership among the *Greek* states for over four hundred years. But after that time, as they little by little began to relax each one of the institutions and to turn to luxury and indifference, and as they grew so corrupted as to use coined money and to amass wealth, they lost the leadership." [*Diodorus Siculus*. 7.12.8]

"Now it remains we should speak of the *Tyrrhenians:* they were antiently very valiant, and enjoyed a large country, and built many famous cities, and having a great navy, were long masters at sea, and called the sea lying under *Italy* the *Tyrrhenian* sea, after their own name…At last they threw off their former sobriety, and now live an idle and debauched life, in riot and drunkenness; so that it is no wonder that they have lost the honour and reputation their forefathers gained by warlike achievements." [Idem. 5.2]

As a *Pelasgian* progeny, the *Lacedæmonians* and the *Spartans* utilized their native language, akin to *Thracian, Scythian,* and *Turkic.* From *Plutarch,* we learned a number of words used by the *Dorian* race. Both in shape and meaning, they are in perfect match with the *Turkic* lexical units that yet again proves our assertion that they were of *Turkic* origin:

"So eager was *Lycurgus* for the establishment of this form of government, that he obtained an oracle from *Delphi* about it, which they call a "rhetra." And this is the way it runs: "When thou hast built a temple to *Zeus Syllanius* and *Athena Syllania,* divided the people into 'phylai' and into 'obai,' and established a senate of thirty members, including the 'archagetai,' then from time to time 'appellazein' between *Babyca* and *Cnacion,* and there introduce and rescind measures; but the people must have the deciding voice and the power." In these clauses, the "phylai" and the "obai" refer to divisions and distributions of the people into clans and phratries, or brotherhoods; by "archagetai" the kings are designated, and "appellazein" means to assemble the people, with a reference to *Apollo,* the *Pythian* god, who was the source and author of the polity. The *Babyca* is now called *Cheimarrus,* and the *Cnacion Oenus;* but *Aristotle* says that *Cnacion* is a river, and *Babyca* a bridge." ["*Lycurgus*." 6.1-2]

"Nor was this all; one of the noblest and best men of the city was appointed paedonome, or inspector of the boys, and under his directions the boys, in their several companies, put themselves under the command of the most prudent and warlike of the so-called *Eirens*. This was the name given to those who had been for two years out of the class of boys, and *Melleirens,* or *Would-be Eirens,* was the name for the oldest of the boys. This *eiren*, then, a youth of twenty years, commands his subordinates in their mimic battles, and in doors makes them serve him at his meals. He commissions the larger ones to fetch wood, and the smaller ones potherbs." [Idem. 17.2-3]

"*Hippias the Sophist* says that *Lycurgus* himself was very well versed in war and took part in many campaigns, and *Philostephanus* attributes to him the arrangement of the *Spartan* cavalry by "oulamoi," explaining that the "oulamos," as constituted by him, was a troop of fifty horsemen in a square formation." [Idem. 23.1]

A simple glance at these words brings us to a conclusion that they are not of *Greek* origin. Both the structural and semantic aspects of these *Spartan* vocables imminently lead to their *Turkic* counterparts:

❖ *Eiren* = Εἴρην "warrior, man" > *Erən* "warrior, hero, man" in *Turkic*.

❖ *Melleiren* = Μελλείρην "would-be eiren" > *Bəlli Erən* 'evident, would-be warriors" in *Turkic* (*Melle* > *Bəlli* 'evident, would be').

❖ *Paedonome*, or correctly *Paidonomos* = Παιδονόμος "inspector of the boys": *Pae, Pai* > *Pai* 'man' + *Donome* > *Denetmen* 'inspector' in *Turkish*, + *Os* > *Us* 'master', meaning "main inspector of men" in *Turkic*.

❖ *Obai*, or correctly *Obá* = ὠβά "clan" > *Obá* "tribe, clan" in *Turkic*.

❖ *Phylai*, or correctly *Phulé* = Φυλή "division, group" > *Pölək* "group, division", *Pöl* "divide" in *Turkic*.

❖ *Oulamoi*, or correctly *Oulamos* = Οὐλαμός "horse warrior, cavalry" > *Ulan* "horse warrior, cavalry" in *Turkic*.

❖ *Archagetai*, or correctly *Arkhegetes* = Ἀρχηγέτης "those who appoint a king": *Archa, Arkhe* > *Arxa* 'protector' + *Getes* > *Gətir* 'bring, invite', meaning "those who invite, summon a protector" in *Turkic*. The *Arkegetes* represented a senate of thirty members who would designate kings.

❖ *Appellazein* = Ἀπελλάζειν: *Appella* 'Apollo' > *Əplə* 'compose, create, ponder, contemplate' + *Zein* > *-Sin, -Sın* 'an affix of possession', meaning "belongs to *Apollo*" in *Turkic*. The name of the *Pythian* god *Appella, Apollo* originated from the *Turkic* word *Əplə* 'compose, create, ponder, contemplate', whereas the word *Apollon* originated from the same root by adding the *Turkic* affix *-N* that converts the verb into a noun. As such, *Apollon* > *Əplən* means "creator, author, composer, ponderer" in *Turkic*.
Plutarch indicated the word *Appellazein* both as a noun "…then from time to time 'appellazein' between *Babyca* and *Cnacion*, and there introduce and rescind measures…" and a verb – "appellazein" means to assemble the people, with a reference to *Apollo*, the *Pythian* god, who was the source and author of the polity. Therefore, this word has two meanings: "1) belonging to *Apollo;* 2) ponder, contemplate."

❖ *Troizen* = Τροιζήν: *Troy* + *Zen* > *-Sin, -Sın* 'an affix of possession', meaning "*Trojan*", "belongs to *Trojans*" in *Turkic*. This name was given to the city in *Peloponnesus* by its ruler *Pittheus* to honor *Troy*. The word *Troizen* was included here to compare with the afore-mentioned word *Appellazein,* as well as to demonstrate the formation of the *Spartan* words with the help of affixes, like in *Turkic*.

❖ *Krupteia* = Κρυπτεία "secret mission to kill": *Kr* > *Qir* 'destroy, kill' + *Upt* > *Abit* 'hide, conceal oneself' + *-Eia* > *-A* 'an affix, converting a verb into a verbal adjective or adverb', meaning "kill

195

in hiding" in *Turkic*. The *Spartans* had a special military task to destroy their enemies, called *Krupteia*, as *Plutarch* described it below:

> "The so-called "krupteia," or secret service, of the *Spartans,* if this be really one of the institutions of *Lycurgus,* as *Aristotle* says it was, may have given *Plato* also this opinion of the man and his civil polity. This secret service was of the following nature. The magistrates from time to time sent out into the country at large the most discreet of the young warriors, equipped only with daggers and such supplies as were necessary. In the daytime they scattered into obscure and out of the way places, where they hid themselves and lay quiet; but in the night they came down into the highways and killed every *Helot* whom they caught. Oftentimes, too, they actually traversed the fields where *Helots* were working and slew the sturdiest and best of them. So, too, *Thucydides,* in his history of the *Peloponnesian* war, tells us that the *Helots* who had been judged by the *Spartans* to be superior in bravery, set wreaths upon their heads in token of their emancipation, and visited the temples of the gods in procession, but a little afterwards all disappeared, more than two thousand of them, in such a way that no man was able to say, either then or afterwards, how they came by their deaths. And *Aristotle* in particular says also that the ephors, as soon as they came into office, made formal declaration of war upon the *Helots,* in order that there might be no impiety in slaying them." [Idem. 28.1-4]

❖ *Caddichus,* or correctly *Kaddikhos* = Κάδδιχος "bowl, jar" > *Kədik* "bowl, dish, utensil" in *Turkic*. *Plutarch's* description of the *Spartan* food – a broth from meat with pieces of bread in it, served in a bowl reminds the main course, similarly plated up and known under different names, such as *dizi, piti* among the *Turkic* nations:

> "The candidate thus rejected is said to have been "caddished," for "caddichus" is the name of the bowl into which they cast the pieces of bread. Of their dishes, the black broth is held in the highest esteem, so that the elderly men do not even ask for a bit of meat, but leave it for the young men, while they themselves have the broth poured out for their meals." [Idem. 12.6]

❖ *Phiditia* = Φιδίτια, or *Philitia,* correctly *Philios* = Φίλιος "public mess conducive to friendship, friendliness" > *Pilis* "be friends, buddy up"; "friend, acquaintance" in *Turkic*.

> "As for the public messes, the *Cretans* call them "andreia," but the *Lacedaemonians*, "*phiditia*," either because they are conducive to friendship and friendliness, "*phiditia*" being an equivalent of "*philitia*"; or, because they accustom men to simplicity and thrift, for which their word is "*pheido*." But it is quite possible, as some say, that the first letter of the word "*phiditia*" has been added to it, making "*phiditia*" out of "*editia*," which refers merely to meals and eating. They met in companies of fifteen, a few more or less, and each one of the mess-mates contributed monthly a bushel of barley-meal, eight gallons of wine, five pounds of cheese, two and a half pounds of figs, and in addition to this, a very small sum of money for such relishes as flesh and fish. Besides this, whenever anyone made a sacrifice of first fruits, or brought home game from the hunt, he sent a portion to his mess. For whenever anyone was belated by a sacrifice or the chase, he was allowed to sup at home, but the rest had to be at the mess." [Idem. 12.1-2]

❖ *Pheido* = Φειδώ "thrift, prosperity" > *Paidak* 'bountiful' > *Pai* "feast" in *Turkic*.

❖ *Prodikoi,* correctly *Prodikos* = Πρόδικος, or Προδίκως "guardian of a king": *Pr* > *Pir* 'king' + *Odikos* > *Odağası* 'elder, master', meaning "overseer of a king" in *Turkic*. According to *Plutarch,* young, orphaned *Lacedæmonian* kings would have a caretaker assigned to them:

> "Now the guardians of fatherless kings are called "prodikoi" by the *Lacedaemonians*." [Idem. 3.1]

❖ *Leschai*, correctly *Leskhe* = Λέσχη "place of exercise": *Les* > *İliş* 'tussle with someone, meet up' + *Chai, Khe* > *Qəy* 'a lot', meaning "place where men meet, tussle with each other" in *Turkic*.

> "And it was disreputable for the elderly men to be continually seen loitering there, instead of spending the greater part of the day in the places of exercise that are called "leschai". For if they gathered in these, they spent their time suitably with one another, making no allusions to the problems of money-making or of exchange, nay, they were chiefly occupied there in praising some noble action or censuring some base one, with jesting and laughter which made the path to instruction and correction easy and natural." [Idem. 25.1-2]

❖ *Taygetus*, or *Taugeton* = Ταΰγετον "Mount *Taugeton*" > *Taugetes* = Ταϋγέτης: *Tay, Tau* > *Tau* 'mountain' + *Get* > *Kete, Güt* 'guard' [91] + *Es* > *Us* 'master', meaning "main guardian of the mountain" in *Turkic*.

Mount Taygeton was named after the mountain nymph *Taygete*, or *Taugetes*, the mother of *Lacedæmon*. As it is known, nymphs were commonly deemed as embodiments of nature and oversaw a specific landform or waterbody. *Taugetes* protected the mountain, and her appellation signified her ties to this mountain: *Tau* 'mountain' + *Getes* 'master guard'. According to *Plutarch*, the ill-formed and sickly *Spartan* infants were left at the foot of *Mount Taygeton* (translated into *English* as *Taÿgetus*):

> "Offspring was not reared at the will of the father, but was taken and carried by him to a place called *Lesche*, where the elders of the tribes officially examined the infant, and if it was well-built and sturdy, they ordered the father to rear it, and assigned it one of the nine thousand lots of land; but if it was ill-born and deformed, they sent it to the so-called *Apothetae*, a chasm-like place at the foot of *Mount Taÿgetus*, in the conviction that the life of that which nature had not well equipped at the very beginning for health and strength, was of no advantage either to itself or the state." [16.1-2]

❖ *Eurotas* = Εὐρώτας "name of the king of *Laconia*; name of the river in *Laconia*": *Euro* > *Əiri* 'stand still' + *Tas* 'stone', meaning "firm as a stone" in *Turkic*. The *Pelasgian* king of *Laconia Eurotas* named the local river after himself:

> "He led down to the sea by means of a trench the stagnant water on the plain, and when it had flowed away, as what was left formed a river-stream, he named it *Eurotas*."
> [*Pausanias*. 3.1.1]

❖ *Lycophon*, or correctly *Lukophonas* = Λυκόφονας "thistledown": *Luc, Luk* > *Tük* 'down, fluff' + *Ophonas, Ophon* > *Ofan* 'be small', meaning "small fluff" in *Turkic*. As the letter *L* can change to the letter *T* in *Turkic* languages without affecting the semantical content, such as in the following *Turkic* words — *Küslə* = *Küstə*, *Aimaklı* = *Aimaktı*, there should not be any reasonable doubt about the *Luk* to *Tük* modification. According to *Plutarch*, the ancient *Spartans* used the fluff of thistle for their pallet-beds to keep them warm during cold winter nights:

> "They slept together, in troops and companies, on pallet-beds which they collected for themselves, breaking off with their hands — no knives allowed — the tops of the rushes which grew along the river *Eurotas*. In the winter-time, they added to the stuff of these pallets the so-called "lycophon," or thistle-down, which was thought to have warmth in it." [16.7]

❖ *Perioeci*, or correctly *Periokos* = Περίοικος "free provincial": *Peri* > *Pəri* 'this side, here' + *Oec, Oik* > *Öi, Üg* 'dwelling, house' + *I, Os* > *Us* 'master', meaning "independent people who live nearby" in *Turkic*. The *Periokos* were non-citizens of *Sparta*, engaged in commercial and

---
[91] *Egorov V.G.* "Etimologicheskiy slovar chuvashskogo yazika." [110].

money-making activities, considered unworthy to genuine *Spartans*. They lived within the limits of *Sparta* but were free to visit other countries and lands:

> "Suiting the deed to the word, he distributed the rest of the *Laconian* land among the "perioeci," or free provincials, in thirty thousand lots, and that which belonged to the city of *Sparta,* in nine thousand lots, to as many genuine *Spartans*." [Idem. 8.3]

❖ *Scytale, Skutale* = Σκυτάλη "pole, club": *Scy, Sku* > *Soku* 'pole, club' + *Tale* > *Dola* [92] 'wrap around', meaning "wrapped around a club" in *Turkic*.
From the narration of *Plutarch,* we learned that the *Spartans* would send their messages to another party in the form of parchment wrapped around a club, or a *Skutale:*

> "The dispatch-scroll is of the following character. When the ephors send out an admiral or a general, they make two round pieces of wood exactly alike in length and thickness, so that each corresponds to the other in its dimensions, and keep one themselves, while they give the other to their envoy. These pieces of wood they call "scytalae." Whenever, then, they wish to send some secret and important message, they make a scroll of parchment long and narrow, like a leathern strap, and wind it round their "*scytale*", leaving no vacant space thereon, but covering its surface all round with the parchment. After doing this, they write what they wish on the parchment, just as it lies wrapped about the "*scytale*"; and when they have written their message, they take the parchment off, and send it, without the piece of wood, to the commander. He, when he has received it, cannot other get any meaning of it, — since the letters have no connection, but are disarranged, — unless he takes his own "*scytale*" and winds the strip of parchment about it, so that, when its spiral course is restored perfectly, and that which follows is joined to that which precedes, he reads around the staff, and so discovers the continuity of the message. And the parchment, like the staff, is called "*scytale*", as the thing measured bears the name of the measure." [Idem. 19.5-7]

❖ *Kothon* = Κώθων "drinking-cup" > *Kutu* 'jar, container" in *Turkic*. Among the utensils used by the *Spartans, Plutarch* mentioned a container to drink out of, named *Kothon*. The word has a distinctive *Turkic* derivation.

> "In this way it came about that such common and necessary utensils as bedsteads, chairs, and tables were most excellently made among them, and the *Laconian* "*kothon*", or drinking-cup, was in very high repute for usefulness among soldiers in active service, as *Critias* tells us." [Idem. 9.4]

❖ *Retra* = Ρήτρα "law, decree, truths" > *Rairət* "power, authority" in *Turkic*. In *Plutarch's* interpretation, *Retra* meant a decree descended from heaven:

> "And this was the special grievance which they had against King *Agesilaüs* in later times, namely, that by his continual and frequent incursions and expeditions into *Boeotia* he rendered the *Thebans* a match for the *Lacedaemonians*. And therefore, when *Antalcidas* saw the king wounded, he said: "This is a fine tuition-fee which thou art getting from the *Thebans,* for teaching them how to fight, when they did not wish to do it, and did not know how." Such ordinances as these were called 'rhetras' by *Lycurgus,* implying that they came from the god and were oracles." [Idem. 13.6]

❖ *Klaria* = Κλαρια "allotment pledges": *Kl* > *Kol* 'signature' + *Aria* > *Ara* 'mediator', meaning "signed mediation agreement" in *Turkic*. From the words of *Plutarch,* it appears clearly that the *Spartan* society was advanced and utilized key economic instruments, such as mortgages and loans:

---

[92] *Musayev O.I.* "Azərbaycanca-İngiliscə lüğət." [160].

198

"So they caused mortgages (the *Spartans* call them "klaria", or allotment pledges) to be brought into the marketplace, heaped them altogether, and set fire to them."
["Comparison of *Agis* and *Cleomenes* and the *Gracchi*." 13.3]

The *Lacedemonians* had several derivative branches, such as the *Æolians*, the *Melians*, the *Minyai*, the *Sabini* with their offshoots:

➢ *Sabines*, aka *Sabinoi* = Σαβῖνοι, aka *Sabini*, aka *Sevini* > *Səbin, Sevin* "love, worship, idolize, adore" in *Turkic*.

There were two main theories about the meaning of the *Sabini*'s name. According to *Pliny the Elder*, the *Sabini* were called as such due to their diligent worship of and devotion to their deities:
"The *Sabini* (called, according to some writers, from their attention to religious observances and the worship of the gods, *Sevini*) dwell on the dew-clad hills in the vicinity of the Lakes of the *Velinus*." [3.17]

The first version includes two words *Sabini* and *Sevini*, and both have a perfect match in *Turkic* – *Səbin, Sevin*.

The second explanation of the name provided by *Silius Italicus* in "Punica" also makes sense, according to which the *Sabini* were named after their leader *Sabus*:
"Ibant et laeti pars *Sancum* uoce canebant
auctorem gentis, pars laudes ore ferebat,
Sabe, tuas, qui de proprio cognomine primus
dixisti populos magna dicione *Sabinos*." [8.420-423]
"They trooped, half-singing in tribute to *Sancus*,
their forefather, whilst others sang the praises of you, *Sabus*,
Who bestowed his name to the great dominion of the *Sabines*." [93]

"Κάτων δὲ Πόρκιος τὸ μὲν ὄνομα τῷ Σαβίνων ἔθνει τεθῆναί φησιν ἐπὶ Σάβου τοῦ Σάγκου δαίμονος ἐπιχωρίου, τοῦτον δὲ τὸν Σάγκον ὑπό τινων πίστιον καλεῖσθαι Δία."
[Dionysi Halicarnasensis. "Antiquitatum Romanarum quae supersunt." 2.49.2]
"Although, *Porcius Caton* says that the *Sabines* obtained their name from *Sabus*, the son of *Sankus*, a deity of that country, and, according to some, that *Sancus* was called *Zeus Fidius*." [94]

In either case, the root remains unchanged – *Sab*, or *Sev*, that means "love, worship" in *Turkic*. And the same root was observed in the alternative name of the *Sabini* – *Sabelli* that was also proved to be of *Turkic* origin, as well as in the name of a *Scythian* tribe of the *Sabiri*, aka *Saviri*, aka *Saberioi* (*Sab, Sav* > *Səb, Səv, Sev* 'love' + *Ir, Eri* > *İr* 'warrior, man', meaning "friendly warrior, or man" in *Turkic*). They represented a *Hunnic* branch of the *Scythians* who dwelled in the region of the *Caucasus*.

Moreover, there was a *Turkic* tribe *Səbi*, or the *Sabi* [Radlov. 4.1.500], who lived near the river *Kondoma* (an ancient *Turkic* territory, currently a part of *Russia*). It is possible that this *Turkic* tribe of the *Sabi* was the remnant of the *Sabiri*, or the *Saviri*.

The *Sabini* were the *Pelasgians* related to the *Lacedæmonians*, who occupied the mountain country in *Central Italy*:
"Now the *Sabines* were a numerous and warlike people, and dwelt in unwalled villages, thinking that it behoved them, since they were *Lacedaemonian* colonists, to be bold and fearless." [Plutarch. "Romulus." 16.1]

"And at all events, *Numa* [95] was of *Sabine* descent, and the *Sabines* will have it that they were colonists from *Lacedaemon*." [Idem. "Numa." 1.3]

---

[93] This excerpt was translated from *Latin* by the author of the current work.
[94] The translation into *English* was made by the author of the present book.
[95] In the original *Greek* text, it is *Nomas* = Νομάς and proceeds from *Nom* "law" in *Turkic* [R.3.1.695].

However, *Strabo* considered them the native inhabitants of *Italy:*

> "The race of the *Sabini* is extremely ancient, they are *Autochthones*. The *Picentini* and *Samnitæ* descend from them, as do the *Leucani* from these latter, and the *Bruttii* again from these. A proof of their antiquity may be found in the bravery and valour which they have maintained till the present time. *Fabius,* the historian, says that the *Romans* first knew what wealth was when they became masters of this nation." [5.3.1]

These seemingly contradicting statements got clarification from *Dionysius of Halicarnassus,* who reported about the *Aborigines,* from whom the *Romans* originally descended. These very *Aborigines* were the *Autochthones* of *Strabo,* also known as the *Sabini:*

> "There are some, who affirm that the *Aborigines,* from whom the *Romans* are originally descended, were natives of *Italy,* a people sprung from no other; (for I call *Italy,* all that shore, which is surrounded by the *Ionian* and *Tuscan* gulphs; and, in the third place, by the *Alps* on the side of the land); and these authors say that they were first called *Aborigines* from their having been the origin of their posterity; as we should call them, *genearchai* or *prôtogonoi.* Others pretend that certain vagabonds without house or home, gathered together out of many places, met one another there by chance, and seated themselves in the fastnesses, living by robbery and feeding of cattle. For this reason, those, who are of this opinion, change their name also to one more suitable to their condition, calling them *Aberrigines,* to shew they were wanderers; and, according to these, the *Aborigines* are in danger of being confounded with those, the ancients called *Leleges:* For this is the name they, generally, give to a vagabond and mixed people, who have no fixed abode they can call their country." [1.10.1-2]

> "But the most learned of the *Roman* historians, among whom is *Porcius Cato,* who has collected, with the greatest care, the origins of the *Italian* cities; *Caius Sempronius,* and a great many others, say, they were *Greeks;* part of those, who, formerly, inhabited *Achaia,* and, many generations before the *Trojan* war, left that country: But they do not point out either the *Greek* nation, to which they belonged, the city, from which they removed, the time, when, the leader, under whom, or, from what turns of fortune, they left their mother country; and, founding their account on a *Greek* relation, they have quoted no *Greek* author to support it: It is therefore uncertain how the truth stands. If, what they say be true, they can be a colony of no other people, but of those, who are now called *Arcadians:* For these are the first of all the *Greeks,* who crossed the *Ionian* gulph under the conduct of *Oenotrus,* the son of *Lycaon,* and settled in *Italy*. This *Oenotrus* was the fifth from *Azius* and *Phoroneus,* who were the first kings of *Peloponnesus*. For *Niobe* was the daughter of *Phoroneus,* and *Pelasgus* is said to have been the son of *Jupiter* and *Niobe; Lycaon* was the son of *Æzius,* whose daughter was *Deianira;* and *Deianira* and *Pelasgus* were the parents of another *Lycaon,* whose son, *Oenotrus,* was born seventeen generations before the *Trojan* expedition. And this was the time, when the *Greeks* sent this colony into *Italy*. *Oenotrus* left *Greece* as dissatisfied with his portion of land: For *Lycaon,* having two and twenty sons, it was necessary to divide *Arcadia* into as many shares: This inducing *Oenotrus* to depart out of *Peloponnessus,* he prepared a fleet, and crossed the *Ionian* gulph with *Peucetius* one of his brothers: They were followed by many of their own people, (for this nation is said to have been very populous in early times) and by as many other *Greeks,* as had less land, than was sufficient for them. *Peucetius,* therefore, landing his men above the cape *Iapygia,* which was the first part of *Italy* they made, settled there; and, from him, the inhabitants of these places were called *Peucetians*."
> [Idem. 1.11.1-4]

> "Now, let us, also, shew how considerable a nation the *Oenotri* were from the testimony of *Pherecydes,* the *Athenian,* another ancient historian, and a genealogist inferior to none: He thus expresses himself concerning the kings of *Arcadia:* "*Lycaon* was the son of *Pelasgus* and *Deianeira:* This man married *Cyllene,* a *Naid* nymph, from whom the mountain *Cyllene* took

its name." Then, having given an account of their children, and what places each of them inhabited, he mentions *Oenotrus* and *Peucetius*, saying, thus: "And *Oenotrus*, from whom those, who inhabit *Italy*, are called *Oenotri;* and *Peucetius,* from whom those, who live near the *Ionian* gulph, are called *Peucetii*." These, therefore, are the accounts given by the ancient poets and historians, concerning the settlement and origin of the *Oenotri;* by whose authority, I am convinced that, if the *Aborigines* were, in reality, a *Greek* nation, according to the opinion of *Cato, Sempronius,* and many others, they were descendants of these *Oenotri:* For I find that the *Pelasgi* and *Cretenses,* and the other nations, that inhabited *Italy,* came thither afterwards; neither can I discover that any other colony, more ancient than this, came from *Greece* to the western parts of *Europe*. I am of opinion that the *Oenotri* made themselves masters of many other places in *Italy*, some of which were desert, and others ill inhabited; and that they possessed themselves, also, of some part of the country belonging to the *Umbri,* and were called *Aborigines* from their dwelling on mountains (for the *Arcadians* are fond of such situations) in the same manner, as, at *Athens,* some are called *Hyperacrii,* and, others, *Paralii*." [1.13.1-3]

The *Aborigines* of *Dionysius of Halicarnassus* and the *Sabines,* or the *Autochtones* of *Strabo,* dwelled in the mountainous region and built the same cities and towns, such as *Reate, Tribula*:

> "Of the cities, first inhabited by the *Aborigines,* few remain at this time; but, the greatest part of them, having been laid waste both by wars, and other destructive calamities, are abandoned. These cities were in the *Reatine* territory, not far from the *Apennine* Mountain (as *Terentius Varro* writes in his Antiquities) the nearest being one day's journey from *Rome;* the most celebrated of which I shall give an account of after him. *Palatium,* five and twenty stadia distant from *Reate,* which city is still inhabited by the *Romans* near the *Quintian* way. *Trebula,* distant from the same city about sixty stadia, and standing upon an easy ascent. *Vesbola,* at the same distance from *Trebula*." [*Dionysius of Halicarnassus*. 1.14.1-2]

> "The *Sabini* occupy a narrow country, its length from the *Tiber* and the small city of *Nomentum* to the *Vestini* being 1000 stadia. They have but few cities, and these have suffered severely in their continual wars [with the *Romans*]. Such are *Amiternum* and *Reate,* which is near to the village of *Interocrea* and the cold waters at *Cotyliæ*, which are taken by patients, both as drink and as baths, for the cure of various maladies. The rocks of *Foruli,* likewise, belong to the *Sabini;* fitted rather for rebellion than peaceable habitation. *Cures* is now a small village, although formerly a famous city: whence came *Titus Tatius* and *Numa Pompilius,* kings of *Rome*. From this place is derived the name of *Quirites,* which the orators give to the *Romans* when they address the people. *Trebula, Eretum,* and other similar places, must be looked upon rather as villages than cities." [*Strabo*. 5.3]

Dionysius of Halicarnassus pointed out that both the *Aborigines* and the *Pelasgians* shared the same heritage:

> "Afterwards, some of the *Pelasgi,* who inhabited *Thessaly,* as it is, now, called, being obliged to leave their country, settled among the *Aborigines;* and these, with joint forces, made war upon the *Siceli*. It is possible the *Aborigines* might receive them from the hopes of their assistance, but I rather believe it was chiefly on account of their affinity. For the *Pelasgi* were, also, a *Greek* nation, anciently, of *Peloponnesus:* They were unfortunate in many things, but, particularly, in wandering much, and having no fixed abode. For they, first, lived in the neighbourhood of the *Achaian Argos,* as it is now called, being, in the opinion of many, natives of the country." [1.17.1-2]

With this, the author meant to say that both the *Aborigines,* aka the *Sabines,* and the *Pelasgians* were the citizens of *Greece,* not ethnic *Greeks*. He also brought to a surface another version of connection between the *Sabini* and the *Lacedæmonians,* according to which the latter resettled among the former and established their *Spartan* traditions in their society. Certainly, this could not happen if they did not have kinship:

"There is, also, another account given of the *Sabines* in the histories of that country, which says that a colony of *Lacedaemonians* settled among them, when *Lycurgus,* being guardian to his nephew *Eunomus,* gave laws to *Sparta:* That some of them, disliking the severity of his laws, and separating from the rest, quitted the city intirely; and, after a long navigation in the main sea, made a vow to the gods (for they were desirous to land anywhere) to settle in the first place they should arrive at: That, at last, they made that part of *Italy,* which lies near the *Pomentine* plains, and called the place, where they first landed, *Feronia* [*Foronia*], in memory of their being carried through the main; and built a temple to the goddess *Feronia* [*Foronia*], to whom they had addressed their vows; which goddess, by the alteration of one letter, they, now, call *Feronia:* That some of them, going from thence, cohabited with the *Sabines:* And, for this reason, many of their institutions are *Laconic;* particularly, their inclination to war, their frugality, and a severity in all their actions." [Idem. 2.49.1-5]

Furthermore, the *Sabini,* aka the *Aborigines,* inhabited the unwalled settlements, similar to their *Spartan* brethren, most likely, a long time prior to the arrival of the new *Lacedæmonian* colony:

"At the distance of eighty stadia from *Reate,* on the *Jurian* way near the mountain *Coritus,* stood *Corsula,* lately destroyed: There, an island is to be seen, called *Issa,* surrounded with a lake; which island is said to have been inhabited by the *Aborigines,* without any artificial fortification, the inhabitants relying, for their security, on the bogs of the lake, instead of walls." [Idem. 1.14]

As a *Pelasgian* posterity of *Lacedæmonians,* the *Sabini* are expected to speak if not the same but similar language, akin to *Turkic*. Judging from the glosses as the second-hand evidence left by a number of ancient scholars, the fact appears to be that the *Sabini,* indeed, spoke the language cognate with *Turkic*. Let us take a look at these words claimed to belong to the *Sabine* language:

- *Teba* "hill" > *Töbe, Tepe, Təpə* "hill" in *Turkic*.
  This gloss was explained by *Marcus Terentius Varro,* a prominent *Latin* scholar of the 1st c. BCE in connection with *Thebes,* the name of the land in *Bœotia, Greece*:

  "The name of *Thebes,*[96] too, no less clearly shows that the country is more ancient, in that the name given it comes from a type of land, and not from the name of the founder. For the old language, and the *Aeolians* of *Boeotia* in *Greece* as well, use the word *Teba* for hill, leaving out the aspirate; and among the *Sabines,* a country which was settled by the *Pelasgians* from *Greece,* up to this day they use the same word; there is a trace of it in the *Sabine* country on the *Via Salaria,* not far from *Reate,* where a slope of a mile in length is called *Tebae*." [*Varro*. "On agriculture." 3.1.6]

  Remarkably, this very name *Thebes,* or *Thebae,* or *Thebe,* was given to a number of cities and towns beyond *Greece* as well, such as *Thebes* as a capital of *Egypt* under the 11th, early 12th, 17th, and early 18th Dynasties; *Phthiotic,* or *Thessalian Thebes; Cilician Thebae* (presently, in *Turkey*); *Ionian Thebes* in *Asia Minor; Trojan Thebe,* and even *Thebes* village in *Illinois, USA.*

- *Cyprum* "good" > *Kapər* "beautiful, good-looking", *Kepmer* "good, gorgeous" [97] in *Turkic*. Clearly, the *Turkic* words *Kapər* and *Kepmer* are two variants of the same lexeme. In his work "On the *Latin* language", *Varro* unveiled the meaning of the street in *Rome – Vicus Cyprius* by deriving its etymology from the *Sabine* language:

  "The *Vicus Cyprius* "Good Row", from *cyprum,* because the *Sabines* who were taken in as citizens settled, and they named it from the good omen: for *cyprum* means "good" in *Sabine*." [5.159]

---

[96] It is *Thebae* in the original *Latin* text.
[97] *Ashmarin N.I.* "Slovar chuvashskogo yazika." [75, 190].

- *Alpus* "white", "high":
  - *Alpus*, aka *Albus* "white": *Al* > *Ala* 'blue' + *Pus, Buz* 'ice' (*Buz* 'white, whitish, grey'), meaning "blue ice", or "bluish-white" in *Turkic*. The *Alps* mountains are notorious for their snow-covered, icy tops with a blue undertone.
  - *Alpus* "high" > *Alıp, Alp* "giant", *Al* "great, high" in *Turkic*. Radlov V.V. indicated an old *Turkic* expression *Al Taiğa* "great (or high) rocky mountains" [1.1.349].
  - *Alpus, Albus* "high and white": *Al* 'high' + *Pus* > *Buz* 'white', meaning "high and white" in *Turkic*.

The ancient scholarship was divided in their opinion about the meaning of *Alpus*, or *Albus*. The *Sabine* gloss in *Paul's* epitome expresses the meaning "white":

"*Album*, quod nos dicimus, a *Graeco*, quod est ἀλφόν, est appellatum. *Sabini* tamen *Alpum* dixerunt. Unde credi potest, nomen *Alpium* a candore nivium vocitatum.
[*Sexti Pompei Festi*. "De verborum significatione quae supersunt cum Pauli epitome." *Album*]

"What we termed *Albus* is called *Alphon* (ἀλφόν) in *Greek*. However, the *Sabines* called it *Alpus*. Possibly, the name of the *Alps* is derived from the whiteness of its snowy summits."[98]

Other men of letters, such as the grammarian of 4th–5th c. *Maurus Servius Honoratus*, in his "Commentary on the *Aeneid* of *Vergil*", asserted that all high mountains were called *Alps* by the *Gauls*:

"Sane omnes altitudines montium licet a *Gallis Alpes* vocentur…" [2.10.13]
"Even though all the tall mountains are called the *Alps* by the *Gauls*…" [99]

It is important to note that there are several inconclusive attempts to find the *Indo-European* etymology of the name *Alpus*, or *Albus*. However, only in *Turkic*, both meanings – "white" and "high" in both variants – *Alpus, Albus* exist without any semantic distortion or adding, omitting the letters, or dragging them back and forth. This very fact proves the genuine *Turkic* origin of the word.

- *Coena*, aka *Cena* "dinner, banquet, feast" > *Kenə* "satisfy hunger and/or thirst" in *Turkic*.
  "Scensas Sabini *coenas* dicebant. Quae autem nunc prandia sunt, *coenas* dicebant…"
  [*Sexti Pompei Festi*. "Pauli Diaconi Excerpta." 17.149.338]
  "The *Sabines* called *scensa* for *coena* 'dinner'. And they said *coena* for what is now *prandium* 'breakfast'…" [100]

- *Scensa* "evening meal": *S* > *Sı* 'regale, food, meal' + *Cen* > *Kenə* 'satisfy hunger and/or thirst' + *Sa* > *-Si* 'an affix that modifies a verb without changing its definition', meaning "meal to satisfy hunger and thirst" in *Turkic*. An example of *Turkic* words with the added affix *-Si* that lacks any modifying properties, was indicated in "Drevneturkskiy Slovar":
  Em "suck" = *Emsi* "suck" [662].

- *Nero* "person of unsurpassed courage", "brave" > *Nər* "brave, courageous", "brave, courageous man" in *Turkic*. This *Turkic* root got preserved mostly in *Azerbaijani* under these main meanings.[101] The *Sabinian* gloss had multiple derivatives:
  - *Nerio* "valor, courage" > *Nər* "brave" in *Turkic*.
  - *Neronis*, or *Neronas* = Νέρωνας "strong, valiant, courageous": *Ner* > *Nər* + *Onis, Onas* > *Ön* 'core', meaning "brave to the core" in *Turkic*.
  - *Neron* = Νέρων "strong man": *Ner* > *Nər* + *On* > *Ön* 'core', meaning "brave to the core" in *Turkic*.

---

[98] This text was translated from *Latin* into *English* by the author of the current work.
[99] This excerpt was translated into *English* from *Latin* by the author of the present book.
[100] This *Latin* text was rendered into *English* by the author of the present work.
[101] *Musayev O.I.* "Azərbaycanca-İngiliscə lüğət." [436].

- *Nerienes* "valor, courage": *Ner* > *Nər* 'brave' + *Ienes* > *İyən* 'bender, subduer' (*İy* 'bend, subdue' + *-ən* 'an affix, denoting constant action'), meaning "brave subduer" in *Turkic*.
- *Nereides* = Νηρεΐδες "bravery": *Ner* > *Nər* 'brave man' + *Eides* > *İdə* 'power, might', meaning "brave man of power" in *Turkic*.
- *Nerienemque*: *Ner* > *Nər* 'brave' + *Ien* > *İyən* 'bender, subduer' + *Em* > *Um* 'front',[102] meaning "brave conqueror at the frontline" in *Turkic*. *Que* is a *Latin* termination.
- *Nerine* = Νερίνη "1.bravery; 2.goddess of courage": *Ner* > *Nər* 'brave' + *Ine* > *İnə* 'matriarch', meaning "mother of courage" or "brave matriarch" in *Turkic*.

The *Roman* historian *Gaius Suetonius Tranquillus* reviewed the *Sabinian* gloss primarily as a name – *Neronis*:

> "Amongst other cognomina, they assumed that of *Nero*,[103] which in the *Sabine* language signifies strong and valiant."
>
> ["The Lives of The Twelve Caesars" – *Tiberius Nero Caesar*. 1]

Aulus Gellius also assessed the word as a name describing the god of war *Mars* – *Nerienemque Martis*, while pointing out that *Marcus Varro* spelled it as *Nerienes*:

> "Prayers to the immortal gods, which are offered according to the *Roman* ritual, are set forth in the books of the priests of the *Roman* people, as well as in many early books of prayers. In these we find: *Lua* of *Saturn*; *Salacia* of *Neptune*; *Hora* of *Quirinus*; the *Virites* of *Quirinus*; *Maia* of *Vulcan*; *Heries* of *Juno*; *Moles* of *Mars*, and *Nerio* of *Mars*. Of these I hear most people pronounce the one which I have put last with a long initial syllable, as the *Greeks* pronounce Νηρεΐδες (*Nereides*). But those who have spoken correctly made the first syllable short and lengthened the third. For the nominative case of the word, as it is written in the books of early writers, is *Nerio*, although *Marcus Varro*, in his Menippean Satire entitled Σκιομαχία, or Battle of the Shadows, uses in the vocative *Nerienes*, not *Nerio*, in the following verses:
>
> "Thee, *Anna* and *Peranna*, *Panda Cela*, *Pales*,
> *Nerienes* and *Minerva*, Fortune and likewise *Ceres*."
>
> From which it necessarily follows that the nominative case is the same. But *Nerio* was declined by our forefathers like *Atnio*; for, as they said *Aniēnem* with the third syllable long, so they did *Neriēnem*. Furthermore, that word, whether it be *Nerio* or *Nerienes*, is *Sabine* and signifies valour and courage. Hence among the *Claudii*, who we are told sprang from the *Sabines*, whoever was of eminent and surpassing courage was called *Nero*."
>
> ["The Attic Nights of *Aulus Gellius*." 13.23.1]

The 6th c. *Byzantian* writer on antiquarian subjects, *Johannes Laurentius Lydus*, aka *John Lydus*, brought an example of the *Sabinian* gloss by evoking the name of the warrior goddess *Nerine*:

> "On the 10th day before the *Kalends of April*, there is trumpet-purification and movement of the weapons, and honors for *Ares* and *Nerinê* — a goddess so named in the *Sabine* language, who they understood to be *Athena* or else *Aphrodite*. For *nerinê* means "courage" and the *Sabines* call the courageous *nerônas*. And *Homer* demonstrates that she does take the lead in warfare, along with *Ares*: "All these things will be the concern of quick *Ares* and *Athena*." For those who consider *Nerinê* to be *Aphrodite* are mistaken, and *Homer* is equally a witness on this point: "My child [i.e., *Aphrodite*], warlike deeds have not been given to you.""
>
> ["The Months." – March. 60]

The author also confirmed the etymology of another *Sabinian* word – *Neron* (Νέρων):

> "*Neron* is the strong man in the *Sabine* language." [Idem. January. 23.2]

Notwithstanding the multiple variants and derivatives of the *Sabinian* word, the lexical and etymological analysis confirms that all their roots run back to the *Turkic* source.

---

[102] *Egorov V.G.* "Etimologicheskiy slovar chuvashskogo yazika." [p.274].
[103] In the original *Latin* text, it is *Neronis*.

- *Multa = Multæ* "fine, monetary punishment": *Mul > Mal* 'assets, goods' + *Ta > Tıy* 'withhold, deduct', meaning "deduction from the assets", or "fine" in *Turkic*.
  The *Latin* grammarian *Aulus Gellius*, invoking another fellow scholar, asserted the *Sabinian* origin of the word *Multa*:
  > "Furthermore, *Marcus Varro*, in the twenty-first book of his Human Antiquities, also says that the word for fine (multa) is itself not *Latin*, but *Sabine*, and he remarks that it endured even to within his own memory in the speech of the *Samnites*, who are sprung from the *Sabines*." ["The *Attic* Nights of *Aulus Gellius*." 11.1.1]

- *Hernae, Herna* "rock, cliff": *Her > Yar* "rock, steep cliff" + *Nae, Na > Ana* 'piece of land', meaning "rocky land" in *Turkic*.
  Maurus Servius Honoratus, in his commentary to the work by *Virgil* "The *Aeneid*" – "Commentariorum *Servii G.* in *Aeneidos Vergili*," [7.684] made an etymological annotation about the *Sabinian* gloss *Hernæ*:
  > "Sabinorum lingua saxa hernae vocantur. Quorum quidam dux magnus Sabinos de suis locis elicuit et habitare secum fecit in saxosis montibus, unde loca Hernica dicta sunt et populi Hernici." [100]

  > "In the *Sabine* language, rocks are called *Hernae*. A great leader directed a part of *Sabines* from their homeland to the rocky mountains where he made them live with him. For that reason, the place is called *Hernica* and the people – the *Hernici*." [104]

  Paul the Deacon derived the etymology of *Hernæ* from *Marsian*, which was a language akin to the *Sabinian*, as both the *Marsi* and the *Sabini* were related:
  > "Hernici dicti a saxis, quae Marsi herna dicunt." ["De verborum significatione quae supersunt cum Pauli epitome." 8.100.74]

  > "The *Hernici* were denominated after stones, called *Herna* by the *Marsi*." [105]

- *Hirpi*, or *Irpon* = Ιρπον, or *Hirpus*, or *Irpus* "wolf" > *Irbis* "lynx" in *Turkic*. There is a great probability that in ancient *Turkic*, the word *Irbis* also carried the meaning of wolf. There is plenty of examples, provided by *Radlov V.V.*, when one *Turkic* word signified two or three absolutely different animals, such as *Pars* "tiger, panther, lynx" [4.2.1158], *Borta* "deer, horse" [4.2.1665]. According to *Maurus Servius Honoratus*, *Hirpi* meant "wolf" in the language of the *Sabines* [11.785.564].
  However, *Paul the Deacon* glossed the word as a borrowing from *Samnite*, which is, practically, the same as *Sabine*:
  > "Irpini appellati nomine lupi, quem irpum dicunt Samnites; eum enim ducem secuti agros occupavere." [9.106.78]

  > "The *Irpini* were denominated after a wolf, called *Irpus* by the *Samnites*." [106]

  Strabo shared the same opinion about the origin of *Irpus*:
  > "For the *Samnites* call the wolf *irpus*." [5.4.12]

- *Terenus* "soft": *Tere* 'skin' + *Nus > Niş* 'frailness',[107] meaning "frail skin or shell" in *Turkic*. The definition perfectly matches the description of the word provided by the *Latin* grammarian *Ambrosius Aurelius Theodosius Macrobius* in "The Saturnalia" – a collection of ancient *Roman* religious lore along with the direct reference to earlier scholars' opinions on this matter:
  > "Nux terentina dicitur quae ita mollis est ut vix adtrectata frangatur...Item quod quidam Tarentinas oves vel nuces dicunt, quae sunt terentinae a tereno, quod est Sabinorum lingua molle: unde Terentios quoque dictos putat Varro ad Libonem primo." [3.18.13]

---

[104] The excerpt was translated from *Latin* into *English* by the author of the current work.
[105] The translation from *Latin* into *English* was performed by the author of the present book.
[106] The *Latin* text was rendered into *English* by the author of the current work.
[107] Egorov V.G. "Etimologicheskiy slovar chuvashskogo yazika." [140].

"The nut *Terentina* is said to be so soft that can be easily crushed. Also, some call sheep or nuts *Tarentine*, which is correctly *Terentine*, from *Terenus* that stands for "soft" in the language of the *Sabines*. In his first book "To *Libo*", *Varro* surmised that the *Terentii* were named from this word."[108]

As we see, the meaning of *Terenus* is not only "soft" but also "frail", and it applies to both the skin of an animal or the shell of a nut. Hence, the etymological derivation of the *Sabinian* word from the *Turkic* source is both semantically and lexically justified. Whereby, all the travails that proponents of the *Indo-European* origin of the word put themselves through, are a simple waste of time and sweat, as the lexemes remotely resembling the *Sabinian* gloss that they piled up, such as *Greek Teren* "soft", *Teru* "weak, delicate", *Vedic Taruna* "young, tender", *Avestan Tauruna* "young", *Ossetic Tæryn* "boy", *PIE *Ter-* are nothing short of a desperate effort to prove the unprovable that usually ends in digging up fool's gold.

- *Tesqa, Tesca, Tesqua* "empty, harsh": *Tes* > *Tas* 'bare, empty' + *Qa, Ca, Qua* > *Kou* 'dry', meaning "empty, dry land" in *Turkic*.
  The *Latin* satirist of the 2nd c. BCE, *C. Lucili* derived the origin of the word *Tesqua* from the *Sabine* language:
    "…Loca deserta et difficilia lingua Sabinorum sic dicuntur…"
    [*C. Lucili*. "Saturarum reliquiae". 2.3.21]
    "…this is how the deserted and rugged places are called in the *Sabinian* language…" [109]

- *Sankos* = Σάγκος "sky": *San* > *Sağ* 'pure' + *Kos* > *Köi, Göy* 'sky', meaning "pure sky" in *Turkic*. The transition of the letter -*S*- to -*I*- in *Kos* to *Köi* is a well-expected lexical phenomenon, frequently observed in *Turkic*. For instance, the *Turkic* word *Pos* "body" is alternatively spelled as *Poi* [R.4.2.1262].
  John Lydus claimed the *Sabinian* etymology of the word *Sankos*:
    "The [word] *Sancus*[110] signifies "sky" in the *Sabine* language." ["The Months." – June. 90]

The *Sabini* had numerous offshoot tribes. Among them were the *Claudi*, the *Hernici*, the *Marsi*, the *Marrucini*, the *Vestini*, the *Peligni*, the *Picentes*, the *Sabelli*, the *Saunitai*, the *Bruttii*, the *Leucani*, the *Frentani*, the *Hirpini*:

> *Claudi* > *Clausus*: *Claus* > *Kolauz* 'a guide' + *Us* 'master', meaning "leading guide" in *Turkic*. The name of the *Claudi*, a tribe of the *Sabini*, was bestowed to them by their leader *Clausus*, who later renamed himself into a *Latin* nomen *Claudius*:
>   "Then *Clausus* came, who led a num'rous band
>   Of troops embodied from the *Sabine* land,
>   And, in himself alone, an army brought.
>   'T was he, the noble *Claudian* race begot,
>   The *Claudian* race, ordain'd, in times to come,
>   To share the greatness of imperial *Rome*." [*Virgil*. "Aeneid." 7]

> *Hernici*, aka *Ernikoi* = Ἕρνικοι, aka *Ernikes* = Ερνικες: *Her, Er* > *Yar* "rock, steep cliff" + *Ni* > *Ana* 'piece of land' + *C, K* > -*G* 'an affix, denoting a noun', meaning "mountaineer" in *Turkic*. In the present example, the affix -*G* does not add or deduct any lexical or grammatical content, similar to the *Turkic* word *Kişi* "man" > *Kişig* "man" [Dr.Sl.651]. By referring to several reputable ancient

---

[108] The text was translated from *Latin* into *English* by the author of the present work.
[109] The *Latin* text was translated into *English* by the author of the present work.
[110] It should be rendered as *Sankos*, not *Sancus*, in accordance with the original *Greek* text: τὸ Σάγκος ὄνομα οὐρανὸν σημαίνει τῇ Σαβίνων γλώσσῃ.

scholars, *William Smith* confirmed that the *Hernici* were a branch of the *Sabine* with the roots stretching back to the *Pelasgians*:

> "We are told that their name was derived from an old *Sabine* or *Marsic* word "*herna*", signifying a rock, an appellation well suited to the character of their country, the "*Hernica* saxa" of *Virgil*. (Virg. Aen. 7.684; Serv. ad loc.; Festus, v. Hernici.) This derivation would seem to point to their being a race akin to the *Sabines;* and *Servius* distinctly calls them a *Sabine* colony (Serv. ad Aen. l.c.): nor does there seem to be any reason to reject this statement, although the authority of that commentator is in itself of little weight (Niebuhr, vol. i. [p. 1.1060] p. 102). An older commentator on *Virgil* assigns them a *Marsic* origin (Schol. Veron. ad Aen. l.c.), which comes to much the same thing, as the *Marsi* were certainly closely related to the *Sabines*. [MARSI] On the other hand, *Julius Hyginus* (ap. Macrob. 5.18) affirmed that the *Hernicans* were a *Pelasgic* race; and *Macrobius* regards the description of their arm and attire given by *Virgil* as pointing to the same conclusion." [*Hernici*]

➢ *Marsi*, aka *Marsoi* = Μάρσοι, aka *Marsikos* = Μαρσικός, aka *Marsicus*:
  o *Marsi, Marsoi* > *Marsa* "love" in *Turkic*.
  o *Marsikos, Marsicus* > *Marsak* "loving, merciful" in *Turkic*.

From *Pliny the Elder's* commentary, based on a fellow scholar – *Gellianus's* opinion, one can deduce that the name of the *Marsi* traces to their leader *Marsyas*, who was a *Lydian*. As we already know, the *Lydians* were a branch of the *Leleges* related to the *Pelasgians,* in general, and *Spartans,* in particular:

> "From *Gellianus* we learn that *Archippe,* a town of the *Marsi*, built by *Marsyas*, a chieftain of the *Lydians*, has been swallowed up by *Lake Fucinus…*" [3.17]

William Smith came to the conclusion that the *Marsi* belonged to the *Sabini* family by constructing a logical train of thoughts that were heavily relied on the statements of the ancient historians:

> "There can be no doubt that they were, in common with the other inhabitants of the upland valleys of the central *Apennines,* a race of *Sabine* origin; though we have no direct testimony to this effect. Indeed the only express statement which we find concerning their descent is that which represents them as sprung from a son of *Circe*, obviously a mere mythological fable arising from their peculiar customs. (Plin. Nat. 7.2; Solin. 2.27.) Another tradition, equally, fabulous, but obscurely known to us, seems to have ascribed to them a *Lydian* origin, and derived their name from *Marsyas*. (Gellianus, ap. Plin. 3.12. s. 17; Sil. Ital. 8.503.) But the close connection of the four nations of the *Marsi, Marrucini, Peligni* and *Vestini,* can leave no reasonable doubt of their common origin; and the *Sabine* descent of the *Peligni* at least is clearly attested. [PELIGNI] It may be added that the *Marsi* are repeatedly mentioned by the *Roman* poets in a manner which, without distinctly affirming it, certainly seems to imply their connection with the *Sabine* race (Hor. Epod. 17. 29; Juv. 3.169; Verg. G. 2.167.)" [*Marsi*]

➢ *Marrucini*, aka *Marroukinoi* = Μαρρουκῖνοι, Μαρρουκινοί: *Mar* 'hill' + *Ru, Rou* > -*Ri,* -*Li* 'an affix, converting a noun into an adjective and equivalent to the preposition *From*' + *Cin, Kin* > *Kın* 'fan, devotee', meaning "fan of mountains" in *Turkic*. Akin to their *Sabinian* comrades, the *Marrucini* loved mountainous areas and preferred to live there, to which their nomen stands attested. Just like any and all the *Trojan, Scythian, Hunnic, Turkic,* and other related nations, the *Marrucini* were united into a confederate with their related tribes, predominantly with the *Sabinian* shoots – the *Marsi,* the *Peligni,* and the *Vestini,* and later they became loyal supporters of the *Romans,* especially, of the *Roman* emperor *Claudius Nero,* who had a clear-cut *Sabinian* origin:

> "The *Marrucini* were, undoubtedly, like the other tribes in their immediate neighbourhood, of *Sabine* origin, and appear to have been closely connected with the *Marsi;* indeed, the two names are little more than different forms of the same, a fact which appears to have been already recognized by *Cato* (ap. Piscian. ix. p. 871). But, whether the *Marrucini* were an offset of the *Marsi,* or both tribes were separately derived from the common *Sabine* stock, we have no

information. The *Marrucini* appear in history as an independent people, but in almost constant alliance with the *Marsi, Peligni,* and *Vestini*. There is, indeed, little doubt that the four nations formed a kind of league for mutual defence [p. 2.279] Liv. 8.29; Niebuhr, vol. i. p. 101); and hence we find the *Marrucini* generally following the lead and sharing the fortunes of the *Marsi* and *Peligni*. But in B.C. 311 they appear to have taken part with the *Samnites,* though the other confederates remained neuter; as in that year, according to *Diodorus,* they were engaged in open hostilities with *Rome*. (Diod. 19.105.) No mention of this is found in *Livy,* nor is their name noticed in B.C. 308, when the *Marsi* and *Peligni* appear in hostility to *Rome;* but a few years after, B.C. 304, all three nations, together with the *Frentani,* united in sending ambassadors to sue for peace, and obtained a treaty of alliance on favourable terms. (Liv. 9.41, 45; Diod. 20.101.) From this time the *Marrucini* became the firm and faithful allies of *Rome;* and are repeatedly mentioned among the auxiliaries serving in the *Roman* armies. (Dionys. xx. Fr. Didot.; Pol. 2.24; 59.44.40; Sil. Ital. 8.519.) During the Second Punic War their fidelity was unshaken, though their territory was repeatedly traversed and ravaged by *Hannibal* (Liv. 22.9, 26.11; Pol. 3.88); and we find them, besides furnishing their usual contingent to the *Roman* armies, providing supplies for *Claudius Nero* on his march to the *Metaurus,* and raising a force of volunteers to assist *Scipio* in his expedition to *Africa*." (Liv. 27.43, 28.45.) [*William Smith. – Marrucini*]

> *Vestini*, aka *Ouestinoi* = Οὐηστῖνοι: V, Ou > Öv 'home, house' + Estin > Estən 'be calm', meaning "calm, collected tribe" in *Turkic*. The *Vestini* were a part of the confederation, consisting of the major *Sabinian* tribes:
>> "Moreover the race as a whole was fully equal to the *Samnites* in military power, comprising, as it did, the *Marsi,* and the *Paeligni* and *Marrucini,* — all of whom must be had for enemies, should the *Vestini* be molested." [*Titus Livius*. "The History of *Rome*." 8.29.4]

> *Peligni*, aka *Pelignoi* = Πελίγνοι: Peli 'its mountain ridge' (*Pel* 'mountain ridge' + -*i* 'an affix of possession') + Gn > Günü 'lit by sunlight', meaning "people of the sunny mountain ridge" or "people inhabiting an area around a mountain ridge, lit by sunlight" in *Turkic*. The word construction of this ethnic group screams in favor of its *Turkic* origin also due to the geographical position of the *Peligni,* who, according to *William Smith,* populated the region along the mountain ridge:
>> "Their territory was of very small extent, being confined to the valley of the *Gizio,* a tributary of the *Aternus,* of which the ancient name is nowhere recorded, and a small part of the valley of the *Aternus* itself along its right bank. The valley of the *Gizio* is one of those upland valleys at a considerable elevation above the sea, running parallel with the course of the *Apennines,* which form so remarkable a feature in the configuration of the central chain of those mountains [APENNINUS]. It is separated from the *Marsi* and the basin of the lake *Fucinus* on the W. by a narrow and strongly marked mountain ridge of no great elevation; while towards the S. it terminates in the lofty mountain group which connects the central ranges of the *Apennines* with the great mass of the *Majella*. This last group, one of the most elevated in the whole of the *Apennines,* attaining a height of 9100 feet above the sea, rises on the SE. frontier of the *Peligni;* while the *Monte Morrone,* a long ridge of scarcely inferior height, runs out from the point of its junction with the *Majella* in a NW. direction, forming a gigantic barrier, which completely shuts in the *Peligni* on the NE., separating them from the *Frentani* and *Marrucini*." [*Peligni*]

> *Picentes* = Πίκεντες, aka *Pikentinoi* = Πικεντῖνοι, aka *Picentini*:
> o *Picentes*: Picen > Pəkinə 'expeditious, dexterous' + Tes 'quick', meaning "expeditious and quick" in *Turkic*.
> o *Pikentinoi, Picentini*: Piken, Picen > Pəkinə 'expeditious' + Tin > Təŋ 'people', meaning "expeditious people" or "people of a woodpecker" in *Turkic*.
> In his geographic and historical manuscript, *Strabo* included the *Picentes,* or as he called them, the *Pikentinoi,* into the family of the *Sabini* [5.3.1]. The ancient geographer also explained the meaning

of their name from a woodpecker – *Pikon* (*Πικον*), wrongfully translated into *English* as *Picus,* in their language:

> "The *Picentini* proceeded originally from the land of the *Sabini*. A woodpecker led the way for their chieftains, and from this bird they have taken their name, it being called in their language *Picus,* and is regarded as sacred to *Mars*." [5.4.2]

Most likely, the *Sabinian* word *Pikon* proceeded from the *Turkic Pəkinə* "dexterous" to describe a skillful and quick to find its food woodpecker.

> *Sabelli,* aka *Sabelles* = *Σαβέλλες:* Sab > Səb, Səv 'love, worship' (noun) + *Elli* 'belonging to a nation of' (*El* 'nation, people' + *-Li* 'an affix, equivalent to the preposition *From*'), meaning "nation of worship" in *Turkic*. This word construction is still in existence in the *Turkic* languages, i.e., *Yad Elli* "from a foreign nation".
>
> Moreover, this very word *Elli* with the variation *Illi* is the solid evidence of the *Turkic* origin (both variants exist in *Turkic*) and continues to exist in the last names of modern *Italians*. For instance, *Tinelli, Balotelli, Cimorelli, Verzilli.*
>
> The *Sabelli* were acknowledged by *Strabo* as a *Sabinian* branch of the *Samnites*. According to the legend narrated by the ancient scholar, the *Sabelli* obtained their name ("nation of worship") due to their religious devotion, or worship of their deity *Mars,* or *Aries:*

> "The following is the tradition concerning the [origin of the] *Samnites*. The *Sabines* having been engaged for a long period in war with the *Ombrici,* made a vow, common with some of the *Grecian* nations, that they would consecrate to the gods the productions of the year. They were victorious, and accordingly of the productions, the one kind were sacrificed, the other consecrated. However, in a time of scarcity, someone remarked, that they ought likewise to have consecrated the children. This then they did, and the children born at that period were called the sons of *Mars.* When these had grown up to manhood, they were sent forth, a bull leading the way, to found a colony. The bull lay down to rest in a place belonging to the *Opici;* a people dwelling in villages. These they drove out, and established themselves in the place. The bull, according to the direction of the diviners, they sacrificed to *Mars,* who had given him to them as a leader. It seems to have been in allusion to this that their parents called them by the diminutive form of *Sabelli.*" [5.4.12]

> *Saunitai* = *Σαυνίται,* aka *Savnitae,* aka *Safnitae,* aka *Samnites,* aka *Samnitai* = *Σαμνίται:* Saun, Savn, Safn, Samn > Səbin, Sevin 'love, worship, idolize, adore' + *Itai, Itae, Ites* > *It* 'move away', meaning "the *Sabini* who moved away" in *Turkic*. The alternative spelling of *Saunitai* as *Samnitai* with *U* and *M* letter variation is, clearly, a *Turkic* phenomenon; for instance, the *Turkic* word *Ev* "house" also has the variations *Eb, Ef, Əm, Əü*. *William Smith* was also in support of the conjecture about the same root in the name of the *Sabini* and the *Samnitai:*

> "All ancient writers agree in representing the *Samnites* as a people of *Sabine* origin, and not the earliest occupants of the country they inhabited when they first appear in history, but as having migrated thither at a comparatively late period. (Varr. L. L. 7.29; Appian, Samnit., Fr. 4, 5; Strab. v. p.250; Fest. s. v. Samnites, p. 326; A. Gel. 11.1.) This account of their origin is strongly confirmed by the evidence of their name; the *Greek* form of which, Σαυνίται, evidently contains the same root as that of *Sabini* (*Sav-nitae* or *Saf-nitae,* and *Sab-ini* or *Saf-ini*); and there is reason to believe that they themselves used a name still more closely identical. For the *Oscan* form "Safinim", found on some of the denarii struck by the *Italian* allies during the Social War, cannot refer to the *Sabines* usually so called, as that people was long before incorporated with the *Romans,* and is, in all probability, the *Oscan* name of the *Samnites*. (Mommsen, Unter Ital. Dialekte, p. 293; Friedländer, Oskische Muünzen, p. 78.)." [*Samnium*]

The *Samnites,* in their turn, produced more subsidiary tribes, such as the *Frentani,* the *Leucani,* the *Bruttii,* and the *Hirpini*.

- *Bruttii*, aka *Brettioi* = Βρέττιοι, aka *Brettios* = Βρέττιος: *Bru, Bre* > *Barı* 'run, escape' + *Ut, Et* > *Üt, Öt* 'pass, get away' + *Ti* > *Tüyə* 'tribe', meaning "escaped, departed people" in *Turkic*. The current etymological conclusion is impacted by *William Smith's* clarification of the name rendered in *Greek* as *Drapetai* = δραπέται "escapee":

  "The name of *Bruttii* (Βρέττιοι) was given them, it seems, not by the *Greeks*, but by the *Lucanians*, and signified in their language fugitive slaves or rebels (δραπέται, ἀποστάται). But though used at first as a term of reproach, it was subsequently adopted by the *Bruttians* themselves, who, when they had risen to the rank of a powerful nation, pretended to derive it from a hero named *Bruttus* (Βρέττος), the son of *Hercules* and *Valentia*. (Diod. 16.15; Strab. vi. p.255; Justin 23.1; Steph. Byz. s. v. Βρέττος.) *Justin*, on the other hand, represents them as deriving their name from a woman of the name of *Bruttia*, who figured in their first revolt, and who, in later versions of the legend, assumes the dignity of a queen. (Justin. l.c.; Jornand. de Reb. Get. 30; P. Diac. Hist. 2.17.)." [*Brutti*]

- *Lucanians*, aka *Leucani*, aka *Leukanoi* = Λευκανοί, aka *Loukanoi* = Λουκανοί: *Luc, Leuc, Leuk, Louk* > *Loka* 'vagabond' + *An* > *Ən* 'settle', meaning "settled wanderers" in *Turkic*. Though there is no testimony left about the meaning of this people's name, it is easily deduced from the fact that they were colonists of the *Pelasgian* stock from *Greece*, who left their country in pursuit of a better life, and after wandering a while, they reached land in *Italy* that had already been occupied by other *Pelasgian* tribes – the *Oenotrians* and the *Chones*, renamed it into *Lucania* and settled in there:

  "The *Lucanians* were, according to the general testimony of ancient writers, a *Sabellian* race, an offshoot or branch of the *Samnite* nation, which, separating from the main body of that people, in the same manner as the *Campanians*, the *Hirpini*, and the *Frentani* had severally done, pressed on still further to the south, and established themselves in the country subsequently known as *Lucania*. (Strab. vi. p.254; Plin. Nat. 3.5. s. 10.) The origin of their name is unknown; for the derivation of it from a leader of the name of *Lucius* (Plin. xxx. l.c.; Etym. Magn. s. v. Λευκανοί) is too obviously a mere etymological fiction of late days to deserve attention."
  [*William Smith. – Lucania*]

  Strabo asserted their *Samnite* roots and mentioned that they used to run their society based on democratic principles:

  "The *Leucani* are of *Samnite* origin. Having vanquished the *Posidoniates* and their allies, they took possession of their cities. At one time the institutions of the *Leucani* were democratic, but during the wars a king was elected by those who were possessed of chief authority: at the present time they are *Roman*." [6.1.4]

- *Frentani*, aka *Frentanoi* = Φρεντανοί, aka *Ferentanoi* = Φερεντανοί: *Fren, Feren* > *Farın* 'employ full force' + *Tan* > *Təŋ* 'people', meaning "those who employ full force" or "people of *Feronia*" in *Turkic*. Most likely, the *Fren, Feren* signified *Feronia*, or *Foronia* – the *Sabinian* goddess of abundance, who was known to use all her power to answer the prayers of her worshippers. *Dionysius of Halicarnassus* gave an account of the *Spartans*, who settled in *Italy* among the *Sabini* and named their city in honor of this very deity *Feronia* [2.49.4-5].
  The only thing left out by the historian was the probable fact that these *Spartans*, the founders of the *Sabini*, assumed a new name – the *Ferentanoi* to honor their goddess.
  Strabo characterized this small nation as exceptionally bold and fearless that also justifies the meaning of their name "from those who employ full force":

  "Above *Picenum* are the *Vestini*, the *Marsi*, the *Peligni*, the *Marucini*, and the *Frentani*, a *Samnitic* nation possessing the hill-country, and extending almost to the sea. All these nations are small, but extremely brave, and have frequently given the *Romans* proofs of their valour, first as enemies, afterwards as allies; and finally, having demanded the liberty and rights of citizens, and being denied, they revolted and kindled the *Marsian* war." [5.4.2]

- *Hirpini, aka Irpinoi = Ιρπίνοι*: *Hirp, Irp > Irbis* 'lynx; possibly, wolf' + *In > İn* 'house', meaning "house of a wolf" or "the wolf dynasty" in *Turkic*. *Strabo* narrated a captivating legend, according to which the *Hirpini* owed their name to a wolf that had led their tribe to a new place of settlement:
    "Beyond are the *Hirpini*, who are also *Samnites*: their name they take from the wolf, which conducted their colony; a wolf being called by the *Samnites hirpos*: these people border on the *Leucani* in the interior." [5.4.12]

- *Tarantini, aka Tarantinoi = Ταραντίνοι, aka Tarentini:* *Tarant > Taranta* 'selected' + *In > İn* 'house', meaning "tribe of the selected ones" or "the house of *Taranta*" in *Turkic*.
  According to *Strabo*, the *Tarantini* "originally migrated from *Laconia*...", later known as *Sparta* [6.1.15]. They settled in the city of *Tarentum* that "was named from a certain hero" [Idem. 5.3.2]. *Pausanias*, in his turn, clarified the name of this hero – *Taranta (Τάραντα)*, incorrectly translated into *English* as *Taras*:
    "And so on that night he took from the barbarians *Tarentum*, the largest and most prosperous city on the coast. They say that *Taras* the hero was a son of *Poseidon* by a nymph of the country, and that after this hero were named both the city and the river. For the river, just like the city, is called *Taras*." [10.10.8]
  The *Greek* geographer also indirectly confirmed the *Lacedæmonian* origin of the *Tarantini*:
    "*Tarentum* is a colony of the *Lacedaemonians*, and its founder was *Phalanthus*, a *Spartan*. On setting out to found a colony *Phalanthus* received an oracle from *Delphi*, declaring that when he should feel rain under a cloudless sky *Aethra*, he would then win both a territory and a city." [10.10.6]
  In addition to the city of *Tarentum* and the river *Taras*, the name of *Taranta* was applied to the *Spartan* colonists – the *Tarantini*. *Justin* called them the *Tarentini*, surnamed *Spurii* "bastards":
    "What are the *Tarentines*,[111] whom we understand to have come from *Lacedaemon*, and to have been called *Spurii*? The city of *Thurii* they say that *Philoctetes* built; and his monument is seen there to this day, as well as the arrows of *Hercules*, on which the fate of *Troy* depended, laid up in the temple of *Apollo*." [20.1]

- *Melians, aka Melioi = Μήλιοι > Molo* "undefeated" in *Turkic*. *Herodotus* characterized this tribe as an offshoot of the *Lacedæmonians* and as a freedom-loving, audacious people, who refused to surrender to their *Persian* adversary:
    "Also the *Seriphians*, the *Siphnians* and the *Melians* served with the rest; for they alone of the islanders had not given earth and water to the Barbarian." [8.46]

    "The *Melians*, who are descended from the *Lacedemonians*, furnished two; and the *Siphnians*, with the *Seriphians*, both *Ionians*, of *Athenian* original, two more." [Idem. 8.48]

- *Minyai, aka Minúai = Μινύαι > Miɲí* "eternal" in *Turkic*. Though there are two more meanings — "joy" and "brain", the most appropriate ought to be "eternal" to commemorate the everlasting deeds of the ancestors of the *Minyai*. *Herodotus* delivered a story about this *Lacedæmonian* tribe, who came to *Lacedæmon* to reintegrate into their ancestral society:
    "The children's children of those who voyaged in the *Argo*, having been driven forth by those *Pelasgians* who carried away at *Brauron* the women of the *Athenians*, having been driven forth I say by these from *Lemnos*, had departed and sailed to *Lacedemon*, and sitting down on *Mount Taÿgetos* they kindled a fire. The *Lacedemonians* seeing this sent a messenger to inquire who they were and from whence; and they answered the question of the messenger saying that they were *Minyai* and children of heroes who sailed in the *Argo*, for these, they said, had put into *Lemnos* and propagated the race of which they sprang. The *Lacedemonians* having heard the

---

[111] In the original *Latin* text, it is *Tarentini*.

story of the descent of the *Minyai,* sent a second time and asked for what purpose they had come into the country and were causing a fire to blaze. They said that they had been cast out by the *Pelasgians,* and were come now to the land of their fathers, for most just it was that this should so be done; and they said that their request was to be permitted to dwell with these, having a share of civil rights and a portion allotted to them of the land. And the *Lacedemonians* were content to receive the *Minyai* upon the terms which they themselves desired, being most of all impelled to do this by the fact that the sons of *Tyndareus* were voyagers in the *Argo.* So having received the *Minyai* they gave them a share of land and distributed them in the tribes; and they forthwith made marriages, and gave in marriage to others the women whom they brought with them from *Lemnos.* However, when no very long time had passed, the *Minyai* forthwith broke out into insolence, asking for a share of the royal power and also doing other impious things: therefore the *Lacedemonians* resolved to put them to death; and having seized them they cast them into a prison." [4.145-146]

➢ *Æolians,* aka *Aiolians,* aka *Aiolees* = Αἰολέες: *Æ, Ai > Ai, Ay* 'lead' + *Ol, Olees > Iol, Yol* 'way', meaning "lead the way" in *Turkic.* The name of the *Æolians* was imposed on them by *Æolus* – the son of the *Pelasgian* sovereign *Hellen* [*Apollodorus.* "Library." 1.7.3]. The nation of the *Æolians* was initially known as the *Pelasgians,* who became *Hellenized* and converted into *Greeks:*

"The *Aiolians* supplied sixty ships; and these were equipped like *Hellenes* and used to be called *Pelasgians* in the old time, as the *Hellenes* report." [*Herodotus.* 7.95]

"As for the *Pelasgi,* almost all agree, in the first place, that some ancient tribe of that name spread throughout the whole of *Greece,* and particularly among the *Aeolians of Thessaly.*" [*Strabo.* 5.2.4]

➢ *Boeotians,* aka *Boiotoi* = βοιωτοί > *Boiotos*=Βοιωτός: *Boe, Boi > Boi* 'tribe' + *Ot > Öt* 'crush' + *Os > Us* 'master', meaning "chief who crushes other nations" in *Turkic.* Accordant with *Pausanias,* the *Boeotians* were indebted to their founder *Boiotos* (translated into *English* as *Boeotus*) for their name:

"The *Boeotians* as a race got their name from *Boeotus,* who, legend says, was the son of *Itonus* and the nymph *Melanippe,* and *Itonus* was the son of *Amphictyon.*" [*Pausanias.* 9.1.1]

Boiotos was a great-grandson of the *Pelasgian* King *Hellen.* The *Boeotians,* an *Aeolian* people, left *Thessaly,* also known as *Aeolia* – the main habitation of the *Pelasgi* and established a new presence in the region that they named *Boeotia,* or *Boiotia,* or *Beotia* [*Thucydides.* "The History of the Grecian* War". 1.12].

➢ *Phocians,* aka *Phokeoi* = Φωκεοί > *Phocos*=Φῶκος: *Phoc > Pök* 'tall' or *Pökö* 'courageous, strong' + *Os > Us* 'master', meaning "tall or brave leader" in *Turkic.* The *Phocians* were the tribe of the mixed extraction – both from the *Aeolians* and the *Achaeans.* The *Phocian* tribe, as well as of the country *Phocis* they lived in, obtained their name after the *Aeolian* King *Phocus,* or *Phocos,* on the report of *Pausanias:*

"This name had already been given to the land, at the time when *Phocus,* son of *Ornytion,* came to it a generation previously. In the time, then, of this *Phocus* only the district about *Tithorea* and *Parnassus* was called *Phocis,* but in the time of *Aeacus* the name spread to all from the borders of the *Minyae* at *Orchomenos* to *Scarphea* among the *Locri.*" [2.29.3]

In the *Trojan* War, the *Phocians* joined the *Greco-Danaan* forces against the *Trojans:*

"*Phocis* is said to have been originally inhabited by several of those tribes who formed the population of *Greece* before the appearance of the *Hellenes.* Among the earliest inhabitants we find mention of *Leleges* (Dicaearch. p. 5), *Thracians* (Strab. ix. p.401; Thuc. 2.29; comp. Paus. 1.41.8), and *Hyantes.* (Strab. l.c.) The aboriginal inhabitants were conquered by the *Phlegyae* from *Orchomenus.* (Paus. 8.4.4, 10.4.1.) The country around *Tithorea* and *Delphi* is said to have been first called *Phocis* from *Phocus*, a son of *Ornytion*, and grandson of *Sisyphus of Corinth;* and the name is said to have been afterwards extended to the whole country from *Phocus*, a son of *Aeacus*, who arrived there not long afterwards. (Paus. 2.29.3, 10.1.1.) This statement would seem to show that the *Phocians* were believed to be a mixed *Aeolic* and *Achaean* race, as *Sisyphus* was one of the *Aeolic* heroes, and *Aeacus* one of the *Achaean*. In the *Trojan* War the inhabitants appear under the name of *Phocians*, and were led against *Troy* by *Schedius* and *Epistrophus*, the sons of *Iphitus*. (Hom. Il. 2.517.)" [*William Smith. – Phocis*]

➢ *Magnetes* = *Μάγνητες*, aka *Magnesians*, aka *Magnes* = *Μάγνης*:
  o *Magnetes*: Magne > Məŋgi 'shrine' + Et 'do' + Es > Us 'master', meaning "master who builds shrines" in *Turkic*.
  o *Magnes*: Magne > Məŋgi 'shrine + Es > Us 'master', meaning "master of shrines" in *Turkic*.

The *Magnetes*, as well as their land *Magnesia*, located in *Thessaly*, got their identifying appellation from *Magnetes* – the first king of *Magnesia* and son of *Aeolus* [*Pausanias*. 6.21.11] and the grandson of *Hellen* [*Apollodorus*. 1.7.3]. They were the *Pelasgians* of the *Aeolian* branch.

St. Jerome reported that *Magnesia* was founded in 1053 BCE. *Strabo* noted that *Magnesia* was populated by the *Pelasgi* and, among the enumerated *Pelasgian* cities, listed *Magnetis* as well:
  "*Hieronymus* assigns a circuit of 3000 stadia to the plain country in *Thessaly* and *Magnesia*, and says, that it was inhabited by *Pelasgi*, but that these people were driven into *Italy* by *Lapithæ*, and that the present *Pelasgic* plain is that in which are situated *Larisa, Gyrton, Pheræ, Mopsium, Bœbeis, Ossa, Homole, Pelion*, and *Magnetis*." [9.5.23]

The *Pelasgian* beginning of the ethnonym and toponym is additionally proved by the existence of *Magnesia* both in *Lydia* (modern *Manisa* in *Turkey*) and *Thessaly*. Radlov V.V. indicated the city of *Manissa*, the equivalent of *Magnesia* [4.2.2019].

Curiously, the name of this *Pelasgian* tribe was bestowed to a lodestone, found in *Magnesia*, and known as a magnet that exhibits the properties of magnetism, and the city's name applied to the chemical element *Magnesium*.

The *Magnetes* were included in "the *Thessalian* catalogue of the poet" [*Strabo*. 9.5.22] by *Homer*, who introduced them as the fighting side against the *Trojans* in the *Trojan* War.

➢ *Thessalians*, aka *Thessaloi* = *Θεσσαλοί*: Thes > Tes 'agile' + Sal 'fierce', meaning "agile and fierce tribe" in *Turkic*.

The *Pelasgian* nation and the country of the *Pelasgians* – *Thessaly* were named after *Thessalos*=*Θεσσαλός* ("agile and fierce leader" in *Turkic*), the son of *Hercules* [*Homer*. 2.679]. In conformity with *Xenophon*, the *Thessalians* comprised of the people inhabiting *Pelasgian* cities:
  "When he had passed through *Macedonia* and reached *Thessaly*, the people of *Larisa, Crannon, Scotussa* and *Pharsalus*, who were allies of the *Boeotians*, all the *Thessalians*, in fact, except those who happened to be in exile at the time, followed at his heels and kept molesting him." ["*Agesilaus*". 2.2]

Thucydides stated that the *Thessalians* were a part of the ancient confederation with other *Pelasgian* nations:
  "This aid of the *Thessalians* was upon an ancient League with the *Athenians*, and consisted of *Larissaeans, Pharsalians, Parasians, Cranonians, Peirasians, Gyrtonians, Pheraeans*."
  ["The History of the *Grecian* War". 2.22]

Like any other *Pelasgian, Trojan, Scythian, Turkic* nations, the *Thessalians* were famous for their unsurpassed skill of taming the horses:
  "Men declare that amongst the *Thessalians* this is counted honourable, to cut up a bull neatly and to manage steeds." [*Euripides*. "*Electra*". 770-841]

➢ *Pheraeans*, aka *Pheraioi* = *Φεραῖοι* > *Pheres*=*Φέρης*: Pher > Pir 'one' + Es > Əs 'intellect', meaning "person of unique brainpower" in *Turkic*. Both the *Pherœans* and their city *Pherae* (*Φεραί*)

– one of the most ancient cities of *Thessaly*, were named after the *Pelasgian* hero *Pheres*, who was a great-grandson of *Hellen*, a grandson of *Aeolus*, the uncle of the *Argonaut Jason*, and the father of another *Argonaut* – *Admetus*, mentioned by *Apollodorus* ["Library." 1.8.2].

The *Pheræans* were the participants in the *Trojan* War against the *Trojans*, as recorded by *Homer* ["The Iliad." 2].

➤ *Iberians, aka Iber = Ἴβηρ, aka Iberes = Ἴβηρες, aka Ibersi = Ἴβηροι:*
  o *Iberians, Iber: Ib > İba* 'courtesy' + *Er* 'man, warrior', meaning "courteous, suave man/warrior" in *Turkic*.
  o *Iberians, Iber: Ib > Öp* 'wealth' + *Er* 'man, warrior', meaning "wealthy men/warriors" in *Turkic*.
  o *Iberes, Ibersi: Ib > İba* 'courtesy' + *Er* 'man, warrior' + *Es, Si > Soi* 'tribe', meaning "tribe of courteous, suave men/warriors" in *Turkic*.

The *Iberians* are the best example to demonstrate the link between the *Scythians* and the *Pelasgians*, as they belong to both these nations. *Strabo* expressly noted that the *Iberians* were related to the *Scythians*:

"Those who inhabit the mountainous country, and they are the most numerous, are addicted to war, live like the *Sarmatians* and *Scythians*, on whose country they border, and with whom they are connected by affinity of race." [11.3.3]

When going to war, they could rely on the military help from the *Scythian* tribes as well:

"These people however engage in agriculture also, and can assemble many myriads of persons from among themselves, and from the *Scythians* and *Sarmatians*, whenever any disturbance occurs." [Idem ibid]

However, in contrast to the *Scythian* wagon-lifestyle, the *Iberians* preferred to build and live in houses with tile roofs. This sophistication came mostly from their *Pelasgian* roots. *Cornelius Tacitus* described them as the people who proudly asseverated their *Thessalian* lineage:

"They claim to have been descended from the *Thessalians*, at the period when *Jason*, after the departure of *Medea* and the children born of her, returned subsequently to the empty palace of *Æetes*, and the vacant kingdom of *Colchi*." ["The Annals." 6.34]

This means that some of the *Iberians*, like their *Pelasgian* brethren – the ancient *Armenians* and the *Albanians*, were the direct descendants of *Jason* and his *Argonauts* from *Thessaly* – the country of the *Pelasgians*.

As we know, the *Scythians* and the *Pelasgians*, as well as the *Thracians*, shared the same heritage. And the *Iberians* serve as a vivid example of the kinship between the *Scythian* and *Pelasgian* nations. Being the natives of the *Caucasus*, a portion of the *Iberians* spread out to *Europe* (*Spain* was anciently known as *Iberia*) and *Asia Minor*, from where their colony returned to *Iberia* to resettle.

The *Iberians* split into two main groups: the *Caucasian* and the *Western*. The *Caucasian Iberians* were the direct progeny of the *Scythians*, while the *Western Iberians*, aka *Ibersi*, intermingled with other kin nations, such as the *Keltic, Gallic, Germanic, Thracian, Pelasgian* nations, and their derivatives.

➤ *Caucasian Albanians, aka Albani, aka Albanoi = Ἀλβανοὶ, aka Arnaut, aka Arnavut, aka Alwan, aka Aluank, aka Gargarians, aka Gargareis = Γαργαρείς, aka Gargareas = Γαργαρέας:*
  o *Albani, Albanoi: Alb > Albı* 'hero' + *Ani, Anoi > An* 'land',[112] meaning "land of heroes" in *Turkic*. *Ptolemy* enumerated many places with the names, containing the *Turkic* root *Albı*, such as *Albiana* (Ἀλβίανα) "land of heroes" in *Corsica* Island, the city of *Albana* (Ἀλβανα) and the river *Albanus* (presently, *Samur* in *Azerbaijan*) in the country of *Albania* (Ἀλβανία).

---

[112] *Egorov V.G.* "Etimologicheskiy slovar chuvashskogo yazika." [26].

- o *Arnaut, Arnavut: Arna* 'send someone' + *Ut, Vut* > *-Ut* 'an affix, converting a verb into a verbal noun', meaning "the dispatched; those who were sent" in *Turkic*.
- o *Alwan, Aluank* "different" in *Arabic*.
- o *Gargarians, Gargareis, Gargareas: Gar* > *Qara* 'great, high' + *Qari, Qare* > *Qara* 'land' + *Eis, Eas* > *Əs* 'lord, master', meaning "masters of the highland" in *Turkic*. The *Albanian* tribe of the *Gargareis* acquired their name from the highest peak of the *Mount Ida* – *Gargaron=Γάργαρον* ("great highland" in *Turkic*) that also gave its name to the *Pelasgian*, or *Æolian*, city *Gargara=Γάργαρα*:

  "In speaking of the projections like feet on each side of *Ida*, as *Lectum*, and *Zeleia*, he distinguishes in proper terms the summit *Gargarum*, calling it the top (of *Ida*), for there is now in existence in the higher parts of *Ida* a place, from which the present *Gargara*, an *Æolian* city, has its name." [*Strabo*. 13.1.5-6]

  "*Gárgara* (*Γάργαρα* or *Γάργαρον*) one of the heights of *Mount Ida* in *Troas* (Hom. Il. 8.48, 14.292), which continued to bear this name even in the time of *Strabo* (xiii. p.583; comp. Plin. Nat. 5.32; Macr. 5.20; Steph, B. s. v.). Its modern name is said to be *Kazdag*. (*Walpole's* Memoirs relating to *Turkey*, p. 120.) A town of the same name existed from early times upon that height, or rather on a branch of it forming a cape on the north of the bay of *Adramyttium*, between *Antandrus* and [p. 1.977] *Assus*. In the earliest times it is said to have been inhabited by *Leleges*, but afterwards to have received *Aeolian* colonists from *Assus*, and others from *Miletupolis*. (Strab. l.c. pp. 606, 610; Mela, 1.18; Ptol.5.2.5.) The name of this town is in some authors misspelt *Ίάργανον*, as in *Ptolemy*, and *Σάγαρα*, as in *Hierocles*. The territory round *Gargara* was celebrated for its fertility. (Verg. G. 1.103; Senec. Phoen. 4.608.) The modern village of *Iné* probably occupies the site of ancient *Gargara*." [*William Smith. – Gargara*.]

All three variants of the name of the *Caucasian Albanians* reflect the historical, legendary, and ethnic peculiarities of this nation. The *Albani*, or the *Albanians*, were considered heroes, as their founders participated in the heroic actions performed by *Jason* the *Argonaut* (correctly, *Iason=Ίάσων*) on his mission to gain control of the golden fleece and prove his bravery to the world. There is absolutely no doubt about the *Turkic* origin of the name *Albani, Albanoi, Albanians*, as there was an ancient *Turkic* tribe of the *Alban*, the posterity of which still exist under the same name in *Kazakhstan*:

  "The *Kazakh* ethnos structurally consists of three *Zhuzes* (unions). The *Younger Zhuz* includes three large confederations: *Alimuls, Bayuly* and *Zhetiru*. The *Middle Zhuz* includes such clans as *Argyn, Kipshak, Kerey, Naiman, Uak, Konyrat*. The *Elder Zhuz* includes clans like *Sary-Uysun, Dulat*, **Alban**, *Su-An, Ysty, Shaprashty, Oshakty, Shanyshkyly, Srgels, Kanly, Zhalair*." [113]
  [Zhaksylyk M. Sabitov. "O proiskhojdenii kazakhskikh rodov Sari-Uysun, Dulat, Alban, Suan, Isti, Shaprashti, Oshakti, Srgeli." Russian Journal of Genetic Genealogy. Vol.3. №3 (2011)/Vol. 4. № 1 (2012). 94]

This *Alban* clan was genealogically proven to belong to the *Turkic* family of the *Kazakhs* by the researcher *Zhaksylyk M. Sabitov*. Moreover, *Alban* was recorded as an ancient *Turkic* male and the founder of the *Alban* dynasty in *Central Asia* [Idem. 95].

Among the *Turkic* nations, predominantly, the *Azerbaijanis*, the *Albanians* were also known under other *Turkic* names – *Arnaut*, or *Arnavut* ("the dispatched"), according to *Radlov V.V.* [1.1.304], and as *Ərnaud, Ərnavud, Ərnod*, on the report of *Lazar Budagov* [1.33], who derived their etymology from *Turkish*. Nothing is surprising here if one takes two important matters into consideration – *Jason* was sent after the golden fleece, and he was the nephew of the *Pelasgian* king in *Thessaly* with the ancient *Pelasgian* name – *Pelias*, which was initially given to the whole nation of the

---

[113] The text was translated into *English* by the author of the present book.

Pelasgi. Marcus Junianus Justinus confirmed this in his book "History of the World, Extracted from *Trogus Pompeius.*":

> "...*Jason of Thessaly*, whom King *Pelias*, wishing to procure his death from dread of his extraordinary ability, which was dangerous to his throne, despatched on a prescribed expedition to *Colchis*, to bring home the fleece of the ram so celebrated throughout the world; hoping that the man would lose his life, either in the perils of so long a voyage, or in war with barbarians so remote. But *Jason*, having spread abroad the report of so glorious an enterprise, at which the chief of the youth from almost all the world came flocking to him, collected a band of heroes, who were called *Argonauts*." [42.2]

Diodorus Siculus, in his work "The Library of the History", also stated:

> "*Jason* (they say) was the son of *Aeson*, and the nephew to *Pelias*, king of the *Thessaly*, and being a man of strong body and of a high spirit, far above any of his age, was ambitious to perform some memorable and remarkable action; for knowing that *Perseus* his ancestor, and some others, (by their expeditious and admirable achievements in foreign countries), had purchased eternal honour and renown, he resolved to imitate them in the like heroic undertakings..." [4.40.1-3]

Obviously, the *Arnaut*, or *Arnavut*, aka the *Albanians* – the progeny of the legendary *Argonauts*, who sailed from the *Pelasgian* shores of *Thessaly*, belonged to the *Pelasgian* stock of *Turkic* origin:

> "*Jason*, now launching forth his ship, completely furnished with all things necessary, made choice of four-and-fifty of the greatest persons of quality out of the number of those who were desirous to go along with him: amongst whom the most remarkable were *Castor* and *Pollux*,[114] *Hercules* and *Telamon*, *Orpheus* and *Atalanta* the daughter of *Scheneus*, the sons of *Thespius*, and *Jason* himself the head and captain of the expedition to *Colchis;* he called the ship *Argo*, before he took her from the builder, whose name was *Argus*, (as some fabulous writers report), who (they say) embarked with them to repair the ship, as occasion might require: but others say it was so called from its swift sailing, for that *Argou* among the antient *Greeks* signified swift.[115] Being all on board, they unanimously chose *Hercules*, for his extraordinary valour, to be their general." [Idem. 4.41.1-3]

In the *Armenian* medieval books, the *Albanians*, aka the *Arnaut/Arnavut*, were called the *Alwan*, or the *Aluank*, meaning "different" in *Arabic*. The *Armenian* historian of the 10th c., *Movses Kalankatuatsi*, in his book "History of the Country of *Aluank*", constated the kindred ties of the *Albanians* with the *Hun:*

> "Thus, the courageous *Djuansher* sat quietly on his throne when the following year, on the day of the winter equinox, the king of the *Huns* advanced with the horsemen of many thousands. And even before [*Djuansher*] ordered his country to be wary and strengthened, however, the invading *Huns* crossed this side of the *Kura* (*Cyrus*) River, reached the bank of *Eraskh*, and hijacked not only the residents of *Aluank*, but also the locals of *Ayrarat* and the country of *Syunik*, stole sheep and herds of cattle, descending for the winter to the valleys on pastures, and drove them to their camp.
>
> Then the king of the *Hun* wished to see *Djuansher*. And he sent his brothers to [him] [and through them] asked for a meeting so that the brotherly love could be established between them. And the brave and courageous sovereign did not think to be afraid of him; [although] none of the *Persian* kings dared to face the King of *Turkestan* face to face.
>
> Boldly, with a fearless heart, he fell down before the Savior's cross and said:
>
>> "Although I go to the shadows of death, I'm not afraid of evil even a bit because you, *Lord*, are with me."

---

[114] It should be *Poludeukes* = Πολυδεύκης.

[115] Both *Argos* [Ἄργος] as a personal name and *Argos* "swift" are undoubtedly of *Turkic* origin. They could be derived from ərik "swift"; or Arg > ərik 'swift' + Os > Us 'master'; or Ar 'man, warrior' + Gos > Kəs 'swift' = "quick man"; or Ar 'man, warrior' + Gos > Qos 'erupt, disgorge' = "the one who produces warriors".

And he went on his way to him with the royal retinue. And the king of the *Huns* [in turn] went out to meet him and, sailing on the canoe to this bank of the river, stopped in calm and deep waters. Having agreed on peace between themselves, they decided to stop the strife and, most importantly, establish a brotherly friendship. And having concluded the contract, each returned to his camp.

But what valor my brave lord showed the next day! Having crossed with seventeen men to the other side of the river, he came to the *Hun* camp and took the royal daughter as his wife, he returned from captivity one hundred and twenty thousand cattle, seven thousand horses and stallions and [freed] at least one thousand two hundred prisoners. Thus, with joy in his heart, he went back home." [116] [2.26]

As later indicated by the same author, the name of the king of *Turkestan*, the *Hun*, was *Alp-Ilituer*, that has undoubtedly the *Turkic* origin: *Alp* 'courageous' + *Ilit* 'lead' + *Er* 'warrior, hero', meaning "leading courageous warrior, or hero".

As it was earlier established, based on the testimonies of the ancient *Roman* authors, the *Hun* were a *Scythian*, aka a *Turkic* nation. The *Armenian* writer also indirectly confirmed this by indicating that the king of the *Hun* was the sovereign of *Turkestan* – the land of the *Turkic* nations. Moreover, the *Armenian* historian ascertained the fact that both the *Hun* and the *Albanians* were of the same stock and used an unusual otherwise combination of words – "brotherly love", "brotherly friendship" between these two nations. The author never mentioned anything of this kind between the *Albanians* and the *Armenians* or the *Persians*, which proves the point that they had different ethnic and linguistic extractions.

Meanwhile, *Movses Khorenatsi* described the language of the leading tribe of the *Albanians* – the *Gargar* as "guttural, absurd, barbarous, rude language". And this assertion resonated with *Strabo's* and *Tacitus's* version of the origin of the *Albanians* from the *Thessalians*, aka the *Pelasgians*.

Pliny the Elder was very specific when describing the origin of the *Albanians*, or the *Albani*, as well as the territory they occupied:

"At the entrance, on the right-hand side, dwell the *Udini*, a *Scythian* tribe, at the very angle of the mouth. Then along the coast there are the *Albani*, the descendants of *Jason*, it is said; that part of the sea which lies in front of them, bears the name of '*Albanian*.' This nation, which lies along the *Caucasian* chain, comes down, as we have previously stated, as far as the river *Cyrus*, which forms the boundary of *Armenia* and *Iberia*." [6.15]

And it is from the "land of the *Argives*" the *Argonauts*, aka the *Pelasgians*, sailed away in search of the golden fleece, resettled in the country that they established – *Albania* at the territory of present-day *Azerbaijan*, *Armenia*, and some areas of *Georgia*, and became known as the *Albanians*, or the *Arnaut/Arnavut* – the scions of the *Argonauts*.

Remarkably, the ancient *Albanian* capital – *Cabala* (*Khabala* = Χαβάλα) indicated by *Ptolemy* [5.11], or *Cabalaca* – by *Pliny the Elder*, has retained its name as of nowadays and signifies both the region and the city of *Gabala* (*Qəbələ*) in the *Azerbaijan Republic*:

"The whole plain which extends away from the river *Cyrus* is inhabited by the nation of the *Albani*, and, after them, by that of the *Iberi*, who are separated from them by the river *Alazon*, which flows into the *Cyrus* from the *Caucasian* chain. The chief cities are *Cabalaca* in *Albania*, *Harmastis*, near a river of *Iberia*, and *Neoris*; there is the region also of *Thasie*, and that of *Triare*, extending as far as the mountains known as the *Paryadres*." [*Pliny the Elder*. 6.11]

---

[116] It was translated into *English* by the author of the present work from the book *Movses Kalankatuatsi* "Istoriya strani Aluank". The *Russian* translation from old *Armenian* was done by *Sh. V. Smbatyan*.

Figure 22. The ruins of the gates of the Albanian capital Cabala in Azerbaijan. Credit: Emin Bashirov. (CC BY-SA 3.0)

The name of the ancient *Albanian* city *Cabala* proceeds from the *Turkic* word *Kabal* "get locked", which means the city had gates and would be locked at all times. *Radlov V.V.* even used several examples to show that this word *Kabal* applied mostly to the fortresses and citadels [2.1.445]. The ruins of the *Albanian* gates of *Cabala* still exist in the *Gabala* region of *Azerbaijan*.

In slight contrast to *Pliny the Elder* and *Strabo,* who asserted that the *Albanians* were the descendants of the *Argonaut Jason* from *Thessaly,* another *Roman* historian – *Justin* asserted the *Trojan* origin of the *Albanians* – the liegemen of *Hercules* from *Italy*:

"With the *Albanians* he formed an alliance, a people who are said to have followed *Hercules* out of *Italy,* from the *Alban* mount, when, after having killed *Geryon,* he was driving his herds through *Italy,* and who, remembering their *Italian* descent, saluted the soldiers of *Pompeius* in the *Mithridatic* war as their brothers." [42.3.4]

According to *Justin,* the *Albanians* were the *Trojans* from the *Italian* metropolis *Alba Longa* founded by the *Trojan* refugee *Ascanius*. Afterward, the *Albanians* joined *Hercules* and established a new country with the name *Albania* near the *Caspian Sea*:

"Of an illicit connection between a daughter of *Faunus* and *Hercules,* (who, having killed *Geryon* about that time, was driving his herds, the prize of his victory, through *Italy*), was born *Latinus,* in whose reign *Aeneas* came from *Ilium* into *Italy,* after the destruction of *Troy* by the *Greeks*. *Aeneas,* being confronted by an immediate war, led out his troops into the field, but being first invited to a conference, raised such admiration of himself in *Latinus,* that he was both admitted to a share of his throne, and became his son-in-law by a marriage with his daughter *Lavinia*. After this event, they had to carry on war in concert against *Turnus,* king of the *Rutuli,* because he had been disappointed of marrying *Lavinia;* and in the war both *Turnus* and *Latinus* were killed. *Aeneas,* in consequence, becoming by right of victory master of both nations, built a city, which he called *Lavinium,* from the name of his wife. Some time afterwards, he went to war with *Mezentius,* king of the *Etruscans,* and when he was killed in it, *Ascanius* his son succeeded him. *Ascanius* moved out of *Lavinium,* and built *Alba Longa,* which for three hundred years was the metropolis of his kingdom." [43.1]

However, there is no contradiction in any of the aforementioned statements, as *Hercules* joined *Jason* and the team of the *Argonauts* with his followers from *Italy*. Both the *Argonauts* from *Thessaly* and the *Trojans* from *Italy,* as well as their leaders – *Jason* and *Hercules,* were indeed the *Pelasgians,* a part of the greater *Thracian* nation. And *Justin* also acknowledged the fact that all the subdued by *Jason* nations of the *Caucasus* considered him as their founder:

"He then carried on great wars with the neighbouring nations; and of the cities which he took, he added part to the kingdom of his father-in-law, to make amends for the injury that he had done him in his former expedition, in which he had carried off his daughter *Medea* and put to death his son *Aegialeus,* and part he assigned to the people that he had brought with him; and he is said to have been the first of mankind, after *Hercules* and *Bacchus* (whom tradition declares to have been kings of the east), that subdued that quarter of the world. Over some of these nations he appointed *Recas* and *Amphistratus,* the charioteers of *Castor* and *Pollux,* to be their rulers…Hence almost the whole east appointed divine honours, and erected temples, to *Jason,* as their founder; temples which *Parmenio,* one of the generals of *Alexander the Great,* caused many years after to be pulled down, that no name might be more venerated in the east than that of *Alexander.*" [42.3]

Certainly, not all the *Albanians* left *Italy,* as during the time of *Procopius of Caesarea* – 6th c. of our era, they lived on the land called *Langoubilla* (rendered into *English* as *Langovilla*) near the river *Po* in *Italy:*

"And to the north of them live the *Albani* in an exceedingly good land called *Langovilla,*[117] and beyond these are the nations subject to the *Franks,* while the country to the west is held by the *Gauls* and after them the *Spaniards.*" ["History of the Wars." 5.15.25]

When describing the character of the *Albanian* nation, *Strabo* reported that they led a nomadic lifestyle:

"The *Albanians* pursue rather a shepherd life, and resemble more the nomadic tribes, except that they are not savages, and hence they are little disposed to war. They inhabit the country between the *Iberians* and the *Caspian Sea,* approaching close to the sea on the east, and on the west border upon the *Iberians*…To the country of the *Albanians* belongs *Caspiana,* and has its name from the *Caspian* tribe,[118] from whom the sea also has its appellation; the *Caspian* tribe is now extinct." [11.4.1-5]

The centuries-old *Caucasian* and *Turkic* tradition to respect the elderly that is still prevalent in the *Caucasus* was noted by *Strabo* in the *Albanians:*

"The *Albanians* pay the greatest respect to old age, which is not confined to their parents, but is extended to old persons in general. It is regarded as impious to show any concern for the dead, or to mention their names. Their money is buried with them, hence they live in poverty, having no patrimony." [11.4.8]

➢ <u>Arcadians, aka Arkades</u> = Ἀρκάδες > *Arcas, Arkas: Ar* > *Er* 'man, hero, warrior' + *Cas, Kas* > *Kas* 'cultivate', meaning "man who cultivates" in *Turkic*. Just like the *Argives,* the *Arcadians* were named after their own wise leader *Arcas* (Ἀρκάς), who provided much-needed knowledge to his people about husbandry, taught them artisan skills, according to *Pausanias:*

"After the death of *Nyctimus, Arcas* the son of *Callisto* came to the throne. He introduced the cultivation of crops, which he learned from *Triptolemus,* and taught men to make bread, to weave clothes, and other things besides, having learned the art of spinning from *Adristas.* After this king the land was called *Arcadia* instead of *Pelasgia* and its inhabitants *Arcadians* instead of *Pelasgians.*" [8.4.1]

St. Jerome indicated the year of 1483 BCE when the son of *Jove* and *Callisto – Arcas* named *Pelasgia* after himself.

However, *Strabo,* relying on the authority of an ancient *Greek* historian *Ephorus,* traced the *Arcadian* lineage from the king of *Arcadia Lycaon* to *Pelasgus:*

"*Ephorus,* when he supposes that they were a tribe of *Arcadians,* follows *Hesiod,* who says,
"The sons born of the divine *Lycaon,* whom formerly *Pelasgus* begot."'" [5.2.4]

---

[117] In the original *Greek* text, it is Λαγγουβιλλα = *Langoubilla.*
[118] This tribe is also known as the *Kaspioi* = *Kaspioi* = Κάσπιοι.

Amazingly, both *Pelasgian* names – *Argos* and *Arcas,* due to their structural composition, demonstrate their uncanny resemblance to the *Turkic* male names:
- *Argos > Ar + Gos*
- *Arcas > Ar + Kas*
- *Erbey > Er + Bey* "noble warrior".
- *Erçin > Er + Çin* "true warrior".
- *Ergün > Er + Gün* "hero of his time".
- *Ergüneş > Er + Güneş* "stellar warrior".
- *Erhun, Erqun > Er + Hun, Qun* "a *Hun* warrior".
- *Erxan > Er + Xan* "royal warrior".
- *Erol > Er + Ol* "son of a warrior".
- *Ersoy > Er + Soy* "warrior dynasty".
- *Erşad > Er + Şad* "prince warrior".
- *Erşan, Erşed > Er + Şan, Şed* "respected warrior".
- *Erşen > Er + Şen* "cheerful warrior".
- *Ertac > Er + Tac (Taj)* "crown of all the warriors".
- *Ertay, Ertekin > Er + Tay, Tekin* "like a warrior".
- *Erteper > Er + Teper* "destroyer of warriors".
- *Ertoğrul > Er + Toğrul* "warrior-eagle".
- *Ertur, Ertürk > Er + Tur, Türk* "*Turkic* warrior", "*Turian* warrior".
- *Erturan > Er + Turan* "hero of *Turan* (country)".
- *Eruz > Er + Uz* "hero of the *Az* nation".
- *Eryavuz > Er + Yavuz* "hot-tempered warrior".

> *Orchomenians, aka Orkhomenioi = Ὀρχομενίοι > Orkhomenos = Ὀρχομενός*: *Orcho, Orkho > Orka, Arxa*[119] 'backbone, protector' + *Men* 'I' + *Os > Us* 'master', meaning "I am the chief protector" in *Turkic*. *Orkhomenos* was the son of the *Arcadian* King *Lycaon*. The *Orchomenians* and their city *Orchomenus* derived their name after him:
> "*Orchomenus* became founder of both the town called *Methydrium* and of *Orchomenus*, styled by *Homer* "rich in sheep."" [*Pausanias*. 8.3.3]
> *Homer* listed them as a part of the *Greco-Danaan* contingent in the *Trojan* War.

> *Ionians, aka Iones = Ἴωνες, aka Attikoi = Ἀττικοι, aka Athenians, aka Athenaioi = Ἀθηναῖοι, aka Cranian Pelasgians, aka Pelasgoi Kranaoi = Πελασγοί Κραναοί, aka Cecropians, aka Kekropidai = Κεκροπίδαι, aka Ægialeans, aka Pelasgoi Aigialees = Πελασγοὶ Αἰγιαλέες:*
> o *Ionians, Iones > Ion > İon, Yon* "people" in *Turkic*. The name of the grandson of *Hellen* – *Ion* (Ἴων) was applied to the nation of the *Ionians* [*Apollodorus*. 1.7.3]. *Pausanias* was also in favor of this version:
>> "*Ion*, while gathering an army against the *Aegialians* and *Selinus* their king, received a message from *Selinus*, who offered to give him in marriage *Helice*, his only child, as well as to adopt him as his son and successor. It so happened that the proposal found favour with *Ion*, and on the death of *Selinus* he became king of the *Aegialians*. He called the city he founded in *Aegialus Helice* after his wife, and called the inhabitants *Ionians* after himself." [7.1.3-4]
> The etymology of the appellation *Ion* remains undetermined by modern scholars, which is odd, given the widespread opinion about the *Ionians* as the *Greek* nation. This is the second major evidence in favor of its *Turkic* extraction in addition to the etymological connection described above.

---

[119] *Musayev O.I.* "Azərbaycanca-İngiliscə lüğət." [28]

- *Attikoi > Atthis: Atthi > Attı* 'famous' + *Is > İs* 'trace', meaning "eminent mark" in *Turkic*. In consonance with *Pausanias* and *Apollodorus*, the *Ionians*, aka the *Attikoi*, as well as the country *Attica* (Ἀττικός), were named as such after the *Pelasgian* princess *Atthis* (Ἀτθίς):

  "It is said that *Actaeus* was the first king of what is now *Attica*. When he died, *Cecrops*, the son-in-law of *Actaeus*, received the kingdom, and there were born to him daughters, *Herse, Aglaurus* and *Pandrosus*, and a son *Erysichthon*. This son did not become king of the *Athenians*, but happened to die while his father lived, and the kingdom of *Cecrops* fell to *Cranaus*, the most powerful of the *Athenians*. They say that *Cranaus* had daughters, and among them *Atthis*; and from her they call the country *Attica*, which before was named *Actaea*.[120] And *Amphictyon*, rising up against *Cranaus*, although he had his daughter to wife, deposed him from power." [*Pausanias*. 1.2.6]

  "When *Cecrops* died, *Cranaus* came to the throne; he was a son of the soil, and it was in his time that the flood in the age of *Deucalion* is said to have taken place. He married a *Lacedaemonian* wife, *Pedias*, daughter of *Mynes*, and begat *Cranae, Menaechme*, and *Atthis*; and when *Atthis* died a maid, *Cranaus* called the country *Atthis*." [*Apollodorus*. 3.14.5]

- *Athenians, Athenaioi > Athana*=Ἀθάνα *> Asana*=Ἀσάνα: *Ath, As > Əs* 'mind, intellect' + *Ana* 'goddess, matriarch, mother', meaning "mother of wisdom", "goddess of wisdom" in *Turkic*. There was *Humay Ana* "goddess of fertility" in *Turkic* mythology, whose name reveals similarity in word construction and meaning to *Athana*, or *Asana*.

  The *Athenians* borrowed this appellation from the *Pelasgian* goddess of wisdom *Asana*, later corrupted into *Athana*, and then *Athena* (Ἀθηνᾶ) by the *Greeks*. The ancient *Greek* lyric poet of the 1st c., *Pindar*, in his work, consistently used *Athana* instead of *Athena*:

  "μόλεν Δανάας ποτὲ παῖς, ἀγεῖτο δ' Ἀθάνα ἐς ἀνδρῶν μακάρων ὅμιλον"
  [*Fennell.C.A.M.* "The *Olympian* and *Pythian* Odes". – *Pythia*. 10.45]
  "One fine day, the offspring of *Danae* came to that assembly of the sacred beings, led there by *Athana*." [121]

  The original name of the goddess *Athena* was *Asána*, a *Pelasgian* name, introduced by *Aristophanes* in "Lysistrata" in the pronunciation of the *Lacedæmonians*:

  "Χορὸς Λακεδαιμονίων.
  Ταΰγετον αὖτ' ἐραννὸν ἐκλιπῶα,
  Μῶα μόλε Λάκαινα πρεπτὸν ἁμὶν
  κλέωα τὸν Ἀμύκλαις [Ἀπόλλω] σιὸν
  καὶ χαλκίοικον Ἀσάναν." [line 1300]
  "Chorus of *Lacedaemonians*.
  O *Muse of Laconia*, after leaving the lovely *Taygetus*,
  Appear again to see and meet us
  To *Amyclæn Apollo* singing praises,
  To *Asana* abiding in a house of bronze." [122]

  The ancient scholars and men of letters, starting from *Homer* and onwards, were not shy to expose the *Pelasgian* roots of *Zeus* and *Hera*. Logically, it will make sense to apply the same principle to the rest of the gods in the mythology, incorrectly attributed to the *Greeks*. Thereby,

---

[120] *Actæa*, or correctly *Aktaie* (Ἀκταίη) had the name of its first king *Actæus*, aka *Actaios*=Ἀκταῖος "master of white stallions" in *Turkic*. There is a *Turkic* male name that is still in use, mainly in *Azerbaijani*, – *Oktai* or *Oktay* (*Ok* 'arrow' + *Tai* 'stallion') resembling *Actaios* (*Ac > Ak* 'white' + *Tai* 'stallion' + *Os > Us* 'master').
[121] The line was translated into *English* from *Greek* by the author of the present work.
[122] This poetic excerpt was rendered into *English* from *Greek* by the author of the current book.

both the divine ancestors of *Zeus* and *Hera,* including 12 Titans, as well as their progeny, including *Athena,* must be accounted as the *Pelasgian* pantheon of gods, not *Greek.*

The definition of *Athena's* name as "goddess of wisdom" in *Turkic* has *Plato's* indirect support:

"…for most of these, in commenting on the poet, say that he represents *Athena* as mind (νοῦς) and intellect (διάνοια); and the maker of her name seems to have had a similar conception of her, but he gives her the still grander title of "mind of God" ἡ θεοῦ νόησις, seeming to say that she is a ἁ θεονόα; here he used the alpha in foreign fashion instead of eta, and dropped out the iota and sigma. But perhaps that was not his reason; he may have called her *Theonoe* because she has unequalled knowledge of divine things (τὰ θεῖα νοοῦσα). Perhaps, too, he may have wished to identify the goddess with wisdom of character (ἐν ἤθει νόησις)." ["Cratylus." 407b]

o *Cecropians, Kekropidai > Cecrops=Κέκροψ, Kekropos=Κέκροπος: Cecro, Kekro > Kəkri, Kəkrü* 'bandy, crooked, arcuate, bended' + *Ps, Pos > Pos* 'body', meaning "crooked body" in *Turkic*. The *Athenians,* aka the *Ionians,* were also known as the *Cecropians* in honor of their autochthonous King *Cecrops* who, according to *Apollodorus,* had a crooked, serpentine body, just like his name suggests:

"*Cecrops,* a son of the soil, with a body compounded of man and serpent, was the first king of *Attica,* and the country which was formerly called *Acte* he named *Cecropia* after himself." ["The Library." 3.14.1]

Pausanias reminded that *Cecrops* became a king by decision of his father *Xuthus,* the son of *Hellen:*

"On the death of *Erechtheus Xuthus* was appointed judge to decide which of his sons should succeed him. He decided that *Cecrops,* the eldest of them, should be king, and was accordingly banished from the land by the rest of the sons of *Erechtheus*." [7.1.2]

o *Cranian Pelasgians, Pelasgoi Kranaoi > Kranaos=Κραναός: Crana, Krana > Küran* 'tribe, people' + *Os > Us* 'master', meaning "chief of people" in *Turkic*. From *Herodotus,* it became clear that the *Pelasgian* nation of the *Athenians* carried numerous appellations, and at one time, they were known as the *Cranian Pelasgians,* or the *Kranaoi* [8.44], after their sovereign *Cranaus,* as asserted by *Apollodorus* [3.14.5].

o *Ægialeans, Ægialean Pelasgi, Pelasgoi Aigialees > Aigialeos=Αἰγιαλέως: Ægi, Aigi > Aiğa* 'smooth' + *Iale > Iələ, Yələ* 'hair' + *Os > Us* 'master', meaning "smooth-haired chief" in *Turkic*. Though *Pausanias* provided two versions of the *Ægialeans'* name creation – from the king *Aigialeos* or a *Greek* word *Aigialos* (αἰγιαλός), given the fact that the *Ionians,* previously known as the *Aigialean Pelasgi,* were constantly renamed exclusively after their kings, besides the goddess *Athena,* it seems highly probable that the *Pelasgian* nation of the *Ægialeans* received their appellation from their king *Aigialeos:*

"The land between *Elis* and *Sicyonia,* reaching down to the eastern sea, is now called *Achaia* after the inhabitants, but of old was called *Aegialus* and those who lived in it *Aegialians*. According to the *Sicyonians* the name is derived from *Aegialeus,* who was king in what is now *Sicyonia;* others say that it is from the land, the greater part of which is coast (aigialos)." [*Pausanias*. 7.1.1]

Herodotus was the first to state that the *Ionians* were also identified as the *Pelasgoi Aigialees,* translated into *English* also as "*Pelasgi* of the Sea-shore":

"The *Ionians* furnished a hundred ships, and were armed like the *Greeks*. Now these *Ionians,* during the time that they dwelt in the *Peloponnese* and inhabited the land now called *Achaea* (which was before the arrival of *Danaus* and *Xuthus* in the *Peloponnese*), were called, according to the *Greek* account, *Ægialean Pelasgi,* or "*Pelasgi* of the Sea-shore", but afterwards, from *Ion* the son of *Xuthus,* they were called *Ionians*." [7.94]

The *Ionians* had many tribal branches, such as the *Eretrians*, the *Keïans*, the *Naxians*, the *Siphnians*, the *Seriphians*, enumerated by *Herodotus*:

"After the *Eginetans* came the *Chalkidians* with the twenty ships which were at *Artemision*, and the *Eretrians* with their seven: these are *Ionians*. Next the *Keïans*, furnishing the same as before and being by race *Ionians* from *Athens*. The *Naxians* furnished four ships, they having been sent out by the citizens of their State to join the *Persians*, like the other islanders; but neglecting these commands they had come to the *Hellenes*, urged thereto by *Democritos*, a man of repute among the citizens and at that time commander of a trireme. Now the *Naxians* are *Ionians* coming originally from *Athens*. The *Styrians* furnished the same ships as at *Artemision*, and the men of *Kythnos* one ship and one fifty-oared galley, these both being *Dryopians*. Also the *Seriphians*, the *Siphnians* and the *Melians* served with the rest; for they alone of the islanders had not given earth and water to the Barbarian." [8.46]

"All the rest who served in the fleet furnished triremes, but the *Melians*, *Siphnian* and *Seriphians* fifty-oared galleys: the *Melians*, who are by descent from *Lacedemon*, furnished two, the *Siphnians* and *Seriphians*, who are *Ionians* from *Athens*, each one." [Idem. 8.48]

- *Eretrians*, aka *Eretriees* = Ἐρετριέες: *Er* 'man, warrior, hero' + *Etri* > *Oturu* 'staging post, place of halt', *Otur* 'live, stay', meaning "sedentary men" in *Turkic*. The name of the area – *Eritrea* was subsequently meant "place of stay for men/warriors/heroes" in *Turkic*. There is a wide-spread opinion that the name came from the *Greek Eretes* = ἐρέτης, erétēs "rower", which renders *Eretria* as the "City of the rowers". However, this view is flawed as it does not explain etymologically or lexically the missing -R- in *Eret*r*ia*. Considering the fact that the *Eretrians* were the *Ionians*, who, in their turn, were of the *Pelasgian* descent identified as a *Turkic* stock, the *Turkic* origination of the name *Eretria* (or *Eretriees*) does not deliver any doubt. Compare:
    - *Eret*r*iees*: *Er* 'man, warrior, hero' + *Et*r*i* > *Otu*r*u* 'place of stay' in *Turkic*.
    - *Eret*r*iees* > *Eretes* "rower" in *Greek*.
  Moreover, there was an ancient *Turkic* tribe *Otrar*, as well as a city *Otrar* in *Turkestan*, listed by *Radlov V.V.* [1.2.1112] that lexically resembles the ethnonym *Eretriees*:
    - *Eretriees*: *Er* 'man' + *Etri* > *Otur* 'live, stay' in *Turkic*.
    - *Otrar*: *Otr* > *Otur* 'live, stay' + *Ar* > *Ar*, *Er* 'man' in *Turkic*.

- *Keïans*, aka *Keioi* = Κήιοι > *Köi*, *Kök* "free" in *Turkic*. Evidently, this *Ionian* branch considered itself independent, judging by the name.

- *Naxians*, aka *Naksioi* = Νάξιοι > *Nağıs* "strong" in *Turkic*. The *Naxians* preferred to display their strength. Thus, they went under the name declaring that ability.

- *Siphnians*, aka *Siphnioi* = Σίφνιοι > *Siphnos*=Σίφνος: *Siphn* > *Səpən* 'the one who loves' + *Os* > *Us* 'master', meaning "the chief who cares" in *Turkic*. According to *Stephanus Byzantinus*, the *Siphnians* derived their name from *Siphnos*, the son of *Sunius*. Possibly, this king was a loving, caring ruler, as his name suggests.

- *Seriphians*, aka *Serifioi* = Σερίφιοι > *Şərif* "noble" [123] in *Turkic*. Apparently, the *Seriphians* obtained their name after a noble act done by one of them – a fisherman *Dictys* who saved notable *Danaë* and nurtured her son *Perseus*, washed up ashore of the island *Seiphos*, or *Serifos*:

"*Ser'phos* or *Seri'phus* (Σέριφος: Eth. Σερίφιος: Serpho), an island in the *Aegaean* sea, and one of the *Cyclades*, lying between *Cythnos* and *Siphnos*. According to *Pliny* (4.12. s. 22) it is 12

---
[123] *Radlov V.V.* [4.1.1007]

miles in circumference. It possessed a town of the same name, with a harbour. (Scylax, p. 22; Ptol. 3.15.31,) It is celebrated in mythology as the place where *Danaë* and *Perseus* were driven to shore in the chest in which they had been exposed by *Acrisius,* where *Perseus* was brought up, and where he afterwards turned the inhabitants into stone with the *Gorgon's* head. (Apollod. 2.4.3; Pind. P. 10.72, 12.18; Strab. x. p.487; Ov. Met. 5.242) *Seriphos* was colonised by *Ionians* from *Athens,* and it was one of the few islands which refused submission to *Xerxes.* (Hdt. 8.46, 48.)" [*William Smith. – Seriphos*].

- *Kynurians,* aka *Cynurians,* aka *Kunourioi* = Κυνούριοι: *Kyn, Cyn, Kun > Kün* 'Sun' + *Uri, Ouri > Ürü* 'tribe', meaning "sunny, cheerful tribe" in *Turkic. Herodotus* identified the *Kynurians* as an *Ionian* stock:

    "The *Kynurians,* who are natives of the soil, seem alone to be *Ionians,* but they have become *Dorians* completely because they are subject to the *Argives* and by lapse of time, being originally citizens of *Orneai* or the dwellers in the country round *Orneai.*" [8.73]

    The historian also noted that the *Kunourioi,* or the *Kynurians,* were considered to be the native inhabitants of *Peloponnesus,* in addition to the *Arcadians* and the *Achaeans:*

    "Now *Peloponnesus* is inhabited by seven races; and of these, two are natives of the soil and are settled now in the place where they dwelt of old, namely the *Arcadians* and the *Kynurians;* and one race, that of the *Achaians,* though it did not remove from the *Peloponnese,* yet removed in former time from its own land and dwells now in that which was not its own." [Idem. 8.73]

- *Hellespontii,* aka *Hellespontins,* aka *Ellespontioi* = Ἑλλησπόντιοι, aka *Mysians,* aka *Olympenoi:* *Helles, Elles > Ellas*=Ἑλλάς *> Elləş* '1.a female name; 2.make peace' in *Turkic* + *Pontii, Pontins, Pontioi > Pontos* 'sea' in *Greek,* meaning "strait of *Ellas*". The *Hellespontii* were a colony of the *Thracians,* acknowledged as the *Olympenoi* – a subsidiary branch of the *Thracians* through the *Leleges,* who comprised the third dynasty of the *Trojans* and were also identified as the *Mysians,* as well as the *Bithynians* and the *Thyni* [*Strabo.* 12.4.10]. The second appellation as the *Hellespontii,* this *Thracian* nation obtained after the strait of *Hella* dividing *Europe* from *Asia.* However, according to *Strabo,* the ancient scholars diverged in their opinion about the *Hellespont:*

    "All writers do not agree in their description of the *Hellespont,* and many opinions are advanced on the subject. Some describe the *Propontis* to be the *Hellespont;* others, that part of the *Propontis* which is to the south of *Perinthus;* others include a part of the exterior sea which opens to the *Ægæan* and the *Gulf Melas,* each assigning different limits. Some make their measurement from *Sigeum* to *Lampsacus,* and *Cyzicus,* and *Parium,* and *Priapus;* and one is to be found who measures from *Singrium,* a promontory of *Lesbos.* Some do not hesitate to give the name of *Hellespont* to the whole distance as far as the *Myrtoan Sea,* because (as in the Odes of *Pindar*) when *Hercules* sailed from *Troy* through the virgin strait of *Hella,* and arrived at the *Myrtoan Sea,* he returned back to *Cos,* in consequence of the wind *Zephyrus* blowing contrary to his course. Thus some consider it correct to apply the name *Hellespont* to the whole of the *Ægæan Sea,* and the sea along the coast of *Thessaly* and *Macedonia,* invoking the testimony of *Homer,* who says,

    "Thou shalt see, if such thy will, in spring,
    My ships shall sail to *Hellespont.*"

    But the argument is contradicted in the following lines,

    "*Piros, Imbracius'* son, who came from *Ænos.*"

    Piros commanded the *Thracians,*

    "Whose limits are the quick-flowing *Hellespont.*""

    So that he would consider all people settled next to the *Thracians* as excluded from the *Hellespont.*" [Idem. 7.58]

The name *Hellespont* was rather fluid as it was used in several forms, such as the strait of *Hella, Pontus Helles,* and currently as the *Dardanelles.* This fact vividly demonstrates that the symbiosis

of two words that belonged to two different language families was not very accommodating. It eventually fell apart, and a new name emerged – *Dardanelles* that was of pure *Turkic* origin:
- *Dardanelles* > *Dardanos* 'name of the ancestor of the *Trojan* people' + *Elles* 'name of the daughter of *Boeotian* King *Athamas*, drowned in the *Hellespont*'.
- *Dardanos*: *Dardan* 'garner glory' + *Os* > *Us* 'master' + *Elles* > *Elləş* 'make peace' in *Turkic*.

As a reminder, the name *Dardanus*, aka *Dardanos* = Δάρδανος, was also the name of the *Scythian* king [*Diodorus Siculus*. 4.43.3] that proves the underlying linguistic and ethnic connection between the *Thracians* and the *Scythians*.

The *Hellespontii* were the *Mysians* of *Olympus*, according to *Strabo*:

"...the *Mysians* round *Olympus* (who by some are called the *Olympeni* and by others the *Hellespontii*) ..." [12.4.10]

Furthermore, they were considered as the descendants of both the *Ionians* and the *Dorians*, as asserted by *Herodotus*:

"The *Hellespontians*, excepting those of *Abydos* (for the men of *Abydos* had been appointed by the king to stay in their place and be guards of the bridges), the rest, I say, of those who served in the expedition from the *Pontus* furnished a hundred ships, and were equipped like *Hellenes*: these are colonists of the *Ionians* and *Dorians*." [7.95]

The testimony of the two highly acclaimed ancient *Greek* scholars about the *Hellespontian* background brings to the surface the logical conclusion that the *Ionians* and the *Dorians*, as well as their ancestor *Hellen* were the *Thracians*, aka the *Trojans* of the *Pelasgian* extraction. This means that the *Hellespontii* were neither ethnic *Greeks* nor *Indo-Europeans*.

➢ *Islanders* were an *Ionian* branch of *Pelasgian* extraction. *Herodotus* called attention to the similarity of their military equipment with the *Hellenes*:

"The islanders furnished seventeen ships, and were armed like *Hellenes*, this also being a *Pelasgian* race, though afterwards it came to be called *Ionian* by the same rule as the *Ionians* of the twelve cities, who came from *Athens*." [7.95]

➢ *Chians*, aka *Khioi* = Χῖοι > *Khios*=Χίος: *Khi* > *Köi*, *Köy* '1.pour down, come down; 2.sky' + *Os* > *Us* 'master', meaning "chief that came down from sky" or "chief who was born when it was pouring down" in *Turkic*. Most likely, *Khios* was the name of the founder of the *Khioi*, the son of *Poseidon*, after whom both the *Pelasgian* tribe and the island got their names. However, there is also another interpretation of the name linking it to the *Greek* word *Khioni*=Χιόνι "snow". This was suggested by *Pausanias* who referred to a fellow man of letters:

"...*Ion* the tragic poet says in his history that *Poseidon* came to the island when it was uninhabited; that there he had intercourse with a nymph, and that when she was in her pains there was a fall of snow (chion), and that accordingly *Poseidon* called his son *Chios*." [7.4.8]

Strabo noted that the *Chians*, or the *Khioi*, were the *Pelasgian* progeny:

"The *Chians* also say, that the *Pelasgi* from *Thessaly* were their founders." [13.3.3]

The *Chians* were a part of the *Ionian* confederacy, according to *Pausanias*, who, nonetheless, was unable to furnish the reason why they were classified as related nations. Although the answer lies on the surface – they were both *Pelasgians*:

"Three generations from *Amphiclus*, *Hector*, who also had made himself king, made war on those *Abantes* and *Carians* who lived in the island, slew some in battle, and forced others to surrender and depart. When the *Chians* were rid of war, it occurred to *Hector* that they ought to unite with the *Ionians* in sacrificing at *Panionium*. It is said that the *Ionian* confederacy gave him a tripod as a prize for valor. Such was the account of the *Chians* that I found given by *Ion*. However, he gives no reason why the *Chians* are classed with the *Ionians*." [7.4.9-10]

- *Tyrrheni*, aka *Turreni*, aka *Turrenoi* = Τυρρηνοὶ, aka *Tursenoi* = Τυρσηνοί, aka *Troskoi* = Τροσκοι, aka *Etrusci*, aka *Etrouskoi* = Ἐτροῦσκοι, aka *Etrurians*, aka *Touskoi* = Τόυσκοι, aka *Toskoi* = Τοσκοι, aka *Tusci*, aka *Thusci*, aka *Rasenna* = Ῥασέννα, aka *Rasena* = Ῥασένα, aka *Raeti*, aka *Rhaeti*, aka *Raitoi* = Ῥαιτοί:
  - *Tyrrheni, Turreni, Turrenoi, Tursenoi*: *Tyrr, Turr, Turs > Tur* 'ascend' + *En > -An* 'an affix, denoting constant action', meaning "ascending" in *Turkic*.
  - *Tusci, Thusci, Touskoi, Troskoi > Tuskan* "a relative" (*Tu* 'be born' + *-S* 'an affix, denoting an order' + *-Kan* 'an affix, converting a verb into a noun') in *Turkic*.
  - *Etrusci, Etrouskoi*: *Etr > Er* 'warrior, man' + *Trusci, Trouskoi > Tusci > Tuskan* 'a relative', meaning "warrior kinsman" in *Turkic*.
  - *Etrurians*: *Etr > Er* 'warrior, man' + *Trur > Tur* 'the *Tur* nation', meaning "warrior nation of the *Tur*" in *Turkic*.
  - *Rasenna, Rasena*: *Ra* 'reputation' + *Sen > San* 'respect, esteem' + *Na > -Ni* 'an affix, similar to the word *Having*', meaning "highly esteemed" in *Turkic*.
  - *Raeti, Rhaeti, Raitoi > Riayət* "esteem, honor" in *Turkic*.

An extensive discourse and analysis were already provided earlier in this book about the *Turreni* and their offshoots as a part of the *Thrace-Trojan-Pelasgian* family. There are only a few points left to add to complete the picture.

It is important to note that while some of the *Pelasgi* switched their identity, ethnic name, and language to *Greek*, others stayed loyal to their *Trojan* kindred and called themselves *Turrenians* after the *Trojan* prince *Turrenus*, when in the 2nd millennium BCE they moved with him to the new land of *Turrenia*, aka *Etruria*, which is in present-day *Italy*. *Sophocles* was the first to identify the *Pelasgi* and the *Turrenians* as one unified entity. In a fragment from "*Inachus*", or Ἴναχος Σατυρικός in *Greek*, *Sophocles* introduced *Inachus* as a king of the *Tyrrhene Pelasgi*, aka *Turrenian Pelasgians*, aka *Tursenoi Pelasgoi* (Τυρσηνοὶ Πελασγοὶ in *Greek*):

Ἴναχε νᾶτορ, παῖ τοῦ κρηνῶν
πατρὸς Ὠκεανοῦ, μέγα πρεσβεύων
Ἄργους τε γύαις Ἥρας τε πάγοις
κἂν Τυρσηνοῖσι Πελασγοῖς.
[*Sir Richard C. Jebb*. "Commentary on *Sophocles: Electra*." line 5-5]

"Father *Inachus*, son of the fountains of old Ocean,
who art held in great veneration in the streets of *Argos*,
and the hills of *Juno*, and among the *Tyrrhene Pelasgi*."
[*Dionysius of Halicarnassus*. "*Roman* Antiquities". 1.25.4]

The fact that the *Pelasgi* renamed themselves into *Turrenians* was attested by other ancient authors as well, such as the 5th c. historians *Hellanicus of Lesbos* and *Thucydides*:

"*Hellanicus the Lesbian*, says that the *Tyrrhenians*, who were, before, called *Pelasgi*, received the name they are now known by after they had settled in *Italy*. These are his words, in his *Phoronis*;

"*Phrastor* was the son of *Pelasgus*, their king, by *Menippe* the daughter of *Peneus*; his son was *Amyntor*; *Amyntor's Teutamides*; whose son was *Nanas*: In whose reign, the *Pelasgi* were driven out of their country by the *Greeks*; and, leaving their ships in the river *Spines* in the *Ionian* gulph, took *Croton*, an inland town; from whence, advancing, they peopled the country, now called, *Tyrrhenia*."

But the account *Myrsilus* gives is the reverse of that given by *Hellanicus*: "The *Tyrrhenians*", says he, "after they had left their own country, were, from their wandering, called *Tenapyon*, that is, Storks, as resembling, in that respect, the birds, called by that name, that come over in flocks both into *Greece*, and the country of the Barbarians;" and he adds, that these people built the

> wall round the citadel of *Athens,* which is called the *Pelargian* wall." [*Dionysius of Halicarnassus.* "*Roman* Antiquities." 1.28.3-4]

> "And the same people, from the name of the country, out of which they had been driven, and, also, in memory of their ancient extraction, were called by the rest of the world, both *Tyrrhenians,* and *Pelasgi;* which I have mentioned for this reason, that, when the poets, and historians call them *Tyrrhenians,* and *Pelasgi,* none may wonder how the same people should have both these names. For *Thucydides* speaks of them as living in that part of *Thracia* called *Acte,* and of the cities there as inhabited by men, who spoke two languages: He, then, makes mention of the *Pelasgian* nation in the following: "There are some *Chalcidians,* but the greatest part are *Pelasgi,* the same nation with the *Tyrrhenians,* who, once, inhabited *Lemnos,* and *Athens.*"" [Idem. 1.251-5]

According to *Anticlides,* to whose authority *Strabo* referred below, the father of the *Trojan* leader *Turrenus* was the king of *Lydia Atys* (*Atus* = Ἄτυς):

> "*Anticlides* says, that they first colonized about *Lemnos* and *Imbros,* and that some of their number passed into *Italy* with *Tyrrhenus,* the son of *Atys.*" [5.2.4]

By the way, the *Lydian* name *Atys,* or correctly *Atus* (*At* 'horse' + *Ys, Us* > *Us* 'master', meaning "horse tamer" in *Turkic*), channels a *Turkic* male name – *Atış* "shootout" listed by *Mahmud Kashgari* in "The Corpus of the *Turkic* Lexicon" [1.176]. The *Lydians,* like any other *Trojan-Thracian* nation, were known to be passionate about their horses.

Major Conder also confirmed the *Turkic* roots of the *Turrenians* in his work "The Early Races of Western Asia":

> "The general consensus of ancient authority also derives the *Etruscans* from *Asia Minor* as relations of the *Lydians.* We have seen that the *Etruscan* language is *Turanian,* and this race was known to the *Greeks* as *Tyrrhenians.* There is no reason therefore to doubt that in *Lydia* a people of *Ugric* affinities must have very early existed".

["The Journal of the Anthropological Institute of *Great Britain* and *Ireland.*" 19.37]

➤ *Cretans,* aka *Kretes* = Κρήτης, aka *Curetes,* aka *Kouretes* = Κουρῆτες:
  o *Kretes: Kr > Kır* 'cut off' + *Et > Ət* 'own, belonging', meaning "cut off one's own (hair)" in *Turkic.*
  o *Curetes, Kouretes: Cur, Kour > Kır* 'cut off' + *Et > Ət* 'own, belonging', meaning "cut off one's own (hair)" in *Turkic.*
  o *Ciris, Kiris, Ker: Cir, Kir, Ker > Kır* 'cut off' + *Is > İs* 'own, belonging', meaning "cut off one's own (hair)" in *Turkic.*

Both the *Turkic* word *Ət* and its variant *İs* "own, belonging" were reflected in the toponym *Crete* and eponym *Ciris* respectively. This is a hefty argument in favor of the *Turkic* provenance of these words.

The *Cretans* and the *Curetes* seemed to be one nation and acquired their names after the ancient ritual of cutting their locks to show their devotion to the *Cretan* goddess *Ker,* or *Kiris,* or *Ciris.*

As the legend goes, *Ciris* ("cutter"), also known as *Scylla,* was King *Nisus's* daughter, who cut off the magical purple lock of her father's hair that would guarantee him the preservation of his life and his kingdom, in exchange for the love of *Minos,* who ultimately rejected her:

> "While *Scylla* said this, night that heals our cares
> came on, and she grew bolder in the dark.
> And now it is the late and silent hour
> when slumber takes possession of the breast.
> Outwearied with the cares of busy day;
> then as her father slept, with stealthy tread
> she entered his abode, and there despoiled,
> and clipped his fatal lock of purple hair.

> Concealing in her bosom the sad prize
> of crime degenerate, she at once went forth
> a gate unguarded, and with shameless haste
> sped through the hostile army to the tent
> of *Minos,* whom, astonished, she addressed:
> "Only my love has led me to this deed.
> The daughter of King *Nisus,* I am called
> the maiden *Scylla*. Unto you I come
> and offer up a power that will prevail
> against my country, and I stipulate
> no recompense except yourself. Take then
> this purple hair, a token of my love. —
> Deem it not lightly as a lock of hair
> held idly forth to you; it is in truth
> my father's life." And as she spoke
> she held out in her guilty hand the prize,
> and begged him to accept it with her love.
> Shocked at the thought of such a heinous crime,
> *Minos* refused, and said, "O execrable thing!
> Despised abomination of our time!
> May all the Gods forever banish you
> from their wide universe, and may the earth
> and the deep ocean be denied to you!
> So great a monster shall not be allowed
> to desecrate the sacred Isle of *Crete,*
> where *Jupiter* was born." So *Minos* spoke…
> Meanwhile, the Gods had changed her father's form
> and now he hovered over the salt deep,
> a hawk with tawny wings. So when he saw
> his daughter clinging to the hostile ship
> he would have torn her with his rending beak; —
> he darted towards her through the yielding air.
> In terror she let go, but as she fell
> the light air held her from the ocean spray;
> her feather-weight supported by the breeze;
> she spread her wings, and changed into a bird.
> They called her "*Ciris*" when she cut the wind,
> and "*Ciris*" — cut-the-lock — remains her name."
> [*Ovid.* "Metamorphoses." 8.81-151]

As per *Diodorus Siculus, Crete* as an island was named after the princess of the *Curetes* – *Cretê* (Κρήτη) [3.4]

The definition of the *Cretans'* and the *Curetes'* name as "cut off one's hair" is rather consistent with the assertions brought forward by *Archemachus of Euboea,* though the hair-cutting ritual sprung from a different cause:

> "But *Archemachus of Euboea* says that the *Curetes* had their settlement at *Chalcis,* but being continually at war about the plain *Lelantum,* and finding that the enemy used to seize and drag them by the hair of the forehead, they wore their hair long behind, and cut the hair short in front, whence they had the name of *Curetes,* (or the shorn,) from *cura* (κουρά), or the tonsure which they had undergone; that they removed to *Ætolia,* and occupied the places about *Pleuron;* that

others, who lived on the other side of the *Achelous,* because they kept their heads unshorn, were called *Acarnanians.*" [124] [*Strabo.* 10.3.6]

In either case, the names point towards their *Turkic* source. Interestingly, there is a derived word in modern *Greek Koureus* = Κουρεύς "hair-cutter, barber" (*Kour* > *Kır* 'cut off' + *Eus* > *Us* 'master' in *Turkic*). Notably, the ancient *Turkic* word *Kır* retained its meaning "cut off" only in *Azerbaijani*.[125]

In the opinion of *Strabo*, the *Curetes* were an *Ætolian* tribe [9.4.18]. However, it seems clear overall that the celebrated geographer did not derive their origin from the *Ætolians*, as he narrated how the latter conquered the land of the *Curetes* and forced them to be called the *Ætolians:*

"With respect to the *Curetes,* some facts are related which belong more immediately, some more remotely, to the history of the *Ætolians* and *Acarnanians*. The facts more immediately relating to them, are those which have been mentioned before, as that the *Curetes* were living in the country, which is now called *Ætolia*, and that a body of *Ætolians* under the command of *Ætolus* came there, and drove them into *Acarnania;* and these facts besides, that *Æolians* invaded *Pleuronia*, which was inhabited by *Curetes,* and called *Curetis*, took away their territory, and expelled the possessors." [Idem. 10.3.6]

Apollodorus and *Pausanias* also confirmed how the country of the *Curetes* got renamed after their conqueror:

"*Endymion* had by a *Naiad* nymph or, as some say, by *Iphianassa*, a son *Aetolus*, who slew *Apis*, son of *Phoroneus*, and fled to the *Curetian* country. There he killed his hosts, *Dorus* and *Laodocus* and *Polypoetes*, the sons of *Phthia* and *Apollo*, and called the country *Aetolia* after himself." [*Apollodorus*. 1.7.6]

"*Aetolus*, who came to the throne after *Epeius*, was made to flee from *Peloponnesus*, because the children of *Apis* tried and convicted him of unintentional homicide. For *Apis*, the son of *Jason*, from *Pallantium* in *Arcadia*, was run over and killed by the chariot of *Aetolus* at the games held in honor of *Azan*. *Aetolus*, son of *Endymion*, gave to the dwellers around the *Achelous* their name, when he fled to this part of the mainland." [*Pausanias*. 5.1.8]

Homer also distinguished the *Curetes* from the *Ætolians* when giving an account about the legendary quarrel over the *Calydonian Boar:*

"The *Curetes* and the *Aetolians* were fighting and killing one another round *Calydon* – the *Aetolians* defending the city and the *Curetes* trying to destroy it. For *Diana* of the golden throne was angry and did them hurt because *Oeneus* had not offered her his harvest first-fruits. The other gods had all been feasted with hecatombs, but to the daughter of great *Jove* alone he had made no sacrifice. He had forgotten her, or somehow or other it had escaped him, and this was a grievous sin. Thereon the archer goddess in her displeasure sent a prodigious creature against him – a savage wild boar with great white tusks that did much harm to his orchard lands, uprooting apple-trees in full bloom and throwing them to the ground. But *Meleager* son of *Oeneus* got huntsmen and hounds from many cities and killed it – for it was so monstrous that not a few were needed, and many a man did it stretch upon his funeral pyre. On this the goddess set the *Curetes* and the *Aetolians* fighting furiously about the head and skin of the boar." ["The Iliad." 10]

While being in agreement with *Homer, Strabo* also added that the war between the *Curetes* and the *Ætolians* broke not only over the boar but most importantly, over the territory:

"*Thestius* however, father-in-law of *Œneus*, and father of *Althea*, chief of the *Curetes*, was master of *Pleuronia*. But when war broke out between the *Thestiadæ, Œneus,* and *Meleager* about a boar's head and skin, according to the poet, following the fable concerning the boar of

---

[124] From *Akarnan* = Ἀκαρνάν: A > Al, O 'he/she' + Kar > Kır 'cut off' + Nan > -Mayán 'does not' (-Ma 'an affix of negation' + Yan 'an affix, denoting constant action'), meaning "the one who does not cut off" in *Turkic*.

[125] *Musayev O.I.* "Azərbaycanca-İngiliscə lüğət." [367].

Calydon, but, as is probable, the dispute related to a portion of the territory; the words are these, *Curetes* and *Ætolians,* firm in battle, fought against one another." [10.3.7]

Several offshoots of the *Curetes* resided in *Eubœa, Ætolia,* and *Acarnania,* besides *Crete:*

"But since even the historians, through the similarity of the name *Curetes,* have collected into one body a mass of dissimilar facts, I myself do not hesitate to speak of them at length by way of digression, adding the physical considerations which belong to the history. Some writers however endeavour to reconcile one account with the other, and perhaps they have some degree of probability in their favour. They say, for instance, that the people about *Ætolia* have the name of *Curetes* from wearing long dresses like girls, (κόραι,) and that there was, among the *Greeks,* a fondness for some such fashion. The *Ionians* also were called tunic-trailers, and the soldiers of *Leonidas,* who went out to battle with their hair dressed, were despised by the *Persians,* but subjects of their admiration in the contest. In short, the application of art to the hair consists in attending to its growth, and the manner of cutting it, and both these are the peculiar care of girls and youths; whence in several ways it is easy to find a derivation of the name *Curetes.* It is also probable, that the practice of armed dances, first introduced by persons who paid so much attention to their hair and their dress, and who were called *Curetes,* afforded a pretence for men more warlike than others, and who passed their lives in arms, to be themselves called by the same name of *Curetes,* I mean those in *Eubœa, Ætolia,* and *Acarnania. Homer* also gives this name to the young soldiers…" [Idem. 10.3.8]

Legend has it that the *Curetes* were the first *Cretans* who were half-mythical, half-human creatures nurturing *Zeus* in the island of *Crete:*

"There are others more remote from the subject of this work, which have been erroneously placed by historians under one head on account of the sameness of name: for instance, accounts relating to *Curetic* affairs and concerning the *Curetes* have been considered as identical with accounts concerning the people (of the same name) who inhabited *Ætolia* and *Acarnania.* But the former differ from the latter, and resemble rather the accounts which we have of *Satyri* and *Silenes, Bacchæ* and *Tityri;* for the *Curetes* are represented as certain dæmons, or ministers of the gods, by those who have handed down the traditions respecting *Cretan* and *Phrygian* affairs, and which involve certain religious rites, some mystical, others the contrary, relative to the nurture of *Jupiter* in *Crete;* the celebration of orgies in honour of the mother of the gods, in *Phrygia,* and in the neighbourhood of the *Trojan Ida.* There is however a very great variety in these accounts. According to some, the *Corybantes, Cabeiri, Idœan Dactyli,* and *Telchines* are represented as the same persons as the *Curetes;* according to others, they are related to, yet distinguished from, each other by some slight differences; but to describe them in general terms and more at length, they are inspired with an enthusiastic and *Bacchic* frenzy, which is exhibited by them as ministers at the celebration of the sacred rites, by inspiring terror with armed dances, accompanied with the tumult and noise of cymbals, drums, and armour, and with the sound of pipes and shouting; so that these sacred ceremonies are nearly the same as those that are performed among the *Samothracians* in *Lemnus,* and in many other places; since the ministers of the god are said to be the same. The whole of this kind of discussion is of a theological nature, and is not alien to the contemplation of the philosopher." [*Strabo.* 10.3.8]

Most definitely that the *Curetes,* aka the *Cretans,* who were in charge of keeping *Zeus* safe, were the *Pelasgians,* as the ancient men of letters, such as *Hesiod* and *Homer,* gave *Zeus* the surname "*Pelasgian*". As claimed by *Dante,* the mother of *Zeus Rhea* decisively selected *Crete* to safeguard her issue from his murderous father:

"So then he said, "bearing the name of *Crete,*
Under whose monarch once the world was chaste.
A mountain rises there which once was glad
With wood and water – *Ida* it is nam'd –
Now desert, like a thing worn out and old,
This *Rhea* chose a cradle fit and safe

> For her newborn, and better to conceal
> When the babe wept, with noise she drown'd his cries.'" ["Inferno." 14.94 -102]

The renowned lexicographer *William Smith* also opined his conclusion about the *Pelasgian* roots of the *Curetes*:

> "The original inhabitants of *Aetolia* are said to have been *Curetes*, who according to some accounts had come from *Euboea*. (Strab. x. p.465.) They inhabited the plains between the *Achelous* and the *Evenus*, and the country received in consequence the name of *Curetis*. Besides them we also find mention of the *Leleges* and the *Hyantes*, the latter of whom had been driven out of *Boeotia*. (Strab. pp. 322, 464.) These three peoples probably belonged to the great *Pelasgic* race, and were at all events not *Hellenes*." [*Aetolia*]

In addition to the *Curetes*, or the *Cretans*, *Crete* was the cradleland of the *Trojans*, the *Romans*, and ultimately, of the *Pelasgians*. Initially, the non-*Greek* peoples inhabited it:

> "...for in old time the whole of *Crete* [126] was possessed by Barbarians..." [*Herodotus*. 1-173]

The *Trojan* nations of the *Lycians* and the *Teucrians* issued forth from *Crete*, as reported by *Herodotus* [1.173], *Ovid* ["Metamorphoses." 13.705], and *Virgil* ["The Aeneid." 3.69-120]. The founder of the *Trojans* and the ancestor of the *Romans*, *Teucer* was, evidently, a native *Cretan*, besides his *Pelasgian* background.

Homer in "The Odyssey" introduced the *Cretans* as *Eteokretes* (Ἐτεόκρητες), aka the *Eteocretans*:

> "There is a fair and fruitful island in mid-ocean called *Crete*; it is thickly peopled and there are ninety cities in it: the people speak many different languages which overlap one another, for there are *Achaeans*, brave *Eteocretans*, *Dorians* of three-fold race, and noble *Pelasgi*."
> [Translated by *Samuel Butler*. 19.168-171]

The fact that the *Cretans* and the *Curetes* were the same people was asserted by *Virgil* and *Silicus Italicus*:

> "Nauticus exoritur vario certamine clamor:
> hortantur socii Cretam proavosque petamus.
> Prosequitur surgens a puppi ventus euntis,
> et tandem antiquis Curetum adlabimur oris." [*P. Vergili Maronis*. Aeneidos. [3.128-131]
> "The seamen's clamour rises in emulous dissonance; each cheers his comrade: "Seek we *Crete* and our forefathers." A wind rising astern follows us forth on our way, and we glide at last to the ancient *Curetean* coast." [*Virgil*. "The Aeneid." Translated by *J.W. Mackail*. 3.122-154]

> "Cres erat, aerisonis Curetum aduectus ab antris..." [*Silicus Italicus*. "Punica." 2.93]
> "Being a *Cretan* himself, from the caves of the *Curetes*..." [127]

There were several *Cretan* traditions that other nations took note of and followed, besides their religious rites:

> "For of all the many nations of men, both *Greek* and foreign, the only people who refrain from drinking-bouts and the jesting that occurs where there is wine, are the *Cretans*, and after them the *Spartans*, who learnt it from the *Cretans*. In *Crete* it is one of their laws which *Minos* ordained that they are not to drink with each other to intoxication. And yet it is evident that the things he thought honorable were what he ordained as lawful for his people as well."
> [*Plato*. "*Minos*." 320a]

> "The *Cretans*, again, either by land or sea, in ambushes and piratical excursions, in deceiving the enemy, in making night attacks, and in fact in every service which involves craft and separate action, are irresistible; but for a regular front to front charge in line they have neither the courage nor firmness; and the reverse again is the case with the *Achaeans* and *Macedonians*."
> [*Polybius*. "Histories." 4.8]

---

[126] *Crete* has been known as *Kirid* among the *Turkic* nations [*Radlov V.V.* 2.2.1358].
[127] The translation into *English* from *Latin* was done by the author of the present work.

The *Cretans* also partook in the *Trojan* War against the house of *Priam,* as confirmed by *Homer:*
"The famous spearsman *Idomeneus* led the *Cretans,* who held *Cnossus,* and the well-walled city of *Gortys; Lyctus* also, *Miletus* and *Lycastus* that lies upon the chalk; the populous towns of *Phaestus* and *Rhytium,* with the other peoples that dwelt in the hundred cities of *Crete.* All these were led by *Idomeneus,* and by *Meriones,* peer of murderous *Mars.* And with these there came eighty ships." ["The Iliad." 2]

§ 11-5-1. PELASGIAN CITIES AND DISTRICTS.

The *Pelasgi* played a fundamental role in the antique world. As one of the most ancient nations, they founded numerous cities, mainly in *Greece* and *Italy*. They introduced a new kind of architecture, called *Pelasgian,* or *Cyclopean,* by erecting enormous buildings with heavy stones, some weighing 2 tons and standing tall against all odds and elements even nowadays. Masonry of the *Pelasgi* involved massive boulders from limestone that fitted each other without any mortar, leaving hardly any space between the stones. The major locations of the *Pelasgian* structures include *Athens* in *Greece, Sicily, Ciprus, Sardinia, Alatri* acropolis near *Rome,* as well as the walls of the ancient city of *India Rajgriha.* The megalithic structures throughout *Greece* and *Italy* present a distinct map of the *Pelasgian* movement from place to place, country to country. The existence of similar constructions in *India* is another proof of the wandering nature of the *Pelasgi,* who reached the far shores of the *Indian Ocean* to leave their trace in the history and culture of yet another nation.

Strabo described some major *Pelasgian* cities and towns found by the *Pelasgi,* aka the *Turrenians,* by providing specific details and facts about them. Several of them were built on the island of *Corsica* (the birthplace of the famous military leader of *France* – Napoleon Bonaparte, currently a part of *France*), previously known under a *Turkic* name of *Cyrnus,* or *Kurnos.* The etymological analysis of the *Pelasgian* city names leaves no doubt about their *Turkic* roots:

❖ *Cyrnus* or *Kurnos* (Κύρνος) > *Kurnaz* "deceitful, delusive" in *Turkic*. Perhaps, its name the island earned due to the treacherous and vicious inhabitants:
"*Cyrnus* is called by the *Romans Corsica;* it is poorly inhabited, being both rugged and in many parts entirely inaccessible, so that the mountaineers, who live by plunder, are more savage than wild beasts…" [*Strabo.* 5.2.7]
This island had a number of cities with the names of notably *Turkic* origin, such as *Sulchi, Caralis.*

❖ *Sulchi* or *Soulkhoi* (Σοῦλχοι) > *Suluk* "having river" in *Turkic*.

❖ *Caralis* or *Karalis* (Κάραλις): *Caral, Karal* > *Karal* 'become dark, black, turn bad' + *Is* > *-Iş* 'an affix, converting a verb into a noun', meaning "darkness" in *Turkic*. The unsettling meaning of the city *Caralis* was indirectly explained by *Strabo,* who noticed the evil, unhealthy environment of the place:
"There are many cities, some are considerable, as *Caralis* and *Sulchi.* There is however an evil, which must be set against the fertility of these places; for during the summer the island is unhealthy, more particularly so in the most fertile districts; in addition to this, it is often ravaged by the mountaineers, whom they call *Diagesbes,* who formerly were named *Iolaënses*. For it is said that *Iolaus* brought hither certain of the children of *Hercules,* and established himself amongst the barbarian possessors of the island, who were *Tyrrhenians.*" [5.2.7]

❖ *Dodona* or *Dodone* (Δωδώνη) or *Dodón* (Δωδών) or *Dodonaios* (Δωδωναῖος): *Dod* > *Dat* 'meaning; soul' + *Ona, One, On, Onai* > *Ona* 'mother, matriarch', meaning "carrier of meaning" or "mistress of soul" in *Turkic*.

Dodona was one of the most ancient and famous *Pelasgian* towns, celebrated for its oracle of *Zeus*, the oldest *Pelasgic* divination place, later replaced by the one at *Delphi*. According to *St. Jerome*, *Greece* first used the *Dodonean* oracle in 639 BCE.

Strabo gave an interesting account about *Dodona* and its population – the *Helli*, or the *Selli*, in line with a number of ancient authors:

"…and *Hesiod*,
"He went to *Dodona*, the dwelling of the *Pelasgi*, and to the beech tree." [7.7.10]

"With respect to *Dodona*, *Homer* clearly intimates that the people who lived about the temple were barbarians, from their mode of life, describing them as persons who do not wash their feet, and who sleep on the ground. Whether we should read *Helli*, with *Pindar*, or *Selli*, as it is conjectured the word existed in *Homer*, the ambiguity of the writing does not permit us to affirm confidently. *Philochorus* says, that the country about *Dodona* was called, like *Euboea, Hellopia*; for these are the words of *Hesiod*, "There is a country *Hellopia*, rich in corn-fields and pastures; at its extremity is built *Dodona*." It is supposed, says *Apollodorus*, that it had this name from the "hele," or marshes about the temple. He is of opinion that the poet did not call the people about the temple *Helli*, but *Selli*, adding, that *Homer* mentions a certain river (near) of the name of *Selleis*. He specifies the name in this line, "At a distance far from *Ephyra*, from the river *Selleis*."" [7.7.10]

The *Turkic* origin of the names – the river *Selleis* and the *Selli* people is as clear as it gets. Both words originated from *Sel* "stream, torrent, flood" in *Turkic*. The same people – the *Selli* were mentioned by *Sophocles* in "The *Trachiniae*":

"I wrote them down in the grove of the *Selli*, dwellers on the hills, whose couch is on the ground; they were given by my Father's oak of many tongues…" [1170]

Homer called them the prophets of *Zeus* living on the ground of *Dodona*:

"…lord of *Dodona*, god of the *Pelasgi*, who dwellest afar, you who hold wintry *Dodona* in your sway, where your prophets the *Selli* dwell around you with their feet unwashed and their couches made upon the ground…" ["The Iliad." 16]

❖ *Hormiae* or *Ormiai* (Ορμίαι) or *Formiae* or *Formiai* (Φορμίαι) > *Hörmə, Örme* "structure", *Hörmək* "to build" in *Turkic*. Notably, this word exists only in *Turkish* (as *Örme*) and *Azerbaijani* (as *Hörmə*) and not in other *Turkic* languages.

The city near *Rome*, built by the descendants of the *Pelasgi* – the *Lacedæmonians*, had a name that was a classic example of the word modification, inherent to the *Turkic* languages – from *Hormiæ* to *Formiæ*, as stated by *Strabo*:

"Near to *Tarracina*, advancing in the direction of *Rome*, a canal runs by the side of the *Via Appia*, which is supplied at intervals by water from the marshes and rivers…Beyond is *Formiæ*, founded by the *Lacedæmonians*, and formerly called *Hormiæ*, on account of its excellent port. Between these [two cities], is a gulf which they have named *Caiata*, in fact all gulfs are called by the *Lacedæmonians Caietæ*: some, however, say that the gulf received this appellation from [*Caieta*], the nurse of *Æneas*." [5.3.6]

❖ *Caiata* or *Kaiete* (Καίητη): *Cai, Kai* > *Koi* 'bay, gulf' + *Ata, Ete* > *Atau* 'landmass', meaning "gulf surrounded by land" in *Turkic*.

❖ *Europus* or *Europos* (Εὐρωπός): *Eur* > *Er* 'warrior' + *Opu, Opo* > *Oba* 'race' + *Us, Os* > *Us* 'master', meaning "master of the warrior race" or "master of the *Arian* race" in *Turkic*. It is an unknown fact that the name *Europe* has *Turkic* origins – the continent acquired its name after the *Pelasgian* King *Europus*. The *Latin* historian *Justin* made it known that *Europe* was a *Pelasgian* land ruled by King *Europus*:

"The inhabitants were called *Pelasgi,* the country *Pæonia*...In the region of *Paeonia,* which is now a portion of *Macedonia,* is said to have reigned *Pelegonus,* the father of *Asteropaeus,* whose name we find, in the *Trojan* war, among the most distinguished defenders of the city. On the other side a king named *Europus* held the sovereignty in a district called *Europa.*" [7.1]

Furthermore, *Europos* was also noted as a city in *Media* by *Ptolemy* [6.2].

- ❖ *Roma* or *Rome* (Ῥώμη) or *Romanus* or *Romaios* (Ῥωμαῖος) > *Urum* "mastery in war" in *Turkic*. In ancient times, the *Turkic* people would call *Rome* "*Urum*". This was also confirmed by the *German* etymologist *Radlov V.V.,* who provided two variants of the name in *Turkic: Rum* and *Urum* [3.1.724].

  Among the ancient scholars, there were several postulates about the origin of *Rome's* name. However different they were – whether that was the name of the *Trojan* female *Roma* or a *Trojan* male *Romus,* all of them had the *Trojan,* or *Pelasgian,* beginning. The most plausible is the version below, reported by *Plutarch* that also defines the name *Rome:*

  "Some say that the *Pelasgians,* after wandering over most of the habitable earth and subduing most of mankind, settled down on that site, and that from their **strength in war** they called their city *Rome.*" [*Romulus.* 1.1]

  The *Turkic* word *Urum* "mastery in war" perfectly matches the definition stated by *Plutarch.* Hence, the name of *Rome* has a *Turkic* origin, as it was founded by the *Turkic* nation of the *Pelasgians,* aka the *Trojans. Justin* called them "the *Trojans,* the authors of the *Roman* race" and confirmed their mutual pride of the ancestral origins:

  "Preparations for a contest were in consequence made on both sides; and when the *Romans,* having entered *Asia,* had reached *Troy,* mutual gratulations took place between the *Trojans* and the *Romans;* the *Trojans* observing that "*Aeneias,* and the other leaders that accompanied him, had gone forth from them;" the *Romans* telling them that "they were their children"; and such joy was among them all as is wont to be between parents and children met after a long separation. The *Trojans* were delighted that their descendants, after having conquered the west and *Africa,* were now laying claim to *Asia* as their hereditary domain, remarking that "the ruin of *Troy* had been an event to be desired, since it was so happily to revive again." On the other hand, an insatiable longing to gaze on their ancient home, the birthplace of their ancestors, and the temples and images of the gods, had taken possession of the *Romans.*" [31.8.1-4]

  In the opinion of *St. Jerome* and several *Roman* writers, *Rome* was established in 755 BCE.

  All other possible sources that gave birth to the name *Rome,* such as the *Trojan* names *Romus, Roma,* even *Romulus,* had the same *Turkic* root – *Rum,* or *Urum:*
  - *Romus: Rom > Urum* 'mastery in war' + *Us* 'master', meaning "skillful in war leader" in *Turkic.*
  - *Romulus: Rom > Urum* 'mastery in war' + *Ulus* 'people', meaning "skillful in war nation" in *Turkic.*

- ❖ *Thessaly* or *Thessalia* (Θεσσαλία) or *Thettalia* (Θετταλία) or *Thettalos* (Θετταλός) or *Thessalos* (Θεσσαλός) or *Thessalus* or *Thessalis* (Θεσσαλίς) or *Thettalis* (Θετταλίς) > *Thessalos:*

  Thes, Thet > Tes 'agile' + *Sal, Tal > Sal* 'fierce' + *Os, Is, Us > Us* 'master', meaning "agile and fierce leader" in *Turkic.*

  The country of the *Pelasgians* – *Thessaly* was named after *Thessalos* (Θεσσαλός), the son of *Hercules* [Homer. "The Iliad." 2], not *Thettalos* (Θετταλός), the son of *Hercules* or *Hæmon,* as suggested by *Strabo:*

  "In general we say, that it was formerly called *Pyrrhœa,* from *Pyrrha,* the wife of *Deucalion; Hæmonia,* from *Hæmon;* and *Thettalia,* from *Thettalus,* the son of *Hæmon.* But some writers, after dividing it into two portions, say, that *Deucalion* obtained by lot the southern part, and called it *Pandora,* from his mother; that the other fell to the share of *Hæmon,* from whom it was called *Hæmonia;* that the name of one part was changed to *Hellas,* from *Hellen,* the son of *Deucalion,* and of the other to *Thettalia,* from *Thettalus,* the son of *Hæmon.* But, according to

some writers, it was the descendants of *Antiphus* and *Pheidippus*, sons of *Thettalus*, descended
from *Hercules*, who invaded the country from *Ephyra* in *Thesprotia*, and called it after the name
of *Thettalus* their progenitor. It has been already said that once it had the name of *Nessonis*, as
well as the lake, from *Nesson*, the son of *Thettalus*." [*Strabo*. 9.5.23]

Given the fact that *Homer* lived 10-12 centuries earlier than *Strabo*, his version of the name
Thessalos seems more genuine in comparison to the corrupted *Thettalus*.

❖ *Pelasgiotis* (Πελασγιῶτις): *Pelasgi* 'teach, train' (*Pelas* > *Pilis* 'knowledge' + *Ga* > -*Gə* 'an affix, converting a noun into a verb') + *Otis* > *Otai* 'dwelling, camp', meaning "training camp" or "abode of the *Pelasgi*" in *Turkic*. *Pelasgiotis* was the district inhabited by the *Pelasgians*, or the *Pelasgiotai*. There were numerous *Pelasgian* cities, including the capital – *Larissa*, as well as *Armenium, Elatea, Mopsium, Gyrton, Argura*, and the like.

❖ *Larissa* (Λάρισσα) or *Lárisa* (Λάρισα) or *Láreisa* (Λάρεισα) or *Larissaios* (Λαρισσαῖος) or *Larisaois* (Λαρισαῖος) or *Larasa* (Λαρασα): *Lar* > *Lala* 'chief officer' + *Issa, Isa, Eisa, Asa* > *Əs* 'property', meaning "overlord's land" in *Turkic*. The replacement of *R* by *L* in *Lar, Lala* is a natural linguistic process in *Turkic* and can be observed in the words *İlik* = *İrik* "race", *Pur̲ta* = *Bal̲ta* "axe". As claimed by *Pausanias*, the city *Larisa* was named after the daughter of *Pelasgus*:

"The citadel they call *Larisa*, after the daughter of *Pelasgus*. After her were also named two of the cities in *Thessaly*, the one by the sea and the one on the *Peneus*." [2.24.1]

This was a rather frequently observed act of naming places and countries after a female among the *Pelasgians*. One can recall *Sparta, Athene* – female names bestowed to a city and even to a nation. The name of *Larissa* was common not only to many *Pelasgian* towns. There was *Larsa* – an *Akkadian* city, *Larasa* – a city in *Media* [*Ptolemy*. 6.2] The first component of the name – *Lar* meant "chief" in *Etruscan* and was a part of the *Etruscan* name *Larke* (*Lar* 'chief' + *Ke* > *Kə* 'great mind'), meaning "leading great mind" in *Turkic*. The fact of this name's existence in *Akkadian, Etruscan, Median*, in addition to *Pelasgian*, proves that there was one and only source uniting these nations – *Turkic*.

❖ *Armenium* or *Armenion* (Ἀρμένιον) or *Ormenion* (Ὁρμένιον) or *Orminion* (Ὁρμίνιον): *Ar, Or* > *Ar, Ör* 'warrior' + *Men, Min* > *Men, Min* 'I', meaning "I am a warrior" in *Turkic*. This *Pelasgian* town was the birthplace of *Armenus*, the *Argonaut*, who named both the country of *Armenia* and its inhabitants – the *Armenians* after himself:

"*Armenus*, they say, was a native of *Armenium*, one of the cities on the lake *Boebeis*, between *Pheræ* and *Parisa*, and that his companions settled in *Acilisene*, and the *Suspiritis*, and occupied the country as far as *Calachene* and *Adiabene*, and that he gave his own name to *Armenia*." [*Strabo*. 11.4.8]

On a separate occasion, *Strabo* also called it *Ormenium*. Evidently, in the time of *Strabo*, it was known under several variants. The *Turkic* origin of the name is also proved by the existing variations of all its components – *Ar, Or* (*Ör*) and *Men, Min* in *Turkic*.

The name of this *Pelasgian* city was established after *Armenus*, or *Ormenus*, the great-grandson of *Hellen*, grandson of *Æolus*:

"*Ormenium* is now called *Orminium*. It is a village situated below *Pelion*, near the *Pagasitic Gulf*, but was one of the cities which contributed to form the settlement of *Demetrias*, as I have before said. The lake *Bœbeis* must be near, because both *Bœbe* and *Ormenium* belonged to the cities lying around *Demetrias. Ormenium* is distant by land 27 stadia from *Demetrias*. The site of *Iolcus*, which is on the road, is distant 7 stadia from *Demetrias*, and the remaining 20 from *Ormenium. Demetrius of Scepsis* says, that *Phoenix* came from *Ormenium*, and that he fled thence from his father *Amyntor*, the son of *Ormenus*, to *Phthia*, to king *Peleus*. For this place was founded by *Ormenus*, the son of *Cercaphus*, the son of *Æolus*. The sons of *Ormenus* were

Amyntor and *Eumæmon;* the son of the former was *Phœnix,* and of the latter, *Eurypylus.*" [*Strabo*. 9.5.18]

Homer included the inhabitants of *Ormenium,* or correctly *Ormenion* (Ορμένιον) in the Catalogue of fighters against the *Trojans* in the *Trojan* War ["The Iliad." 2], whom *Apollodorus* presented as the *Ormenians* [E3.12-15]:

"And (those) who did-possess *Ormenium,* and (those) who (did possess) (the) fountain *Hyperia,* and (those) who did-possess *Asterius,* and (the) white heights of *Titanus,* these *Eurypylus* did command, (the) illustrious son of *Euaemon:* and together with him forty black ships did follow." ["The Iliad of *Homer:* With an Interlinear Translation..." Translated verbatim by *Thomas Clark*. 2.240]

❖ *Elatea* or *Elatia* or *Elateia* (Ἐλάτεια) or *Elateus* (Ἐλατεύς) > *Elatus:*
- *Elateus, Elatus: El* 'nation' + *At* 'glory' + *Us* 'master', meaning "leading glory of the nation" in *Turkic*.
- *Elatea, Elatia, Elateia: El* 'nation' + *At* 'glory', meaning "glory of the nation" in *Turkic*.

The inhabitants of this *Pelasgian* town claimed to be *Arcadians,* deriving their name from *Elatus,* the son of *Arcas,* as reported by *Pausanias:*

"This nymph they call *Erato,* and by her they say that *Arcas* had *Azan, Apheidas* and *Elatus.* Previously he had had *Autolaus,* an illegitimate son.

When his sons grew up, *Arcas* divided the land between them into three parts, and one district was named *Azania* after *Azan;* from *Azania,* it is said, settled the colonists who dwell about the cave in *Phrygia* called *Steunos* and the river *Pencalas.* To *Apheidas* fell *Tegea* and the land adjoining, and for this reason poets too call *Tegea* "the lot of *Apheidas.*"

Elatus got *Mount Cyllene,* which down to that time had received no name. Afterwards *Elatus* migrated to what is now called *Phocis,* helped the *Phocians* when hard pressed in war by the *Phlegyans,* and became the founder of the city *Elateia.*" [8.4.2-4]

❖ *Mopsium* or *Mopsion* (Μόψιον) or *Mopsios* (Μοψιος) or *Mopseieus* (Μοψειεύς) or *Mopsieus* (Μοψιεύς) > *Mopsos: Mops* > *Müşö* 'eight body parts' + *Os* > *Us* 'master', meaning "master of his faculties" in *Turkic*.

This *Pelasgian* town in *Thessaly* owed the origin of its name to a *Pelasgian* from the *Lapithae* tribe, called *Mopsus* or *Mopsos* (Μόψος), who was a famous seer, as believed by *Strabo:*

"*Mopsium* has not its name from *Mopsus,* the son of *Manto* the daughter of *Teiresias,* but from *Mopsus,* one of the *Lapithæ,* who sailed with the *Argonauts.*" [9.5.23]

❖ *Gyrtón* or *Gurton* (Γυρτών) or *Gyrtona* or *Gurtóne* (Γυρτώνη) or *Gurtónios* (Γυρτώνιος) > *Gyrton, Gurton* (Γυρτών), *Gurtonos* (Γυρτῶνος):
- *Gyrton, Gurton, Gyrtona, Gurtone: Gyr, Gur* > *Gür* 'powerful' + *Ton, Tona, Tone* > *Toη* 'strong', meaning "powerful and strong" in *Turkic*.
- *Gurtonios, Gurtonos: Gyr, Gur* > *Gür* 'powerful' + *Ton* > *Toη* 'strong' + *Ios, Os* > *Us* 'master', meaning "powerful and strong chief" in *Turkic*.

In the opinion of *Stephanus of Byzantium,* the city of *Gyrton* got its appellation after its *Pelasgian* founder *Gyrton,* aka *Gurtonos.*

Being the original abode of the *Phlegyae,* this was "a town of *Perrhaebia* in *Thessaly,* situated in a fertile plain between the rivers *Titaresius* and *Peneius.* Its site is represented by the modern village of *Tatári.*" [*William Smith. – Gyrton*] The *Turkic* roots of the name of the ancient *Pelasgian* town of *Gyrton* are evident partially due to its modern appellation – *Tatári* that needs no further discussion about its etymology.

❖ *Argura* (Ἄργυρα) or *Argoura* (Ἄργουρα) or *Argouraios* (Ἀργουραῖος) or *Argourios* (Ἀργούριος) or *Argousa* (Ἄργουσα) or *Argissa* (Ἄργισσα):

- *Argura, Argoura*: *Ar* 'warrior' + *Gura, Goura* > *Qorı* 'guard, defend', meaning "defended by warriors" in *Turkic*.
- *Argousa, Argissa*: *Ar* 'warrior' + *Gous, Gis* > *Qıs* 'impel' + *Sa* 'power, force', meaning "the force to impel warriors" in *Turkic*.
- *Argouraios, Argourios*: *Ar* 'warrior' + *Goura, Gouri* > *Qorı* 'guard, defend' + *Ios, Os* > *Ös* 'motherland', meaning "motherland of the protecting warriors" in *Turkic*.

Initially introduced by *Homer* as *Argissa* [2.738], this town in *Pelasgiotis* in *Thessaly* had several corrupted and modified names. On the authority of *Stephanus of Byzantium*, the *Pelasgian* city *Argoura*, aka *Argissa*, was affiliated with the ethnicon *Argourios* (Ἀργούριος), and most likely, derived from it.

§ 11-5-2. PELASGIAN ORIGINS OF THESEUS, HERCULES, ACHILLES, AND ALEXANDER THE GREAT.

There is a deliberately forgotten, slowly buried under the weight of lies and ages, but still withstanding the barrage of falsehoods, indestructible truth, strongly attested by the most reputable scholars of ancient times. This unvarnished truth was rarely, if ever, brought to the surface by any late or modern researchers. However clear and obvious it was to a naked eye, the medieval and contemporary scholars preferred to turn a blind eye to it, as the fact would make them very uncomfortable and disrupt their illogical and biased conjectures.

In accord with the testimonies of the ancient *Greek* authors, this ever-lasting truth concerns the noble lineage of the famous heroes – *Theseus, Hercules, Achilles,* and *Alexander* the *Great*. All of them shared one source – *Pelasgi-Thrace-Phryge-Trojan* heritage, not *Greek*, as it is commonly believed.

Theseus, the founder of the megalopolis *Athens*, traced his lineage to the *Pelasgian* King *Erechtheus* from his father's side and the *Phryge-Thrace-Pelasgian* ruler *Pelops* from his mother's side:

> "The lineage of *Theseus*, on the father's side, goes back to *Erechtheus* and the first children of the soil; on the mother's side, to *Pelops*. For *Pelops* was the strongest of the kings in *Peloponnesus* quite as much on account of the number of his children as the amount of his wealth. He gave many daughters in marriage to men of the highest rank, and scattered many sons among the cities as their rulers. One of these, named *Pittheus*, the grandfather of *Theseus*, founded the little city of *Troezen*, and had the highest repute as a man versed in the lore of his times and of the greatest wisdom. Now the wisdom of that day had some such form and force as that for which *Hesiod* was famous, especially in the sententious maxims of his "Works and Days." One of these maxims is ascribed to *Pittheus*, namely:
> "Payment pledged to a man who is dear must be ample and certain."
> At any rate, this is what *Aristotle* the philosopher says, and *Euripides*, when he has *Hippolytus* addressed as "nursling of the pure and holy *Pittheus*," shows what the world thought of *Pittheus*." [*Plutarch*. "*Theseus*." 3.1-3]

Plutarch also determined the *Pelasge-Thrace-Phryge-Trojan* extraction of the legendary *Hercules*, or *Heracles*, and his close affinity to *Theseus*:

> "In like manner *Theseus* admired the valour of *Heracles*, until by night his dreams were of the hero's achievements, and by day his ardour led him along and spurred him on in his purpose to achieve the like. And besides, they were kinsmen, being sons of cousins-german. For *Aethra* was daughter of *Pittheus*, as *Alcmenea* was of *Lysidice*, and *Lysidice* and *Pittheus* were brother and sister, children of *Hippodameia* and *Pelops*." [6.7-7.1]

The following diagram can help get a clear picture of the genealogy of both *Hercules* and his next of kin, *Theseus:*

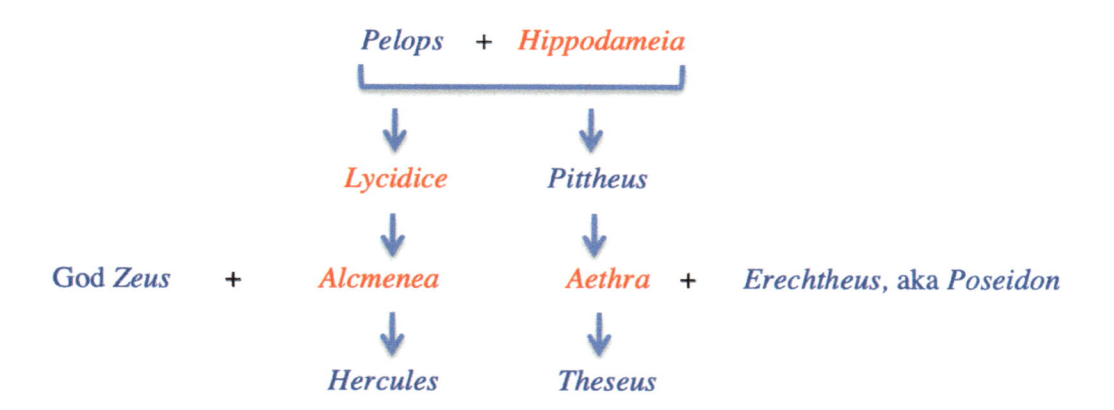

```
                    Pelops  +  Hippodameia
                   ┌────────────────────┐
                   ↓                    ↓
                Lycidice             Pittheus
                   ↓                    ↓
God Zeus  +    Alcmenea             Aethra   +   Erechtheus, aka Poseidon
                   ↓                    ↓
                Hercules             Theseus
```

Another equally important fact was ignored and never brought to the public attention by any ancient or modern historian or expert in antiquity, though it was in plain view and openly declared by *Homer*. The praised hero of *Greece*, the "sacker of cities, fleet-footed" *Achilles* was, in fact, not a *Greek*. He was of *Pelasgian* origin, a son of King *Peleus*, who ruled *Phthia* in *Thessaly,* the land of the *Pelasgi*. As it was stated earlier, the *Pelasgi* derived their denomination from this *Turkic* name – *Peleus,* or *Pilə* "reign, rule, know". The name of *Achilles,* or *Akhilleus* (Ἀχιλλεύς), was also of *Turkic* origin:

- *Achilles, Akhilleus:* Ach, Akh > Ak, Ağ 'pure, honest' + *Ille* > *İlle* 'from nation' (*Il* > *İl* 'nation, people' + *Le* > *-Li* 'an affix, equivalent to the preposition *From*') + *Es, Us* > *Us* 'master', meaning "chief of the honest people" in *Turkic*.

The name of the whole country – *Agylla* that the *Pelasgi* established and the nation populating it – the *Agyllæi,* also shared the same *Turkic* lexical components:

"However, amongst the *Greeks* this city was highly esteemed both for its bravery and rectitude of conduct; for they refrained from piracy, with favourable opportunities for engaging in it, and dedicated at *Delphi* the treasure, as it was called, of the *Agyllæi;* for their country was formerly named *Agylla*, though now *Cærea*. It is said to have been founded by *Pelasgi* from *Thessaly*." [*Strabo*. 5.2.3]

Repeatedly, *Homer* implied that *Achilles* was different from the rest of the *Greeks*. Due to his constant quarrel with King *Agamemnon* over a *Trojan* Queen *Briseis,* he remained non-combatant. Only after his beloved friend *Patroclus* got killed by the *Trojan* hero *Hector, Achilles* sprung back into the war action. And even though he killed *Hector* and dragged his body incessantly, he gave the body of "noble *Hector*", as he put it, back to the *Trojan* King *Priam* after "the servants had washed the body and anointed it, and had wrapped it in a fair shirt and mantle, *Achilles* himself lifted it on to a bier, and he and his men then laid it on the waggon." ["The Iliad." 24] Addressing his adversary *Priam* with respect, *Achilles* also negotiated 12 days of truce and restrained the *Greco-Danaan* army, allowing the *Trojans* to mourn *Hector*'s death in accordance with their traditions.

Out of known gods of the so-called *Greek* pantheon, *Achilles* would exclusively pray to *Zeus,* or *Jove,* whom he called "god of the *Pelasgi*":

"Then *Achilles* went inside his tent and opened the lid of the strong chest which silver-footed *Thetis* had given him to take on board ship, and which she had filled with shirts, cloaks to keep

out the cold, and good thick rugs. In this chest he had a cup of rare workmanship, from which no man but himself might drink, nor would he make offering from it to any other god save only to father *Jove*. He took the cup from the chest and cleansed it with sulphur; this done he rinsed it [with] clean water, and after he had washed his hands he drew wine. Then he stood in the middle of the court and prayed, looking towards heaven, and making his drink-offering of wine; nor was he unseen of *Jove* whose joy is in thunder. "King *Jove*," he cried, "lord of *Dodona*, god of the *Pelasgi*, who dwellest afar, you who hold wintry *Dodona* in your sway, where your prophets the *Selli* dwell around you with their feet unwashed and their couches made upon the ground – if you heard me when I prayed to you aforetime, and did me honour while you sent disaster on the *Achaeans*, vouchsafe me now the fulfilment of yet this further prayer.'"
["The Iliad." 16]

In addition to *Homer*, *Virgil*, in "*Aeneid*", pointed out his *Pelasgian* origin by describing him as "*Larissean Achilles*", whereas *Larissa* was the chief city of the *Pelasgi*. As such, all these facts allow confidently proclaiming that *Achilles* was a *Pelasgian* of *Turkic* blood.

While on the subject of the famous *Pelasgians*, *Alexander the Great*, the legendary *Macedonian* conqueror was also a *Pelasgian* and related to *Achilles* by blood, as claimed by the *Armenian* historian *Movses Khorenatsi*:

"*Alexander the Great*, the son of *Philip* and *Olympia*, the twenty-fourth descendant of *Achilles*, having taken over the whole universe, dies, after commanding his state to many, in order to be considered everywhere as rulers of the *Macedonians*." [2.1]

Another ancient chronicler, *Arrian of Nicodemia*, also made it known numerous times in his "The Anabasis of *Alexander*" that the great military mind and the vanquisher of *Asia*, *Alexander* hailed from the *Pelasgian* soil of *Argos* and was the progeny of *Hercules*, who, in his turn, was the posterity of the legendary *Phryge-Pelasgian* king *Pelops*:

"Therefore it was unseemly to begin this discussion, when thou oughtest to have remembered that thou art not associating with and giving advice to *Cambyses* or *Xerxes*, but to the son of *Philip*, who derives his origin from *Heracles* and *Aeacus*, whose ancestors came into *Macedonia* from *Argos*, and have continued to rule the *Macedonians*, not by force, but by law." [4.11]

Incidentally, more than 300 years after the death of *Alexander the Great*, *Pliny the Elder* still identified *Macedonia* as the original and then-current land of the *Thracians*, aka the *Pelasgians*:

"Formerly the territory they possessed was more extensive, although even now the barbarians possess a large part of the country, which, without dispute, is *Greece*. *Macedonia* is occupied by *Thracians*, as well as some parts of *Thessaly*…" [7.7.1]

The truth about the *Pelasgian*, not the *Greek* origin of *Alexander the Great*, should be accepted, as *Alexander the Great* derived his lineage from the *Pelasgi*, aka the *Thracians*, related to the *Scythians*, the *Medes*, and ultimately, the *Turkic* nations. As a reminder, the *Scythians* also claimed to have descended from *Hercules*.

Arrian of Nicodemia, aka *Lucius Flavius Arrianus*, continued his discussion about *Alexander*'s ancestry:

"Nor do I by any means commend him for changing the *Macedonian* style of dress which his fathers had adopted, for the *Median* one, being as he was a descendant of *Heracles*." [4.7]

> "An arrangement was made between *Alexander* and the *Sophists* in conjunction with the most illustrious of the *Persians* and *Medes* who were in attendance upon him, that this topic should be mentioned at a wine-party. *Anaxarchus* commenced the discussion by saying that he considered *Alexander* much more worthy of being deemed a god than either *Dionysus* or *Heracles*, not only on account of the very numerous and mighty exploits which he had performed, but also because *Dionysus* was only a *Theban*, in no way related to *Macedonians;* and *Heracles* was an *Argive*, not at all related to them, except that *Alexander* deduced his descent from him. He added that the *Macedonians* might with greater justice gratify their king with divine honours, for there was no doubt about this, that when he departed from men they would honour him as a god. How much more just then would it be to worship him while alive, than after his death, when it would be no advantage to him to be honoured." [Idem. 4.10]

Meanwhile, *Alexander* considered his father to be *Zeus*, or *Ammon* – as the *Egyptians* and the *Medes* would call this *Pelasgian* god:

> "There is also a current report that *Alexander* wished men to prostrate themselves before him as to a god, entertaining the notion that *Ammon* was his father, rather than *Philip;* and that he now showed his admiration of the customs of the *Persians* and *Medes* by changing the style of his dress, and by the alteration he made in the general etiquette of his court. There were not wanting those who in regard to these matters gave way to his wishes with the design of flattering him; among others being *Anaxarchus*, one of the philosophers attending his court, and *Agis*, an *Argive* who was an epic poet." [Idem. 4.9]

Herodotus also acknowledged the event when the *Greeks* disputed the *Grecian* origins of *Alexander the Great*:

> "Moreover the *Hellanodicai*, who manage the games at *Olympia*, decided that they were so: for when *Alexander* wished to contend in the games and had descended for this purpose into the arena, the *Hellenes* who were to run against him tried to exclude him, saying that the contest was not for Barbarians to contend in but for *Hellenes*: since however *Alexander* proved that he was of *Argos*, he was judged to be a *Hellene*, and when he entered the contest of the foot-race his lot came out with that of the first." [5.22]

Congruent with a well-known saying – "there is no smoke without fire", the claims that *Alexander the Great* was not *Greek* could be easily justified by many factors, such as his lineage reaching *Achilles* and *Hercules*, who were *Pelasgians*, as well as his *Argive* heritage. His ancestors initially came from *Argo* that used to be *Pelasgian*, as confirmed by *Strabo*:

> "Almost everyone is agreed that the *Pelasgi* were an ancient race spread throughout the whole of *Greece*, but especially in the country of the *Aeolians* near to *Thessaly*…And that portion of *Thessaly* between the outlets of the *Peneius* and the *Thermopylae*, as far as the mountains of *Pindus*, is named *Pelasgic Argos*, the district having formerly belonged to the *Pelasgi*. The poet himself also gives to *Dodonaean Jupiter*, the epithet of *Pelasgian*:
> "*Pelasgian, Dodonaean Jove* supreme."
> Many have likewise asserted that the nations of the *Epirus* are *Pelasgic*, because the dominions of the *Pelasgi* extended so far. And, as many of the heroes have been named *Pelasgi*, later writers have applied the same name to the nations over which they were the chiefs. Thus *Lesbos* has been called *Pelasgic*, and *Homer* has called the people bordering on the *Cilices* in the *Troad Pelasgic*:
> "*Hippothous* from *Larissa*, for her soil
> Far-famed, the spear-expert *Pelasgians* brought."

> *Ephorus,* when he supposes that they were a tribe of *Arcadians,* follows *Hesiod,* who says,
> "The sons born of the divine *Lycaon,* whom formerly *Pelasgus* begot."
> Likewise *Aeschylus* in his *Suppliants,* or *Danaids,* makes their race to be of *Argos* near *Mycenae.*
> *Ephorus* likewise says that *Peloponnesus* was named *Pelasgia*..." [5.2.4]

Justin also corroborated the *Pelasgian* roots of *Alexander the Great* through his mother, who was from *Thessaly:*

> "In the course of his march he had exhorted the *Thessalians* to peace, reminding them of the kindnesses shown them by his father *Philippus,* and of his mother's connection with them by the family of the *Aeacidae.*" [11.3.1]

From the notes left by the translator of the book Rev. *John Selby Watson,* M.A., it appears that the *Aeacidae* were the progeny of *Aeacus,* the father of *Peleus* and the grandfather of *Achilles.*

Alexander the Great could not be considered *Greek* from his father's side as well, as King *Phillipus* traced his ancestry to *Hercules* – the great-grandson of the *Pelasgi-Phrygian* King *Pelops,* as stated by *Arrian of Nicodemia* [4.11]. Even a fable about *Alexander's* father being *Zeus* in the shape of a serpent, based on which *Phillipus* rejected his paternity and divorced his wife, also points towards the *Pelasgian* primogenitor – God *Zeus,* or *Ammon,* or *Jupiter,* who was recognized as a *Pelasgian* deity by the authors of ancient times:

> "He then went to the temple of *Jupiter Ammon,* to consult the oracle about the event of his future proceedings, and his own parentage. For his mother *Olympias* had confessed to her husband *Philippus,* that "she had conceived *Alexander,* not by him, but by a serpent of extraordinary size." *Philippus,* too, towards the end of his life, had publicly declared that "*Alexander* was not his son;" and he accordingly divorced *Olympias,* as having been guilty of adultery. *Alexander,* therefore, anxious to obtain the honour of divine paternity, and to clear his mother from infamy, instructed the priests, by messengers whom he sent before him, what answers he wished to receive. The priests, as soon as he entered the temple, saluted him as the son of *Ammon.* *Alexander,* pleased with the god's adoption of him, directed that he should be regarded as his son." [*Justin.* 11.11]

While on the subject about the *Pelasgian* origin of the famous heroes ascribed to *Greeks,* we ought to throw bright limelight upon the irrefutable fact, completely ignored or purposefully omitted to conceal the earth-shattering truth about the participants of the *Trojan War.* We already unveiled the *Pelasgian* background of *Achilles.* However, the shocking matter is that both sides, inaccurately presented as the *Greeks* and the *Trojans,* were genuinely the wolves from the same pack. In actuality, the war started between two *Pelasgian* nations – the *Trojans* and the *Spartans.* The dispute was over the *Lacedæmonian* wife of the *Spartan* King *Menelaus,* who eloped with the *Trojan* Prince *Paris.* Furthermore, *Menelaus* and his royal brother *Agamemnon* were the grandsons of *Pelops* – the *Phryge-Thrace-Pelasgian* hero who founded *Peloponnesus.* And this was explicitly emphasized by *Sophocles* in his play "*Ajax*", or correctly *Aias* "Αἴας":

> "δύστηνε, που βλέπων ποτ' αυτά και θροείς;
> ουκ οίσθα σου πατρός μεν ὃς προύφυ πατήρ
> αρχαίον όντα Πέλοπα βάρβαρον Φρύγα;
> 'Ατρέα δ', ὃς αν σ' έσπειρε, δυσσεβέστατον
> προθέντ' αδελφῷ δείπνον οικείων τέκνων;
> αυτός δε μητρός εξέφυς Κρήσσης, εφ' ή
> λαβών έπακτον άνδρ' ο φιτύσας πατήρ
> έφηκεν έλλοϊς ιχθύσιν διαφθοράν." [1290-1297]

> "Despicable man you are! Dare to look at me while spreading lies!
> Don't you know that *Pelops* – the father of your father was a *Phrygian*? A barbarian?
> And *Atreus*, your father, was the wickedest of all the men, who set the feast
> For his brother – an execrable repast made from the flesh of his brother's sons.
> And your *Cretan* mother, who gave you birth – the fornicating adulteress whom
> Your father caught in the act and cast her into a sea to feed the grateful fish." [128]

For some odd reason, the name *Aias* was practically unanimously rendered into *English* as *Ajax*, while even the original *Greek* text has it as *Aias* = *Αἴας*. (This applies to the works by *Homer* and other *Greek* intellectuals as well.) The only scholar, who used the correct version, was the professor of *Greek* at the University of *St. Andrews, Lewis Campbell*, M.A., LL.D. ["The Death and Burial of *Aias*. A tragedy of *Sophocles*". 1826]. It is only left to say that *Aias* was a *Turkic* name *Aias*, or *Ayas*, meaning "pure, clear" ["Drevneturkskiy slovar." 27]. *Mahmud Kashgari* also noted that the name *Ayas* was usually given to those with beautiful faces [Idem ibid].

Going back to the discussion about the participants of the *Trojan* war, on the *Trojan* side, there were the *Thracians*, the *Pelasgians*, and related to them big and small tribes, as well as the *Scythians*, such as the *Halizones*, aka the *Chalybes*, the *Amazones* (the latter were mentioned by *Diodorus Siculus*).

On the so-called *Greek* side, or as *Homer* called them – "the chiefs and princes of the *Danaans*", the poet enumerated predominantly *Pelasgian* tribes, such as the *Argives*, the *Achaeans*, the *Locrians*, the *Abantes* (a *Thracian* people), the *Spartans* and the *Lacedæmonians*, the *Arcadians*, the *Cretans*, the *Magnetes*, as well as the inhabitants of the *Pelasgian* cities in *Pelasgiotis* – *Argissa, Gyrtone*, and the like, along with a handful of *Greek* tribes, who fought against the *Trojans*, and due to their presence the assailing side was named *Greek* by the scholars and translators of much later age:

> "Then King *Agamemnon* rose, holding his sceptre. This was the work of *Vulcan*, who gave it to *Jove* the son of *Saturn*. *Jove* gave it to *Mercury*, slayer of *Argus*, guide and guardian. King *Mercury* gave it to *Pelops*, the mighty charioteer, and *Pelops* to *Atreus*, shepherd of his people. *Atreus*, when he died, left it to *Thyestes*, rich in flocks, and *Thyestes* in his turn left it to be borne by *Agamemnon*, that he might be lord of all *Argos* and of the isles. Leaning, then, on his sceptre, he addressed the *Argives*." ["The Iliad." 2]

> "*Ajax*,[129] the fleet son of *Oileus*, commanded the *Locrians*. He was not so great, nor nearly so great, as *Ajax* the son of *Telamon*. He was a little man, and his breastplate was made of linen, but in use of the spear he excelled all the *Hellenes* and the *Achaeans*. These dwelt in *Cynus, Opous, Calliarus, Bessa, Scarphe*, fair *Augeae, Tarphe*, and *Thronium* about the river *Boagrius*. With him there came forty ships of the *Locrians* who dwell beyond *Euboea*." [Idem ibid]

> "The fierce *Abantes* held *Euboea* with its cities, *Chalcis, Eretria, Histiaea* rich in vines, *Cerinthus* upon the sea, and the rock-perched town of *Dium*; with them were also the men of *Carystus* and *Styra; Elephenor* of the race of *Mars* was in command of these; he was son of *Chalcodon*, and chief over all the *Abantes*. With him they came, fleet of foot and wearing their hair long behind, brave warriors, who would ever strive to tear open the corslets of their foes with their long ashen spears. Of these there came fifty ships." [Idem ibid]

> "And those that dwelt in *Lacedaemon*, lying low among the hills, *Pharis, Sparta*, with *Messe* the haunt of doves; *Bryseae, Augeae, Amyclae*, and *Helos* upon the sea; *Laas*, moreover, and *Oetylus*; these were led by *Menelaus* of the loud battle-cry, brother to *Agamemnon*, and of them there were sixty ships, drawn up apart from the others." [Idem ibid]

---

[128] This poetic excerpt was rendered into *English* from *Greek* by the author of the present book.
[129] In the original *Greek* text, it is *Aias* (*Αἴας*), not *Ajax*. ["The Iliad of *Homer*" with an interlinear translation, for the use of schools and private learners, on the *Hamiltonian* system." *Philadelphia*. 1888]

"And those that held *Arcadia,* under the high mountain of *Cyllene,* near the tomb of *Aepytus,* where the people fight hand to hand; the men of *Pheneus* also, and *Orchomenus* rich in flocks; of *Rhipae, Stratie,* and bleak *Enispe;* of *Tegea* and fair *Mantinea;* of *Stymphelus* and *Parrhasia;* of these King *Agapenor* son of *Ancaeus* was commander, and they had sixty ships. Many *Arcadians,* good soldiers, came in each one of them, but *Agamemnon* found them the ships in which to cross the sea, for they were not a people that occupied their business upon the waters." [Idem ibid]

"The famous spearsman *Idomeneus* led the *Cretans,* who held *Cnossus,* and the well-walled city of *Gortys; Lyctus* also, *Miletus* and *Lycastus* that lies upon the chalk; the populous towns of *Phaestus* and *Rhytium,* with the other peoples that dwelt in the hundred cities of *Crete.*" [Idem ibid.]

"Those again who held *Pelasgic Argos, Alos, Alope,* and *Trachis;* and those of *Phthia* and *Hellas* the land of fair women, who were called *Myrmidons, Hellenes,* and *Achaeans;* these had fifty ships, over which *Achilles* was in command." [Idem ibid]

"*Tlepolemus,* son of *Hercules,* a man both brave and large of stature, brought nine ships of lordly warriors from *Rhodes*. These dwelt in *Rhodes* which is divided among the three cities of *Lindus, Ielysus,* and *Cameirus,* that lies upon the chalk. These were commanded by *Tlepolemus,* son of *Hercules* by *Astyochea,* whom he had carried off from *Ephyra,* on the river *Selleis,* after sacking many cities of valiant warriors." [Idem ibid]

"Those that held *Argissa* and *Gyrtone, Orthe, Elone,* and the white city of *Oloosson,* of these brave *Polypoetes* was leader. He was son of *Pirithous,* who was son of *Jove* himself, for *Hippodameia* bore him to *Pirithous* on the day when he took his revenge on the shaggy mountain savages and drove them from *Mt. Pelion* to the *Aithices*. But *Polypoetes* was not sole in command, for with him was *Leonteus,* of the race of *Mars,* who was son of *Coronus,* the son of *Caeneus*. And with these there came forty ships." [Idem ibid]

"Of the *Magnetes, Prothous* son of *Tenthredon* was commander. They were they that dwelt about the river *Peneus* and *Mt. Pelion. Prothous,* fleet of foot, was their leader, and with him there came forty ships." [Idem ibid]

Apollodorus in "Epitome" also compiled a detailed list of the anti-*Trojan* forces that confirmed *Homer's* testimony about their mostly *Pelasgian* background – the *Boeotians, Orchomenians, Phocians, Locrians, Euboeans,* aka *Abantes, Argives, Mycenaeans, Lacedaemonians, Arcadians, Rhodians* (*Heracleidae*), *Pheraeans, Ormenians, Gyrtonians, Magnesians,* aka *Magnetes,* sprinkled with the *Greek* militaries:

"The men who went to the *Trojan* war were as follows. Of the *Boeotians,* ten leaders: they brought forty ships. Of the *Orchomenians,* four: they brought thirty ships. Of the *Phocians,* four leaders: they brought forty ships. Of the *Locrians, Ajax,* son of *Oeleus*: he brought forty ships. Of the *Euboeans, Elephenor,* son of *Chalcodon* and *Alcyone*: he brought forty ships. Of the *Athenians, Menestheus*: he brought fifty ships. Of the *Salaminians, Telamonian Ajax*: he brought twelve ships. Of the *Argives, Diomedes,* son of *Tydeus,* and his company: they brought eighty ships. Of the *Mycenaeans, Agamemnon,* son of *Atreus* and *Aerope*: a hundred ships. Of the *Lacedaemonians, Menelaus,* son of *Atreus* and *Aerope*: sixty ships. Of the *Pylians, Nestor,* son of *Neleus* and *Chloris*: forty ships. Of the *Arcadians, Agapenor*: seven ships. Of the *Eleans, Amphimachus* and his company: forty ships. Of the *Dulichians, Meges,* son of *Phyleus*: forty

ships. Of the *Cephallenians, Ulysses,* son of *Laertes* and *Anticlia:* twelve ships. Of the *Aetolians, Thoas,* son of *Andraemon* and *Gorge:* he brought forty ships. Of the *Cretans, Idomeneus,* son of *Deucalion:* forty ships. Of the *Rhodians, Tlepolemus,* son of *Hercules* and *Astyoche:* nine ships. Of the *Symaeans, Nireus,* son of *Charopus:* three ships. Of the *Coans, Phidippus* and *Antiphus,* the sons of *Thessalus:* thirty ships. Of the *Myrmidons, Achilles,* son of *Peleus* and *Thetis:* fifty ships. From *Phylace, Protesilaus,* son of *Iphiclus:* forty ships. Of the *Pheraeans, Eumelus,* son of *Admetus:* eleven ships. Of the *Olizonians, Philoctetes,* son of *Poeas:* seven ships. Of the *Aeanianians, Guneus,* son of *Ocytus:* twenty-two ships. Of the *Triccaeans, Podalirius:* thirty ships. Of the *Ormenians, Eurypylus:* forty ships. Of the *Gyrtonians, Polypoetes,* son of *Pirithous:* thirty ships. Of the *Magnesians, Prothous,* son of *Tenthredon:* forty ships. The total of ships was one thousand and thirteen; of leaders, forty-three; of leaderships, thirty."
[E3.11-15]

§ 11-5-3. Pelasgian mythology and pantheon of gods.

In addition to building beautiful cities adorned with amazing architecture, the *Pelasgi* were the nation that introduced the pantheon of gods to the *Greek* and *Latin* world.

The famous temple of *Dodona* established and served by the *Pelasgian* priestesses and oracles was the first place of worship in the ancient *Pelasgian* and later *Greek* world. *Strabo* mentioned it, invoking *Homer,* and indicated that the temple was right below the mountain *Tomaros* (Τόμαρος), or *Tmaros* (Τμάρος):

> "*Dodona* was formerly subject to the *Thesproti,* as was the mountain *Tomarus,* or *Tmarus,*[130] (both names are in use,) below which the temple is situated. The tragic writers and *Pindar* give the epithet of *Thesprotis* to *Dodona.* It was said to be subject, in later times, to the *Molotti.* Those called by the poet *Jove*'s interpreters, and described by him as men with unwashen feet, who slept on the ground, were, it is said, called *Tomuri*[131] from *Mount Tomarus,* and the passage in the *Odyssey* containing the advice of *Amphinomus* to the suitors not to attack *Telemachus* before they had inquired of *Jupiter* is as follows,
> "If the *Tomuri* of great *Jove* approve, I myself will kill him, and I will order all to join in the deed;
> but if the god forbid it, I command to withhold."
> For it is better, it is asserted, to write *Tomuri* than *Themistæ,*[132] because in no passage whatever are oracles called by the poet *Themistæ,* this term being applied to decrees, or statutes and rules of civil government; and the persons are called *Tomuri,*[133] which is the contracted form of *Tomaruri,*[134] or guardians of *Tomarus.*" [7.7.10-12]

The name of the mountain *Tomaros* urges an investigative mind to compare it with the appellation of the legendary *Scythian* Queen of the *Massagetes* – *Tomuris,* who annihilated the *Persian* army and beheaded its bloodthirsty King *Cyrus.* This name in many variations – as *Tomiri, Thomryis, Tomiride, Tomaris, Tamrus,* and *Tomris* – is still in use in *Turkey, Kazakhstan,* the *Azerbaijan Republic, Southern*

---

[130] In the original *Greek* text, it is *Tomaros* = Τόμαρος and *Tmaros* = Τμάρος.
[131] It is *Tomouroi* = Τομοῦροι in the *Greek* text.
[132] It should be *Themistos* = θεμιστός.
[133] In the *Greek* text, it is *Tomouroi* = Τομοῦροι.
[134] It should be *Tomarofulakas* = Τομαροφύλακας. This is a *Turkic* word: *Tomaro* 'mountain *Tomaros*' + *Ful* > *Pül* 'manage' + *Akas* > *Aka* 'caretaker', meaning "caretakers being in charge of the mountain *Tomaros*".

Azerbaijan in *Iran* to honor the brave queen who was not afraid to stand up against the powerful enemy and crush him.

This unisexual appellation, found in several variants, was also the name of the *Thracian* king *Thamyris*, or correctly *Thamuris* (Θάμυρις), as specified by *Strabo:*

> "*Mount Athos* is pap-shaped, and so lofty that the husbandmen on the summit are already weary of their labour, the sun having long since risen to them, when to the inhabitants of the shore it is the beginning of cockcrowing. *Thamyris*, the *Thracian*, was king of this coast, and followed the same practices as *Orpheus*." [7.35]

Obviously, *Strabo* drew his knowledge from *Homer* in his report involving *Thamyris*, the *Thracian*. *Homer* described *Thamyris*, or *Thamuris*, as a divine singer who had no match among mortals and immortals:

> "...*Dorium*, where the *Muses* met *Thamyris*, and stilled his minstrelsy forever. He was returning from *Oechalia*, where *Eurytus* lived and reigned, and boasted that he would surpass even the *Muses*, daughters of aegis-bearing *Jove*, if they should sing against him; whereon they were angry, and maimed him. They robbed him of his divine power of song, and thenceforth he could strike the lyre no more."
> ["The Iliad." 2]

The analysis of the names of the mountain *Tomaros*, the *Scythian* Queen *Tomuris*, the *Thracian* singer *Thamuris* (*Thamyris*) brings additional clarity to the question about the direct kinship between the *Pelasgi*, *Scythians*, the *Thracians*, and the *Turkic* nations. All of these names contain one *Turkic* root – *Tömür*, or *Temir*, or *Təmir* "metal", meaning "strong, invincible as metal" in *Turkic*:

- o   Pelasgian <u>Tomaros</u> = Scythian <u>Tomuris</u> = Thracian <u>Thamuris</u> = Turkic <u>Tamrus</u>.

There are numerous ancient *Turkic* names with this root that continue staying in use among the *Turkic* nations, such as *Təmrus, Tomris, Temir, Təhmiras, Təhmuraz, Timur, Teymur*.

As stated earlier, *Greek* mythology was founded entirely on the beliefs and religion presented by the *Pelasgi* and their derivatives to the *Greeks* and surrounding them nations, including the *Latins*. The polytheistic religion was a vital link, connecting the *Pelasgi* with the *Trojan* nations. God *Zeus*, also known as *Jove* and *Jupiter*, was considered to be the originator of the *Pelasgians* and also called "*Pelasgian Zeus*", "*Pelasgian Dodonœan Jove*" by *Ephorus*, "*Pelasgian Lord Zeus*" by *Homer*, "*Pelasgic Jupiter*" by *Suidas*.

Strabo, along with *Sexti Properti*, seconded this assertion and attributed *Pelasgian* pedigree to *Zeus's* wife *Juno*, or *Hera*, as well:

> "*Suidas*, in order to court the favour of the *Thessalians* by fabulous stories, says, that the temple was transported from *Scotussa* of the *Thessalian Pelasgiotis*, accompanied by a great multitude, chiefly of women, whose descendants are the present prophetesses, and that hence *Jupiter* had the epithet *Pelasgic*." [*Strabo*. 7.7.12]

> "An contempta tibi Iunonis templa Pelasgae?" [*Sexti Properti*. "Elegiarum." 28a]
> "Or did you pay no regard to *Pelasgian Juno's* shrine?" [135]

Ovid in "*Fasti*" went even further and asserted that the *Pelasgi*, aka the *Arcadians*, were more ancient than *Zeus* himself:

---

[135] The translation from *Latin* into *English* was provided by the author of the present work.

"Before the birth of *Jupiter* the *Arcadians* are said to have inhabited the earth, and that nation existed before the moon." [Translated by *R. Mongan*. 2.267]

The poet also emphasized that the *Romans* bowed down before the deities, introduced to them by the *Pelasgi*:

"The ancient *Arcadians* are reported to have worshipped *Pan* (as) god of cattle; he is chiefly found on the *Arcadian* hills…In consequence of this, we revere this god and the sacred rites imported from the *Pelasgians*…" [Idem ibid]

Herodotus, on the authority of the *Pelasgian* priestesses themselves, testified that the *Pelasgi* first established and practiced the religion that later was taught to the *Greeks* and known today as *Greek* mythology instead of *Pelasgian*:

"… the *Grecians*…learnt of the *Pelasgians* to make the image of *Hermes* with an erected priapus, the *Athenians* having been the first, who practis'd this manner, and others by their example. For these *Pelasgians* were inhabitants of *Samothracia,* before they came into the country of *Attica,* and had instructed the *Samothracians* in the orgian rites as they afterwards did the *Athenians,* who by that means were the first of all the *Grecians* that form'd the images of *Mercury* in the manner above-mention'd: for which the *Pelasgians* pretend certain sacred reasons, explain'd in the *Mysteries of Samothracia*. They had formerly sacrific'd and pray'd to gods in general, as I was inform'd at *Dodona,* without attributing either name or surname to any deity, which in those times they had never heard. But they call'd them by the name of gods, because they dispos'd and govern'd all actions and countries. After a long time, the names of the other gods were brought among them from *Ægypt,* and last of all that of *Bacchus:* upon which they consulted the oracle of *Dodona,* still accounted the most ancient, and then the only oracle in *Greece;* and having enquir'd, whether they should receive these names from barbarians, the oracle answer'd, they should. So from that time they invok'd the gods in their sacrifices, under distinct names, and the same were afterwards receiv'd by the *Grecians* from these *Pelasgians*. But what original is to be assign'd to each of those gods; whether they always were, and of what form, was utterly unknown till of late, and, to use a common expression, of yesterday. For I am of opinion, that *Hesiod* and *Homer,* who liv'd not above four hundred years before my time, were the persons that introduc'd the genealogy of the gods among the *Grecians;* impos'd names upon each; assign'd their functions and honours; and cloath'd them in their several forms. As to the other poets, suppos'd to be more ancient, I think they liv'd after these. And this is my sense touching *Hesiod* and *Homer;* but the rest, which I related before, I had from the priestesses of *Dodona*." [2.51]

Herodotus confirmed the *Pelasgian* lineage of the gods by confidently relying on the authority of *Hesiod* and *Homer*. The latter was the one who determined the origins of these gods by giving a *"Pelasgian"* attribute to them, such as *"Pelasgian Zeus",* as well as ascribed the divine lineage to the *Trojan* nations. In assent with *Homer*, the *Pelasgian* leader *Pylaeus* was from the *Arian* race – the scion of *Ares*, or *Mars,* the god of war:

"*Hippothous* led the tribes of *Pelasgian* spearsmen, who dwelt in fertile *Larissa* – *Hippothous*, and *Pylaeus* of the race of *Mars,* two sons of the *Pelasgian Lethus,* son of *Teutamus.*"
["The Iliad." 2]

The *Dardanian* headman *Aeneas* was conceived by the goddess *Venus,* or *Aphrodite:*

> "The *Dardanians* were led by brave *Aeneas,* whom *Venus* bore to *Anchises,* when she, goddess though she was, had lain with him upon the mountain slopes of *Ida*. He was not alone, for with him were the two sons of *Antenor, Archilochus* and *Acamas,* both skilled in all the arts of war." [Idem ibid]

The legendary founder of the *Trojan* nation *Dardanus* was considered to be the son of *Zeus* and a mortal woman:

> "In the beginning *Dardanus* was the son of *Jove,* and founded *Dardania,* for *Ilius* was not yet established on the plain for men to dwell in…" [Idem. 20]

> "It is fated, moreover, that he should escape, and that the race of *Dardanus,* whom *Jove* loved above all the sons born to him of mortal women, shall not perish utterly without seed or sign. For now indeed has *Jove* hated the blood of *Priam,* while *Aeneas* shall reign over the *Trojans,* he and his children's children that shall be born hereafter." [Idem ibid]

The *Maeonian* strongmen also sprung from the heavenly entity – the sprite of the *Gygaean Lake:*

> "*Mesthles* and *Antiphus* commanded the *Meonians,* sons of *Talaemenes,* born to him of the *Gygaean* lake. These led the *Meonians,* who dwelt under *Mt. Tmolus*." [Idem. 2]

Sophocles in *Electra* gave *Apollo* an attribute *Lycean* to honor the *Trojan* nation – *Lycians,* also known as the *Aphneii,* or the *Aphneian Trojans:*

> "O *Lycean Apollo,* graciously hear these prayers, and grant them to us all, even as we ask!" [Translated by *R.C. Jebb.* 655-656]

The attribute of "godlike" was used numerous times by *Homer* when describing the *Trojan* heroes, such as *Mestor, Priam*'s son *Polydorus,* while *Hector* was depicted as "a god among men, so that one would have thought he was son to an immortal" ["The Iliad." 24].
    Homer repeatedly demonstrated that the divine pantheon – *Zeus* himself, *Apollo,* and *Ares* mostly rooted for the *Trojans* in the *Trojan* war. These were the most worshipped gods by the *Trojans* and the *Scythians*. The god of war, *Ares* or *Mars,* was the chief god, put on the highest pedestal by the *Scythians*. It was from *Ares* the *Trojan* female *Ilia* birthed the founding fathers of *Rome* – *Romulus* and *Remulus*. The *Scythians* considered themselves to be the descendants of *Hercules* and *Zeus*. These additional shreds of evidence provided by the mythology also help establish the kinship between the *Trojans,* the *Scythians,* and the *Turrenians* of *Rome*.
    Herodotus was the first to constate that the *Greeks* obtained their pantheon of gods from the *Pelasgi,* or correctly, the *Ægyptians* of the *Pelasgian* descent:

> "*Jupiter* is by the *Ægyptians* call'd *Ammon*. For the same reason the ram is accounted a sacred animal, and never kill'd by the *Thebans,* except once in every year on the Festival of *Jupiter;* when, after they have slay'd the body, and put the skin upon the image of the god, they bring a statue of *Hercules* into his presence: which done, all the assistants give a blow to the ram, and afterwards bury him in a consecrated coffin. I have been inform'd, that this *Ægyptian Hercules* is one of the twelve gods; but of the other, who is known to the *Grecians,* I could never hear the least mention in any part of *Ægypt*. And I have many good reasons to believe, that the *Ægyptians* did not borrow this name from the *Grecians;* but rather the *Grecians,* and especially those who gave it to the son of *Amphitryon,* from the *Ægyptians*. Principally, because *Amphitryon* and *Alcmena,* father and mother to the *Grecian Hercules,* were both of *Ægyptian* descent. Besides; the *Ægyptians* affirm, they know not the names of *Neptune, Castor* and *Pollux,* nor ever received

them into the number of their gods: Yet if they had borrow'd the name of any deity from the *Grecians,* they would certainly have mention'd these in the first rank, had any of the *Grecians* then frequented the sea, and been acquainted with the use of shipping, as I believe they were. And therefore the *Ægyptians* must have known the names of these gods, rather than that of *Hercules*. But however this be, *Hercules* is one of the ancient gods of the *Ægyptians* who say, that seventeen thousand years before the reign of *Amasis,* the number of their gods, which had been eight, was increas'd to twelve, and that *Hercules* was accounted one of these. Concerning which things, being desirous to know with certainty as much as might be discover'd, I sail'd to *Tyre* in *Phœnicia,* because I had heard there was a temple dedicated to *Hercules*. That temple I saw, enrich'd with many magnificent donations, and among others with two pillars, one of fine gold, the other made of a smaragdus, which shines by night in a surprizing manner. Conversing with the priests of this god, and inquiring how long this temple had been built, I found these also to differ from the *Grecians*. For they assur'd me that the temple was built at the same time with the city, and that two thousand three hundred years were already past since the foundation of *Tyre*. In this city I saw another temple dedicated to *Hercules* by the name of *Thasian;* and when I arriv'd in *Thasus,* I found there also a temple of the same god, built by those *Phœnicians,* who founded that city during the expedition they made in search of *Europa* which was five generations before *Hercules,* the son of *Amphitryon* appear'd in *Greece*. All these things evidently prove, that the *Ægyptian Hercules* is a god of great antiquity; and therefore, in my opinion, those *Grecians* act most rationally, who build temples to both; sacrificing to the first, as to an immortal being, under the name of *Olympian,* and honouring the other as a hero."
[2.42-44]

Evidently, the *Pelasgi* did not borrow the names of the *Egyptian* gods; they just accepted the concept of functionality for some gods. *Pelasgian Zeus* or *Jupiter* is *Egyptian Ammon,* while *Hercules* is *Thasian.* As such, the *Pelasgi* gave their gods specific names, using their own lexical reservoir. Out of 12 main *Egyptian* gods – *Amun, Anubis, Horus, Ra, Thoth, Osiris, Isis* (the *Thrace-Pelasgian* princess *Io*), *Seth, Sekhmet, Ptah, Hathor,* and *Hephthys* - which one corresponds to *Hercules* is still to be determined. The *Greeks,* however, quickly appropriated both the names of the gods and their designation from the *Pelasgi*.

An unexpected and strong affiliation between the *Egyptians* and the *Pelasgians* was defined by the ancient *Greek* tragedian of 463-7 BCE *Aeschylus* in "Suppliant Women". The *Pelasgian* King *Pelasgus* of *Argos* received a group of *Egyptian* refugees from *Egypt,* seeking his protection from their cousins, who forcefully wanted to marry them, and in response to his question about their lineage, these women claimed to be of *Pelasgian* origin. This drew opposition from the king:

"Foreign maidens, your tale is beyond my belief — how your race can be from *Argos*. For you are more similar to the women of *Libya* and in no way similar to those native to our land. The *Nile,* too, might foster such a stock, and like yours is the *Cyprian* impress stamped upon female images by male craftsmen. And of such aspect, I have heard, are nomad women, who ride on camels for steeds, having padded saddles, and dwell in a land neighboring the *Aethiopians*. And had you been armed with the bow, certainly I would have guessed you to be the unwed, flesh-devouring *Amazons*. But inform me, and I will better comprehend how it is that you trace your race and lineage from *Argos*." [274-290]

Having accepted the challenge to prove their lineage, the *Egyptian* refugees told a story about their founder *Io,* who kept the keys of *Hera*'s shrine. As *Zeus* slept with *Io* and "this entanglement was not secret from *Hera*", "the goddess of *Argos*" transformed *Io* into a cow. But this did not stop *Zeus,* who continued to pursue this heifer by "making his form that of a bull lusting for a mate." In return, the vengeful *Hera* sent a gadfly and drove *Io* out of her fatherland to *Canobus* and *Memphis*. The story made the king *Pelasgus of Argos* acknowledge that the *Egyptians* indeed shared ancient ties with *Argos* from old times [Idem. 320-340].

And it was from this *Thrace-Pelasgian* dynasty of *Io,* the *Egyptians* learned about the *Pelasgian* gods and deities.

Aside from the beautiful legend about how the *Pelasgi* ended up in *Egypt,* there is another account – down-to-earth and historically sound. *Diodorus Siculus* narrated in his work that the *Egyptians* would bring the conquered nations to their land and make them work for them in ancient times. Unlike other nations, the *Trojans* refused to be slaves for the *Egyptians* and stayed free:

> "*Sesostris* having now disbanded his army, gave leave to his companions in arms, and fellow victors, to take their ease, and enjoy the fruits of their conquest. But he himself, fired with an earnest desire of glory, and ambitious to leave behind him eternal monuments of his memory, made many fair and stately works, admirable both for their cost and contrivance, by which he both advanced his own immortal praise, and procured unspeakable advantages to the *Egyptians,* with perfect peace and security for the time to come. For, beginning first with what concerned the gods, he built a temple in all the cities of *Egypt,* to that god whom every particular place most adored; and he employed none of the *Egyptians* in his works, but finished all by the labours of the captives; and therefore he caused an inscription to be made upon all the temples thus – "None of the natives were put to labour here." It is reported that some of the *Babylonian* captives, because they were not able to bear the fatigue of the work, rebelled against the king; and having possessed themselves of a fort near the river, they took up arms against the *Egyptians,* and wasted the country thereabouts: but at length having got a pardon, they chose a place for their habitation, and called it after the name of that in their own country, *Babylon.* Upon the like occasion, they say, that *Troy,* situated near the river *Nile,* was so called: for *Menelaus,* when he returned from *Ilium* with many prisoners, arrived in *Egypt,* where the *Trojans* deserting the king, seized upon a certain strong place, and took up arms against the *Greeks,* till they had gained their liberty, and then built a famous city after the name of their own. But I am not ignorant how *Ctesias the Cretan* gives a far different account of these cities, when he says, that some of those who came in former times with *Semiramis* into *Egypt,* called the cities which they built after the names of those in their own country. But it is no easy matter to know the certain truth of these things: yet it is necessary to observe the different opinions concerning them, that the judicious reader may have an occasion to inquire, in order to pick out the real truth." [1.4]

Of course, not all the *Egyptian* wars would end up with the enslaved *Trojans*. One of them, known in history as the *Battle of Kadesh,* produced the first recorded peace treaty and the royal marriage between the fighting sides – the ancient *Turkic* nation of the *Hittites* and the *Egyptians*.

The *Hittites*, as an ancient non-*Semitic*, non-*Indo-European* people of *Turkic* origin, were another essential chain that connected them with the *Pelasgi* and related *Trojan, Thracian, Scythian* nations, and made a lasting impact on all of them, as well as on the *Egyptians*. The *Hittites* had an empire that used to encompass the territory of modern *Turkey, Syria,* and *Lebanon* and flourished in the *Bronze Age* from c.1700 to 1200 BCE. In the famous *Battle of Kadesh* that took place near the modern *Lebanon-Syria* border in 1274 BCE, the *Trojan* nations, such as the *Lycians,* the *Maeonians,* the *Mysians,* joined the *Hittites* as allies to settle their grievances with the *Egyptians*. Unable to have a decisive win over the *Hittite Empire,* the *Egyptian* Pharaoh *Ramses II* offered a truce to the *Hittites:*

> "The treaty of peace was yet further confirmed by the marriage of *Rameses* with the daughter of *Kheta-Sar.* A relief in the temple of *Abu-Simbel,* dating from the thirty-fourth year of this king, depicts the *Hittite* king wearing the high tiara, and accompanied by the Prince of *Keti* (perhaps *Cataonia*), leading his child, in the attire of an *Egyptian* princess, to the Pharaoh. The daughter of *Rameses* appears to have married a *Syrian* prince; for on the granite statue which her father

erected as a pendent to his own before the second pylon of the temple of *Luxor,* she is distinguished by a *Syrian* name, *Bant-Anat* ('daughter of the goddess *Anat*). Similarly the *Hittite* wife of *Rameses* received the *Egyptian* name, *Ra-măa-ar-nefru*. A tablet between two pillars of the first hall of the temple of *Abu Simbel* bears a eulogium of *Rameses,* in the form of an address of the god *Ptah-Totunen*. It was also engraved on the pylon of the temple of *Rameses III* at *Medinet-Abu*."
["A History of All Nations from the Earliest Times Being a Universal Library by Distinguished Scholars. – *Egypt* and *West Asia* in Antiquity." *F. Justi,* et al. 1906. 276-277]

From the works of ancient historians, it is evident that most of the time, when going to war against another nation, a fighting side would gather forces from the kindred tribes and nations. This was the case with the *Scythians* against the *Persians* and true with the *Trojans* against the *Egyptians*. The fact that the *Trojan* nations participated in the war against the *Egyptians* on the side of the *Hittites* is another proof that they were closely related by blood, language, culture, and religious beliefs.

In addition to their own gods, the *Egyptians* kept in high esteem the deities of the *Hittites,* as stated by *Major Conder:*

"The *Egyptians* revered *Hittite* gods, for *Istar* and *Set* were both adored in the land of *Khemi.*"
["*Altaic* Hieroglyphs and *Hittite* Inscriptions." 240]

He also added that the *Turkic* nation of the *Hittites* made a tremendous impact on the religion of the *Phoenicians* as well:

"On the *Phoenicians* the *Hittites* seem to have had great influence. It is not the case that the latter worshipped *Semitic* gods. On the contrary, it was from the *Altaic* race that much of the civilization of the *Semitic* people was derived, and the *Phoenician* pantheon is in great measure of *Hittite* origin." [Idem. 145]

The cartouche of the *Egyptian* Pharaoh *Rameses* II, discovered in 1882, demonstrated that the ancient *Altaic* (read *Turkic*) hieroglyphs were dated around the 14th c. BCE or older than that:

"Dr. *Gollob's* discovery of the cartouche of *Rameses* II on the weeping *Niobe* gives us a clear indication that the *Altaic* emblems on that monument are older than about 1350 B.C.: the characters in this case do not seem to be marked by any peculiarities of archaic nature. We may, therefore, fairly assume that the *Hamath* and *Carchemish* stones are at least as old as *Moses,* and perhaps as old as *Abraham;* and there is good reason to suppose that they are the oldest monuments yet found in *Asia*." [Idem. 156-157]

Conder compared the hieroglyphs used by the ancient *Turkic* nations, that he grouped under the name *Altaic,* with the *Egyptian* characters, as seen below, and revealed an incredible closeness of the two writing systems:

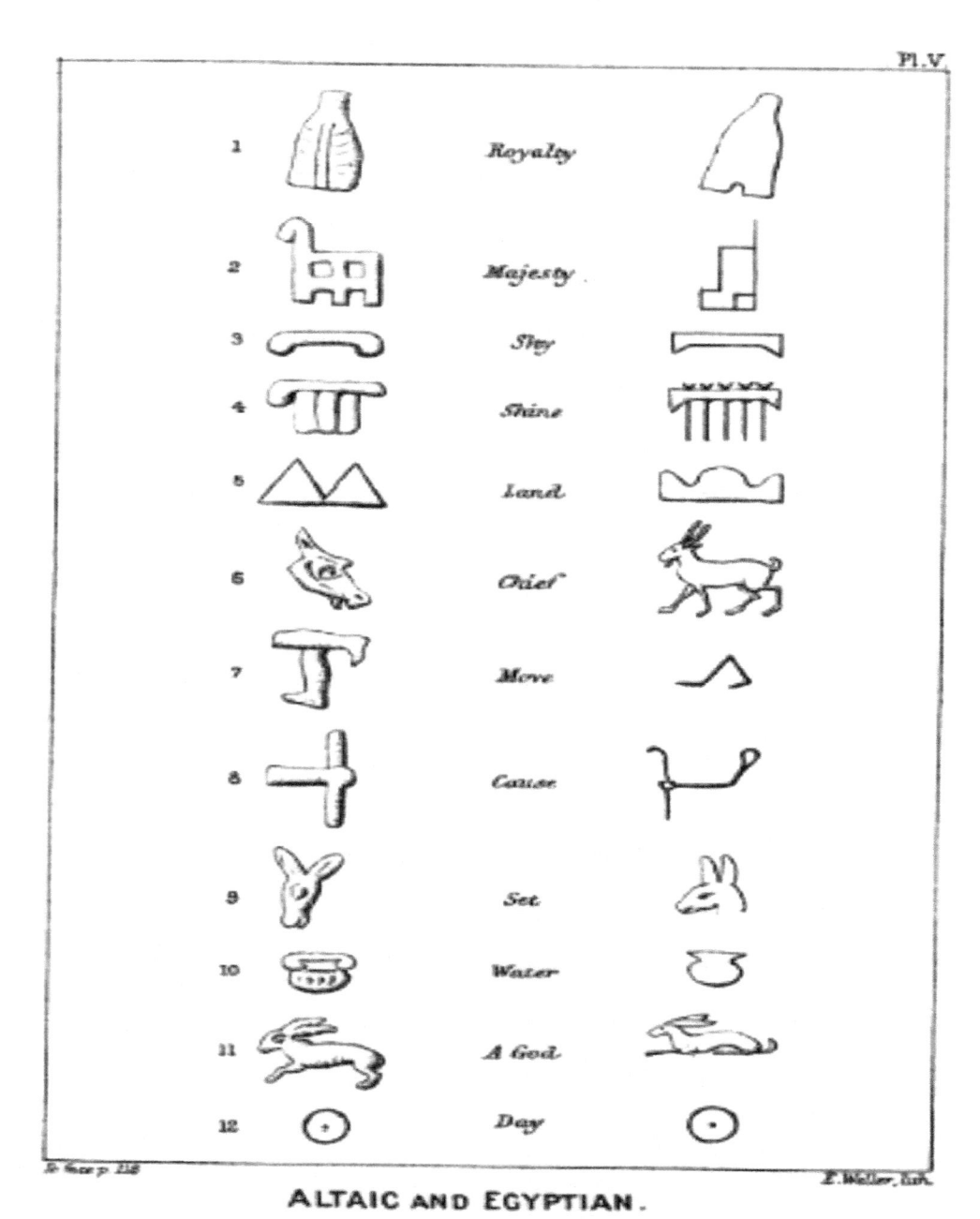

Figure 23. Altaic hieroglyphs on the left, Egyptian ones - on the right. "Altaic Hieroglyphs and Hittite Inscriptions." [119].

Based on the authority of the renowned Egyptologists of the 19th c., *Conder* asserted that both the *Egyptian* and *Hittite* hieroglyphs originated from the same source in spite of the fact that these were two languages that belonged to different language systems:

> "Professor *de Lacouperie* (Babylonian Record, December, 1866, p. 27) has recently written as follows: "There are strong reasons to believe that the *Babylonian* and *Egyptian* writings have sprung from a former system. They have many symbols in common, with similar phonetic values which are not loan signs"...I find that there are cogent reasons to believe that both writings have come from an older system, which has also produced the *Hittite* hieroglyphs, and the pictorial figures and symbols which were preserved on the black stone of *Susa*, the boundary-stones of *Babylonia*, and also preserved in some later symbols." [Idem. 115-116]

Some Egyptologists deduced the origin of the hieroglyphs from the ancient *Turkic* nation that resided in *Egypt:*

> "Many Egyptologists have supposed that a *Turanian Asiatic* stock existed in *Egypt,* and to them possibly the origin of the hieroglyphics may be due. It is in this manner, perhaps, that we may best explain the connection between *Altaic* and *Egyptian* hieroglyphics. The connection may be due to a common *Asiatic* origin in a picture-writing whence the *Egyptian* and the so-called *Hittite* both developed. The *Egyptian* is of immense antiquity, and far more complex, since it consists of about 400 symbols against the *Altaic* 110 to 140 emblems. The *Egyptian* is a double system of determinatives and syllables; the *Altaic* represents a simpler stage when the pictorial ideograph with a monosyllabic value is accompanied, not by determinatives, but only by conventionalized symbols of particles and grammatical forms. I might even suggest that the *Egyptian* double system arose from the fact that the emblems were applied to a language other than that to which they belonged in the first instance; just as in Cuneiform the old *Akkadian* ideograph got a new phonetic value when it came to be used in a *Semitic* language. Determinatives may have served to fix the true value of syllables which at first had another sound in another language." [Idem. 121-122]

Numerous 12 thousand-years-old pictographs on the rocks in the *Qobustan* reserve in *Azerbaijan,* especially with the jointly dancing circle of people, shows a striking resemblance to the *Egyptian* pictorial symbols of a dancing round of humans, discovered in 2019 inside the *South Sinai* caves in *Egypt.*

Figure 24. On the left: a pictograph of dancing people in a circle. Gobustan, Azerbaijan. © Credit: Kaetana/stock.adobe.com On the right: a pictogram of dancing people in a circle. Egypt. © Credit: Ministry of Tourism and Antiquities of Egypt.

The renowned Orientalist of the 19th c., *Isaac Taylor,* went even further by asserting that "The <u>ancient *Egyptian* is a *Turanian* [136] language</u> which rivals the *Etruscan* in antiquity." ["*Etruscan* Researches." 163].

Moreover, according to *Conder,* the ancient *Turkic* writing system was first used by the *Greeks, Babylonians,* and *Syrians:*

---

[136] Read *Turkic.*

252

"The *Aryans* in *Greece,* the *Semitic* tribes in *Babylonia* and in *Syria,* used first the *Altaic* syllabaries, and afterwards adopted the alphabets which had the same original derivation. In fact, no *Asiatic* system of writing can, on this theory, be distinguished as having other than an *Altaic* origin. The genealogy of these systems would, therefore, be as follows:

```
1st stage—Picture-writing   -   -   Altaic
2nd   „   —Hieroglyph   -  Egyptian   Proto-Medic, etc.
3rd   „   —Syllabary    -  Hieratic   Cypriote   Cuneiform
4th   „   —Pure alphabet-  Phœnician
```

The Eastern branches never reached the fourth stage, and their late syllabaries were in time superseded by the various alphabets which sprang from the *Phoenician;* but both *Cypriote* and *Cuneiform* were still in use as late as 300 B.C; *Persian* Cuneiform with thirty-six letters still retained a few ideograms." [Idem. 124]

Diodorus Siculus gave the same account, except for using the term *Pelasgian* instead of the *Altaic,* though both stand for *Turkic:*

"He says that *Linus* was the first that invented rhimes and music in *Greece:* and that *Cadmus* brought letters out of *Phœnicia,* and was the first who taught the *Grecians* to pronounce them, and gave them their several names, and formed their distinct characters: hence these letters are all generally called *Phœnician* letters, because they were brought over out of *Phœnicia* into *Greece:* but they were afterwards called *Pelasgian* characters, because the *Pelasgians* were the first that understood them after they were brought over." [3.4]

The upcoming chapter will provide a detailed discourse about the ancient *Turkic* alphabet and its irreplaceable impact on the *Indo-European* and *Semitic* languages.

Getting back to the subject of the religion practiced by the *Pelasgians,* including the *Thracians* and other *Trojan* nations in comparison to their brethren – the *Scythians,* one could notice that the *Pelasgian* gods were the same as the *Scythians* used to worship, except for their names. As *Herodotus* asserted:

"They worship no other gods than these. In the first place *Vesta* who is their principal deity. Then *Jupiter;* and the *Earth,* which is accounted his wife. After them *Apollo, Venus, Urania, Hercules,* and *Mars.* All these are generally acknowledg'd: but those who go under the name of *Royal Scythians,* sacrifice likewise to *Neptune. Vesta,* in the *Scythian* language is call'd '*Tahiti', Jupiter* is, in my opinion, rightly nam'd '*Papœus*', the *Earth* '*Apia*', *Apollo* '*Oetosyrus*', the celestial *Venus* '*Artimpasa*', and *Neptune* '*Thamimasades*'. They erect no images, altars, or temples, to any other god, except *Mars* alone…" [4.59]

Customarily, the *Scythians* denominated some of their towns in honor of the *Pelasgian* goddess *Aphrodite,* such as *Aphrodisias,* in conformity with the *Roman* author *Pliny the Elder:*

"All this country was formerly possessed by the *Scythians,* surnamed *Aroteres;* their towns were Aphrodisias, Libistos, Zygere, Rocobe, Eumenia, Parthenopolis, and Gerania…" [4.18.1306]

On the testimony of *Herodotus,* the *Scythians* claimed their divine origin from *Jupiter:*

> "The first man that appear'd in *Scythia*, then an uninhabited desert, was *Targitaus* concerning whom they relate things incredible to me. For they affirm that he was born of *Jupiter* and a daughter of the river *Borysthenes:* that he had three sons who went by the names of *Lipoxais, Apoxais,* and *Colaxais.*" [4.5]

As attested by *Strabo*, the *Pelasgi* were considered "to be the most ancient people". According to *Herodotus*, their kith and kin – the *Phrygians* were also ruled as the most ancient nation in the world [2.2]. Furthermore, the *Scythians* too were declared as the earliest nation that ever inhabited the Earth:

> "The nation of the *Scythians* was always regarded as very ancient; though there was long a dispute between them and the *Egyptians* concerning the antiquity of their respective races... The *Egyptians* being confounded with these arguments, the *Scythians* were always accounted the more ancient."
> [*Justinus*. "*Justin's* History of the World, Extracted from *Trogus Pompeius.*" 2.1.5-21]

As we see, all three nations – the *Pelasgi*, the *Phrygians*, and the *Scythians* were recognized as the most primordial nations on *Earth*. And the verdict is true on all accounts, as the *Pelasgi*, related to the *Phrygians* through *Thracian* and *Trojan* ties, led the lifestyle similar to the *Scythians* and belonged to the greater *Scythian* family, which was *Turkic* in essence.

The *Scythian* affinity with the *Pelasgi* got its confirmation in "The Encyclopædia *Britannica:* Or, Dictionary of Arts, Sciences, and General Literature", 1842:

> "...the *Pelasgians* certainly descended from the north-east into *Greece,* and thus came from, or at least through, a country which had been overspread by the *Scythians* long before the period of their descent into *Hellas,* it may be inferred that they were of the same origin and race with the inhabitants of *Thrace, Thessaly,* and the other countries where they first made their appearance; a conclusion, we may observe, which, whether it be well or ill founded, does not necessarily follow from the premises, because the circumstance of a roving or migratory tribe passing through a particular country in its progress towards other settlements, by no means warrants the supposition either of identity or diversity of origin with reference to the prior inhabitants of such country...At a very early period *Pelasgian* settlements were established on the *Hellespont;* that, in the days of *Homer,* and even much later, a district in *Thessaly* was named *Pelasgia;* that the people of *Macedonia* were anciently called *Pelasgians;* that the *Thracians,* who, under *Eumolpus,* colonized *Attica,* were by *Herodotus* denominated *Pelasgians;* and that *Plutarch* describes the same people as a roving or migratory race, who, having subdued the inhabitants, settled in the countries they had conquered, — a description which, he thinks, can only apply to the *Scythians*. Besides, *Herodotus, Thucydides,* and *Strabo,* all state that the *Pelasgians* came originally from *Thessaly* into *Greece;* and as *Thessaly* was anciently accounted a part of *Thrace,*...the *Pelasgians* were *Thracians,* that is, *Scythians...*" [17.177]

§ 11-5-4. The Turkic word Tatar, or Tartar, used by the Greeks, Romans, Hittites, Armenians.

There is another vital link, more like the unbreakable chain that joins the *Hittite*, the *Pelasgi*, the *Scythians*, and other *Trojan* nations into a circle with the *Turkic* nations – the ancient *Turkic* name *Tatar*, or *Tartarus*, or *Tartaro* (Ταρτάρῳ in *Greek*). Some kings of the *Hittites* were called as such – *Tiatar*, *Tatar*, *Tetar*, *Totar*, *Tatir*:

> "The northern half of the west side shows the pursuit into the river. Here the lists name *Tetar*, chief of domestics, brother of the king *Masrima*; *Rebasununa*, prince of the people of *Anunas*; and *Suaas*, prefect of *Tanis*, who is being drawn from the water. On the water girt fortress are inscribed the words "the Fortress *Kadesh*." Eventually, *Mutnara*, by a truly *Oriental* euphemism, 'succumbed to his destiny'— i.e., was probably murdered by his brother *Kheta-Sar*, who succeeded him."
> [*Justi F*. et al. "A History of All Nations…*Egypt* and *Western Asia* in Antiquity." 1.274]"

The close resemblance of the *Hittites* with the *Tatars* and other *Turkic* nations of *Central Asia* was noted by *Conder*:

> "With this list the personal appearance of the *Hittites* as represented at *Karnak* is in complete accord. They are a hairless people with long thin moustache — like that of the *Chinese* — light complexion, the head partly shaven, and a clear and unmistakable pigtail. The eyes seem to have a slight inclination; the facial angle is oblique. This was pointed out to me in 1882 by the late Dr. *Birch*, and my remark on the subject in '*Heth* and *Moab*' has been reproduced by several later writers. *Perrot* has given a couple of heads from the drawings of *Rosellini*, which Dr. *Birch* showed me. I submit that we can have no doubt that the *Hittites* were an *Altaic* tribe, and that since we know them to have lived in *Carchemish* [137] and *Hamath*, and find in both places texts which are shown independency to be written in an *Altaic* language, the result is clear. Dr. *Wright* was right when in 1874 he announced as a new idea that the *Hamath* stones were of *Hittite* origin." ["*Altaic* Hieroglyphs and *Hittite* Inscriptions." 130-131]

Notably, the king of *Macedon* and *Greece*, *Alexander the Great* (356 BC-323 BCE), also fought with the descendants of the *Hittites*, or the *Kheta*, called as *Cathaeans*, or correctly *Kathaioi* (Καθαῖοι), who resettled in *India*. [Arrian of Nicomedia. "The Anabasis of *Alexander* or, the History of the Wars and Conquests of *Alexander the Great*." 5.22.2]

The ancient *Turkic* word *Tatar*, or *Tartar*, served as a male name among the *Hittites*, the *Kheta*, or *Khatioi*, the *Armenians* of the *Phrygian* extraction, and the *Turkic* nations. In the *Behistun* inscription, King *Darius* mentioned his *Armenian* general *Tatarşis* [Column 2, line 7 of the *Median* text] [138]. *Tatar* is an ancient ethnonym of a *Turkic* people, as well as a toponym, an oronym detected in many places around the world, such as the river *Tartaro* in *Italy*, a village *Tatári* in *Greece*, *Tartar* region in *Azerbaijan*, *Tatarstan Republic* (currently, a part of *Russia)*, and the like.

However, for the *Pelasgians*, *Trojans*, and subsequently, the *Greeks* and *Romans*, *Tartarus* had a mythical connotation and a dual meaning – as a deity and as a place in the underworld, where souls were judged. *Hesiod* in "The *Theogony*" used *Tartarus* in both meanings:

---

[137] The word *Carchemish* is, undoubtedly, of *Turkic* origin and means "cursed". The suffix –*Mish* is observed in some *Turkic* names, such as the *Tatar* khan *Tokhtamish*. The latter gained notoriety in history for defeating the *Russians* and keeping them under the *Tatar* rule.
[138] *Edwin Norris*. "Memoir on the *Scythic* Version of the *Behistun* Inscription." [110].

"But when *Zeus* had driven the *Titans* from heaven, huge *Earth* bare her youngest child *Typhoeus* of the love of *Tartarus,* by the aid of golden *Aphrodite.*" [820]

"And in the bitterness of his anger *Zeus* cast him into wide *Tartarus.*" [Idem. 853]

Sophocles also followed *Hesiod*'s suit in "*Oedipus* at *Colonus*":

"So I pray and call
On the ancestral gloom of *Tartarus*
To snatch thee hence, on these dread goddesses
I call, and *Ares* who incensed you both
To mortal enmity." [1390]

"Hear, Goddess dread, invisible!
Monarch of the regions drear,
Aidoneus, hear, O hear!
By a gentle, tearless doom
Speed this stranger to the gloom,
Let him enter without pain
The all-shrouding *Stygian* plain.
Wrongfully in life oppressed,
Be he now by Justice blessed.
Queen infernal, and thou fell
Watch-dog of the gates of hell,
Who, as legends tell, dost glare,
Gnarling in thy cavernous lair
At all comers, let him go
Scathless to the fields below.
For thy master orders thus,
The son of earth and *Tartarus;*
In his den the monster keep,
Giver of eternal sleep." [Idem. 1560-1570]

In the interpretation of *Homer* and other *Greek, Latin* authors of antiquity, *Tartarus* was the abyss or hell where even the gods were scared to be in:

"...*Jove* called the gods in council on the topmost crest of serrated *Olympus*. Then he spoke and all the other gods gave ear. "Hear me," said he, "gods and goddesses, that I may speak even as I am minded. Let none of you neither goddess nor god try to cross me, but obey me every one of you that I may bring this matter to an end. If I see anyone acting apart and helping either *Trojans* or *Danaans*, he shall be beaten inordinately ere he come back again to *Olympus;* or I will hurl him down into dark *Tartarus* far into the deepest pit under the earth, where the gates are iron and the floor bronze, as far beneath *Hades* as heaven is high above the earth, that you may learn how much the mightiest I am among you." [*Homer*. "The Iliad." 8]

"'Tis here, in different paths, the way divides;
The right to *Pluto*'s golden palace guides;
The left to that unhappy region tends,
Which to the depth of *Tartarus* descends;
The seat of night profound, and punish'd fiends." [*Virgil*. "The Aeneid." 6]

"I come not
down here because of curiosity
to see the glooms of *Tartarus* and have
no thought to bind or strangle the three necks
of the *Medusan* Monster, vile with snakes." [*Ovid*. "Metamorphoses." 10.1-85]

"After these, *Earth* bore him the *Cyclopes,* to wit, *Arges, Steropes, Brontes,* of whom each had one eye on his forehead. But them *Sky* bound and cast into *Tartarus,* a gloomy place in *Hades* as far distant from earth as earth is distant from the sky." [*Apollodorus*. "Library." 1.1.2]

"And amongst the foremost *Cottus* and *Briareos* and *Gyes* insatiate for war raised fierce fighting: three hundred rocks, one upon another, they launched from their strong hands and overshadowed the *Titans* with their missiles, and hurled them beneath the wide-pathed earth, and bound them in bitter chains when they had conquered them by their strength for all their great spirit, as far beneath the earth as heaven is above earth; for so far is it from earth to *Tartarus*. For a brazen anvil falling down from heaven nine nights and days would reach the earth upon the tenth: and again, a brazen anvil falling from earth nine nights and days would reach *Tartarus* upon the tenth. Round it runs a fence of bronze, and night spreads in triple line all about it like a neck-circlet, while above grow the roots of the earth and unfruitful sea."
[*Hesiod*. "Theogonomy." 713-730]

"The first to introduce *Titans* into poetry was *Homer,* representing them as gods down in what is called *Tartarus;* the lines are in the passage about *Hera's* oath."
[*Pausanias*. "Description of *Greece*." 8.37]

"One of the chasms of the earth is greater than the rest, and is bored right through the whole earth; this is the one which *Homer* means when he says: "Far off, the lowest abyss beneath the earth;" and which elsewhere he and many other poets have called *Tartarus*."
[*Plato*. "Phaedo." 111e-112a]

"Now in the time of *Cronos* there was a law concerning mankind, and it holds to this very day amongst the gods, that every man who has passed a just and holy life departs after his decease to the *Isles of the Blest,* and dwells in all happiness apart from ill; but whoever has lived unjustly and impiously goes to the dungeon of requital and penance which, you know, they call *Tartarus*." [*Plato*. "Gorgias." 523a-523b]

"*Prometheus*. Oh if only he had hurled me below the earth, yes beneath *Hades,* the entertainer of the dead, into impassable *Tartarus,* and had ruthlessly fastened me in fetters no hand can loose, so that neither god nor any other might have gloated over this agony I feel!"
[*Aeschylus*. "Prometheus Bound." PB152]

Meanwhile, *Sophocles* and *Hesiod's* vision of *Tartarus* as a living deity, who had children with *Earth*, was echoed by *Apollodorus* and *Aristophanes:*

"When the gods had overcome the giants, *Earth,* still more enraged, had intercourse with *Tartarus* and brought forth *Typhon* in *Cilicia,* a hybrid between man and beast."
["Library." 1.6.3]

"Before the creation of Æther and Light,
Chaos and Night together were plight
In the dungeon of *Erebus* foully bedight.

> Nor Ocean, or Air, or Substance was there,
> Or solid or rare, or figure or form,
> But horrible *Tartarus* ruled in the storm." [*Aristophanes*. "The Birds." 701-706]

A quick look at the names of *Tartarus*, or *Tartaros* (Τάρταρος), his beloved *Earth*, aka *Ge* (Γῆ), and their offspring *Typhon*, or *Tufon* (Τυφῶν), brings an immediate association with their *Turkic* counterparts, thereby, confirms their *Turkic* origin:

- ❖ *Tartarus*, aka *Tartaros* > *Tartar, Tatar*: *Tart, Tat* 'rip, tear' + *Ar* 'warrior, hero, man', meaning "hero/warrior who rips others apart" in *Turkic*. The existence of two variants of the name – *Tartar* and *Tatar* is explained by the presence of both options in *Turkic*. The *Turkic* words *Tart* and *Tat* share the same definition [*Radlov*. 3.1.857, 901].

- ❖ *Ge* > *Çer, Çör, Sir, Jer, Yer* "Earth" in *Turkic*.

- ❖ *Typhon, Tufon* > *Tufan* "typhoon" in *Turkic*. By the way, the *English* word *Typhoon* was borrowed from *Turkic*.

Tartarus left its trace in the name of the river in *Italy*, presently known as *Tartaro*, according to *Tacitus*, *Pliny the Elder*, and *William Smith*:

> "Soon afterwards, *Cæcina* strongly fortified a camp between *Hostilia*, a village belonging to *Verona*, and the marshes of the river *Tartarus*, where his position was secure, as his rear was covered by the river, and his flank by intervening marshes." [*Tacitus*. "The History." 3.9]

> "We next come to the overflowing mouths of *Carbonaria*, and the *Fosses of Philistina*, by some called *Tartarus*, all of which originate in the overflow of the waters in the *Philistinian Canal*, swollen by the streams of the *Atesis*, descending from the *Tridentine Alps*, and of the *Togisonus*, flowing from the territory of the *Patavini*." [*Pliny the Elder*. "The Natural History." 3.20]

> "*Tartarus* (*Tartaro*), a river of *Venetia*, near the borders of *Gallia Transpadana*. It is intermediate mediate between the *Athesis* (*Adige*) and the *Padus* (*Po*); and its waters are now led aside by artificial canals partly into the one river and partly into the other, so that it may be called indifferently a tributary of either… The river is here still called the *Tartaro*: lower down it assumes the name of *Canal Bianco*, and after passing the town of *Adria*, and sending off part of its waters right and left into the *Po* and *Adige*, discharges the rest by the channel now known as the *Po di Levante*." [*William Smith*. – *Tartarus*]

Tartarus was also considered to be one-third of the physical, real world, in the opinion of *Ovid*:

> "The Gods of Heaven
> are overcome by thee; and *Jupiter*,
> and all the Deities that swim the deep,
> and the great ruler of the Water-Gods:
> why, then, should *Tartarus* escape our sway —
> the third part of the universe at stake —
> by which thy mother's empire and thy own
> may be enlarged according to great need." ["Metamorphoses." 5.378-385]

Strabo also supported *Ovid's* view of *Tartarus* as the tangible land on the map, not a poetic myth:

> "Now, since it is evident that night is ominous, and near to *Hades*, and *Hades* to *Tartarus*, it seems probable that [*Homer*], having heard of *Tartessus*, took thence the name of *Tartarus* to distinguish the farthest of the places beneath the earth, also embellishing it with fable in virtue of the poetic licence." [3.2.12]

This ancient *Turkic* name *Tartarus* was well known in *Biblical* times, too. It was mentioned in the *Hebrew* scriptures – Septugint of *Job*, *Enoch* dated 400-200 BCE, as well as in The First Epistle of *Peter* of the New Testament in the meaning of "hell":

> "*Uriel*, one of the holy angels, who is over the world and over *Tartarus*."
> ["The Book of *Enoch*, or 1 *Enoch*." 20.2]

> "For if God didn't spare angels when they sinned, but cast them down to *Tartarus,* and committed them to pits of darkness, to be reserved for judgment."
> [2. Peter. 2:4.WEB (The World English Bible)]

Under the name of *Tatár* "warrior/hero who tears to pieces", the ancient *Turkic* nation still exists and populates the *Republic* of *Tatarstan* in *Russia*. This *Tatar* nation ruled *Russia* until the 17th c. when Tsar *Petr* the *First* renamed *Moskoviya* into *Rus* (not to confuse with *Rus,* currently known as *Ukraine)*. On a side note, this tsar's mother was a *Tatar* princess *Naryshkina*.

In *Azerbaijan*, both options of this word – *Tartar* and *Tatar* exist as toponyms: the region of *Tartar* (*Tərtər*) and the village of *Tatar*. Back in the 19th c., the *Azerbaijanis* were also called "the *Caucasian Tatars*" by the *Russians*.

Moreover, it was the name of the large, if not the largest empire of the 18th c. in the world, known as *Grand Tartaria*, or *Tartary Magna*, or *Grande Tartarie*. The map "*Le Carte de l'Asie*", published in 1755 in *London* and shown below, as well as "Encyclopedia Britannica", dated 1771, confirm the existence of the 18th c. *Great Tartary:*

> "*Tartary*, a vast country in the northern parts of *Asia*, bounded by *Siberia* on the north and west: this is called *Great Tartary*. The *Tartars* who lie south of *Muscovy* and *Siberia,* are those of *Astracan, Circassia,* and *Dagistan,* situated north-west of the *Caspian*-sea; the *Calmuc Tartars*, who lie between *Siberia* and the *Caspian*-sea; the *Usbec Tartars* and *Moguls*, who lie north of *Persia* and *India;* and lastly, those of *Tibet*, who lie north-west of *China.*"
> ["Encyclopedia Britannica." 1771.3.887]

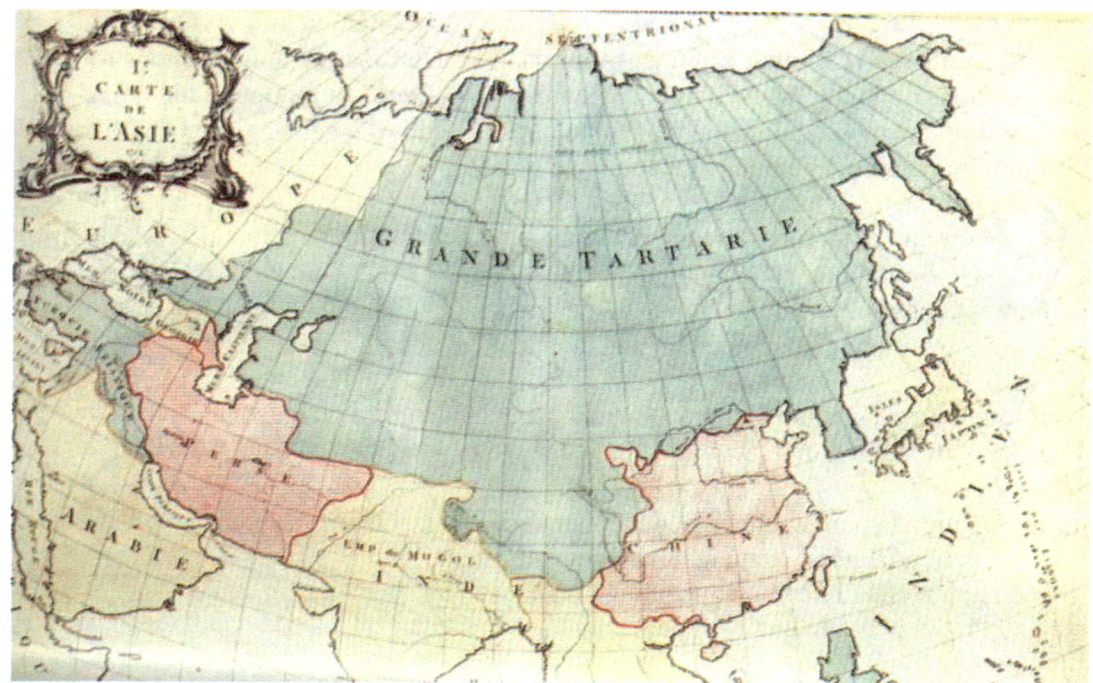

Figure 25. The map of Great Tartary. Palairet J. "Atlas Methodique, Compose pour l'Usage de son Altesse Serenissime Monseigneur le Prince d'Orange et de Nassau Stadhouder des Sept Provinces-Unis, etc. Par Jean Palairet, Agent de LL. HH. PP., Les Etats Generaux, a la Cour Britannique." Se Trouve a Londres, Chez Mess. J. Nourse & P. Vaillant dans le Strand; J. Neaulme a Amsterdam & a Berlin & P. Gosse a La Haye. 1755 [CCO]

This map reveals the greatest cover-up in the world history – how the *Russian* historians falsified their history by presenting the *Turkic* lands – *Tartary* as their own. Not a single history book or school textbook in *Russia*, and prior to that in the USSR, and prior to that in *Tsar Russia* of the 19th c. ever mentioned the name of this great *Turkic* country – *Tartary*, currently known as *Russia*. It is evident that around 300 years ago there was no *Russia* on the map. There was *Muscovy* – a small country of the *Russians* that occupied the territory of present-day *Moscow* and *Moscow* region.

The inhabitants of *Great Tartary* were mostly the *Turkic* peoples, known under the unanimous name of the *Tartars*, or *Tatars*. *Great Tartary* was one of many empires established by the *Turkic* nations.

Back in the 18th c., the *Turkic* nations controlled a major part of the world. At the time of *Great Tartary*'s existence, there were also other *Turkic* empires, such as the *Turkish Osman Empire* that spread from *Southeastern Europe*, *Western Asia*, the *Middle East* to *North Africa*, the *Turkic Moghul* (*Mogol*) Empire in *South Asia*, controlling *India*, *Bangladesh*, *Afghanistan*, and the *Turkic* Empire of the *Azerbaijanis* who ruled *Persia*, the *Caucasus*, and the surrounding territories. *China* was also under the subjection of the *Turkic* might by the *Uyghurs* and other related *Turkic* nations of that time.

Furthermore, out of 51 countries existing in the 10th c., reported by the anonymous *Persian* author of "Hudud Al-Alam" ("The Boundaries of the World"), 22 were populated and run by the *Turkic* peoples – *Adharbadhagan*, aka *Azerbaijan*, *Sarir*, *Alan*, *Khazar*, *Saqlab*, *Khazarian Pecheneg*, *M.rvat*, aka *Mirvat*, *Inner Bulghar*, *Majghar*, *Turkish Pecheneg*, *B.radas*, aka *Biradiz*, *Burtas*, aka *Bulghar*, *Khiphjaq*, *Ghuz*, *Kimak*, *Chigil*, *Tukhs*, *Khallukh*, *Yaghma*, *Tokuzghuz*, *Khyrkhyz*, *Transoxiana* (modern *Uzbekistan* with the cities *Bukhara*, *Paykand*, *Samarqand*, *Farghana* that was named "the Gateway of *Turkistan*" by the enigmatic author: *Kath* – "the capital of *Khowarazm* and the gateway of the *Ghuz Turkistan*. It is the hub of the goods of the *Turks*, *Turkistan*, *Transoxiana*, and the *Khazar*." [25.1-22]):

"The populated lands of the world ("ecumene") consist of fifty-one countries, of which five are located south of the Equator, viz., *Zaba*, *Zangistan*, *Habasha*, *Buja*, and *Nuba*. One western country, *Sudan,* is partly north and partly south, as it is crossed by the Equator. Forty-five countries are located on the northern side of the Populated Quarter, viz., *China, Tibet, Hindustan, Sindh, Khorasan* with its border regions, *Transoxiana* with its border areas, *Kirman, Pars,* the *Kargas-kuh* desert (spelled: *Karas-kuh*), *Daylaman, Khuzistan,* the *Jibal* province, *Iraq,* the lands of the *Arabs, Jazira, Adharbadhagan, Syria, Egypt, Maghrib, Spain, Rum,* the *Sarir,* the *Alan,* the *Khazar,* the *Saklab,* the *Khazar Pecheneg,* the *M.rvat,* the *Inner Bulgar,* the *Rus,* the *Madjgar,* the *N.ndr* (*V.n.nd.r*), the *Turkic Pecheneg,* the *B.radas,* the *Burtas,* the *Khiphjaq,* the *Ghuz,* the *Kimak,* the *Chigil,* the *Tukhs,* the *Khallukh,* the *Yagma,* the *Tokuzghuz,* and the *Khyrkhyz.* Each of these countries is subdivided into provinces, each of which has numerous cities." [139] [8.6]

We did not include *China* (the *Khotan, Kashghar* regions), *Tibet* (ruled by the *Tubbat* Khagan of *Turkic* ethnicity), *Khorasan* (the *Tukharistan* region, *Sakalkand, Sari*), country of *Rum* (modern *Turkey,* the *Bulghari), Sind* (modern *Pakistan* – the *Turan* region), *Daylaman* (*Gurgan, Abaskun, Turji, Kalar, Damghan*), *Rus* (ruled by *Rus* Khagan) in spite of the dominant *Turkic* presence in these countries.

The historical falsifications, revisions, and outright fraud with the only purpose in mind – to trash the *Turkic* nations, downgrade their importance in the world history, and even brazenly erase their history from the books by aggrandizing themselves and concocting new history for themselves by replacing the *Turkic* names with their own – these were the tools in the *Russian* and *Soviet* political box since the early 19th c. And CIA – (the Central Intelligence Agency) bore witness to this. The declassified CIA report "National cultural development under communism", dated 1957, states:

"Or let us take the matter of history, which, along with religion, language and literature, constitute the core of a people's cultural heritage. Here again the Communists have interfered in a shameless manner. For example, on 9 August 1944, the Central Committee of the Communist Party, sitting in *Moscow,* issued a directive ordering the party's *Tartar* Provincial Committee "to proceed to a scientific revision of the history of *Tartaria,* to liquidate serious shortcomings and mistakes of a nationalistic character committed by individual writers and historians in dealing with *Tartar* history." In other words, *Tartar* history was to be re-written –- let us be frank, was to be falsified —in order to eliminate references to Great *Russian* aggressions and to hide the facts of the real course of *Tartar-Russian* relations. And this was no isolated case. In every Muslim area within the *USSR,* historians, on orders of the Communist Party, have written history to distort the facts so that the *Russians* appear always in good light. Needless to say, histories which present the facts truthfully have been withdrawn and destroyed, so that the present and future generations of Muslims are forever denied the chance of learning the true facts of their nations' past."
[Document Number (FOIA) /ESDN (CREST): CIA-RDP78-02771R000200090002-6. p.9]
https://www.cia.gov/library/readingroom/document/cia-rdp78-02771r000200090002-6

This highly reputable CIA report also accused "Great *Russian* chauvinism" of "contempt for the rights of the minority people of the *Soviet Union*", the genocide of the entire peoples who were of *Turkic* extraction – the *Crimean Tatars, Balkars, Karachais, Kalmyks,* as well as other *Caucasian* peoples, such as the *Chechens, Ingushes:*

"Thus, already at the end of 1943…a decision was taken and executed concerning the deportation of all the *Karachai* from the lands on which they lived. In the same period, at the end of December 1943, the same lot befell the whole population of the *Autonomous Kalmyk Republic.* In March 1944 all the *Chechen* and *Ingush* peoples were deported and the *Chechen-Ingush Autonomous Republic* was liquidated. In April 1944 all *Balkars* were deported to faraway

---

[139] The text was translated into *English* by the author of the present book.

places. The *Ukrainians* avoided meeting this fate only because there were too many of them and there was no place to which to deport them." [Idem. 10-11]

Actually, the *Azerbaijanis* were also set to be deported to the *Kazakhstan* steppes. Luckily, the whole nation was saved by *Mirjafar Bagirov,* the First Secretary of the *Azerbaijan* Communist Party, the leader of the *Azerbaijan Republic*. After he learned about the imminent deportation of the *Azerbaijanis,* he flew to *Moscow* and met with *Stalin,* who had given this directive. *Bagirov* was the only person who was allowed to enter *Stalin's* office with his gun on him. According to *Bagirov's* recollections long after *Stalin's* passing, he rushed to exhort *Stalin* not to deport his people – the *Azerbaijanis*. In case if he failed, he was going to shoot *Stalin* down with his gun and sacrifice his own life to prevent the deportation and liquidation of the whole nation. Luckily, he managed to persuade *Stalin* to change his mind and keep the *Azerbaijani* nation in their native lands.

By the way, the *Azerbaijanis* were able to save another *Caucasian* people from imminent deportation – the *Dagestanis* thanks to the petition of the First Secretary of *Dagestan Aziz Aliyev* – the grandfather of the modern President of *Azerbaijan Ilham Aliyev*.

The CIA report also gave an account of the language discrimination in the *Soviet Union* that has a chilling resemblance to what has been happening towards the *Azerbaijanis* in *Iran* since the *Persian* chauvinists – *Reza Shah* and then *Ayatollah Khomeini* came to power in the 20th c., as well as towards the *Uyghurs* and other *Turkic* minority in *China*. Perhaps, the leading class in both countries studied well the *Russian* tactics and have been successfully applying them as of today against 40 million *Azerbaijanis* in *Iran* and 12 million *Uyghurs* in *China:*

> "Today, *Russian* is not only taught in all schools but also, through the force of political, economic and legal pressures, become the language of all business and social life in every part of the *Soviet Union*. Every *Soviet* citizen, regardless of his national origin, is compelled to make use of it if he is to achieve any success in his career, whatever that may be." [Idem. 7]

It will be naïve to say that the mistreatment of the *Turkic* nations took place only during the *Tsar* and *Communist* regimes. In "The Voyage of Master *Antony Jenkinson,* Made from the Citie of *Mosco* in *Russia,* to the Citie of *Boghar* in *Bactria,*[140] in the Yeere 1558: Written by Himselfe to the Merchants of *London* of the *Moscouie* Companie", *British* gentleman uncovered an ugly truth about cruelty and horrific acts of malice against the *Turkic* peoples in *Russia* of the 16th c.:

> "And at my being at the sayd *Astracan,* there was a great famine and plague among the people, and specially among the *Tartars* called *Nagayans,* who the same time came thither in great numbers to render themselves to the *Russes* their enimies, & to seeke succour a their hands, their countrey being destroyed, as I said before: but they were but ill entertained or relieved, for there died a great number of them for hunger, which lay all the Island through in heapes dead and like to beasts unburied, very pitifull to behold: many of them were also sold by the *Russes,* and the rest were banished from the Island. At that time it had bene an easie thing to have converted that wicked Nation to the *Christan* faith, if the *Russes* themselves had bene good *Christians*: but how should they shew compassion unto other Nations, when they are not mercifull unto their owne?" ["*Hakluyt's* Collection of the Early Voyages, Travels, and Discoveries, of the English Nation." 1.364]

---

[140] Present day city of *Bukhara* in *Uzbekistan*.

§ 11-6. THE SOLYMI, MILYAE, TERMILAE, LYCIANS, XANTHIOI, APHNEII.

Strabo considered the *Lycians*, also known as the *Aphneii*, or the *Aphneian Trojans*, as the sixth dynasty of the *Trojans*, quoting *Homer* on this matter:

> "...then the *Lycians* under the command of *Pandarus* he calls *Trojans;*
> "*Aphneian Trojans*, who inhabited *Zeleia* at the farthest extremity of *Ida*,
> who drink of the dark waters of *Æsepus*, these were led by *Pandarus*, the
> illustrious son of *Lycaon*." This is the sixth dynasty." [13.1.7]

> "These people he calls also *Lycians*. They had the name of *Aphneii*, it is thought, from the lake *Aphnitis*, for this is the name of the lake *Dascylitis*." [Idem. 3.1.10]

The *Lycians* inhabited a region on the southern coast of what is today modern *Turkey*, where the river *Æsepus* flowed from the foothills of the mountain *Ida*, at the present site of *Kurşuntepe* in *Turkey*, and emptied into the *Hellespont* in the vicinity of *Zeleia* – a city of *Lycian* foundation. *Homer* classified the *Lycians* as *Trojans:*

> "They that dwelt in *Telea* under the lowest spurs of *Mt. Ida,* men of substance, who drink the limpid waters of the *Aesepus*, and are of *Trojan* blood - these were led by *Pandarus* son of *Lycaon,* whom *Apollo* had taught to use the bow." ["The Iliad." 2]

Known in ancient times as the *Termilae,* the *Lycians* came to that region from *Crete,* as stated by *Herodotus:*

> "The *Lycians* furnished fifty ships. Their crews wore greaves and breastplates, while for arms they had bows of cornel wood, reed arrows without feathers, and javelins. Their outer garment was the skin of a goat, which hung from their shoulders; their head-dress a hat encircled with plumes; and besides their other weapons they carried daggers and falchions. This people came from *Crete*, and were once called *Termilae;* they got the name which they now bear from *Lycus*, the son of *Pandion,* an *Athenian*." [7.92]

However, *Herodotus* elucidated the matter by stating that back in the old times, *Crete* belonged to non-*Greeks:*

> "The *Lykians* however have sprung originally from *Crete* (for in old time the whole of *Crete* was possessed by Barbarians): and when the sons of *Europa, Sarpedon* and *Minos,* came to be at variance in *Crete* about the kingdom, *Minos* having got the better in the strife of parties drove out both *Sarpedon* himself and those of his party: and they having been expelled came to the land of *Milyas* in *Asia*, for the land which now the *Lykians* inhabit was anciently called *Milyas*, and the *Milyans* were then called *Solymoi*. Now while *Sarpedon* reigned over them, they were called by the name which they had when they came thither, and by which the *Lykians* are even now called by the neighbouring tribes, namely *Termilai;* but when from *Athens Lycos* the son of *Pandion* came to the land of the *Termilai* and to *Sarpedon*, he too having been driven out by his brother namely *Aigeus*, then by the name taken from *Lycos* they were called after a time *Lykians*." [1.173]

Strabo also confirmed that *Lycians* had many more ancient names, such as *Milyae* and before that – *Solymi:*

"...*Sarpedon*, brother of *Minos* and *Rhadamanthus*...gave the name of *Termilae* to the people formerly called *Milyae,* and still more anciently *Solymi.*" [12.8.5]

The *Lycians* were recognized under several appellations that proved to be of *Turkic* extraction:

➢ *Lukioi* = Λύκιοι > *Lükə* "rain drop" in *Turkic*.

➢ *Aphneioi* = Ἀφνειοί: *Aph* > *Əp* 'hurry, move with haste' + *Nei* > *-Ən* 'an affix, denoting constant action', meaning "those who hasten" in *Turkic*.

➢ *Milúai* = Μιλύαι, aka *Milyae* > *Milí* "brainy, intelligent" in *Turkic*.

➢ *Termilai* = Τερμίλαι, aka *Termilae:* *Ter* > *Tərə* 'fresh, new' + *Milai, Milae* > *Milí* 'brainy, intelligent', meaning "new smart tribe" in *Turkic*. As *Strabo* noted, *Termilai* was a new name of the *Miluai*. Both of them carry the same *Turkic* root *Milí*. With the added *Ter* at the beginning of the name, the tribe acquired an additional connotation – "new". As such, the name of the *Termilai* signified that they were a new division of the *Miluai*.

➢ *Solumoi* = Σόλυμοι, aka *Solymi: Sol* > *Söl* 'wilderness' + *Um, Ym* > *Uma* 'people', meaning "people from the wilderness" in *Turkic*.

➢ *Xanthioi* = Ξάνθιοι, aka *Cisianthi,* aka *Dahæ: Ks, Cis* > *Kis* 'cut, slash' + *An, Ian* > *-Ən* 'an affix, denoting constant action' + *Thi* > *Tui* 'people', meaning "tribe of slashers or slayers" in *Turkic*. The nation of the *Xanthioi,* also known as the *Dahæ* and the *Cisianthi,* was initially a *Scythian* tribe, recognized later as the *Thracians* and the *Trojans*.
In "The Iliad", *Homer* named two armed forces of *Lycians,* who participated in the *Trojan* war – one was led by *Pandarus* and the other – by *Sarpedon:*
"*Sarpedon* and *Glaucus* led the *Lycians* from their distant land, by the eddying waters of the *Xanthus*." [2]
In the opinion of *Herodotus,* the *Lycians,* who inhabited *Xanthos,* were acknowledged as the *Xanthioi:*
"After a time the *Pedasians* were conquered; and the *Lykians,* when *Harpagos* marched his army into the plain of *Xanthos,* came out against him and fought, few against many, and displayed proofs of valour; but being defeated and confined within their city, they gathered together into the citadel their wives and their children, their property and their servants, and after that they set fire to this citadel, so that it was all in flames, and having done so and sworn terrible oaths with one another, they went forth against the enemy and were slain in fight, that is to say all the men of *Xanthos:* and of the *Xanthians* who now claim to be *Lykians* the greater number have come in from abroad, except only eighty households; but these eighty households happened at that time to be away from their native place, and so they escaped destruction." [1.176]
According to *Strabo's* observations, there were several *Xanthian*-related *Thracian* and *Trojan* ethnonyms, toponyms, and hydronyms:
"There are many names common to *Thracians* and *Trojans,* as *Scei*, a *Thracian* tribe, a river *Sceus,* a *Scæn* wall, and in *Troy, Scæan* gates. There are *Thracians* called *Xanthii,* and a river *Xanthus* in *Troja...*" [13.1.21]
Xanthus was not only the name of the river in *Troy* – it was the capital city of ancient *Lycia* – present-day *Kınık* near the river *Eşen Çayı* on the southern coast of *Turkey*.
The fact that besides the *Lycian* tribe, *Xanthioi* was also the name of *Thracian* and *Scythian* tribes, (the latter is additionally known as the *Dahæ*), confirms the point that all three tribes were the bees from the same hive.

Strabo also ascertained that the *Lycians* were split into two tribes under the same name:

> "Two tribes bearing the name of *Lycians*, lead us to suppose that they are the same race; either the *Trojan Lycians* sent colonies to the *Carians*, or the *Carian Lycians* to the *Trojans*. Perhaps the same may be the case with the *Cilicians*, for they also are divided into two tribes; but we have not the same evidence that the present *Cilicians* existed before the *Trojan* times. *Telephus* may be supposed to have come with his mother from *Arcadia;* by her marriage with *Teuthras,* (who had received them as his guests,) *Telephus* was admitted into the leges, it is said, settled on the continent with the assistance of the *Cretans*. They built *Miletus*, of which the founder was *Sarpedon* from *Miletus* in *Crete*. They settled the colony of *Termite* in the present *Lycia*, but, according to *Herodotus*, these people were a colony from *Crete* under the conduct of *Sarpedon*, brother of *Minos* and *Rhadamanthus*, who gave the name of *Termilae* to the people formerly called *Milyae*, and still more anciently *Solymi;* when, however, *Lycus* the son of *Pandion* arrived, he called them *Lycii* after his own name. This account shows that the *Solymi* and *Lycians* were the same people, but the poet distinguishes them. He represents *Bellerophon* setting out from *Lycia,* and "fighting with the renowned *Solymi*." He says *Peisander*, his son, *Mars* "slew when fighting with the *Solymi*," and speaks of *Sarpedon* as a native of *Lycia*." [12.8.4-5]

One particular custom of the *Lycians* was similar to that of the *Etruscans,* according to *Herodotus:*

> "The customs which these have are partly *Cretan* and partly *Carian;* but one custom they have which is peculiar to them, and in which they agree with no other people, that is they call themselves by their mothers and not by their fathers; and if one asks his neighbour who he is, he will state his parentage on the mother's side and enumerate his mother's female ascendants: and if a woman who is a citizen marry a slave, the children are accounted to be of gentle birth; but if a man who is a citizen, though he were the first man among them, have a slave for wife or concubine, the children are without civil rights." [1.173]

As far as the gods that the *Trojans,* in general, and the *Lycians,* in particular, worshipped and sought help from, *Apollo* – the god of arts and the lyre, was the most devoted to them and tried to help them win by all available means over the *Danaans* in the *Trojan* War, as asserted by *Homer* and *Ovid:*

> "When, therefore, *Minerva* saw these men making havoc of the *Argives*, she darted down to *Ilius* from the summits of *Olympus*, and *Apollo*, who was looking on from *Pergamus*, went out to meet her; for he wanted the *Trojans* to be victorious."
> ["The Iliad." 7]
>
> "*Mulciber* was arrayed against *Troy;*
> *Apollo* was for *Troy*…"
> [*Ovid*. "Tristia." 1.2.1-10]

Homer in "The Iliad" called this god "*Lycian Apollo*":

> "He laid the arrow on the string and prayed to *Lycian Apollo,* the famous archer, vowing that when he got home to his strong city of *Zelea* he would offer a hecatomb of firstling lambs in his honour."
> ["The Iliad." 4]

§ 11-7. THE PAPHLAGONIANS, CAUCONIANS, MARIANDYNI, LIGUES, MATIENOI, CAPPADOCIANS, HENETI.

Entitled by *Homer* as "the brave *Paphlagonians*", they were the ones who came to the rescue of the brotherly nation of *Troy* in their epic war against the *Greco-Danaans*:

> "And the *Paphlagonians* were commanded by stout-hearted *Pylaemenes* from the land of the *Enetoi*, where the mules run wild in herds. These were they that held *Cytorus* and the country round *Sesamon*, with the cities by the *Parthenius, Cromna, Aegialus,* and lofty *Erythini*."
> ["Iliad." 2.850-855]

Homer did not enounce the name of the place where they came from by limiting himself to "the land of the *Enetoi*" without going into any further detail. The *Enetoi* were the most prominent tribe among the *Paphlagonians*:

> "But the account most generally received is, that the *Heneti* were the most considerable tribe of the *Paphlagonians*; that *Pylaemenes* was descended from it; that a large body of this people accompanied him to the *Trojan* war; that when they had lost their leader they passed over to *Thrace* upon the capture of *Troy*; and in the course of their wanderings arrived at the present *Henetic* territory. Some writers say that both *Antenor* and his sons participated in this expedition, and settled at the inner recess of the gulf of *Adria*, as we have said in the description of *Italy*. It is probable that this was the cause of the extinction of the *Heneti*, and that they were no longer to be found in *Paphlagonia*." [*Strabo.* 12.3.8]

As reported by *Herodotus*, the *Enetoi* (translated into *English* as the *Henetes*) were the descendants of the *Medes*:

> "Next adjoining to these, are the *Henetes*, who dwell in *Adria*, and say they are a colony of the *Medes*." [5.9]

In view of this fact, the *Paphlagonians* and their other branches – the *Cauconians*, the *Ligues*, the *Matienoi*, the *Mariandunoi*, the *Cappadocians*, or the *Kappadokai*, should all be considered as the *Median* progeny.

While narrating about the *Mede-Thrace-Trojan* nation of the *Paphlagonians* and the people related to them, it will be a sin not to mention an interesting fact, unearthed by the translator of *Strabo's* book – *Horace Leonard Jones*. According to him, *Strabo* himself was a *Paphlagonian* "of *Asiatic* blood". He was not a pure *Greek,* though his learned tongue and educational background were:

> "A further proof of the existence of *Asiatic* blood in the veins of *Strabo* is the name of his kinsman *Tibius*; for, says *Strabo*, the *Athenians* gave to their slaves the names of the nations from which they came, or else the names that were most current in the countries from which they came; for instance, if the slave were a *Paphlagonian*, the *Athenians* would call him *Tibius*. Thus it appears that *Strabo* was of mixed lineage, and that he was descended from illustrious *Greeks* and *Asiatics* who had served the kings of *Pontus* as generals, satraps, and priests of *Ma*. But by language and education he was thoroughly *Greek*." [1.xiv]

When considering the above-mentioned inference about the *Paphlagonians* as the colony of the *Medes*, who were of *Turkic* origin, a clear-cut conclusion emerges out of it that *Strabo* had *Turkic* blood running in his veins.

The etymological and lexical dissection of the tribal names belonging to the currently discussed group of the *Trojan* nations swiftly exposed their *Turkic* roots:

- *Paphlagones* = Παφλαγόνες, aka *Paphlagonians*, aka *Pylaimenes* = Πυλαιμένης, aka *Pylæmenes:*
  - *Paphlagones*: Paphla > Pəpilə 'pamper, coddle' + Gon > Kon 'live', meaning "people, leading pampered life" or "comfort-loving people" in *Turkic*.
  - *Pylaimenes, Pylæmenes*: Pulai, Pylæ > Pülə 'light' + Men > Men, Mən 'I', meaning "I am the light" in *Turkic*. The name of this *Paphlagonian* tribe, obtained from the *Trojan* hero, was built on the same principle as other names of *Turkic* origin, enumerated below:

Pylaimenes	>	Pylai	+ Men + -Es
Markomanoi	>	Marko	+ Man = -Oi
Turkmən	>	Turk	+ Mən
Naimən	>	Nai	+ Mən
German	>	Ger	+ Man
Burman	>	Bur	+ Man
Ottoman	>	Otto	+ Man

The *Paphlagonian* tribe, as well as its country, obtained their name after their leader *Paphlagon* (Παφλαγών "leading pampered life" in *Turkic*), who was a great-great-grandson of the *Pelasgi-Thracian Io* through his father *Phineus* (Φινεύς) – son of *Belos*, who, in his turn, was the son of *Libya* – the daughter of *Epaphos*, or *Apis*, and a granddaughter of *Io*.

However, earlier than that, the country of *Paphlagonia* and the name of the tribe used to be known as *Pylaimenia* (or *Pylæmenia*) and *Pylaimenes* respectively after *Pylaimenes* – the commander of the *Paphlagonians* during the *Trojan* War:

> "Beyond this river begins the nation of *Paphlagonia*, by some writers called *Pylæmenia*; it is closed in behind by the country of *Galatia*." [Pliny the Elder. 6.2]

The way how the *Paphlagonians* were equipped for the war, based on *Herodotus's* testimony, shows close similarities with the *Phrygians*, the *Lydians*, the *Mysians*, the *Scythians*, the *Thracians*, the *Medes*, the *Bactrians*, as well as the *Ligyes*, the *Matieni*, the *Mariandyni*, and the *Cappadocians*, who had the exact military equipment as the *Paphlagonians*:

> "The *Paphlagonians* in the army had woven helmets on their heads, and small shields and short spears, and also javelins and daggers; they wore their native shoes that reach midway to the knee. The *Ligyes* and *Matieni* and *Mariandyni* and *Syrians* were equipped like the *Paphlagonians*. These *Syrians* are called by the *Persians Cappadocians*. *Dotus* son of *Megasidrus* was commander of the *Paphlagonians* and *Matieni*, *Gobryas* son of *Darius* and *Artystone* of the *Mariandyni* and *Ligyes* and *Syrians*." [7.72]

The *Paphlagonians* carried small shields, like the *Lydians* and the *Mysians*; short spears, like the *Bactrians*, the *Parthians*, the *Chorasmians*, the *Sogdians*, the *Gandatians*, and the *Dadicans*; the javelins like the *Thracians* and the *Mysians*; the daggers like the *Thracians*, the *Scythians*, and the *Medes* [7.62-74]. By the way, though the *Persians* were dressed and equipped in the same manner as the *Medes*, *Herodotus* pointed out that it was not their native clothing or weapons, as they copied it all directly from the *Medes* [7.62].

Xenophon in "Anabasis" described the *Paphlagonian* helmets as tiaras, the design of which matched the same of the *Medes*:

> "They wore short tunics which did not reach their knees and were as thick as a linen bag for bedclothes, and upon their heads leathern helmets just such as the *Paphlagonian* helmets, with a tuft in the middle very like a tiara in shape; and they had also iron battle-axes." [5.4.13]

Judging from the remnants of the *Scythian* burial in *Kazakhstan*, discussed earlier in this book, it seems that the *Paphlagonians* were donned in indigenous boots that matched the *Scythian* design – reaching up to the middle of the shin, worn by the *Scythians*. This fact presents vivid evidence of the profound path leading the *Paphlagonians* to their *Scythian* forefathers. This should not strike as a shocker, for one of the *Paphlagonian* tribes – the *Caucones* were considered by some ancient experts as the *Scythians:*

> "The *Caucones,* who, according to history, inhabited the line of sea-coast which extends from the *Mariandyni* as far as the river *Parthenius,* and to whom belonged the city *Tieium,* are said by some writers to be *Scythians,* by others a tribe of *Macedonians,* and by others a tribe of *Pelasgi."* [*Strabo.* 12.3.5]

Actually, all the ancient experts who considered them to be of *Pelasgian* or *Macedonian* origin were right, as these nations were related to each other, sharing the same *Scythian* root, which is equal to the *Turkic* one.

According to *Xenophon,* the *Paphlagonians* had an excellent cavalry which was a common feature for all the *Scythian* descendants – from the *Medes* to the *Thracians* nations:

> "Secondly, I know that they have plains and a cavalry which the barbarians themselves regard as superior to the whole of the King's cavalry." [5.6.8]

➢ *Caucones = Καύκωνες,* aka *Cauconians,* aka *Kaukoniatai = Καυκωνιάται,* aka *Cauconiatae,* aka *Kaukoensioi = Καυκοηνσιοι,* aka *Caucoenses:*

- *Cauconians, Caucones: Cau > Kav* 'drive out' + *Con > Kon* 'live', meaning "drive others away and settle in their places" in *Turkic.* Most likely, the *Cauconians* were named after their chief *Caucon,* as it was customary in ancient times. *Strabo* confirmed this possibility:

  > "But *Caucones* were masters of both these tracts, and even of the *Macistus,* which some call *Platanistus.* The town has the same name as the territory. It is said, that in the *Lepreatis* there is even a monument of a *Caucon,* who had the name of the nation, either because he was a chief, or for some other reason." [8.3.16]

- *Cauconiatae, Kaukoniatai: Cau > Kav* 'drive out' + *Con > Kon* 'live' + *Atae, Atai > Atai* 'patriarch', meaning "leading tribe that drives others away and settles in their places" in *Turkic.* By the way, there were a number of the *Scythian, Germanic, Illyrian,* and *Turkic* tribes that contained the lexical component *Atai* in their tribal names, such as *Zakatai, Zaratai, Aukatai, Paralatai, Karatai* (*Scythians* and *Sarmats*); *Rakatai* (a *Germanic* tribe); *Dalmatai* (an *Illyrian* tribe); *Karatai, Chagatai* (*Çağatai*) – the *Turkic* tribes, the appellation of which also served as a *Turkic* male name [*Radlov.* 4.1.15]).

- *Kaukoensioi, Caucoenses: Kau, Cau > Kav* 'drive out' + *Koen, Coen, Kon > Kon* 'live' + *Sioi, Ses > Soi* 'tribe', meaning "tribe that drives others away and settles in their places" in *Turkic.* The *Dacian* tribe of the *Kaukoensioi* and the *Trojan* tribe of the *Caucones,* as well as their derivative – the *Cauconiatae,* represented the same ethnic group of the *Scythian* extraction.

The *Paphlagonian* tribe of the *Caucones* was a part of the *Trojan* contingent against the *Greco-Danaan* forces, mentioned separately from the *Paphlagonians* by *Homer.* Though *Homer* did not include them into the list of "The *Trojan* leaders and contingents", the poet stated their presence in few remarks:

> "To the seaward lie the *Carians,* the *Paeonian* bowmen, the *Leleges,* the *Cauconians,* and the noble *Pelasgi."* ["The Iliad." 10]

In comparison to *Homer's* scarce notes, *Strabo* was generous enough to put the *Cauconians* in a larger frame and described them as a nomadic tribe akin to their *Pelasgic* brethren:

> "There are several accounts of the *Cauconians;* for it is said that, like the *Pelasgians,* they were an *Arcadian* tribe, and, again like the *Pelasgians,* that they were a wandering tribe. At any rate, the poet tells us that they came to *Troy* as allies of the *Trojans.* But he does not say whence they come, though they seem to have come from *Paphlagonia;* for in *Paphlagonia* there is a people called *Cauconiatae* whose territory borders on that of the *Mariandyni,* who are themselves *Paphlagonians.* But I shall speak of them at greater length when I come to my description of that region. At present I must add the following to my account of the *Cauconians* in

Triphylia. Some say that the whole of what is now called *Eleia*, from *Messenia* as far as *Dymê*, was called *Cauconia*. *Antimachus*, at any rate, calls all the inhabitants both *Epeians* and *Cauconians*. Others, however, say that the *Cauconians* did not occupy the whole of *Eleia*, but lived there in two separate divisions, one division in *Triphylia* near *Messenia*, and the other in *Buprasis* and *Coelê Elis* near *Dymê*. And *Aristotle* has knowledge of their having been established at this latter place especially." [8.3.17]

"This disposition, however, showed itself before the time of the *Trojan* war; for there existed then tribes of *Pelasgi*, *Caucones*, and *Leleges*, who are said to have wandered, anciently, over various parts of *Europe*. The poet represents them as assisting the *Trojans*, but not as coming from the opposite coast." [12.8.4]

Strabo first asserted that "...the race of the *Caucones* has everywhere entirely disappeared..." [12.3.9], but later added that during his time the *Cauconian* remnants still existed:

"But the tribe of the *Caucones* about *Tieium* extends to the *Parthenius*; that of the *Heneti*, who occupy *Cytorum*, immediately follows the *Parthenius*, and even at present some *Caucones* are living about the *Parthenius*." [12.3.5]

➤ *Mariandyni*, aka *Mariandunoi* = Μαριανδυνοί: Mar 'hill' + Ian > Yan 'side' + Dyn, Dun > Dan 'from', meaning "from the hillside" or "mountaineer" in *Turkic*. The leader of the *Trojan* tribe – *Mariandynos* (Μαριανδυνός) in line with an ancient custom, imparted his name on his tribe and the land it occupied:

"*Theopompus* says that *Mariandynos*, who governed a part of *Paphlagonia*, which was subject to many masters, invaded and obtained possession of the country of the *Bebryces*, and that he gave his own name to the territory which he had before occupied. It is also said that the *Milesians* who first founded *Heracleia*, compelled the *Mariandyni*, the former possessors of the place, to serve as *Helots*, and even sold them, but not beyond the boundaries of their country. For they were sold on the same conditions as the class of persons called *Mnoans*, who were slaves to the *Cretans*, and the *Penestæ*, who were slaves of the *Thessalians*." [*Strabo*. 12.3.4]

Strabo asserted that "the *Mariandyni*, who are themselves *Paphlagonians*" [8.3.17] were acknowledged by some of his peers as the *Caucones* – "the next to the *Mariandyni* (by some also called *Caucones*)" [12.3.4].

He also noted that both the *Mariandyni* and the *Caucones* resembled the *Bithynians* in everything and spoke the language identical to *Bithynian*. By this, the renowned scholar gave us a strong signal that all the *Paphlagonian* tribes of the *Trojan* group automatically should be considered as *Thracians*:

"There is not, however, the same agreement among writers with regard to the *Mariandyni*, and the *Caucones*. For they say that *Heracleia* is situated among the *Mariandyni*, and was founded by *Milesians*. But who they are, or whence they came, nothing is said. There is no difference in language, nor any other apparent national distinction between them and the *Bithynians*, whom they resemble in all respects. It is probable therefore the *Mariandyni* were a *Thracian* tribe." [12.3.4]

"Even the *Phrygians* themselves are the same as the *Briges*, a people of *Thrace*, as also are the *Mygdones*, the *Bebryces*, the *Maedobithyni*, the *Bithyni*, the *Thyni*, and, as I consider, also are the *Mariandyni*." [7.3.2]

The same principle applies to other tribes – the *Ligues*, the *Matienoi*, and the *Cappadocians*, mentioned by *Herodotus* in the conjunction with the *Mariandyni* and the *Paphlagonians* [7.72].

➤ *Ligues* = Λίγυες > Liq "brimful, jampacked" in *Turkic* [*Schwarz*. 866] and [R.3.1.756]. From the definition serving as a cue, it becomes clear that this tribe had much manpower.

- *Matienoi* = Ματιηνοì: *Mat* 'honest' + *Ien* > *Yən* 'soul', meaning "honest tribe" in *Turkic*.

- *Cappadocians*, aka *Kappadokai*= Καππαδόκαι, aka *Suroi* = Σύροι, aka *Surioi* = Σύριοι, aka *Syrians*, aka *Leucosyri*, aka *Leukosuroi* = Λευκόσυροι:
  - *Kappad* > *Kappidə* 'suddenly' [141] + *Doc, Dok* > *Doğ* 'appear, be born, ascend', meaning "swiftly ascending tribe" in *Turkic*.

  - *Syrians, Suroi, Surioi* > *Sur* "reign" in *Turkic*. According to *Plutarch*, the *Suroi* were named after their founder, *Apollo's* son *Syros*, or *Suros* (Σύρος):
    > "These *Syrians* who were in possession of the city were descended, as it is said, from *Syros*, the son of *Apollo* and *Sinopé*, the daughter of *Asopis*." ["*Lucullus*." 23]

  - *Leucosyri, Leukosuroi*: *Leuco, Leuko* 'white' in *Greek* + *Sur* 'reign', meaning "tribe of the white *Syri*" in *Turkic*.

The *Cappadocians* are classified as a *Paphlagonian* tribe due to *Herodotus's* report about these two tribes, dressed and equipped similarly and grouped into one military division. However, *Herodotus* also acknowledged them as the *Syrians*. Moreover, the author also recognized another nation – the *Assyrians* as the *Syrians*:

> "The *Assyrians* served with helmets about their heads made of bronze or plaited in a Barbarian style which it is not easy to describe; and they had shields and spears, and daggers like the *Egyptian* knives, and moreover they had wooden clubs with knobs of iron, and corslets of linen. These are by the *Hellenes* called *Syrians*, but by the Barbarians they have been called always *Assyrians*: and the commander of them was *Otaspes* the son of *Artachaies*." [7.63]

> "Now the *Cappadokians* are called by the *Hellenes Syrians*; and these *Syrians*, before the *Persians* had rule, were subjects of the *Medes*, but at this time they were subjects of *Cyrus*." [1.72]

The dubious statements provided by *Herodotus* about two types of *Syrians* – the *Cappadocians* and the *Assyrians*, were effortlessly explained by *Strabo*. He documented them as two distinct nations, distinguished by the color of their skin – the *Cappadocians* being of light skin and consequently, obtained the appellation 'white', or *Leucosyri*, while the other *Syrians* had a dark complexion:

> "The boundary of the *Paphlagonians* to the east is the river *Halys*, which flows from the south between the *Syrians* and the *Paphlagonians*; and according to *Herodotus*, (who means *Cappadocians*, when he is speaking of *Syrians*,) discharges itself into the *Euxine Sea*. Even at present they are called *Leuco-Syrians*, (or White *Syrians*,) while those without the *Taurus* are called *Syrians*. In comparison with the people within the *Taurus*, the latter have a burnt complexion; but the former, not having it, received the appellation of *Leuco-Syrians* (or White *Syrians*). *Pindar* says that the *Amazons* commanded a *Syrian* band, armed with spears with broad iron heads; thus designating the people that lived at *Themiscyra*. *Themiscyra* belongs to the *Amiseni*, and the district of the *Amiseni* to the *Leuco-Syrians* settled beyond the *Halys*." [12.3.9]

Strabo also noted that the *Greeks*, just like the *Persians*, as recorded by *Herodotus*, recognized these *Syrians* as the *Cappadocians*:

> "We have already spoken of these people elsewhere. *Callisthenes* in his comment upon the enumeration of the ships inserts after this verse,
> "*Cromna, Aegialus,* and the lofty *Erythini,*"
> these lines,
> "The brave son of *Polycles* led the *Caucones*,
> Who inhabited the well-known dwellings about the river *Parthenius*,"

---

[141] *Schwarz H.G.* "*An Uyghur-English* Dictionary." [674].

for the territory extends from *Heracleia,* and the *Mariandyni* as far as the *Leucosyri,* whom we call *Cappadocians."* [12.3.5]

The renowned *Greek* geographer also called attention to the fact that the *Cappadocians* used the *Paphlagonian* names in abundance:

"Nor is there any foundation for the opinion, that all the ancients agree that no people from the country beyond the *Halys* took part in the *Trojan* war. Testimony may be found to the contrary. *Mæandrius* at least says that *Heneti* came from the country of the *Leuco-Syrians* to assist the *Trojans* in the war; that they set sail thence with the *Thracians,* and settled about the recess of the *Adriatic;* and that the *Heneti,* who had no place in the expedition, were *Cappadocians.* This account seems to agree with the circumstance, that the people inhabiting the whole of that part of *Cappadocia* near the *Halys,* which extends along *Paphlagonia,* speak two dialects, and that their language abounds with *Paphlagonian* names, as *Bagas, Biasas, Æniates, Rhatotes, Zardoces, Tibius, Gasys, Oligasys,* and *Manes.* For these names are frequently to be found in the *Bamonitis,* the *Pimolitis,* the *Gazaluitis,* and *Gazacene,* and in most of the other districts. *Apollodorus* himself quotes the words of *Homer,* altered by *Zenodotus;* from *Henete,* whence comes a race of wild mules, and says, that *Hecatæus* the *Milesian* understands *Henete* to mean *Amisus.* But we have shown that *Amisus* belongs to the *Leuco-Syrians,* and is situated beyond the *Halys.* He also somewhere says that the poet obtained his knowledge of the *Paphlagonians,* situated in the interior, from persons who had travelled through the country on foot, but that he was not acquainted with the seacoast any more than with the rest of the territory of *Pontus;* for otherwise he would have mentioned it by name. We may, on the contrary, after the description which has just been given of the country, retort and say that he has traversed the whole of the seacoast, and has omitted nothing worthy of record which existed at that time. It is not surprising that he does not mention *Heracleia, Amastris,* or *Sinope,* for they were not founded; nor is it strange that he should omit to speak of the interior of the country; nor is it a proof of ignorance not to specify by name many places which were well known, as we have shown in a preceding part of this work." [12.3.25-26]

The *Paphlagonian* names with the endings *-Es, -Us, -Os, -As* (from *Us* "master, chief" in *Turkic*), enumerated above by *Strabo* expose their *Turkic* roots:

- *Bagas* = Βάγας: Baga > Baǧa 'courageous' + As > Us 'master', meaning "courageous master" in *Turkic*. This name was a part of the *Turkic* name *Baǧatur* "courageous *Tur*", "hero".
- *Biasas* = Βιάσας: Bi 'wise' + As > Əs 'mind' + As > Us 'master', meaning "master of wise mind" in *Turkic*.
- *Æniates,* or *Ainiates* = Αινιάτης: Aeni, Aini > Aini 'equal' + At 'glory' + Es > Us 'master', meaning "fair and glorious master" in *Turkic*.
- *Rhatotes* = Ρατώτης: Rhat > Ört 'light, flame' + Ot 'fire' + Es > Us 'master', meaning "master of light and fire" in *Turkic*. The available *Turkic* equivalent *Rat* "remove" is not suitable for this occasion.
- *Zardoces* = Ζαρδώκης: Zar 'strong hope'[142] + Doc > Dök 'pour, disseminate' + Es > Us 'master', meaning "chief that instills strong hope" or "chief that inspires" in *Turkic*.
- *Tibius,* or *Tibios* = Τίβιος: Tibi > Tip 'very straight' + Us, Os > Us 'master', meaning "honest master" in *Turkic*.
- *Gasys, Gasus* = Γάσυς: Gas > Qazi 'fearless, brave' + Ys, Us > Us 'master', meaning "brave master" in *Turkic*.
- *Oligasys* = Ὀλίγασυς: Oli > Ölö 'great' + Gas > Qazi 'brave' + Ys > Us 'master', meaning "great, brave master" in *Turkic*.
- *Manes* = Μάνης: Man 'great, big'[143] + Es > Us 'master', meaning "great master" in *Turkic*.

---

[142] *Schwarz H.G.* "An *Uyghur-English* Dictionary." [550].
[143] *Egorov V.G.* "Etimologicheskiy slovar chuvashskogo yazika." [130].

As far as the *Leuco-Syrians* and the *Syrians* of *Strabo*, as well as the *Syrians* and the *Assyrians* of *Herodotus*, it is evident that the *Leuco-Syrians* of *Strabo* and the *Syrians* of *Herodotus* were of the *Scythe-Thrace-Turkic* origin, while the *Syrians* of *Strabo* and the *Assyrians* of *Herodotus* belonged to the *Semitic* family. This assertion is based on the work of the renowned linguist of the 19th c. *Major C.R. Conder*, published in the highly reputable "Journal of the Anthropological Institute of Great Britain and Ireland." The *British* scholar discovered two races that lived in *Syria* as far back as the 16th c. BCE – the *Semitic* (*Arabic*) and the *Turkic*:

> "…As early as 1600 B.C., at least, there were two races in *Syria* and *Palestine* known to the *Egyptians*. One of these was a *Semitic* race, speaking a language akin to *Hebrew* and *Phoenician*, and represented with *Semitic* features on the monuments…It is not, however, with this *Semitic* population — the existence of which is proven beyond dispute — that we are now concerned, but with that other population, the contemporary existence of which, especially in the north between *Damascus* and *Aleppo*, is equally undoubted. The names of the towns conquered by *Thothmes III*, about 1600 B.C., in this region, are (as *Chabas* pointed out) not *Semitic* and not *Aryan*…Several very distinctive *Turko-Tatar* words form often repeated elements of these names, among which I may mention as perhaps most clear: <u>Tami</u> for a "building", <u>Su</u> for "water", and <u>Tep</u> for a "hill." In this respect, therefore, the *Syria* of 3,500 years ago differs little from the *Syria* of to-day, when the same mixed nomenclature, *Arab* and *Turkoman*, is recognisable in the geographical names…" [32]

As a reminder, this was stated back in the 19th century. Today, in the 21st century, nothing has changed – both the *Arabs* and the *Turkomans* (the *Turkic* nation) inhabit the currently war-torn land of *Syria*, just like many thousand years ago their ancestors did.

➤ <u>Heneti, aka *Veneti*, aka *Ouenetoi* = Ουενετοι, aka *Enetoi* = Ἐνετοί, aka *Enetii*, aka *Henetes*:</u> Hen, Ven, Ouen, En > En 'mark' + Et 'do, make', meaning "tribe that leaves its mark" in *Turkic*.
Strabo considered the *Paphlagonians* and the *Cauconians* of the same stock, inhabiting the land of the *Heneti*, or the *Henetes* – the colony of the *Medes*, by the river *Parthenius*.
As earlier mentioned, this tribe was introduced by *Herodotus* as the *Enetoi* – a colony of the *Medes* [5.9], by *Gotus Iordanus* – as the *Enetii* [29.148-149], by *Strabo* and *Ptolemy* as a *Galatian* tribe of the *Ouenetoi*, by *Pliny the Elder*, adverting to another scholar – *Cornelius Nepos*, as the *Veneti* – the forefathers of the *Veneti* of *Italy*:

> "In it are *Mastya*, a town founded by the *Milesians*, and then *Cromna*, at which spot *Cornelius Nepos* also places the *Heneti*, from whom he would have us believe that the *Veneti* of *Italy*, who have a similar name, are descended." [6.2]

Apparently, it is from their name *Venice* got its denomination. And lastly, *Apollonius Rhodius* confirmed in his work "The Argonautica" that the *Thracian* nation of the *Paphlagonians* and the *Enetoi*, aka *Veneti*, were related [2.341-359].

Now, let us put the facts together. The *Heneti* were the colony of the *Medes* and a part of the greater *Scythian* nation. The kindred relations between the *Scythians* and the *Medes* were already established due to the accounts of the ancient authors and the artifacts. As the *Henetes* were related to the *Paphlagonians*, being their most prominent tribe, and to the *Cauconians* for living on their lands with the equal kindred rights, we reach the conclusion that both the *Paphlagonians* with their offshoots – the *Mariandyni*, the *Ligues*, the *Matienoi*, the *Cappadocians*, and the *Cauconians*, shared the same *Scythian* and *Median* heritage, which was *Turkic* on its essence. No wonder why they came to fight for the *Trojans*, as the latter were also of *Turkic* blood!

§ 11-8. THE HALIZONES, CHALYBES, ARMENOCHALYBES, AMAZONES.

Homer introduced this *Scythian* tribe of the *Halizones* as a *Trojan* people, who inhabited the land of *Alybe* (Ἀλύβη) and fought at the side of the *Trojans*, being a part of the *Trojan* contingent:

> "*Odius* and *Epistrophus* were captains over the *Halizoni* from distant *Alybe*, where there are mines of silver." ["The Iliad." 2]

The *Halizones* were known under many other appellations, such as the *Alazonians, Alizones, Alubes, Khalubes, Khaluboi, Chaldæi, Khaldaioi, Chaldeans*. Referring to *Strabo*'s expertise on this matter, it is reasonable to expect that the country *Alybe*, mentioned by *Homer*, was the same as *Chalybe*, and the people were called the *Chalybes*, known as the *Khaldaioi* in the time of *Strabo*:

> "The present *Chaldaei* [144] were anciently called *Chalybes*. It is in their territory chiefly that *Pharnacia* is situated…These I suppose are the people who are called by *Homer Halizoni*, who in his *Catalogue* follow the *Paphlagonians*.
>   "But *Odius* and *Epistrophus* led the *Halizoni*
>   Far from *Alybe*, where there are silver mines;"
> whether the writing was changed from "far from *Chalybe*," or whether the people were formerly called *Alybes* instead of *Chalybes*. We cannot at present say that it is possible that *Chaldaei* should be read for *Chalybes*, but it cannot be maintained that formerly *Chalybes* could not be read for *Alybes*, especially when we know that names are subject to many changes, more especially among barbarians. For example, a tribe of *Thracians* were called *Sinties*, then *Sinti*, then *Saii*, in whose country *Archilochus* is said to have thrown away his shield:
>   "One of the *Saii* exults in having a shield, which, without blame, I involuntarily left behind in a thicket."
> This same people have now the name of *Sapaei*. For all these people were settled about *Abdera*, they also held *Lemnos* and the islands about *Lemnos*. Thus also *Brygi, Briges*, and *Phryges* are the same people; and *Mysi, Maeones*, and *Meones* are the same people. But it is unnecessary to multiply instances of this kind." [*Strabo*. 12.3.19-20]

The ancient man-of-arts, *Aeschylus*, in his composition of 467 BCE "Seven Against *Thebes*", revealed that the *Chalybes* were of *Scythian* extraction:

> "A stranger distributes their inheritance, a *Chalybian* immigrant from *Scythia*, a bitter divider of wealth, savage-hearted iron that apportions land for them to dwell in, as much as they can occupy in death when they have lost their share in these wide plains." [727-733]

Herodotus recognized them as the *Alazones* (Ἀλαζόνες) and situated them right next to the land-cultivating *Scythians*:

> "The third river is the *Hypanis*, which starts from *Scythia* and flows from a great lake round which feed white wild horses; and this lake is rightly called "Mother of *Hypanis*". From this then the river *Hypanis* takes its rise and for a distance of five days' sail it flows shallow and with sweet water still; but from this point on towards the sea for four days' sail it is very bitter, for there flows into it the water of a bitter spring, which is so exceedingly bitter that, small as it is, it changes the water of the *Hypanis* by mingling with it, though that is a river to which few are equal in greatness. This spring

---

[144] In the original *Greek* text, it is *Khaldaioi* = Χαλδαῖοι.

is on the border between the lands of the agricultural *Scythians* and of the *Alazonians*, and the name of the spring and of the place from which it flows is in *Scythian Exampaios* [Ἐξαμπαῖος], and in the *Hellenic* tongue *Hierai Hodoi* [Ἱραὶ ὁδοί]. Now the *Tyras* and the *Hypanis* approach one another in their windings in the land of the *Alazonians*, but after this each turns off and widens the space between them as they flow." [4.52]

"Beginning with the trading station of the *Borysthenites*, for of the parts along the sea this is the central point of all *Scythia*, beginning with this, the first regions are occupied by the *Callipidai*, who are *Hellenic Scythians;* and above these is another race, who are called *Alazonians*. These last and the *Callipidai* in all other respects have the same customs as the *Scythians*, but they both sow corn and use it as food, and also onions, leeks, lentils and millet. Above the *Alazonians* dwell *Scythians* who till the ground, and these sow their corn not for food but to sell." [4.17]

Most likely, by the time of *Strabo, Pliny the Elder*, and *Aeschylus*, the colony of the *Halizones* resettled in *Pontus* and *Cappadocia* (the territory of present *Turkey*), where they became known as the *Chalybes*, or the *Alybes*, and later, as the *Chaldæi*. Furthermore, *Aeschylus* characterized them as wild brutes to stay away from, who were metal workers similar to *Homer's* description of the *Halizones* as silver-miners and as iron-miners by *Apollonius Rhodius*:

"First, from this spot, turn yourself toward the rising sun and make your way over untilled plains; and you shall reach the *Scythian* nomads, who dwell in thatched houses, perched aloft on strong-wheeled wagons and are equipped with far-darting bows. Do not approach them, but keeping your feet near the rugged shore, where the sea breaks with a roar, pass on beyond their land. On the left hand dwell the workers in iron, the *Chalybes*, and you must beware of them, since they are savage and are not to be approached by strangers." [*Aeschylus*. "*Prometheus* Bound." 707-720]

"That folk have no care for ploughing with oxen or for any planting of honey-sweet fruit; nor yet do they pasture flocks in the dewy meadow. But they cleave the hard iron-bearing land and exchange their wages for daily sustenance; never does the morn rise for them without toil, but amid bleak sooty flames and smoke they endure heavy labour."
[*Apollonius Rhodius*. "The *Argonautica*." 2.1002-1008]

"Onward from thence the bend of a huge and towering cape reaches out from the land, next *Thermodon* at its mouth flows into a quiet bay at the *Themiscyreian* headland, after wandering through a broad continent. And here is the plain of *Doeas*, and near are the three cities of the *Amazons*, and after them the *Chalybes*, most wretched of men, possess a soil rugged and unyielding – sons of toil, they busy themselves with working iron." [Idem. 2.360]

Pliny the Elder positioned the *Chalybes* near the city of *Themiscyra* founded by the *Amazons*:

"Upon the coast there is the river *Thermodon*, which rises at the fortified place called *Phanaroea*, and flows past the foot of *Mount Amazonius*. There was formerly a town of the same name as the river, and five others in all, *Amazonium, Themiscyra, Sotira, Amasia*, and *Comana*, now only a *Manteium*. We find here the nations of the *Genetae*, the *Chalybes*, the town of *Cotyorum*, the nations of the *Tibareni* and the *Mossyni*, who make marks upon their bodies, the people called *Macrocephali*, the town of *Cerasus*, the port of *Chordule*, the nations called the *Bechires* and the *Buzeri*, the river *Melas*, the people called the *Macrones*, and *Sidene* with its river *Sidenus*, by which the town of *Polemonium* is washed, at a distance from *Amisus* of one hundred and twenty miles." [6.4]

Surprisingly, when stating the participation of the *Halizones* in the *Trojan* war, *Homer* missed a remarkable chance to tell the story about the queen of the *Amazons Penthesileia*, who came to aid the *Trojans* and fought against the *Greeks*. According to *St. Jerome*, this happened in 1185 BCE. *Diodorus Siculus* was among a few historians to bring this up:

> "For a few years after *Hercules's* time, the *Trojan* war broke forth, at which time *Penthesilea*, queen of those *Amazons* that were left, and daughter of *Mars,* having committed a cruel murder among her own people, for the horridness of the fact fled, and after the death of *Hector,* brought aid to the *Trojans;* and though she bravely behaved herself, and killed many of the *Greeks,* yet at last she was slain by *Achilles,* and so in heroic actions ended her days. This, they say, was the last queen of the *Amazons,* a brave-spirited woman, after whom the nation (growing by degrees weaker and weaker) was at length wholly extinct." [2.3]

The *Greek* poet of the late 4th c. BCE, *Quintus Smyrnaeus,* in his epic work "The Fall of *Troy*", gave a poetic description of the *Amazonian* warrior queen:

> "Then from *Thermodon,* from broad-sweeping streams,
> Came, clothed upon with beauty of Goddesses,
> *Penthesileia* – came athirst indeed for groan-resounding battle, but yet more
> Fleeing abhorred reproach and evil fame,
> Lest they of her own folk should rail on her
> Because of her own sister's death, for whom
> Ever her sorrows waxed, *Hippolyte,*
> Whom she had struck dead with her mighty spear,
> Not of her will – 'twas at a stag she hurled.
> So came she to the far-famed land of *Troy*…
> And with her followed twelve beside, each one
> A princess, hot for war and battle grim,
> Far-famous each, yet handmaids unto her:
> *Penthesileia* far outshone them all.
> As when in the broad sky amidst the stars
> The moon rides over all pre-eminent,
> When through the thunderclouds the cleaving heavens
> Open, when sleep the fury-breathing winds;
> So peerless was she mid that charging host.
> *Clonie* was there, *Polemusa, Derinoe,*
> *Evandre,* and *Antandre,* and *Bremusa,*
> *Hippothoe,* dark-eyed *Harmothoe,*
> *Alcibie, Derimacheia, Antibrote,*
> And *Thermodosa* glorying with the spear.
> All these to battle fared with warrior-souled
> *Penthesileia:* even as when descends
> Dawn from *Olympus'* crest of adamant,
> Dawn, heart-exultant in her radiant steeds
> Amidst the bright-haired hours;
> And o'er them all, how flawless-fair soever these may be,
> Her splendour of beauty glows pre-eminent;
> So peerless amid all the *Amazons*
> Unto *Troy*-town *Penthesileia* came." [1.20-60]

Justin, the *Latin* historian, also gave an account describing the sad demise of the *Amazon* queen in the *Trojan* war:

> "After *Orithyia*, *Penthesilea* occupied the throne, of whose valour there were seen great proofs among the bravest heroes in the *Trojan* war, when she led an auxiliary force thither against the *Greeks*. But *Penthesilea* being at last killed, and her army destroyed, a few only of the *Amazons*, who had remained at home in their own country, established a power that continued (defending itself with difficulty against its neighbours), to the time of *Alexander the Great*. Their queen *Minithya*, or *Thalestris*, after obtaining from *Alexander* the enjoyment of his society for thirteen days, in order to have issue by him, returned into her kingdom, and soon after died, together with the whole name of the *Amazons*." [2.4.31-33]

Hailing originally from the *Caucasus*, as attested by *Procopius of Caesarea* in "History of the Wars." [8.3.2-7], *Aeschylus* in "*Prometheus* Bound." [707], the *Amazones* also founded a *Scythian* nation of the *Sarmatai*, or *Sauromatai*, that occupied a vast territory across the river *Tanaïs* (the *Don* River), reaching the *Caspian Sea*, including the lands of modern *Russia*, *Ukraine*, part of the *Balkans* and around *Moldova*. The *Sarmatai* were an offshoot of the *Medes*, and both the *Amazons* and the *Scythians* were related to them. The courageous warrior princesses of the *Caspian* and *Black Seas* were the fearless partners in battle and life of the *Scythians*, who cherished and highly valued the *Amazons* for their freedom-loving nature, heroic endeavors, and commendable military skills.

Based on several factors, such as close geographical proximity, the *Scythian* kinship, as well as matching names, it becomes clear that the *Trojan* nation of the *Halizones*, or *Alazones*, and the *Caucasian Amazones* were related. Both their names can easily be deduced from *Turkic*:

➢ *Amazones* = Ἀμαζόνες, aka *Amazon* = Ἀμαζών: *Ama* 'female' + *Azon* > *Əzən* 'destroyer' (*Əz* 'destroy, crush' + *-Ən* 'an affix, denoting constant action'), meaning "female who slays" in *Turkic*. It is important to note that both components of the ethnonym *Amazon* still continue to exist as independent *Turkic* words. Moreover, there is even a matching combination of these words in *Turkic*, for instance, *Ama Çelen* "female biter, female snake" [145] (*Çel* 'bite' + *-En* 'an affix, denoting constant action'). Compare:
- *Amazon* > *Ama* 'female' + *Azon* > *Əzən* 'destroyer'.
- *Ama Çelen* > *Ama* 'female' + *Çelen* 'biter'.
- *Alazon* > *Al* 'powerful' + *Azon* > *Əzən* 'destroyer'.

➢ *Alazones* = Ἀλαζόνες, aka *Alazonians*, aka *Halizones*, aka *Alizones* = Ἀλιζῶνες, aka *Alubes* = Ἀλύβης, aka *Khalubes* = Χάλυβες, aka *Khaluboi* = Χάλυβοι, aka *Chaldæi*, aka *Khaldaioi* = Χαλδαῖοι, aka *Chaldeans*:
  o *Alazones*, *Alazonians*: *Al* 'powerful' + *Azon* > *Əzən* 'destroyer' (*Əz* 'destroy' + *-Ən* 'an affix, denoting constant action'), meaning "powerful destroyer" in *Turkic*.
  o *Halizones*, *Alizones*: *Hal*, *Al* 'powerful' + *Izon* > *İzən* (*İz* 'destroy' + *-Ən* 'an affix, denoting constant action'), meaning "powerful, robust tribe" in *Turkic*.
  o *Alubes*, *Khalubes*, *Khaluboi*: *Al*, *Khal* > *Al*, *Xal* 'powerful' + *Ub* > *Oba* 'tribe', meaning "powerful tribe" in *Turkic*.
  o *Khaldaioi*, *Chaldæi*, *Chaldeans*: *Khal*, *Chal* > *Xal* 'powerful' + *Dai*, *Dœi* > *Dəü* 'great', meaning "powerful, big tribe" in *Turkic*.

All the name variations of the *Halizones* perfectly match their *Turkic* counterparts that happened to have similar variations for both components, such as *Al*, *Xal*, *Hal* "powerful" for *Al*, *Khal*, *Hal* [*Radlov*. 1.1.349; 2.21674] and *İzən*, *Əzən* "destroyer" for *Izon*, *Azon* [*Radlov*. 1.2.1536].

---

[145] Ashmarin.N.I. "Slovar chuvashskogo yazika." [1.185].

- *Armenochalybes:* Armen (*Ar* 'warrior' + *Men* 'I') + *Chal* > *Xal* 'powerful' + *Yb* > *Oba* 'tribe', meaning "powerful warrior tribe of *Armenia*" in *Turkic*.

  This was a derivative tribe of the *Chalybes*, called the *Armenochalybes*, who were spotted living right next to the *Greater Armenia*, adjoining the *Albanians* and the *Iberians*, as specified by *Pliny the Elder:*

  > "We next come to the river *Iasonius* on the site of the older city of *Side*, at the mouth of the *Sidenus* and *Melanthius*, and at a distance of eighty miles from *Amisus*, the town of *Pharnacea*, the fortress and river of *Tripolis*; the fortress and river of *Philocalia*, the fortress of *Liviopolis*, but not upon a river, and at a distance of one hundred miles from *Pharnacea*, the free city of *Trapezus*, shut in by a mountain of vast size. Beyond this town is the nation of the *Armenochalybes* and the *Greater Armenia*, at a distance of thirty miles." [6.4]

  > "The whole plain which extends away from the river *Cyrus* is inhabited by the nation of the *Albani*, and, after them, by that of the *Iberi*, who are separated from them by the river *Alazon*, which flows into the *Cyrus* from the *Caucasian* chain. The chief cities are *Cabalaca*,[146] in *Albania*, *Harmastis*, near a river of *Iberia*, and *Neoris*; there is the region also of *Thasie*, and that of *Triare*, extending as far as the mountains known as the *Paryadres*. Beyond these are the deserts of *Colchios*, on the side of which that looks towards the *Ceraunian Mountains* dwell the *Armenochalybes*…" [Idem. 6.11]

  The *Armenochalybes* were the descendants of the *Chalybes* – the *Scythians*. Most likely, they added the attribute *Armen* to their name in honor of the *Pelasgian* hero *Armenus*, who gave his name to the country of *Armenia* and its inhabitants – the *Armenians*, as well as to emphasize their kinship. However, they should not be confused with the modern *Armenians*, as these two were not related to each other whatsoever.

The *Chalybes*, aka the *Chaldeans*, had their own script and used it to create historical books and chronicles in their language. The *Armenian* annalist *Movses Khorenatsi* indirectly confirmed this in his work:

> "I don't want to leave without mentioning and censure the uninquisitive disposition of our ancient ancestors, but here, at the beginning of our enterprise, I will say words of condemnation about them. For if in all verity, those of the kings who, in writing, in stories, fixed the course of events of their time and perpetuated all the wise and valiant deeds in tales and stories, and after them those who worked hard in the archives to create books, thanks to which we gain knowledge of worldly laws and civil orders by reading their writings when we especially read the wise speeches and stories of the *Chaldeans* and the *Assyrians*, the *Egyptians*, and the *Hellenes*, and at the same time it seems we envy the wisdom of the men, who have undertaken such work, then, of course, we all are aware of the ignorance of our kings and other ancestors in the sciences and the immaturity of their mind." ["The History of Armenia." 1.3]

---

[146] It still exists in the *Azerbaijan Republic* as the city and the region of *Gabala*.

§ 11-9. The Cilicians, or Hypachaeans, Tracheiotae, Pisidians, Selgeis, Sagalasseis, Clitae.

Finally, we complete our discourse about the *Trojan* nations with the *Cilicians*. They did not participate in the *Trojan* war, as prior to the war, the lands of the *Cilicians* were destroyed, and their ruler got killed by the *Greco-Danaan* contingent. From *Strabo*, we learn that the *Cilicians* represented the second *Trojan* dynasty:

> "*Andromache*, daughter of the magnanimous *Eetion*, *Eetion* king of the *Cilicians*, who dwelt under the woody *Placus* at *Thebe Hypoplacia*.
> This is the second *Trojan* dynasty after that of *Mynes*, and in agreement with what has been observed are these words of *Andromache*;
>> "*Hector*, wretch that I am; we were both born under the same destiny; thou at *Troja* in the palace of *Priam*, but I at *Thebe*."
>
> The words are not to be understood in their direct sense, but by a transposition; "both born in *Troja*, thou in the house of *Priam*, but I at *Thebe*."" [13.1.7]

The *Cilicians* became a part of the *Trojan* house of *Priam* due to the marriage between the king *Priam*'s son *Hector* and the *Cilician* princess *Andromache*. They had a son *Scamandrius*, whom the *Trojans* called *Astyanax*, that meant "Lord protector" in tribute to his father, *Hector*:

> "*Hector* hurried from the house when she had done speaking, and went down the streets by the same way that he had come. When he had gone through the city and had reached the *Scaean* gates through which he would go out on to the plain, his wife came running towards him, *Andromache*, daughter of great *Eetion* who ruled in *Thebe* under the wooded slopes of *Mt. Placus*, and was king of the *Cilicians*. His daughter had married *Hector*, and now came to meet him with a nurse who carried his little child in her bosom – a mere babe. *Hector's* darling son, and lovely as a star. *Hector* had named him *Scamandrius*, but the people called him *Astyanax*, for his father stood alone as chief guardian of *Ilius*." [*Homer*. "The Iliad." 6]

The name *Astyanax*, or *Astuanaks* (Αστυάναξ), is of pure *Turkic* origin. It consists of two words:

> *Astyanax, Astuanaks: As* > *Әs* 'lord, chief' + *Tyanax, Tuanaks* > *Tayanak* 'supporter, stronghold, protector' (*Tayan* 'rely, support' [147] + *-Ak* 'an affix, converting a verb into a noun'), meaning "lord protector", "chief guardian" in *Turkic*.

By the way, after the *Greco-Danaans* took over *Troy*, they murdered this little boy by hurling him down from the city tower to prevent him from restoring the kingdom of *Troy* in the future. *Ovid*, in "Metamorphoses.", described in detail the sack of *Troy* and the killing spree that did not discriminate *Trojan* women and children:

> "Great *Troy* was burning: while the fire still raged,
> *Jove's* altar drank old *Priam's* scanty blood.
> The priestess of *Apollo* then, alas!
> Was dragged by her long hair, while up towards heaven
> she lifted supplicating hands in vain.
> The *Trojan* matrons, clinging while they could
> to burning temples and ancestral gods,

---

[147] *Egorov V.G.* "Etimologicheskiy slovar chuvashskogo yazika." [234].

victorious *Greeks* drag off as welcome spoil.
Astyanax was hurled down from the very tower
from which he often had looked forth and seen
his father, by his mother pointed out,
when *Hector* fought for honor and his country's weal." [13]

Euripides, in "*Andromache*", also depicted the horrors and the aftermath of the *Trojan* war:

"O city of *Thebes,* glory of *Asia,* whence on a day I
came to *Priam's* princely home with many a rich and costly
thing in my dower, affianced unto *Hector* to be the mother
of his children, I *Andromache,* envied name in days of
yore, but now of all women that have been or yet shall be
the most unfortunate; for I have lived to see my husband
Hector slain by *Achilles,* and the babe *Astyanax,* whom I
bore my lord, hurled from the towering battlements, when
the *Hellenes* sacked our *Trojan* home; and I myself come
to *Hellas* as a slave, though I was esteemed a daughter of a
race most free, given to *Neoptolemus* that island-prince, and
set apart for him as his special prize from the spoils of *Troy.*" [1-19]

According to *Herodotus,* the *Cilicians* were known as the *Hypachaens* in ancient times:

"The *Cilicians* furnished a hundred ships. The crews wore upon their heads the helmet of their country, and carried instead of shields light targes made of raw hide; they were clad in woollen tunics, and were each armed with two javelins, and a sword closely resembling the cutlass of the *Egyptians*. This people bore anciently the name of *Hypachaeans,* but took their present title from *Cilix,* the son of *Agenor* (Ἀγήνωρ), a *Phoenician*." [7.91]

On the testimony of *Apollodorus,* it turns out that the *Cilicians* took their beginning from the *Pelasgian-Thracian* king *Inachus* and his daughter *Io,* who was the queen of *Egypt*. From her great-grandson *Agenor* – the king of *Phoenicia* – descended the son *Cilix,* who became the founder of the *Cilicians:*

"Having now run over the family of *Inachus* and described them from *Belus* down to the *Heraclids,* we have next to speak of the house of *Agenor*. For as I have said, *Libya* had by *Poseidon* two sons, *Belus* and *Agenor*. Now *Belus* reigned over the *Egyptians* and begat the aforesaid sons; but *Agenor* went to *Phoenicia,* married *Telephassa,* and begat a daughter *Europa* and three sons, *Cadmus, Phoenix,* and *Cilix*. But some say that *Europa* was a daughter not of *Agenor* but of *Phoenix*. *Zeus* loved her, and turning himself into a tame bull, he mounted her on his back and conveyed her through the sea to *Crete*. There *Zeus* bedded with her, and she bore *Minos, Sarpedon,* and *Rhadamanthys;* but according to *Homer, Sarpedon* was a son of *Zeus* by *Laodamia,* daughter of *Bellerophon*. On the disappearance of *Europa* her father *Agenor* sent out his sons in search of her, telling them not to return until they had found *Europa*. With them her mother, *Telephassa,* and *Thasus,* son of *Poseidon,* or according to *Pherecydes,* of *Cilix,* went forth in search of her. But when, after diligent search, they could not find *Europa,* they gave up the thought of returning home, and took up their abode in divers places; *Phoenix* settled in *Phoenicia; Cilix* settled near *Phoenicia,* and all the country subject to himself near the river *Pyramus* he called *Cilicia;* and *Cadmus* and *Telephassa* took up their abode in *Thrace* and in like manner *Thasus* founded a city *Thasus* in an island off *Thrace* and dwelt there." [3.1.1]

Similar to the fellow *Trojan* tribe – the *Lycians*, and unlike any other people of *Pelasgian*, *Thracian*, or *Scythian* extraction, the *Cilicians* were split into two tribes under the same name, unwilling to assign another appellation to their colony, according to *Strabo*'s observation:

> "Two tribes bearing the name of *Lycians*, lead us to suppose that they are the same race; either the *Trojan Lycians* sent colonies to the *Carians*, or the *Carian Lycians* to the *Trojans*. Perhaps the same may be the case with the *Cilicians*, for they also are divided into two tribes; but we have not the same evidence that the present *Cilicians* existed before the *Trojan* times. *Telephus* may be supposed to have come with his mother from *Arcadia*; by her marriage with *Teuthras*, (who had received them as his guests,) *Telephus* was admitted into the family of *Teuthras*, was reputed to be his son, and succeeded to the kingdom of the *Mysians*." [12.8.4-5]

> "Since the *Cilicians* in the *Troad* whom *Homer* mentions are far distant from the *Cilicians* outside the *Taurus*, some represent those in *Troy* as original colonisers of the latter, and point out certain places of the same name there, as, for example, *Thebê* and *Lyrnessus* in *Pamphylia*, whereas others of contrary opinion point out also an *Aleïan Plain* in the former." [14.5.21]

Having said that, *Strabo* also narrated about several tribes that were related to the *Cilicians*, such as the *Pisidians* and their derivatives – the *Selgeis*, the *Sagalasseis*. The *Cilicians* of the post-*Homeric* era turned into full-blown marine gangsters, according to the testimony of *Strabo*:

> "…it was *Tryphon*, together with the worthlessness of the kings who by succession were then reigning over *Syria* and at the same time over *Cilicia*, who caused the *Cilicians* to organise their gangs of pirates; for on account of his revolutionary attempts others made like attempts at the same time, and thus the dissensions of brethren with one another put the country at the mercy of any who might attack it. The exportation of slaves induced them most of all to engage in their evil business, since it proved most profitable; for not only were they easily captured, but the market, which was large and rich in property, was not extremely far away, I mean *Delos*, which could both admit and send away ten thousand slaves on the same day; whence arose the proverb, "Merchant, sail in, unload your ship, everything has been sold."" [14.5.2]

The *Pisidians* shared the same unsavory traits inherent to the *Cilicians*:

> "All the rest of the mountain tribes of the *Pisidians* whom I have spoken of are divided into states governed by tyrants, and follow like the *Cilicians* a predatory mode of life. It is said that anciently some of the *Leleges*, a wandering people, were intermixed with them, and from the similarity of their habits and manners settled there." [Idem. 12.7.2-3]

Strabo considered the *Selgeis* and the *Sagalasseis* to be the most notable among the rest of the *Pisidians*:

> "Contiguous to these, among other tribes of the *Pisidians*, are the *Selgeis*, the most considerable tribe of the nation. The greater part of the *Pisidians* occupy the summits of *Taurus*, but some tribes situated above *Side* and *Aspendus*, which are *Pamphylian* cities, occupy heights, all of which are planted with olives. The parts above these, a mountainous country, are occupied by the *Catennenses*, who border upon the *Selgeis* and the *Homonadeis*. The *Sagalasseis* occupy the parts within the *Taurus* towards *Milyas*. *Artemidorus* says that *Selge*, *Sagalassus*, *Petnelissus*, *Adada*, *Tymbrias*, *Cremna*, *Pityassus*, (*Tityassus?*) *Amblada*, *Anabura*, *Sinda*, *Aarassus*, *Tarbassus*, *Termessus*, are cities of the *Pisidians*. Of these some are entirely among the mountains, others extend on each side even as far as the country at the foot of the mountains, and reach to *Pamphylia* and *Milyas*, and border on *Phrygians*, *Lydians*, and *Carians*, all of whom are disposed to peace, although situated to the north." [12.7.1-2]

In his turn, *Cornelius Tacitus* wrote about another troublesome *Cilician* tribe – the *Clitae:*

> "Not long afterwards some tribes of the wild population of *Cilicia*, known as the *Clitae*, which had often been in commotion, established a camp, under a leader *Troxobor*, on their rocky mountains, whence rushing down on the coast, and on the towns, they dared to do violence to the farmers and townsfolk, frequently even to the merchants and ship-owners.
> They besieged the city *Anemurium*, and routed some troopers sent from *Syria* to its rescue under the command of *Curtius Severus;* for the rough country in the neighbourhood, suited as it is for the fighting of infantry, did not allow of cavalry operations.
> After a time, *Antiochus*, king of that coast, having broken the unity of the barbarian forces, by cajolery of the people and treachery to their leader, slew *Troxobor* and a few chiefs, and pacified the rest by gentle measures." ["The Annals." 12.55]

The analysis of the *Cilician* tribal names confirms their well-expected *Turkic* origin:

➤ <u>*Cilicians*, aka *Kilikes* = Κίλικες:</u> *Cil, Kil* > *Kiləü* 'courageous' + *Iki, Ike* > *İkə* 'lord', meaning "brave noblemen" in *Turkic*. The name of the *Cilicians* and the country of *Cilicia* (Κιλικία) was obtained after their ruler *Kiliks*, or *Cilix* = Κίλιξ "brave lord". Although there is another variant – *Kilik* "temper, character" in *Turkic*, the offered etymology consisting of two components seems much more precise, as it was prompted by the name of *Kilix's* brother *Phoenix* (*Phoiniks* = Φοῖνιξ):
  o *Cilix, Kiliks:*   *Cil, Kil*   > *Kiləü* 'courageous'   +   *Ix, Iks*   >   *İkə* 'lord'.
  o *Phoenix, Phoiniks: Phoen, Phoin* > *Puian, Puyan* 'gorgeous' + *Ix, Iks* > *İkə* 'lord'.

Evidently, similar to *Egypt* and *Libya*, the country of *Phoenicia* (Φοινίκη) and its inhabitants received their names after the *Thrace-Pelasgian* king from *Io's* dynasty – *Phoenix*.

Incidentally, the father of *Cilix* and *Phoenix* was King *Agenor*, the founder of the city *Tyre* around 1500 c. BCE, whose name screams about its *Turkic* pedigree:
  o *Agenor: Agen* > *Ağın* 'fast' + *Or* > *Ör* 'warrior, man', meaning "swift warrior/man" in *Turkic*.

Earlier in this book, we gave an extensive analysis of the word *Tyre* and the root *Tur* observed in the names of the *Turkic* tribes, proper names, toponyms, hydronyms. This *Turkic* word *Tur* has three primary meanings – 1."direct"; 2."ascend"; 3.the name of the ethnos - *Turks*. It turns out the same word is also the base of many *Pelasgian, Thracian, Trojan* toponyms, hydronyms, ethnonyms spread all over three continents - *Europe, Asia, Africa* in ancient and modern times. The examples below were taken chiefly from "Dictionary of *Greek* and *Roman* Geography" by *William Smith* and "Ethnica" by *Stephanus of Byzantium*:

1) <u>*Tyre*</u>, or <u>*Turos*</u>=Τύρος — an ancient city in *Phoenicia* (presently *Lebanon*) found by the *Thrace-Pelasgians*.
2) <u>*Tyro*</u>=Τυρώ, a *Thessalian* princess, according to the *Pelasgian* mythology; the wife of the *Thrace-Pelasgian* king *Agenor* who gave her name to the city of *Tyre* in *Phoenicia*.
3) <u>*Tyracia*</u>, or <u>*Tyracina*</u>, or <u>*Turakinai*</u>=Τυρακῖναι, or <u>*Tyraciensis*</u> — an ancient city of *Sicily*.
4) the <u>*Tyracinae*</u>, or the <u>*Tyracienses*</u> — a people of *Sicily*.
5) <u>*Tyracinus*</u> — a male name.
6) the <u>*Turgesh*</u>=*Türgəş* — an ancient tribe of the western *Turks*.
7) <u>*Tyrallis*</u>, or <u>*Turallis*</u>=Τυραλλίς — a place in *Cappadocia*.
8) <u>*Tyrambae*</u>, or <u>*Turambai*</u>=Τυράμβαι — a people of *Asiatic Sarmatia*, whose chief city was <u>*Tyrambe*</u> (Τυράμβη).

9) the *Tyragetae*, *Tyrangitae*, or *Turangeitai*=Τυραγγεῖται, *Turangetai*=Τυραγγέται, or *Turegetai*=Τυρεγέται — the *Getae* of the *Tyras*, *Turanian Getai* – a *Scythe-Sarmatian* tribe in *European Sarmatia*, dwelling east of the river *Tyras*.
10) *Tyras*=Τύρας, or *Turis*=Τύρις — one of the principal rivers in *European Sarmatia*. Its modern name is the *Dniester*, though the *Turks* still call it the *Tural*.
11) *Tyras*=Τύρας — a town in *European Sarmatia*, situated at the mouth of the river *Tyras*.
12) *Tyras*, or *Turas*=Τύρας — a city and a river near the *Black Sea*.
13) *Turanoi*=Τυρανοί — a *Scythian* tribe.
14) *Turites*=Τυριτης, or *Tyritai*, or *Turitai* — a *Pelasgian* people that lived in the city of *Tyras* near the *Black Sea*.
15) *Tyritake*, or *Turitake*=Τυριτάκη — a city in the *Pontic* region, presently eastern *Black Sea* region of *Turkey*.
16) the *Tyritakaios*=Τυριτακαῖος, or *Turitakenos*=Τυριτακηνός — a people who inhabited the city of *Turitake*.
17) *Tyriaeum*, or *Turiaion*=Τυριαῖον, or *Tyrienses* — a town of *Lycaonia*, on the eastern frontier of *Phrygia*.
18) *Tyrictaca*, or *Turiktake*=Τυρικτάκη, or *Toriktake*=Τωριτάκη — a town in the *Chersoneses Taurica*.
19) *Tyrissa*, or *Turissa*=Τύρισσα, or *Tyrissaeus* — a town of *Emathia* in *Macedonia*.
20) the *Tyritae*, or *Turitai*=Τυρῖται — a *Scythe-Pelasgian* tribe that settled at the mouth of the river *Tyras*.
21) *Turrenia*=Τυρρηνία — a country established by the *Lydians* of *Pelasgian* extraction in *Italy*.
22) the *Turreni*, or the *Etruscans* — a nation of *Italy* who founded *Turrenia* after the name of their leader *Turrenos*.
23) the *Tyrrhenian Sea* — a part of the *Mediterranean Sea* that connects the islands of *Corsica*, *Sardinia*, and *Sicily*.
24) *Turaniana* — a place in *Hispania Baetica*.
25) *Turba* — a town of the *Edetani* in *Hispania Tarraconensis*, also it was a capital of *Aquitania*.
26) *Turbula*, or *Tourboula*=Τούρβουλα — a town of the *Bastetani* in *Hispania Tarraconensis*.
27) the *Turcae*, or *Tourkoi*=Τοῦρκοι, or *Turuk*, or *Turk* — a *Scythian* people of *Asiatic Sarmatia*, the ancestors of the modern *Turkic* nations.
28) *Siagathourgoi* — a *Sarmatian* tribe.
29) the *Turcilingi* — a tribe in northern *Germany*.
30) the *Turdetani*, or *Tourdetanoi*=Τουρδητανοί — the principal people of *Hispania Baetica*.
31) *Turdetania*, or *Tourdetania*=Τουρδητανία, or *Tourtutania*=Τουρτυτανία — the ancient country in *Hispania Baetica*.
32) *Turduli*, or *Tourdouloi*=Τουρδοῦλοι — a people in *Hispania Baetica*, very closely connected with the *Turdetani*.
33) *Turia*, or *Turium* — a river in the territory of the *Edetani* in *Hispania Tarraconensis*.
34) *Turi* — a city in *Italy*.
35) *Turin* — a city in *Italy*.
36) *Turiaso*, or *Touriaso*=Τουριασώ, or *Touriasso*=Τουριασσώ, or *Turiasson*, or *Turiasonensis* — a town of the *Celtiberi* in *Hispania Tarraconensis*.
37) *Turicum*, or *Turegum* — an ancient name of *Zurich* in *Switzerland*.
38) *Thur* — a river in north-eastern *Switzerland*.
39) *Turku* — the first capital and the oldest city of *Finland*.
40) *Turiga* — a city of the *Celtici* in *Hispania Baetica*.
41) *Turissa* — a town of the *Vascones* in *Hispania Tarraconensis*.
42) the *Turmodigi* — a people in *Hispania Tarraconensis*.
43) *Turmogum*, or *Tourmogon*=Τούρμογον — a town in the interior of *Lusitania*.
44) *Turmuli* — a town of *Lusitania* on the *Tagus*.

45) *Turnacum*, or *Tornacum* — a city of *North Gallia*.
46) *Turobrica* — a town of *Hispania Baetica*.
47) the *Turodi*, or *Tourodoi=Τουροδοί* — a people in *Hispania Tarraconensis*.
48) the *Turones*, or *Turoni*, or *Turonii* — a people of *Western Gallia*.
49) *Touraine* — a province of *France* named after the *Turones*.
50) *Tours* — the capital of *Touraine*.
51) *Turoni*, or *Touronoi* — a German tribe.
52) *Turoqua*, or *Turaqua* — a town of the *Callaici* in *Hispania Tarraconensis*.
53) *Turres* — a place in the interior of *Moesia Superior*; a town of the *Oretani* in *Hispania Tarraconensis*; a town in the territory of the *Contestani* in the same province.
54) *Turris Caesaris* — a place in *Numidia*.
55) *Turris Hannibalis* — a strong fortress in the territory of *Carthage*.
56) *Turris Tamalleni* — in *Africa Proper*.
57) *Turris Libyssonis* — a town of *Sardinia*.
58) *Turris Stratonis* — an ancient maritime town of *Palestine*.
59) *Turrus* — a river in *Aquileia*, which was the capital of the province of *Venetia* in *Italy*.
60) *Turriga* — a town of the *Callaici Lucenses* in *Hispania Tarraconensis*.
61) *Turulis*, or *Touroulis=Τούρουλις* — a river in the territory of the *Edetani* in *Hispania Tarraconensis*.
62) *Turum*, or *Turinus*, or *Turi* — a town of *Apulia* in *Italy*.
63) *Turuntus*, or *Tourountos=Τουρούντος* — a river of *European Sarmatia*.
64) *Turuptiana*, or *Tourouptiana=Τουρουπτίανα* — a town of the *Callaici Lucenses* in *Hispania Tarraconensis*.
65) *Turan* — a city in the *Turkic Republic* of *Tyva* in *Russia*.
66) *Turinsk* — a city in *Russia*.
67) *Turkestan* — a city in *Kazakhstan*.
68) *Tura Beach* — a city in *Australia*.
69) *Turakurgan* — a city in *Uzbekistan*.
70) *Turbach* — a city in *Switzerland*.
71) *Turbenthal* — a city in *Switzerland*.
72) *Turgau* — a canton in *Switzerland*.
73) *Turgi* — a municipality in *Switzerland*.
74) *Tyrodiza=Τυρόδιζα* — an ancient city in *Thrace*.
75) *Tyrmeidai*, or *Turmeidai=Τυρμεῖδαι*, or *Turmidai=Τυρμίδαι* — an ancient place in *Attica*.

- *Hypachaeans*, aka *Upakhaioi* = Ὑπαχαιοὶ: *Hypa, Upa > Up* 'waste, destroy' + *Chae, Khai > Kai* 'cut, obliterate', meaning "tribe that destroys and obliterates" in *Turkic*.

- *Pisidians*, aka *Pisidai* = Πισίδαι: *Pis* 'have skills' + *Idi, Id > İdi* 'lord, noble', meaning "skillful noblemen" in *Turkic*.

- *Selgians*, aka *Selgeis* = Σελγεῖς: *Selg > Silig* 'prominent' + *Eis > Əs* 'lord, master', meaning "prominent noblemen" in *Turkic*. The second component of the name *Eis* is not a *Greek* ending, to which the name of the city *Selge* (Σέλγη) stands attested. It is an independent word observed at the end of the *Thracian, Pelasgian, Scythian* ethnonyms and toponyms:
    - *Gargareis* = Γαργαρεὶς (a *Caucasian Albanian* tribe).
    - *Auseis* = Αὐσεῖς (a *Scythian* tribe).
    - *Norosbeis* = Νοροσβεῖς (a *Scythian* tribe).
    - *Boebeis* = Βοιβηῒς (a lake in *Thessaly*).

- *Bris<u>eis</u>* = Βρισηῖς (a daughter of *Briseus*=Βρισεύς, or *Brises*=Βρίσης, and the wife of King *Mynes*, representing the first *Trojan* dynasty).
- *Sard<u>eis</u>* = Σάρδεις (the *Trojan* capital of *Lydia*, also known as *Sardis*=Σάρδις).
- *Sagalass<u>eis</u>* = Σαγαλασσεῖς (a *Trojan-Cilician* tribe).

> *Sagalasseis* = Σαγαλασσεῖς, aka *Sagalassenes*, aka *Sagalasseni*:
>   o *Sagalasseis*: *Sag* > *Sağ* 'healthy' + *Alass* > *Alaşa* 'horse' + *Eis* > *Əs* 'lord, master', meaning "masters of vigorous horses" in *Turkic*.
>   o *Sagalassenes, Sagalasseni*: *Sag* > *Sağ* 'healthy' + *Alass* > *Alaşa* 'horse' + *Enes, Eni* > *En* 'house', meaning "the house of vigorous stallions" in *Turkic*.
> *Titus Livius* characterized this *Pisidian* branch of the *Cilicians* as the finest fighters of the region, who lived in the fortress town *Sagalassos* (Σαγαλασσός, or *Sagalasseus*=Σαγαλασσεύς, or *Sagalassmeos*= Σαγαλασσμνός):
>> "Then they entered the country of the *Sagalassenes*, rich and abounding in all kinds of crops. *Pisidians* inhabit it, by far the best warriors in this region." [38.15.8]

> *Clitae*, aka *Klitai* = Κλιταί: *Cli*, *Kli* > *Kiləü* 'courageous' + *Tae, Tai* > *Tai* 'steed', meaning "brave steeds" in *Turkic*. Remarkably, *Clitae*, or *Klitai*, was also an inland town in *Bithynia*, presented as a part of *Greater Asia* by *Ptolemy* [5.1].

The country of *Cilicia* was situated along the *Aegean* coast from *Pamphylia* to *Mount Amanus* in the territory of present-day *Turkey*. Split into two main parts, *Cilicia* had *Greek* surnames, such as *Tracheiotis* "rugged" and *Pedias* "plain", and the *Cilicians* residing in the rugged area of *Cilicia* were named accordingly by the *Greeks* – the *Tracheiotae*:

"As for *Cilicia* outside the *Taurus*, one part of it is called *Tracheia* and the other *Pedias*. As for *Tracheia*, its coast is narrow and has no level ground, or scarcely any; and, besides that, it lies at the foot of the *Taurus*, which affords a poor livelihood as far as its northern side in the region of *Isaura* and of the *Homonadeis* as far as *Pisidia*; and the same country is also called *Tracheiotis*, and its inhabitants *Tracheiotae*. But *Cilicia Pedias* extends from *Soli* and *Tarsus* as far as *Issus*, and also to those parts beyond which, on the northern side of the *Taurus*, *Cappadocians* are situated; for this country consists for the most part of plains and fertile land." [*Strabo*. 14.5.1]

§ 11-10. MITOCHONDRIAL DNA DATA CONNECT THE TROJANS, THE SCYTHIANS, THE ETRUSCANS, THE TURRENIANS, THE PELASGIANS TO THE TURKIC NATIONS.

Modern science gave its indisputable verdict substantiating the truthfulness of the ancient scholars and writers about the ancient *Turkic* nations. Several genetic studies proved the kinship of the *Trojans*, *Turrenians*, *Etruscans* to *Turks* and provided indisputable evidence that the language of the *Etruscans* was non-*Indo-European*.

According to the extensive study "Mitochondrial DNA Variation of Modern *Tuscans* Supports the Near Eastern Origin of *Etruscans*" done by *Alessandro Achilli* et al., the *Etruscans*, aka the *Turrenians* (*Tyrrehnians*), arrived from the territory of present-day *Turkey* [www.ncbi.nlm.nih.gov/pmc/articles/PMC1852723/]. The imprints of this arrival are still evident in modern *Tuscany* – a region in central *Italy*, also known as *Etruria*, *Tyrrhenia*, western *Umbria*, and northern *Latium*. The culture of the *Etruscans,* aka the *Trojans,* aka the *Turks,* was much more advanced than the culture of the *Greeks* and *Latins* back in the 9th c. BCE.

The testimonies of the ancient historians were declared to be historically correct due to the latest breakthrough in genetics. For instance, *Herodotus* stated the truth about the *Lydians,* a part of which resettled in the land of present-day *Italy,* created a kingdom of *Turrenia* and called themselves *Turrenians,* later known as the *Tusci, Etruscans,* who were the *Trojans* of the *Scythian* extraction and *Turkic* blood. In the article "Ancient *Etruscans* Were Immigrants from *Anatolia,* Or What Is Now *Turkey*" published by the *European* Society of Human Genetics, one of the study researchers, Professor *Piazza* confirmed that the *Tuscans* or *Etruscans* descended from the people of *Turkey* (read, *Turks*). Out of all the *Italian* DNA samples, the ones obtained from subjects of *Murlo* municipality and mountaintop town *Volterra* in the *Tuscany* region demonstrated their strongest and closest proximity with individuals in *Turkey.* Furthermore, the genetic variant detected in *Murlo* was found only in *Turkish* people. From professor *Piazza's* statements, it becomes clear that both the *Turks* and the *Tuscans* were closely related to the *Pelasgians* from *Lemnos.* This genetic research serves as serious scientific evidence corroborating *Herodotus's* stories about the *Lydians,* who immigrated to *Italy* and built a great *Turrenian* realm, and were later recognized as the *Etruscans,* or *Tuscans* [www.sciencedaily.com/releases/2007/06/070616191 637.htm].

Another research, "The *Etruscans:* A Population-Genetic Study", completed by *Cristiano Vernesi, David Caramelli* et al. in 2004, based its results on the bone samples obtained from the *Etruscans* of the 7th - 3rd c. BCE. This study determined that the *Etruscans* did not belong to the *Indo-European* population and had a non-*Indo-European* language [www.sciencedirect.com/science/article/pii/S0002929707618 941]. This genetic study confirms the fact that has been long ignored or purposefully distorted by the proponents of the *Indo-European* inception of *Europe* and *Asia*: the language of the *Etruscans, Turrenians,* as well as their progenitors and kinsmen, such as the *Thracians,* the *Trojans,* the *Phrygians,* the *Pelasgians,* the *Scythians,* and greater *Scythian* family, including the *Medes,* the *Parthians,* the *Bactrians,* the *Getae,* the *As,* the *Turcae,* was, firstly, non-*Indo-European,* and secondly, of *Turkic* origin. The gene pool of the *Etruscans* showed their much closer affinity with *Turks* and *North Africans* than any other populace. It was also established that the *Turkish* component in the *Etruscan* gene pool was prevalent, three times as much as that of any other populace.

The *North African* component in the *Etruscans'* gene pool proves their *Egyptian* connection due to the *Thrace-Pelasgian* dynasty of *Io* that ruled *Egypt, Libya,* and nearby countries for centuries and from where the repatriation process took place through the *Pelasgian* branch of the *Danaii,* or the *Danaans.* Yes, the ones who organized and led the multinational forces against the *Trojans* in the famous *Trojan* war. Hereby, the DNA research attested to the testimonies of the ancient *Greek* and *Roman* scholars, historians, intellectuals, who corroborated the existence of the nations and tribes derived from the *Thracians,* the *Pelasgians,* and the *Trojans* in the *North African* countries – *Egypt, Libya,* and others.

Another interesting fact revealed by this genetic study serves as additional proof that both the *Kelts* and the *Germans* belonged to the *Scythian* family of *Turkic* origin. The *Etruscans* shared four haplotypes with the *Turks,* five haplotypes with the *Cornish* and seven haplotypes with the *Germans.* This means that the *Etruscans* were genetically close to the *Celtic* ethnic group – the *Cornish* and the *Germans.*

Here come to mind the words of the 18th c. *Swedish* professor *Sven Lagerbring,* the founder of the *Swedish* historiography:

"We, the *Germanic* people, by origin, are *Turks.*"

From this genetic study, it also became obvious that the *Etruscans* and most, if not all, the *European* lineages share a common ancestral origin – the *Turkic* genetic base.

There is another genetic research, "The mystery of *Etruscan* origins: novel clues from Bos taurus mitochondrial DNA", done by a group of *Italian* geneticists – *Marco Pellecchia* et al. in 2007. It brought to a focus the fact mentioned by *Plutarch, Ovid,* and many other ancient authors that the *Etruscans,* or the *Trojans,* were the founders of *Rome* and the *Roman* empire [www.ncbi.nlm.nih.gov/pmc/articles/PMC 2189563/]. Developed in the 1st millennium BCE, the *Etruscan* culture formed the civilization of the neighboring *Indo-European* peoples. The *Etruscans* brought with them not only their artistic and political acumen, religion, traditions but also their alphabet, based on which they helped create the *Latin* alphabet for the *Latins* and subsequently for other *European* nations.

The results of the sequenced bovine DNA from 11 breeds of *Italian* livestock helped the researchers conjecture the arrival timeframe of the *Etruscan* settlers with their cattle in the Late Bronze Age (13th to 12th c. BCE), as well as serve as evidence confirming the statements of *Herodotus* and *Thucydides* about the *Trojan* background of the *Turrenians*, aka the *Etruscans*. The research strongly supported the genetic closeness of the *Tuscan* bovines to those in *Turkey* and, like other reputable genetic studies, proclaimed the non-*Indo-European* origin of the *Etruscans*. The glorious words about the *Etruscan's Asian* roots, once said by the renowned *Roman* writer *Lucius Annaeus Seneca,* come to mind:

"Tuscos Asia sibi vindicat." ["Ad Helviam Matrem de Consolatione." 7.2]
"*Asia* claims the *Etruscans* as her own".[148]

All the conducted genetic studies related to the *Etruscans* revealed the ultimate truth, purposefully hidden for centuries from the public worldwide. The *Etruscans,* who were the *Trojans* from *Lydia,* were a *Turkic* nation. This fact entails the following verified statements, supported by archeological, linguistic, genetic evidence:

- The *Turkic* presence in *Asia Minor* and *Europe* was much earlier than 13th–12th c. BCE.

- The *Trojans,* as well as the *Pelasgians,* the *Thracians,* the *Scythians,* the *Germanic* nations, were of *Turkic* origin, i.e., the *Turks.*

- All the nations akin to the *Trojans* belonged to the *Turkic* family. This includes the *Phrygians,* the *Carians,* the *Lydians,* the *Lacedemonians* and *Spartans,* the *Thracians,* the *As,* the *Pelasgians,* and consequently, the *Scythians* and *Scythian* tribes – the *Getae,* the *Massagetae,* the *Amazons,* the *Sarmatians,* the *Turcae,* other nations related to the *Scythians,* such as the *Medes,* the *Parthians,* the *Bactrians,* the *Albanians,* the *Hun,* as well as the *Germans, Celts,* and the *Gauls.*

- Most, if not all, the *Europeans* are the descendants of the ancient *Turks* and the *Turkic* nations, such as the *Scythians,* the *Medes,* the *Pelasgians.* They once used the same language, shared the same culture, religion, even the alphabet, only later to forget and destroy any traces and knowledge about their *Turkic* past.

The detailed analysis of the discussed nations and tribes in this work revealed the undeniable and irrefutable fact that all of them had a *Turkic* pedigree, and in some cases, they were the progenitors of modern *Turkic* peoples.

In order to get a better understanding of the correlation between the *Medes*, the *Turks*, the *Scythians,* the *Pelasgians*, the *Thracians*, and their offshoots, a table below was created. Only major nations and tribes are indicated here, skipping the enumeration of several hundreds of *Scythian* tribes, as well as other small tribes - derivatives of the *Thracians*, the *Medes*, the *Trojans*, the *Pelasgians*, and the like.

---

[148] The text was translated from *Latin* into *English* by the author of the current work.

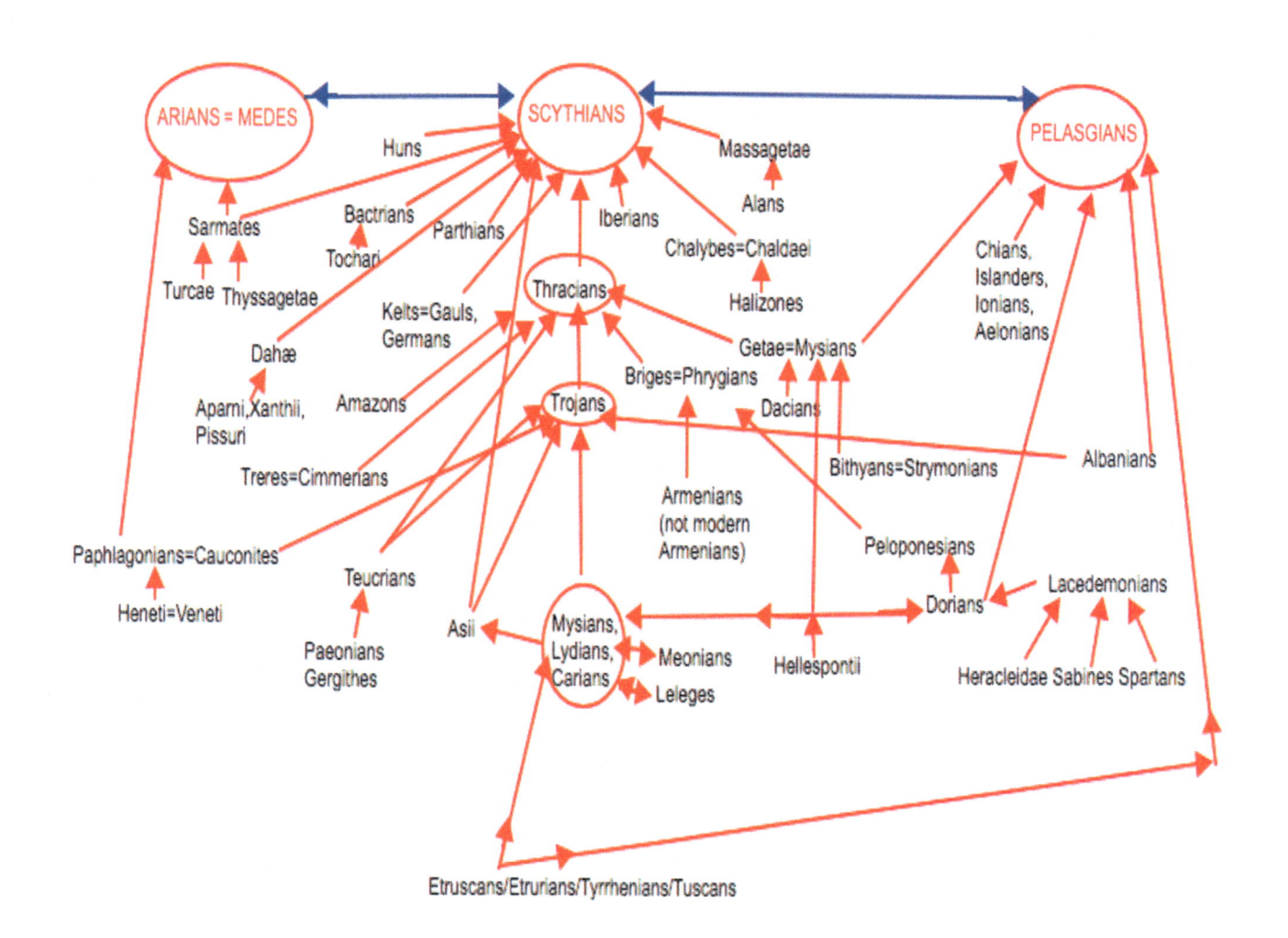

Diagram: Relationships among ancient peoples

Main groups (circled): ARIANS = MEDES ↔ SCYTHIANS ↔ PELASGIANS

Feeding into SCYTHIANS:
- Huns
- Bactrians
- Tochari
- Parthians
- Iberians
- Massagetae
- Alans
- Chalybes = Chaldaei
- Halizones
- Sarmates
- Thyssagetae
- Kelts = Gauls, Germans
- Amazons
- Dahæ
- Treres = Cimmerians

Feeding into ARIANS = MEDES:
- Turcae
- Paphlagonians = Cauconites
- Heneti = Veneti
- Aparni, Xanthii, Pissuri (→ Dahæ)

Feeding into PELASGIANS:
- Chians, Islanders, Ionians, Aelonians
- Albanians
- Dorians
- (via Etruscans route)

Thracians (intermediate) ← Getae = Mysians, Briges = Phrygians, Dacians, Bithyans = Strymonians
- Thracians → Scythians

Trojans (intermediate) ← Teucrians, Paeonians, Gergithes, Asii
- Trojans → Scythians / Thracians

Mysians, Lydians, Carians (intermediate)
- → Meonians
- → Leleges
- ← Hellespontii
- ↔ Dorians

Dorians ← Heracleidae, Sabines, Spartans, Lacedemonians
- ← Peloponesians

Armenians (not modern Armenians) → Trojans

Etruscans / Etrurians / Tyrrhenians / Tuscans → Trojans, → Pelasgians

---

<<<<<<<<<<<<<<<<<<<<<<< ⋄ >>>>>>>>>>>>>>>>>>>>>>

Chapter VI.

The Ancient Turkic alphabet and its close similarity to the Pelasgian, Lydian, Lycian, Phrygian, Carian, Etruscan/Turrenian, Scythian scripts.

It's already been established through the testimonies of the ancient historians, geographers, and scholars, as well as the genetic studies that the *Trojans*, aka the *Turrenians*, aka the *Etruscans*, belonged to the greater *Turkic* family.

It was also determined that the *Trojan* nations, including the *Pelasgians*, the *Lydians*, the *Leleges*, and the like were the *Thracians*.

In its turn, the *Thracians* belonged to a greater *Scythian* family that included hundreds of large and small tribes and nations, such as the *Medes*, the *Turcae*, the *Parthians*, the *Getae*, the *Bactrians*, and others.

Finally, it was ruled that all these nations and tribes traced back to the same origin – *Turkic*. However, there is an additional tool to corroborate the *Turkic* lineage of these nations – the alphabet. Some of these peoples developed their written system of characters or signs, and others never had it.

We conducted a comparative analysis based on the following alphabets – *Iberian, Lycian, Phrygian, Celtiberian, Lydian, Caucasian Albanian, Etruscan, Pelasgian, Carian, Khazarian, Scythian, Phoenician, Kharosthi, Greek, Latin* versus *Turkic* runic alphabet. Table No.1 below indicates the letters of each alphabet that have their equivalents in the *Turkic* alphabet. The *Turkic* alphabet, presented here, contains all available versions: the *Yenisey, Orkhon, Talas, Don, Kuban, Achiktash, Isfar, S. Yenisey* scripts. Another two alphabets – *Phoenician* and *Kharosthi* are used here for controlling purposes to determine whether they were the source of the letters found both in the *Turkic* and other alphabets. According to the ancient historian *Diodorus Siculus*, the *Greeks* built their alphabet on the base of the *Phoenician* alphabet and used some additional components from the *Pelasgian* alphabet. As far as the *Kharosthi* script, it was claimed to supply the blueprint material to the alphabets in *Central Asia*.

The *Scythian* alphabet indicated here was constructed from the letters inscribed on the *Issyk* silver cup dated 5-6th c. BCE, whereas the *Hunnic* alphabet is completely based on the *Hunne-Scythic* alphabet, reconstructed by *Matthias Bel*, aka *Matthiae Belii*, in his book "De Vetere Litteratura *Hunno-Scythica* Exercitatio", written in *Latin* and published in 1718. The *Pelasgian* alphabet used here was recreated by the *Turkish* linguist *P. Kaya*.

**Figure 26. A marble stele with a Lydian inscription. 6th c. BCE. The Metropolitan Museum of Art, USA. [OA].
Credit: Gift of The American Society for the Excavation of Sardis, 1926.**

Table No.1.

Turkic	Iberian	Lycian	Phrygian	Celtiberian	Lydian	Caucasian Albanian	Etruscan	Pelasgian	Phoenician	Kharosthi / Khazarian	Greek	Scythian	Hunnic	Carian

Turkic	Iberian	Lycian	Phrygian	Celtiberian	Lydian	Caucasian Albanian	Etruscan	Pelasgian	Phoenician / Kharosthi	Khazarian	Greek	Scythian	Hunnic	Carian
ᑫ ᑫᑫᑫ ᑫᑫᑫ	ᑫᑫ ᑫ	P ᑫP	ᑫᑫ	P ᑫ	ᑫ ᑫ	ᑫP	ᑫ	ᑫ	---	---	ᑫ P	---	---	ᑫ/P
NHN ПN ИNИ HИN HH HH	NHN N	N	H	---	---	---	---	---	日	H	HHN	NN	NN	H
ᖕ ᖕᖕ ᖕᖕ	---	---	ᖕ	---	ᖕ	ᖕ	ᖕ	ᖕ	ᖕ	---	ᖕ	ᖕᖕ	---	---
↓↑↑ ↑	↑ ᴪ	↑	---	↑	↑	---	↓	↓↑	↑	---	Ψ↑	↑	↑	↑V
ᖀ ᖀ ᖀᖀ	᙭᙭	K	K	---	᙭	K	᙭	᙭	᙭	---	᙭ K	---	x	---
▷△ △▽ △▲ ᐁᐁ ᐁᐁ	▷ △▷ △▲	△	◁◁	▷ ▽ ◁	---	---	---	---	△ △	᙮	△ △	---	ᘔ	▽
B B B B	---	B	B	---	B	ꓭ	B B	---	---	B	B B	---	ꓯ	B M

Turkic	Iberian	Lycian	Phrygian	Celtiberian	Lydian	Caucasian Albanian	Etruscan	Pelasgian	Phoenician / Kharosthi	Khazarian	Greek	Scythian	Hunnic	Carian

Turkic	Iberian	Lycian	Phrygian	Celtiberian	Lydian	Caucasian Albanian	Etruscan	Pelasgian	Phoenician / Kharosthi	Khazarian	Greek	Scythian	Hunnic	Carian
	⋀													
	------	------	------	------	ℏ	------	------	------	ℏ	ℵ		------	⋈	------
	Φ	------	------	------	------	------	------	------	------	৭		------	------	------
	⚹	------	------	------	------	------	------	------	------	------		⨍	✕	------
	Ψ	------	Ψ	Ψ	⋎	⋏	Ψ	Ψ	------	Ψ	Ψ λ	⋏	Ψ	Ψ
	⬦ ⊤	◇ ⊤	⊢ ⊤	⊤ ⊤	⊢ ⊤	T	T	T	⋏ / T ⋎	▱ ⊤	T	⊻	⊤	T
	∩ ⋀ A	⋀	⋀ A	A	ꟻ ⋂	A		✕ ⋏	⋀ ⋀ ⋂ A	(	⋀ ⋀	⋂ ⋀ ⋀ ⋀ A

Turkic	Iberian	Lycian	Phrygian	Celtiberian	Lydian	Caucasian Albanian	Etruscan	Pelasgian	Phoenician / Kharosthi	Khazarian	Greek	Scythian	Hunnic	Carian
∩∩ ∩∩ ∧∧														
⌗⌗ ▢▢	▢	-----	▢	----	▢	⊞		▢	----	▢	-----	-----	⌶▢	
ᛖᛖ ᛖ	ᛖ ᛖ	M	ᛖ M	ᛖ M	-----	M M	ᛖ	M	M M	ᛖ	M	M		
ʒʒ ʒʒ	ʒ ʒ	-----	ʒʒʒ	-----	Σ	-----	ʒ	-----	ʒ 3	Σ	Ʒ	-----		
⋈ ⋈8 ✕	⋈ ⋈	----	----	8	8	-----	-----	-----	⋈ ⋈ ᙰ	----	----	⋈	⋈⋈	
⬤⬤ ⬤⬤ ⬤⬤	⬤ ⊙	O	O	⊙ O	O-	O⊙	O⊙	⊙⊙	O O punctuation mark	o	O Θ θ O	-----	⊙	OΘ
11 ⟩	1	1	1	1	1	1	1	1	1	1	1	-----	-----	-----
⟩⟩3 Ɛ3	------	------	------	------	------	------	------	------	------	---	ξ			
Ω	------	------	------	------	------	------	------	------	------	Ω	Ω	------	------	Ω

The comparative analysis of the given alphabets with *Turkic* provided anticipated results. It is determined that there are letters that do not have their match in the *Phoenician* alphabet – the main source of alphabet creation in ancient languages of *Asia Minor*. However, they exist in *Turkic* and other scripts that we examined. These letters fall into the following categories:

Ψ **The exact or close match in both shape and sound with Turkic:**

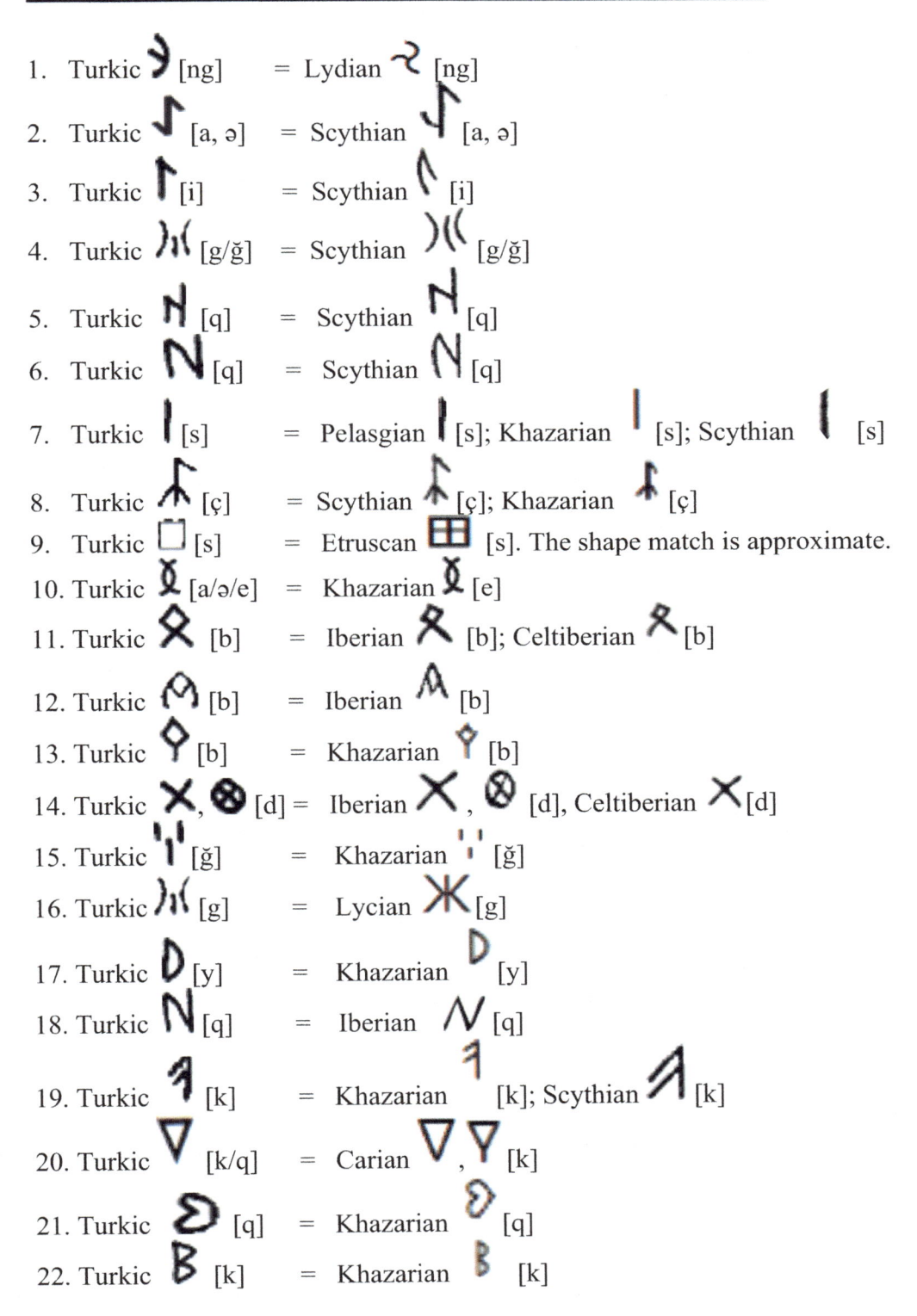

1. Turkic [ng] = Lydian [ng]
2. Turkic [a, ə] = Scythian [a, ə]
3. Turkic [i] = Scythian [i]
4. Turkic [g/ğ] = Scythian [g/ğ]
5. Turkic [q] = Scythian [q]
6. Turkic [q] = Scythian [q]
7. Turkic [s] = Pelasgian [s]; Khazarian [s]; Scythian [s]
8. Turkic [ç] = Scythian [ç]; Khazarian [ç]
9. Turkic [s] = Etruscan [s]. The shape match is approximate.
10. Turkic [a/ə/e] = Khazarian [e]
11. Turkic [b] = Iberian [b]; Celtiberian [b]
12. Turkic [b] = Iberian [b]
13. Turkic [b] = Khazarian [b]
14. Turkic ✕, ⊗ [d] = Iberian ✕, ⊗ [d], Celtiberian ✕ [d]
15. Turkic [ğ] = Khazarian [ğ]
16. Turkic [g] = Lycian [g]
17. Turkic [y] = Khazarian [y]
18. Turkic [q] = Iberian [q]
19. Turkic [k] = Khazarian [k]; Scythian [k]
20. Turkic [k/q] = Carian [k]
21. Turkic [q] = Khazarian [q]
22. Turkic [k] = Khazarian [k]

295

23. Turkic ↲ [L] = Etruscan ↲ [L] = Pelasgian ↲ [L] = Khazarian) [L]; Greek ↲ [L]

24. Turkic Ұ [L] = Scythian У [L]

25. Turkic) [n] = Khazarian) [n] = Hunnic ᘯ [n]

26. Turkic ⋀ [t] = Carian ⋀ [tⱨ]

27. Turkic ⋀ [t] = Scythian ⋇ [t]

28. Turkic ⅄ [z] = Scythian ⅄ ⱶ [z]

29. Turkic ∩ [ş] = Khazarian ∩ [ş]

30. Turkic ⁀ [nç] = Pelasgian ⁀ [nç]

31. Turkic M [Lt] = Khazarian M [Lt]

32. Turkic ⋂ [ot] = Carian Ω [t]

Ψ The exact or close match in shape with Turkic, absent in Phoenician:

1. Turkic ⌐ < Iberian ✓ ; Phrygian ⌐ ; Celtiberian ✓

2. Turkic ⱨ < Carian ↄ ; Greek ↄ

3. Turkic X < Lycian X ; Carian)(

4. Turkic ⱷ < Hunnic ⌯ ; Carian ↄ ; Khazarian ⱷ

5. Turkic N < Carian N ; Khazarian N

6. Turkic M < Phrygian M ; Iberian M ; Celtiberian M ; Etruscan M

7. Turkic ⁚ (a word separator) = Pelasgian ⁚ ; Khazarian ⁚ ; Lycian ⁚ ; Etruscan ⁚

8. Turkic ⊗ < Etruscan ⊗ ; Iberian ⊗ ; Hunnic ⊗ ; Greek ⊗

9. Turkic ׀׀ < Carian ׀׀ ; Khazarian ׀׀

10. Turkic Є < Iberian ℉ ; Phrygian E ; Carian E ; Lycian E ; Etruscan E ; Greek E

11. Turkic Є < Iberian Ɛ

12. Turkic F < Lycian F ; Phrygian F ; Celtiberian ⋜ ; Etruscan Ռ

13. Turkic Ɛ < Celtiberian ⱶ ; Iberian ℉, ⱶ

14. Turkic ⊃ < Lydian ⊃ ; Iberian ⊃ ; Carian ⊃

15. Turkic D < Carian D ; Etruscan D ; Khazarian D

16. Turkic H < Carian H ; Iberian H ; Celtiberian H ; Greek H

17. Turkic H < Iberian N ; Greek H

18. Turkic N < Iberian N ; Lycian N ; Khazarian H ; Greek N ; Hunnic N ; Scythian N

19. Turkic ҺҺ < Caucasian Albanian ҺҺ ; Khazarian ҺҺ ; Hunnic ҺҺ

20. Turkic ⅎ, ⅎ < Phrygian ⅎ ; Etruscan ⅎ ; Greek ⅎ ; Lydian ⅎ ; Pelasgian ⅎ ; Khazarian ; Scythian ⅎ

21. Turkic ↓ < Pelasgian ↓ ; Etruscan ⋁ ; Lycian ⋁ ; Carian ⋁ ; Greek ψ

22. Turkic ↑ < Iberian ↑ ; Lycian ↑ ; Lydian ↑ ; Celtiberian ↑ ; Carian ↑ ; Pelasgian ↓ ; Hunnic ↑ ; Scythian ↑

23. Turkic ↑ < Iberian ↑ ; Scythian ↑, ↑ ; Hunnic ↑

24. Turkic ⋀ < Iberian ⋀ ; Celtiberian ⋀ ; Hunnic ⋀ ; Carian ⋀

25. Turkic Ə < Khazarian Ə ; Hunnic Ə

26. Turkic K < Phrygian K ; Lycian K ; Hunnic X ; Etruscan K ; Greek K

27. Turkic ▷,◁ < Phrygian ◁/▷ ; Iberian ▷,◁ ; Celtiberian ▷,◁

28. Turkic △ < Greek △ ; Iberian △△ ; Lycian △

29. Turkic ▽ < Celtiberian ▽ ; Carian ▽

30. Turkic B < Phrygian B ; Carian B, ⋀⋀ ; Lycian B ; Greek B, ß ; Etruscan B, ß ; Khazarian B ; Hunnic ß ; Lydian B ; Caucasian Albanian ჻

31. Turkic ↲, ↳ < Etruscan ↲ ; Pelasgian ↲ ; Khazarian ↲ ; Hunnic ↲ ; Greek ↲

32. Turkic Y < Hunnic Y ; Caucasian Albanian ჻ ; Lydian ჻ ; Khazarian ჻

33. Turkic Ч < Celtiberian Ч

34. Turkic ☦ < Hunnic ☦

35. Turkic ⊃ < Etruscan ⊃ ; Iberian ʔ ; Lydian ⊃ ; Caucasian Albanian ⊃ ; Hunnic ⊃, ⊃ ; Khazarian ⊃

36. Turkic > < Caucasian Albanian ⟩ ; Khazarian >

37. Turkic ʃ < Caucasian Albanian ʃ

38. Turkic ʃ < Scythian ʃ ; Hunnic ʃ, ʃ

39. Turkic 6 < Iberian G

40. Turkic C < Caucasian Albanian [; Kharosthi ʃ ; Carian C/C ; Etruscan C

41. Turkic Ψ < Lydian Ψ ; Lycian Ψ ; Iberian Ψ ; Celtiberian Ψ ; Khazarian Ψ

42. Turkic Ψ < Khazarian M

43. Turkic Ψ < Phrygian Ψ ; Lydian Ψ ; Etruscan Ψ ; Pelasgian Ψ ; Carian Ψ ; Iberian Ψ ; Celtiberian Ψ ; Greek Ψ ; Hunnic Ψ ; Khazarian Ψ

44. Turkic ʎ < Lydian ʎ

45. Turkic ʎ, ♣ < Caucasian Albanian ʎ ; Greek λ

46. Turkic ⚹ < Khazarian ⚹ ; Scythian ⚹, ⚹, ⚹

47. Turkic Λ < Iberian Λ ; Lycian Λ ; Phrygian Λ ; Greek Λ ; Hunnic Λ ; Carian ⊓ ; Etruscan ⊓ ; Scythian (

48. Turkic ⊓ < Iberian ⊓ ; Khazarian ⊓ ; Greek Π

49. Turkic □ < Carian □ ; Pelasgian ■ ; Iberian □ ; Celtiberian □ ; Khazarian □ ; Etruscan ⊞

50. Turkic M < Etruscan M ; Iberian M ; Celtiberian M ; Khazarian M ; Greek M

51. Turkic M < Lycian M ; Lydian M ; Carian M ; Greek M ; Latin M ; Hunnic M

52. Turkic ⋈ < Carian ⋈

53. Turkic ⋈ < Iberian ⋈

54. Turkic 8 < Hunnic X

55. Turkic ҍ < Scythian ҍ

298

56. Turkic ⏳ < Carian ⏳ ; Iberian ⏳ ; Celtiberian ⏳ ; Khazarian ⏳ , ✕

57. Turkic 8 < Lydian 8 ; Caucasian Albanian 8 ; Khazarian 8

58. Turkic ⋈ < Iberian ⋈ ; Hunnic ⋈

59. Turkic ↑,ᒋ < Iberian ↑,↗ ; Celtiberian ↑ ; Khazarian ᒋ ; Carian ⌒ ; Lycian ⌐ ; Scythian Ⲩ

60. Turkic ⌐ < Carian Γ ; Celtiberian Γ ; Greek Γ

61. Turkic ⏀ < Iberian ⏀, ⏀, ✵ ; Celtiberian ⏀

62. Turkic ⏀ < Carian ∇ ; Iberian ⏀,⏀ ; Caucasian Albanian ⏀ ; Etruscan ⏀ ; Khazarian ⏀

63. Turkic ⏀ < Carian ⏀

64. Turkic ⏀ < Iberian Ⱥ

65. Turkic ⇉ < Khazarian ⇉

66. Turkic ✕ < Iberian ✕ ; Lycian ✕ ; Celtiberian ✳ ; Scythian)((

67. Turkic P < Iberian P, P ; Lycian P ; Phrygian P ; Carian P ; Etruscan P ; Greek P

68. Turkic ◈ < Iberian ◈

69. Turkic ◇ < Lycian ◇ ; Celtiberian ◯ ; Khazarian ◇ ; Hunnic ◇'

70. Turkic ✦ < Iberian ◈

71. Turkic ⊣ < Caucasian Albanian ⊣ ; Hunnic ✝ ; Lydian Y ; Khazarian Y ; Scythian Y

72. Turkic ⟨ < Iberian ⟨ ; Phrygian Ξ ; Caucasian Albanian Σ ; Greek Σ

73. Turkic ε < Greek ξ

74. Turkic ⟩ < Iberian ⟩ ; Phrygian ⟩ ; Khazarian ⟩ ; Pelasgian ⟩

75. Turkic Ʒ < Hunnic Ʒ

76. Turkic ⊙ < Iberian ⊙ ; Celtiberian ⊙ ; Pelasgian ⊙ ; Etruscan ⊙ ; Hunnic ⊙ ; Carian ⊖ ; Greek ⊖

77. Turkic ⟳ < Khazarian Ω ; Carian Ω ; Greek Ω
78. Turkic ⟨K < Iberian A ; Phrygian A ; Lydian A ; Etruscan Я ; Pelasgian A ; Greek A ; Carian A
79. Turkic ⟨X < Hunnic α

Ψ **The exact or close match in shape with Turkic and Greek, absent in Phoenician:**

1. Turkic ⌐ < Greek Γ
2. Turkic ⊗ < Greek ⊗
3. Turkic ⊓ < Greek Π
4. Turkic ϵ < Greek ξ
5. Turkic Λ < Greek Λ
6. Turkic N < Greek N
7. Turkic H < Greek H
8. Turkic H < Greek H
9. Turkic K < Greek K
10. Turkic B < Greek B
11. Turkic ⟨ < Greek ζ
12. Turkic ϵ < Greek E
13. Turkic M < Greek M
14. Turkic P < Greek P
15. Turkic ⅂ < Greek ⅂
16. Turkic Δ < Greek Δ
17. Turkic J < Greek J
18. Turkic Ψ < Greek Ψ
19. Turkic K < Greek A
20. Turkic ⟨ < Greek Σ
21. Turkic ⊙ < Greek Θ
22. Turkic ⟳ < Greek Ω

300

23. Turkic [symbol] < Greek λ

Ψ The exact or close match in shape with Turkic, absent in Greek, Phoenician, Kharosthi:

1. Turkic X < Lycian X ; Carian)(
2. Turkic ⌀ < Hunnic ⌇ ; Carian ϛ ; Khazarian ⌀
3. Turkic N, ⋔ < Carian N ; Khazarian N ; Phrygian ⋔ ; Iberian ⋔ ; Celtiberian ⋔ ; Etruscan N
4. Turkic • (a word separator) = Pelasgian • ; Khazarian • ; Lycian • ; Etruscan •
5. Turkic ⵊ < Carian ⵊ ; Khazarian ⵊ
6. Turkic ◖ < Lydian ◖ ; Iberian ◖ ; Carian ◖
7. Turkic D < Carian D ; Etruscan D ; Khazarian D
8. Turkic ↑ < Iberian ↑ ; Lycian ↑ ; Lydian ↑ ; Celtiberian ↑ ; Carian ↑ ; Pelasgian ↑ ; Hunnic ∱ ; Scythian ↑
9. Turkic ⯒ < Iberian ⯒ ; Scythian ⯒, ↑ ; Hunnic ∱
10. Turkic ⌃ < Iberian ⌃ ; Celtiberian ⌃ ; Hunnic Λ ; Carian ⌃
11. Turkic Y < Hunnic Y ; Caucasian Albanian ၆ ; Lydian ʕ ; Khazarian ʕ
12. Turkic ѱ < Lydian ѱ ; Lycian ѱ ; Iberian ѱ ; Celtiberian ѱ ; Khazarian Υ
13. Turkic ⋔ < Khazarian ⋔
14. Turkic ⌇ < Lydian ⌇
15. Turkic ⯒ < Khazarian ⯒ ; Scythian ⯒, ⯒, ⯒
16. Turkic □ < Carian □ ; Pelasgian □ ; Iberian □ ; Celtiberian □ ; Khazarian □ ; Etruscan ⊞
17. Turkic ⋇ < Carian ⋇
18. Turkic ⋎ < Iberian ⋎
19. Turkic 8 < Hunnic ⋊
20. Turkic ҺҺ < Scythian ҺҺ

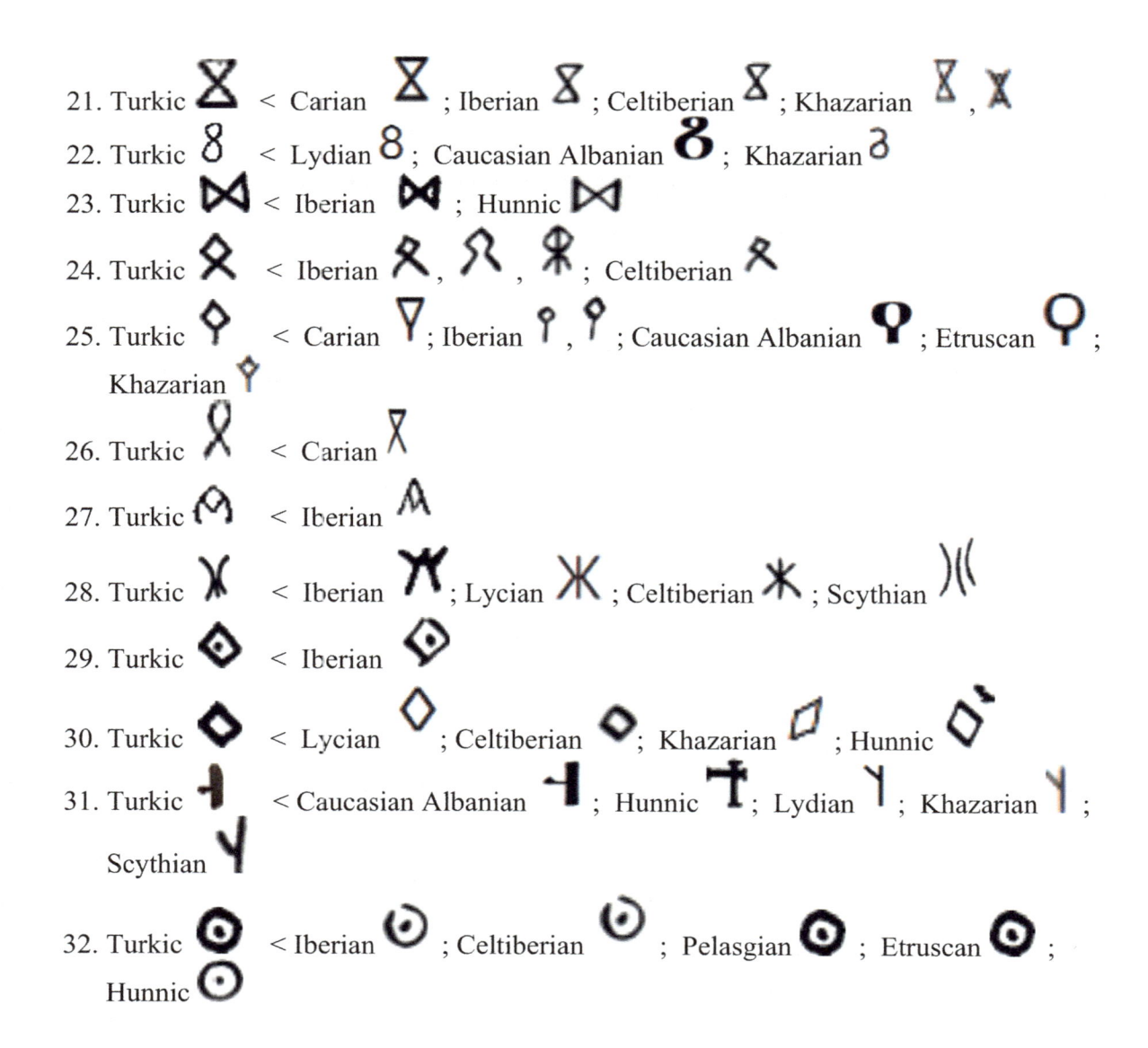

21. Turkic ⧖ < Carian ⧖ ; Iberian ⧖ ; Celtiberian ⧖ ; Khazarian ⧖ , ⧖

22. Turkic 8 < Lydian 8 ; Caucasian Albanian 8 ; Khazarian 8

23. Turkic ⋈ < Iberian ⋈ ; Hunnic ⋈

24. Turkic ⚦ < Iberian ⚦, ⚦, ⚦ ; Celtiberian ⚦

25. Turkic ♀ < Carian ♀ ; Iberian ♀, ♀ ; Caucasian Albanian ♀ ; Etruscan ♀ ; Khazarian ♀

26. Turkic ⚧ < Carian ⚧

27. Turkic ᠓ < Iberian A

28. Turkic ✕ < Iberian ✕ ; Lycian ✕ ; Celtiberian ✶ ; Scythian)((

29. Turkic ⊙ < Iberian ⊙

30. Turkic ◇ < Lycian ◇ ; Celtiberian ◇ ; Khazarian ◇ ; Hunnic ◇

31. Turkic ⊢ < Caucasian Albanian ⊢ ; Hunnic ⊤ ; Lydian Y ; Khazarian Y ; Scythian Y

32. Turkic ⊙ < Iberian ⊙ ; Celtiberian ⊙ ; Pelasgian ⊙ ; Etruscan ⊙ ; Hunnic ⊙

The *Indo-European* proponents have long asserted that the ancient *Greek* alphabet was created solely from the *Phoenician* alphabet. However, they humbly keep silent about 23 *Greek* characters that do not have their exact counterparts in *Phoenician*. The more puzzling fact is that all these letters match the letters of the ancient *Turkic* alphabet!

Table No.1 with 16 alphabets comparing the ancient *Turkic* alphabet with 15 others, uncovered the undeniable truth – all these mysterious 23 letters in the *Greek* alphabet are of *Turkic* origin. And this is the fact, not a fairy-tale story or wishful thinking.

The *Phoenician* alphabet was introduced to the *Greeks* by the son of the *Phoenician* king *Agenor* – *Cadmos*, who had the *Thrace-Pelasgian* extraction and belonged to the legendary dynasty of *Io* – the *Thracian* princess deified in *Egypt* as the goddess *Isis*. It seems evident that the *Phoenicians* owed the creation of their alphabet to *Io*, who brought the script to *Egypt* from *Thrace*. This alphabet in its basic form was already in use by the *Thracians* but continued to develop after *Io's* departure.

The *Thracian* royalty, who, according to the legend, was turned into a cow by *Zeus* and found refuge in *Egypt*, is identified with the *Egyptian* deity *Isis*. The approximate time of her arrival on the *Egyptian* soil can be established from the 5th dynasty onward when her name as *Isis* was mentioned in the Pyramid Texts, dated c. 2350 – c. 2100 BCE. However, *Saint Jerome* chronicled her as a documented goddess venerated in *Egypt* in 1852 BCE.

Evidently, by that time, the *Thrace-Pelasgian* alphabet would have existed in its basic version, that later was brought to *Greece* by *Cadmos,* the great-great-grandson of *Io:*

> "And therefore it is believed, that, many ages after, *Cadmos* the son of *Agenor* brought the knowledge of letters out of *Phœnicia* first into *Greece…*" [*Diodorus Siculus.* 5.3]

Furthermore, *Diodorus Siculus* made a note of the way how *Cadmos* introduced the letters to the inhabitants of *Greece:*

> "Not long after, *Cadmos,* the son of *Agenor,* being commanded by the king to seek after *Europa,* made for *Rhodes;* and in the voyage, being overtaken with a violent storm, made a vow to build a temple to *Neptune.* Having therefore escaped the danger, according to his vow, he dedicated a temple to this god in the island, and left some of the *Phœnicians* to be overseers of the sacred mysteries, who were made members of the city with the *Ialysians,* and out of their families, they say, from time to time, were chosen the priests. *Cadmos,* at that time devoted many rich gifts to *Minerva Lindia,* amongst which was a brass caldron, a most excellent piece of curious antient workmanship; it had an inscription upon it in *Phœnician* letters, which were therefore called *Phœnician,* because, they say, they were first brought out of *Phœnicia* into *Greece.*" [Idem ibid]

Diodorus Siculus asserted that at the beginning, the *Greek* alphabet was called *Pelasgic* (read *Turkic*), as it was the *Pelasgians* who first received the script from their *Phoenician* kin of the *Thrace-Pelasgian* extraction – *Cadmus* and utilized the letters to satisfy the need for a *Greek* alphabet:

> "…Hence these letters are all generally called *Phœnician* letters, because they were brought over out of *Phœnicia* into *Greece:* but they were afterwards called *Pelasgian* characters, because the *Pelasgians* were the first that understood them after they were brought over." [3.4]

Furthermore, in accordance with another highly esteemed scholar *Dionysius,* "who composed a history of the antient stories and fables: for he has written a history of *Bacchus,* of the *Amazons,* of the expedition of the *Argonauts,* and the war of *Troy,* and many other things; annexing thereunto several poems of the antient mythologists and poets", *Diodorus Siculus* stated that the ancient musician *Linos,* or *Linus,* processed the letters brought by *Cadmos* and created the alphabet for the *Greeks* by further developing their shape and assigning a name to each of the symbols:

> "…*Linus* was the first that invented rhimes and music in *Greece:* and that *Cadmos* brought letters out of *Phœnicia,* and was the first who taught the *Grecians* to pronounce them, and gave them their several names, and formed their distinct characters…" [Idem ibid]

Linos (Λίνος), recognized as *Linus of Thrace,* was not an ethnic *Greek.* His *Thrace-Pelasgian* roots are evident due to the commonly accepted fact that he and the *Thracian* singer *Orpheus* were brothers. *Strabo* was firm in his belief that *Orpheus* was a *Thracian* [10.3.17].

Diodorus Siculus also asserted that the alphabet brought by *Cadmus* from *Phoenicia* was first utilized by the *Pelasgians,* who later compiled the *Greek* alphabet for the *Greeks.* As a side note, both the *Greek* and *Latin* alphabets were created by the *Pelasgians,* and the *Etruscans,* who founded the *Latin* script, also belonged to the *Pelasgian* family.

According to "The Chronicle" by the *Latin* historian of the 4th c. *Saint Jerome, Linos* was a contemporary of *Cadmus,* who founded and reigned the city *Thebes* (correctly, *Thebae* "hill" in *Turkic*) in *Bœotia, Greece,* in 1429 BCE.

However, the earliest known fragmentary *Greek* inscriptions date from 770–750 BCE. This means that *Linus* first crafted a *Pelasgic* alphabet, which was utilized by the *Greeks* around seven centuries later. This conjecture is in perfect alignment with *Diodorus Siculus's* statement about the *Pelasgic* alphabet, as the early *Greek* literary and poetic writings were in the *Pelasgic* alphabet:

> "This *Linus* (they say) wrote in *Pelasgian* letters, the acts of the first *Bacchus*, and left other stories in his writings behind him. *Orpheus,* likewise, it is said, used the same characters, and *Pronapides, Homer's* master, an ingenious musician. *Thymætes* also, the son of *Thymætus,* the son of *Leomedon,* who lived in the time of *Orpheus,* and travelled through many parts of the world, as far as to the western parts of *Libya* to the very ocean: this *Thymætes* visited likewise (they say) *Nysa,* the place where *Bacchus* was brought up, as is reported by the antient inhabitants; where being instructed by the *Nysians,* he wrote a poem called *Phrygia,* of the particular actions of this god, in very old language and character." [Idem ibid]

Further discourse, provided by *Diodorus Siculus,* confirms the antediluvian age of the *Pelasgian* alphabet and the existence of the written *Pelasgian* monuments long before the famous repatriation voyage of *Cadmus* to *Greece* in the 15th c. BCE:

> "Afterwards, when most of the inhabitants of *Greece* were destroyed by the flood, and all records and antient monuments perished with them, the *Egyptians* took this occasion to appropriate the study of astrology solely to themselves; and whereas the *Grecians* (through ignorance) as yet valued not learning, it became a general opinion that the *Egyptians* were the first that found out the knowledge of the stars. And so even the *Athenians* themselves, though they built the city *Sais,* in *Egypt,* yet by reason of the flood, were led into the same error of forgetting what was before. And therefore it is believed, that, many ages after, *Cadmus* the son of *Agenor* brought the knowledge of letters out of *Phœnicia* first into *Greece;* and after him, it is supposed the *Grecians* themselves added some letters to those they learned before; but a general ignorance, however, still prevailed amongst them." [5.3]

Let us not forget that back then *Greece* was primarily inhabited and ruled by the *Pelasgians,* a branch of which – the *Athenians* – became *Hellenized* in 1333 BCE and changed their appellation to *Ionians* after their new ruler *Ion* [Saint Jerome. "The Chronicle."].

As far as the *Phoenicians,* they did not invent their alphabet either – they simply borrowed it from the same source as the *Pelasgians* did, accordant with *Diodorus Siculus:*

> "But there are some who attribute the invention of letters to the *Syrians,* from whom the *Phœnicians* learned them, and communicated them to the *Grecians* when they came with *Cadmus* into *Europe:* whence the *Grecians* called them *Phœnician* letters. To these that hold this opinion, it is answered, that the *Phœnicians* were not the first that found out letters, but only changed the form and shape of them into other characters, which many afterwards using, the name of *Phœnician* grew to be common." [5.4]

Even if we agree with the erroneous opinion of some ancient scholars about the *Syrian* origin of the *Phoenician* letters, then it is important to remind that under the *Syrians,* the *Greeks* recognized the *Cappadocians* [Herodotus. 1.72]. In that case, knowing that the *Cappadocians* were a *Thracian* people, it becomes clear that the *Thrace-Pelasgians* of *Turkic* blood invented the alphabet and the letters.

As it was determined earlier, the letters of the *Greek* alphabet were very similar to the *Turkic* tamgas, and the *Pelasgians* used the letters identical with those of the *Turkic* alphabet, up to the punctuation mark, or a sentence separator ⁑

It seems clear on the whole that both the *Pelasgians* and the *Turkic* nations drew their scripts from the common pool. In order to establish the parental source of the *Pelasgian* letters and the ancient *Turkic* tamgas, it is necessary to embark on a search after this mysterious alphabet. With that purpose in mind, we created Table No. 2 that includes 7 alphabets – *Turkic, Turdaş, Linear A, Linear B, Cypriot, Phoenician,* and *Greek*.

Table No. 2.

Turkic	Turdaş 60 c. BCE	Linear A 18 c. BCE	Linear B 15 c. BCE	Cypriot 15 c. BCE	Phoenician 11 c. BCE	Greek 8 c. BCE

		--------			--------	
		--------	--------	--------	--------	-----
	--------	-----	----------	--------	--------	-----
			----------		--------	------
					--------	--------
			----------		--------	--------

305

Turkic	Turdaş 60 c. BCE	Linear A 18 c. BCE	Linear B 15 c. BCE	Cypriot 15 c. BCE	Phoenician 11 c. BCE	Greek 8 c. BCE
✕✕ ✕✶✕ ✕⊛	✕ ⊗⊕ ✺ ✕ ✕'✕	⊕ ✕	⊕ ✕	✕ ⊖	⊕ ✕	✕ ✕ ⊗
(various)	⟊ ✳	⊤ ✳	⊤ ⟊	)(	------	------
ϵϵϵ	ϵ ⊻E	F	E	F	ㅋ	⇁ E
D D D	D G	------	▷	------	------	----
9 9 q q P	P	q	ᛈ	-----	⊲	⊲
H H И И И Н Н Н Н	⊤ ⊞	H ⊞	⊟	⊢	------	⊟ H N
⊤ ⊤ ⊤ ⊐	⊤	⊤	⊤ ⇉	✕	------	⊤

Turkic	Turdaş 60 c. BCE	Linear A 18 c. BCE	Linear B 15 c. BCE	Cypriot 15 c. BCE	Phoenician 11 c. BCE	Greek 8 c. BCE

		------	-------			
			--------	--------	--------	

	(	--------	-----	-----		-----
			-------	-------	--------	
		------	-------	-------		

Turkic	Turdaş 60 c. BCE	Linear A 18 c. BCE	Linear B 15 c. BCE	Cypriot 15 c. BCE	Phoenician 11 c. BCE	Greek 8 c. BCE
					--------	-----
		--------			--------	-----
		------			--------	-----
		------		--------	--------	-----
		--------	--------	--------	--------	-----
		--------	--------	--------	--------	-----

308

Turkic	Turdaş 60 c. BCE	Linear A 18 c. BCE	Linear B 15 c. BCE	Cypriot 15 c. BCE	Phoenician 11 c. BCE	Greek 8 c. BCE
					--------	Ψ λ
					--------	T
						Λ Π A
				--------	--------	-----
				--------	--------	M M Μ Σ
			--------	--------	--------	Σ
		--------		-------	--------	-----

309

Turkic	Turdaş 60 c. BCE	Linear A 18 c. BCE	Linear B 15 c. BCE	Cypriot 15 c. BCE	Phoenician 11 c. BCE	Greek 8 c. BCE
⊙⊙ ⊙⊙ ⊙	○ ⊙	⊙	⊜	⊕	O	O Θ θ O
11 ⟩	1	冘	-----	)⟨	1	1
⋚ ⋚ ⋛ ⋛ ⋳	⋛	⋛	-----	-----	....	ξ
⌒	☷	-----	Ω			Ω

Table No.2 yielded fascinating results – except for a punctuation mark, all the main *Turkic* alphabet letters found their ideal or close match with the majority of *Turdaş*, or *Vinča*, alphabet letters. None of the other displayed alphabets – *Linear A, Linear B, Cypriot* had this many characters similar to the *Turkic* tamgas.

Radiocarbon-dated as early as around 6,000 BCE, the artifacts with *Turdaş* symbols were first unearthed in the 19th c. in a region of *Romania* with a strikingly familiar *Turkic* name *Turdaş*. Though modified from *Tordos*, this name still shows its undeniable *Turkic* roots: *Tor=Tur* 'Turk' + *Dos=Daş* 'stone', meaning "*Turkic* stone". Interestingly, the tablets with this script were also found in a *Romanian* village with a typical *Turkic* name – *Tartaria*. Later, similar inscriptions were uncovered in *Vinča* – a suburban area of the *Serbian* city *Belgrade*. Since then, this script has been known as *Turdaş* (or *Vinča*). As of today, more than a thousand fragments inscribed with this script have been discovered throughout *Europe*, including *Greece, Bulgaria, Moldova, Hungary, Ukraine, Romania*, and *Serbia*.

Figure 27. Monument for the Neolithic Tărtăria tablets, dated to 5500-5300 BCE and discovered in 1961 at Tărtăria, Alba County, Romania by the archaeologist Nicolae Vlassa. The clay tables are associated with the Turdaş-Vinča culture. The monument has been created near the discovery location. [CC BY-SA 3.0] Credit: Țetcu Mircea Rareș.

The following Table No.3 presents a lineup of the *Turkic* and *Turdaş* characters.

Table No.3.

Turkic tamgas	...
Turdaş symbols	...

The analysis of all three Tables comparing the ancient *Turkic* alphabet to 19 other ancient scripts allowed us to reach the following conclusions:

1. The *Turdaş* alphabet is the mother of the *Turkic* alphabet – the direct and indirect source of creation of other scripts, such as *Phoenician, Greek, Latin, Carian, Etruscan, Iberian, Celtiberian, Lycian, Lydian, Pelasgian, Phrygian, Kharosthi, Scythian, Khazarian,* and *Caucasian Albanian*, to some extent.

2. The *Turkic* tamgas, or letters, exhibited here represent one of the most ancient writings known to the scientific world as of today.

3. The *Turkic* script surpasses all other scripts, such as the *Phoenician, Greek, Latin,* and the *Linear A, Linear B, Cypriot,* in antiquity – it is much older than the rest and was created from within, without any external assistance of other nations.

4. The existence of the *Turdaș* alphabet throughout *Europe,* its uniqueness, and the antediluvian age confirms that the *Turkic* nations were among the first, if not the first, inhabitants of the *European* territory. The radioactive analysis of the unearthed artifacts with the *Turdaș* inscriptions dated them as far back as 6,000-5,000 BCE and showed the rise of the ancient *Turkic* culture contrary to the official scientific belief that during that period, there was nobody but cave dwellers on Earth with a few smart ones among them, trying to invent the wheel.

5. The *Turkic* alphabet originated in *Europe* and then spread throughout the *Caucasus, Central Asia* up to *North Africa.*

6. Both the *Phoenician* script, dated 11th c. BCE, and *Kharosthi* script that appeared in the 3rd c. BCE, adopted the elements of the *Turkic* alphabet with no or slight modification, such as changing the direction of a letter from left to right or vice versa. There are 9 characters borrowed by *Phoenician* and 11 characters that *Kharosthi* loaned from the *Turdaș/Turkic* alphabet:

    The *Turdaș/Turkic* characters in *Phoenician*:

    The *Turdaș/Turkic* characters in *Kharosthi*:

7. Except for one letter, all 9 *Phoenician* letters borrowed from the *Turdaș/Turkic* source were adopted by the *Aramaic* language, which was the main language of the *Persian, Babylonian,* and *Assyrian* empires. The *Early Aramaic* alphabet, created from the *Phoenician* script around the late 10th–9th c. BCE served as a replacement for the cuneiform, used in the *Assyrian* empire.

8. Ancient *Greek* writing system transferred some characters directly from the *Etruscan, Lydian,* and *Pelasgian* (which are closely related languages), leaving out the *Phoenician* symbols:

    Greek ⊗ > *Etruscan* ⊗ ≠ *Phoenician* ⊕

    Greek ⌐ > *Etruscan* or *Pelasgian* ⌐ ≠ *Phoenician* L

    Greek A > *Lydian* A, *Pelasgian* A ≠ *Phoenician*

    Greek M > *Etruscan* M ≠ *Phoenician*

    Greek M > *Lydian* M ≠ *Phoenician*

    This means that long before the *Phoenician* set of letters appeared, there were the *Etruscan, Pelasgian, Lydian* alphabets that gave life to the *Phoenician, Greek,* and later *Latin* scripts. The *Latins* benefited from the *Etruscan* alphabet in the 11th c. BCE after the fall of *Troy* that, according to *Saint Jerome,* took place around 1206 BCE. The defeated *Trojans,* later known as the *Etruscans,* fled their motherland and resettled in new lands, bringing their advanced civilization, including their script.

9. All 15 scripts of Table No.1 revealed characters of the *Turkic/Turdaș* origin:

    ❖ *Iberian* - 54 characters
    ❖ *Lycian* – 15 characters and a word separator :
    ❖ *Phrygian* – 21 characters
    ❖ *Celtiberian* – 21 characters

- *Lydian* – 17 characters
- *Caucasian Albanian* – 12 characters
- *Etruscan* – 18 characters and a word separator
- *Pelasgian* – 18 characters and a word separator
- *Khazarian* – 33 characters and a word separator
- *Greek* – *Cretan* and *Attic* versions – 31 characters
- *Scythian* – 18 characters (the source – the *Issyk* silver cup)
- *Carian* – 38 characters
- *Hunnic* – 26 characters

10. All 12 scripts of Table No.1 unveiled *Turkic/Turdaş* characters that were absent in other 3 alphabets – *Greek, Phoenician, Kharosthi* and could not be borrowed from them:

    - *Lycian* – 6 characters
    - *Carian* – 13 characters
    - *Hunnic* – 10 characters
    - *Khazarian* – 16 characters
    - *Phrygian* – 1 character
    - *Iberian* – 19 characters
    - *Celtiberian* – 10 characters
    - *Etruscan* – 6 characters
    - *Pelasgian* – 4 characters
    - *Lydian* – 7 characters
    - *Scythian* – 8 characters
    - *Caucasian Albanian* – 4 characters

11. The numbers 0,1, 2, 3, 4, 5, 7, 8, 9, currently called *Hindu-Arabic* numerals, originally came from the *Turkic/Turdaş* alphabet. They should be called *Turkic* numbers. Compare the set of 10 symbols below:

Turdaş	O	٦	Z	ろ	⋆	५	5	ь	ㄱ	8	∽
Turkic	O	1	2	3	4	ﾉ	6	ㄱ	8	9
Hindu-Arabic	0	1	2	3	4	5	6	7	8	9

12. The same applies to the *Roman* numerals. There is no doubt in their *Turkic/Turdaş* origin. There are practically only 3 main *Turkic* symbols – I, Y, X that were used in different combinations to create *Roman* ciphers. Most definitely, the following *Turdaş* symbols were used to develop the *Roman* numerals: I, II, III, ∨, X. There is nothing extraordinary in this if one takes into account a very important fact – it was the *Etruscans* of the *Turkic* origin who brought both the alphabet and the numerals to *Rome* and presented them to the *Indo-European* nation of the *Latins* who eagerly accepted this innovation.

13. The punctuation mark **:** which was used to mark the end of a sentence, has a *Turkic* origin.

14. The infamous swastika sign, fallen into disgrace after World War II, did not originate from *Vedic Sanscrit,* dated 1500 BCE, as assumed worldwide. The main and only source of this sign is the *Turdaş/Turkic* 卍 卐 ☩ symbol found on the artifacts as far back as 5300 BCE. This is a pure *Turkic* sign, used for religious and tribal distinguishing purposes, as well as a letter of the alphabet.

    The *Turkic* alphabet is the only script in the world that contains this logogram as a letter 卍 ; ⚇ representing the Z sound. Among ancient *Turkic* nations, this symbol had several names: *Az, Oz,* and several meanings – "fate", "4 elements". Its religious meaning is *Tengri,* or *Tanri* – the name of *God* in *Turkic*.

    The ancient *Turkic* symbol *Tengri* 卍 卐 ☩ was discovered in all the regions that were populated by ancient *Turkic* nations – on *Trojan* pottery (*Turkey*), on *Qobustan* rocks (*Azerbaijan*), etched on the rocks in *Khakassiya* (a *Turkic* land, currently in *Russia*), in a *Celtic* chieftain's burial chamber dated 550 BCE near *Hochdorf* in *Southern Germany,* engraved on a pot in *Arkaim* (the *Kazakh* steppe, currently in *Russia*), on the rocks in *Kazakhstan,* on the rugs of *Native American* tribe of *Navajo* (*United States*), and many others. As a side note, it was genetically established that the *Navajo* tribe had *Turkic* roots.

    The *Turkic* tribe of the *Afshars* that belongs to the *Oguz* branch – the union of several *Turkic* nations, such as the *Azerbaijanis,* the *Turks,* the *Turkmens,* or the *Turkomans,* had this *Tengri* tamga. It served as an indicator of this *Turkic* tribe distinguishing it from other *Turkic* peoples. As a reminder, the *Turkic* monarch of *Persia* in the 18th c. – *Nader Shah,* emerged from this *Afshar* tribe. The *Afshars* have preserved their name and identity intact up until modern times, living primarily in *Turkey*.

<<<<<<<<<<<<<<<<<<<<< ⚇ >>>>>>>>>>>>>>>>>>>>>

Chapter VII.

§ 1. THE ANCIENT TURKIC TAMGAS.

Since times immemorial, people had a tendency to distinguish their property, identity, tribe, dynasty with an identifying symbol, mark, or logo. The ancient *Turkic* nations were very fond of marking their territory, possessions, cattle with their respective brand, called *Tamga*, or *Ongon*, in *Turkic*. The famed chronicler and statesman *Rashid ad-Din* who served in the court of the *Turkic* ruler of *Persia* from the *Ilkhanid* dynasty brought to light the circumstances that led to the emergence of these distinction symbols:

> "After *Oguz's* death, in accordance with his will, *Kun-khan* sat on the throne and reigned for seventy years; his father [*Oguz*] had a governor named *Eryangi-Kent Irkyl-khodja*. He was an adviser, vizier, and manager of affairs for the *Kun-khan*. Once, he said to *Kun-khan:*
>> "*Oguz* was a great sovereign; he conquered all the states of the world; had countless treasury, [all kinds of] property and livestock; and he left all this to you, his sons. Each of you, with divine help, had four worthy sons. God forbid so that later these sons begin to quarrel and argue over the kingdom! It will be good to determine and assign a title, path, name, and cognomen to each of them so that each has [his] own sign and tamga to specially mark [his] orders, treasury, herds, and flocks with that sign and tamga so that no one could quarrel and argue with each other, and each of the children, their descendants, would know their name, cognomen, and path, so that [this] would be the reason for the stability of the state and the constancy of their good name."
>
> *Kun-khan* favored these words, and *Eryangi-Kent Irkyl-Khodja* took up this matter. And after the six sons were given the cognomen *Bozuk* and *Uchuk* and the sides of the right and left wings of the army were individually assigned to them, he again appointed and approved the cognomen, name, tamga, and sign to each of their children, and a certain animal was assigned to each branch of these twenty-four branches to be their *Ongon* (*Tamga*). This word comes from *Inak*, and *Inak* in the *Turkic* language means "Blessed", as they say: "Inak bulsun!" – that is, "Blessed be!" And there is such a custom – they do not attack anything that bears the *Ongon* of any tribe, they do not resist it, and they do not eat its meat, since they have appropriated it as an auspicious omen. Until our time, the significance of this remains in force, and each of those tribes knows its own *Ongon*." [149]
>
> ["Jāmiʿ al-tawārīkh." – "A Compendium of Chronicles." 1.86-87]

According to the classification, provided by the *Azerbaijani* linguist *Araz Qurbanov* in his research "Damğalar, rəmzlər...mənimsəmələr" ("The Tamgas, Symbols...Appropriations"), the *Turkic* tamgas were marked on different kinds of objects, on live and dead persons:

- ❖ on battle flags and banners;
- ❖ as a headline on top of the royal decree;
- ❖ on armor, helmets and shields, on cutting tools;
- ❖ on poles or other demarcation objects specifying the boundaries of a given territory;
- ❖ on carpets, rugs, any fabric – silk, plaid, wool;
- ❖ on decorative items, such as pottery, jewelry, ornaments, accessory;
- ❖ as tattoo on the body, forehead, arm, wrist, hand, and the like;
- ❖ on clothes – military and everyday headgear, wedding dresses, children garments;

---

[149] This excerpt was translated into *English* by the author of this book.

- inside and outside of the house – on the walls of the tents or houses, on the roofs, on the doors and gates;
- on gravestones;
- in religious places, places of worship;
- on religious and spiritual objects;
- on forehead, ears, tails, thighs of the large and small hoofed domestic animals, such as cows, horses, camels;
- on the carts, wagons, wains, carriages;
- at the entrance to warehouses, stables.

These ancient *Turkic* logograms, or tamgas, served several purposes:

- to indicate the ethnicity and culture of a given *Turkic* nation, tribe;
- to identify the royal or vassal status of a nation, or tribe;
- to mark the territorial affiliation of a tribe or nation;
- to be used like characters of the *Turkic* writing system;
- to represent whole words;
- to demonstrate the religious and mythological affiliation;
- for branding livestock.

Remarkably, most of the *Turkic* tamgas were represented by the letters of the *Turkic* alphabet that, in addition to serving their primary purpose, also denominated a word, carried a certain definition, notion. For example:

1) ⤻ – the *M* sound.
   'wolf's mouth', 'wolf's head' (according to the *Oguz* nations).

2) ↥, ↦ – the *P* sound.
   'hook', 'tong', 'hack'.

3) ▷, ◁, △ – the *K* sound.
   1. '*Humay Ana* – the goddess of fertility'; 2. 'evil eye' (an ornament representing the evil eye on *Turkic* carpets). 3. In the form of ▽, it was called *Qalxan* "shield" in *Turkic*.

4) ∨, √, ∫ – the *L* sound.
   1. 'corner'; 2. 'hook'.

5) ⋀ – the *Ş* (*Sh*) sound.
   'tent door', 'hut door'.
   It has another variants ⊓, ⌒ – recognized as *Bosaqa* "door frame" in *Turkic*. This tamga is a frequently met ornament on the carpets of *Azerbaijan, Turkey, Central* and *Western Asia*. In conjunction with its another form, the tamga ∨⋀ used to identify the *Turkic* tribe – the *Tutirqa*. As a modified tamga ⊓, it served as an identifier for the *Turkic* tribe of *Yaparli* from the *Oguz Confederation,* while in another reshaped form, this tamga ⋔ was used to distinguish a *Turkic*

316

tribe of the *Oguz Confederation* – the *Bugduz*. There is a couple of close matches in the *Turdaş* writing: ⊓̂; ⋔; ⊓; ⊓; ⊓; ⩙.

6) ⟩ – the *O, U* sounds.

'corner'. This tamga was employed in other forms as well, like these ones: V; ⟨.

7) ℭ, Ɛ – the *G* sound.
'supreme power over vassals'.

8) ☻, ◉, ⊙, O – the *Nd, Nt* sounds.
1.'oath'; 2. 'brotherhood'; 3.'indestructible union'.

9) Y – the *L* sound.
1.'craft'; 2. 'large jug with a long narrow neck and handle'; 3. 'pitchfork'.
This is a national emblem of the *Turkic* nation of *Karaim*, also known as the *Crimean Karaites*, or Krymkaraylar, or *Garays*, who, like their progenitors – the *Khazars*, profess Judaism as their religion. This tamga was used as an ethnic symbol in the *Golden Horde* and the *Crimean Khanate*.

10) ꟼ, Ͱ – the *Ŋ, ŋ (Ng)* sound.
1.'ten'; 2. 'right' – *Ong, On* in *Turkic*. In a slightly modified form ⌐, this tamga served as an identifying symbol of the *Oguz* tribe – *Kizik*.

11) P, ꟼ – the *Y* sound, as in the word <u>Y</u>es.
'ax'.

12) ✕, † – the *D* sound.
1.'a cross'; 2. 'a cross of the *Turkic* goddess *Humay Ana*'. This also was a tribal emblem of the *Afshars* – a *Turkic* tribe of the *Oguz* branch. This tamga was detected in the ancient artifacts of *Media, Manna*, at the territory of *Azerbaijan* – in *Gobustan*, in *Central Asia*.

13) ⚭ – the *B* sound.
'house', 'home'. It is also used in another form – ⚯.

14) ⱨ – the *T* sound.
1.'ram'; 2. 'goat'.

15) Ч – the *R* sound.
'cross with a hook'.

16) ☽,☾ – the *Y* sound, like in a word *Yes*.
   1. 'moon'; 2. 'bow'.

17) | – the *S* sound.
   1. 'one tribe'; 2. 'one generation'; 3. 'spear'; 4. 'knife'.

18) ᛉ – the *R* sound.
   1. 'warrior'; 2. 'man'.

19) ⚜ – the *Z* sound.
   1. '*God Tanri*'; 2. 'four elements'; 3. 'the *Az* tribe'.

20) ∫, ↕, ✕, ∽ – the *A, E, Ə* sounds.
   'hook'.

21) ⋀ – the *T* sound.
   1. 'cavalier', 'horseman'; 2. 'horse'.

22) ⋈, ⊠ – the *V* sound, also the words *Baş, Aş*.
   1. 'head'; 2. 'valley'; 3. 'two mountains in a valley'.

23) □, ▯ – the *Ş (Sh)* sound.
   1. 'threshhold'; 2. 'door'; 3. 'door frame'. In the modified form ▭, this tamga acquired one more meaning – 'cradle', or *Beşik* in *Turkic*.

24) ◈, ◇ – the *Ḍ,ŋ (Ng)* sound.
   'eye of a camel's calf'.

25) ⅂ – the *K* sound.
   1. 'musical wind instrument called *Ney* – a flute', played mainly by the *Azerbaijanis*; 2. 'musical wind instrument called *Kuray*', played mostly by the *Bashkirs*. It was used as a tamga in another version ᛋ.

26) ⋙ – the *D* sound.
   1. 'legs'; 2. 'support'; 3. 'stronghold'.

27) ᛉ – the *Ç (Ch)* sound.
   1. 'central, supporting pole of the house or a hut'; 2. 'sacred tree of the family'; 3. 'superior'; 4. a sign of royalty; 5. 'tree of life'.

28) ↓, ↑ – the *Q* sound.
    'arrow'.

29) H – the *Q* sound.
    1.'prosperity'; 2.'harvest'; 3.'power'.

30) ꓛ – the *N* sound.
    1.'the Moon'; 2.'summer'; 3. 'domination'.

31) M – the *Lt* sound, also the *Turkic* word *Alt*.
    'bottom', 'ground'.

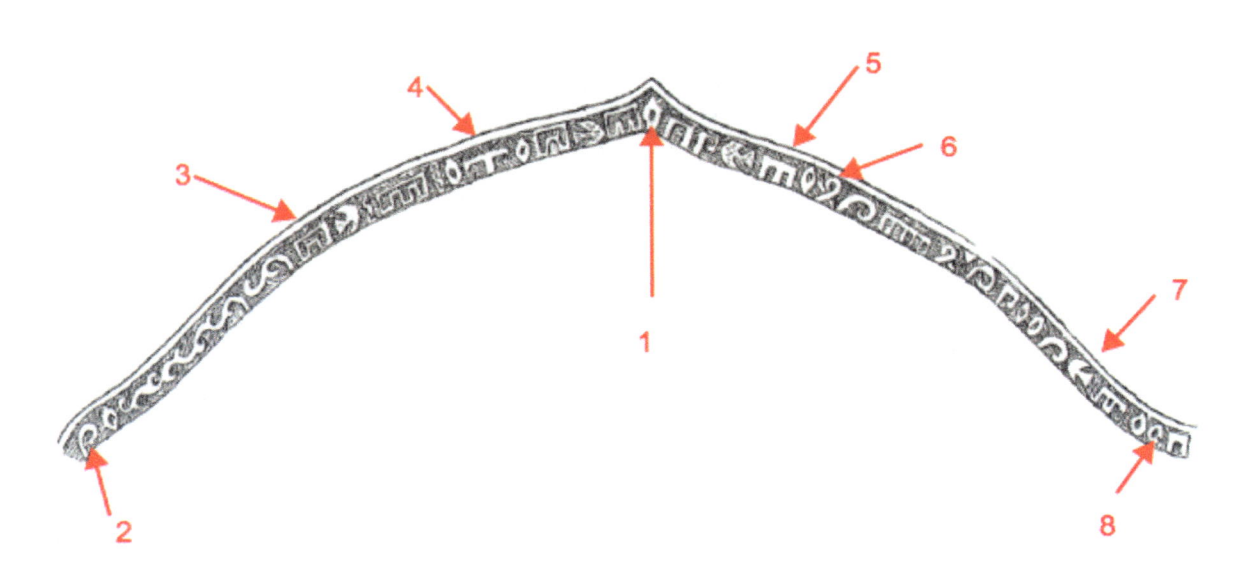

32) ○ ⋏ – the logogram *Ot*, also the *Turkic* word *Ot*.
    'grass'. The tamga resembles the *Turdaş* symbol ⌂.

Figure 28. A Scythian artifact with the Turkic tamgas, found in a kurgan. The Kuban region, Russia. The Turkic tamgas: 1. ◇ 'motherland'; 2. P 'ax'; 3. ⊓ 'door'; 4. T 'two-edge Scythian ax'; 5. ⊓⊓ 'vassal' ; 6. ⏃ 'home' ; 7. ← 'tribe'; 8. ○ 'indestructible union'; 'the Sun God'. Credit: Smirnov I.I. "Vostochnoye serebro…" [267].

In addition to the logograms used primarily for writing purposes, ancient *Turkic* nations developed and utilized tamgas, or signs, for a wide range of applications.

319

Prior to getting into details about other *Turkic* tamgas, a little-known fact asks to be revealed. Since ancient times, particular *Turkic* tamgas have been used worldwide as astrological and planetary signs, as follows:

Turkic Tamgas	*Turdaş Signs*	*Planetary and Zodiac Symbols*
⊛	⊕	⊕ Earth
)ı(	⊢⁊ı	♅ Uranus
Ч	⩊	♃ Jupiter
⌂	↑	♂ Mars
Ψ	Ψ	♆ Neptune
☉	☉	☉ Sun
⊃	(	☽ Moon
♄	⊓	♄ Saturn
⚥	⚥	♀ Venus
⚹	✳	♇ Pluto
⋈	⟡	☿ Mercury
⚲	⚳	Ψ Vulcan
♈	⋀	♈ Ares

Furthermore, according to the 11th c. linguist *Mahmud Kashgari*, it was the *Turks* who invented the 12-year cycle of years called *Chak* (*Çağ*, or *Çak*) and denominated each cycle year with the name of an animal:

"The *Turks* named twelve successive years with the names of twelve animals. They calculate the year of birth, the time of battles, and so on through this cycle. This chronology arose as follows: one of the kings needed to know the time of the battle that took place several years before him. But when calculating the year in which the battle took place, an error was made, then the sovereign's people consulted each other and said: "We made a mistake in determining this date; others will also make mistakes in the future. Let's give names to twelve years, the number of which is equal to the number of months and constellations in the sky, to keep a calendar for this cycle and leave the eternal memory." That is what they said to him.

And that king went out to hunt and ordered to drive wild animals into the river *Ili*. It is a big river. They drove the animals into the water. Twelve of them crossed over it. After each of them, a year was named.

The first one is *Sıçğan* – the Mouse. It was the first to pass over, so its name stands at the head of the cycle. The years follow in this order: *Sıçğan Yılı* – the Year of the Mouse. Then after it, *Ud Yılı* – Year of the Cattle. Then *Bars Yılı* – the Year of the Leopard. Then *Tavışğan Yılı* – the Year of the Hare. Then *Nək Yılı* – the Year of the Crocodile. Then *Yılan Yılı* – the Year of the Snake. Then *Yund Yılı* – the Year of the Horse. Then *Qoy Yılı* – the Year of the Sheep. Then *Biçin Yılı* – the Year of the Monkey. Then *Taqağu Yılı* – the Year of the Chicken. Then *İt Yılı* – the Year of the Dog. Then the Year of the Pig, it is called *Tonquz Yılı*. After the Year of the Pig, the score restarts again with the mouse…They say that if it is the Year of the Cow, there are many wars because the cows butt heads. In the Year of the Chicken, food is abundant, but there is a disorder among the people since the chicken's food is grain, and it constantly searches the dregs. The Years of the Snake and the Crocodile are rainy and fruitful, as they live in water. The Year of the Boar is cold, snowy, and vague. Thus, they see something peculiar in each year." [150] [1.174]

Most likely, the *Chinese* adopted this calendar cycle from the *Turks* and, with small replacements, such as a dragon instead of a crocodile, a rooster instead of a chicken, to name a few, presented it to the world as their own creation.

Figure 29. Zodiac symbols on the Hunnic artifact. From the book "De vetere literature Hunno-Scythica Exercitatio" by Matthiae Belii.

Each and every *Turkic* tribe and nation had its own tamga, exclusively belonging to them and distinguishing them as a separate entity. We are not going to enumerate them all here, as initially, being 20 tribes, they split into a myriad of different branches. Quoting *Mahmud Kashgari*, "Each tribe has offshoots the number of which only *Allah* knows. I enumerate only the main tribes and leave out the insignificant ones, except for the divisions of the *Turkman-Oguz* …as people ought to know them." [151] [1.20]

Based on the accounts provided by the *Turkic* linguist *Mahmud Kashgari* in his book "Divanü Lüğat-it-Türk" ("The Corpus of the *Turkic* Lexicon"), by the *Turkish* writer of the 15th c. *Yazichioglu Ali* in his "Tevârih-i Al-i Selçuk" ("Seljukname"), and by *Seyyid Lokman* of the 16th c. in his work "Hünername" ("Book of Skills"), the following tamgas signify 22 tribes of the *Oguz* branch of the *Turkic* nations. As stated by *M. Kashgari*,

> "The *Oguz* – one of the tribes of the *Turks,* they are the *Turkman*. They comprise twenty-two divisions. Each division has a mark and tamga on its animals by which they distinguish them. Their foremost and leading (division) is *Qiniq*." [152] [1.40]

---

[150] The excerpt was translated from the *Russian* version: Makhmud al-Kashgari. "Divan lugat at-Turk." – "Svod turkskikh slov." into *English* by the author of this book.
[151] Translated by the author of the present book.
[152] The translation into *English* was provided by the author of the current work.

Turkic Tribe	Divanu Lugat-it Turk XI c.	Seljukname XV c.	Hunername XVI c.
Qınıq			
Qayıq, aka Qayığ, aka Qayı			
Bayundur, aka Bayındır			
Iva, aka Yıva, aka İyva			
Salğur, aka Salur			
Afşar			
Bəktili, aka Bektili			
Bügdüz, aka Büğdız			
Bayat			
Yazğır, aka Yazır			
Əymür, aka İmur			
Qara Bölük, aka Qaraüyli			
Alqa Bölük, aka Alqaüyli			
İgdır, aka Bekdir			
Yürəgir, aka Ürəgir, aka Urkiz			
Tutırqa, aka Dodırğa			
Ula Yundluğ, aka Alaüyintili			
Tügər, aka Tögər, aka Dögər			
Bəçənək, aka Bejene			
Çuvuldar, aka Zhauındır, aka Zhauıldır			
Çəpni, aka Şebni			

In the 11th c., the twenty-second tribe *Çaruqluğ* was few in numbers, and their brand was unknown to the *Turkic* authors.

It is important to note that while some of the tamgas remained as symbols and did not become letters in the ancient *Turkic* or *Turdaş* alphabets, they were adopted as characters in *Greek, Latin*, even *Russian*, for instance:

T ; Ͱ ; W ; Φ .

In general, the *Turkic* tamgas can be grouped in accordance with the aspects they signified, including political, religious, military qualities of the *Turkic* society, as well as the nature and the animal world.

§ 2. THE POLITICAL TAMGAS, INDICATING STATEHOOD, LEVEL OF INDEPENDENCE OF A STATE, AND ITS SUBJECTS.

1) Ψ – the sign of the royalty, 'a khan', 'an emperor'. It is known as *Eltəbər, Baltavar, Baysanak, Baytörə, Dirək* in *Turkic*. This was the emblem of the *Parthian Empire* and was on a flag of the *Great Hun Empire*. It had numerous modifications, including ⊃⚹⊂ that has several meanings, one of which stands for the dominion of the *Turkic Empire* over four sides of the world. This is a very ancient tamga, found in the *Turdaş* artifacts and dated 6-5 millennium BCE in the form Y. Later, it was used in different variants by the *Cimmerians*, the *Medes*, the *Caucasian Albanians*, the *Khazarian Khaganate*, by the *Mongol* Empire of *Chinghiz Khan*, the *Turkic* dynasty of the *Safavids* in *Iran*, the *Golden Horde*, by the *Turkic* nations in *Central* and *Western Asia*, in the *Caucasus, Crimea, Azerbaijan, Asia Minor, Ukraine, Russia, Bulgaria* as a state attribute, or the statehood tamga on the coins and flags:

Ψ, Ψ, Ψ, Ψ, Ψ, Ψ, Ψ, Ψ, Ψ, Ψ, Ψ, Ψ, Ψ,
Ψ, Ψ, Ψ, ⋔, ⋔, ⋔, ⋔, ⋔, ⋔, ⋔, ⋔, ⋔.

This tamga, known among the *Turkic* people as *Qaba Ağac, Dirilik Ağacı*, also has another meaning – "tree of life". The *Turkic* tamgas Ψ, ⋔ were used in the *Sassanian* Empire that ruled in *Persia* from 224 to 651c.

Figure 30. A two-edged ax-shaped obelisk in Göbekli Tepe, Turkey. 11,500 BCE. The Turkic tamga of higher power ⌂ and the tamga of protection, also denoting land, motherland ◇ © Credit: Kenan Yelken/"Her Yönü ile Göbekli Tepe."

Figure 31. A stone tablet dated 10th millennium BCE, found in Göbekli Tepe with 3 Turkic tamgas from left to right – a Snake, denoting wisdom; an Emperor; a Vassal, meaning "wise ruler over a subjected nation". © Credit: Kenan Yelken/"Her Yönü ile Göbekli Tepe".

2) Ψ, ∪, ⊔, ⋈, Ψ, Ш – 1. 'two-headed eagle'; 2. 'double-edged ax'. This tamga was used in both meanings as an attribute of state. Known in *Turkic* as *Toğrul*, one head of the eagle represented the monarch, while the other stood for religion. In *Turdaş* artifacts, it is seen as ⚶. The signs similar to this symbol, such as this one – 🦅, were reflected on the flags or coins of the *Sumerians*, the *Hittites*, the *Medes*, the *Golden Horde*, the *Turkic khanates* of the *Atabeks*, the *Seljuks*, in *Crimea*, and one hundred years after the dissolution of the *Golden Horde* – on the flag and coins of *Russia*.

3) ⊃, ⊂, D, Ʒ, Ð, ⌐ – 'higher power, authority, independence'. The *Sassanian* Empire in *Persia* used these tamgas – ƷÐ.

4) ⌒, ⋔, ⚭ – 'lesser power, lesser authority'. The *Turkic* tamga ⋔ was in use in the *Achaemenid* Empire, known as the First *Persian* Empire, founded by *Cyrus*, a *Mede* on his mother's side and a *Pelasgian* through his paternal lineage.

5) ↑, ⊓, ⊓, ⊓, ш, ⋔, ⊓, ⋔, ⋔ – 'subordinate to a higher power, a vassal'. The tamga ⊓ was used in the *Sassanian* Empire too. There is a matching *Turdaş* symbol – ⊓ with an exact counterpart – the *Turkic* tamga ⊓ called *Daraq* "comb".

6) ⊞ – 'double subordinate to two separate powers'. A similar symbol was in the *Turdaş* writing – 🜲.

7) Ψ – 'monarch and his/her army'. The tamga is a combination of two symbols:) – 'bow', or *Yay* in *Turkic*, and ↑ – 'arrow', or *Ox* (*Ok*) in *Turkic*, and has several variations, such as Ɵ, ϑ, ⋊, ꝛ. A bow stands for a khan, and an arrow – for the warriors. There is an ancient symbol in the *Turdaş* culture presented in several forms – ϵ, ϵ, ⋁ that match this tamga.

8) I – 'one tribe', or 'one arrow', or *Bir Ok* (*Ox*) in *Turkic*, II – 'two tribes', or *Qoşa Ok* (*Ox*) 'two arrows' in *Turkic*. Both these tamgas were in use in the *Sassanian* Empire.

9) III – 'confederation, tribal union', known as *Üç Ok* (*Ox*) 'three arrows' in *Turkic*.

10) IYI – 'support of one power', or *Qoşa oxlu sənək* in *Turkic*. It was the identifying tamga of the *Qayıq* tribe in the *Oguz Confederation*. It has several variants: ⋔, ⋔, ⋔, ⋓, used by the *Turkic* nations in *Southern* and *Northern Azerbaijan*, the *Caucasus*, *Central Asia*, *Siberia*, *Central* and *Western* part of *Russia*, *Ukraine*, *Serbia*, and *Macedonia*. This tamga was also reflected in the *Turdaş* culture – ⋔.

§ 3. THE RELIGIOUS TAMGAS, INDICATING MYSTICAL, MAGICAL, SPIRITUAL SIGNS.

1) 卍, 卐, 卍, ✠, ✺, ✣, ✣, ⊕, ▨, ▨ – 'domain of *Tengri* over four directions, four dimensions, and four elements.' These are the tamgas of protection, frequently

325

observed on *Turkic* amulets, charms, talismans, carpets in *Azerbaijan, Turkey, Central Asia*. There is also a matching *Turdaş* symbol 卍.

2) ⟦symbols⟧ – the tamgas of protection from the evil eye, reflected as an ornament on the carpets of the *Turkic* nations, such as the *Azerbaijanis*, the *Turks*, the *Bashkirs*, the *Karachai*, the *Kazakhs*, the *Crimean Tatars*, the *Bulgars* along the *Volga* River, the *Kirghiz*, the *Turkmens*, the *Khakass*. There are similar *Turdaş* symbols: ⟦symbols⟧.

3) ⟦symbols⟧ – 'scorpion', called *Əqrəb* in *Turkic*. These tamgas served to protect from evil forces, evil magic, and the evil eye. They were detected as ornaments on the *Turkish* and *Azerbaijani* carpets, as well as on a monument in *Göbekli Tepe*.

Figure 32. The tamga of a scorpion on a stela. Göbekli Tepe, Turkey. © Credit: Kenan Yelken/"Her Yönü ile Göbekli Tepe".

4) ★, ☆ – 1. 'man from Heaven', 'God *Tengri*', called *Göy Adamı, Tengri* in *Turkic*; 2. 'the Sun', or *Günəş* in *Turkic*; 3. 'a star' – *Ulduz* in *Turkic*. These sacral signs denoted protection from evil forces and evil eyes among the *Turkic* nations.

5) ⟦symbols⟧ – 'first man'. According to *Turkic* mythology, the name of the first man on *Earth* was *Manas*. This name is still in use by the *Turkic* nations as *Manas* and *Manaf,* and even by the *Arabic* nations as *Manaf,* whom they consider a pre-Islamic deity. This ancient name *Manas* as

Manes (*Μάνης*) was also a *Phrygian* name, mentioned by *Strabo*. It was also the name of the *Lydian* King *Manes,* the grandfather of *Asias,* after whom the continent of *Asia* was named.

6) ⚹⚹⚹⚹⚹ ⚹⚹⚹ Y – 'tree of life', or *Qaba Ağac, Dirilik Ağacı, Həyat Ağacı* in *Turkic*. In *Turkic* mythology, the leaves of this tree represent the souls of shamans and unborn children. The *Turdaş* artifacts have a similar symbol in several forms: ⚹, ⚹, ⚹, ⚹.

Figure 33. Antique Turkic carpets. National Museum of Kazakhstan. From the author's collection.

7) +, ⊕, ✣ – 'a cross', one of the most sacral symbols, known as *Xaç, Açamay, Aça* in *Turkic*. It denotes the *Turkic* goddess *Humay Ana's* cross. It also denotes the equal power of God *Tengri* over 4 elements, 4 worlds, 4 directions.

8) ⊕ ⊛ ⊗ ⊕ ⊗ – 'wheel', called *Təkər* in *Turkic*. The symbol with its variants bears the same meaning as the cross, including 'unity of a family', 'motherland'. The *Turdaş* artifacts contain similar tamgas: ⊕ ⊗.

9) ○ – 'a sky deity representing the Sun, the Sun-God', or *Tengri Xan-Günəş* in *Turkic*. According to the ancient *Turkic* religion called *Tengriism*, there was God – *Tengri*, or *Tanri*, and Goddess – *Humay Ana*. This tamga was on the flag of the *Azerbaijani* ruler of *Persia* from the *Safavid* dynasty – Shah Tahmasib II.

10) ◉ – this tamga has several names. As a tamga of protection, it is called *Abak* in *Turkic*. Known as *Ana* 'mother' in *Turkic,* this tamga also denotes a mother and her child in the womb, as well as two worlds – macro and micro. This logogram was used in a number of variations ✺, ◉, ◉, ⊙ by the *Turkic* nations, such as the *Azerbaijanis,* the *Kirghiz,* the *Uyghurs,* the *Yakuts,*

327

the *Crimea Tatars*, the *Kipchaks*, the *Caucasian Albanians*, the *Hun*, and the *Kazakhs*. The ancient language system – *Turdaş* incorporated the signs ☼ and ⊙.

Figure 34. The Turkic tamga *Təkər* in the artifacts from left to right: A Scythian artifact. Unknown date. Found in a Turkic village Kulagish, Russia. Credit: Smirnov I.I. "Vostochnoye serebro..." [50]; Gobustan National Preserve Park, Azerbaijan. Credit: www.gobustan-rockart.az/en/photogallery/18; The gold bowl with the Turkic inscriptions. Western Siberia. Unknown date. Credit: Smirnov I.I. "Vostochnoye serebro..." [20]

Figure 35. The Turkic tamga *Təkər* in Saymaluu Tash. Kyrgyzstan. 3,000 BCE. © Credit: Kenan Yelken/"Her Yönü ile Göbekli Tepe".

11) ▲△⛰🛡🔺🔻⚠️▷ – 'protection from magic, evil eye, curse'. In *Turkic*, it is called *Tumar, Tumarça, Bitik*. *Turdaş* artifacts also have the resembling symbol △.

12) ⧖ – 'double protection from evil', known as *Qoşa Tumar* in *Turkic*. The exact same form was found in the *Turdaş* artifacts: ⧖ with its variation – ⧖.

13) 🌶 – the tamga of protection, embodying pure fire that repels evil eye, diseases. This symbol *Buta,* or *Puta,* had a dual meaning: one had a religious and magical connotation, while the other served a military purpose as a shooting target.

14) **H** – the tamga of prosperity, harvest, power. This is an ancient *Turkic* sign, also found in *Göbekli Tepe, Turkey.*

Figure 36. The Turkic tamga of prosperity **H** with the surrounding signs of Moon – waning and waxing. Göbekli Tepe, Turkey. © Credit: Kenan Yelken/"Her Yönü ile Göbekli Tepe".

15) ✶ – 1. 'prosperity'; 2. 'a star' – *Ulduz* in *Turkic;* 3. 'an eye' – *Göz* in *Turkic*. It serves to protect from the evil eye. It is mostly detected as an ornament on *Turkic* carpets.

16) ◆ – in *Azerbaijan* and *Turkish* mythology, this tamga stands for 'a dragon' – *Əjdaha* in *Azerbaijani* and embodies prosperity. In *Central Asia*, it has a modified form – ▦, ⊞ called *Balıq Gözü* 'fish eye'. There are several matching *Turdaş* symbols: #, #, ⊚, ⊞.

17) # – 'hearth', called *Ocaq* in *Turkic*. It was mostly used as an ornament on clothes or carpets of the *Turkic* nations in *Azerbaijan, Turkey,* the *Caucasus, Central Asia,* and *Europe*. This tamga was the identifying symbol of the *Turkic* tribe *Alayuntlu,* which was a part of the *Oguz Confederation*. The *Turdaş* sign system includes the exact symbol: #.

329

18) **H U** – 1. 'union of the worldly and spiritual power'; 2. 'two-headed eagle'.

19) **⋔** – 'an eagle with one head', or *Bir-başlı Qartal* in *Turkic*. It is the tribal symbol of the *Dodurqa* tribe in *Turkey*.

Figure 37. From left to right: A Mayan bird ornament. 7th -8th c. The Metropolitan Museum of Art in New York, USA. [OA]. Credit: The Michael C. Rockefeller Memorial Collection, Purchase, Mrs. Gertrud A. Mellon Gift, 1963; A Scythian artifact with an eagle and its prey. Unknown date. Credit: Smirnov I.I. "Vostochnoye serebro..." [88]; A Parthian belt adornment with an eagle and its prey. 1st–2nd century CE. The Metropolitan Museum of Art in New York, USA. [OA]. Credit: Gift of J. Pierpont Morgan, 1917.

20) – these tamgas were found on the carpets made in the *Karabakh* region of *Azerbaijan*, *Central Asia*, the *Northern Caucasus*, *Siberia*, *Crimea*, *Eastern Europe*. They consist of two symbols: the lower section represents the Moon and *Tengri*, and the upper portion embodies the tree of life, both serving as a protective sign.

21) – 'a ram', known as *Qoç* in *Turkic*. This symbol embodies two sacral notions: 'prosperity and abundance' and 'a sacred entity that delivers the souls of the deceased to the domain of *Tengri*'. Similar symbols are found in the *Turdaş* symbolic system: .

22) – a sign of the universe, 'a spiral', known as *Dolanqaç* in *Turkic*.

23) – 'hands on the waist', called *Əli Belində* in *Turkic*. This is one of the ancient *Turkic* tamgas, reflected in the *Turdaş* cultural heritage as well – . In *Turkic* mythology, it stands for the goddess *Humay Ana*. It also represents the eternal nature of a soul and

its reincarnation. Similar symbols were found in a number of *Scythian* artifacts throughout *Azerbaijan, Turkey,* the *Caucasus, Central Asia,* as far as the *Americas.* The recently discovered *Göbekli Tepe* archeological site dated 11th-10th c. BCE has a monument strikingly similar to the ones in *Ukraine, Mexico,* and *Bolivia.*

Figure 38. From left to right: A statue of a Scythian with the hands on the waist. Dnipropetrovsk, Ukraine. Muzey Starozhytnostey [CC BY-SA 4.0]. Credit: Nataliya Shestakova; A statue with the hands on the waist, Göbekli Tepe, Turkey. Credit: Kenan Yelken/"Her Yönü ile Göbekli Tepe"; A figure of an Aztec with the hands of the waist. Mexico. 14-15c. Metropolitan Museum of Art. [OA] Credit: Museum Purchase, 1900; A megalithic statue with the hands on the waist. Tiwanaku, Bolivia. [CC BY-SA 2.0]. Credit: wallygrom.

24) ◆, ◇ – 'eye of a camel's calf', or *Kösək Gözü* in *Turkic*. It is used for protection from the evil eye.

§ 4. THE TAMGAS, INDICATING MILITARY AND STATE ATTRIBUTES.

1. ⸫, ⸪, ⊙, △, ⊙ – 'an oath', called *And* in *Turkic*. These symbols were used by many *Turkic* nations, such as the *Scythians*, the *Khazars*, the *Oguz*, the *Kipchak*, to indicate a solemn oath. They served as a seal to confirm the military alliance, brotherhood, indestructible union between the *Turkic* tribes, nations. In the form of ⸫ , the sign served as a state emblem and

a symbol on the flag of the *Timurid* Empire in the 14th c., founded by the *Turkic* Emperor – *Amir Timur*, aka *Tamerlane*. The symbol denominates a withstanding union, camaraderie.

2. ⊔⊓ ⊔⊓ ⌒ ⊔⊓ ⊔⊔ ⊔⊔ – 'a camel' – *Dəvə* in *Turkic* and means 'wealth, prosperity'. This was the state emblem and the symbol on the flag of the *Aq Qoyunlu* dynasty of the *Turkic* rulers in *Persia* from 1378 to 1501. It is also a symbol of the *Turkic* tribe – the *Bayandur*.

3. ☐ – 'door, outside' – *Qapı, Eşik* in *Turkic*. It was the emblem on the flag of the *Jalairid Sultanate*, which ruled over the western part of *Persia* and *Iraq* in the 14th c. This tamga was used by the *Turkic* nations in *Central Asia*, along the *Volga* riverside, in *Crimea*, including the *Oguz* and the *Kipchak*.

4. ↑ ↑ ↑ – 'a warrior, a man, a hero', known as *Ar, Er, Ər, Ir, Ör* in *Turkic*.

5. ⋀ – 'a horseman', or *Atlı* in *Turkic*. This tamga was widely used by the *Turkic* nations inhabiting the *Caucasus*, along the *Atıl*, or *Volga* River, *Crimea*, *Central Asia*, *Siberia*. In its modified form ⋂, the tamga serves as an identifying sign of the *Kumik* tribe – *Djandar*, as well as the *Chuvuldar* from the *Oguz Confederation*. In conjunction with another tamga ☐⋂, it stands to distinguish a *Turkic* tribe from the *Oguz Confederation* – the *Qara Boluk*.

6. ⋃⫲, Ↄ, Ⴙ, Ψ, ⤬, ⋏, ℓ, θ, θ – this tamga with its multiple variations has several meanings: 1.'bow and arrows', or *Yay-Ox* in *Turkic*; 2.'invitation to fight'; 3.'a *Turkic* leader and his/her warriors'. The tamga is reflected in the *Turdaş* culture as ↳ that has a strong resemblance to the *Turkic* tamga θ. The *Turdaş* symbol has a number of variants, such as ↓, ⋁, ⫰, D, ∈, ∈.

7. ↑, ⤊ – the tamga is called *Ok* (*Ox*) 'arrow' in *Turkic* and was a very ancient and popular tamga among the *Turkic* nations. It was a distinguishing symbol of the *Turkic* tribes from the *Oguz Confederation* – the *Bayat* and the *Qiniq*. The roots of this tamga are tracked to the *Turdaş* culture – ↓, ⋁.

8. T, T – 1. 'an ax', or *Balta* in *Turkic*; 2. 'hammer', or *Çəkic* in *Turkic*; 3. 'a two-edged *Scythian* ax', or *Sakar* in *Turkic*. This tamga was mostly spread among the *Turkic* nations in *Central Asia*, the *North Caucasus*, and *Crimea*. It also served as an identifying tamga of the *Chepni* tribe, a part of the *Oguz Confederation*, as well as of the *Nogay* tribes – the *Toymas* and the *Saray*. There is a corresponding *Turdaş* symbol – T.

9. P, ٩ – another variation of 'ax', or *Balta* in *Turkic*. It is an identifying symbol of the *Turkic* tribe in *Kazakhstan* – the *Baltali*. The name literally means "having an ax".

10. ⌇ – the tamga *Qılınc* 'sword' in *Turkic* was observed in the *Turkic* artifacts found in *Central* and *Western Asia, in Europe.*

Figure 39. A Scythian bow and arrow case. There are 2 inscriptions on the sword consisting of Turkic letters: vertically ↑ ᶜ)ᒋIᏞ (əl Sab Göq – "people of the Sab tribe"), horizontally ⊓ Y (El Üş – "a confederation of 3 tribes"). 4th c. BCE. Most likely, these people were the Sabines of the Scythe-Pelasgian extraction. There was a Turkic tribe of the Sabi, mentioned by Radlov V.V. [4.1.500], that lived near the river Kondoma, modern Russia. [CC BY 2.0]. Credit: Peter Kudlacz.

11. ⌇ , ⌇ – 'a sword', or *Aybulat, Aypolad* in *Turkic*. This tamga was the official emblem of *Caucasian Albania.*

12. | – 'a spear, a lance', or *Nizə* in *Turkic*.

13. ▽ – 'a shield', or *Qalxan* in *Turkic* was a preferred weapon among the horsemen of *Caucasian Albania*. This tamga was also popular among the *Turkic* people of *Central Asia.*

14. ⌇ , ⌇ – 'a pitchfork', called *Hənək, Sənək* in *Turkic*, used both as an agrarian tool and a weapon by the ancient *Turkic* nations. In the modified form – Y, it was accepted as the distinguishing symbol of the *Turkic* tribe – *Bektili*. Another reshaped variant ૪ was the identifying sign of the *Turkic* tribes from the *Oguz Confederation* – *Bayandur* and *Eymur*. The altered form of the same tamga Y was the distinguishing symbol of the *Bichenek* tribe, which was a part of the *Oguz Confederation.*

15. ⌽ – this tamga was observed in the artifacts found in *Azerbaijan, Central Asia*. It was utilized in ancient *Media*, as well as by the *Turkic* nations, such as the *Kumiks*. This sign also has other

333

versions: ⌀, ⌀, ⌀. In the form ⌀, the tamga served to differentiate the *Turkic* tribe *Botash* from the *Karachai*. It is also an ethnic *Azerbaijan* tamga. There is one more version of this tamga – ⌀, which was the identifying symbol of the *Turkic* tribe *Suvar*, or *Suan*, in *Kazakhstan*. It also represents the *Uyghur* letters *Ö, O*.

16. ⊔ – 'a two-edged ax', or *İkiağızlı Balta, Baltavar, Toskur* in *Turkic*. The tamga was used by the *Bulgars*, the *Crimea Tatars*, the *Nogays*, and the *Turkic* nations of *Central Asia*.

17. ◌ – known since ancient times as *Buta, Puta* in *Turkic*, it was used as a shooting target to improve archery skills. It is mostly observed as an ornament on the *Turkic* carpets, especially on the *Azerbaijan* carpets, clothes, scarfs in numerous modifications: ◌◌◌◌◌, as well as in *Central Asia*, *Crimea*, along the *Volga* river. Some *Turdaş* artifacts include similar symbols: ◌, ◌.

18. ♀, ♀ – 1. 'earring'; 2. 'the Moon with a tail', known as *Alban, Atban, Sırğa, Quyruqlu Ay* in *Turkic*; 3. 'the Ram-Sun', or *Qoç-Günəş* in *Turkic*; 4. 'God *Tengri*-Sun', or *Tengri-Günəş* in *Turkic*. This tamga has numerous variations: ♀, ♀, ♀, ♀, ♀, ♂, ♂, ♂, ♂, ♂, ♂, ♂, ♂. It served as an identifying sign in the *Hunnic* Empire, in *Central Asia*, while in *Azerbaijan*, *Asia Minor*, the *Caucasus* it mostly stood for the symbols 'the Ram-Sun' and 'God *Tengri*-Sun'. There are derivative variants ♂, ♂ called *Açar* 'key', that was a popular tamga in the *Caucasus*, *Crimea*, *Tatarstan*, *Central Asia*. It was first depicted in the form of ♂ on *Turdaş* artifacts, dated 55th c. BCE.

19. ▼ – the tamga of the *Turkic* tribe of the *Iqdir* from the *Oguz Confederation*, as well as a distinguishing symbol of the *Shilbir* tribe in *Kazakhstan*.

20. ⋏ – the tribal emblem of the *Chebni* – a *Turkic* tribe from the *Oguz Confederation*.

21. ⊥ – the identifying tamga of the *Afshar* tribe in *Turkey*.

22. ✕, ✕, ✕, ✕, ✕ – these tamgas come in other shapes as well – ⋈, ✕ that signify the same notion 'head'. They were in use as ✕ and ✕ in ancient *Media*. The *Turkic* tribe *Chebni* had a slightly different version – ⋏. There are numerous *Turdaş* symbols matching these tamgas: ✕, ✕, ✕, ✕, ✕.

334

23. ⨀ – 'a saddle strap', or *Quşqun* in *Turkic*. This tamga also has another form and meaning – 'double-edged spear', or *İkidişli Nizə* in *Turkic*.

24. ⊥ – 'finger', or *Barmaq* in *Turkic*. This tamga was the identifier of the *Baybakti* tribe in *Kazakhstan*. It has another version ⊥, utilized by the *Uyghurs* as a letter *N*.

25. ⋀, ⋁⋀ – the tamgas symbolize settlement, building one's house, hut, yurt. They turned up in a number of artifacts in *Azerbaijan*, *Caucasian Albania*, and the *Golden Horde*. They are called *Barxan* in *Central Asia*. In the *Turdaş* culture, there are resembling matches – ⋀, △.

26. ◊ – the tamga bears the notion of 'land, motherland'.

27. Ɋ, Ɋ – discovered on the artifacts of *Gobustan* rocks in *Azerbaijan*, on the rocks surrounding Lake *Baikal* in *Siberia*, this tamga is the modification from the *Turdaş* symbols ⋊ ⋊. It bears the same meaning as the previous tamga – 'settlement', 'house'.

§ 5. The tamgas, representing nature and animals.

1. ☽☉ ⚓ ⚓⚓ ⚓⚓ ⚓ ⚓⚓⚓○ ⊕ ☉ ☽ ⌒
☽ ☾ ☪ – 1. 'the Moon-Sun' – *Ay-Günəş* in *Turkic*; 2. 'the Moon-Star' – *Ay-Ulduz* in *Turkic*. Most of these tamgas were observed on the rock carvings in the *Gobustan* National Park in *Azerbaijan*, *Central Asia*, *Eastern Siberia*, the land of the *Uyghurs* – former *East Turkestan*, currently the *Xinjiang* province of *China*, *Göbekli Tepe* – *Turkey*.

Figure 40. On the left, the Moon-Sun ☉ ☽ tamga in Göbekli Tepe, Turkey. On the right – the Uyghur temple shaped as the Moon-Sun tamga. East Turkestan (Xinjiang). Around 1,000 BCE. © Credit: Kenan Yelken/«Her Yönü ile Göbekli Tepe».

2. ✳✶🔵❀✿❉✦★☆★ – 1. 'the Sun' – *Günəş* in *Turkic;* 2. 'a star' – *Ulduz* in *Turkic*. In *Turdaş* culture, similar symbols were detected: ✳, ✶, ☼. The most popular *Turkic* tamga ✳ was spotted in *Azerbaijan, Central Asia, Crimea,* along the *Volga* River.

3. ↲ – 1. 'flowing water' – *Axar Su* in *Turkic;* 2. 'hook' – *Qarmaq* in *Turkic;* 3. 'fish hook' – *Çəngəl* in *Turkic*. Mostly frequented as an ornament on the *Azerbaijan* and *Turkish* carpets, it was used to depict a neck of a camel's calf or a goose; a dog's tail; the back of an ant in *Central Asia*. This is a very ancient tamga that was a part of the *Turdaş* writing in several forms – Z, ट, ?, ⌐,工, ⥂, ⑥. The *Scythian* artifacts of the 6th – 4th c. BCE contain a different modification of the tamga: ∾, also observed in the *Turkic* countries of *Central Asia*, such as *Uzbekistan* and *Turkmenistan*.

4. C D ᴗ ⊔ ⊍ – 'the Moon' – *Ay* in *Turkic*. It is also known in the form ⋃ that stands for 'the brave Moon', or *Ürəkli Ay*. This shape is observed on the *Göbekli Tepe* obelisk as well.

The two other versions ⊔ and ⊍ stand for 'a boat', or *Qayıq* in *Turkic*.

Figure 41. Göbekli Tepe, Turkey. A symbol of the Brave Moon ⋃.
© Credit: Adobe Stock.

336

Figure 42. A Sarmatian roundel with a horned animal, lions, and griffins. 3rd-1st c. BCE. The Metropolitan Museum of Art, USA. [OA] Credit: Purchase, Florance Waterbury Bequest, 1970

5. ∫ – 1. 'sickle', or *Oraq* in *Turkic*; 2. 'the Moon with tail', or *Kuyruktu Ay* in *Turkic*. It was the tribal symbol of the *Salur* from the *Oguz Confederation*.

6. ⵦ – 'the Moon with tail', or *Quyruqlu Ay* in *Turkic*. It has a couple of variations – Y , Ψ, mostly used in *Central Asia*.

7. ⩓ – 'horse', or *At* in *Turkic*.

8. ∩, ⌣ – 'horseshoe', or *Nal* in *Turkic*. This tamga is widespread among the *Turkic* nations of *Central Asia* and *Siberia*.

9. ⊃ – the tamga represents letters *T, D* in *Uyghur* and has a similar match in the *Turdaş* alphabet – ⌒. Most likely, it stands for 'a horse'.

10. ⤜, ⩓, △, ⩓, ⩓ – 'a head of a wolf', or *Qurd Başı* in *Turkic*. In *Tatarstan*, currently a part of *Russia*, this tamga is called *İskəndər Damğası* – "the seal of *Alexander the Great*" in *Turkic*. There is a symbol in the *Turdaş* sign system that shows a close resemblance to this tamga – ↭.

11. A, ∀ – 'a bear's head', or *Ayı Başı* in *Turkic*.

12. ↑ – 'fish', or *Balıq* in *Turkic*.

337

13. **🐏** – 'ram', or *Qoç* in *Turkic*. In its modified form ⌒, it stands for the tribal emblem of the *Yaparli* from the *Oguz Confederation*. This form closely resembles the *Turdaş* symbol ∨. This tamqa has a modified form that carries an additional meaning in the *Uyghur* culture – 'ram's neck', or *Kuldya, Qoç Müyüz* in *Turkic*. As ϒ shape, it was the ethnic emblem displayed by the *Turkic* tribes – the *Nayman* and the *Qarakirey* in *Kazakhstan*. There is one more version of this tamga that stands for 'pair of horns', or *Qoşa Buynuz* in *Turkic*.

14. ∨ – 1. 'bird's claw' – *Quş Caynağı* in *Turkic*; 2. 'goose feet' – *Qaz Ayağı* in *Turkic*. The *Turdaş* symbol completely matches this tamga – ∨. There are modified variants of this tamga – ⋀, as well as the signs distinguishing the *Turkic* tribe of the *Bichenek* – , and of the tribe *Salgur* .

15. ✕,✕ – 'crow tracks', or *Qarğa İzi* in *Turkic*. It was observed in the *Turkic* artifacts found in *Central* and *Western Asia*, in *Europe*. This also was a tribal symbol of the *Yazirs* from the *Oguz Confederation*. There is a close *Turdaş* match – ✕, ✕.

16. ⋈ – 'wolf tracks', or *Qurd Izi* in *Turkic*.

17. ▷▷ – 'mouse tracks', or *Tuşqan İzi, Siçan İzi* in *Turkic*.

18. ⊔, E, ∃ – this tamga serves as an ornament called *Dəvə* 'camel' in *Turkic*. It is also common in *Central Asia* and *Turkey*.

19. ✦ – the tamga *Gül* 'flower' was a welcome guest on any *Turkic* carpets, including *Azerbaijan, Turkish, Central Asian* ones. It signifies 'family happiness', 'love', and 'loyalty'.

20. – depicting a swan, the tamga has several names in *Turkic: Ağ Quş, Su Sonası, Ak Kaz*. This symbol represents the *Turkic* goddess *Humay Ana*, a co-creator of the universe, the protector of a family and children.

21. – 'a rooster', or *Xoruz* in *Turkic*. As an ornament, it is a regular sign on the carpets of *Azerbaijan*. Usually depicted as a couple, this tamga signifies the notion of evil versus good.

Interestingly, the *Turdaş* symbol system also has a similar sign ⼅ – a rooster on top of a tree or a pole.

22. ⊙–⊙ – 1. 'pair of eyes' – *Qoşa Göz* in *Turkic;* 2. 'blister', or *Suluk* in *Turkic*. This tamga embodies eyes, vision. It is an identifying sign of the *Turkic* tribes – *Mayjenli* and *Mingkuba*. It also comes in another version – ⊙⊙ to identify the *Turkic* tribes of *Central Asia* and *Crimea* – the *Argun* and the *Altin*.

23. ～, ～, ～ – 'a snake', or *İlan* in *Turkic*. This is an identifying tamga of a *Turkic* tribe *Yaparli* from the *Oguz Confederation*. It reminds the *Turdaş* symbol ～～ and was also detected on a *Göbekli Tepe* artifact.

24. T – 1. 'shrub', or *Kol* in *Turkic;* 2. 'arm', or *Qol* in *Turkic*. It is used in *Central Asia*. It also serves as the identifier of the *Turkic* tribe – the *Shanishkili* in *Kazakhstan*.

@@@@@@@@@@@@@@ ⋀⋀ @@@@@@@@@@@@@@

Chapter VIII.

§ 1. THE TURKIC NATIONS IN THE AMERICAS.

It has been long asserted by the linguists and experts in *Turkic* Studies that the *Americas* were known to the *Turkic* nations since ancient times. The latter not only did visit both *American* continents but stayed there, spread their roots all over the continents, left their tracks in the names of the places – lands, mountains, rivers, in the architecture they built, the culture they created, the religion they professed, the language they spoke. However, this topic still remains rather undeveloped in the scientific world. Luckily, the genetic research under the auspices of National Geographic proved the theory, once brought forward by the brightest mind of his time *Isaac Taylor* that it was the *Turkic* nations who crossed the *Bering* strait and settled in the *Americas*.

"A Dissertation upon the peopling of *America*" written by *John Swinton* for the encyclopedia "The Universal History from the Earliest Account of Time", published in 1748 in *London*, gave an extensive account of the *Turkic* ancestors of the *Native Americans* who first populated *America*:

"Now no country can be pitched upon so proper and convenient for this purpose as the northeastern part of *Asia*, particularly *Great Tartary, Siberia,* and more especially the peninsula of *Kamtschatka*. That probably was the tract through which many *Tartarian*[153] colonies passed into *America,* and peopled the most considerable part of the new world. This at present is the most prevailing opinion among the learned; nor will any sober intelligent person, we persuade ourselves, refuse his assent to it, after he has maturely weighed the following observations:

1. The genius, manners, and customs, of the *Americans,* have, little affinity with those of the *Europeans,* the more civilized *Asiatics,* or any of the *African* nations. It if, therefore, reasonable to suppose, that their progenitors were seated in some of the barbarous parts of *Asia*. Now, as the northeastern *Asiatic Tartars, Siberians,* and the people of *Kamtschatka,* had such a situation; from them, as from their proper source, we must derive the greatest part of the *American* tribes.

2. Many of the *Americans,* in their idolatry, savage disposition, barbarous qualities, and singular customs, vastly resemble the north-eastern *Asiatics,* particularly the *Tartars,* and natives of *Kamtschatka*. The *Algonkins,* according to *La Hontan,* rove about from one spot of ground to another, like the *Scenite Arabs* and *Tartars,* having neither cities, towns, nor any fixed habitations. The *Peruvians* hang their dead on tree, as do the people of *Kamtschatka*. The *West-Indians* live in houses, or huts, erected on four posts, into which they ascend by a ladder; and in such cottages as these dwell the inhabitants of *Kamtschatka*. The men of *California* go naked, are of a swarthy complexion, and live chiefly upon fish; all which holds true of the *Kamtschatkians*. The *Tungusi, Ostiacks,* and other neighbouring nations, worship the devil with their inchanting drums; and that the ancient inhabitants of *Virginia* paid divine honours to infernal spirits, and were addicted to inchantments and conjurations…

3. There is great reason to believe, that some of the western provinces of *North America* must either be continuous to, or at no great distance from, the north-eastern part of *Asia*…However, it is highly probable, that to the east of *Kamtschatka,* or, as the *Chinese* call it, *Jecco,* and the *Germans Jedso,* there is an immense tract approaching to north *America;* and that even to this day there remains at least a kind of communication between them, by means of a chain of islands. It may also be supposed, that *Asia* and *America* were formerly connected by an isthmus, which might have been destroyed by an earthquake.

4. That part of *America* next to *Asia* is much more populous than the remoter eastern provinces, or kingdoms; which is a manifest indication, that this was first planted by colonies coming from the

---

[153] Under *"Tartarian"*, the author meant *Turkic* nations.

nearest parts of *Asia*, who settled here, and afterwards spread themselves gradually over the new world. From whence we may conclude, that the bulk of the *Americans* are descended from the *Tartars, Siberians,* and people of *Kamtschatka.*

5. …though the *Spaniards* found the continent of *America* full of wild beasts, yet none of them were to be met with in any of the islands which lay remote from that continent. This *Acosta* asserts to be true, on strict examination, of *Cuba, Hispaniola, Margarita, Dominica, Jamaica,* etc. And this has been observed in other islands discovered since *Acosta's* time. *J. De Lact* also says, that there were no such birds in any of these islands as could not fly far, such as partridges, etc. From whence it may be inferred, that *America* received many of its animals, and even men too, from some part of the world nearer to its continent than were *Cuba, Hispaniola, Jamaica,* etc. Now, as this must have been some of the north-eastern districts or provinces of *Asia,* it undoubtedly was, in a great measure, peopled, and stocked with animals, from thence.

6. The people inhabiting the extreme north-eastern part of *Asia* entirely want horses, those animals not being able to live in so cold a region. Now no horses were found in *America,* at the first discovery of it by the *Spaniards;* so that in several places the natives used rein-deer, and large mastiff-dogs, instead of them, as many of the posterity of the ancient most northern *Scythians* or *Tartars* did.

7. The *Chichimecæ,* a barbarous people, in their roving manner of life, and many of their customs, much resembling the *Tartars,* came into *Mexico,* according to the *Americans* themselves, about seven hundred years after the birth of *Christ*. As, therefore, about the year of *Christ* 400 the *Scythians* or *Tartars* so overstocked their country, that they were obliged to disperse into various parts of the world, some of them at that time probably found their way into *America,* over a considerable part of which they might spread themselves in 300 years. This they might do, either by advancing westward to the *Frozen Sea,* and *Nova Zemla,* from whence they might easily pass over to *Greenland,* separated from north *America* only by *Davis's Streights;* or by moving in an eastern direction towards the peninsula of *Kamtschatka*. But, for various reasons that might be assigned, it is not likely, that any great number of people could attempt the former passage; and therefore it must be allowed, that the most considerable body of planters migrated out of the north-eastern part of *Asia* into the new world.

8. It appears from *Solinus, Ammianus Marcellinus,* and *Paulas Venetus,* that *Scythia,* or *Tartary,* and *Hyrcania,* abounded with tigers, lions, bears, and deer. Nay, we learn from *Pliny,* that there was a vast variety, as well as multitude, of wild beasts, in the great *Tartarian* solitudes; and that the country, in many places, was rendered a desert by those beasts. As, therefore, these animals are found in *America,* we may reasonably presume, that they came from thence, though how this passage was effected, we cannot pretend to determine, till we see what relation the eastern extremity of *Asia* bears to the western one of *America*…so that the multitude of strange beasts, as well as birds, to be met with in *America,* may be easily conceived to have got thither from *Tartary* by the eastern passage. This will amount to a reasonable presumption, that such a passage was the most natural, and consequently that the largest number of planters came to the new world from *Tartary, Siberia, Kamtschaka,* and the other most northeastern regions of *Asia.*

9. Nor can any objection to what has been advanced be drawn from the supposed impossibility of the *Scythians* or *Tartars* being ever induced to undertake so long and dangerous a migration. For we are informed by *Pliny* and *Ammianus Marcellinus,* that the *Scythian Cannibals,* or man-eaters, depopulated all the neighbouring country, obliging the inhabitants to fly to the remotest regions, in order to seek out new habitations. The names of these cannibal nations have long been, in a great measure, lost; though there are the remains of two of them, according to *Hornius,* still in *America;* which may possibly give some light into the origin of some of the *American* tribes. About *Florida* we meet with a people called *Apalatci* and *Apalcheni,* which appear, by the affinity of their names, to have been the *Apalai* of *Solinus*. That author joins these *Apalai* with the *Mossagetæ,* some of whose descendents likewise probably migrated into the new world. For we find the *Mazateca,* or *Masateca,* constituting one of the four nations of *New Spain,* and the *Massachaseta, Massachuseta,* or *Massagaseta* (which is still nearer to *Massageta*), situated in *New England*. The *Tambi,* an ancient

people of *Peru*, according to *Hornius*, came from the *Tabieni of Ptolemy*, from whom the promontory of *Tabis*, or *Tabin*, received its name. Hence, we may conclude, that these *Tabieni* pretty nearly corresponded with the present *Jukagri, Koraiki, Tschucktshi, Liutori, Kamtscbadali*, and *Kurili*, inhabiting the extremity of the northeastern tract of *Asia* towards the aforesaid promontory; and consequently that the north-eastern *Asiatic Tartars, Siberians*, and inhabitants of *Kamtschatka*, not a little contributed towards peopling the new world.

10. That there was a second migration of the *Huns, Alans, Avares, Turks, Tartars, Moguls, Parians*, and other *Scythian* nations, into *America*, we learn from *Hornius*. The *Huns*, or at least a branch of that people placed in the farthest part of *Asia*, had the appellation of *Cunadani*, or *Canadani*, from *Cunad*, a place not far from the sea, where some of them had their situation. Hence, we find a city in the *Upper Hungary*, built by their dependents, denominated *Chonad*, or *Chunad* the inhabitants of which, and those of the neighbouring district, still retain the name of *Chonadi*, or *Cunadi*. From these *Hornius* believes the natives of *Canada* to have deduced both their origin and denomination. And, as an author of good credit assigns the *Huyrones* habitations in the neighbourhood of the *Moguls*, he thinks, that these *Huyrones* were the progenitors of the *Hurons*, seated not far from *Canada;* and that the *Hunni*, or *Chuni*, in conjunction with the *Alani*, to whom they were neighbours, were likewise the ancestors of the *Chonsuli*, a people about *Nicaragua*. The same writer also supposes the *Parii*, an ancient *Scythian* nation, to have spread themselves over the region of *Paria* in *America*. Farther, as *Herodotus* mentions a *Scythian* or *Tartar* people called *Napa*, and another denominated *Pali*, he conjectures, that the *Nepi*, in the island of *Trinidada*, came from the former, and the *Otapali* in *Florida* from the latter. The *Turks* seem to have been called *Iyrca* by *Herodotus*, and were, according to *Hornius*, the fathers of the *Iroquoi*, or *Iroquois;* nay, as the *Hyrcanians*[154] were descended from the *Iyrca*, and in their own language had the name of *Tzuruki*, he takes the *Souriquoi* to have been also their posterity. The *Mexican* words *Teu* and *Tepec*, importing *God* and a mountain, had likewise the same signification in the ancient *Turkish;* which he considers as a confirmation of the truth of his opinion. Some traces of the *Moguls* may be observed in the *Tamogali*, and the *Mogoles* about the *Rio de la Plata*. *Choten*, or *Chotena, Baita*, and *Tangur*, or *Tanguth*, are local proper names in *Great Tartary;* and with these *Coton* in *Chili, Paita* in *Peru*, and *Tangora* in the same country, very well correspond. The *Mexican* local proper names generally end in *-an*, as *Teutitlan, Coatlan, Hazatlan, Quezatlan, Petutlan*, etc. as do also those of the *Tartars, Indians*, and other eastern nations. Many of the *Scythian*, or *Hunnian*, etc. proper names, had the particle *Al* prefixed to them; which frequently happened to those of *Yucatan*,[155] and the adjacent parts of *North America*. An *American* king named *Tatarax* reigned formerly in *Quivira*, who seems to have been of *Tartar* extraction. For, the antient *Turks* and *Tartars* frequently annexed the particle *ax* to the proper names of their princes, and the word *Tatar* or *Tartar* occurs in that of this monarch. Nay, that the *Americans* imitated the *Turks* and *Tartars* in the aforesaid particular, appears from those *American* kings called *Stalderax, Almorax, Merebax*, and *Naguatax;* as also from *Atzlan*, an ancient name in the kingdom of *Mexico*, answering exactly to that of *Atzlan Beg*, a *Turkish* prince in *Natolia*, about the year of *Christ* 1300. From all which we may infer, to omit other instances of this kind which might be produced, that the greatest part of the ancient inhabitants of the new world deduced their original from the above-mentioned north-eastern *Asiatic* nations.

11. The *Epicerini*, a people of *Canada*, when the *Europeans* first came among them, asserted, that, very far from them, in a western direction, there lived a nation who affirmed, that foreign merchants, without beards, in great ships, frequently visited their coasts....it appears, that the *Japanese* had also an intercourse with the *Americans*. The *Chiapaneca*, a nation in this vast region that came from *Nicaragua*, but originally from *Mexico* and *California*, by their name appear to be descended from some people left in *America* by the *Japanese*. The river, province, and lake of *Chiapa*, in the kingdom of *Mexico*, as well as *Ker-Japan* in the island of *Trinidada*, afford some

---

[154] *Hyrkania* – modern *Shirvan*, a region of the *Azerbaijan Republic*.
[155] The word *Yucatan* consists of 2 *Turkic* words – *Yuk* 'load, cargo' and *Atan* 'throwing', meaning "the resting place" in *Turkic*.

traces of the *Japanese*. The *Tartars* anciently called the *Japanese Zipangri;* and, when *Columbus* arrived at *Hispaniola,* and heard that part of this place was called *Zipangi* by the natives, he imagined himself to have come to the proper *Japan*. The word *Montezuma,* or *Motezume,* the usual title of the emperors of *Mexico,* is plainly of *Japanese* extraction, *Motazaiuma,* according to *Hornius,* being the common appellation of the *Japanese* monarchs. But though, from what is here observed, it seems probable, that the *Japanese* left some people on this vast continent, yet we are apt to believe, that not many natives of *Japan* remained here. For that nation, being originally *Chinese,* undoubtedly retained the customs, and political maxims, prevailing in *China*. However, as, under the name of *Chinese,* several *Oriental* writers comprehended the *Manchew Tartars,* who were quite of a different political constitution from the true *Chinese,* we may reasonably suppose, that the former attended the latter, as well as the *Japanese,* to *America,* and made several settlements there. From whence we may collect, that the new world was principally supplied with inhabitants by the eastern and north-eastern *Asiatic Tartary*.

    12. The founder of the *Peruvian* empire was one *Manco,* or *Mancu,* if we will believe the *Americans* themselves, who certainly must have been the best acquainted with the traditional knowledge of their own antiquities. Now *Manco,* or *Mancu,* evidently alludes to *Manchew,* or rather is the same word with it. This is an additional proof, that some *Manchew* colonies settled in *America,* and particularly *Peru;* so that, as this was the politest part of the new world, together with *Mexico,* we may naturally suppose the *Chinese* to have been the most conversant with the inhabitants of it, and, if anywhere, to have planted colonies in it. But, from what is here observed, it is likely enough, that the *Manchew Tartars,* who probably were introduced by the *Chinese,* founded the *Peruvian* empire; as those of the same nation who attended the *Japanese* did that of *Mexico*. So that the *Chinese* and *Japanese* seem only to have traded with the *Americans,* transported in their ships the *Manchew Tartars* hither, and communicated some of their names, customs, manners, etc. to them. The northeastern and eastern *Tartars,* therefore, of which the *Manchews* were a branch, must greatly, if not above all other nations, have contributed towards the peopling at least of a considerable part of the new world.

    13. Father *Jartoux* has obliged the learned world with a most accurate description of the celebrated plant *Ginseng,* which he first committed to writing in the year 1709. At the time it was gathered, when he had it exhibited to his view in the utmost perfection. This plant is a native of *Manchew Tartary;* and then it was not known, that any other part of the world produced it. Father *Lafitau,* a missionary *Jesuit* in *Canada,* being hereby excited to an inquiry after the *Ginseng,* after three months search, found it there. The *Americans* had, for a long time, been acquainted with its virtues; and, among them, it all along went under the name of *Garentoguen,* which signified the thighs of a man. However, he inferred from thence, and in our opinion very justly, that north *America* was joined to *Tartary,* or at least to some tract continuous to it; since it is almost impossible, that the *Tartars* and *Americans* could both have hit upon those names without a communication of ideas. Nor do we doubt, but many similar arguments, in favour of a connection of *Asia* and *America,* would be suggested to us, by a nice inspection into, and examination of, the plants and animals, as well as customs, religions, languages, etc. of those two immense continents, which, with the seas appertaining to them, form the most considerable part of the terraqueous globe.

    14. ...So that, from the tract lately discovered, to the east of *Japan* and *Kamtschatka,* and the people settled there, we may infer the probability of *America's* being planted in part by colonies drawn from the north-eastern regions of *Asia*. For, by such discovery, a nearer approach is made from *Japan* and *Kamtschatka* to the coast of *California;* and, from this approach, a presumptive argument is drawn in favour of our opinion; according to which, all the islands and continents between *Japan, Kamtschatka,* and *California,* as well as a considerable part of *America,* at least, were peopled from *Siberia* and *Tartary*." [20.4.33.162-172]

Among the most enduring, withstanding the pressure of time markers of ancient nations are the names of the people and tribes, as well as the names of land, cities, and villages they built, mountains, hills, canyons, rivers they inhabited or used to derive their everyday food. Now, we will discuss the following main topics to confirm the presence of the ancient *Turkic* race in the *American* continents:

1. The names of the *Native American* tribes and places of *Turkic* origin.
2. The religion of the *Native Americans*, compatible with *Turkic Tengriism*.
3. The similarities of the *Native American* artifacts, petroglyphs, mounds, tamgas on clothes and carpets, rugs with the *Turkic* ones.

§ 2. THE NAMES OF THE NATIVE AMERICAN TRIBES THAT HAVE A TURKIC ORIGIN.

There are a lot of native *American* tribes, the names of which strike the cord of any *Turkic* speaker, as it is clear as a day that their name is of *Turkic* origin. The following list of the *Native-American* names with the attested definition and their comparison to the *Turkic* lexical units is provided to determine their *Turkic* roots and set aside any doubts about the *Turkic* origin of these tribes:

- *Bayougoula, aka Ischenoca:*
  - *Bayougoula* "people of marshy waterbody": *Bayoug > Batak* 'marshy, stagnant water body' + *Oul* 'offspring; son' + *-A > -I* 'an affix of possession, equivalent to the preposition *Of*', meaning "people of marshy water body" in *Turkic*. The structure of the word is unmistakably *Turkic* – first comes a noun *Bayoug* followed by the noun *Oul* with the added affix of possession at the end.
  - *Ischenoca* "our people": *Ischen > İçin* 'internal; inside' + *Oca > Aka* 'man', meaning "our people" in *Turkic*. This was the native name of the *Bayougoula* tribe.

- *Pascagoula:*
  This tribe was known as "bread people" in the language of the *Choktaw*. The name stems from the *Turkic* words:
  - *Pascagoula* "bread people": *Pascag > Boğoz* 'bread' + *Oul* 'son, offspring' + *-A > İ* 'an affix of possession', meaning "bread people" in *Turkic*.

- *Choctaw:*
  Nobody knows the exact meaning of the tribal name. However, based on the legend surrounding the *Choctaw* nation, according to which these people originated from a sacred hill in *Mississippi*, their name reflects not only their place of origination from a mountain but also demonstrates their mound-building culture. As such, it can be easily deduced from *Turkic*:
  - *Choctaw: Choc > Çok* 'great' + *Taw > Tau* 'mountain', meaning "great mountain".

- *Catawba, aka Kotaha, aka Issa, aka Essa:*
  - *Catawba* "divided, separated": *Cat > Kət* 'leave, go away' + *Awba > Oba* 'tribe', meaning "separated tribe" in *Turkic*.
  - *Kotaha* "robust men": *Kot > Köt* 'health' + *Aha > Aka* 'man', meaning "healthy, robust men" in *Turkic*.
  - *Issa, Essa* "river people": *Is, Es > İş, Eş* 'friend, companion' + *Sa > Su* 'river', meaning "river people" in *Turkic*. This was the native name of the *Catawba* tribe.

- *Comanche*, aka *Nermurnuh*, aka *Nimenim*, aka *Nemene*, aka *Nuumu:*
  - *Comanche* "anyone who wants to fight me": *Com > Kam, Kem, Kim* 'who, anyone' + *Man > Men, Mən* 'I' + *Che > Çır* 'tear apart', meaning "anyone who fights me" in *Turkic*. Again, the structure of the name strictly follows the *Turkic* word structural pattern. This tribal name was bestowed to the *Comanche* by the *Ute* tribe.
  - *Nermurnuh* "true human being": *N > Ən* 'most' + *Er > Aru* 'pure' + *Murnuh > Murki* 'ancestor', meaning "the truest ancestor" in *Turkic*. This is the self-name with many variants.
  - *Nimenim, Nemene, Nuumu* "true human being" > *Nəmə* "being" in *Turkic*.

- *Delaware, aka Lenape:*
  The self-name of this tribe was *Lenape* "original people; true men; grandfathers". It consists of two *Turkic* words:
  - *Lenape: Le > Ulu* 'great; grand' + *Nape > Nəbə* 'being', meaning "great men; grandfathers" in *Turkic*.

- *Illinois*, aka *Illiniwek*, aka *Illinik*, aka *Illini*, aka *Aliniouek*, aka *Aliniwek*, aka *Eriniouai*, aka *Hileni*, aka *Illiniouck*, aka *Ilinoue*, aka *Inoca:*
  Illinois is the *French* variety of their original name *Illiniwek, Illinik* "men, people". The name sprang from the *Turkic* word *İl* "people; tribe" that has a derivative *İlin* "of people; belonging to people". By the way, the state of *Illinois* owes its name to this *Native American* tribe of *Turkic* extraction.

- *Ottawa, aka Odawa:*
  - *Ottawa, Odawa* "at home anywhere people": *Ot, Od > Ota, Oda* 'tent, yurt' + *Ta > -Ta* 'an affix, similar to the prepositions *In, Inside*' + *Awa > Oba* 'tribe', meaning "at home people" in *Turkic*.

  The *Ottawa* were the *Algonquians* of *Great Lakes* and a part of the confederation called the *Council of Three Fires* that included the *Ojibwe* and the *Potawatomi* tribes.

  There is also another suggested meaning of the tribal name – "to trade". However, the *Ottawa* became known as traders only after the arrival of *Europeans*. Most likely, the already existing name *Ottawa* became a denominative of their trading activity that made this tribe notable. By the way, the tribe *Ottawa* gave its name to the capital of *Canada* and the river that separates *Ontario* from *Quebec* in *Canada*. The *Ottawa* tribe became noted for its famously courageous, prominent leader *Pontiac*. Fascinatingly, the name of the *Ottawa* tribal leader *Pontiac*, or *Bwandiag* in the native form, could be deciphered as a combination of the *Turkic* words:

  Bwandiag: Bwan > Buvın 'generation' + *Diag > Dayaq* 'support', meaning "defender of the nation" in *Turkic*.

  The *Americans* honored the *Ottawan* chief *Pontiac* by assigning his name to the automobile brand and the city in *Michigan*, near which he was buried.

- *Potawatomi*, aka *Potawatami*, aka *Pottawatami*, aka *Pottawatomie:*
  - *Potawatomi, Potawatami, Pottawatami, Pottawatomie* "people of the place of fire": *Po* 'here, this' + *Ot* 'fire' + *Awa > Oba* 'tribe' + *Tomi, Tami > Təmi* 'earth, clay'[156] (*Təm* 'earth' + *-İ* 'an affix of possession, equivalent to the preposition *Of*'), meaning "this is the place of the fire nation" in *Turkic*.

  As a part of the union, including two other tribes – the *Algonquians* and the *Chippewa* (*Ojibway*), this tribe was reported to live in what is today *Michigan*.

---

[156] *Egorov V.G.* "Etimologicheskiy slovar chuvashskogo yazika." [236].

- *Ojibwe, aka Otchipwa, aka Chippewa, aka Anishinaabe, aka Anishinabe:*
  - *Ojibwe, Otchipwa, Chippewa* "pointed skin": *Oj, Otch, Chi > Uj, Uc* 'edge' + *I > -İ* 'an affix of the possessive pronoun, equivalent to *Its'* + *Bwe, Pwa, Ppewa > Büz* 'pucker', meaning "puckered edge" in *Turkic*. This tribe acquired its name due to the puckered seam of moccasins [157] and pointed at the bottom shirts worn by the tribesmen. The name of this tribe *Ojibwe* or *Chippewa* comes from the *Algonquin* word "*Otchipwa*", meaning 'to pucker' which perfectly resonates with the *Turkic* words.
  - *Anishinaabe, Anishinabe* "original people": *Ani > An* 's/he' + *Shin > Şın* 'genuine, original' + *Aabe, Abe > Oba* 'tribe, race', meaning "they are original people" in *Turkic*. This is the native name of the tribe *Anishinabe* that points to its *Turkic* pedigree.

  This *Northern Athabascan* tribe used to be the largest and most influential in *North America*, with the preferred territory of habitation around the western *Great Lakes*.
  Being a confederate of the *Council of Three Fires*, they had an offshoot *Algonquin* branch called *Athabascan* that became an encompassing word, defining all *Native American* peoples of the *Athabascan* or *Athapascan* language family.

- *Athabascan, aka Athapaskan, aka Tinneh, aka Déné:*
  - *Athabascan, Athapaskan* "there are reeds one after another": *Atha > Ota* 'by grass' (*Ot* 'grass' + *-A* 'an affix, equivalent to the preposition *By*') + *Bas, Pas* 'cover, spread' + *Can, Kan > -Kan* 'an affix, converting a verb into an adjective', meaning "covered by grass" in *Turkic*. The *Athabascans* acquired this name from another *Native American* tribe – the *Cree*, who named a lake *Athabasca* in *Canada* to depict the grassy surrounding of this waterway.
  - *Tinneh, Déné* "the people" > *Təŋ* "crowd, people" in *Turkic*.

  The *Athapascans* swelled in numbers and split into the *Northern, Southern,* and *Alaskan Athapascans*.
  The *Northern Athapascans* were divided into the *Subarctic Athapascans* populating the western part of the *Subarctic*; the *Canadian Rocky Athapascans* living near the *Rocky Mountains*; the *Lake Athapascans* inhabiting ancestral lands near *Great Slave* and *Great Bear Lakes*.
  The *Southern Athapascans* acquired new names – the *Apache*, the *Navajo*, who occupied the *American Southwest*, while other tribes migrated far away and settled among the *Plateau Indians*, the *California Indians*.
  The *Alascan Athapascans* resided in *Alaska* with some adjoining lands of *Canada*.

- *Navajo:*
  This *Native American* people call themselves *Dine,* or *Tinneh,* or *Dinaa,* or *Dena,* or *Dene* "people". The name takes its roots from the *Turkic* word *Təŋ* "crowd, people". They are the *Southern Athabascans*.

- *Apache, aka Nde, aka Ndee:*
  The native name *Nde,* or *Ndee* "the people", is a modified form from *Dene,* or *Tinneh,* and has the same *Turkic* root *Təŋ* "people". This tribe belongs to the *Southern Athabascan* branch of the *Native Americans*.

- *Thlingchadinne, aka Tli Cho, aka Tlicho, aka Dogrib:*
  - *Thlingchadinne* "dog-flank people": *Thling, Tli > Tula* 'dog' + *Cha, Cho > Çörü* 'edge, side' + *Dinne > Təŋ* 'people', meaning "dog-flank people" in *Turkic*.

  These *Northern Athabascan* people obtained their name after their sorcerer, who, as their legend says, would retain his human body by day and transform into a dog at night.

---

[157] The word *Moccasin* proceeds from the *Turkic* word *Maksi* – shoes made from soft leather [*Radlov. 4.2.1999*].

- *Kawchottine*, aka *Kawchodinne*, aka *Nigottine*, aka *Nniotinné*, aka *Kattagottine*, aka *Krathagotinné*, aka *Katchogottine*, aka *Krachogotinne*, aka *Satchotugottine*, aka *Sachothugotinné*, aka *Nellagottine*, aka *Nnellagotinné*, aka *Hare:*
    - *Kawchottine, Kawchodinne* "people of the great hare": *Kaw > Koyan* 'hare' + *Cho > Çok* 'plenty' + *Ttine, Dinne > Tǝŋ* 'people', meaning "people having many hares" in *Turkic*. This tribe was named after an arctic hare which was their source of food and clothing. The *Kawchottine* had 5 offshoot tribes. All the names of these tribes originated from the *Turkic* source:
    - *Nigottine, Nniotinné* "people of the moss": *Nig, Nni > Nǝm* 'humid area' + *Ot* 'plant' + *Tine, Tinne > Tǝŋ* 'people', meaning "people from the humid area covered with plant" in *Turkic*. Obviously, moss is a plant that grows in humid, shady areas.
    - *Kattagottine, Krathagotinné* "people among the hares": *Kat, Kra > Kodan* 'hare' + *Tago, Thago > Takal* 'be nearby' + *Ttine, Tinne > Tǝŋ* 'people', meaning "people with hares nearby" in *Turkic*.
    - *Katchogottine, Krachogotinne* "people of the big hares": *Kat, Kra > Kodan* 'hare' + *Cho > Çok* 'very' + *Ogo > Okar* 'tall, big' + *Ttine, Tinne > Tǝŋ* 'people', meaning "people having very big hares" in *Turkic*.
    - *Satchotugottine, Sachothugotinné* "people of *Great Bear Lake*": *Sa > Sai* 'river' + *Tcho, Cho > Çok* 'great' + *Otugo > Adığ* 'bear' + *Ttine, Tinne > Tǝŋ* 'people', meaning "people of the *Great Bear River*" in *Turkic*.
    - *Nellagottine, Nnellagotinné* "people of the end of the world": *Nella, Nnella > Nǝ El* 'all countries, all people' + *Ago > Akır* 'end' + *Ttine, Tinne > Tǝŋ* 'people', meaning "people of the end of all countries" in *Turkic*.

  This *Northern Athapascan* tribe populated the lands near the *Mackenzie River* and *Great Bear Lake* in *Canada*.

- *Hupa*, aka *Natinookwa*, aka *Natinixwe:*
    - *Natinookwa, Natinixwe* "where the trails return": *Na > Uŋai* 'right path' + *Tinoo, Tini > Dönü* 'return' + *Kwa, Xwe > Kaya* 'where', meaning "the place where true trails return" in *Turkic*.

  These were the *Southern Athapascans*.

- *Tolowa:*
    - *Tolowa* "people of lake": *Tol > Talai* 'lake' + *Owa > Oba* 'tribe', meaning "people of lake" in *Turkic*.

- *Dakelh*, aka *Takulli*, aka *Carriers:*
    - *Dakelh* "people who go upon the water": *Dak > Dǝk* 'tribe' + *Elh > Ilai* 'murky water', meaning "people of murky water" in *Turkic*.
    - *Takulli* "people who go upon the water": *Tak > Tǝk* 'tribe' + *Ulli > Ilai* 'murky water', meaning "people of murky water" in *Turkic*.

  The endonym of the *Northern Athapascan* tribe consists of the components in two variants that meet their match in *Turkic*, such as *Dǝk, Tǝk*. The *Dakelh* were known as the *Carriers* due to the cultural tradition of carrying the charred bones of the deceased husband by a widow for three years.

- *Etchareottine*, aka *Etchaottine*, aka *Slavey*, aka *Awokanek*, aka *Tinneh*, aka *Dine:*
    - *Etchareottine, Etchaottine* "people dwelling in the shelter": *Etchare, Etcha > İçəri* 'inside' + *Ot > Otau* 'yurt, dwelling' + *Tine > Tǝŋ* 'people', meaning "people in the dwelling" in *Turkic*. This was the name of the *Northern Athapascan* tribe given to them by the *Chipewyan*.
    - *Tinneh, Dine* "people" > *Tǝŋ* "people" in *Turkic*. The *Etchareottine* called themselves the *Tinneh*, or *Dine*, similar to other *Athapascan* people.

- *Tatsanottine, aka Yellowknife:*
  - *Tatsanottine* "people of the scum of water": *Tat* 'stain, rust' + *Sano* > *Sai* 'river' + *Ttine* > *Təŋ* 'people', meaning "people of the stain of the river" in *Turkic*.

  The *Northern Athabaskan* tribe was named as such after a copper residue along the *Coppermine River*.

- *Tanaina, aka Denaina, aka Knaiakhotana, aka Kaniakhotana, aka Kenaitze:*
  - *Tanaina, Denaina* "people" > *Təŋ* "people" in *Turkic*.
  - *Knaiakhotana, Kaniakhotana, Kenaitze* "people of the *Kenai Peninsula*": *Knaia, Kania, Kenai* > *Kenai* + *Kho* > *Koi* 'bay, narrow passage' + *Tana, Tze* > *Təŋ* 'people', meaning "people of the narrow passage *Kenai*" in *Turkic*.

- *Paiute, aka Numa, aka Nuwuvi, aka Numu:*
  - *Numa, Nuwuvi, Numu* "people" > *Umu* "people" in *Turkic*.

  This is an endonym – the *Northern Paiute* call themselves *Numa*, or *Numu*, whereas the *Southern Paiute* recognize themselves as *Nuwuvi*. The tribe is also called *Paiute* "water *Ute*" or "true *Ute*".

- *Ute, aka Utes, aka Uteas, aka Noochee:*
  - *Ute* "mountain people" > *Uca, Yüce* "high" in *Turkic*. *Ute* and the related name *Utah* are the *Navajo* words, meaning "upper, higher up".
  - *Utes, Uteas* "upper people": *Ut* > *Uca* 'high' + *Es, Eas* > *Əs* 'host, master', meaning "lord of the highlands" in *Turkic*.
  - *Noochee* "people" > *Nark* "people" in *Turkic*. This is the endonym of the *Ute* people.

  The *American* state of *Utah* is named after this *Native American* tribe of the *Turkic* extraction.

- *Spokan, aka Spokane:*
  - *Spokan, Spokane* "people of the Sun": *Spo* > *Sıbai* 'neighboring' + *Kan, Kane* > *Kün, Gün* 'the Sun', meaning "close to the Sun" in *Turkic*. Interestingly, the word *Kün* also means "people" in *Turkic*.

  This *Native American* tribe gave its name to the *Spokane River* and the city of *Spokane* in the state of *Washington*.

- *Tionontati,* aka *Khionontateronon:*
  - *Khionontateronon* "where the mountain stands": *Khiono* > *Kanı* 'where' + *On* > *Ol* 'that' + *Ta* > *Tau, To, Tu* 'mountain' + *Teronon* > *Turan* 'standing', meaning "where that mountain stands" in *Turkic*.
  - *Tionontati* "where the mountain stands": *Tion* > *Kanı* 'where' + *On* > *Ol* 'that' + *Ta* > *Tau, To, Tu* 'mountain' + *Ti* > *Tur* 'stand', meaning "where that mountain stands" in *Turkic*.

  This was an *Iroquoian*-speaking tribe with ancestral lands in *Ontario, Canada*.

- *Tohono Oodham,* aka *Papago,* aka *Ppahvio Oodham:*
  - *Tohono Oodham* "desert people": *Tohono* > *Tala* 'desert' + *Oodham* > *Adam* 'person', meaning "desert people" in *Turkic*.
  - *Papago, Ppahvio Oodham* "bean people" > *Paxla* [158] *Adam* "bean person" in *Turkic*.

  The ancestral territory of this tribe extended to the *Sonoran Desert* near the *Gulf of California*.

- *Olmecatl,* aka *Olmec,* aka *Olmecah:*
  - *Olmecah, Olmec* "inhabitant of the rubber country": *Ol* > *Oləi* 'oil' + *Mecah* > *Manka* 'crowd', meaning "people of oil" in *Turkic*.

---

[158] *Musayev O.I.* "Azərbaycanca-İngiliscə lüğət." [457].

- *Olmecatl* "inhabitant of the rubber country": *Ol > Olǝi* 'oil' + *Mecah > Manka* 'crowd' + *Tl > Tal* 'part, branch', meaning "part of people of oil" or "person of the oil" in *Turkic*.

This tribe was known for extracting latex out of rubber trees and creating rubber. The name reflected this activity – "inhabitant of the rubber country". The ancient *Turkic* nations recognized the milky substance found in a rubber tree as oil. There are several derivatives pointing to the extraction of oil from a tree in *Turkic*:

Olǝi "oil".
Oluk "chute". After tapping a rubber tree, its bark serves as a chute to extract the latex.
Oliva "tree oil".

The *Olmecs* were the cultural founders of *Mesoamerica* from 1200 BCE through 300 CE, with ancestral lands covering the *Gulf* coast until modern-day *Mexico City*.

Figure 43. An Olmec – a kneeling bearded figure. 900-400 BC. Mexico. Metropolitan Museum of Art. [OA]
Credit: Gift of Stephanie Bernheim, in memory of Leonard H. Bernheim Jr., and in celebration of the Museum's 150th Anniversary, 2017

- *Chichimeca,* aka *Chichimecah,* aka *Chichimecatl:*
  - *Chichimecah* "sons of dogs": *Chichi > Küçük* 'whelp' + *Mecah > Manka* 'crowd', meaning "people of dogs" in *Turkic*.
  - *Chichimecatl* "sons of dogs": *Chichi > Küçük* 'whelp' + *Mecah > Manka* 'crowd' + *Tl > Tal* 'part, branch', meaning "branch of the dog people" in *Turkic*.
  - *Chichiman* "area of milk": *Chichi > Çigǝn* 'fermented milk' + *Man > Maŋ* 'area', meaning "area of milk" in *Turkic*.
  - *Chichimecah* "people from the milk area": *Chichi > Çigǝn* 'fermented milk' + *Mecah > Manka* 'crowd', meaning "people of the milk" in *Turkic*.
  - *Chichimecatl* "people from the milk area": *Chichi > Çigǝn* 'fermented milk' + *Mecah > Manka* 'crowd' + *Tl > Tal* 'part, branch', meaning "branch of the people of the milk" in *Turkic*.

As we see, there are several variants offered as the definition of the tribal name. All of them have their match in *Turkic*. These people led a life of a wanderer, who followed their God *Huitzilpochtli* to the shores of *Lake Texcoco*. In the 20th volume of "An Universal History, from Earliest Account of Time", it is established that the *Chichimeca* were the progeny of the *Turkic* nation of *Tatars:*

> "…the *Chichimecæ,* a barbarous people, in most of their customs resembling the antient *Scythians,* found their way into *Mexico* about the 700th year of *Christ*. The first of these migrations seems to have been occasioned by the embroiled state of *Tartary,* which was greatly agitated by bloody wars and intestine commotions, as well as overstocked with people, about the beginning of the fifth century. And the latter was probably effected by the descendents of the first migrators, who in the space of 300 years might have peopled the most northern parts of *America*. This is likewise confirmed by the account the *Americans* themselves give us of the *Chichimecæ,* and their first arrival in *Mexico*. Nor can it well be doubted, but that since the year 700 the *Tartars* have performed several other such migrations." [20.4.33.190]

- *Toltec, aka Toltecah, aka Toltecatl:*
  - *Toltecah, Toltec* "people of the reeds": *Tol > Tonnuz* 'reed' + *Tecah, Tec > Tək* 'race, dynasty', meaning "people of the reeds" in *Turkic*.
  - *Toltecatl* "people of the reeds", "inhabitants of *Tollan*": *Tol > Tonnuz* 'reed' + *Teca > Tək* 'race' + *Tl > Tal* 'part, branch', meaning "branch of people of the reeds", "inhabitants of *Tollan*" in *Turkic*.
  - *Tollan* "place of the reeds": *Tol > Tonnuz* 'reed' + *Lan > Maŋ* 'area', meaning "place of the reeds" in *Turkic*.

  These people were a branch of the *Chichimec* family that dominated central and southern *Mexico* prior to the *Aztecs*. *Tollan* was the name of their city and meant "place of reeds", where *Tol* stood for "reed". Both the city and the tribal name have irrefutable *Turkic* whence.

- *Aztec, aka Aztecah, aka Aztecatl, aka Mexica:*
  - *Aztecah, Aztec* "people of *Aztlan*": *Az = Aztlan + Tecah, Tec > Tək* 'race', meaning "people of *Aztlan*" in *Turkic*.
  - *Aztecatl* "people of *Aztlan*": *Az = Aztlan + Tecah, Tec > Tək* 'race' + *Tl > Tal* 'part, branch', meaning "part of the *Aztec* tribe" or "part of *Aztlan's* people" in *Turkic*.

  This *Native American* tribe was a side-shoot of the *Chichimec* tribe. Being a nomadic tribe, they first settled in the city of *Aztlan,* from where they migrated into the central highlands of *Mexico*. The meaning of the name *Aztlan* is uncertain, with some suggesting "place of egrets", and others – "place of whiteness". However, the remaining component of the name is *Turkic* by shape and meaning. The definition of the appellation *Mexica* is not clear, though some claim it to be named after the *Aztec* deity of war *Huitzilopochtli's* secret name *Mexitl* or *Mexi* "place of *Mexi*" or "land of the war god". The name can be derived from the *Turkic Mak* or *Mağu* "glory".
  The *Aztecs* created a highly civilized society with well-designed cities, magnificent architecture, including pyramids. Their civilization was destroyed by the *Europeans,* namely the *Spanish*.

- *Maya:*
  - *Maya > Maya* 'power, vigor', meaning "nation of power" in *Turkic*.

  The nation of the *Maya* was the most fascinating among the *Native American* peoples due to its mind-boggling architecture, art, mathematical and astronomical achievements, and above them all – its writing system.
  According to the genetic research under the auspices of *National Geographic*, led by *Spencer Wells,* the *Mayans,* like many other *Native Americans,* also bear the *Turkic* markers that stem from the 40,000 years long DNA of the *Turkic* man *Zakirjan Niyazov* from *Central Asia*.

- *Kiche*:
  - *Kiche > Kişi* "man" in *Turkic*.

  The *Kiche* tribe was of the *Mayan* descent that resettled in *Guatemala*.

- *Anasazi:*
    - *Anasazi* "enemy ancestors", "ancient non-*Navajos*": *A* 'grandfather' + *Na* > *Nayı* 'friend' + *Sazi* > *-Siz* 'an affix, indicating the word *Without*', meaning "friendless ancestors" in *Turkic*.
    - *Anasazi* "ancient ones who are not among us": *Ana* 'female ancestor' + *Sazi* > *Sazi* > *Siz* 'an affix, indicating the preposition *Without*', meaning "being without a female ancestor" in *Turkic*.

  The *Anasazi* were the ancestors of the *Hopi* and the *Pueblo* tribes. Their name in *Navajo* bears several meanings – "enemy ancestors", "ancient non-*Navajos*", "ancient ones who are not among us".

- *Tunica,* aka *Tonica,* aka *Tonnica,* aka *Thonnica:*
    - *Tunica, Tonica, Tonnica, Thonnica* "people", "those who are the people" > *Tanık* "friend, acquaintance" in *Turkic*. This *Native American* tribe initially lived in the *Mississippi River Valley*.

- *Inuk,* aka *Inuit:*
    - *Inuk* "person" > *Inak* "friend" in *Turkic*.
    - *Inuit* "people" > *Inak* + *-İt* 'an affix, indicating plural form', meaning "friends" in *Turkic*. The word *Inak* was subjected to modification by removing a portion of the word *-Ak* and replacing it with the affix *-İt* to accommodate the transition into plurality. The *U* sound replaced *A* in *Inuit* to maintain the harmony of the word.

  These people were from the *Canadian Arctic,* officially known as the *Inuit*. They were previously called *Eskimos*, which stands for "eater of raw meat".

- *Haudenosaunee,* aka *Iroquois:*
    - *Haudenosaunee* "people of the longhouse": *Hau* > *O* 's/he' + *Den* > *Təŋ* 'people' + *Osaun, Oshoun* > *Usun* 'long' + *Ee* > *İv, Ev* 'house', meaning "they are the people of the long house" in *Turkic*.
    - *Iroquois* – there is not any reliable definition of the tribal name *Iroquois,* as some consider it a *French* word, others propose unsubstantiated meanings.

  Following the tradition set by their *Turkic* ancestors, the *Haudenosaunee* got organized into a confederation and selected a longhouse as their totem.

  As it is known, unlike some nations, such as the ancient *Persians,* the *Semitic* people, and the *Egyptians,* the *Turkic* nations always assembled into tribal unions, or confederations, called *El* (with the derivatives *Ellə* "create confederation", *Ellig* "being a member of a confederation" in *Turkic*). The confederation structure of society was built by the peoples of *Turkic* extraction from ancient times, including the *Scythians,* the *Hun,* the *Thracians,* the *Trojans,* the *Turrenians,* the *Pelasgians,* the *Spartans,* the *Germanic* tribes, and their offshoots.

  The *Native American* tribe of the *Haudenosaunee* was also a part of the confederation called "the *Iroquois Confederacy"* that included five other tribes – the *Cayuga, Mohawk, Oneida, Onondaga,* and *Seneca*.

  Remarkably, the forefathers of the *USA* – *Thomas Jefferson, George Washington, Benjamin Franklin,* adopted the ancient *Turkic* political and structural blueprint of society from this *Native American* confederacy.

  The *Haudenosaunee* currently occupy the reservations, mainly in *New York, Quebec,* and *Ontario,* with some inhabiting the states of *Wisconsin* and *Oklahoma*.

- *Cayuga,* aka *Guyohkohnyoh:*
    - *Cayuga, Guyohkohnyoh* "people of the place where the boats were taken out": *Cayug, Guyohk* > *Qayiq, Kayik, Kayık* 'boat' + *Ohn* > *An* 'piece of land' + *Yoh* > *Üyə* 'stock, progeny', meaning

"people of the place where boats are" in *Turkic*. Evidently, *Cayuga* was the shortened version of *Guyohkohnyoh*.

This was one of the six main tribes of the *Iroquois League,* primarily located along *Cayuga Lake,* named after them in the *New York* State.

Remarkably, the name of a *Turkic* tribe from the *Oguz* branch was also *Qayığ* "boat" [*Mahmud Kashgari*. 1.55], resembling the *Native American Cayuga* both in meaning and form.

- *Onondaga:*
  - *Onondaga* "on the hill": *Onon > Onun* 'his/her' + *Daga > Dağı* 'hill, mountain' (*Dağ* 'hill' + -*I* 'an affix of possession, equivalent to the pronoun *His/Her*'), meaning "their mountain" in *Turkic*.

  This nation populated the vicinity of *Onondaga Lake* and the *Oswego River* near the state of *New York*. They were held in high esteem as the leading tribe of the *Iroquois Confederacy,* also known as the Keepers of the Council Fire. Their village under the same name, *Onondaga*, was the place of meeting for the Great Council of the *Iroquoian* confederates.

  Judging by the lexical peculiarity of the tribal name, i.e., *Onun* instead of *Anın*, *Dağ* instead of *Tau*, it becomes clear that its components belong to the *Oguz* branch of the *Turkic* languages. The *Oguz* division primarily includes the *Turkish,* the *Azerbaijani,* and the *Turkmen*.

- *Onondowagah,* aka *Nundawaono*, aka *Osininka*, aka *Seneca:*
  - *Ononondowagah, Nundawaono* "people of the great hill": *Onon, Nun > Onun* 'his/her' + *On > Ön* 'great' + *Dowagah, Dawaono > Dağı* 'hill, mountain' (*Dağ* 'hill' + *-I* 'an affix of possession, equivalent to the pronoun *His/Her*'), meaning "their great mountain" in *Turkic*. The native name of this tribe was very similar to the *Onondaga*, with the added *Turkic* word *Ön* "great" and modified *Dowagah* for *Dağ* "hill".
  - The names *Osininka* and *Seneca* were given to this tribe by the non-related peoples.

  The ancestral homeland of this member of the *Iroquois Confederacy* extended from *Seneca* Lake to the *Allegheny* River in *New York*.

- *Onayotekaona,* aka *Oneida:*
  - *Onayotekaona* "people of the upright stone": *Onayo > Onun* 'his/her' + *Tek > Tik* 'upright' + *Kaona > Kantar* 'boulder, stone', meaning "their upright stone" in *Turkic*.
  - *Oneida* "people of the upright stone": *Onei > Onun* 'his/her' + *Da* 'hill, mountain', meaning "their hill" in *Turkic*. *Oneida* was the shortened form of the tribal self-name.

  This tribe was named after a large rock within their territory. It was a member of the *Iroquois Confederacy* and also resided in the territory of present-day *New York* State.

- *Kanienkahagen,* aka *Kanienkehaka,* aka *Mohawk:*
  - *Kanienkahagen, Kanienkehaka* "people of the place of flint": *Kani > Kanı* 'where' + *Enkah, Enkeh > Yaŋ* 'ignite' + *Agen, Aka > Aka* 'man, elder, lord', meaning "people of the place that ignites" in *Turkic*.
  - *Mohawk* "man-eaters". This was an exonym, an external name of this *Native American* tribe.

  The place where the *Kanienkehaka* lived was abundant with the stone called flint that was regularly used to ignite a fire. They were the members of the *Iroquois Confederacy*.

- *Tuscarora,* aka *Skaruhreh:*
  - *Tuscarora, Skaruhreh* "shirt-wearing people", "people of shirt": *Tus, S > Üs* 'upper', 'upper part' + *Car > Kərkə* 'cloth garment' + *Ora, Uhreh > Ör* 'man, warrior', meaning "people of the upper garment" or "people of shirt" in *Turkic*. Incidentally, there was a similar archaic word combination in *Turkic – Üst Kürkü* "fur coat" or "upper coat" [*Radlov*. 2.2.1457].

  These people were the last confederate who joined the *Iroquois Confederacy*.

- *Cherokee*, aka *Ani-Yunwiya:*
  - *Ani-Yunwiya* "principal people": *Ani* > *Ən* 'most' + *Yun* 'important' + *Wiya* > *Üyə* 'stock, progeny', meaning "principal people" in *Turkic*. This was the self-name of the tribe, also known under the exonym *Cherokee*.

  This tribe occupied the lands in the *Southeast* of the *USA*, in some parts of *North* and *South Carolina, Virginia, Tennessee, Georgia, Alabama,* and *Kentucky*.

- *Cheyenne*, aka *Tsetchestahase*, aka *Tsistsistas*, aka *Dzitsistas:*
  - *Tsetchestahase* "beautiful people", "our people": *Tsetches* > *Çiçək* 'flower, beauty' + *Tahase* > *Taş* 'fellow', meaning "beautiful fellow" in *Turkic*.
  - *Tsistsistas*: *Tsistsis* > *Çiçək* 'flower, beauty' + *Tas* > *Taş* 'fellow', meaning "beautiful fellow" in *Turkic*.
  - *Dzitsistas*: *Dzitsis* > *Çiçək* 'flower, beauty' + *Tas* > *Taş* 'fellow', meaning "beautiful fellow" in *Turkic*.

  Initially, this tribe lived in the territory of present-day *Minnesota*.

- *Chickasaw*, aka *Chikasha*, aka *Chicaza:*
  - *Chickasaw, Chikasha, Chikaza* "rebel, "leave": *Chick, Chik* > *Çık* 'leave, rise, rebel' + *Asaw. Asha, Aza* > *-Asan* 'an affix, denoting a modal auxiliary verb, equivalent to *Can*', meaning "free to leave, rise, rebel" in *Turkic*.

  Having been classified as the *South-East Indians*, they mainly inhabited *Mississippi, Tennessee, Kentucky,* and *Arkansas*.

- *Chimariko:*
  - *Chimariko* > *Chimar, Djimar* "person": *Chima, Djima* > *Çıma* 'people' + *Ariko, Ar* > *Ar* 'man', meaning "people's man" in *Turkic*. This tribe derived its name from the word *Chimar* or *Djimar* "person".

  Currently extinct, this *Native American* tribe used to inhabit the land across the *Trinity River* in what is now *Northern California*.

- *Coosan*, aka *Kusan*, aka *Coos:*
  - *Coosan, Kusan, Coos* "inland bay", "lake": *Coos, Kus* > *Kaş* 'shore, riverbank' [159] + *An* > *Ən* 'piece of land', meaning "part of the shore" in *Turkic*. There are also other *Turkic* words close to *Coos*, such as *Koi* "bay", *Kat* "riverbank", *Kəm* "river", *Köl* "lake".

  There was a *Turkic* people with the matching name – a *Tatar* tribe of *Kuzan* (*Küzən*) that used to inhabit the shores of the river *Biy* in the *Altai* region (currently, a part of *Russia)*. Furthermore, a *Turkic* city of *Kusan* (*Küsən*) was mentioned by *Mahmud Kashgari* in *East Turkestan* [1.404].

  This *Native American* tribe used to live in the currently known state of *Oregon*.

- *Absaroka*, aka *Apsaslooka*, aka *Crow:*
  - *Absaroka, Apsaslooka* "bird people": *Ab, Ap* > *Oba* 'tribe' + *Saroka, Saslooka* > *Saskan* 'magpie', meaning "crow people" or "bird people" in *Turkic*.

  Magpie and crow belong to the same family of corvids, and both prefer living in open woodland areas. This habitation preference was the reason why the *Absaroka*, or the *Crow* tribe, acquired their name. These people used to live originally in upper *Missouri*, presently *North Dakota*, from where they migrated to the territory around the *Yellowstone River*, which is now part of *Montana* and *Wyoming*. Their native name *Absaroka*, or *Apsaslooka*, takes its origin from the *Turkic* source.

---

[159] *Budagov L.* "Sravnitelniy slovar turetsko-tatarskikh narechiy." [2.15].

- *Chumash:*
  - *Chumash* "bead makers", "seashell people": *Chuma > Çumın* 'immerse into the water' + *Ash > Aş* 'arise', meaning "tribe that gets something out of water" in *Turkic*.

The true meaning of their name reflects their daily activities, such as fishing, hunting marine creatures that involved immersion into water. The *Turkic* source seems to be the most opportune to explain the name.

Having lived for thousands of years on the coast of present-day *Southern California*, the *Chumash* were noted for their excellent maritime skills. Being very crafty, the *Chumash* were the only *North American* natives who built boats out of planks. The rock art created by them on the cave walls, currently preserved as *Chumash Painted Cave* State Historic Park, demonstrates the signs and symbols that match the *Turkic* tamgas.

Figure 44. Turkic tamgas ✲ 'tree of life', ⊕ ✦ ✦ 'unity; motherland'; ✝ '4 dominions of God Tengri' at Chumash Painted Cave State Historic Park. Library of Congress. Credit: The Jon B. Lovelace Collection of California Photographs in Carol M. Highsmith's America Project, Library of Congress, Prints and Photographs Division.

- *Duwamish:*
  - *Duwamish* "inside people": *Duwam > Dam* 'house' + *Ish > İç* 'inside', meaning "inside home" or "inside people" in *Turkic*.

Like most *Native American* and *Turkic* nations, this tribe preferred to dwell along the waterways. It occupied the lands along the waterways of the territory, which is a present-day city of *Seattle* in the state of *Washington*. Due to living inland, this tribe was named accordingly "people of the inside".

- *Havasupai, aka Hualapai, aka Yavapai, aka Baja:*
  - *Havasupai* "people of the blue-green water": *Hava > Kəvak* 'blue' [160] + *Su* 'water' + *Pai > Pai, Pi* 'lord, noble', meaning "noble people of the air-colored water" in *Turkic*.
  - *Hualapai* "pine tree people": *Huala > Khırıya* 'pine tree' + *Pai > Pai, Pi* 'lord, noble', meaning "noble people of the pine tree" in *Turkic*.

---

[160] *Egorov V.G.* "Etimologicheskiy slovar chuvashskogo yazika." [96].

- *Yavapai* "people of the Sun": *Yava* > *Xövel* 'the Sun' [161] + *Pai* > *Pai, Pi* 'lord, noble', meaning "noble people of the Sun" in *Turkic*. Remarkably, there was the *Yava*, aka the *Ava* tribe, a *Turkic* people of the *Oguz* branch [*Kashgari*. 3.27].
- *Baja* > *Bəy, Pai, Pi* 'lord, noble', meaning "noble people" in *Turkic*.

These people are a part of the *Yuman*-speaking *Pai* tribal union that includes the following tribes – *Hualapai, Yavapai, Baja*. They had their ancestral homeland in the territory of present-day northwestern *Arizona*.

> *Yokuts:*
- *Yokuts* "person", "people" > *Yakut* "the name of the *Turkic* people, currently residing in *Yakutiya*, aka the *Republic of Sakha, Russia*": *Yok, Yak* > *Yək* 'wonderful, noble' + *Uts, Ut* > *İgit* 'youth, young male', meaning "noble young people" in *Turkic*.

The *Yokuts* were one of several *Native American* tribes of *California*. Their ancestral territory included the lands along the *San Joaquin River*.

> *Iowa*, aka *Ayuhwa*, aka *Ioway*, aka *Bahkhoje*, aka *Pahodja*, aka *Paxoje:*
- *Iowa, Ioway, Ayuhwa* "sleepy ones": *I, A* > *A* 'man' + *Oway, Yuhwa* > *Yuki, Yuxu* 'sleep', meaning "sleepy man" in *Turkic*.
- *Bahkhoje, Pahodja, Paxoje* "dusty noses": *Bahkh, Pah, Pax* > *Bok, Pox* 'filth, dirt' + *Oj, Odj* > *Uc* 'tip, edge' + *E, A* > *-I* 'an affix of possession', meaning "dirty tip of the nose" in *Turkic*.

For most of recorded history, these people lived in the territory, now a part of the *American* state bearing their name – *Iowa*.

These were just a selected few *Native American* tribal names analyzed here. And all of them revealed *Turkic* traces. Many *Native American* tribes have names that are very similar to the *Turkic* tribes and people:

- *Yokuts* — *Yakut*
- *Chumash* — *Chuvash*
- *Yavapai* — *Yava*
- *Towa* — *Tuwa*
- *Kusan* — *Kuzan*.

§ 3. RELIGION AND THE KURGAN BUILDING CULTURE OF THE NATIVE AMERICANS.

The *Turkic* ancestry of many *Native Americans* revealed itself on many levels – language, religion, architecture, the mound-building culture.

The religion professed by all the *Native Americans* had a very close spiritual, shamanistic connection to the animistic belief practiced by the pre-Islamic *Turkic* nations. Both *Native Americans* and the *Turkic* people worshipped the creator – the Master Spirit by the former and *Tengri* – "the Sky Man" by the latter.

The *Mayan* belief resonated with the *Turkic* religion – the names of the sacred places were undoubtedly *Turkic* by origin. In *Mayan* belief, there were two realms – *Xibalba* and *Tamoanchan*. The dead would start their journey to *Tamoanchan*, the paradise with blooming flowers from beneath the earth, called *Xibalba* – a dark realm from whence the Tree of Life grew through the earth and after

---
[161] Idem [297].

passing thirteen levels of the heavens would reach the promised land – *Tamoanchan*. The mind-boggling fact is that both these names have very close counterparts in *Turkic* that serves as solid proof of their *Turkic* roots:

- *Xibalba (Shibalba)* "place of fear" > *Shibaldai (Şibəldəi)* "evil spirit living beneath the earth" in *Turkic* [Radlov. 4.1.10.89].
- *Tamoanchan* "place of the misty sky": *Tamoan* > *Tuman* 'mist' + *Chan* > *Kan* 'place', meaning "misty place" in *Turkic*.

According to the *Mayan* faith, *Xibalba* was inhabited by evil spirits ready to trick and wreck a soul. Therefore, the meaning of *Xibalba* should be interpreted as "place of evil spirits" and "evil spirits of the underworld".

The *Maya* worshipped the Sun God called *Kinich Ahau*. The name has a clear *Turkic* pedigree. Furthermore, this *Mayan* Sun God *Kinich Ahau* was known as *Kün Təngri* in *Turkic* mythology ["Drevneturkskiy slovar." 326]. Both in the *Mayan* and *Turkic* languages, the word denoting the Sun comes first followed by another one indicating God:

- *Kinich Ahau*: *Kinich* > *Künəş* 'Sun' + *Ahau* > *A, Ağa* 'lord', meaning "the Sun God" in *Turkic*.
- *Kün Təngri*: *Kün* 'the Sun' + *Təngri* 'God', meaning "the Sun God" in *Turkic*.

Just like the *Turkic* nations and related to them ancient cultures of *Europe* and *Asia* – the *Scythians*, the *Medes*, the *Pelasgians*, and others, the *Native Americans* also had a strong passion for horses – "the wings of the *Turks*", as the 11th c. *Turkic* scholar *Mahmud Kashgari* noted [1.36].

Similar to the *Turkic* people, the *Native Americans* built thousands of kurgans, mostly in the eastern part of *North America*. As we know, the word *Kurgan* has a *Turkic* origin and means "mound". The scholars distinguished four cultural groups – *Poverty Point, Adena, Hopewell,* and *Mississippian*. The mounds at the *Poverty Point* sites detected in *Arkansas, Louisiana, Mississippi, Florida, Missouri,* and *Tennessee* were reported to be built between 1800 to 500 BCE. The *Adena* burial mounds were constructed between 1000 BCE until 200 CE in present-day *Kentucky, West Virginia, Pennsylvania, Indiana, New York,* and *Ohio*. The legendary *Serpent Mound* in *Ohio*, built in the shape of an enormous snake, was one of the creations of the *Adena* culture. Lasted from 200 BCE until 700 CE, the *Hopewell* culture left its trace along the *Ohio* valley, the *Illinois* and *Mississippi* river valleys, as well as many other river valleys of the *East* and *Midwest*.

And the youngest mound-building culture, centered along the *Mississippi* river, the *Mississippian* culture emerged around 700 CE.

With the arrival of the *European* civilization in the face of the *Spanish* and *British* colonizers in *America*, the *Native American* civilization was brought to the brink of extinction, including mound building that ceased by 1550.

§ 4. THE GEOGRAPHICAL NAMES OF THE TURKIC ORIGIN IN THE AMERICAS.

Among the *Native American* toponyms, hydronyms, there are numerous geographical names of mountains, rivers, regions that reveal *Turkic* roots. The problem with the *Native American* names is that most of them have uncertain meanings. This makes it difficult to determine the right counterpart in *Turkic*. The deciphering process mostly depends upon several factors: historical events that could prompt the appearance of a name; geographical peculiarities of a given location; spiritual, religious, ritualistic importance of a locale. We are not going to discuss all of these place names here. Separate research should be devoted to this matter.

The following most significant and popular *Native American* toponyms, hydronyms demonstrate their *Turkic* whence:

1) *Yukatán: Yuk > Yük* 'bale, pack load' + *Atán* 'throwing', meaning "settled down" in *Turkic*. This is the name of the *Yukatan* peninsula where the *Maya* emerged around 2600 BCE. Clearly, the seafaring *Turkic* ancestors of the *Maya* first arrived by the *Atlantic* Ocean from the *European* continent to the *Yukatan* peninsula, where they first settled down. The *Turkic* origin of *Yukatán* is also supported by the typical for the *Turkic* words stress mark that always falls on the last syllable in the *Turkic* languages.

2) *Atacama: Ata* 'father, elder' + *Cama > Kam* 'shaman', meaning "father shaman" or "elder shaman" in *Turkic*. Undoubtedly, the *Atacama* Desert owes its name to this largest in the world prehistoric geoglyph depicting a shaman. This anthropomorphic figure served as an astronomical calendar. Depending on the points of alignment of the shaman's head with the Moon, the *Native Americans* could determine a day, a season, and a crop cycle.

Figure 45. The Atacama Shaman. The Atacama Desert, Chile. [CC BY-SA 2.0] Credit: Emilio Erazo-Fischer.

3) *Saskatchewan,* or *Kisiskatchewanisipi,* or *Kissiskatcheswanisipi* "rapid flowing river": *Sas, Kisis, Kissis > Kizək* 'suddenly, swiftly' + *Katchewan, Katcheswan > Kaçan* 'running' + *Sipi > Sup* 'river', meaning "swiftly running river" in *Turkic*. This is the name of the *Canadian* province and the river running through it, from *Cree (Algonquian) Kissiskatcheswanisipi* "rapid flowing river".

4) *Coba > Kopa* "lake with the reeds" in *Turkic*. *Coba* is an ancient *Mayan* city on the *Yucatan* Peninsula of *Mexico*, named after *Lake Coba*, located nearby.

5) *Cusco* or *Cuzco* or *Qusqu > Küskü, Güzgü* "mirror" in *Turkic*. Currently the capital of the *Cusco* region and a province in *Peru, Cusco* was the historic capital of the *Inca* Empire from the 13th to the 16th c. There are several interpretations of the name: some assert that it comes from the local *Quechua* language and means "navel of the world", while others seek its origin from the phrase *Qusqu Wanka* "rock of the owl" in the *Aymara* language. However, *Cusco* emerged under

this name as the result of the beautiful legend about a mystical mirror owned by the *Incan* emperor *Pachacuti*. A round mirror is said to have fallen from the sky into the spring to the east of *Cusco*. When *Pachacuti* lifted it from the water, he saw an image of the god *Viracocha*. The phantom told him that *Pachacuti* would win many wars. The legend says that *Pachacuti* conquered a vast territory and established a powerful empire within the next 10 years. He always held the mirror with him and consulted it to learn about future events.

6) *Caracol: Cara > Kara* 'great' + *Col > Kol* 'valley without a river', meaning "great valley" in *Turkic*. *Caracol* is the name of the important political center of the *Maya* Lowlands that rests in the foothills of the *Maya* Mountains. There are many ridiculous efforts to derive the origin of the name from *Vulgar Latin Cochleār, Latin Cochlea* "snail", from ancient *Greek Kokhlías* "spiral, snail shell", even laughable *Cuyar* "spoon" in a pathetic struggle to tie it to the pre-*Roman Indo-European* source. Meanwhile, there are many *Turkic* city, town, village names that ideally match the *Mayan Caracol*, such as *Caracol* town in *Kyrgyzstan*, village *Karakol* in *Iran*, *Qorakol* town in *Uzbekistan*.

7) *Illinois* "men, people" > *İl* "people; tribe", *İlin* "of people; belonging to people". The state of *Illinois* owes its name to the *Native American* tribe of *Turkic* origin, known under several appellations –*Illiniwek, Illinik Illini, Aliniouek, Aliniwek, Eriniouai, Inoca, Hileni, Illiniouck, Ilinoue.*

8) *Ottawa* or *Odawa* "at home anywhere people": *Ot > Ota, Oda* 'tent, yurt' + *Ta > -Ta* 'an affix, similar to the prepositions *In, Inside*' + *Awa > Oba* 'tribe', meaning "at home people" in *Turkic*. Presently, it is the name of the capital of *Canada*.

9) *Canada* "village, town" > *Kənd, Kent* "village, town" in *Turkic*. The name of *Canada* is said to be a *Latinized* form of a word for "village" in a now-extinct *Iroquoian* language of the *St. Lawrence* valley and the still-spoken *Iroquoian* language of *Mohawk* as *Kanata* "town".

10) *Utah* "high" > *Uca, Yüce* "high" in *Turkic*. The *Native American* name of the state of *Utah* has a distinct *Turkic* origin.

11) *Spokane* "people of the Sun": *Spo > Sıbai* 'neighboring' + *Kan, Kane > Kün, Gün* 'the Sun', meaning "close to the Sun" in *Turkic*. This *Native American* tribal name retained its trace in the name of the modern *American* city of *Spokane*.

12) *Iowa*, or *Ioway*, or *Ayuhwa* "sleepy ones": *I, A > A* 'man' + *Oway, Yuhwa > Yuki, Yuxu* 'sleep', meaning "sleepy man" in *Turkic*. The state of *Iowa* obtained its name from this *Native American* tribe, which is, ultimately, of *Turkic* origin.

13) *Copán > Kopán* "magnificent, great" in *Turkic*. *Copán* was the capital of the *Maya* kingdom from the 5th through 9th centuries CE. Currently, it is an archaeological site of the *Maya* civilization in *Honduras*.

14) *Palenque*, or *Otulún*, or *Bàak'*, or *Lakamha* "big water" was a *Maya* city-state in the 7th c., currently a part of *Mexico*. The name *Palenque* is a *Spanish* calque from the *Chol* word *Otulún*. All three names of this administrative center point to their *Turkic* whence:
    ❖ *Bàak > Böyük* "big" in *Turkic*. This name comes from the *Yucatec Maya* language.
    ❖ *Lakamha* "big water": *Laka > Yekə, Ulkan* 'big' + *Amha > Akhar* 'stream of water', meaning "big water" in *Turkic*. This was the ancient name of *Palenque*.
    ❖ *Otulún* "fenced or fortified place" > *Oturú* "camp" in *Turkic*.

15) *Bally* or *Bully* "spirit": *Bal, Bul > Bəl* 'mountain spirit' + *Ly > -Lı* 'an affix, equivalent to the word *Having*', meaning "having mountain spirits" in *Turkic*. According to *Radlov V.V.*, the ancient *Turks* believed in mountain spirits called *Bal* [4.2.1607]. *Bally*, or *Bully*, is the *Native American* name of the mountain in *Shasta* County, *California*, near the *Trinity* line.

16) *Bully Choop* or *Bally Chup: Bal, Bul > Bəl* 'mountain spirit' + *Ly > -Lı* 'an affix, equivalent to the word *Having*' + *Choop, Chup > Çüp* 'place', meaning "place full of mountain spirits" in *Turkic*. *Bully Choop* is a mountain in *Shasta* County, *California*.

17) *Un Bully: Un* 'ten' + *Bal, Bul > Bəl* 'mountain spirit' + *Ly > -Lı* 'an affix, equivalent to the word *Having*', meaning "having ten mountain spirits" in *Turkic*. The *Un Bully* Mountain is located between *Siskiyou* and *Trinity* counties of *California*.

18) *Yallo Bally* or *Yolla Bolly: Yallo, Yolla > Yəlli* 'windy' (*Yəl* 'wind' + *-Li* 'an affix, equivalent to the word *Having*') + *Bally, Bolly* 'having mountain spirits' (*Bal, Bul > Bəl* 'mountain spirit' + *Ly > -Lı* 'an affix, equivalent to the word *Having*'), meaning "windy place with mountain spirits" in *Turkic*. *Yallo Bally, Yolla Bolly* Mountains are situated between *Trinity* and *Tehama* Counties in *California*. In the *Native American* language of *Wintun*, *Yola* means "snow" and *Boli* "spirit". Just like the ancient *Turkic* nations, the *Native Americans* believed that there were mountain spirits. Interestingly, there is an ancient male name *Yollu* "windy, stormy" in *Turkic*.

19) *Bohemotash: Bohem > Boilu* 'great', *Böyük* 'large' + *Tash > Taş* 'rock', meaning "large rock" in *Turkic*. *Bohemotash* mountain in *Shasta* County, *California*, is said to be named from a northern *Wintun* word, where *Bohem* is "big" and the second part of the word remains uncertain. There is a similar *Turkic* word combination – *Kaya Taşı* "rock" [*Radlov*. 3.1.933].

20) *Cahto, Kato* "lake" > *Kat* "small lake" in *Turkic*. This *Native American* name, meaning "lake", applies both to the *Cahto* tribe and the land in *Mendocino* County between *San Francisco Bay* and the *Oregon* border.

21) *Cayucos* "boat" > *Kayık* "boat" in *Turkic*. This *Native American* name of the *Californian* town and beach is *Turkic*, in essence.

22) *Caicos* "canoe, boat" > *Kayık* "boat" in *Turkic*. This is the name of the island, also known as the *Turks* and *Caicos*, with the *Grand Turk* Island in the tropical *Atlantic*, southeast of the *Bahamas* and north of the *Dominican Republic*. Obviously, these islands were first visited by the *Turkic* nations, who left their trace in the name of this territory. *Caicos* means "canoe, boat" in the language of the *Lucayan*, the aborigines of the islands.

23) *Chemehuevi: Chemehu > Çıma* 'people' + *Evi* 'home' (*Ev* 'home' + *-İ* 'an affix of possession, equivalent to the preposition *Of*'), meaning "home of people" in *Turkic*. The *Native American* tribe of the *Chemehuevi* extended its name to the valley and mountains in *San Bernardino* County of *California*.

24) *Koip Peak* "mountain sheep" > *Koi* "sheep" in *Turkic*. *Koip Peak* is situated between *Mono* and *Tuolumne* counties of *California*. *Koip* means "mountain sheep" in the *Northern Paiute* dialect.

25) *Ojai* "nest" or *Ahwai* "moon": *Ojai > Ojaq, Ocaq* "nest", *Ahwai > Ai* "moon". Both names of the small town in *Ventura* County of *California* – *Ojai* and *Ahwai* take their origin from the *Turkic* source.

26) *Otay* "brushy" > *Otai* "covered in the grass; grassy" in *Turkic*. Presently, this *Native American* name designates the *Otay* subregional plan area, the *Otay* reservoir, and the *Otay Ranch* in *San Diego* County.

27) *Shasta* or *Úytaahkoo* "white mountain":
    ❖ *Shasta > Şəstli* "majestic" in *Turkic*.
    ❖ *Úytaahkoo: Uy > U* 'that' + *Ta* 'mountain' + *Ahkoo > Ak* 'white', meaning "that mountain is white" in *Turkic*. This variant of the name is derived from *Karuk*, an endangered *Native American* language of *Turkic* pedigree.

    Shasta is the name of the mountain and county in *California*. There is no definitive etymology of this name. However, it is most likely appeared to describe the majestic mountain.

28) *Saboba* or *Soboba: Sab, Sob > Sıbı* 'fir-tree' + *Oba* 'tribe', meaning "people of fir-trees" in *Turkic*. *Soboba* is currently the name of the *Indian* reservation in *Riverside* County of *California*. As the name suggests, the area was widely populated by fir trees, or white fir, the common tree growing in *California*.

29) *Tolowa* or *Tallowa: Tol, Tall* > *Talai* 'lake' + *Owa* > *Oba* 'tribe', meaning "people of the lake" in *Turkic*. Lake of *Tolowa* in *Del Norte* County of *California* was named after the *Native American* tribe of *Tolowa Deeni'* "*Tolowa* people".

30) *Toowa: Too* 'mountain' + *Owa* > *Oba* 'tribe', meaning "people of the mountain" in *Turkic*. There is a *Toowa Range* – a ridge in *Tulare County* of *California*, as well as *Toowa* – a valley and a lake in *Sierra Nevada, California*. Apparently, there was a *Native American* tribe *Toowa* that later went extinct.

31) *Tolay* > *Talai* "lake" in *Turkic*. Some derive the name of *Tolay Lake* from the chief of the *Native American* tribe *Hukalaka Tolay* who resided nearby. However, it does not change the meaning of the word *Tolay* as "lake", especially given the fact that this chief inhabited the vicinity of the lake.

32) *Topa Topa* or *Topatopa* > *Töpə-töpə* "mountain after mountain" or "many mountains" in *Turkic*. The *Topotopa* Mountains represent a mountain range in *Ventura County* of *California*. There were a couple of weak attempts to derive the etymology from the *Chumash* word meaning "reed" or "rush", as well as "gopher". However, the *Turkic* version makes the best sense, as it describes the existence of many mountains standing next to each other.

33) *Machu Picchu* "old mountain": *Machu* > *Muçi* 'old person, elderly' + *Pikchu* > *Pikçə* 'peak' (*Pik* 'high' + -*Çə* 'an affix, converting an adjective into a noun'), meaning "old peak" in *Turkic*. The word *Picchu=Pikçə* has a construction similar to another *Turkic* word *Akça* "money, silver coins". By adding an affix -*Ça*, -*Çə,* an adjective turns into a noun.

A scoop of the *Native American* toponyms, hydronyms of *Turkic* origin, introduced here, also helped us recognize familiar *Turkic* word formation patterns inherent to the *Turkic* languages. Some of the names were created by adding affixes to the end, such as in -*Chu* (-*Ça*) in *Macho Picchu*, -*Ly* (-*Li*) in *Bally*.

Other examples include an affix -*Chi* (-*Çı*, -*Çi*) denoting a status, or occupation in the following *Native American* tribal names: *Monachi, Yaudanchi, Heuchi, Pitkachi, Wakichi, Dalinchi, Apiachi, Pohonichi,* and *Tachi.*

A *Turkic* affix of possession -*İ* is also observed in the name of the *Native American* tribe *Chemehuevi* (*Chemehu* > *Çıma* 'people' + *Ev* 'home' + -*İ* 'an affix of possession').

The *Turkic* affix -*Ta*, equivalent to the preposition of place *At* in *English*, was noted by *Kroeber A.L.* in the *Native American* place name *Oleta*:

"*Oleta,* in *Amador* County, is in *Miwok Indian* territory. A stem *Ole* appears in several *Miwok* dialects with the meaning "coyote" – compare *Olema,* -and -*ta* or -*to* means "at.""
["*California* place names of *Indian* origin." – UC publications in *American* archaeology and ethnology. 2.2.52]

And lastly, a typical *Turkic* language phenomenon of paired words, when a lexeme doubles itself in one word, exists in the *Native American* languages, such as *Topatopa* (*Topa* + *Topa*).

§ 5. THE TURKIC ETYMOLOGY OF THE MAYAN VOCABULARY.

Language is the soul of a nation, its foundation, and its true source of inspiration. The analysis of 54 *Maya* words taken from the mythological work of art "*Popol Vuh*", literally translated by *Allen J. Christenson,* divulged the highly anticipated truth about their *Turkic* whence. The table below compares the lexemes from both languages and confirms their close kinship.

	***Mayan* words**	***Turkic* words**
1.	*Amaq* 'nation'	*Aimaq* 'tribe, nation'
2.	*Aqab* 'night'	*Kara* 'night'
3.	*Bi* 'name'	*Abır* 'name, honor'
4.	*Chob* 'divisions of people, group'	*Çub* 'division of people'
5.	*Chuti* 'small'	*Cuzi* 'small' or *Cüllüt* 'small'
6.	*Che* 'tree'	*Ağaç, Ağac, Ağaş* 'tree'
7.	*Chi* 'mouth'	*Çənə, Çene* 'jaw'
8.	*Chikutun* 'reveal!'	*Çıkartın* 'pull out, reveal!'
9.	*Choqik* 'cry out'	*Çığlık* 'cry'
10.	*Chuch* 'mother'	*Çecə, Çaça* 'stepmother'
11.	*Ja* 'house'	*Yıv, Uy, Av* 'house'
12.	*Jab'* 'rain'	*Jaan, Yağış, Yağmur* 'rain'
13.	*Jok* 'pathway'	*Yol* 'pathway'
14.	*Jul* 'cave'	*Köhül* 'cave'
15.	*Jul* 'hole'	*Yalaq* 'hole'
16.	*Jun* 'one'	*Ön* 'first, front'
17.	*Jupacha* 'how'	*Necə* 'how'
18.	*Kate utz chikoje* "then good there shall be"	*Anta uca çıkar* "then great [there] will be": *Kate > Anta* 'then' + *Utz > Uca* 'great' + *Chikoje > Çıkar* 'will be'
19.	*Kuxlay* 'heart'	*Könül* 'heart'
20.	*Kaam* 'bush'	*Kol* 'bush'
21.	*Kajol* 'boy'	*Ol, Oğul* 'boy, son'
22.	*Kajol* 'servant'	*Kul* 'servant'
23.	*Kiche* 'people, men'	*Kishi* 'man'
24.	*Kurib* 'gathered itself'	*Kurub* 'set up, built'
25.	*Ka* 'second'	*Ikinci* 'second'
26.	*Kaib'* 'two'	*Iki, Eki, Ikke* 'two'
27.	*Kaj* 'sky'	*Köy, Köi, Göy, Kök* 'sky'
28.	*Kiej* 'deer'	*Kiyik* 'deer'
29.	*Kochoch* 'home'	*Koch* 'nomadic camp', *Koş* 'tent'
30.	*Ma* 'not'	*Nə, Emas* 'not'
31.	*Naqi* 'why; what'	*Neqe* 'why'
32.	*Nima, Nim* 'great'	*Önəmli* 'great'
33.	*Palo* 'sea'	*Talai* 'sea'
34.	*Qaq* 'fire, bonfire'	*Ocaq* 'bonfire'
35.	*Qequm* 'darkness'	*Karangu, Qaranlik* 'darkness'
36.	*Qij* 'day'	*Gün* 'day'
37.	*Qajaw* 'father'	*Akka* 'father'
38.	*Qatit* 'grandmother'	*Katun* 'mother', *Qadın* 'female'
39.	*Saq* 'white'	*Aq* 'white'
40.	*Ta chikis* – "when will be completed"	*Ta çıka* "when will be done": *Ta* 'until' + *Çıka* 'will be done; will come out'
41.	*Tepew* 'sovereign'	*Tepe* 'sovereign'
42.	*Tikil* 'to plant'	*Tik* 'build'

	Mayan words	*Turkic* words
43.	*Tukel* 'alone'	*Tek* 'alone'
44.	*Tzikin* 'bird'	*Çükə* 'jackdaw' – a bird
45.	*Tzuk* 'corner'	*Burçak, Bucaq* 'corner'
46.	*Tzuk* 'germination'	*Çıkış* 'germination', *Çık* 'germinate'
47.	*U* 'he; its; his'	*U* 'he, she; it'
48.	*Ulew* 'earth'	*Ul* 'ground, foundation'
49.	*Utz* 'good'	*Uca* 'great'
50.	*Waral* 'here'	*Bura* 'here'
51.	*Wi* 'home'	*Iv* 'home'
52.	*Winaq* 'people'	*Inak* 'friend'
53.	*Xepichicharik* 'insides'	*İç, Iç içalat* 'inside, insides'
54.	*Yan* 'shame'	*Uyat* 'shame'

§ 6. THE NATIVE AMERICAN WORDS OF TURKIC ORIGIN.

In addition to *Maya*, seven other *Native American* languages, such as *Lacandon, Guarijio, Tarahumara, Navajo, Cochimi, Huasteco, Chuj*, also proved to carry many *Turkic* words, as seen on the following table.

TURKIC	LACANDON	GUARIJIO	TARAHUMARA	NAVAJO	COCHIMI	HUASTECO	CHUJ	MAYA
Bir, Perre, Ön 'one', 'first'	Hun	Pire	Bire			Juun	Ju'un	Hun, Jun, Jump'ejl, Untu
Iki, Eki 'two'		Gohka	Osa	Naaki	Kuak			Ka'a, Ka, Ka'i
Üç, Üş, Uçta, Üs, İç, Öç, Oza 'three'	Ox, Oş				Oox, Ooş		Oxe', Oşe	Oox [Ooş], 'Ox [Oş], Oxi' [Oşi], Uxp'ejl [Uşpeyl], Uxtu [Uştu]

TURKIC	LACANDON	GUARIJIO	TARAHUMARA	NAVAJO	COCHIMI	HUASTECO	CHUJ	MAYA
It, Et, Juta, Kopek 'dog'	Pek'				Ethat		Tz'i'	Peek', Pek', Tz'i', Ts'i'
Gün, Kün 'sun'	K'in					Q'uiichaa	K'u	
Su, Uu, Şu, Şıv, Axar 'water', 'flow'	Ha'	Pa'wi	Ba'wi	To	Tasi	Ja'	Ha'	Ha', Ja', Ya'
Ak, Ağ 'white'				Ligaii				Sak, Səq, Sək
Ana, Nənə 'mother'						Naana		
Ata, Dədə 'father'						Taata		
Ye 'eat'				Yiya				
Gör 'see'					Gir			
Uquu, Qulaq as, Duy 'hear'					Decui			U'uy, U'yaj, Ubintel, Ubin
Oku, Oxu 'sing'					Kanopai			K'ay, K'aay

363

§ 7. The Turkic tamgas, petroglyphs and Native American artifacts.

A comparative analysis of the *Turkic* tamgas with the petroglyphs, pictographs, and other artifacts ascribed to the *Native American* nations, revealed an expected connection of the latter with the *Turkic* peoples. These *Native American* images carved or painted onto rocks, stones, as well as imprinted, sewn on clothes, rugs, can be divided into two main categories:

1. depicting nature and everyday human life, including the Sun, the Moon, people, animals.
2. reflecting abstract notions, such as religion, power, etc.

The examples of the first group of signs can be the following rock art:

Figure 46. The Native American petroglyphs depicting people on the left, and an animal on the right. Newspaper Rock. Petrified Forest National Park, USA. Credit: NPS.

Now, compare the *Native American* petroglyphs above to similar ones in the *Gobustan* National Park, *Azerbaijan,* below:

Figure 47. Gobustan rock carvings depicting people with a ship on the left. Credit: Bruno Girin [CC BY-SA 2.0]. An animal on the right. [CC BY-SA 3.0]. Credit: Interfase. Cropped.

364

The second category of the pictographs etched on stone are much more complex. The stunning match of the *Turkic* tamgas, as well as the *Turdaş* marks to the *Native American* symbols, is an undeniable proof of close affinity between these two civilizations – so far out in the distance and so close in culture.

1) The *Turkic* tamga ⋈ 'a wolf's mouth' and the similar *Turdaş* symbol ⋈⋈.

Figure 48. The Native American petroglyph. Petrified Forest National Park, USA. 60th c. BCE – 14th c. CE. Credit: NPS.

2) The *Turkic* tamga ⋂ signifying 'tent-door', as well as 'horseshoe'. It also represents the Ş sound.

Figure 49. The Native American petroglyphs. Petrified Forest National Park, USA. Credit: NPS.

3) The *Turkic* tamga of royalty Ψ and the *Turdaş* symbol Υ. It also represents the *Ç* sound.

Figure 50. The Native American petroglyph. Petrified Forest National Park, USA. Credit: NPS.

4) The *Turkic* tamga ⊃ 'higher authority, independence' or 'the waxing Moon', also represents the *N* sound.

Figure 51. The Native American petroglyph. Petrified Forest National Park, USA. Credit: NPS.

5) The *Turkic* sign of the universe, called 'Dolanqaç' – 🌀🌀.

Figure 52. The Native American petroglyph. Petrified Forest National Park, USA. Credit: NPS.

6) The *Turkic* tamgas $\mathbf{3}$ – the consonant cluster *Nç*, ✝ – 'cross of the goddess *Humay Ana*'; Ш, ᵯ – 'subordinate to a higher power'; △ – the *K* sound, 'protection from evil forces', 'the goddess *Humay Ana*'; 〰 – 'snake'; ☥ – 'the Sun God', or *Kün Tengri*.

Figure 53. The Native American petroglyphs. Petrified Forest National Park, USA. Credit: NPS.

1. $\mathbf{3}$; 2. ✝ ; 3. Ш, ᵯ ; 4. △ ; 5. 〰 ; 6. ☥.

367

7) The *Turkic* tamgas ![tree] 'tree of life'; ★ 'God *Tengri*'; ⌒ 'lesser authority'; ▢ 'door, threshold'; Ч – the *R* sound, 'cross with a hook'; ↳ and ↱ – the *A, E, Ə* sounds, 'hook'; Y – the *L* sound, 'pitchfork';)Ӄ – the *G* sound, 'ram's head' or the *Turdaş* symbols – ЬЯ, ✵.

Figure 54. The Native American petroglyphs. Petrified Forest National Park, USA. Credit: NPS.
1. ![tree]; 2. ★; 3. ⌒; 4. ▢; 5. Ч; 6. ↳, ↱; 7. Y; 8.)Ӄ; 9. ✵.

8) The *Turkic* tamgas ⭘ 'Tanrı-Qoç', or 'God Tengri-Ram'; ◉ – 'mother with a child','macro and micro worlds' with the matching symbol in *Turdaş* – ◉; ◇ – 'protection from the evil eye'; ⋀,⋀̰ –'settlement'; | – 'one tribe'; ||| – 'confederation, tribal union'; 8 'eyes'; ¤ or *Turdaş* ☼ – the *M* sound, '*Tengri-Sun*'.

Figure 55. The Native American petroglyphs. Lava Beds National Monument, USA. Credit: NPS.
1. ⭘; 2. ◉; 3. ◇; 4. ⋀,⋀̰; 5. |, |||; 6. OO; 7. ¤ or Turdaş ☼.

9) The *Turkic* tamgas ◇ – the *Ŋ; Ng* sound; 'protection from evil eye'; X – the *A, E, Ə* sounds, 'hook'; Ч – the *R* sound; O – the consonant clusters *Nt, Nd*, '*Tengri-Sun*'.

Figure 56. The Olmec ceramic sculpture. Mexico. 12th -9th c. BCE. The Metropolitan Museum of Art, USA.
1. X; 2. Ч; 3. O; 4. ◇
[OA] Credit: The Michael C. Rockefeller Memorial Collection, Bequest of Nelson A. Rockefeller, 1979

10) The *Turkic* tamgas ∨ 'corner'; ✕ – the *D* sound, 'a cross of the goddess *Humay Ana*'; ⊞ or *Turdaş* ⊕ 'prosperity'.

Figure 57. The Olmec ceramic bird vessel. 12th-9th c. BCE. Mexico, Mesoamerica. The Metropolitan Museum of Art, USA. 1. ∨; 2. ✕; 3. ⊞. [OA] Credit: Rogers Fund, 1986.

Compare this *Olmec* bird vessel with the *Etruscan* terracotta vase in the shape of a cockerel below:

Figure 58. The Etruscan vase with the Etruscan alphabet, 650-600 BCE. The Metropolitan Museum of Art, USA. [OA] Credit: Fletcher Fund, 1924.

370

11) The *Turkic* letter ⊞ – the *Q* sound, 'prosperity, harvest, power'; the tamga of protection ⊙.

Figure 59. The Nasca vase, Peru. 2000 BCE -200 CE. The Cleveland Museum of Art, USA. 1. ⊞; 2. ⊙
[CC0 1.0] Credit: James Albert Ford Memorial Fund.

12) The *Turkic* letters ↯, ↗ – the *A, E, Ə* sounds, 'hook'; ⋙ – the *D* sound.

Figure 60. The Xochipala female figurine, Mexico. 1500 – 500 BCE. The Cleveland Museum of Art. [CC0 1.0]
Credit: John L. Severance Fund.

371

13) The *Turkic* tamgas ⌒ – the *T* sound, 'horse', horseman'; ◁ – the *Q, K* sounds, 'the goddess *Humay Ana*', 'shield', 'protection'; ᠑, ᠒ – the *B* sound, 'the waxing Moon', 'domination'; Y – the *Ṣ* sound, 'pitchfork', 'the Moon with tail'; ⌐ – the *L* sound, 'corner', 'ax'; O – the consonant clusters *Nd, Nt*, 'oath', '*Tengri-Sun*'; ᠌ – 'the waning Moon'.

Figure 61. The Native American container, Cupisnique culture, Peru. 12c.-2c. BCE. The Cleveland Art of Museum, USA.
1. ⌒; 2. ◁; 3. ᠑; 4. Y; 5. ⌐; 6. O; 7. ᠌; 8. ᠒. [CC0 1.0] Credit: Purchase from the J. H. Wade Fund.

372

14) The *Turkic* tamga ◈ 'dragon', 'prosperity'.

Figure 62. The Native American serape, 1820. The Cleveland Museum of Art, USA. [CC0 1.0]
Credit: Gift of Mrs. John A. Hadden

15) The *Turkic* tamga ⊙, ⊙ – the consonant clusters *Nd, Nt,* 'oath', 'mother with a child', 'macro and micro worlds'; ⚘ – the *Turkic* symbol 'hands on the waist' (*Əli belində*) signifies the goddess *Humay Ana;* ⊞ – 'fish eye'.

Figure 105. The Native American pestle, Chavin culture, Peru. 7th c. BCE.
1. ⊙ ; 2. ⊙ ; 3. ⚘ ; 4. ⊞
The Cleveland Museum of Art, USA. [CC0 1.0] Credit: In memory of Mr. and Mrs. Henry Humphreys, gift of their daughter Helen.

Figure 63. The Etruscan bronze disk with ivory, 7th-6th c. BCE. The symbol ⊙.
The Metropolitan Museum of Art, USA. [OA]
Credit: Purchase, 1896.

Figure 64. The artifacts, similar to Turkic ⚭ 'hands on the waist' (*әli belindә*). On the left: the Native American ceramic whistle as a standing figure with the hands on the waist, Ecuador. 2nd c. BCE-3rd c. CE. The Metropolitan Museum of Art, USA. [OA] Credit: Gift of Margaret B. Zorach, 1980. On the right: the Aztec figure with the hands on the waist, Mexico. 14th –15th c. CE. The Metropolitan Museum of Art, USA. [OA] Credit: Museum Purchase, 1900.

16) The *Turkic* tamgas ℰ – the *G* sound, 'supreme power'; ⊙ – the consonant clusters *Nd, Nt*, 'mother with child', 'macro and micro world'; ◁ – the *G, K* sounds, 'protection from evil'; ◈ – the *Ḍ, Ng* sound, 'protection from the evil eye'; ⊗ 'unity of a family, motherhood'; ▭ – the *S* sound, 'cradle'; ‡ – 'tree of life'; ⚓ – 'a star and the Moon'; H – the *Q* sound, 'prosperity', 'harvest', 'power'; ✕ – 'eagle'; ↙ – the *A, E, Ә* sounds, 'hook'.

Figure 65. The Native American figure of a mother with a child, Recuay culture, Peru. 1st c. – 7th c. The Cleveland Museum of Art, USA. 1. ‡ ; 2. ℰ ; 3. ⊙ ; 4. ◁ ; 5. ▭ ; 6. ⊗ ; 7. ◈ ; 8. ⚓ ; 9. H ; 10. ✕ ; 11. ↙ [CC0 1.0] Credit: Severance and Greta Millikin Purchase Fund.

17) The *Turkic* tamga ![symbols] – '*Tengri*', signifying the domain of God *Tengri* over 4 directions.

Figure 66. From left to right symbols, similar to Turkic 卍: the Apache ceramic jar, 1800-1900. The Cleveland Museum of Art, USA. [CC0 1.0] Credit: Gift of I. T. Frary; the Mogollan bowl, 11th -12th c. CE. The Cleveland Museum of Art, USA. [CC0 1.0] Credit: Charles W. Harkness Endowment Fund; the Anasazi ceramic vessel, 15th – 16th c. CE. The Cleveland Museum of Art, USA. [CC0 1.0] Credit: Purchase from the J. H. Wade Fund.

Figure 67. On the left: the Sioux beaded vest, 1876. 1. ⊕ – the Turkic tamga 'Tengri'; 2. ◇ – 'protection from the evil eye'; 3. ⟁ – 'yurt, settlement'. From the author's collection. On the right: the Turkic carpet with a rounded ⊕ tamga. The National Museum of Kazakhstan. From the author's collection.

From the dawn of history as of nowadays, one consistent pattern has been observed. Ancient *Turkic* nations – the *Scythians, Akkadians, Trojans, Turrenians, Kitay, Medes, Hittites, Tatars, Mongols, Hun, Moguls*, even most of the *Native Americans,* who were of *Turkic* extraction, – all of them founded great empires and countries only to be gradually replaced or destroyed by other nations. In most cases, the *Turkic* inventions, culture, architecture, history, religious belief were credited to false claimants, and the *Turkic* nations were rendered down to the level of the barbarian tribes descended from the *Altai* mountains.

Who knows nowadays that the founder of the *Roman* empire and the city of *Rome* was from the *Turkic* nation of the *Trojans*? Who believes now that the *Medes* were of *Turkic* origin and were not the *Persians*, as the latter claim? Who can recall that the first *Persian* Empire was established by the descendant of the *Turkic* blood – *Cyrus*, the founder of the *Achaemenid* Empire? Who admits the fact that the world-famous architecture, such as *Taj-Mahal* in *India*, was built by the *Turkic* ruler from the *Mogul* dynasty? What about the *Russian* empire? Who realizes now that it was established by the *Turkic* nation of the *Tatars*, to whom *Russians* used to pay tributary up until the 17th c.? Can any *Ukrainian* accept the fact that old *Kievan Rus* was built by the *Turkic* nation of the *Khazars*, later renamed into *Ashkenazi Jews?* Do the *Chinese* openly recognize that the *Turkic* nation of the *Uyghurs* once ruled *China* with their king in *Beijing?* How many *Europeans*, including the royal houses, can stomach the truth that their predecessors were of *Turkic* origin?

Thanks to the greatest invention of the humankind – Internet and the safekeepers of eternal wisdom, such as *Google,* who digitalized the works of the ancient authors, the truth about the *Turkic* nations will never be buried and sent to oblivion. Long passed the times when the history books about *Turks* were burned in the middle of the streets in *Persia;* when the *Turkic* historians were killed or tortured to prevent them from safeguarding the truth for the upcoming generations; when the ancient *Turkic* monuments, books about the *Turkic* nations were destroyed by order of the clergy to erase any memory of the *Turkic* presence in the *European* continent; when the names of the *Turkic* cities, villages, places were replaced by *Russian, Armenian, Chinese, Persian* and other names. The times passed, but not forgotten. Alas! There is not much left to recover. What was done to most of the *Turkic* nations and their history could be described by invoking *Xerxes,* the *Persian* king (from the *American* movie "300") who threatened the *Spartan* king *Leonidas* to expunge the name of *Sparta* and *Spartans* from the historical records and execute anyone who would dare not only to write or retell the history of this *Pelasgian* nation but even mention its name in order to wipe out all the traces of its existence in the world.

There is a famous saying: if you can eliminate the people's past, it is easy to control their future. Luckily, despite all the efforts, the past of the *Turkic* nations was not completely eradicated, though their history was molded to fit the needs of the predetermined narrative. Many *Turkic* peoples have become extinct, yet still there are too many existing nowadays to enumerate. Here is an incomplete list of the modern *Turkic* nations living worldwide:

- in *Central Asia* – the *Kazakh, Kyrgyz, Uzbek, Turkmen, Khalaj;*
- in the *Caucasus* – the *Azerbaijani, Karachai, Balkar;*
- in *Russia* – the *Bashkir, Tatar, Cherkess, Chagatai, Chelkan, Chuvash, Kalmyk, Karakalpak, Khakass, Kumyk, Nogay, Salar, Shor, Soyot, Teleut, Tofa, Tuvali, Yakut, Dolgan, Altay, Siberian Tatar, Dukha, Yakut;*
- in *China* – the *Uyghur, Aynu, Taglig, Dolan, Sarig Yugur;*
- in *Europe* – the *Bosnians, Hungarians, Turks, Abdal;*
- in *Moldova* – the *Gagauz;*
- in *Ukraine* – the *Karaim, Krym Tatar, Krymchak, Urum;*
- in the *Middle East* – the *Turkoman;*
- in *Iran* – the *Azerbaijani, Kashgai, Afshar, Kadjar, Shakhsevan, Bayati, Turkmen;*
- in *Mongolia* – the *Yugur, Khoton.*

In the end, we would like to address all the nations of this world with the (slightly modified) wise words of Emperor *Wen* from the *Han* dynasty:

> "The sky covers all, distinguishing none, and the earth bears all, favoring none. Thus, let's forget the previous great and minor troubles, go along the Great Path, destroy the past evil in the interests of a long future so that the peoples of our world become like children of one family!"

Bibliography.

1. *Annales Bertiniani.* Scriptores Rerum Germanicarum in usum scholarum ex monumentis Germanie hitsorics recusi. Hannoverae. 1883. In public domain.
https://www.google.com/books/edition/Annales_Bertiniani/RCsKAAAAIAAJ?hl=en&gbpv=1
2. *The book of Enoch, or 1 Enoch.* Translated by Robert Henry Charles from the Editor's Ethiopic Text and Edited with the Introduction, Notes and Indexes of the First Edition Wholly Recast, Enlarged and Rewritten, Together with a Reprint from the Editor's Text of the Greek Fragment. Oxford. 1912. In public domain.
https://www.google.com/books/edition/The_Book_of_Enoch/BAVPMjUouiQC?hl=en&gbpv=0
3. *The Book of Yasher. Referred to in Joshua and Second Samuel.* Salt Lake City. 1887 https://www.sacred-texts.com/chr/apo/jasher/index.htm
4. *The Encyclopædia Britannica: Or, Dictionary of Arts, Sciences, and General Literature.* 7th edition. Volume 17. Edinburgh. 1842. In public domain.
https://play.google.com/store/books/details?id=dk-g2bOzKrkC&rdid=book-dk-g2bOzKrkC&rdot=1
5. *The Encyclopaedia Britannica.* 11th edition. New York. 1911
6. *The Illustrated London News.* Volume 37. In public domain. 1860.
https://play.google.com/books/reader?id=Y5g0AQAAMAAJ&hl=en&pg=GBS.PA570
7. *The Jew in the Medieval World: A Sourcebook.* Translated by Jacob Marcus. 315-1791. New York: JPS, 1938. 227-232. In public domain. https://en.wikisource.org/wiki/Khazar_Correspondence
8. *Abul Ghazi Bahader.* History of the *Turks, Moguls,* and *Tatars,* Vulgarly Called *Tartars* together with a Description of the Countries They Inhabit. London. 1730
9. *Achilli, A., Olivieri, A., Pala, M., Metspalu, E., Fornarino, S., Battaglia, V., Accetturo, M., Kutuev, I., Khusnutdinova, E., Pennarun, E., Cerutti, N., Di Gaetano, C., Crobu, F., Palli, D., Matullo, G., Santachiara-Benerecetti, A. S., Cavalli-Sforza, L. L., Semino, O., Villems, R., Bandelt, H. J., ... Torroni, A. (2007).* Mitochondrial DNA variation of modern Tuscans supports the near eastern origin of Etruscans. American journal of human genetics, 80(4), 759–768. https://doi.org/10.1086/512822
10. *Aeschylus.* Persians. Translated by Herbert Weir Smyth. Volumes 1-2. Cambridge, MA.1926. (CC BY-SA 3.0 US)
https://www.perseus.tufts.edu/hopper/text?doc=Perseus:text:1999.01.0012
11. *Aeschylus.* Prometheus Bound. Translated by Herbert Weir Smyth, Ph. D. Volumes 1-2. Cambridge, MA. Harvard University Press. 1926. In public domain. (CC BY-SA 3.0 US)
http://www.perseus.tufts.edu/hopper/text?doc=Perseus%3Atext%3A1999.01.0010%3Acard%3D1
12. *Aeschylus.* Seven against Thebes. Translated by Herbert Weir Smyth, Ph. D. Cambridge, MA. Harvard University Press. 1926. (CC BY-SA 3.0 US)
http://www.perseus.tufts.edu/hopper/text?doc=Perseus%3Atext%3A1999.01.0014%3Acard%3D1
13. *Aeschylus.* Suppliant Women. Translated by Herbert Weir Smyth. Volumes 1-2. Cambridge, MA.1926. (CC BY-SA 3.0 US) https://www.perseus.tufts.edu/hopper/text?doc=Perseus:text:1999.01.0016
14. *Ala-ad-Din Ata-Malik Juvaini.* The History of the World Conqueror. Translated by Boyle J.A. Harvard. 1958
15. *Alau D-Din Atâ Malik-i- Juwayni.* Tarīkh-i Jahān-gushā (Containing the History of Chingiz Khan and His Successors.) Leyden, London. 1912.
https://archive.org/details/in.ernet.dli.2015.322637/page/n1/mode/2up
16. *Alexander von Humboldt.* Views of Nature Or Contemplations on the Sublime Phenomena of Creation, with Scientific Illustrations. Translated from German by Otte E.C. and Bohn H.G. London.1850
17. *Alexey Kassian.* Lexical Matches between *Sumerian* and *Hurro-Urartian:* Possible Historical Scenarios. (CC BY-SA 3.0)
http://ancientworldonline.blogspot.com/2011/08/open-access-journal-cuneiform-digital_891.html]
18. *Ammiani Marcellini.* Historiae. Vol. 4-31. www.thelatinlibrary.com
19. *Ammianus Marcellinus.* The Roman History of Ammianus Marcellinus: During the Reigns of the Emperors Constantius, Julian, Jovianus, Valentinian, and Valens. Translated by C.D. Yonge. London.1894. In public domain.
https://www.google.com/books/edition/The_Roman_History_of_Ammianus_Marcellinu/hh8NAAAAIAAJ?hl=en&gbpv=0
20. *An Universal History from the Earliest Account of Time. Compiled from Original Authors. The History of the Turks, Tartars, and Moguls.* Volume 20. Book 4. London. 1748. In public domain.
21. *Apollodorus.* The Library. Translated into English by Sir James George Frazer. Vol. 1-2. Cambridge, MA, Harvard University Press; London, William Heinemann Ltd. 1921 (CC BY-SA 3.0 US)
http://www.perseus.tufts.edu/hopper/text?doc=Perseus:text:1999.01.0022
22. *Apollonius Rhodius.* The Argonautica. Translated by Robert Cooper Seaton. London, New York. 1912. In public domain.
https://www.google.com/books/edition/The_Argonautica/ipANAAAAIAAJ?hl=en&gbpv=0

23. *Appian.* The Foreign Wars. Horace White. New York. 1899. (CC BY-SA 3.0 US) http://www.perseus.tufts.edu/hopper/text?doc=Perseus%3Atext%3A1999.01.0230%3Atext%3DPref.
24. *Appianus of Alexandria.* The Roman History of Appian of Alexandria. Translated from Greek by Horace White. Volumes 1-2. London. 1899
25. *Archibald Henry Sayce.* Lectures on the Origin and Growth of Religion: As Illustrated by the Religion of the Ancient Babylonians. London. 1891. In public domain. https://www.google.com/books/edition/Lectures_on_the_Origin_and_Growth_of_Rel/c0ROAAAAYAAJ?hl=en&gbpv=0
26. *Ariodante Fabretti.* Corpus inscriptionum italicarum antiquioris aevi ordine geographico digestum, et glossarium italicum in quo omnia vocabula continentur ex umbricis, sabinis, oscis, volscis, etruscis aliisque monumentis quae supersunt collecta... cura et studio. Aug. Taurinorum: Ex officina Regia. 1867
27. *Aristophanes.* Comoediae. Volume 2. Indiana University. 1835 https://www.google.com/books/edition/Aristophanes_comoediae/DyAjAQAAMAAJ?hl=en&gbpv=0
28. *Aristophanes.* The Birds. Translated by J.H. Frere. Cambridge. 1883 In public domain. https://www.google.com/books/edition/The_Birds_of_Aristophanes_tr_by_J_H_Frer/UMEDAAAAQAAJ?hl=en&gbpv=0
29. *Aristotle.* Politics. Translated by H. Rackham. Cambridge, MA, Harvard University Press; London, William Heinemann Ltd. 1944 (CC BY-SA 3.0 US) http://www.perseus.tufts.edu
30. *Arrian the Nicomedian.* The Anabasis of Alexander; Or, The History of the Wars and Conquests of Alexander the Great. Translated by E.A. Chinnock. London, New York. 1884. In public domain. https://www.google.com/books/edition/The_Anabasis_of_Alexander_Or_The_History/rlcIAAAAQAAJ?hl=en&gbpv=0
31. *Asko Parpola.* The Roots of Hinduism: the Early Aryans and the Indus Civilization. Oxford. 2015
32. *Aulus Gellius.* The Attic Nights. Translated into English by John Carew Rolfe. John C. Rolfe. Cambridge. Cambridge, Mass., Harvard University Press; London, William Heinemann, Ltd. 1927. (CC BY-SA 3.0 US) https://www.perseus.tufts.edu/hopper/text?doc=Perseus:text:2007.01.0072
33. *Bailkey N. M., Lim R.* Readings in Ancient History. Boston, 2002
34. *Bartomeu Obrador Cursach.* Lexicon of the Phrygian Inscriptions. Barselona. 2018.
35. *Black J.* A Concise Dictionary of Akkadian. Edited by J. Black, A. George, N. Postgate. Wiesbaden. 2000
36. *Bury J.B.* History of the Later Roman Empire from the Death of Theodosius I to the Death of Justinian (A. D. 395 to A. D. 565). Volume 1. London. 1923. https://play.google.com/books/reader?id=Xw4fAAAAMAAJ&hl=en&pg=GBS.PR2
37. *C. Julius Caesar.* The Gallic War. Translated into English by W. A. McDevitte, W. S. Bohn. New York. 1869. In public domain. (CC BY-SA 3.0 US) http://www.perseus.tufts.edu/hopper/text?doc=Perseus%3Atext%3A1999.02.0001%3Abook%3D1%3Achapter%3D1
38. *C. Iuli.* Commentarii Rerum in Gallia Gestarum. VII A. Hirti Commentarius VII. T. Rice Holmes. Oxonii. e Typographeo Clarendoniano. 1914. Scriptorum Classicorum Bibliotheca Oxoniensis. In public domain. https://www.perseus.tufts.edu/hopper/text?doc=Perseus%3Atext%3A1999.02.0002%3Abook%3D1%3Asection%3D1
39. *C. Suetonius Tranquillus.* The Lives of the Caesars. Translated by Alexander Thompson. Philadelphia. Gebbie & Co. 1889. (CC BY-SA 3.0 US) https://www.perseus.tufts.edu/hopper/text?doc=Perseus:text:1999.02.0132
40. *C. Lucili.* Saturarum reliquiae. In public domain. Lipsiae.1872 https://play.google.com/books/reader?id=yZB_0MF4liAC&hl=en&pg=GBS.PR1
41. *C. Plinius Secundus.* The Historie of the World. Commonly called the Naturall historie of C.Plinius Secundus. Translated by Philemon Holland. Volumes 1-15. London. 1601
42. *Carolus Müllerus.* Geographi graeci minores. E codicibus recognovit prolegomenis annotatione indicibus instruxit. Vol. 2. Paris. 1861. In public domain. https://play.google.com/books/reader?id=OiX6abSvHUIC&hl=en
43. *Cassius Dio Cocceianus.* Dio's Roman history. Translated by Earnest Cary. Vol. 1-9. London, New York. 1917. In public domain. https://play.google.com/books/reader?id=kL9LAAAAYAAJ&hl=en&pg=GBS.PA2
44. *Charles de Secondat baron de Montesquieu.* Persian Letters. Vol. 2. Translated by John Davidson. London. 1899. In public domain. https://play.google.com/books/reader?id=cOM_AQAAMAAJ&printsec=frontcover&pg=GBS.PR3
45. *Charles M. Andrews, John Fiske, Theodor Flathe, F. Justi,* et al. A History of All Nations from the Earliest Times Being a Universal Library by Distinguished Scholars. - Egypt and Western Asia in Antiquity. Volumes 1-24. In public domain. https://play.google.com/books/reader?id=FHTdDWLB6tQC&hl=en&pg=GBS.PR3
46. *Christopher A. Straughn.* Sakha-English Dictionary. Chicago.2006
47. *Chronicles of Jerahmeel.* Translated by Moses Gaster. 1899. https://www.sacred-texts.com/bib/coj/index.htm

48. *Claudii Ptolemaei.* Geographia. Lipsiae.1843
49. *Claudio Ottoni, Giuseppina Primativo, Baharak Hooshiar Kashani, Alessandro Achilli, Cristina Martínez-Labarga, Gianfranco Biondi, Antonio Torroni,* and *Olga Rickards*. Mitochondrial Haplogroup H1 in *North Africa:* An Early Holocene Arrival from *Iberia*. Published online 2010 Oct 21. doi: 10.1371/journal.pone.0013378 (Copyright: © 2010 Ottoni et al. This is an open-access article distributed under the terms of the Creative Commons Attribution License, which permits unrestricted use, distribution, and reproduction in any medium, provided the original author and source are credited.)
50. *Claudius Ptolemy.* The Geography. Translated by E.L. Stevenson. New York. 1991. Reprint from Geography of Claudius Ptolemy. New York.1932.
51. *Cohen R.* Israel is Real: An obsessive quest to understand the *Jewish* nation and its history. New York. 2009
52. *Conder C.R.* The Early Races of Western Asia. The Journal of the Anthropological Institute of Great Britain and Ireland. Vol. 19 (1890), pp. 29-51. London. 1890.
https://www.google.com/books/edition/The_Journal_of_the_Anthropological_Insti/R88EAAAAYAAJ?hl=en&gbpv=0
53. *Conder C.R.* The First Bible. London. 1902. In public domain.
https://play.google.com/store/books/details?id=5kw2AAAAMAAJ&rdid=book-5kw2AAAAMAAJ&rdot=1
54. *Conder C.R.* Altaic Hieroglyphs and Hittite Inscriptions. Published for the committee of the Palestine exploration fund by A.P. Watt. 1889. In public domain.
https://play.google.com/store/books/details?id=2jcCf80uQR8C&rdid=book-2jcCf80uQR8C&rdot=1
55. *Cornelius Tacitus.* The Annals of Tacitus. Translated by Alfred John Church, William Jackson Brodribb. London, New York. 1888 In public domain.
https://www.google.com/books/edition/Annals_of_Tacitus/5n0JAQAAIAAJ?hl=en&gbpv=0
56. *Cornelius Tacitus.* The Agricola and Germany of Tacitus. Translated Into English by A. J. Church and W. J. Brodribb. London. 1868. In public domain.
https://play.google.com/store/books/details?id=P9pUAAAAcAAJ&rdid=book-P9pUAAAAcAAJ&rdot=1
57. *Cornelius Tacitus.* The History. Translated into English by A. J. Church, W. J. Brodribb. With Notes and a Map. (Life of Tacitus.). London. 1873. In public domain.
https://www.google.com/books/edition/The_History_of_Tacitus_Translated_Into_E/xuvP6ikxhJQC?hl=en&gbpv=0
58. *Cristiano Vernesi, David Caramelli, Isabelle Dupanloup, Giorgio Bertorelle, Martina Lari, Enrico Cappellini, Jacopo Moggi-Cecchi, Brunetto Chiarelli, Loredana Castrì, Antonella Casoli, Francesco Mallegni, Carles Lalueza-Fox, Guido Barbujani.* The Etruscans: A Population-Genetic Study. The American Journal of Human Genetics. Volume 74, Issue 4, 2004. Pages 694-704. ISSN 0002-9297.
https://doi.org/10.1086/383284.(https://www.sciencedirect.com/science/article/pii/S0002929707618941)
59. *Curtius Rufus, Quintus.* Historiarum Alexandri Magni Macedonis libri qui supersunt. Lipsiae. 1908.
60. *Dante Alighieri.* The Divine Comedy. A translation of Dante's Inferno. Translated by David Johnston. Oxford University. 1867. In public domain.
https://www.google.com/books/edition/A_translation_of_Dante_s_Inferno_Purgato/LBdcAAAAQAAJ?hl=en&gbpv=0
61. *David Rohl.* Pharaohs and Kings: A Biblical Quest. New York. 1995
62. *Diodorus Siculus.* The Historical Library of Diodorus the Sicilian: In Fifteen Books. The First Five, Contain the Antiquities of Egypt, Asia, Africa, Greece, the Islands, and Europe. The Last Ten, an Historical Account of the Affairs of the Persians, Grecians, Macedonians, and Other Parts of the World. To which are Added, the Fragments of Diodorus that are Found in the Bibliotheca of Photius: Together with Those Publish'd by H. Valesius, L. Rhodomannus, and F. Ursinus. Translated by Edward Jones. London. 1700
63. *Diodorus Siculus.* The Library of History. Translated by C.H. Oldfather (Vol.1-6), by C.L. Sherman (Vol.7), by C. Bradford Welles (Vol.8), by Russel M. Geer (Vol.9-10), by F. R. Walton (Vol. 11). In public domain.
https://penelope.uchicago.edu/Thayer/E/Roman/Texts/Diodorus_Siculus/home.html
64. *Diodorus Siculus*. Bibliotheca Historica. Books 9-17. Translated by C.H. Oldfather. Leipzig. 1888-1890. In public domain. (CC BY-SA 3.0 US)
http://www.perseus.tufts.edu/hopper/text?doc=Perseus%3Atext%3A1999.01.0084%3Abook%3D9%3Achapter%3D1%3Asection%3D1
65. *Diodorus Siculus.* The Historical Library of Diodorus the Sicilian, In Fifteen Books. To which are Added the Fragments of Diodorus, and Those Published by H. Valesius, I. Rhodomannus, and F. Ursinus. Translated by G. Booth. Volume 1. Books 1-14. London. 1814. In public domain.
https://play.google.com/books/reader?id=oysUAAAAYAAJ&hl=en&pg=GBS.PR1
66. *Diodorus Siculus.* The Historical Library of Diodorus the Sicilian in Fifteen Books to which are added the Fragments of Diodorus, and those published by H. Valesius, I. Rhodomannus, and F. Ursinus. Translated by G. Booth. Volume 2. Books 15-20. London. 1814. In public domain.
https://play.google.com/store/books/details?id=keautnyHFpkC&rdid=book-keautnyHFpkC&rdot=1
https://play.google.com/books/reader?id=oysUAAAAYAAJ&hl=en&pg=GBS.PA15

67. *Dionysius of Byzantium.* Anaplous of the Bosporos. Translated with lapses and confusions by Brady Kiesling for ToposText (or any other noncommercial use that does not require consistency, accuracy, or elegance), from the 1874 Greek/Latin edition of Carolus Wechsler, Anaplous Bosporou. Dionysii Byzantii De Bospori navigatione quae supersunt, digitized by Google at Archive.org. https://topostext.org/work/619
68. *Dionysius of Halicarnassus.* Roman Antiquities. Translated by Edward Spelman. Volume 1. London. 1758. In public domain. https://www.google.com/books/edition/The_Roman_Antiquities_of_Dionysius_Halic/NwEMAAAAYAAJ?hl=en&gbpv=1
69. *Dionysi Halicarnasensis.* "Antiquitatum Romanarum quae supersunt. Germany: in aedibus B. G. Teubneri, 1867. In public dmain. https://www.google.com/books/edition/Dionysi_Halicarnasensis_Antiquitatum_Rom/RQ8MAAAAYAAJ?hl=en&gbpv=0
70. *Dionysiou Halikarnaseos.* Ta heuriskomena, historika te kai rhetorika, syngrammata. 1586. In public domain. https://archive.org/details/dionysiouhalikar00dion/page/n99/mode/2up
71. *Dr. Julius Oppert.* The *Median* version of the *Behistun* inscription of *Darius Hystaspes.* Records of the Past: Being *English* Translations of the *Assyrian* and *Egyptian* Monuments. 1874. In public domain. https://www.google.com/books/edition/Records_of_the_Past/KexfAAAAcAAJ?hl=en&gbpv=0
72. *Edwin Norris.* Memoir on the Scythic Version of the Behistun Inscription. Harrison and Sons, 1853. https://www.google.com/books/edition/Memoir_on_the_Scythic_Version_of_the_Beh/8GI-AAAAcAAJ?hl=en&gbpv=0
73. *Elishe.* Slovo o voyne armyanskoy, isproshennoye iereyem Davitom Mamikoneanom. http://www.vehi.net/istoriya/armenia/egishe/EGISHE.html#_ftnref37
74. *Encyclopædia Britannica: Or a Dictionary of Arts and Sciences Compiled Upon a New Plan. In which the different sciences and arts are digested into distinct treatises or systems; and the various technical terms, etc. are explained as they occur in order of the Alphabet.* By a Society of Gentlemen in Scotland. Volumes 1-3. Edinburgh. 1771. In public domain. https://play.google.com/store/books/details?id=Ko7FweJ5Ue0C&rdid=book-Ko7FweJ5Ue0C&rdot=1
75. *Erendiz Özbayoğlu.* Ancient times. Eyüp Sultan Symposium. 1-8. Selected articles. Istanbul. 2011
76. *Euripides.* The Plays of Euripides. Translated into English by Edward P. Coleridge, B.A. Volume 2. London. 1891 https://www.google.com/books/edition/The_Plays_of_Euripides_Andromache_Electr/H0S7gWIlKugC?hl=en&gbpv=0
77. *European Society of Human Genetics.* (2007, June 18). Ancient Etruscans Were Immigrants from Anatolia, Or What Is Now Turkey. ScienceDaily. Retrieved May 2, 2021 from www.sciencedaily.com/releases/2007/06/070616191637.htm
78. *Ferdowsi,* or *Abul-Qâsem Ferdowsi Tusi.* Shahname. In Persian. Quatremère, Étienne, Ḥāǧǧī ʿAbd-al-Muḥammad Rāzī, Muṣṭafā Qulī Ibn-Muḥammad Hādī Sulṭān Kuǧūrī, Ḥāǧǧī Muḥammad Ḥusain. شاهنامهٔ فردوسی طوسی. Iran: رازی, 1850.
79. *Ferdowsi.* The Epic of Kings. (Shahnameh). Translated into English by Helen Zimmern. 1st edition. London. 1883
80. *Flavii Arriani.* Quae exstant omnias: Alexandri Anabasin continens. V.1-2. Scripta minor et fragmenta. Lipsiae. 1907.
81. *Flavius Josephus.* The complete works of Flavius Josephus. Translated by William Whiston, M.A. London. 1851. In public domain. https://www.google.com/books/edition/The_Complete_Works_of_Flavius_Josephus_T/Z1eDk09sNoIC?hl=en&gbpv=0
82. *Forlong J.G.R.* Faiths of Man: A Cyclopedia of Religions. Vol. 1-3. London. 1906. In public domain.
83. *Gaius Julius Hyginus.* Fabulae. - The Myths. Translated and edited by Mary Grant. University of Kansas Publications in Humanistic Studies, no. 34., now in the public domain, with thanks to www.theoi.com for making the text available online. https://topostext.org/work/206
84. *Gaius Plinius Secundus.* Historia mundi, denvo emendata, non paucis locis ex diligenti ad pervetusta et optimæ fidei exemplaria collatione, nunc primũ animaduersis castigatisq[ue], quemadmodum cuidenter in Sigismundi Gelenij Annotationibus operi adnexis apparet. Adiunctus est Index copiosissimus. (Joan. Camertis.). 1563.
85. *Gaius Suetonius Tranquillus,* aka *Suetonius.* The Lives Of The First Twelve Caesars. Translated by Alexander Thomson. London. 1796
86. *Gaius Valerius Flaccus.* Argonauticon. In public domain. (CC BY-SA 3.0) https://www.perseus.tufts.edu/hopper/text?doc=Perseus%3Atext%3A2007.01.0058%3Abook%3D1%3Acard%3D1
87. *George Grote.* History of Greece. Volume 3. Boston. 1852. https://www.loc.gov/law/mlr/Lieber_Collection-pdf/HistoryOfGreece-III.pdf
88. *Goodrich S.G.* A History of All Nations, from the Earliest Periods to the Present Time: or, Universal History: in Which the History of Every Nation, Ancient and Modern, is Separately Given. Vol. 1. Boston. 1851 https://play.google.com/books/reader?id=YewLAAAAYAAJ&printsec=frontcover&pg=GBS.PA1
89. *Grugni V.* et al. Ancient Migratory Events in the *Middle East:* New Clues from the Y-Chromosome Variation of Modern Iranians. Published on July 18, 2012

https://journals.plos.org/plosone/article?id=10.1371/journal.pone.0041252 [Open access]
90. *Gurbanov A.* Damğalar, rəmzlər...mənimsəmələr. Baku. 2013
91. *H.W. Bell; W.H. Buckler; Howard Crosby Butler; Charles Densmore Curtis; Enno Littmann; Charles Rufus Morley; Theodore Leslie Shear.* Sardis. American Society for the Excavation of Sardis. Volume 6. Lydian Inscriptions. Part 1 by Enno Littmann. Leyden. 1916
92. *Haber, M., Mezzavilla, M., Xue, Y. et al.* Genetic evidence for an origin of the Armenians from Bronze Age mixing of multiple populations. Eur J Hum Genet 24, 931–936 (2016). https://doi.org/10.1038/ejhg.2015.206 (CC BY 4.0)
https://www.nature.com/articles/ejhg2015206#citeas
93. *Henry Bradley.* The Story of the Goths from the Earliest Times to the End of the Gothic Dominion in Spain. New York, London. 1888. In public domain.
https://play.google.com/store/books/details?id=1DWXIerPxJ8C&rdid=book-1DWXIerPxJ8C&rdot=1
94. *Herodotus.* The History of Herodotus. Translated by George Rawlinson. Vol. 1-4. London.1858. In public domain.
95. *Herodotus.* The History of Herodotus. Parallel English/Greek. Translated by G. C. Macaulay, 1890. www.sacred-texts.com
96. *Herodotus.* The History of Herodotus. Translated by Isaac Littlebury. Oxford. 1824
97. *Hesiod.* The Homeric Humns and Homerica. Translated by Hugh G. Evelyn-White, M.A. London, New York. 1914. In public domain.
https://play.google.com/store/books/details?id=GvLfAAAAMAAJ&rdid=book-GvLfAAAAMAAJ&rdot=1
98. *Hippocrates.* Collected works. Translated by W. H. S. Jones. Cambridge. 1868. In public domain. (CC BY-SA 3.0)
http://www.perseus.tufts.edu/hopper/text?doc=Perseus%3Atext%3A1999.01.0251%3Atext%3Dintro
99. *Homer.* The Iliad of Homer: With an Interlinear Translation, for the Use of Schools and Private Learners, on the Hamiltonian System. Translated by Thomas Clark. Philadelphia. 1888. In public domain.
https://www.google.com/books/edition/The_Iliad_of_Homer/jFo7AQAAMAAJ?hl=en&gbpv=0
100. *Homer.* The Iliad. Translated by Samuel Butler. 1898. (CC BY-SA 3.0)
https://en.wikisource.org/wiki/The_Iliad_(Butler)
101. *Homer.* The Iliad. Translated by A.T. Murray, Ph.D. Vol. 1-2. Cambridge, MA., Harvard University Press; London, William Heinemann, Ltd. 1924. (CC BY-SA 3.0)
http://www.perseus.tufts.edu/hopper/text?doc=Perseus:text:1999.01.0134
102. *Homer.* The Iliad of Homer. Rendered into English prose for the use of those who cannot read the original. Samuel Butler. Longmans, Green and Co. 39 Paternoster Row, London. New York and Bombay. 1898. In public domain. (CC BY-SA 3.0)
http://www.perseus.tufts.edu/hopper/text?doc=Perseus%3Atext%3A1999.01.0217%3Abook%3D1%3Acard%3D1
103. *Homer.* The Odyssey. Translated by Samuel Butler. London. 1900. In public domain.
https://en.wikisource.org/wiki/The_Odyssey_(Butler)
104. *Ibn Fadlan.* Ibn Fadlan and the Land of Darkness. *Arab* Travellers in the Far North. Translated with an Introduction by *Paul Lunde* and *Caroline Stone.* Penguin Books Ltd. *England.* 2012.
105. *Iñigo Olalde, Swapan Mallick, Nick Patterson,* et al. The genomic history of the *Iberian Peninsula* over the past 8000 years. Science. Vol. 363. Issue 6432. pp.1230-1234. 2019. https://science.sciencemag.org/content/363/6432/1230.full
106. *Iordanes Gotus.* De Getorum, sive Gothorum Origine et rebus gestis. Isidori Chronicon Gothorum ... Procopii Fragmentum, de priscis fedibus et migrationibus Gothorum, Graece et Latine. Leiden. 1597
107. *Iordanes Gotus.* Incipit de Origine actibusque Getarum. 1848
https://books.google.com/books/about/Incipit_de_Origine_actibusque_Getarum.html?id=cHlVAAAAcAJ
108. *Isaac Taylor.* Etruscan Researches. London. 1874
109. *J. Wentworth Webster.* Les Basques. Translated into English by Jno. Davenport Wheeler. The New Englander. Vol. 41. New Haven. 1882. In public domain.
https://play.google.com/store/books/details?id=N_EaAAAAYAAJ&rdid=book-N_EaAAAAYAAJ&rdot=1
110. *Jesus Rodriguez Ramos.* La lectura de las inscripciones sudlusitano-tartesias. 21-48. Faventia 22/1. 2000
111. *Johannes Laurentius Lydus.* De Mensibus. Lipsiae. 1898
112. *John Francis Gemelli Careri.* A Voyage Round the World in six parts. From A Collection of Voyages and Travels, Some Now First Printed from Original Manuscripts. Others translated out of foreign languages, and now first publish'd in English. Vol. 1-4. London. 1704
113. *John Gast.* (Archdeacon of Glandelagh.) The History of *Greece,* Properly so Called, to the Accession of *Alexander* of Macedon." Vol. 1-2. Dublin. 1793. In public domain.
https://play.google.com/store/books/details?id=afpNAAAAcAAJ&rdid=book-afpNAAAAcAAJ&rdot=1
114. *John Jackson.* Chronological Antiquities: Or, the Antiquities and Chronology of the Most Ancient Kingdoms from the Creation of the World of the Space of Five Thousand Years. Vol. 1-3. London. 1752. In public domain.
https://play.google.com/store/books/details?id=ZysVAAAAQAAJ&rdid=book-ZysVAAAAQAAJ&rdot=1
115. *John Lydus.* The Months. (De Mensibus). Translated by Mischa Hooker for Roger Pearse. The translation has been placed in the public domain by Roger Pearse.
https://penelope.uchicago.edu/Thayer/E/Roman/Texts/Lydus/de_Mensibus/home.html
116. *John Malcolm Russell.* The writing on the wall. Indiana. 1999

117. *John Swinton*. A Dissertation upon the Peopling of America – The Universal History from the Earliest Account of Time. Compiled from original authors and illustrated with maps, cuts, notes, etc.". Vol. 20. Chapter 33. p.157-195. London. 1748. In public domain.
https://www.google.com/books/edition/An_Universal_History_from_the_Earliest_A/n1xjAAAAMAAJ?hl=en&gbpv=0

118. *John Pinkerton*. A General Collection of the Best and Most Interesting Voyages and Travels in All Parts of the World. London. 1811. In public domain.
https://www.google.com/books/edition/A_General_Collection_of_the_Best_and_Mos/2EtSAQAAIAAJ?hl=en&gbpv=0

119. *Jordanes*. The Origin and Deeds of the Goths". Translated by Charles Christopher Mierow. Prinston. 1908. In public domain.
https://www.google.com/books/edition/Jordanes_The_Origin_and_Deeds_of_the_Got/C5hJAAAAYAAJ?hl=en&gbpv=0

120. *Joseph the Khazar and Hasdai ibn Shaprut*. Khazar Correspondence. Translated by Jacob Marcus. The Jew in the Medieval World: A Sourcebook, 315-1791, (New York: JPS, 1938), 227-232. (CC BY-SA 3.0)
https://en.wikisource.org/wiki/Khazar_Correspondence

121. *Justin*. Justin, Cornelius Nepos, and Eutropius. – Justin's History of the World extracted from Trogus Pompeius. Translated by John Selby Watson. London.1853
https://www.google.com/books/edition/Justin_Cornelius_Nepos_and_Eutropius/7S8W0VgSi1oC?hl=en&gbpv=0

122. *Kitabi-Dədə Qorqud*. Baku. 2004

123. *Kristiina Tambets, Bayazit Yunusbayev*, et al. Genes reveal traces of common recent demographic history for most of the *Uralic*-speaking populations. Genome Biology, Vol. 19, Article #139. 2018. [CC BY 4.0]
https://genomebiology.biomedcentral.com/articles/10.1186/s13059-018-1522-1

124. *Kroeber A.L.* California Place Names of Indian Origin. UC publications in American Archaeology and ethnology. Vol. 12. No.2. p. 31-69. UC Berkeley press. Berkeley. 1916

125. *L.Annaei Senecae*. Opera quae supersunt. Dialogorum". Volume 12. Lipsiae. 1905. In public domain.
https://www.google.com/books/edition/L_Annaei_Senecae_opera_quae_supersunt_fa/kvBDAQAAMAAJ?hl=en&gbpv=0

126. *Larcher P.H.* Larcher's Notes on Herodotus. Historical and Critical Comments on the History of Herodotus, with a Chronological Table". Edited by W.D. Cooley. Vol. 1-2. London. 1844 https://play.google.com/books/reader?id=d24-AAAAcAAJ&hl=en

127. *Latyshev V.V.* Scythica et Caucasica e veteribus scriptoribus graecis et latinis. Vol.1. Saint-Petersburg. 1890

128. *Lily Agranat-Tamir, Shamam Waldman, Mario A.S. Martin, David Gokhman, et al.* The Genomic History of the Bronze Age Southern Levant. Cell. Volume 181, Issue 5. P1146-1157.E11. May 28, 2020.
https://doi.org/10.1016/j.cell.2020.04.024

129. *Louis Figuier*. The Human Race. *London*. 1872

130. *Lucian (of Samosata)*. Selections from Lucian. Translated by Emily James Smith. New York. 1892

131. *Lucius Annaeus Florus*. Epitome of Roman History, from Romulus to Augustus Caesar. Made English from the best editions and corrections of learned men. London. 1725. In public domain.
https://www.google.com/books/edition/L_A_F_his_Epitome_of_Roman_History_made/O75XAAAAcAAJ?hl=en&gbpv=1

132. *M.Iuniano Iustino*. Iustinus Trogi Pompei Historiarum Philippicarum epitoma.
https://www.thelatinlibrary.com/justin/20.html

133. *Macrobii Ambrosii Theodosii*. Opera Quae Supersunt ...: Saturnaliorum. Libri VII. Lipsiae. 1852. In public domain.
https://www.google.com/books/edition/Macrobii_Ambrosii_Theodosii_Opera_Quae_S/xeMNAAAAYAAJ?hl=en&gbpv=0

134. *Mahmud Kaşğari*. Divanü Lüğat-it-Türk (The Corpus of the Turkic Lexicon). Translated into Azerbaijani by Ramiz Askar. Vol. 1-4 Baku. 2006

135. *Henry Creswicke Rawlinson*. The *Persian* Cuneiform Inscription at *Behistun,* Decyphered and Translated; with a Memoir on *Persian* Cuneiform Inscriptions in General, and on that of *Behistun* in Particular. Royal Asiatic Society. London. 1846. In public domain.
https://www.google.com/books/edition/The_Persian_Cuneiform_Inscription_at_Beh/0lE-AAAAcAAJ?hl=en&gbpv=0

136. *H.C. Rawlinson*. Memoir on the Babylonian and Assyrian inscriptions. Journal of the Royal Asiatic Society of Great Britain and Ireland. Vol. 14.1. London. 1851. In public domain.
https://www.google.com/books/edition/Journal_of_the_Royal_Asiatic_Society_of/yoryj6ipPhAC?hl=en&gbpv=1

137. *Marcus Annaeus Lucanus,* aka *Lucan.* De bello civili sive Pharsalia (The Civil War).
http://thelatinlibrary.com/lucan.html

138. *Marcus Terentius Varro.* On Agriculture. (De Re Rustica). Published in the Loeb Classical Library. 1934. Translated by W. D. Hooper and H. B. Ash, printed in the same edition. The translation is in the public domain pursuant to the 1978 revision of the U. S. Copyright Code, since the copyright was not renewed in 1961 or 1962.

https://penelope.uchicago.edu/Thayer/E/Roman/Texts/Varro/de_Re_Rustica/home.html
139. *Marcus Terentius Varro.* On the Latin Language. Volumes 5-7. Translated by Roland Grubb Kent. The Loeb Classical Library. 1938. In public domain. https://topostext.org/work/728
140. *Martial.* The Epigrams of Martial. Books 1-14. London. 1871. In public domain. https://www.google.com/books/edition/The_Epigrams_of_Martial/LzXgAAAAMAAJ?hl=en&gbpv=1
141. *Masudi.* Murūj aḏ-Ḏahab wa-Maʿādin al-Jawhar – The meadows of gold and mines of precious gems". https://www.wdl.org/en/item/7441/
142. *Matthiae Belii.* De vetere literature Hunno-Scythica Exercitatio. Leipzig. 1718. In public domain. https://play.google.com/store/books/details?id=ewJFAAAAYAAJ&rdid=book-ewJFAAAAYAAJ&rdot=1
143. *Michal Feldman, Daniel M. Master, Raffaela A. Bianco, Marta Burri, Philipp W. Stockhammer, Alissa Mittnik, Adam J. Aja, Choongwon Jeong, Johannes Krause.* Ancient DNA sheds light on the genetic origins of early Iron Age Philistines. Science Advances, 2019; 5 (7): eaax0061 DOI: 10.1126/sciadv.aax0061
144. *Movses Khorenatsi.* The History of Armenia. Translated into English by Troy Azelli, A.S. 2020
145. *Musayev O.I.* Azərbaycanca-İngiliscə luğət. Baku. 1998
146. *National cultural development under communism.* June 1957. Document Number (FOIA) /ESDN (CREST): CIA-RDP78-02771R000200090002-6. Approved For Release 1999/08/24: CIA-RDP78-02771 R000200090002-6. https://www.cia.gov/readingroom/document/cia-rdp78-02771r000200090002-6
147. *P. Ovidi Nasonis.* Artis Amatoriae. Vol. 1, 2. www.thelatinlibrary.com
148. *P. Ovidius Nasa.* Metamorphoses. Translated by Brookes More. Boston. 1922 https://www.perseus.tufts.edu/hopper/text?doc=Perseus%3Atext%3A1999.02.0028%3Abook%3D1%3Acard%3D1 (CC BY-SA 3.0 US)
149. *P. Ovidius Nasa.* Ovid's Fasti. Vol. 1-3. Literally translated by Roscoe Mongan. London, Dublin, Liverpool. 1878. In public domain. https://www.google.com/books/edition/Ovid_s_Fasti_tr_into_Engl_prose_by_R_Mon/8eYIAAAAQAAJ?hl=en&gbpv=0
150. *P. Ovidius Nasa.* The Fasti, Tristia, Pontic Epistles, Ibis, and Halieuticon of Ovid. Translated by Henry Thomas Riley. London. 1851. In public domain. https://www.google.com/books/edition/The_Fasti_Tristia_Pontic_Epistles_Ibis_a/V_0pAAAAYAAJ?hl=en&gbpv=0
151. *P. Ovidius Nasa.* Art of Love. https://topostext.org/people/1411
152. *Palairet Jean.* Atlas méthodique: composé pour l'usage de Son Altesse Serenissime Monseigneur le prince D'Orange et de Nassau, stadhouder des sept provinces-unies, etc. etc. etc. par Jean Palairet, Agent de LL. HH. PP., les etats generaux, a la cour Britannique.
153. *Pavel Josef Šafárik.* Slawische Alterthümer. Leipzig. 1843-44.
154. *Pashayev A., Bashirova A.* Azərbaycan şəxs adlarının izahlı lüğəti". Baku. 2011
155. *Pausanias.* "Description of Greece". Vol. 1-4. Translated into English by W.H.S. Jones, Litt.D., and H.A. Ormerod. Cambridge, London. 1918 (CC BY-SA 3.0 US) http://www.perseus.tufts.edu/hopper/text?doc=Perseus%3Atext%3A1999.01.0160%3Abook%3D2%3Achapter%3D18%3Asection%3D7
156. *Pellecchia, M., Negrini, R., Colli, L., Patrini, M., Milanesi, E., Achilli, A., Bertorelle, G., Cavalli-Sforza, L. L., Piazza, A., Torroni, A., & Ajmone-Marsan, P. (2007).* The Mystery of Etruscan Origins: Novel Clues from Bos Taurus Mitochondrial DNA. Proceedings. Biological sciences, 274(1614), 1175–1179. https://doi.org/10.1098/rspb.2006.0258
157. *Philostratus.* The Life of Apollonius of Tyana. The Epistles of Apollonius and the Treatise of Eusebius. Vol. 1. Translated by Frederick Cornwallis Conybeare. London, New York. 1912 https://www.google.com/books/edition/The_Life_of_Apollonius_of_Tyana/ci4jAQAAMAAJ?hl=en&gbpv=1
158. *Pindar.* The Olympian and Pythian Odes of Pindar. Translated by Rev.Francis David Morice, M.A. London. 1849. In public domain. https://archive.org/details/olympianpythitra00pinduoft/page/n5/mode/2up
159. *Pindar.* The Olympian and Pythian Odes. Fennell, Charles Augustus Maude. The Olympian and Pythian Odes: With Notes Explanatory and Critical, Introductions and Introductory Essays. UK: University Press. 1893. https://www.google.com/books/edition/The_Olympian_and_Pythian_Odes/J1w1AQAAMAAJ?hl=en&gbpv=0
160. *Pinkerton J.* A General Collection of the Best and Most Interesting Voyages and Travels in All Parts of the World: Many of which are Now First Translated Into English. Vol. 7. London. 1811
161. *Plato.* Cratylus. Translated by Harold N. Fowler. Vol. 1-12. Cambridge, MA. London. 1921 (CC BY-SA 3.0 US) http://www.perseus.tufts.edu/hopper/text?doc=Perseus%3Atext%3A1999.01.0172%3Atext%3DCrat.%3Asection%3D383a
162. *Plato.* Greater Hippias. Vol. 1-12. Translated by H.N. Fowler, W.R.M. Lamb. Cambridge, MA, Harvard University Press; London, William Heinemann Ltd. 1925. (CC BY-SA 3.0 US) http://www.perseus.tufts.edu/hopper/text?doc=Perseus:text:1999.01.0180
163. *Plato.* The Dialogues of Plato. Translated by Jowett B. Volume 5. Oxford. 1892. In public domain. https://www.google.com/books/edition/Laws_Index/408-AAAAYAAJ?hl=en&gbpv=0

164. *Pliny the Elder*. The Historie of the World, Commonly Called, The Naturall Historie of C. Plinius Secundus". Vol. 1. Books 1-10. Translated by Dr. Philemon Howard. London. 1601. In public domain.
https://www.google.com/books/edition/The_Historie_of_the_World/HiQ6KlZSt8MC?hl=en&gbpv=0
165. *Pliny*. Pliny's Natural History. A translation on the basis of that by Dr. Philemon Holland. 1847.
https://play.google.com/books/reader?id=XrFgAAAAIAAJ&printsec=frontcover&pg=GBS.PR1.w.11.0.0
166. *Pliny the Elder*. The Natural History. Vol. 1-37. Translated by John Bostock, H.T. Riley. London. 1855 (CC BY-SA 3.0 US)
https://www.perseus.tufts.edu/hopper/text?doc=Perseus%3Atext%3A1999.02.0137%3Abook%3D1%3Achapter%3Ddedication
167. *Plinii Secundi*. Historia Mvndi, Denvo Emendata, Non Pavcis Locis Ex Diligenti Ad Pervetvsta Et optimæ fidei exemplaria collatione, nunc primũ animaduersis castigatisq[ue], quemadmodum cuidenter in Sigismundi Gelenij Annotationibus operi adnexis apparet. Adiunctus est Index copiosissimus. 1535.
https://play.google.com/books/reader?id=TtFWAAAAcAAJ&printsec=frontcover&pg=GBS.PA6
168. *Plutarch*. Plutarch's Lives. Translated by Bernadotte Perrin. Cambridge, MA. Harvard University Press. London. William Heinemann Ltd. 1914. 2. (CC BY-SA 3.0 US)
http://www.perseus.tufts.edu/hopper/searchresults?q=plutarch
169. *Polybius*. Histories. Translated by Evelyn S. Shuckburgh. London, New York. Macmillan. 1889. Reprint Bloomington 1962. (CC BY-SA 3.0 US)
http://www.perseus.tufts.edu/hopper/text?doc=Perseus%3Atext%3A1999.01.0234%3Abook%3D1%3Achapter%3D1
170. *Pomponii Melae*. De situ orbis. Vol.1-3. Ghent.1700. In public domain.
171. *Pomponius Mela*. The Worke of Pomponius Mela. The cosmographer, concerninge the situation of the world, wherein every parte, is devided by it selfe in most perfect manner, as appeareth in the table at the end of the booke. Translated by Arthur Golding Gentleman. London. 1585. In public domain.
https://www.google.com/books/edition/The_Worke_of_Pomponius_Mela_Concerninge/W1Y-HfpBcM0C?hl=en&gbpv=0
172. Popol Vuh – Sacred Book of the Quiche Maya people. Translated by Allen J. Christenson. (University of Oklahoma Press, Norman, 2003). www.mesoweb.com/publications/
173. *Procopius of Caesareia*. Buildings. Books 4-5. Translated by Henry Bronson Dewing. 1919, 1940
174. *Procopius of Caesaria*. History of the Wars. Vol. 1-6. Books 1-2. 1964. London, New York. In public domain.
https://babel.hathitrust.org/cgi/pt?id=mdp.39015011291245&view=1up&seq=7
175. *Procopius of Caesaria*. History of the Wars. Translated by H.B. Dewing. Loeb Classical Library. Vol. 2. Books 3-4. London, New York. 1916. In public domain.
https://www.google.com/books/edition/Procopius_Vandalic_war/xmxKAAAAYAAJ?hl=en&gbpv=0https://penelope.uchicago.edu/Thayer/E/Roman/Texts/Procopius/Wars/home.html#BG
176. *Procopius of Caesaria*. History of the Wars. Vol. 3. Books 5-6. Translated by H.B. Dewing. London, New York. 1919. In public domain. 1919.
https://play.google.com/books/reader?id=wW1KAAAAYAAJ&hl=en&pg=GBS.PP9
177. *Quintus Smyrnaeus*. The Fall of Troy. Translated by Arthur S. Way. London, New York. 1913. In public domain.
https://play.google.com/store/books/details?id=DcwFUhDO-XAC&rdid=book-DcwFUhDO-XAC&rdot=1
178. *Rawlinson G*. The Five Great Monarchies of the Ancient Eastern World: Or, The History, Geography, and Antiquities of Chaldæa, Assyria, Babylon, Media, and Persia, Collected and Illustrated from Ancient and Modern Sources. Vol. 2. London. 1879. In public domain.
179. *Redhouse J.W.* Redhouse's Turkish Dictionary in two parts, English and Turkish, and Turkish and English. London. 1880
180. *Richard Hakluyt*. Hakluyt's Collection of the Early Voyages, Travels, and Discoveries, of the English Nation. London. 1809. In public domain.
https://www.google.com/books/edition/Hakluyt_s_Collection_of_the_Early_Voyage/EfpAAQAAMAAJ?hl=en&gbpv=1
181. *Richard Phillips*. A Geographical View of the World: Embracing the Manners, Customs, and Pursuits, of Every Nation; Founded on the Best Authorities. Second American edition, revised, corrected and improved by James G. Percival. M.D. New York.1851. In public domain.
https://play.google.com/store/books/details?id=Z2EBAAAAYAAJ&rdid=book-Z2EBAAAAYAAJ&rdot=1
182. *Russel J.M.* The Writing on the Wall: Studies in the Architectural Context of Late Assyrian Palace Inscriptions (Mesopotamian Civilizations). 1990
183. *Sarkissian A. O.* On the Authenticity of Moses of Khoren's History. Journal of the American Oriental Society 60, no. 1 (1940): 73-81.
184. *Schwarz H.G.* An Uyghur-English Dictionary. East Asian Studies Press. 1992. https://cedar.wwu.edu/easpress/30
185. *Servii Grammatici*. Qui feruntur in Vergilii carmina commentarii: Aeneidos librorum VI-XII commentarii. Vol. 2. 1884. In public domain.
https://www.google.com/books/edition/Servii_Grammatici_qvi_fervntvr_in_Vergil/cYsrLUHwKmAC?hl=en&gbpv=0

186. *Sexti Pompei Festi*. De verborum significatione quae supersunt, cum Pauli epitome. Lipsiae. 1839. In public domain.
https://www.google.com/books/edition/S_P_Festi_de_verborum_significatione_qu/cC1kAAAAcAAJ?hl=en&gbpv=0
187. *Sexti Propertius*. Elegiarum. www.TheLatinLibrary.com
188. *Silius Italicus*. Punica. (in Latin) Corpus Poetarum Latinorum, Vol 2. Walter Coventry Summers. John Percival Postgate. London. Sumptibus G. Bell et Filiorum. 1905. (CC BY-SA 3.0 US)
http://www.perseus.tufts.edu/hopper/text?doc=Perseus:text:2008.01.0674
189. *Sima Qian*. The Account of the Xiongnu. Shi Ji 110. https://canvas.dartmouth.edu/files/5929996/download?download_frd=1
190. *Sir Richard C. Jebb*. Commentary on Sophocles: Electra. Sophocles: The Plays and Fragments, with critical notes, commentary, and translation in English prose. Part VI: The Electra. Sir Richard C. Jebb. Cambridge. Cambridge University Press. 1894. (CC BY-SA 3.0 US)
http://www.perseus.tufts.edu/hopper/text?doc=Perseus%3Atext%3A1999.04.0025%3Atext%3Dintro
191. *Snorra Sturlusonar*. Eða Gylfaginníng, Skáldskaparmál og Háttatal. Reykjavik. 1907. In public domain.
https://play.google.com/store/books/details?id=dicPAAAAQAAJ&rdid=book-dicPAAAAQAAJ&rdot=1
192. *Snorri Sturluson*. The Prose *Edda*. Translated by from the Icelandic by Arthur Gilchrist Brodeur, PhD. New York, London. 1916. In public domain.
https://play.google.com/books/reader?id=_T1cAAAAMAAJ&printsec=frontcover&pg=GBS.PR3
193. *Sophocles*. Oedipus the King. Oedipus at Colonus. Antigone. Translated by F. Storr. B.A. Vol. 1-2. London, New York. 1912. In public domain.
https://play.google.com/books/reader?id=xBg_AQAAMAAJ&hl=en&pg=GBS.PR1
194. *Sophocles*. Sophocles' Ajax. The Death and Burial of Aias. A tragedy of Sophocles. Translated by Lewis Campbell, M.A., LL.D. Edinburgh, London.1826. In public domain.
https://www.google.com/books/edition/Sophocles_Ajax_The_death_and_burial_of_A/o4ICAAAAQAAJ?hl=en&gbpv=0
195. *Sophocles*. The Electra. Translated by Richard Claverhouse Jebb. London, Glasgow. 1894. In public domain.
https://www.google.com/books/edition/Sophocles_The_Electra_1894/Ar8NAAAAIAAJ?hl=en&gbpv=0
196. *Sophocles*. The Plays and Fragments. The Trachiniae. Volume 5. Translated by Sir Richard Claverhouse Jebb. Cambridge. 1908. In public domain.
https://www.google.com/books/edition/Sophocles_The_Trachiniae_1892/DjwZAAAAYAAJ?hl=en&gbpv=0
197. *Sorin Paliga*. The Tablets of Tărtăria. An Enigma? A Reconsideration and Further Perspectives."
198. *St. Jerome*. Chronicon. https://topostext.org/work.php?work_id=530#B1429
199. *Stephani Byzantii*. Ethnicorum Quae Supersunt. Berolini. 1849. In public domain.
https://www.google.com/books/edition/Ethnicorum/2m7Z-jbE8M8C?hl=en&gbpv=0
200. *Stephanus de Urbibus*. Que Primus Thomas de Pinedo Lustanus Latii jure donabat et Observationibus Scrutinio Variarum Linguarum, ac præcipue Hebraicæ, Phœniciæ, Græcæ et Latinæ detectis illustrabat. Amsterdam. 1725
201. *Stephen Oppenheimer*. The Origins of the British: A Genetic Detective Story.
https://www.walesonline.co.uk/news/wales-news/basque-ing-in-welsh-dna-2281798
202. *Strabo*. The Geography of Strabo. Translated by H.C. Hamilton, Esq., W. Falconer, M.A. London 1903. (CC BY-SA 3.0 US)
https://www.perseus.tufts.edu/hopper/text?doc=Perseus%3Atext%3A1999.01.0239%3Abook%3Dnotice
203. *Strabonis*. Geographica. Graece cum versione reficta. Accedit index variantis lectionis et tabula rerum nominumque locupletissima. Parisiis. 1853. In public domain.
https://play.google.com/books/reader?id=RgVBAAAAcAAJ&pg=GBS.PP7
204. *Sven Lagerbring*. Bref till Cancellie Rådet och Riddaren, Herr *Joh. Ihre* om Svenska och *Turkiska* Språkens likhet (A Letter to the Chancellor and the Knight, Mr. Joh. Ihre about the Similarity of the Swedish and Turkish languages.). Lund University. 1764. In public domain.
https://play.google.com/store/books/details/Bref_till_Joh_Ihre_Om_Swenska_och_Turkiska_Spr%C3%A5ken?id=mdZWAAAAcAAJ&hl=lt&gl=US
205. *The Dublin University Magazine*. The theatre of *St. Paul's* activity. Vol. 75. Dublin. 1870
206. *The Translator* (the author is anonymous). An Account of the Present State of the *Northern Asia,* Relating to the Natural History of *Grand Tatary* and *Siberia* and the Manners, Customs, Trade, Laws, Religion and Polity of the Different People Inhabiting the Same together with Some Observations concerning *China, India, Persia, Arabia, Turky,* and *Great Russia*. Vol. 2. London. 1729
207. *Thor Heyerdahl*. Thor Heyerdahl, Norwegian Explorer in Search of Odin. 2010
https://ironlight.wordpress.com/2010/02/20/thor-heyerdahl-norwegian-explorer-in-search-of-odin/
208. *Thucydides*. The History of the Grecian War in 8 books. Translated by Thomas Hobbes of Malmsbury. 2nd edition. London. 1676
https://www.google.com/books/edition/The_History_of_the_Grecian_War_Faithfull/1o9mAAAAcAAJ?hl=en&gbpv=0
209. *Thucydides*. History of the Peloponnesian War. Books 1-8. Translated by Thomas Hobbes of Malmsbury. In public domain. (CC BY-SA 3.0 US)

http://www.perseus.tufts.edu/hopper/text?doc=Perseus%3Atext%3A1999.01.0247%3Abook%3Dintro%3Achapter%3D1

210. *Titus Livius*. The history of Rome. Translated into English by Rev. Canon Roberts. New York. 1912 (CC BY-SA 3.0 US) http://www.perseus.tufts.edu/hopper/searchresults?q=livius
211. *U Roostalu, I Kutuev, E-L Loogväli, E Metspalu, K Tambets, M Reidla, EK Khusnutdinova, E Usanga, T Kivisild, R Villems*. Origin and Expansion of Haplogroup H, the Dominant Human Mitochondrial DNA Lineage in West Eurasia: The Near Eastern and Caucasian Perspective. Molecular Biology and Evolution, Vol. 24, Issue 2, February 2007, Pages 436–448. https://doi.org/10.1093/molbev/msl173
212. *V.Gardthausen*. Coniectanea Ammianea codice adhibito Vaticano scripsit. Kiliae.1869
213. *Virgil*. The Aeneid. Translated into Blank Verse by James Beresford. London.1794. In public domain. [http://www.wdorner.com:8080/xtf/view?docId=aeneid/beresford.xml]
214. *Virgil*. Virgil's Aeneid. Translated by John Dryden. New York.1909. In public domain. https://www.google.com/books/edition/Aeneid/-NE6AAAAMAAJ?hl=en&gbpv=0
215. *Viola Grugni* et al. Ancient Migratory Events in the Middle East: New Clues from the Y-Chromosome Variation of Modern Iranians. https://www.ncbi.nlm.nih.gov/pmc/articles/PMC3399854/
216. *Virgil*. The Aeneid of Virgil. Translated by J.W. Mackail. Oxford. London. 1885. In public domain. https://www.google.com/books/edition/The_Aeneid_of_Virgil/Z-9MAQAAMAAJ?hl=en&gbpv=0
217. *Wales Online*. Basque-ing in Welsh DNA. 2007, 2013. https://www.walesonline.co.uk/news/wales-news/basque-ing-in-welsh-dna-2281798
218. *William Smith*. A Dictionary of *Greek* and *Roman* biography and mythology. Vol. 1-3. London. Boston. 1849. In public domain. https://www.google.com/books/edition/Dictionary_of_Greek_and_Roman_Biography/2ek_AAAAYAAJ?hl=en&gbpv=0
219. www.ancient-origins.net/news-history-archaeology/scythian-empire-0014802
220. www.AncientTurks.org
221. www.AtalarMirasi.org
222. www.BibleHub.com
223. www.Bitig.kz
224. www.gumilev-center.ru
225. www.SacredTexts.com
226. www.TheLatinLibrary.com
227. www.worldenglish.bible/
228. www.вокабула.рф/словари/казахско-русский-словарь
229. *Xenophon*. Vol. 1-7. E.C.Marchant, G.W.Bowersock, tr. Constitution of the Athenians. Harvard University Press, Cambridge, MA; William Heinemann, Ltd., London. 1925 (CC BY-SA 3.0 US) http://www.perseus.tufts.edu/hopper/text?doc=Perseus%3Atext%3A1999.01.0210%3Atext%3DAges.%3Achapter%3D1%3Asection%3D1
230. *Xenophon*. The Whole Works of Xenophon. Translated by Ashley, Spelman, Fielding, et al. London. 1847. In public domain. https://play.google.com/books/reader?id=XfIERBH4_Z4C&hl=en&pg=GBS.PA2
231. *Yazıcıoğlu Ali*. Tevârih-i Al-i Selçuk. Topkapı Sarayı kütüphanesi. Revan Köşkü bölümü no.1391, 233a.
232. *Yusif Balasaqunlu*. Qutadqu Bilik. Translated into Azerbaijani by Xalil Rza Uluturk. Baku. 2003
233. *Zosimus*. The History of Count Zosimus. Sometime Advocate and Chancellor of the Roman Empire. UK. J. Davis. 1814. In public domain. https://www.google.com/books/edition/The_History_of_Count_Zosimus/vXVEAQAAMAAJ?hl=en&gbpv=0
234. *Ашмарин Н.И.* «Словарь чувашского языка». (Ashmarin N.I. Slovar chuvashskogo yazika). Vol.1-2. Cheboksari. 1994.
235. *Байыр-оол А.В., Шагдурова О. Ю.* «Причины развития и способы формирования парных слов в Тувинском языке (в сопоставлении с хакасским языком.» (Bayir-ool A.V., Shagdurova O.Yu. Prichiny razvitiya i sposoby formirovaniya parnikh slov v tuvinskom yazike (v sopostavlenii s khakasskim yazikom.) http://net.knigi-x.ru/24filologiya/114713-1-v-tyurkskih-yazikah-shiroko-rasprostraneni-parnie-slova-parnie-slova-opredeleniyu-ko.php
236. *Башбуг Фират*. "Особенности послеложных конструкций в чулымском языке." (*Bashbug Firat*. Features of Postpositions in Chulym Language.) Nauchniy dialog. 5, 2017. https://www.nauka-dialog.ru/jour/article/view/365
237. *Будагов Л.З.* «Сравнительный словарь турецко-татарских наречий со включением употребительнейших слов арабских и персидских и с переводом на русский язык.» (Budagov L.Z. Sravnitelniy slovar turksko-tatarskikh narechiy so vklucheniyem upotrebitelneyshikh slov arabskikh i persidskikh i s perevodom na russkiy yazik.») Vol. 1-2. Saint Petersburg. 1869.
238. *Егоров В. Г.* «Этимологический словарь чувашского языка.» (Egorov V.G. Etimologicheskiy slovar chuvashskogo yazika.) Cheboksari. 1964.

239. *Жаксылык Муратович Сабитов.* «О происхождении казахских родов сары-уйсун, дулат, албан, суан, ысты, шапрашты, ошакты, сргелы.» (Jaksylyk Muratovich Sabitov. O proiskhojdenii kazakhskikh rodov sari-uysun, dulat, alban, suan, ysty, shaprashty, oshakty, srgely.) Russian Journal of Genetic Genealogy. Vol. 3. №3 (2011)/Vol. 4. № 1 (2012).[94]
240. *Ибн Даста (Руста).* «Известия о Хозарах, Буртасахъ, Болгарахъ, Мадьярахъ, Славянах и Руссах Абу-Али Ахмеда Бенъ Омаръ Ибнъ-Даста, неизвестного доселе Арабского писателя начала X века по рукописи Британского музея.» (Izvestiya o khozarakh, burtasakh, bolgarakh, madiarakh, slavianakh i russakh Abu-Ali Akhmeda Ben Omar Ibn-Dasta, neizvestnogo dosele arabskogo pisatelia nachala X veka po rukopisi Britanskogo muzeia.) Translated by Hvolson D.A. S-Petersburg. 1869
241. *Ибн Хаукаль.* «Книга путей и стран». (Ibn Hawqal. Ṣūrat al-'Arḍ. - Kniga putey i stran.) Древняя Русь в свете зарубежных источников: Хрестоматия, Том III: Восточные источники. М. Русский Фонд Содействия Образованию и Науке. 2009
242. *Ибн Хордадбех.* «Книга путей и стран.» (Ibn Khordadbekh. Kniga putey i stran.) Translated into Russian from Arabic by Nailya Velikhanova. Baku. 1986.
243. *Коркина Е.И.* «Наклонения глагола в якутском языке». (Korkina E.I. Nakloneniya glagola v yakutskom yazike.) Moscow. 1970
244. *Кызласов И.Л.* «Рунические письменности Евразийских степей.» (Kyzlasov I.L. Runicheskie pismennosti Evraziyskikh stepey. Moscow. 1994
245. *Махмуд Ал-Кашгари.* «Диван Лугат Ат-Турк» - «Свод тюркских слов». (Mahmud al-Kashgari. Svod Turkskikh slov.) Translated into Russian by Rustamov A.P. Moscow. 2010
246. *Махмуд Ал-Кашгари.* «Диван Лугат Ат-Турк». (Mahmud al-Kashgari. Divan Lugat At-Turk.) Translated into Russian by Auezova Z.-A.M. Almaati, 2005
247. *Мовсес Каланкатуаци* «История страны Алуанк». (Movses Kalankatuatsi. Istoriya strany Alwank.) Translated into Russian from old *Armenian* by *Sh. V. Smbatyan*. Institute of Ancient Manuscripts named after *Mashtots – Matenadaran. Yerevan.* 1984
248. *Мовсес Хоренаци.* «История Армении» в трех частях. (Movses Khorenatsi. Istoriya Armenii.) Translated from old Armenian by Gagik Sarkisyan. Erevan. Armenia. 1990 ՄՈՎՍԵՍ ԽՈՐԵՆԱՑԻ ՀԱՅՈՑ ՊԱՏՄՈՒԹԻՒՆ
249. *Наделяев В.М., Насилов Д.М., Тенишев Э.Р., Щербак А.М.* «Древнетюркский словарь». (Nadelyaev V.M., Nasilov D.M., Tenishev E.R., Sherbak A.M. Drevneturkskiy slovar.) Leningrad.1969.
250. «Памятная книжка Оренбургской губернии на 1865 год.» (Pamiatnaya knijka Orenburgskoy gubernii na 1865 god.) Orenburg.1865
251. *Пекарский Э.К.* «Краткий русско-якутский словарь.» (Pekarskiy E.K. Kratkii russko-iakutskii slovar.) Petrograd. 1916.
252. *Пекарский Э.К.* «Словарь якутского языка.» (Pekarskiy E.K. Slovar iakutskogo iazyka.) 1899. Iakutsk. 1907–1930. Petersburg.
253. *Радлов В. В.* «Опыт словаря тюркских наречий». (Radlov V.V. Opit slovaria turkskikh narechiy.) Vol.1-4. Saint Petersburg. 1893.
254. *Рашид ад-Дин.* «Сборник летописей". (Rashid ad-Din. Sbornik letopisei.) Том 1. Книга 1. М.-Л. АН СССР. 1952
255. *Сабиров Р. А.* «Татарско-русский полный учебный словарь.» (Sabirov R.A. Tatarsko-russkii polnyi uchebnyi slovar.) Kazan. 2008–2010
256. *Самашев С.К.* «Оғыз таңбалары.» (Samashev S.K. Oguz tanbalary.) p.117. BULLETIN of the L.N. Gumilyov Eurasian National University. Historical Sciences. Philosophy. Religion Series, 4(133)/2020
257. *Себеос.* «История императора Иракла. Сочинение епископа Себеоса, писателя 7 века.» (Sebeos. "Istoriya imperatora Irakla. Sochinenie episkopa Sebeosa, pisatelia 7 veka.) Translated from Armenian into Russian by Patkanian K., Saint-Petersburg, 1862.
258. *Смирнов Я. И.* «Восточное серебро. Атлас древней серебряной и золотой посуды восточного происхождения, найденной преимущественно в пределах Российской империи.» (Smirnov Ia.I. Vostochnoye serebro. Atlas drevney serebrianoi i zolotoi posudi vostochnogo proiskhojdenia, naidennoi preimushestvenno v predelakh Rossiiskoi imperii.) Санкт-Питербург. 1909
259. *Сыма Цянь.* «Исторические записки». (Syma Tsian. Istoricheskie zapiski.) Moscow. http://www.vostlit.info/Texts/Dokumenty/China/I/Syma_Tsjan/index.htm
260. *Татаринцев Б. И.* «Этимологический словарь тувинского языка.» (Tatarintsev V.I. «Etimologicheskii slovar tuvinskogo yazika»). Vol.1-2. Novosibirsk. 2000.
261. *Ураксин З.Г.* «Башкирско-русский словарь.» (Uraksin Z.G. Bashkirsko-russkii slovar.) Moscow. 1996
262. *Усманова М. Г.* «Еще раз о категории времени в башкирском языке.» (Usmanova M.G. "Eshe raz o kategorii vremeni v bashkirskom iazyke"). Vestnik. Ufa. 2016
263. *Федотов М. Р.* «Этимологический словарь чувашского языка.» (Fedotov M.R. Etimologicheskiy slovar chuvashskogo yazika.) Vol. 1-2. Cheboksari. 1996.
264. «Худуд-ал-Алам». (Hudud al-Alam) Created by an anonymous geographer. Translated from Persian into Russian by Minorskiy V.F. 1936

Made in the USA
Columbia, SC
12 December 2022